110  21

FOG 595

# Strategies in Prose

338 - 344

354 - 360

Style — Read in
Deism — God
Utilitarianism — Everthything for purpose

SECOND EDITION

# Strategies in Prose

WILFRED A. FERRELL
NICHOLAS A. SALERNO
*Arizona State University*

HOLT, RINEHART AND WINSTON, INC.

*New York    Chicago    San Francisco    Atlanta    Dallas*

# PREFACE

*E*DITING A new edition of *Strategies in Prose* has been a gratifying experience for us. It has given us the opportunity to improve our reader. In the Second Edition we have not departed from our original design; on the contrary, we have refined it with new selections we found to be more relevant to our purpose in the book. Further, we have produced a *Instructor's Manual* that is more detailed than the first one. For teachers who may prefer a reader with fewer selections than are included in the Second Edition, we have edited a shorter Edition.

In our Second Edition we again followed our commitment to recognized principles and practices that justify the reader as a text for the composition course. These derive from the long-established fact that people best learn to write by writing. But the writing experience serves this purpose only when the student writer has something to say and has a reason for saying it. The student in the freshman composition course may discover the substance for his writing by reading and discussing those writings that lie within the range of his interests and experiences, that engage his intellectual capabilities, and that cause him to make a response. And by analyzing and studying *how* the authors present their ideas, he may develop a sense for stylistics and rhetorical strategy.

The selections in the Second Edition of *Strategies in Prose* reflect the range of interest and experience of freshman composition students. It further reflects what we believe should be the province of their awareness and concerns.

To obtain a desirable range of subjects and viewpoints we have eighty-five selections—approximately one-third of them new—organized into six sections: the individual, modern social problems, science, language, education, and popular culture. Our purpose in each section is to offer a

v

variety of writings about the general area, as well as a number of different styles and rhetorical methods.

As a special feature in each of the six sections we have included a selection by a controversial writer or a chapter from a controversial book. Immediately following each of these we have a *pro* review and a *con* review of the book from which the selection was taken. The reviews lend another dimension to the variety of viewpoints in the sections, as well as give the students an opportunity to analyze critical writing and to examine several forms of the review, a type of essay they may be required to produce many times during their college years.

To provide still another level of diversity in each section, we have included at least one short story. Related in their section by subject or theme, these may be used for an individual study and analysis or for comparison and contrast with the other rhetorical types in the section.

The authors of the selections are, for the most part, all recognized authorities, either as writers or as experts in their field of specialization. We give a brief biographical sketch of the author on the first page of each selection and indicate when and where the selection originally appeared. Several authors have selections in two different sections. Our purpose here is to give the students an opportunity to see how a writer may adjust his style and rhetorical approach to serve different subjects, purposes, and audiences.

In addition to the obvious reasons for selecting known writers, we chose them to emphasize the importance of authority in the prose voice. Our purpose is to help the students recognize that a basic requirement for effective prose is the authority of the voice that has something to say and a compelling reason for saying it. We want to stress the students' need to prepare before they write, not necessarily so that they may speak as experts, but to give genuine thought to their subject before they attempt to write about it.

Although most of our selections come from twentieth-century writers, we do include a few from writers of earlier periods. Most of these latter selections have gained acceptance as classics of their type. Their place in the collection is to demonstrate how many of the issues and ideas of today were the concern of writers in earlier times. They also provide a means for the students to compare and contrast the styles and rhetorical methods of different periods.

The study questions at the end of each selection are intended to help the students read the selection critically and to assist them in analyzing the writer's method and techniques. The questions are not intended to be exhaustive for these purposes, but to suggest ways the students may start their study and analysis.

In the table of contents we have indicated the rhetorical type of each selection. These labels are not to be considered exclusive, since any given essay may incorporate forms of several different rhetorical methods and modes. Our designations are intended to serve as a ready reference for those who wish to examine a particular rhetorical type.

We are deeply grateful to friends and colleagues who kindly offered suggestions and recommendations for the Second Edition of *Strategies in Prose*. In particular we wish to acknowledge the generous assistance of Richard Beal, David Donaldson, Luayn Fleming, Kay Fuller, Del Kehl, Wanda McPherson, James Merrill, Carleton Moore, Paul O'Connell, Dixie Lee Powell, Daniel Quirk, Betty B. Renshaw, Robert V. Wilson, and Terry Withers.

W.A.F.<br>N.A.S.

Tempe, Arizona
November 1969

# CONTENTS

*Preface*                                                                    v

*One/ THE INDIVIDUAL*    "*This Above All*"                               1

*Benjamin Franklin*    A Bold and Arduous Project                         3
(ANALYSIS)

*D. H. Lawrence*    Benjamin Franklin                                    11
(PERSUASION)

*Harvey Cox*    Sex and Secularization                                   21
(ILLUSTRATION)

*Joseph Wood Krutch*    Straight Men in a Crooked                         32
World
(ILLUSTRATION)

*Time*    On Being a Contemporary                                        38
Christian
(DEFINITION)

*Jonathan Swift*    An Argument Against Abol-                             44
ishing Christianity
(REASONED ARGUMENT)

*E. M. Forster*    What I Believe                                        55
(ANALYSIS)

*Martin Buber*    Books and Men                                          63
(COMPARISON AND CONTRAST)

*Nathaniel Hawthorne*    Young Goodman Brown                             65
(NARRATIVE)

ix

The Minister's Black Veil      76
—A Parable
(NARRATIVE)

Thomas E. Connolly    Hawthorne's "Young Good-     87
man Brown": An Attack on
Puritanic Calvinism
(ANALYSIS)

Robert W. Cochran     Hawthorne's Choice: The Veil   92
or the Jaundiced Eye
(ANALYSIS)

Thomas E. Connolly    How Young Goodman Brown       98
Became Old Badman Brown
(REASONED ARGUMENT)

Robert W. Cochran     Reply                        100
(REASONED ARGUMENT)

Harry Golden          For Two Cents Plain          101
(ILLUSTRATION)

Charles Lamb          Dream-Children               106
(NARRATION)

Graham Greene         The Revolver in the Corner   110
Cupboard
(NARRATION)

George Orwell         A Hanging                    114
(NARRATION)

Two/MODERN SOCIAL
PROBLEMS              "Some Must Watch"            119

Norman Mailer         Looking for the Meat and Po-  121
tatoes—Thoughts on Black
Power
(ANALYSIS)

James Baldwin         Unnameable Objects, Un-      133
speakable Crimes
(ANALYSIS)

Ebony                 What Whites Can Learn        139
From Negroes
(PERSUASION)

# Contents

*William Faulkner*    On Fear: Deep South in La-   143
bor: Mississippi
(PERSUASION)

*Flannery O'Connor*    Everything That Rises Must   152
Converge
(NARRATIVE)

*William Styron*    It Is Done (Part IV, *The*   165
*Confessions of Nat Turner*)
(NARRATION)

*C. Vann Woodward*    Confessions of a Rebel: 1831   172
(ANALYSIS)

*Charles V. Hamilton*    Our Nat Turner and William   177
Styron's Creation
(ARGUMENT)

*Eric Sevareid*    The World Still Moves   181
Our Way
(ARGUMENT)

*Jonathan Swift*    A Modest Proposal   188
(PERSUASION)

*Sir Julian Huxley*    The Crowded World   195
(ARGUMENT)

*Arthur Schopenhauer*    On Noise   203
(ILLUSTRATION)

*Three / SCIENCE*    "Brave New World"   207

*Ashley Montagu*    Introducing Anthropology   209
(CLASSIFICATION)

*John James Audubon*    The Wild Turkey   213
(IDENTIFICATION)

*Walter Van Tilburg Clark*    Hook   220
(NARRATION)

*Loren C. Eiseley*    The Bird and the Machine   236
(ILLUSTRATION)

*Joseph Wood Krutch*    He Was There Before Coro-   244
nado
(IDENTIFICATION)

Stephen Vincent Benét    We Aren't Superstitious          252
                         (ILLUSTRATION)

Newsweek                 The New Medicine and Its         264
                         Weapons
                         (IDENTIFICATION)

Rachel Carson            The Obligation to Endure         275
                         (PERSUASION)

Loren C. Eiseley         Using a Plague to Fight a        282
                         Plague
                         (PERSUASION)

William J. Darby         Silence, Miss Carson             286
                         (REASONED ARGUMENT)

Bertrand Russell         The Science to Save Us From      291
                         Science
                         (REASONED ARGUMENT)

Philip Wylie             Science Has Spoiled My           298
                         Supper
                         (PERSUASION)

H. G. Wells              The Lord of the Dynamos          304
                         (NARRATION)


Four / LANGUAGE          "The Soul of Wit"                313

George Orwell            Politics and The English         315
                         Language
                         (ILLUSTRATION)

Dwight MacDonald         The Decline and Fall of          326
                         English
                         (ARGUMENT)

H. L. Mencken            Hell and Its Outskirts           338
                         (IDENTIFICATION)

Wallace E. Stegner       "Good-Bye to All T—T"            344
                         (ILLUSTRATION)

Mark Twain               Buck Fanshaw's Funeral           347
                         (NARRATION)

Max Beerbohm             How Shall I Word It?             354
                         (ILLUSTRATION)

Contents

Phillip B. Gove    Preface to *Webster's Third*    360
*New International Dictionary*
(ANALYSIS)

Wilson Follett    Sabotage in Springfield    369
(ANALYSIS)

Bergen Evans    But What's a Dictionary For?    378
(ARGUMENT)

Five/EDUCATION    *"Unwillingly to School"*    389

Hugh Kenner    Don't Send Johnny to Col-    391
lege
(PERSUASION)

John William Gardner    College and the Alternatives    397
(ARGUMENT)

Harold Taylor    Quality and Equality    407
(ANALYSIS)

J. Edward Dirks    Neo-Knighthood    410
(ANALYSIS)

Graham Greene    The Lost Childhood    413
(ILLUSTRATION)

Paul Goodman    The New Aristocrats    418
(ANALYSIS)

Clark Kerr    The Exaggerated Generation    431
(ANALYSIS)

Paul Woodring    Eros on the Campus    438
(ANALYSIS)

Herbert Gold    Letter From a Far Frat    445
(NARRATION)

Sidney Hook    Academic Freedom and Stu-    451
dent Riots
(ANALYSIS)

Leo Rosten    To An Angry Young Man    459
(ARGUMENT)

Jeremy Larner    Another Plane in Another    463
Sphere: The College Drug
Scene
(ANALYSIS)

Mark Schorer     To the Wind     474
(NARRATION)

Six/POPULAR CULTURE     "The Winter of Our Discon-     485
tent"

How Culturally Active Are     487
Americans?
Elmo Roper     (ANALYSIS)

Frank Lloyd Wright     Taliesin     491
(DESCRIPTION)

Ashley Montagu     Frank Lloyd Wright     500
(PERSUASION)

F. A. Macklin and Charles Webb     ". . . Benjamin Will Sur-     502
vive. . . ." An Interview
with Charles Webb, author of
The Graduate
(IDENTIFICATION)

Hollis Alpert     Mike Nichols Strikes Again     508
(ANALYSIS)

Stanley Kauffmann     Cum Laude     510
(ANALYSIS)

Brendan Gill     The Current Cinema     515
(ANALYSIS)

Stephen Farber and Estelle Changas     The Graduate     517
(ANALYSIS)

Charles Webb     Letter to Stanley Kauffmann     524

Stanley Kauffmann     Second Look     524
(ANALYSIS)

Charles Webb and     Correspondence: "The Grad-     527
Stanley Kauffmann     uate"
(REASONED ARGUMENT. PER-
SUASION)

Hollis Alpert     "The Graduate" Makes Out     529
(ANALYSIS)

John Mason Brown     Disney and the Dane     535
(NARRATION)

Contents

*Marya Mannes*    The Conquest of Trigger   539
Mortis
(PERSUASION)

*Russell Lynes*    What Revolution in Men's   546
Clothes?
(ANALYSIS)

*Tom Wolfe*    The Marvelous Mouth   553
(NARRATION)

*Eudora Welty*    Powerhouse   563
(NARRATION)

*E. H. Lacon Watson*    "Tarzan" and Literature   574
(ANALYSIS)

*Gore Vidal*    The Waking Dream: Tarzan   584
Revisited
(ANALYSIS)

*Joseph Wood Krutch*    Must Writers Hate the Uni-   590
verse?
(PERSUASION)

*Saul Bellow*    Mind Over Chatter   599
(PERSUASION)

*Index of Authors and Titles*   603

# Strategies in Prose

# Section One

# The Individual

## "This Above All"

*Benjamin Franklin*

# A BOLD AND ARDUOUS PROJECT

Benjamin Franklin (1706–1790) was born in Boston, Massachusetts. Perhaps the best representative of the American Enlightenment, he has been
called the founder of America's first circulating library, first colonial hospital, and first learned society. He studied earthquakes, the Gulf Stream, and
electricity and lightning, becoming famous as a scientist with the publication of *Experiments and Observations on Electricity* (1751–1753). His political career was equally distinguished—clerk to the Pennsylvania assembly; member of the Second Continental Congress, the committee which
drafted the Declaration of Independence, and the Constitutional Convention; and ambassador to France. Jefferson, who followed Franklin as ambassador to France, said: "No one can replace him, Sir; I am only his successor." Franklin's *Poor Richard's Almanack* and his *Autobiography* have
earned him a place in American literary history.

IT WAS about this time I conceived the bold and arduous
project of arriving at *moral perfection;* I wished to live
without committing any fault at any time, and to conquer
all that either natural inclination, custom or company, might lead me into.
As I knew, or thought I knew what was right and wrong, I did not see why I
might not *always* do the one and avoid the other. But I soon found I had
undertaken a task of more difficulty than I had imagined: while my attention
was taken up, and care employed in guarding against one fault, I was often
surprised by another: habit took the advantage of inattention; inclination
was sometimes too strong for reason. I concluded at length that the mere
speculative conviction, that it was our interest to be completely virtuous,
was not sufficient to prevent our slipping; and that the contrary habits must
be broken, and good ones acquired and established, before we can have any
dependence on a steady uniform rectitude of conduct. For this purpose I
therefore tried the following method.

In the various enumerations of the *moral virtues* I had met with in my
reading, I found the catalogue more or less numerous, as different writers
included more or fewer ideas under the same name. *Temperance* for exam-

First published 1868.

3

ple, was by some confined to eating and drinking; while by others it was extended to mean the moderating every other pleasure, appetite, inclination or passion, bodily or mental, even to our avarice and ambition. I proposed to myself, for the sake of clearness, to use rather more names, with fewer ideas annexed to each, than a few names with more ideas; and I included under thirteen names of virtues, all that at that time occurred to me as necessary or desirable; and annexed to each a short precept, which fully expressed the extent I gave to its meaning.

These names of *virtues,* with their precepts, were;

1.   TEMPERANCE.—Eat not to dulness: drink not to elevation.
2.   SILENCE.—Speak not but what may benefit others or yourself: avoid trifling conversation.
3.   ORDER.—Let all your things have their places: let each part of your business have its time.
4.   RESOLUTION.—Resolve to perform what you ought; perform without fail what you resolve.
5.   FRUGALITY.—Make no expence but to do good to others or yourself; i. e. Waste nothing.
6.   INDUSTRY.—Lose no time; be always employed in something useful; cut off all unnecessary actions.
7.   SINCERITY.—Use no hurtful deceit; think innocently and justly; and if you speak, speak accordingly.
8.   JUSTICE.—Wrong none by doing injuries, or omitting the benefits that are your duty.
9.   MODERATION.—Avoid extremes: forbear resenting injuries so much as you think they deserve.
10.   CLEANLINESS.—Tolerate no uncleanliness in body, clothes, or habitation.
11.   TRANQUILLITY.—Be not disturbed at trifles, or at accidents common or unavoidable.
12.   CHASTITY.—Rarely use venery, but for health or offspring; never to dulness or weakness, or the injury of your own or another's peace or reputation.
13.   HUMILITY.—Imitate *Jesus* and *Socrates*.

My intention being to acquire the *habitude* of all these virtues, I judged it would be well not to distract my attention by attempting the whole at once, but to fix it on *one* of them at a time; and when I should be master of that, then to proceed to another; and so on till I should have gone through the thirteen. And as the previous acquisition of some, might facilitate the acquisition of certain others, I arranged them with that view as they stand above. *Temperance* first, as it tends to procure that coolness and clearness of head, which is so necessary where constant vigilance was to be kept up, and a guard maintained against the unremitting attraction of ancient habits and the force of perpetual temptations. This being acquired and established, *Silence* would be more easy; and my desire being to gain knowledge at the same time that I improved in virtue; and considering that in conversation it was obtained rather by the use of the ear than of the tongue, and therefore wishing to break a habit I was getting into of prattling, punning and jesting, (which only made me acceptable to trifling company) I gave *Silence* the second place. This and the next, *Order,* I expected would allow me more time for attending to my project and my studies. *Resolution* once become habitual, would keep me firm in my endeavours to obtain all the subsequent virtues; *Frugality* and *Industry* relieving me from my remaining debt and producing affluence and independence, would make more easy the practice of *Sincerity* and *Justice,* &c. &c. Conceiving then, that agreeably to the advice of Pythagoras in his Golden Verses, daily examination would be necessary; I contrived the following method for conducting that examination.

I made a little book in which I allotted a page for each of the virtues. I ruled each page with red ink, so as to have seven columns, one for each day of the week, marking each column with a letter for the day. I crossed these columns with thirteen red lines, marking the beginning of each line with the first letter of one of the virtues; on which line, and in its proper column, I might mark by a little black spot, every fault I found upon examination to have been committed respecting that virtue, upon that day.

FORM OF THE PAGES.

## TEMPERANCE.

Eat not to dulness : drink not to elevation.

|        | Sun. | M. | T. | W. | Th. | F. | S. |
|--------|------|----|----|----|-----|----|----|
| Tem.   |      |    |    |    |     |    |    |
| Sil.   | •    | •  |    | •  |     | •  |    |
| Ord.   | •    | •  | •  |    | •   | •  | •  |
| Res.   |      | •  |    |    |     | •  |    |
| Fru.   |      | •  |    |    |     | •  |    |
| Ind.   |      |    | •  |    |     |    |    |
| Sinc.  |      |    |    |    |     |    |    |
| Jus.   |      |    |    |    |     |    |    |
| Mod.   |      |    |    |    |     |    |    |
| Clea.  |      |    |    |    |     |    |    |
| Tran.  |      |    |    |    |     |    |    |
| Chas.  |      |    |    |    |     |    |    |
| Hum.   |      |    |    |    |     |    |    |

I determined to give a week's strict attention to each of the virtues successively. Thus in the first week, my great guard was to avoid every the least offence against *Temperance;* leaving the other virtues to their ordinary chance, only marking every evening the faults of the day. Thus, if in the first week I could keep my first line marked T. clear of spots, I supposed the habit of that virtue so much strengthened, and its opposite weakened, that I might venture extending my attention to include the next; and for the following week keep both lines clear of spots. Proceeding thus to the last, I could get through a course complete in thirteen weeks, and four courses in a year. And like him who having a garden to weed, does not attempt to eradicate all the bad herbs at once, (which would exceed his reach and his strength,) but works on one of the beds at a time, and having accomplished the first, proceeds to a second; so I should have (I hoped) the encouraging pleasure, of seeing on my pages the progress made in virtue, by clearing successively my lines of their spots; 'till in the end by a number of courses, I should be happy in viewing a clean book, after a thirteen weeks' daily examination.

This my little book had for its motto, these lines from Addison's Cato:

> *"Here will I hold: If there's a Power above us,*
> *(And that there is, all Nature cries aloud*
> *Through all her works,) He must delight in Virtue;*
> *And that which he delights in must be happy."*

Another from Cicero,

*"O Vitæ Philosophia Dux! O Virtutum indagatrix expultrixque vitiorum! Unus Dies bene, et ex præceptis tuis actus, peccanti immortalitati est anteponendus."*

Another from the Proverbs of Solomon, speaking of wisdom or virtue:

*"Length of days is in her right hand, and in her left hand riches and honor. Her ways are ways of pleasantness, and all her paths are peace."*

And conceiving God to be the fountain of wisdom, I thought it right and necessary to solicit his assistance for obtaining it; to this end I formed the following little prayer, which was prefixed to my tables of examination, for daily use.

*"O powerful goodness! bountiful father! merciful guide! Increase in me that wisdom which discovers my truest interest. Strengthen my resolution to perform what that wisdom dictates. Accept my kind offices to thy other children, as the only return in my power for thy continual favors to me."*

I used also sometimes a little prayer which I took from Thomson's Poems, viz.

> *"Father of light and life, thou God supreme!*
> *O teach me what is good; teach me thyself!*
> *Save me from folly, vanity, and vice,*
> *From every low pursuit; and fill my soul*
> *With knowledge, conscious peace and virtue pure;*
> *Sacred, substantial, never-fading bliss!"*

The precept of Order, requiring that *every part of my business should have its allotted time,* one page in my little book contained the following scheme of employment for the twenty-four hours of a natural day.

### SCHEME.

#### Hours.

| | | |
|---|---|---|
| MORNING. | 5 | Rise, wash, and address *Powerful Good-* |
| The *Question.* | 6 | *ness!* contrive day's business and take the |
| What good shall | | resolution of the day; prosecute the present |
| I do this day? | 7 | study and breakfast. |
| | 8 | |
| | 9 | Work. |
| | 10 | |
| | 11 | |
| NOON. | 12, 1 | Read, or look over my accounts and dine. |
| AFTERNOON. | 2, 3, 4, 5 | Work. |
| EVENING. | 6 | Put things in their places. Supper. Music |
| The *Question.* | 7 | or diversion, or conversation. Examination of |
| What good have | 8 | the day. |
| I done today? | 9 | |
| NIGHT. | 10, 11, 12, 1, 2, 3, 4 | Sleep. |

I entered upon the execution of this plan for self-examination, and continued it with occasional intermissions for some time. I was surprised to find myself so much fuller of faults than I had imagined; but I had the satisfaction of seeing them diminish. To avoid the trouble of renewing now and then my little book, which, by scraping out the marks on the paper of old faults to make room for new ones in a new course, became full of holes, I transformed my tables and precepts to the ivory leaves of a memorandum book, on which the lines were drawn with red ink, that made a durable stain; and on those lines I marked my faults with a black-lead pencil; which marks I could easily wipe out with a wet spunge. After a while I went through one course only in a year; and afterwards only one in several years; till at length I omitted them entirely, being employed in voyages and business abroad, with a multiplicity of affairs, that interfered; but I always carried my little book with me. My scheme of *Order* gave me the most trouble; and I found that though it might be practicable where a man's business was such as to leave him the disposition of his time, that of a journeyman printer for instance, it was not possible to be exactly observed by a master, who must mix with the world, and often receive people of business at their own hours. Order too, with regard to places for things, papers, &c. I found extremely difficult to acquire. I had not been early accustomed to *method,* and having an exceeding good memory, I was not so sensible of the inconvenience attending want of method. This article therefore cost me much painful attention, and my faults in it vexed me so much, and I made so little progress in amendment, and had such frequent relapses, that I was almost ready to give up the attempt, and content myself with a faulty character in that respect. Like the man who in buying an axe of a smith my neighbour, desired to have the whole of its surface as bright as the edge: the smith consented to grind it bright for him if he would turn the wheel: he turned while the smith pressed the broad face of the axe hard and heavily on the stone, which made the turning of it very fatiguing. The man came every now and then from the wheel to see how the work went on; and at length would take his axe as it was, without further grinding. No, said the smith, turn on, turn on, we shall have it bright by and by; as yet 'tis only speckled. Yes, said the man, but *"I think I like a speckled axe best."* And I believe this may have been the case with many, who having for want of some such means as I employed, found the difficulty of obtaining good and breaking bad habits in other points of vice and virtue, have given up the struggle, and concluded that *"a speckled axe was best."* For something, that pretended to be reason, was every now and then suggesting to me, that such extreme nicety as I exacted of myself might be a kind of foppery in morals, which if it were known, would make me ridiculous; that a perfect character might be attended with the inconvenience of being envied and hated; and that a benevolent man should allow a few faults in himself, to keep his friends in countenance. In truth I found myself incorrigible with respect to *Order;* and now I am grown old, and my memory bad, I feel very sensibly the want of it. But on the whole, though I never arrived at the perfection I had been so ambitious of obtaining, but fell far short of it, yet I was by the endeavour, a better and a happier man than I otherwise should have been, if I had not attempted it; as those who aim at perfect writing by imitating the engraved copies, though they never reach the wished for excellence of those copies, their hand is mended by the endeavour, and is tolerable while it continues fair and legible.

It may be well my posterity should be informed, that to this little artifice, with the blessing of God, their ancestor owed the constant felicity of his life down to his 79th year, in which this is written. What reverses may attend the remainder is in the hand of Providence: but if they arrive, the reflection on past happiness enjoyed, ought to help his bearing them with more resignation. To *Temperance* he ascribes his long continued health, and what is still left to him of a good constitution. To *Industry* and *Frugality,* the early easiness of his circumstances, and acquisition of his fortune, with all that knowledge that enabled him to be an useful citizen and obtained for him some degree of reputation among the learned. To *Sincerity* and *Justice,* the confidence of his country, and the honorable employs it conferred upon him: and to the joint influence of the whole mass of the virtues, even in the imperfect state he was able to acquire them, all that evenness of temper and that cheerfulness in conversation which makes his company still sought for, and agreeable even to his young acquaintance. I hope therefore that some of my descendants may follow the example and reap the benefit.

It will be remarked that, though my scheme was not wholly without religion, there was in it no mark of any of the distinguishing tenets of any particular sect; I had purposely avoided them; for being fully persuaded of the utility and excellency of my method, and that it might be serviceable to people in all religions, and intending some time or other to publish it, I would not have any thing in it, that should prejudice any one, of any sect, against it. I proposed writing a little comment on each virtue, in which I would have shewn the advantages of possessing it, and the mischiefs attending its opposite vice; I should have called my book THE ART OF VIRTUE, because it would have shewn the means and manner of obtaining virtue, which would have distinguished it from the mere exhortation to be good, that does not instruct and indicate the means; but is like the apostle's man of verbal charity, who without shewing to the naked and hungry, how or where they might get clothes or victuals, only exhorted them to be fed and clothed. *James* II, 15, 16.

But it so happened that my intention of writing and publishing this comment was never fulfilled. I had indeed from time to time put down short hints of the sentiments, reasonings &c. to be made use of in it; some of which I have still by me: but the necessary close attention to private business, in the earlier part of life; and public business since, have occasioned my post-poning it. For it being connected in my mind with *a great and extensive project,* that required the whole man to execute, and which an unforeseen succession of employs prevented my attending to, it has hitherto remained unfinished.

In this piece it was my design to explain and enforce this doctrine, *that vicious actions are not hurtful because they are forbidden, but forbidden because they are hurtful;* the nature of man alone considered: that it was therefore every one's interest to be virtuous, who wished to be happy even in this world: and I should from this circumstance, (there being always in the world a number of rich merchants, nobility, states and princes who have need of honest instruments for the management of their affairs, and such being so rare) have endeavoured to convince young persons, that no quali-ties are so likely to make a poor man's fortune, as those of *probity* and *integrity*.

My list of virtues contained at first but twelve: but a quaker friend having kindly informed me that I was generally thought proud; that my pride shewed itself frequently in conversation; that I was not content with being in the right when discussing any point, but was overbearing, and rather inso-lent; (of which he convinced me by mentioning several instances) I deter-mined to endeavour to cure myself if I could of this vice or folly among the rest; and I added *Humility* to my list, giving an extensive meaning to the word. I cannot boast of much success in acquiring the *reality* of this virtue, but I had a good deal with regard to the appearance of it. I made it a rule to forbear all direct contradiction to the sentiments of others, and all positive assertion of mine own. I even forbid myself, agreeably to the old laws of our Junto, the use of every word or expression in the language that imported a fixed opinion; such as *certainly, undoubtedly &c.* and I adopted instead of them, *I conceive, I apprehend,* or *I imagine,* a thing to be so, or so; or it so *appears to me at present.* When another asserted something that I thought an error, I denied myself the pleasure of contradicting him abruptly, and of shewing immediately some absurdity in his proposition; and in answering I began by observing, that in certain cases or circumstances, his opinion would be right, but in the present case there *appeared* or *seemed to me* some difference &c. I soon found the advantage of this change in my manners; the conversations I engaged in went on more pleasantly. The modest way in which I proposed my opinions, procured them a readier reception and less contradiction; I had less mortification when I was found to be in the wrong, and I more easily prevailed with others to give up their mistakes and join with me when I happened to be in the right. And this mode, which I at first put on with some violence to natural inclination, became at length easy, and so habitual to me, that perhaps for the fifty years past no one has ever heard a dogmatical expression escape me. And to this habit (after my character of integrity) I think it principally owing that I had early so much weight with my fellow-citizens, when I proposed new institutions, or alterations in the old; and so much influence in public councils, when I became a member: for I was but a bad speaker, never eloquent, subject to much hesitation in my choice of words, hardly correct in language, and yet I generally carried my point.

In reality there is perhaps no one of our natural passions so hard to subdue, as *Pride;* disguise it, struggle with it, stifle it, mortify it as much as one pleases, it is still alive, and will every now and then peep out and show itself; you will see it perhaps often in this history. For even if I could conceive that I had completely overcome it, I should probably be *proud* of my *humility*.

### STUDY QUESTIONS

1.   At times, Franklin wondered if his project of arriving at moral perfection "might be a kind of foppery in morals." Do you think the project was a "ridiculous" one? To what extent?

2.   Why was Virtue #3 the most difficult to acquire?

3.   How effective are Franklin's similes about weeding a garden and the man with a new ax?

4.   Why did Franklin deliberately avoid mentioning religion in his project?

5.   Franklin felt he had more success in attaining the "appearance" of Humility than the "reality" of it. Was he, then, a hypocrite?

# D. H. Lawrence   Read

# BENJAMIN FRANKLIN

D. H. Lawrence (1885–1930) was born in Eastwood, near Nottingham, England, and educated at Nottingham University College. He ranks among the most important contemporary novelists for books which include *White Peacock* (1911), *Sons and Lovers* (1913), *The Rainbow* (1915), *Women in*

*Love* (1920), *Aaron's Rod* (1922), *The Plumed Serpent* (1926), and *Lady Chatterley's Lover* (1928). Lawrence made history when, in 1928, he was prosecuted for the obscenity of *Lady Chatterley's Lover* and his paintings, exhibited that year in London. As a writer, he is equally famous for his short stories, such as *The Prussian Officer* (1914); travel books, including *Sea and Sardinia* (1921); his literary criticism, which includes the controversial *Studies in Classical American Literature* (1923); and his volumes of poetry, such as *Pansies* (1929).

THE PERFECTIBILITY of Man! Ah heaven, what a dreary theme! The perfectibility of the Ford car! The perfectibility of which man? I am many men. Which of them are you going to perfect? I am not a mechanical contrivance.

Education! Which of the various me's do you propose to educate, and which do you propose to suppress?

Anyhow I defy you. I defy you, oh society, to educate me or to suppress me, according to your dummy standards.

The ideal man! And which is he, if you please? Benjamin Franklin or Abraham Lincoln? The ideal man! Roosevelt or Porfirio Diaz?

There are other men in me, besides this patient ass who sits here in a tweed jacket. What am I doing, playing the patient ass in a tweed jacket? Who am I talking to? Who are you, at the other end of this patience?

Who are you? How many selves have you? And which of these selves do you want to be?

Is Yale College going to educate the self that is in the dark of you, or Harvard College?

The ideal self! Oh, but I have a strange and fugitive self shut out and howling like a wolf or a coyote under the ideal windows. See his red eyes in the dark? This is the self who is coming into his own.

The perfectibility of man, dear God! When every man as long as he remains alive is in himself a multitude of conflicting men. Which of these do you choose to perfect, at the expense of every other?

Old Daddy Franklin will tell you. He'll rig him up for you, the pattern American. Oh, Franklin was the first downright American. He knew what he was about, the sharp little man. He set up the first dummy American.

At the beginning of his career this cunning little Benjamin drew up for himself a creed that should "satisfy the professors of every religion, but shock none."

Now wasn't that a real American thing to do?

*"That there is One God, who made all things."*

(But Benjamin made Him.)

*"That He governs the world by His Providence."*

(Benjamin knowing all about Providence.)

*"That He ought to be worshipped with adoration, prayer, and thanksgiving."*

(Which cost nothing.)

*"But—"* But me no buts, Benjamin, saith the Lord.

*"But that the most acceptable service of God is doing good to men."*

(God having no choice in the matter.)

*"That the soul is immortal."*

(You'll see why, in the next clause.)

*"And that God will certainly reward virtue and punish vice, either here or hereafter."*

Now if Mr. Andrew Carnegie, or any other millionaire, had wished to invent a God to suit his ends, he could not have done better. Benjamin did it for him in the eighteenth century. God is the supreme servant of men who want to get on, to *produce*. Providence. The provider. The heavenly storekeeper. The everlasting Wanamaker.

And this is all the God the grandsons of the Pilgrim Fathers had left. Aloft on a pillar of dollars.

*"That the soul is immortal."*

The trite way Benjamin says it!

But man has a soul, though you can't locate it either in his purse or his pocket-book or his heart or his stomach or his head. The *wholeness* of a man is his soul. Not merely that nice little comfortable bit which Benjamin marks out.

It's a queer thing, is a man's soul. It is the whole of him. Which means it is the unknown him, as well as the known. It seems to me just funny, professors and Benjamins fixing the functions of the soul. Why the soul of man is a vast forest, and all Benjamin intended was a neat back garden. And we've all got to fit into his kitchen garden scheme of things. Hail Columbia!

The soul of man is a dark forest. The Hercynian Wood that scared the Romans so, and out of which came the white-skinned hordes of the next civilization.

Who knows what will come out of the soul of man? The soul of man is a dark vast forest, with wild life in it. Think of Benjamin fencing it off!

Oh, but Benjamin fenced a little tract that he called the soul of man, and proceeded to get it into cultivation. Providence, forsooth! And they think that bit of barbed wire is going to keep us in pound forever? More fools them.

This is Benjamin's barbed wire fence. He made himself a list of virtues, which he trotted inside like a grey nag in a paddock.

1.   TEMPERANCE   Eat not to dulness; drink not to elevation.
2.   SILENCE   Speak not but what may benefit others or yourself; avoid trifling conversation.

3.   ORDER   Let all your things have their places; let each part of your business have its time.

4.   RESOLUTION   Resolve to perform what you ought; perform without fail what you resolve.

5.   FRUGALITY   Make no expence but to do good to others or yourself—i.e., waste nothing.

6.   INDUSTRY   Lose no time, be always employed in something useful; cut off all unnecessary actions.

7.   SINCERITY   Use no hurtful deceit; think innocently and justly, and, if you speak, speak accordingly.

8.   JUSTICE   Wrong none by doing injuries, or omitting the benefits that are your duty.

9.   MODERATION   Avoid extremes, forbear resenting injuries as much as you think they deserve.

10.   CLEANLINESS   Tolerate no uncleanliness in body, clothes, or habitation.

11.   TRANQUILLITY   Be not disturbed at trifles, or at accidents common or unavoidable.

12.   CHASTITY   Rarely use venery but for health and offspring, never to dulness, weakness, or the injury of your own or another's peace or reputation.

13.   HUMILITY   Imitate Jesus and Socrates.

A Quaker friend told Franklin that he, Benjamin, was generally considered proud, so Benjamin put in the Humility touch as an afterthought. The amusing part is the sort of humility it displays. "Imitate Jesus and Socrates," and mind you don't outshine either of these two. One can just imagine Socrates and Alcibiades roaring in their cups over Philadelphian Benjamin, and Jesus looking at him a little puzzled, and murmuring: "Aren't you wise in your own conceit, Ben?"

"Henceforth be masterless," retorts Ben. "Be ye each one his own master unto himself, and don't let even the Lord put his spoke in." "Each man his own master" is but a puffing up of masterlessness.

Well, the first of Americans practised this enticing list with assiduity, setting a national example. He had the virtues in columns, and gave himself good and bad marks according as he thought his behaviour deserved. Pity these conduct charts are lost to us. He only remarks that Order was his stumbling block. He could not learn to be neat and tidy.

Isn't it nice to have nothing worse to confess?

He was a little model, was Benjamin. Doctor Franklin. Snuff-coloured little man! Immortal soul and all!

The immortal soul part was a sort of cheap insurance policy.

Benjamin had no concern, really, with the immortal soul. He was too busy with social man.

1.  He swept and lighted the streets of young Philadelphia.
2.  He invented electrical appliances.
3.  He was the centre of a moralizing club in Philadelphia, and he wrote the moral humorisms of Poor Richard.
4.  He was a member of all the important councils of Philadelphia, and then of the American colonies.
5.  He won the cause of American Independence at the French Court, and was the economic father of the United States.

Now what more can you want of a man? And yet he is *infra dig,* even in Philadelphia.

I admire him. I admire his sturdy courage first of all, then his sagacity, then his glimpsing into the thunders of electricity, then his common-sense humour. All the qualities of a great man, and never more than a great citizen. Middle-sized, sturdy, snuff-coloured Doctor Franklin, one of the soundest citizens that ever trod or "used venery."

I do not like him.

And, by the way, I always thought books of venery were about hunting deer.

There is a certain earnest naïveté about him. Like a child. And like a little old man. He has again become as a little child, always as wise as his grandfather, or wiser.

Perhaps, as I say, the most complete citizen that ever "used venery."

Printer, philosopher, scientist, author and patriot, impeccable husband and citizen, why isn't he an archetype?

Pioneer, Oh Pioneers! Benjamin was one of the greatest pioneers of the United States. Yet we just can't do with him.

What's wrong with him then? Or what's wrong with us?

I can remember, when I was a little boy, my father used to buy a scrubby yearly almanack with the sun and moon and stars on the cover. And it used to prophesy bloodshed and famine. But also crammed in corners it had little anecdotes and humorisms, with a moral tag. And I used to have my little priggish laugh at the woman who counted her chickens before they were hatched, and so forth, and I was convinced that honesty was the best policy, also a little priggishly. The author of these bits was Poor Richard, and Poor Richard was Benjamin Franklin, writing in Philadelphia well over a hundred years before.

And probably I haven't got over those Poor Richard tags yet. I rankle still with them. They are thorns in young flesh.

Because although I still believe that honesty is the best policy, I dislike policy altogether; though it is just as well not to count your chickens before they are hatched, it's still more hateful to count them with gloating when they *are* hatched. It has taken me many years and countless smarts to get out of that barbed wire moral enclosure that Poor Richard rigged up. Here am I now in tatters and scratched to ribbons, sitting in the middle of Benjamin's America looking at the barbed wire, and the fat sheep crawling under the fence to get fat outside and the watchdogs yelling at the gate lest by chance anyone should get out by the proper exit. Oh America! Oh Benjamin! And I just utter a long loud curse against Benjamin and the American corral.

Moral America! Most moral Benjamin. Sound, satisfied Ben!

He had to go to the frontiers of his State to settle some disturbance among the Indians. On this occasion he writes:

We found that they had made a great bonfire in the middle of the square; they were all drunk, men and women quarrelling and fighting. Their dark-coloured bodies, half naked, seen only by the gloomy light of the bonfire, running after and beating one another with fire-brands, accompanied by their horrid yellings, formed a scene the most resembling our ideas of hell that could well be imagined. There was no appeasing the tumult, and we retired to our lodging. At midnight a number of them came thundering at our door, demanding more rum, of which we took no notice.

The next day, sensible they had misbehaved in giving us that disturbance, they sent three of their counsellors to make their apology. The orator acknowledged the fault, but laid it upon the rum, and then endeavoured to excuse the rum by saying: "The Great Spirit, who made all things, made everything for some use; and whatever he designed anything for, that use it should always be put to. Now, when he had made rum, he said: 'Let this be for the Indians to get drunk with.' And it must be so."

And, indeed, if it be the design of Providence to extirpate these savages in order to make room for the cultivators of the earth, it seems not improbable that rum may be the appointed means. It has already annihilated all the tribes who formerly inhabited all the seacoast. . . .

This, from the good doctor, with such suave complacency is a little disenchanting. Almost too good to be true.

But there you are! The barbed wire fence. "Extirpate these savages in order to make room for the cultivators of the earth." Oh, Benjamin Franklin! He even "used venery" as a cultivator of seed.

Cultivate the earth, ye gods! The Indians did that, as much as they needed. And they left off there. Who built Chicago? Who cultivated the earth until it spawned Pittsburgh, Pa.?

The moral issue! Just look at it! Cultivation included. If it's a mere choice of Kultur or cultivation, I give up.

Which brings us right back to our question, what's wrong with Benjamin, that we can't stand him? Or else, what's wrong with us, that we find fault with such a paragon?

Man is a moral animal. All right. I am a moral animal. And I'm going to remain such. I'm not going to be turned into a virtuous little automaton as

Benjamin would have me. "This is good, that is bad. Turn the little handle and let the good tap flow," saith Benjamin and all America with him. "But first of all extirpate those savages who are always turning on the bad tap."

I am a moral animal. But I am not a moral machine. I don't work with a little set of handles or levers. The Temperance-silence-order-resolution-frugality-industry-sincerity-justice-moderation-cleanliness-tranquillity-chastity-humility keyboard is not going to get me going. I'm really not just an automatic piano with a moral Benjamin getting tunes out of me.

Here's my creed, against Benjamin's. This is what I believe:

*"That I am I."*
*"That my soul is a dark forest."*
*"That my known self will never be more than a little clearing in the forest."*
*"That gods, strange gods, come forth from the forest into the clearing of my known self, and then go back."*
*"That I must have the courage to let them come and go."*
*"That I will never let mankind put anything over me, but that I will try always to recognize and submit to the gods in me and the gods in other men and women."*

There is my creed. He who runs may read. He who prefers to crawl, or to go by gasoline, can call it rot.

Then for a "list." It is rather fun to play at Benjamin.

1. TEMPERANCE  Eat and carouse with Bacchus, or munch dry bread with Jesus, but don't sit down without one of the gods.
2. SILENCE  Be still when you have nothing to say; when genuine passion moves you, say what you've got to say, and say it hot.
3. ORDER  Know that you are responsible to the gods inside you and to the men in whom the gods are manifest. Recognize your superiors and your inferiors, according to the gods. This is the root of all order.
4. RESOLUTION  Resolve to abide by your own deepest promptings, and to sacrifice the smaller thing to the greater. Kill when you must, and be killed the same: the *must* coming from the gods inside you, or from the men in whom you recognize the Holy Ghost.
5. FRUGALITY  Demand nothing; accept what you see fit. Don't wast your pride or squander your emotion.
6. INDUSTRY  Lose no time with ideals; serve the Holy Ghost; never serve mankind.

7.   SINCERITY   To be sincere is to remember that I am I, and that the other man is not me.

8.   JUSTICE   The only justice is to follow the sincere intuition of the soul, angry or gentle. Anger is just, and pity is just, but judgment is never just.

9.   MODERATION  Beware of absolutes. There are many gods.

10.   CLEANLINESS  Don't be too clean. It impoverishes the blood.

11.   TRANQUILLITY  The soul has many emotions, many gods come and go. Try and find your deepest issue, in every confusion, and abide by that. Obey the man in whom you recognize the Holy Ghost; command when your honour comes to command.

12.   CHASTITY   Never "use" venery at all. Follow your passional impulse, if it be answered in the other being; but never have any motive in mind, neither off-spring nor health nor even pleasure, nor even service. Only know that "venery" is of the great gods. An offering-up of yourself to the very great gods, the dark ones, and nothing else.

13.   HUMILITY   See all men and women according to the Holy Ghost that is within them. Never yield before the barren.

There's my list. I have been trying dimly to realize it for a long time, and only America and old Benjamin have at last goaded me into trying to formulate it.

And now I, at least, know why I can't stand Benjamin. He tries to take away my wholeness and my dark forest, my freedom. For how can any man be free, without an illimitable background? And Benjamin tries to shove me into a barbed-wire paddock and make me grow potatoes or Chicagoes.

And how can I be free, without gods that come and go? But Benjamin won't let anything exist except my useful fellow-men, and I'm sick of them; as for his Godhead, his Providence, He is Head of nothing except a vast heavenly store that keeps every imaginable line of goods, from victrolas to cat-o-nine tails.

And how can any man be free without a soul of his own, that he believes in and won't sell at any price? But Benjamin doesn't let me have a soul of my own. He says I am nothing but a servant of mankind—galley-slave I call it—and if I don't get my wages here below—that is, if Mr. Pierpont Morgan or Mr. Nosey Hebrew or the grand United States Government, the great US, US or SOMEOFUS, manages to scoop in my bit along with their lump— why, never mind, I shall get my wages HEREAFTER.

Oh Benjamin! Oh Binjum! You do NOT suck me in any longer.

And why oh why should the snuff-coloured little trap have wanted to take us all in? Why did he do it?

Out of sheer human cussedness, in the first place. We do all like to get things inside a barbed-wire corral. Especially our fellow-men. We love to round them up inside the barbed-wire enclosure of FREEDOM, and make 'em work. *"Work, you free jewel,* WORK!" shouts the liberator, cracking his whip. Benjamin, I will not work. I do not choose to be a free democrat. I am absolutely a servant of my own Holy Ghost.

Sheer cussedness! But there was as well the salt of a subtler purpose. Benjamin was just in his eyeholes—to use an English vulgarism meaning he was just delighted—when he was at Paris judiciously milking money out of the French monarchy for the overthrow of all monarchy. If you want to ride your horse to somewhere you must put a bit in his mouth. And Benjamin wanted to ride his horse so that it would upset the whole apple-cart of the old masters. He wanted the whole European apple-cart upset. So he had to put a strong bit in the mouth of his ass.

"Henceforth be masterless."

That is, he had to break-in the human ass completely, so that much more might be broken, in the long run. For the moment it was the British Government that had to have a hole knocked in it. The first real hole it ever had: the breach of the American rebellion.

Benjamin, in his sagacity, knew that the breaking of the old world was a long process. In the depths of his own under-consciousness he hated England, he hated Europe, he hated the whole corpus of the European being. He wanted to be American. But you can't change your nature and mode of consciousness like changing your shoes. It is a gradual shedding. Years must go by, and centuries must elapse before you have finished. Like a son escaping from the domination of his parents. The escape is not just one rupture. It is a long and half-secret process.

So with the American. He was a European when he first went over the Atlantic. He is in the main a recreant European still. From Benjamin Franklin to Woodrow Wilson may be a long stride, but it is a stride along the same road. There is no new road. The same old road, become dreary and futile. Theoretic and materialistic.

Why then did Benjamin set up this dummy of a perfect citizen as a pattern to America? Of course he did it in perfect good faith, as far as he knew. He thought it simply was the true ideal. But what we *think* we do is not very important. We never really know what we are doing. Either we are materialistic instruments, like Benjamin or we move in the gesture of creation, from our deepest self, usually unconscious. We are only the actors, we are never wholly the authors of our own deeds or works. It is the author, the unknown inside us or outside us. The best we can do is to try to hold ourselves in unison with the deeps which are inside us. And the worst we can do is to try to have things our own way, when we run counter to IT, and in the long run get our knuckles rapped for our presumption.

So Benjamin contriving money out of the Court of France. He was contriving the first steps of the overthrow of all Europe, France included. You can never have a new thing without breaking an old. Europe happens to be the old thing. America, unless the people in America assert themselves too much in opposition to the inner gods, should be the new thing. The new thing is the death of the old. But you can't cut the throat of an epoch. You've got to steal the life from it through several centuries.

And Benjamin worked for this both directly and indirectly. Directly, at the Court of France, making a small but very dangerous hole in the side of England, through which hole Europe has by now almost bled to death. And indirectly in Philadelphia, setting up this unlovely, snuff-coloured little ideal, or automaton, of a pattern American. The pattern American, this dry, moral, utilitarian little democrat, has done more to ruin the old Europe than any Russian nihilist. He has done it by slow attrition, like a son who has stayed at home and obeyed his parents, all the while silently hating their authority, and silently, in his soul, destroying not only their authority but their whole existence. For the American spiritually stayed at home in Europe. The spiritual home of America was and still is Europe. This is the galling bondage, in spite of several billions of heaped-up gold. Your heaps of gold are only so many muck-heaps, America, and will remain so till you become a reality to yourselves.

All this Americanizing and mechanizing has been for the purpose of overthrowing the past. And now look at America, tangled in her own barbed wire, and mastered by her own machines. Absolutely got down by her own barbed wire of shalt-nots, and shut up fast in her own "productive" machines like millions of squirrels running in millions of cages. It is just a farce.

Now is your chance, Europe. Now let Hell loose and get your own back, and paddle your own canoe on a new sea, while clever America lies on her muck-heaps of gold, strangled in her own barbed-wire of shalt-not ideals and shalt-not moralisms. While she goes out to work like millions of squirrels in millions of cages. Production!

Let Hell loose, and get your own back, Europe!

## STUDY QUESTIONS

1.  Clearly, Franklin and Lawrence do not think alike. Nor do they write alike. What are the most obvious differences in their styles? Does the century in which each man lived, by itself, account for the man and his style?

*figure speech based resemblance literal to implied subject.*

*comparison figure speech*

*symbolized*

2.  Franklin used figurative language infrequently. Lawrence used it often. Is the effectiveness of Lawrence's similes and metaphors diminished by the frequency of their occurrence?

3.  For what reasons and in what ways does Lawrence play with the word *venery?* ← *intercourse*

4.  How different are the interpretations which Franklin and Lawrence place on the virtues of Silence, Moderation, and Tranquillity?

5.  According to Lawrence, what motivated Franklin to spring his "snuff-coloured little trap" on us? *Cussedness, wanted NEW*

# Harvey Cox

# SEX AND SECULARIZATION

Harvey Cox (1929–      ) was born in Chester County, Pennsylvania. He received his B.A. (1951) from the University of Pennsylvania, his B.D. (1955) from Yale Divinity School, and his Ph.D. (1963) from Harvard University. Cox has been associated with Oberlin College and the Andover Newton Theological School, but is presently Professor of Divinity at Harvard Divinity School. Among his books are *Festivity and Fantasy* (1960), *God's Revolution and Man's Responsibility* (1965), and *On Not Leaving It to the Snake* (1967). *The Secular City* (1965) made him one of the most influential voices of the 60's. Cox has contributed to the *Christian Century*, the *Baptist Leader, Commonweal, Harper's, Life, Look*, and *Playboy*. An ordained minister of the American Baptist Church, he has been reported wearing a "Jesus-was-a-dropout" button and as calling Vietnam "our own Guernica."

No ASPECT of human life seethes with so many unexorcised demons as does sex. No human activity is so hexed by superstition, so haunted by residual tribal lore, and so harassed by socially induced fear. Within the breast of urban-secular man, a toe-to-toe struggle still rages between his savage and his bourgeois fore-bears. Like everything else, the images of sex which informed tribal and town society are expiring along with the eras in which they arose. The erosion of traditional values and the disappearance of accepted modes of behavior have left contemporary man free, but somewhat rudderless. Abhoring a vacuum, the mass media have rushed in to supply a new code and a new set of behavioral prototypes. They appeal to the unexorcised demons. Nowhere is the persistence of mythical and metalogical denizens more obvious than in sex, and the shamans of sales do their best to nourish them. Nowhere is the humanization of life more frustrated. Nowhere is a clear word of exorcism more needed.

How is the humanization of sex impeded? First it is thwarted by the parading of cultural-identity images for the sexually dispossessed, to make money. These images become the tyrant gods of the secular society, undercutting its liberation from religion and transforming it into a kind of neotribal culture. Second, the authentic secularization of sex is checkmated by an anxious clinging to the sexual standards of the town, an era so recent and yet so different from ours that simply to transplant its sexual ethos into our situation is to invite hypocrisy of the worst degree.

Let us look first at the spurious sexual models conjured up for our anxious society by the sorcerers of the mass media and the advertising guild. Like all pagan deities, these come in pairs—the god and his consort. For our purposes they are best symbolized by The Playboy and Miss America, the Adonis and Aphrodite of a leisure-consumer society which still seems unready to venture into full postreligious maturity and freedom. The Playboy and Miss America represent The Boy and The Girl. They incorporate a vision of life. They function as religious phenomena and should be exorcised and exposed.

## The Residue of Tribalism

Let us begin with Miss America. In the first century B.C., Lucretius wrote this description of the pageant of Cybele:

Adorned with emblem and crown . . . she is carried in awe-inspiring state. Tight-stretched tambourines and hollow cymbals thunder all round to the stroke of open hands, hollow pipes stir with Phrygian strain. . . . She rides in procession through great cities and mutely enriches mortals with a blessing not expressed in words. They straw all her path with brass and silver, presenting her with bounteous alms, and scatter over her a snow-shower of roses.[1]

[1] This is quoted from Lucretius ii, 608f. in T. R. Glover, *The Conflict of Religions in the Early Roman Empire* (Boston: Beacon, 1960), p. 20. It was originally published in 1909 by Methuen & Co. Ltd.

Now compare this with the annual twentieth-century Miss America pageant in Atlantic City, New Jersey. Spotlights probe the dimness like votive tapers, banks of flowers exude their varied aromas, the orchestra blends feminine strings and regal trumpets. There is a hushed moment of tortured suspense, a drumroll, then the climax—a young woman with carefully prescribed anatomical proportions and exemplary "personality" parades serenely with scepter and crown to her throne. At TV sets across the nation throats tighten and eyes moisten. "There she goes, Miss America————" sings the crooner. "There she goes, your ideal." A new queen in America's emerging cult of The Girl has been crowned.

Is it merely illusory or anachronistic to discern in the multiplying pageants of the Miss America, Miss Universe, Miss College Queen type a residuum of the cults of the pre-Christian fertility goddesses? Perhaps, but students of the history of religions have become less prone in recent years to dismiss the possibility that the cultural behavior of modern man may be significantly illuminated by studying it in the perspective of the mythologies of bygone ages. After all, did not Freud initiate a revolution in social science by utilizing the venerable myth of Oedipus to help make sense out of the strange behavior of his Viennese contemporaries? Contemporary man carries with him, like his appendix and his fingernails, vestiges of his tribal and pagan past.

In light of this fertile combination of insights from modern social science and the history of religions, it is no longer possible to see in the Miss America pageant merely an over-publicized prank foisted on us by the advertising industry. It certainly is this, but it is also much more. It represents the mass cultic celebration, complete with a rich variety of ancient ritual embellishments, of the growing place of The Girl in the collective soul of America.

This young woman—though she is no doubt totally ignorant of the fact —symbolizes something beyond herself. She symbolizes The Girl, the primal image, the One behind the many. Just as the Virgin appears in many guises—as our Lady of Lourdes or of Fatima or of Guadalupe—but is always recognizably the Virgin, so with The Girl.

The Girl is also the omnipresent icon of consumer society. Selling beer, she is folksy and jolly. Selling gems, she is chic and distant. But behind her various theophanies she remains recognizably The Girl. In Miss America's glowingly healthy smile, her openly sexual but officially virginal figure, and in the name-brand gadgets around her, she personifies the stunted aspirations and ambivalent fears of her culture. "There she goes, your ideal."

Miss America stands in a long line of queens going back to Isis, Ceres, and Aphrodite. Everything from the elaborate sexual taboos surrounding her person to the symbolic gifts at her coronation hints at her ancient ancestry. But the real proof comes when we find that the function served by The Girl in our culture is just as much a "religious" one as that served by Cybele in hers. The functions are identical—to provide a secure personal "identity" for initiates and to sanctify a particular value structure.

Let us look first at the way in which The Girl confers a kind of identity on her initiates. Simone de Beauvoir says in *The Second Sex* that "no one is *born* a woman." [2] One is merely born a female, and *"becomes* a woman" according to the models and meanings provided by the civilization. During the classical Christian centuries, it might be argued, the Virgin Mary served in part as this model. With the Reformation and especially with the Puritans, the place of Mary within the symbol system of the Protestant countries was reduced or eliminated. There are those who claim that this excision constituted an excess of zeal that greatly impoverished Western culture, an impoverishment from which it has never recovered. Some would even claim that the alleged failure of American novelists to produce a single great heroine (we have no Phaedra, no Anna Karenina) stems from this self-imposed lack of a central feminine ideal.

Without entering into this fascinating discussion, we can certainly be sure that, even within modern American Roman Catholicism, the Virgin Mary provides an identity image for few American girls. Where then do they look for the "model" Simone de Beauvoir convincingly contends they need? For most, the prototype of femininity seen in their mothers, their friends, and in the multitudinous images to which they are exposed on the mass media is what we have called The Girl.

In his significant monograph *Identity and the Life Cycle,* Erik Erikson reminds us that the child's identity is not modeled simply on the parent but on the parent's "super-ego." [3] Thus in seeking to forge her own identity the young girl is led beyond her mother to her mother's ideal image, and it is here that what Freud called "the ideologies of the superego . . . the traditions of the race and the people" become formative. It is here also that The Girl functions, conferring identity on those for whom she is—perhaps never completely consciously—the tangible incarnation of womanhood.

To describe the mechanics of this complex psychological process by which the fledgling American girl participates in the life of The Girl and thus attains a woman's identity would require a thorough description of American adolescence. There is little doubt, however, that such an analysis would reveal certain striking parallels to the "savage" practices by which initiates in the mystery cults shared in the magical life of their god.

For those inured to the process, the tortuous nightly fetish by which the young American female pulls her hair into tight bunches secured by metal clips may bear little resemblance to the incisions made on their arms by cer-

[2] Simone de Beauvoir, *The Second Sex* (New York: Knopf, 1953; London: Cape), p. 41.

[3] Erik Erikson, *Identity and the Life Cycle* (New York: International University Press, 1959).

tain African tribesmen to make them resemble their totem, the tiger. But to
an anthropologist comparing two ways of attempting to resemble the holy
one, the only difference might appear to be that with the Africans the torture
is over after initiation, while with the American it has to be repeated every
night, a luxury only a culture with abundant leisure can afford.

In turning now to an examination of the second function of The Girl—
supporting and portraying a value system—a comparison with the role of
the Virgin in the twelfth and thirteenth centuries may be helpful. Just as the
Virgin exhibited and sustained the ideals of the age that fashioned Chartres
Cathedral, as Henry Adams saw, so The Girl symbolizes the values and aspirations of a consumer society. (She is crowned not in the political capital,
remember, but in Atlantic City or Miami Beach, centers associated with leisure and consumption.) And she is not entirely incapable of exploitation. If
men sometimes sought to buy with gold the Virgin's blessings on their questionable causes, so The Girl now dispenses her charismatic favor on
watches, refrigerators, and razor blades—for a price. Though The Girl has
built no cathedrals, without her the colossal edifice of mass persuasion
would crumble. Her sharply stylized face and figure beckon us from every
magazine and TV channel, luring us toward the beatific vision of a consumer's paradise.

The Girl is *not* the Virgin. In fact she is a kind of anti-Madonna. She
reverses most of the values traditionally associated with the Virgin—
poverty, humility, sacrifice. In startling contrast, particularly, to the biblical portrait of Mary in Luke 1:46–55, The Girl has nothing to do with filling the hungry with "good things," hawking instead an endless proliferation
of trivia on TV spot commercials. The Girl exalts the mighty, extols the
rich, and brings nothing to the hungry but added despair. So The Girl does
buttress and bring into personal focus a value system, such as it is. In both
social and psychological terms, The Girl, whether or not she is really a goddess, certainly acts that way.

Perhaps the most ironic element in the rise of the cult of The Girl is that
Protestantism has almost completely failed to notice it, while Roman Catholics have at least given some evidence of sensing its significance. In some
places, for instance, Catholics are forbidden to participate in beauty pageants, a ruling not entirely inspired by prudery. It is ironic that Protestants
have traditionally been most opposed to lady cults while Catholics have
managed to assimilate more than one at various points in history.

If we are correct in assuming that The Girl *functions* in many ways as a
goddess, then the cult of The Girl demands careful Protestant theological
criticism. Anything that functions, even in part, as a god when it is in fact
not God, is an idol. When the Reformers and their Puritan offspring criticized the cult of Mary it was not because they were anti-feminist. They opposed anything—man, woman, or beast (or dogma or institution)—that

usurped in the slightest the prerogatives that belonged alone to God Almighty. As Max Weber has insisted, when the prophets of Israel railed against fertility cults, they had nothing against fertility. It is not against sexuality but against a cult that protest is needed. Not, as it were, against the beauty but against the pageant.

Thus the Protestant objection to the present cult of The Girl must be based on the realization that The Girl is an *idol*. She functions as the source of value, the giver of personal identity. But the values she mediates and the identity she confers are both spurious. Like every idol she is ultimately a creation of our own hands and cannot save us. The values she represents as ultimate satisfactions—mechanical comfort, sexual success, unencumbered leisure—have no ultimacy. They lead only to endless upward mobility, competitive consumption, and anxious cynicism. The devilish social insecurities from which she promises to deliver us are, alas, still there, even after we have purified our breaths, our skins, and our armpits by applying her sacred oils. She is a merciless goddess who draws us farther and farther into the net of accelerated ordeals of obeisance. As the queen of commodities in an expanding economy, the fulfillment she promises must always remain just beyond the tips of our fingers.

Why has Protestantism kept its attention obsessively fastened on the development of Mariolatry in Catholicism and not noticed the sinister rise of this vampirelike cult of The Girl in our society? Unfortunately, it is due to the continuing incapacity of theological critics to recognize the religious significance of cultural phenomena outside the formal religious system itself. But the rise of this new cult reminds us that the work of the reformer is never done. Man's mind is indeed—as Luther said—a factory busy making idols. The Girl is a far more pervasive and destructive influence than the Virgin, and it is to her and her omnipresent altars that we should be directing our criticism.

Besides sanctifying a set of phony values, The Girl compounds her noxiousness by maiming her victims in a Procrustean bed of uniformity. This is the empty "identity" she panders. Take the Miss America pageant, for example. Are these virtually indistinguishable specimens of white, middle-class postadolescence really the best we can do? Do they not mirror the ethos of a mass-production society, in which genuine individualism somehow mars the clean, precision-tooled effect? Like their sisters, the finely calibrated Rockettes, these meticulously measured and pretested "beauties" lined up on the Boardwalk bear an ominous similarity to the faceless retinues of goose-steppers and the interchangeable mass exercisers of explicitly totalitarian societies. In short, *who* says this is beauty?

The caricature becomes complete in the Miss Universe contest, when Miss Rhodesia is a blonde, Miss South Africa is white, and Oriental girls with a totally different tradition of feminine beauty are forced to display their thighs and appear in spike heels and Catalina swim suits. Miss Universe is as universal as an American adman's stereotype of what beauty should be.

The truth is that The Girl can*not* bestow the identity she promises. She forces her initiates to torture themselves with starvation diets and beauty-parlor ordeals, but still cannot deliver the satisfactions she holds out. She is young, but what happens when her followers, despite added hours in the boudoir, can no longer appear young? She is happy and smiling and loved. What happens when, despite all the potions and incantations, her disciples still feel the human pangs of rejection and loneliness? Or what about all the girls whose statistics, or "personality" (or color) do not match the authoritative "ideal"?

After all, it is God—not The Girl—who is God. He is the center and source of value. He liberates men and women from the bland uniformity of cultural deities so that they may feast on the luxurious diversity of life He has provided. The identity He confers frees men from all pseudo-identities to be themselves, to fulfill their human destinies regardless whether their faces or figures match some predetermined abstract "ideal." As His gift, sex is freed from both fertility cults and commercial exploitation to become the thoroughly human thing He intended. And since it is one of the last items we have left that is neither prepackaged nor standardized, let us not sacrifice it too hastily on the omnivorous altar of Cybele.

The Playboy, illustrated by the monthly magazine of that name, does for the boys what Miss America does for the girls. Despite accusations to the contrary, the immense popularity of this magazine is not solely attributable to pin-up girls. For sheer nudity its pictorial art cannot compete with such would-be competitors as *Dude* and *Escapade*. *Playboy* appeals to a highly mobile, increasingly affluent group of young readers, mostly between eighteen and thirty, who want much more from their drugstore reading than bosoms and thighs. They need a total image of what it means to be a man. And Mr. Hefner's *Playboy* has no hesitation in telling them.

Why should such a need arise? David Riesman has argued that the responsibility for character formation in our society has shifted from the family to the peer group and to the mass-media peer-group surrogates.[4] Things are changing so rapidly that one who is equipped by his family with inflexible, highly internalized values becomes unable to deal with the accelerated pace of change and with the varying contexts in which he is called upon to function. This is especially true in the area of consumer values toward which the "other-directed person" is increasingly oriented.

Within the confusing plethora of mass media signals and peer-group

[4] David Riesman, *The Lonely Crowd* (New Haven: Yale University Press, 1950; Harmondsworth, Middlesex: Penguin).

values, *Playboy* fills a special need. For the insecure young man with newly acquired free time and money who still feels uncertain about his consumer skills, *Playboy* supplies a comprehensive and authoritative guidebook to this forbidding new world to which he now has access. It tells him not only who to be; it tells him *how* to be it, and even provides consolation outlets for those who secretly feel that they have not quite made it.

In supplying for the other-directed consumer of leisure both the normative identity image and the means for achieving it, *Playboy* relies on a careful integration of copy and advertising material. The comic book that appeals to a younger generation with an analogous problem skillfully intersperses illustrations of incredibly muscled men and excessively mammalian women with advertisements for body-building gimmicks and foam-rubber brassière supplements. Thus the thin-chested comic-book readers of both sexes are thoughtfully supplied with both the ends and the means for attaining a spurious brand of maturity. *Playboy* merely continues the comic-book tactic for the next age group. Since within every identity crisis, whether in teens or twenties, there is usually a sexual-identity problem, *Playboy* speaks to those who desperately want to know what it means to be a man, and more specifically a *male,* in today's world.

Both the image of man and the means for its attainment exhibit a remarkable consistency in *Playboy*. The skilled consumer is cool and unruffled. He savors sports cars, liquor, high fidelity, and book-club selections with a casual, unhurried aplomb. Though he must certainly *have* and *use* the latest consumption item, he must not permit himself to get too attached to it. The style will change and he must always be ready to adjust. His persistent anxiety that he may mix a drink incorrectly, enjoy a jazz group that is passé, or wear last year's necktie style is comforted by an authoritative tone in *Playboy* beside which papal encyclicals sound irresolute.

"Don't hesitate," he is told, "this assertive, self-assured weskit is what every man of taste wants for the fall season." Lingering doubts about his masculinity are extirpated by the firm assurance that "real men demand this ruggedly masculine smoke" (cigar ad). Though "the ladies will swoon for you, no matter what they promise, don't give them a puff. This cigar is for men only." A fur-lined canvas field jacket is described as "the most masculine thing since the cave man." What to be and how to be it are both made unambiguously clear.

Since being a male necessitates some kind of relationship to females, *Playboy* fearlessly confronts this problem too, and solves it by the consistent application of the same formula. Sex becomes one of the items of leisure activity that the knowledgeable consumer of leisure handles with his characteristic skill and detachment. The girl becomes a desirable—indeed an indispensable—"Playboy accessory."

In a question-answering column entitled "The Playboy Adviser," queries about smoking equipment (how to break in a meerschaum pipe), cocktail preparation (how to mix a Yellow Fever), and whether or not to wear suspenders with a vest alternate with questions about what to do with girls who complicate the cardinal principle of casualness either by suggesting marriage or by some other impulsive gesture toward a permanent relationship. The infallible answer from the oracle never varies: sex must be contained, at all costs, within the entertainment-recreation area. Don't let her get "serious."

After all, the most famous feature of the magazine is its monthly fold-out photo of a *play*mate. She is the symbol par excellence of recreational sex. When playtime is over, the playmate's function ceases, so she must be made to understand the rules of the game. As the crew-cut young man in a *Playboy* cartoon says to the rumpled and disarrayed girl he is passionately embracing, "Why speak of love at a time like this?"

The magazine's fiction purveys the same kind of severely departmentalized sex. Although the editors have recently dressed up the *Playboy* contents with contributions by Hemingway, Bemelmans, and even a Chekhov translation, the regular run of stories relies on a repetitive and predictable formula. A successful young man, either single or somewhat less than ideally married—a figure with whom readers have no difficulty identifying—encounters a gorgeous and seductive woman who makes no demands on him except sex. She is the prose duplication of the cool-eyed but hot-blooded playmate of the fold-out.

Drawing heavily on the fantasy life of all young Americans, the writers utilize for their stereotyped heroines the hero's schoolteacher, his secretary, an old girl friend, or the girl who brings her car into the garage where he works. The happy issue is always a casual but satisfying sexual experience with no entangling alliances whatever. Unlike the women he knows in real life, the *Playboy* reader's fictional girl friends know their place and ask for nothing more. They present no danger of permanent involvement. Like any good accessory, they are detachable and disposable.

Many of the advertisements reinforce the sex-accessory identification in another way—by attributing female characteristics to the items they sell. Thus a full-page ad for the MG assures us that this car is not only "the smoothest pleasure machine" on the road and that having one is a "love-affair," but most important, "you drive it—it doesn't drive you." The ad ends with the equivocal question "Is it a date?" [5]

*Playboy* insists that its message is one of liberation. Its gospel frees us from captivity to the puritanical "hatpin brigade." It solemnly crusades for "frankness" and publishes scores of letters congratulating it for its unblush-

[5] This whole fusing of sex and machine symbols in contemporary mass media was once brilliantly explored by Marshall McCluhan in *The Mechanical Bride*, now out of print.

ing "candor." Yet the whole phenomenon of which *Playboy* is only a part vividly illustrates the awful fact of a new kind of tyranny.

Those liberated by technology and increased prosperity to new worlds of leisure now become the anxious slaves of dictatorial tastemakers. Obsequiously waiting for the latest signal on what is cool and what is awkward, they are paralyzed by the fear that they may hear pronounced on them that dread sentence occasionally intoned by "The Playboy Adviser": "You goofed!" Leisure is thus swallowed up in apprehensive competitiveness, its liberating potential transformed into a self-destructive compulsion to consume only what is *à la mode. Playboy* mediates the Word of the most high into one section of the consumer world, but it is a word of bondage, not of freedom.

Nor will *Playboy*'s synthetic doctrine of man stand the test of scrutiny. Psychoanalysts constantly remind us how deep-seated sexuality is in the human being. But if they didn't remind us, we would soon discover it ourselves anyway. Much as the human male might like to terminate his relationship with a woman as he would snap off the stereo, or store her for special purposes like a camel's-hair jacket, it really can't be done. And any one with a modicum of experience with women knows it can't be done. Perhaps this is the reason *Playboy*'s readership drops off so sharply after the age of thirty.

*Playboy* really feeds on the existence of a repressed fear of involvement with women, which for various reasons is still present in many otherwise adult Americans. So *Playboy*'s version of sexuality grows increasingly irrelevant as authentic sexual maturity is achieved.

The male identity crisis to which *Playboy* speaks has at its roots a deep-set fear of sex, a fear that is uncomfortably combined with fascination. *Playboy* strives to resolve this antinomy by reducing the proportions of sexuality, its power and its passion, to a packageable consumption item. Thus in *Playboy*'s iconography the nude woman symbolizes total sexual accessibility but demands nothing from the observer. "You drive it—it doesn't drive you." The terror of sex, which cannot be separated from its ecstasy, is dissolved. But this futile attempt to reduce the *mysterium tremendum* of the sexual fails to solve the problem of being a man. For sexuality is the basic form of all human relationship, and therein lies its terror and its power.

Karl Barth has called this basic relational form of man's life *Mitmensch,* co-humanity.[6] This means that becoming fully human, in this case a human male, requires not having the other totally exposed to me and my purposes —while I remain uncommitted—but exposing myself to the risk of encounter with the other by reciprocal self-exposure. The story of man's refusal so to be exposed goes back to the story of Eden and is expressed by man's desire to control the other rather than to *be with* the other. It is basically the fear to be one's self, a lack of the "courage to be."

[6] Karl Barth, *Church Dogmatics* (Edinburgh: T & T Clark, 1957), II/2.

Thus any theological critique of *Playboy* that focuses on its "lewdness" will misfire completely. *Playboy* and its less successful imitators are not "sex magazines" at all. They are basically antisexual. They dilute and dissipate authentic sexuality by reducing it to an accessory, by keeping it at a safe distance.

It is precisely because these magazines are antisexual that they deserve the most searching kind of theological criticism. They foster a heretical doctrine of man, one at radical variance with the biblical view. For *Playboy*'s man, others—especially women—are *for* him. They are his leisure accessories, his playthings. For the Bible, man only becomes fully man by being *for* the other.

Moralistic criticisms of *Playboy* fail because its antimoralism is one of the few places in which *Playboy* is right. But if Christians bear the name of One who was truly man because He was totally *for* the other, and if it is in Him that we know who God is and what human life is for, then we must see in *Playboy* the latest and slickest episode in man's continuing refusal to be fully human.

Freedom for mature sexuality comes to man only when he is freed from the despotic powers which crowd and cower him into fixed patterns of behavior. Both Miss America and The Playboy illustrate such powers. When they determine man's sexual life, they hold him in captivity. They prevent him from achieving maturity. They represent the constant danger of relapsing into tribal thralldom which always haunts the secular society, a threat from which the liberating, secularizing word of the Gospel repeatedly recalls it.

STUDY QUESTIONS

1. Where is the thesis sentence for this section of "Sex and Secularization"?

2. How does the metaphorical language of the first paragraph prepare the reader for the discussion which follows? How is the metaphor related to the subtitle, "The Residue of Tribalism"? Is the basic metaphor extended throughout the essay?

3. What two "religious" functions does Miss America fulfill? Are these functions stated or implied? How much of the discussion of The Girl is related to these functions?

4. According to Cox, what is the reason for *Playboy*'s immense popularity? Does *Playboy* still run stories which rely on "a repetitious and predictable formula"?

5.  Why does Cox call *Playboy*'s doctrine of man "synthetic"? Why does he feel *Playboy*'s version of sexuality "grows increasingly irrelevant"? And why does he conclude that *Playboy* is "basically antisexual"?

*Joseph Wood Krutch*

# STRAIGHT MEN IN A CROOKED WORLD

Joseph Wood Krutch (1893–      ) was born in Knoxville, Tennessee. He received his B.A. (1915) from the University of Tennessee and his M.A. (1916) and Ph.D. (1932) from Columbia University. He has taught English, journalism, and drama at Columbia; lectured at the New School for Social Research; served as drama critic for the *Nation;* and acted as president of the New York Drama Critics Circle. Krutch now lives in Tucson, Arizona, and is a trustee of the Arizona–Sonora Desert Museum. He has edited the works of William Congreve, Eugene O'Neill, Marcel Proust, and Thomas Gray, and written critical studies of Restoration comedy, and of Samuel Johnson, Edgar Allan Poe, and Henry David Thoreau. Other books include *The Modern Temper* (1929), *The Desert Year* (1952), *The Measure of Man* (1954), *Grand Canyon* (1958), and the revised *Baja California, and the Geography of Hope* (1969).

$S$OME YEARS ago a distinguished playwright told me how he had taken his East Side mother-in-law to see Maurice Evans in *Richard III*. The old lady—whose experience with both literature and the theatre was extremely limited—listened intently in silence for half an hour, then waved a derisive thumb in the direction of the mellifluously complaining Richard and announced firmly: "I don't sympathize."

Now this was, of course, a fine tribute to the purely dramatic skill of Shakespeare. He had provoked the reaction he aimed at without any direct indication of what his own attitude was. I remember the anecdote at the moment for a simple reason. "I don't sympathize" vigorously sums up my own response to certain modern Richards, namely those who enlarge with too much self-pity upon their "alienation" from modern society, modern man and, indeed, from the universe as a whole. On the one hand I find myself ready to agree with a good deal of their criticism; on the other I am irritated by their chronic reaction to the things we both abhor.

To take the most obvious and least significant case, consider the beatniks. I dislike—almost if not quite as much as they do—the dominant middle-class and organization-man concept of the Good Life. Although we can't all be philosophers, scholars, artists or monks, I agree that too many moderns aspire to nothing more than the "status symbols" that money can buy, and far too few to what George N. Shuster recently defined as the ultimate aim of education: "sharing the life of the scholar, poet and saint." But to respond to this situation by taking a shot of heroin and driving a car at ninety miles an hour seems unlikely either to improve society or, what is more relevant, lead to a Good Life.

Sympathetic interpreters of the beatniks have described them as "taking a revenge on society." For example, the hero of a recent novel is described by a reviewer thus: "Seeing too well in a world dazed by the bomb, Renaud undertakes an alcoholic strike against humanity." But the phrase "an alcoholic strike," like "a revenge on society," seems to me merely comic. It suggests the popular saying about "biting off your nose to spite your face," that being precisely what some intellectuals (including many somewhat above the beatnik level) are doing—as though turning into a dope addict does not hurt oneself even more than it hurts anyone else. It seems only slightly less obvious that the more respectable intellectuals who devote themselves exclusively to exploring and exploiting their "alienation" are doing much the same thing. Surely it is more productive of personal happiness and even "more useful to society" to be a candle throwing its beams into a naughty world than a beatnik crying "revenge, revenge" from the gutter. We hear a great deal about the responsibility of society toward the individual. The individual also has a responsibility toward society. And if things are as bad as the alienated say, the only way one can discharge that responsibility is by being an honorable man.

I presume that this thesis hardly needs elaboration and is not likely to be contested outside beatnik circles. But a considerable number of the most talented novelists, poets, painters and composers of the present day reveal, even if they do not proclaim, their alienation; and it seems to me that their most frequent response is only less grotesque, not more fruitful, than that of the beatniks. Even granted, as most of them proclaim in some version of Yeats's often quoted words that "Things fall apart; the center cannot hold," is there still nothing for a wise man to do except take heroin with the beatniks or, as is usual among the alienated squares, elaborate in more and more complicated phrases their dark convictions?

To this question the hearty do-gooder will of course reply: "Why obviously the thing to do is to work for social improvement. Join the party of your choice and the church of your choice; be sure to register for all elections and attend the meetings of your local P.T.A." Without entering into any question concerning the ultimate effectiveness of such a method of employing one's time, it must be admitted that your alienated artist or philosopher is no more likely than a beatnik to undertake it. Let us suppose, therefore, that he has, like Thoreau, both "signed off" from the church and wished that he could as easily sign off from society as a whole. Of course he will be thoroughly disapproved of almost everywhere outside the circle of the completely alienated; but he might, like a few others besides Thoreau, find in this determination to stand alone the possibility of making for himself a private world from which he was *not* alienated, instead of devoting himself exclusively to the task of saying just how alienated he is. He could even find a few justifications formulated in the past for doing just what he has done.

I seem to remember somewhere in Plato the opinion that when times are thoroughly bad a wise man will merely stand by the wall. Similarly, it would appear from the *Meditations* of Marcus Aurelius that although the Emperor was no less aware than Yeats of a world in which "things fall apart," he spent relatively little time in either elaborating or bemoaning the lack of wisdom or virtue in society. He determined instead to cultivate them in himself. Then there is even a wholehearted defense of the mere slacker, which is quoted by Montaigne from one Theodorus who held that "It is not just that a wise man should risk his life for the good of his country and imperil wisdom for fools."

As I see it, the question is not so much whether the alienated would do better to imitate Marcus Aurelius rather than Baudelaire and Apollinaire, for it is a larger and, so many will think, an outrageous question. Is it possible that present-day civilization would be in some important respects better than it is if more people had thought less about how to improve society and more about how to improve themselves?

No doubt the medieval monk was too exclusively concerned with his private salvation. But we have gone to the other extreme and are so obsessed with the idea of society as a whole that it no longer seems quite respectable to seek even intellectual or spiritual self-improvement. I am not saying that we are, in actual fact, excessively unselfish. But the cant of the time requires that we should always be asking of any proposed good, "Can everybody have it?" or "Is it an answer to the general problem?" With astonishing regularity I get letters from people who comment on something I have written with a "Well that's the answer so far as you are concerned; I guess it could be the answer so far as I am concerned. But only the privileged, or the lucky, or the well educated, or the intelligent, or the whatnot, can do what you and I can. So what is the answer for society as a whole?"

No doubt it would be fine if we could find a universal formula for salvation. I would welcome a convincing one if I ever heard it. But I never have, and I see no reason why, this being true, the individual should not save himself so long as he is not doing so at somebody else's expense. After all, society is composed of individuals. It cannot be "saved" except insofar as the individuals who compose it are.

I am not preaching universal indifference to society and social action as the highest wisdom. I am saying simply that if and when one individual feels (as so many articulate people do seem to feel) that the world is hopeless, then it is wiser to see what one can do about oneself than to give up all hope of that also. "I came into this world," said Thoreau, "not primarily to make it better but to live in it be it good or bad." If you insist, you may soften that a little by substituting "exclusively" for "primarily," but the meaning will still point in the same direction. Or as the same argument was recently discussed in that excellent "little magazine" called *Manas:* "If an artist can find nothing but bad brushes to paint with, he will not dissipate all his energies leading a revolution against bad brushes—but will develop techniques which make it possible for him to paint with bad brushes. He may even discover things that bad brushes do better than good brushes. It is one thing to fight the good fight for good brushes, and another to start to paint."

During the thirties, when most intellectuals moved leftward, quite a number of those who confessed (at least to their friends) that they had embraced communism were nevertheless engaged in writing movies for Hollywood or advertisements for Madison Avenue, while at the same time professing to regard both the movies and advertising as poisonous exhalations from a deliquescent society. Often (and I report from my own experience) they justified themselves by saying that there was no use trying to be anything but rotten in a rotten society. Comes the revolution and we will all be decent. Meanwhile, since we live in an evil society, we submit to it without any bourgeois nonsense about merely personal decency.

Such an attitude is only a logical extreme of the one taken by those who may not completely renounce either personal integrity or personal happiness, but insist upon our duty to think primarily in terms of what can be done for "society," and who sink into despair if we do not know an answer. I will even go so far as to suggest the possibility that society may be in a bad way partly because we have laid so much stress on public education—to take one example—and so little upon self-education. (Perhaps it also has something to do with the fact that I have met "educators" who were not and made no effort to be educated themselves.)

"Philanthropy," so Thoreau wrote, "is almost the only virtue which is sufficiently appreciated by mankind. . . . The kind uncles and aunts of the race are more esteemed than its true spiritual fathers and mothers. I once heard a reverend lecturer on England, a man of learning and intelligence, after enumerating her scientific, literary and political worthies, Shakespeare, Bacon, Cromwell, Milton, Newton and others, speak next of her Christian heroes, whom, as if his profession required it of him, he elevated to a place far above all the rest, as the greatest of the great. They were Penn, Howard and Mrs. Fry. Everyone must feel the falsehood and cant of this. The last were not England's best men and women; only, perhaps, her best philanthropists." This is a tough-minded opinion. It is stated with characteristic exaggeration. But at least there is something to be said for those who do their best even though they do not see at the moment just what practical good it is going to do "for the common man."

After all the medieval monk did perform a service. Neither the God he served nor the learning he preserved counted for much in the world from which he had retired. But he did exemplify in himself virtues that might otherwise have ceased to exist entirely, and he did preserve learning that without him would have been lost.

What it all comes down to in practice is simply this: if you despair of the world, don't despair of yourself. And it is because so many of the alienated critics of our society with whose criticisms I agree seem unable to do anything of the sort that I find myself alienated from them also.

Thirty years ago when I published a book much more pessimistic than I could possibly write now, I received a good many letters that might have been boiled down to a sentence in one of them: "If these are your convictions why don't you go hang yourself?" The answer was, and has continued to be through all such changes of opinion as I have undergone, that there is a private world of thought and endeavor which society has never been able to take away from me.

Perhaps the most curious and shocking result of the exclusive stress upon social rather than upon private ethics is the disappearance of the concept of honor as distinct from that of morality. One of the differences between the two is simply that honor is relevant to the individual only. True, society may be more affected than some social scientists seem to think by the prevalence or scarcity of honor in the code of the individuals who make it up. But the man of honor always asks first whether or not an action would dishonor him personally, and he is not influenced by an argument that his dishonorable act would have no bad (perhaps even some good) effect upon society and is therefore "moral" even if dishonorable.

The world would not now be as profoundly shocked as it was a generation ago by the phrase "a scrap of paper." We are used to having promises so treated. But the Junkers were merely a little ahead of us in their willingness to believe that since the triumph of Germany would promote the advent of the superman, there was nothing immoral in a broken oath.

Many college students, so the pollsters tell us, see nothing wrong about cheating on examinations. "Everybody does it and it doesn't really *hurt* anyone."

In such statements it is easy to see a reasonable application of the two leading principles of ethics-without-absolutes-and-without-honor, which is sometimes called "socialized morality." These two leading principles are: (1) What everybody does must be permissible since the *mores* determine morality; and (2) "Wrong" can mean only "socially harmful."

If you believe all this and also that the only difference between, let us say, an honest man and a thief is the difference between a man who has been "conditioned" to act honestly and one who has not, then there isn't much basis for argument with the student opinion.

When some scandal breaks in government or journalism or business or broadcasting, the usual reaction of even that part of the public which is shocked by it is to say that it could not have happened if there had been adequate laws supervising this or that activity. But, usually, is it not equally true that it could not have happened if a whole group of men, often including the supposed guardians of public morality, had not been devoid of any sense of the meaning and importance of individual integrity? May one not go further and ask whether any amount of "social consciousness" and government control can make decent a society composed of people who have no conception of personal dignity and honor? It was a favorite and no doubt sound argument among early twentieth-century reformers that "playing the game" as the gentleman was supposed to play it was not enough. But has the time not come to add that it is, nevertheless, indispensable?

If the relevance of all this to the first part of the present discussion is not obvious, please allow me to dot the *i*'s. To those who believe that society is corrupt beyond redemption I propose the ancient but neglected concept of personal integrity, virtue and honor accompanied, if they feel it necessary, with the contempt and scorn recently advocated in a telling article in the [*American*] *Scholar* itself.

Those who hold that "social morality" is the only kind worth considering tend to assume that the end justifies the means. If a broken promise or a cynical invasion of a private right promotes "the greatest good of the greatest number" then it is an act of "higher morality." That seems to me a curiously inverted, soft-hearted and soft-headed Machiavellianism. The man of honor is reluctant to use dishonorable means no matter what ends seem to justify them. And he seems to me to be a safer member of society.

## STUDY QUESTIONS

1. Explain George N. Shuster's definition of the ultimate aim of education. Is that indeed the ultimate aim of education?

2. What responsibility *does* society have toward the individual? The individual toward society?

3. In recent years, what groups have been notably and noticeably alienated from society? The beats? The angry young men? The hippies? The yippies? Hell's Angels? SDS? Black Muslims? How has the behavior of these groups revealed their alienation?

4. Krutch feels that we are in a bad way partly because we have placed too much emphasis on public education and too little on self-education. Has public education contributed to the alienation of contemporary youth? How?

5. Is there anything wrong about cheating on examinations? If there is, who is wronged? If there isn't, what justifications for cheating can you suggest? How does your instructor feel about the matter? Should examinations be proctored?

*Time*

# ON BEING A CONTEMPORARY CHRISTIAN

"WHAT is bothering me is the question what Christianity really is, or indeed who Christ really is, for us today."

So wrote the young Lutheran Theologian Dietrich Bonhoeffer from his Berlin prison cell in April 1944, one year before he was executed by the SS for complicity in the plots against Hitler's life. It is a question that today—for more complicated reasons—concerns countless thousands of U.S. churchgoers, who see about them a Christianity in the midst of change, confusion and disarray.

For Roman Catholics, the religious revolution set loose by the Second Vatican Council has changed many traditional patterns of worship and thought, and seemingly unleashed a legion of priests, nuns and laymen who feel free to cast doubt on every article of defined dogma. Protestants too have been stunned by the spectacle of an Episcopal bishop openly denying the Trinity and the Virgin Birth, and ordained ministers teaching in seminaries proclaiming the news that God is dead. On the theological right, evangelical preachers summon believers back to a strict Biblical orthodoxy; on the left, angry young activists insist that to be a Christian is to be a revolutionary, and propose to substitute picket lines for prayer.

It is not really surprising that the churches should be sounding uncertain trumpets, or that Christians should be insecure as to the meaning and direction of their spiritual commitment. Undeniably, one of the most telling events of modern history has been a revolution in the relationship of religion to Western civilization. The churchgoer could once take comfort in the fact that he belonged to what was essentially a Christian society, in which the existence of an omnipotent God was the focus of ultimate meaning. No such security exists today, in a secular-minded culture that suggests the eclipse rather than the presence of God.

Science and technology have long since made it unnecessary to posit a creative Deity as a hypothesis to explain anything in the universe. From Marxists, existentialists and assorted humanists has come the persistent message that the idea of God is an intellectual bogy that prevents man from claiming his mature heritage of freedom. In the U.S., which probably has a higher percentage of regular Sunday churchgoers than any other nation on earth, the impact of organized Christianity appears to be on the wane. One problem for the future of the churches is the indifference and even hostility toward them on the part of the young. Even those drawn to the person of Christ chafe against outmoded rules, irrelevant sermons, dogmas that apparently have no personal meaning to a generation struggling to understand themselves, to grapple with such concrete issues as sex and social injustice.

### Also a Man

Undeniably, one major task of theology today is to define what it means to be a Christian in a secular society. For millions, of course, there is no real problem. Baptism and church membership are the external criteria of faith, and a true follower of Jesus is one who keeps his beliefs free from heresy and tries to live a decent, upright, moral life. Yet to the most thoughtful spokesmen of modern Christianity, these criteria are not only minimal, they are secondary and even somewhat irrelevant. Instead, they argue that faith is not an intellectual assent to a series of dogmatic propositions but a commitment of one's entire being; ethical concern is directed not primarily toward one's own life but toward one's neighbor and the world. The mortal sins, in this new morality, are not those of the flesh but those of society; more important than the evil man does to himself is the evil he does to his fellow man. "The Christian's role is to bear witness to God in man," says Jesuit

Clinical Psychologist Carlo Weber. "Jesus Christ is the wedding of the divine and the human. Being a Christian for me means bearing witness to the wedding of divinity and humanity, to love God and man—to be involved, therefore, in human affairs."

Although the churches have always taught that Christ was both God and man, Christians have hardly ever seemed to accept his humanity. Historically, preaching has emphasized the Risen Christ, who sits at the right hand of God, and will come in glory to the Last Judgment. This is a basic premise of faith, but it is equally true that Jesus was emphatically a man—a lowly carpenter who walked the earth of Palestine at a specific moment in human history, and whose death fulfilled Isaiah's prophesy of the Suffering Servant. Jesus, as Bonhoeffer memorably put it, was "the man for others."

Summing up his message to man, Jesus asked his followers to love God, and "thy neighbor as thyself." For centuries, Christians have seemed to emphasize the first of those commands—and all too frequently, when there was a conflict between the two, it was love of man that went by the boards. But Biblical scholars point out that the New Testament is a very secular book, and there is an unmistakable social concern in Jesus' moral teachings. In *Matthew 23,* for example, Jesus condemns as hypocrites the scribes and Pharisees who ostentatiously tithe their possessions but neglect "the weightier matters of the law, justice and mercy and faith."

## Christian & Atheist

There is nothing fundamentally new about the insight that Christian ethics are corporate rather than individualistic. The medieval monasteries, for example, were dedicated to serving their communities as well as to praising God in communal prayer; the Mennonites and Quakers have always emphasized brotherly love and peace rather than dogma. The difference is that theologians now take it for granted that Christian love is something that cannot be confined to the church but is directed toward all the world. The commitment of a man who follows Jesus is not to an institution, but to life itself.

Within the churches, there is considerably less agreement on how this commitment should be exercised. Christian radicals—such as the young firebrands who dominated the National Council of Churches' Conference on Church and Society in Detroit last fall—argue that the true follower of Jesus is the revolutionary, siding with forces and events that seek to overthrow established disorder. On the other hand, Protestant Theologian Hans-Joachim Margull of Hamburg University points out that it is not always so easy to identify the secular causes that Christians have a clear moral duty to support.

It is easy enough to argue that Christians have a God-given duty to work for racial equality, or for the eradication of hunger and disease in the world.

The strategies to be followed in achieving these goals do not so easily acquire universal assent. For that reason, Dean Jerald Brauer of the University of Chicago Divinity School argues that churches should not necessarily be engaged in trying to hand down specific solutions to social and political problems from the pulpit. Christian creativity in trying to solve these questions, he says, "won't be a case of the churches poking their noses into areas where they have no right to be. Churches may have no special answers, although they certainly have a responsibility to sensitize their people to the questions. But the answers will have to be worked out by the body politic."

What this means, in essence, is that a commitment to love in worldly life cannot be separated from faith in Christ, who demanded that commitment. One argument against trying to build Christianity on moral action alone is that Jesus' teachings, unlike those of, say, Confucius, make sense only when understood as counsels of perfection in obedience to God rather than as workable guidelines of behavior. The Rev. David H. C. Read, pastor of Manhattan's Madison Avenue Presbyterian Church, points out that in facing many problems of life the behavior of the Christian and the humanist might well be identical. Bertrand Russell and the Archbishop of Canterbury, for example, could equably serve on the same committee to improve housing. "The distinction is not in their action," Read argues. "It is in their motivation and ultimate conviction on the meaning of life." This suggests that the committed Christian who is immersed in the secular world will also be to some extent an anonymous Christian; his light will still shine before the world, but it will not be so easily identified.

Since faith is the reason for commitment, most churchmen regard the idea of a "Christian atheist" or a "Christian agnostic" as something of a contradiction in terms. "I can't see how it is possible to be a Christian atheist," says Episcopal Bishop James A. Pike, who has been accused of being just that by some of his fellow clerics. "You cannot attack the idea of an ultimate and at the same time accept Jesus as an ultimate." Swiss Catholic Theologian Hans Küng points out that "Jesus had no sense of himself without God. He made it clear that his radical commitment to men presupposed a radical commitment to God."

Nonetheless, theologians also acknowledge that only God is the final judge of who can rightly be considered a Christian. Austrian Jesuit Theologian Karl Rahner, for example, suggests that there is today "an invisible Christianity which does indeed possess the justification of sanctifying grace from God. A man belonging to this invisible Christianity may deny his Christianity or maintain that he does not know whether he is a Christian or not. Yet God may have chosen him in grace." Similarly, the late Protestant theologian Paul Tillich contrasted the "manifest church" of confessed believers with what he called the "latent church," whose membership included all men engaged with the ultimate realities of life.

## The Decline of Dogma

Since faith is primarily a way of life rather than a creed to be so proclaimed, it is not something that can be reduced to an articulated set of principles. In an age of ecumenical breakthrough and doctrinal pluralism, sectarian particularities of belief seem largely irrelevant and even a little quaint. What is important is not the doctrine of predestination, for example, but the mystery of man's relationship to God that lies behind it. A Christian must accept the Incarnation—but there is room for differing interpretations of Jesus' unique relationship to God. The Resurrection is, as St. Paul insisted, the cornerstone of faith; but how one defines this unique defiance of death is of less moment.

Even in the Roman Catholic Church, which has traditionally upheld the immutability of dogma, there is widespread recognition by theologians that all formulas of faith are man's frail and imperfect vessels for carrying God's truth, and are forever in need of reformulation. In the light of Christianity's need to respond to the human needs of the earth, many of these ancient formulas hardly seem worth rethinking. "The central axis of religious concern," notes Langdon Gilkey of the University of Chicago Divinity School, "has shifted from matters of ultimate 'salvation,' and of heaven or hell, to questions of the meaning, necessity, or usefulness of religion for this life." In other words, the theological task is to justify Christianity in this world— and let God take care of the next.

The faith commitment of the Christian also implies the need for allegiance to a church—or at least to some kind of community of faith. Theoretically, it may be possible for a Christian to survive without any institutional identity—but the majority of modern theologians would agree that to be "a man for others" there must be others to be with, and that faith is sustained by communal structure. Churchmen would also argue that there is nothing obsolete about the basic necessity for worship and prayer. "Liturgy must be an expression of something that is happening in the community," says the Rev. David Kirk, a Melchite Catholic priest who is founder of a unique interfaith center in Manhattan called Emmaus House. "Without worship, the community is a piece of rubbish." On the other hand, there is little doubt that the churches are in desperate need of new, this-worldly liturgies that reflect present needs rather than past glories.

## A Band of Soul Brothers

While a church—in the sense of a community—may be necessary for a viable Christian life, institutional or denominational churches are not. Today it would be hard to find an atheist whose criticism of religion is any more vociferous than the attack on the irrelevance, stagnation and nonutility of organized Christendom offered by its adherents. "Christianity is like a trip," muses Episcopal Bishop Edward Crowther, a Fellow of the Center for the Study of Democratic Institutions at Santa Barbara, Calif. "The church is like a travel agent with a lot of pictures in her office describing what it's like. But either she's never been there, or was there so long ago that she doesn't remember what it was all about."

Methodist Theologian Van Harvey suggests that the church should not be "a place where men come to be more pious. The church is a place of edification, where one comes to learn to be an honest-to-God person living in dialogue with others." Despite all the yearning for spirituality that may exist in the average American church, it is questionable how many churchgoers can and do live up to this ideal. The stratified irrelevance of the established parish, whether Catholic or Protestant, is a major reason for the growth of what Episcopal Chaplain Malcolm Boyd has dubbed "the underground church" —informal, *ad hoc* gatherings of Christians who cross over and above denominational lines to celebrate improvised Eucharists in each other's homes, and study Scripture or theology together.

To some theologians, the emergence of this underground church is a sign of spiritual health, a harbinger of renewal. To be sure, there is the possibility that these unstructured groups might coalesce into a new kind of gnostic sect—an elect that considers itself set apart from the erring mass of nominal believers. On the other hand, there is the far greater danger that institutional Christianity, without an extraordinary amount of reform, will end up as a monumental irrelevancy. Faced with a choice between the church in its present form and the underground cell, it is likely that a majority of Christian thinkers would opt for the small, unstructured community as a likely model for the future. Jesus never explicitly said that all men would be converted to believe in his word. Far more meaningful is his image of his followers as the "salt of the earth" and "the light of the world"—similes suggesting that the status of Christianity, until God's final reckoning, is properly that of a band of soul brothers rather than a numberless army.

Despite the visible health and prosperity of existing denominations, there is a considerable number of future-oriented theologians who feel that the church, in large parts of the world, is entering a stage of Diaspora—when, like Judaism, it will survive in the form of a scattered few, the hidden remnant. Strangely enough, there are any number of Christians who rejoice at this prospect rather than fear it. This is not because they want to see the fainthearted and the half convinced drift away into unbelief. Rather, they prefer that the choice of being Christian once again become openly, as Kierkegaard puts it, a leap of faith, an adult decision to serve as one of God's pilgrims on the road of life.

It is conceivable that Christianity is heading toward an era in which its

status will be akin to that of the despised minority who proclaimed faith in
the one God against the idolatry of the Roman Empire. To be sure, the
Christian burden in the future will be different from that of the past: less to
proclaim Jesus by word than to follow him in deed and loving service. It may
prove a perilous course, but the opportunity is great: the courage and zeal of
that first despised minority changed the history of the world.

## STUDY QUESTIONS

1.  Does the *TIME* essay answer the question raised in the introductory
    paragraph?

2.  What evidence does *TIME* provide for its statements that Christians have
    "hardly ever seemed to accept" the humanity of Christ, and that
    Christians have failed to love their neighbors as themselves?

3.  What are the implications of the words *to the most thoughtful* in the
    fifth paragraph?

4.  What is accomplished by the frequent quotations from scholars and
    theologians?

5.  What rhetorical devices are used to unify paragraphs? What transitional
    devices are used between paragraphs?

## *Jonathan Swift*

# AN ARGUMENT AGAINST
# ABOLISHING CHRISTIANITY

Jonathan Swift (1667–1745) is one of England's greatest prose writers. He
was born in Dublin, Ireland, and was educated there at Trinity College. The
fact that he took orders in the Church of England did not prevent him from
becoming one of the Tory propagandists. However, Queen Anne disap-

First published 1711.

proved of *A Tale of a Tub* (1704), and Swift was given the deanery of St. Patrick's, Dublin, instead of the English preferment he wanted. Among his now-classic works are *The Battle of the Books* (1704), *Gulliver's Travels* (1726), *A Modest Proposal* (1729), and *The Journal to Stella* (1766).

I AM very sensible what a weakness and presumption it is, to reason against the general humor and disposition of the world. I remember it was with great justice, and a due regard to the freedom both of the public and the press, forbidden upon severe penalties to write or discourse, or lay wagers against the Union, even before it was confirmed by parliament; because that was looked upon as a design, to oppose the current of the people, which, besides the folly of it, is a manifest breach of the fundamental law that makes this majority of opinion the voice of God. In like manner, and for the very same reasons, it may perhaps be neither safe nor prudent to argue against the abolishing of Christianity, at a juncture when all parties appear so unanimously determined upon the point, as we cannot but allow from their actions, their discourses, and their writings. However, I know not how, whether from the affectation of singularity, or the perverseness of human nature, but so it unhappily falls out, that I cannot be entirely of this opinion. Nay, although I were sure an order were issued for my immediate prosecution by the Attorney General, I should still confess that in the present posture of our affairs at home or abroad, I do not yet see the absolute necessity of extirpating the Christian religion from among us.

This perhaps may appear too great a paradox even for our wise and paradoxical age to endure; therefore I shall handle it with all tenderness, and with the utmost deference to that great and profound majority which is of another sentiment.

And yet the curious may please to observe, how much the genius of a nation is liable to alter in half an age. I have heard it affirmed for certain by some very old people, that the contrary opinion was even in their memories as much in vogue as the other is now; and, that a project for the abolishing of Christianity would then have appeared as singular, and been thought as absurd, as it would be at this time to write or discourse in its defense.

Therefore I freely own that all appearances are against me. The system of the Gospel, after the fate of other systems, is generally antiquated and exploded; and the mass or body of the common people, among whom it seems to have had its latest credit, are now grown as much ashamed of it as their betters; opinions, like fashions, always descending from those of quality to the middle sort, and thence to the vulgar, where at length they are dropped and vanish.

But here I would not be mistaken, and must therefore be so bold as to borrow a distinction from the writers on the other side, when they make a difference between nominal and real Trinitarians. I hope no reader imagines me so weak to stand up in the defense of *real* Christianity, such as used in primitive times (if we may believe the authors of those ages) to have an influence upon men's belief and actions. To offer at the restoring of that would indeed be a wild project; it would be to dig up foundations; to destroy at one blow *all* the wit, and *half* the learning of the kingdom; to break the entire frame and constitution of things; to ruin trade, extinguish arts and sciences with the professors of them; in short, to turn our courts, exchanges, and shops into deserts; and would be full as absurd as the proposal of Horace, where he advises the Romans all in a body to leave their city, and seek a new seat in some remote part of the world, by way of cure for the corruption of their manners.

Therefore I think this caution was in itself altogether unnecessary (which I have inserted only to prevent all possibility of caviling), since every candid reader will easily understand my discourse to be intended only in defense of *nominal* Christianity; the other having been for some time wholly laid aside by general consent, as utterly inconsistent with our present schemes of wealth and power.

But why we should therefore cast off the name and title of Christians, although the general opinion and resolution be so violent for it, I confess I cannot (with submission) apprehend the consequence necessary. However, since the undertakers propose such wonderful advantages to the nation by this project, and advance many plausible objections against the system of Christianity, I shall briefly consider the strength of both, fairly allow them their greatest weight, and offer such answers as I think most reasonable. After which I will beg leave to show what inconveniences may possibly happen by such an innovation, in the present posture of our affairs.

First, One great advantage proposed by the abolishing of Christianity is, that it would very much enlarge and establish liberty of conscience, that great bulwark of our nation, and of the Protestant religion, which is still too much limited by priestcraft, notwithstanding all the good intentions of the legislature, as we have lately found by a severe instance. For it is confidently reported, that two young gentlemen of real hopes, bright wit, and profound judgment, who upon a thorough examination of causes and effects, and by the mere force of natural abilities, without the least tincture of learning, having made a discovery, that there was no God, and generously communicating their thoughts for the good of the public, were some time ago, by an unparalleled severity, and upon I know not what *obsolete* law, broke *only* for *blasphemy*. And as it hath been wisely observed, if persecution once begins, no man alive knows how far it may reach, or where it will end.

In answer to all which, with deference to wiser judgments, I think this rather shows the necessity of a *nominal* religion among us. Great wits love to be free with the highest objects; and if they cannot be allowed a *God* to revile or renounce, they will *speak evil of dignities,* abuse the government, and reflect upon the ministry; which I am sure few will deny to be of much more pernicious consequence, according to the saying of Tiberius, *Deorum offensa diis curae.*

As to the particular fact related, I think it is not fair to argue from one instance, perhaps another cannot be produced; yet (to the comfort of all those who may be apprehensive of persecution) blasphemy we know is freely spoken a million of times in every coffeehouse and tavern, or wherever else *good company* meet. It must be allowed indeed, that to break an *English freeborn* officer only for blasphemy, was, to speak the gentlest of such an action, a very high strain of absolute power. Little can be said in excuse for the general; perhaps he was afraid it might give offense to the allies, among whom, for aught I know, it may be the custom of the country to believe a God. But if he argued, as some have done, upon a mistaken principle, that an officer who is guilty of speaking blasphemy, may some time or other proceed so far as to raise a mutiny, the consequence is by no means to be admitted; for, surely the commander of an *English* army is likely to be but ill obeyed, whose soldiers fear and reverence him as little as they do a deity.

It is further objected against the Gospel system that it obliges men to the belief of things too difficult for freethinkers, and such who have shaken off the prejudices that usually cling to a confined education. To which I answer, that men should be cautious how they raise objections which reflect upon the wisdom of the nation. Is not everybody freely allowed to believe whatever he pleases, and to publish his belief to the world whenever he thinks fit, especially if it serves to strengthen the party which is in the right? Would any indifferent foreigner, who should read the trumpery lately written by Asgil, Tindal, Toland, Coward, and forty more, imagine the Gospel to be our rule of faith, and confirmed by parliaments? Does any man either believe, or say he believes, or desire to have it thought that he says he believes one syllable of the matter? And is any man worse received upon that score, or does he find his want of *nominal* faith a disadvantage to him in the pursuit of any civil or military employment? What if there be an old dormant statute or two against him, are they not now obsolete, to a degree, that Empson and Dudley themselves if they were now alive, would find it impossible to put them in execution?

It is likewise urged, that there are, by computation, in this kingdom, above ten thousand parsons, whose revenues added to those of my lords the bishops, would suffice to maintain at least two hundred young gentlemen of wit and pleasure, and freethinking, enemies to priestcraft, narrow principles, pedantry, and prejudices; who might be an ornament to the court and

town. And then, again, so great a number of able (bodied) divines might be a
recruit to our fleet and armies. This indeed appears to be a consideration of
some weight. But then, on the other side, several things deserve to be considered likewise: As, first, whether it may not be thought necessary that in
certain tracts of country, like what we call parishes, there should be *one* man
at least of abilities to read and write. Then it seems a wrong computation,
that the revenues of the Church throughout this island would be large
enough to maintain two hundred young gentlemen, or even half that number, after the present refined way of living; that is, to allow each of them
such a rent, as in the modern form of speech, would make them *easy*. But
still there is in this project a greater mischief behind; and we ought to beware of the woman's folly, who killed the hen that every morning laid her a
golden egg. For, pray what would become of the race of men in the next age,
if we had nothing to trust to beside the scrofulous, consumptive productions,
furnished by our men of wit and pleasure, when, having squandered away
their vigor, health, and estates, they are forced by some disagreeable marriage to piece up their broken fortunes and entail rottenness and politeness
on their posterity? Now, here are ten thousand persons reduced by the wise
regulations of Henry the Eighth, to the necessity of a low diet, and moderate
exercise, who are the only great restorers of our breed, without which the
nation would in an age or two become but one great hospital.

Another advantage proposed by the abolishing of Christianity, is the
clear gain of one day in seven, which is now entirely lost, and consequently
the kingdom one-seventh less considerable in trade, business, and pleasure;
beside the loss to the public of so many stately structures now in the hands of
the clergy, which might be converted into theaters, exchanges, market
houses, common dormitories, and other public edifices.

I hope I shall be forgiven a hard word, if I call this a perfect cavil. I readily own there has been an old custom time out of mind, for people to assemble in the churches every Sunday, and that shops are still frequently shut, in
order as it is conceived, to preserve the memory of that ancient practice; but
how this can prove a hindrance to business or pleasure, is hard to imagine.
What if the men of pleasure are forced one day in the week, to game at home
instead of the chocolate house? Are not the taverns and coffeehouses open?
Can there be a more convenient season for taking a dose of physic? Are
fewer claps got upon Sundays than other days? Is not that the chief day for
traders to sum up the accounts of the week, and for lawyers to prepare their
briefs? But I would fain know how it can be pretended that the churches are
misapplied? Where are more appointments and rendezvous of gallantry?
Where more care to appear in the foremost box with greater advantage of
dress? Where more meetings for business? Where more bargains driven of
all sorts? And where so many conveniences or incitements to sleep?

There is one advantage greater than any of the foregoing, proposed by the abolishing of Christianity: that it will utterly extinguish parties among us, by removing those factious distinctions of High and Low Church, of Whig and Tory, Presbyterian and Church of England, which are now so many grievous clogs upon public proceedings, and dispose men to prefer the gratifying themselves, or depressing their adversaries, before the most important interest of the state.

I confess, if it were certain that so great an advantage would redound to the nation by this expedient, I would submit and be silent. But will any man say, that if the words *whoring, drinking, cheating, lying, stealing,* were by act of parliament ejected out of the English tongue and dictionaries, we should all awake next morning chaste and temperate, honest and just, and lovers of truth? Is this a fair consequence? Or, if the physicians would forbid us to pronounce the words *pox, gout, rheumatism,* and *stone,* would that expedient serve like so many talismans to destroy the diseases themselves? Are party and faction rooted in men's hearts no deeper than phrases borrowed from religion, or founded upon no firmer principles? And is our language so poor that we cannot find other terms to express them? Are envy, pride, avarice, and ambition such ill nomenclators, that they cannot furnish appellations for their owners? Will not *heydukes* and *mamalukes, mandarins* and *potshaws,* or any other words formed at pleasure, serve to distinguish those who are in the ministry from others who *would be in it if they could?* What, for instance, is easier than to vary the form of speech, and instead of the word *Church,* make it a question in politics, whether the *Monument* be in danger? Because religion was nearest at hand to furnish a few convenient phrases, is our invention so barren, we can find no others? Suppose, for argument sake, that the Tories favored Margarita, the Whigs Mrs. Tofts, and the Trimmers Valentini, would not *Margaritians, Toftians,* and *Valentinians* be very tolerable marks of distinction? The *Prasini* and *Veneti,* two most virulent factions in Italy, began (if I remember right) by a distinction of colors in ribbons, which we might do, with as good a grace, about the dignity of the *Blue* and the *Green;* and would serve as properly to divide the court, the parliament, and the kingdom between them, as any terms of art whatsoever, borrowed from religion. Therefore, I think there is little force in this objection against Christianity, or prospect of so great an advantage as is proposed in the abolishing of it.

It is again objected, as a very absurd, ridiculous custom, that a set of men should be suffered, much less employed and hired, to bawl one day in seven against the lawfulness of those methods most in use toward the pursuit of greatness, riches, and pleasure, which are the constant practice of all men alive on the other six. But this objection is, I think, a little unworthy in so refined an age as ours. Let us argue this matter calmly. I appeal to the breast of any polite freethinker, whether in the pursuit of gratifying a predominant passion, he hath not always felt a wonderful incitement, by reflecting it was a thing forbidden; and therefore we see, in order to cultivate this taste, the wisdom of the nation hath taken special care, that the ladies should be furnished with prohibited silks, and the men with prohibited wine. And indeed it were to be wished, that some other prohibitions were promoted, in order to improve the pleasures of the town; which, for want of such expedients, begin already, as I am told, to flag and grow languid, giving way daily to cruel inroads from the spleen.

It is likewise proposed as a great advantage to the public, that if we once discard the system of the Gospel, all religion will of course be banished forever; and consequently, along with it, those grievous prejudices of education, which under the names of virtue, conscience, honor, justice, and the like, are so apt to disturb the peace of human minds; and the notions whereof are so hard to be eradicated by right reason or freethinking, sometimes during the whole course of our lives.

Here first, I observe how difficult it is to get rid of a phrase, which the world is once grown fond of, although the occasion that first produced it, be entirely taken away. For several years past, if a man had but an ill-favored nose, the deep thinkers of the age would some way or other contrive to impute the cause to the prejudice of his education. From this fountain are said to be derived all our foolish notions of justice, piety, love of our country; all our opinions of God, or a future state, Heaven, hell, and the like. And there might formerly perhaps have been some pretense for this charge. But so effectual care has been taken to remove those prejudices, by an entire change in the methods of education, that (with honor I mention it to our polite innovators) the young gentlemen who are now on the scene, seem to have not the least tincture left of those infusions, or string of those weeds; and, by consequence, the reason for abolishing *nominal* Christianity upon that pretext, is wholly ceased.

For the rest, it may perhaps admit a controversy, whether the banishing all notions of religion whatsoever, would be convenient for the vulgar. Not that I am in the least of opinion with those who hold religion to have been the invention of politicians, to keep the lower part of the world in awe by the fear of invisible powers; unless mankind were then very different from what it is now. For I look upon the mass or body of our people here in England, to be as freethinkers, that is to say, as staunch unbelievers, as any of the highest rank. But I conceive some scattered notions about a superior power to be of singular use for the common people, as furnishing excellent materials to keep children quiet when they grow peevish and providing topics of amusement in a tedious winter night.

Lastly, it is proposed as a singular advantage, that the abolishing of Christianity will very much contribute to the uniting of Protestants, by enlarging the terms of communion so as to take in all sorts of dissenters, who are now shut out of the pale upon account of a few ceremonies which all sides confess to be things indifferent: That this alone will effectually answer the great ends of a scheme for comprehension, by opening a large noble gate, at which all bodies may enter; whereas the chaffering with dissenter, and dodging about this or the other ceremony, is but like opening a few wickets, and leaving them ajar, by which no more than one can get in at a time, and that, not without stooping, and sidling, and squeezing his body.

To all this I answer; that there is one darling inclination of mankind, which usually affects to be a retainer to religion, though she be neither its parent, its godmother, or its friend; I mean the spirit of opposition, that lived long before Christianity, and can easily subsist without it. Let us, for instance, examine wherein the opposition of sectaries among us consists, we shall find Christianity to have no share in it at all. Does the Gospel anywhere prescribe a starched, squeezed countenance, a stiff, formal gait, a singularity of manners and habit, or any affected modes of speech different from the reasonable part of mankind? Yet, if Christianity did not lend its name to stand in the gap, and to employ or divert these humors, they must of necessity be spent in contraventions to the laws of the land, and disturbance of the public peace. There is a portion of enthusiasm assigned to every nation, which, if it hath not proper objects to work on, will burst out, and set all in a flame. If the quiet of a state can be bought by only flinging men a few ceremonies to devour, it is a purchase no wise man would refuse. Let the mastiffs amuse themselves about a sheepskin stuffed with hay, provided it will keep them from worrying the flock. The institution of convents abroad, seems in one point a strain of great wisdom, there being few irregularities in human passions, which may not have recourse to vent themselves in some of those orders, which are so many retreats for the speculative, the melancholy, the proud, the silent, the politic, and the morose, to spend themselves, and evaporate the noxious particles; for each of whom we in this island are forced to provide a several sect of religion, to keep them quiet: And whenever Christianity shall be abolished, the legislature must find some other expedient to employ and entertain them. For what imports it how large a gate you open, if there will be always left a number who place a pride and a merit in refusing to enter?

Having thus considered the most important objections against Christianity, and the chief advantages proposed by the abolishing thereof, I shall now with equal deference and submission to wiser judgments as before, proceed to mention a few inconveniences that may happen, if the Gospel should be repealed; which perhaps the projectors may not have sufficiently considered.

And first, I am very sensible how much the gentlemen of wit and pleasure are apt to murmur, and be shocked at the sight of so many draggled-tail parsons, who happen to fall in their way, and offend their eyes; but at the same time, these wise reformers do not consider what an advantage and felicity it is, for great wits to be always provided with objects of scorn and contempt, in order to exercise and improve their talents, and divert their spleen from falling on each other or on themselves; especially when all this may be done without the least imaginable *danger to their persons*.

And to urge another argument of a parallel nature: If Christianity were once abolished, how would the freethinkers, the strong reasoners, and the men of profound learning, be able to find another subject so calculated in all points whereon to display their abilities? What wonderful productions of wit should we be deprived of, from those whose genius by continual practice hath been wholly turned upon raillery and invectives against religion, and would therefore never be able to shine or distinguish themselves upon any other subject! We are daily complaining of the great decline of wit among us, and would we take away the greatest, perhaps the only topic we have left? Who would ever have suspected Asgil for a wit, or Toland for a philosopher, if the inexhaustible stock of Christianity had not been at hand to provide them with materials? What other subject, through all art or nature, could have produced Tindal for a profound author, or furnished him with readers? It is the wise choice of the subject that alone adorns and distinguishes the writer. For, had a hundred such pens as these been employed on the side of religion, they would have immediately sunk into silence and oblivion.

Nor do I think it wholly groundless, or my fears altogether imaginary, that the abolishing of Christianity may perhaps bring the Church into danger, or at least put the senate to the trouble of another securing vote. I desire I may not be mistaken; I am far from presuming to affirm or think that the Church is in danger at present, or as things now stand; but we know not how soon it may be so when the Christian religion is repealed. As plausible as this project seems, there may a dangerous design lurk under it. Nothing can be more notorious, than that the atheists, deists, Socinians, anti-Trinitarians, and other subdivisions of free-thinkers, are persons of little zeal for the present ecclesiastical establishment: Their declared opinion is for repealing the Sacramental Test; they are very indifferent with regard to ceremonies; nor do they hold the *jus divinum* of Episcopacy. Therefore this may be intended as one politic step toward altering the constitution of the Church established, and setting up Presbytery in the stead, which I leave to be further considered by those at the helm.

In the last place, I think nothing can be more plain, than that by this expedient, we shall run into the evil we chiefly pretend to avoid; and that the abolishment of the Christian religion will be the readiest course we can take to introduce popery. And I am more inclined to this opinion, because we know it has been the constant practice of the Jesuits to send over emissaries, with instructions to personate themselves members of the several prevailing sects among us. So it is recorded, that they have at sundry times appeared in the guise of Presbyterians, Anabaptists, Independents, and Quakers, according as any of these were most in credit; so, since the fashion hath been taken up of exploding religion, the popish missionaries have not been wanting to mix with the freethinkers; among whom, Toland the great oracle of the anti-Christians is an Irish priest, the son of an Irish priest; and the most learned and ingenious author of a book called *The Rights of the Christian Church* was in a proper juncture reconciled to the Romish faith, whose true son, as appears by a hundred passages in his treatise, he still continues. Perhaps I could add some others to the number; but the fact is beyond dispute, and the reasoning they proceed by is right; for, supposing Christianity to be extinguished, the people will never be at ease until they find out some other method of worship; which will as infallibly produce superstition, as this will end in popery.

And therefore, if notwithstanding all I have said, it shall still be thought necessary to have a bill brought in for repealing Christianity, I would humbly offer an amendment; that instead of the word *Christianity,* may be put *Religion* in general; which I conceive will much better answer all the good ends proposed by the projectors of it. For, as long as we leave in being a God and his providence, with all the necessary consequences which curious and inquisitive men will be apt to draw from such premises, we do not strike at the root of the evil, although we should ever so effectually annihilate the present scheme of the Gospel. For, of what use is freedom of thought, if it will not produce freedom of action, which is the sole end, how remote soever in appearance, of all objections against Christianity? And therefore, the freethinkers consider it as a sort of edifice, wherein all the parts have such a mutual dependence on each other, that if you happen to pull out one single nail, the whole fabric must fall to the ground. This was happily expressed by him who had heard of a text brought for proof of the Trinity, which in an ancient manuscript was differently read; he thereupon immediately took the hint, and by a sudden deduction of a long sorites, most logically concluded: "Why, if it be as you say, I may safely whore and drink on, and defy the parson." From which, and many the like instances easy to be produced, I think nothing can be more manifest, than that the quarrel is not against any particular points of hard digestion in the Christian system, but against religion in general; which, by laying restraints on human nature, is supposed the great enemy to the freedom of thought and action.

Upon the whole, if it shall still be thought for the benefit of Church and state, that Christianity be abolished; I conceive however, it may be more convenient to defer the execution to a time of peace, and not venture in this conjuncture to disoblige our allies, who, as it falls out, are all Christians, and many of them, by the prejudices of their education, so bigoted, as to place a sort of pride in the appellation. If upon being rejected by them, we are to trust to an alliance with the Turk, we shall find ourselves much deceived:

For, as he is too remote, and generally engaged in war with the Persian emperor, so his people would be more scandalized at our infidelity, than our Christian neighbors. Because the Turks are not only strict observers of religious worship, but, what is worse, believe a God; which is more than is required of us, even while we preserve the name of Christians.

To conclude: Whatever some may think of the great advantages to trade by this favorite scheme, I do very much apprehend, that in six months' time after the act is passed for the extirpation of the Gospel, the Bank and East India stock may fall, at least, one *per cent*. And, since that is fifty times more than ever the wisdom of our age thought fit to venture for the *preservation* of Christianity, there is no reason we should be at so great a loss, merely for the sake of *destroying* it.

## STUDY QUESTIONS

1. By what means does Swift try to convince his readers of his obvious sincerity?

2. What distinction does he make between *real* Christianity and *nominal* Christianity?

3. How does Swift turn to his advantage the argument that the Gospel obliges men to believe things too difficult for freethinkers?

4. What use does Swift make of the seemingly incontrovertible evidence of statistics?

5. How does he appeal to the economic interests of his audience? What is his concluding and most important argument against abolishing Christianity?

E. M. *Forster*

# WHAT I BELIEVE

E. M. Forster (1879–    ) was born in London. He studied at and is an honorary fellow of King's College, Cambridge, and now lives there. Among his degrees and awards is an honorary LL.D. from Aberdeen University. Forster has written a play, a film script, and even the libretto for Benjamin Britten's *Billy Budd*. His fame, however, rests on his novels—*Where Angels Fear to Tread* (1905), *A Room with a View* (1908), *Howard's End* (1910), and *A Passage to India* (1924). His Clark Lectures at Trinity College were published as *Aspects of the Novel* in 1927 and his *Collected Tales* appeared in 1947. Forster is an accomplished amateur pianist, and a member of the Royal Society of Literature and the American Academy of Arts and Letters.

I DO NOT believe in Belief. But this is an age of faith, and there are so many militant creeds that, in self-defence, one has to formulate a creed of one's own. Tolerance, good temper and sympathy are no longer enough in a world which is rent by religious and racial persecution, in a world where ignorance rules, and science, who ought to have ruled, plays the subservient pimp. Tolerance, good temper and sympathy—they are what matter really, and if the human race is not to collapse they must come to the front before long. But for the moment they are not enough, their action is no stronger than a flower, battered beneath a military jack-boot. They want stiffening, even if the process coarsens them. Faith, to my mind, is a stiffening process, a sort of mental starch, which ought to be applied as sparingly as possible. I dislike the stuff. I do not believe in it, for its own sake, at all. Herein I probably differ from most people, who believe in Belief, and are only sorry they cannot swallow even more than they do. My law-givers are Erasmus and Montaigne, not Moses and St. Paul. My temple stands not upon Mount Moriah but in that

Elysian Field where even the immoral are admitted. My motto is: "Lord, I disbelieve—help thou my unbelief."

I have, however, to live in an Age of Faith—the sort of epoch I used to hear praised when I was a boy. It is extremely unpleasant really. It is bloody in every sense of the word. And I have to keep my end up in it. Where do I start?

With personal relationships. Here is something comparatively solid in a world full of violence and cruelty. Not absolutely solid, for Psychology has split and shattered the idea of a "Person," and has shown that there is something incalculable in each of us, which may at any moment rise to the surface and destroy our normal balance. We don't know what we are like. We can't know what other people are like. How, then, can we put any trust in personal relationships, or cling to them in the gathering political storm? In theory we cannot. But in practice we can and do. Though A is not unchangeably A or B unchangeably B, there can still be love and loyalty between the two. For the purpose of living one has to assume that the personality is solid, and the "self" is an entity, and to ignore all contrary evidence. And since to ignore evidence is one of the characteristics of faith, I certainly can proclaim that I believe in personal relationships.

Starting from them, I get a little order into the contemporary chaos. One must be fond of people and trust them if one is not to make a mess of life, and it is therefore essential that they should not let one down. They often do. The moral of which is that I must, myself, be as reliable as possible, and this I try to be. But reliability is not a matter of contract—that is the main difference between the world of personal relationships and the world of business relationships. It is a matter for the heart, which signs no documents. In other words, reliability is impossible unless there is a natural warmth. Most men possess this warmth, though they often have bad luck and get chilled. Most of them, even when they are politicians, *want* to keep faith. And one can, at all events, show one's own little light here, one's own poor little trembling flame, with the knowledge that it is not the only light that is shining in the darkness, and not the only one which the darkness does not comprehend. Personal relations are despised today. They are regarded as bourgeois luxuries, as products of a time of fair weather which is now past, and we are urged to get rid of them, and to dedicate ourselves to some movement or cause instead. I hate the idea of causes, and if I had to choose between betraying my country and betraying my friend, I hope I should have the guts to betray my country. Such a choice may scandalise the modern reader, and he may stretch out his patriotic hand to the telephone at once and ring up the police. It would not have shocked Dante, though. Dante places Brutus and Cassius in the lowest circle of Hell because they had chosen to betray their friend Julius Caesar rather than their country Rome. Probably one will not be asked to make such an agonising choice. Still, there lies at the back of every creed something terrible and hard for which the worshipper may one day be required to suffer, and there is even a terror and a hardness in this creed of personal relationships, urbane and mild though it sounds. Love and loyalty to an individual can run counter to the claims of the State. When they do—down with the State, say I, which means that the State would down me.

This brings me along to Democracy, "even Love, the Beloved Republic, which feeds upon Freedom and lives." Democracy is not a Beloved Republic really, and never will be. But it is less hateful than other contemporary forms of government, and to that extent it deserves our support. It does start from the assumption that the individual is important, and that all types are needed to make a civilisation. It does not divide its citizens into the bossers and the bossed—as an efficiency-regime tends to do. The people I admire most are those who are sensitive and want to create something or discover something, and do not see life in terms of power, and such people get more of a chance under a democracy than elsewhere. They found religions, great or small, or they produce literature and art, or they do disinterested scientific research, or they may be what is called "ordinary people," who are creative in their private lives, bring up their children decently, for instance, or help their neighbours. All these people need to express themselves; they cannot do so unless society allows them liberty to do so, and the society which allows them most liberty is a democracy.

Democracy has another merit. It allows criticism, and if there is not public criticism there are bound to be hushed-up scandals. That is why I believe in the Press, despite all its lies and vulgarity, and why I believe in Parliament. Parliament is often sneered at because it is a Talking Shop. I believe in it *because* it is a talking shop. I believe in the Private Member who makes himself a nuisance. He gets snubbed and is told that he is cranky or ill-informed, but he does expose abuses which would otherwise never have been mentioned, and very often an abuse gets put right just by being mentioned. Occasionally, too, a well-meaning public official starts losing his head in the cause of efficiency, and thinks himself God Almighty. Such officials are particularly frequent in the Home Office. Well, there will be questions about them in Parliament sooner or later, and then they will have to mind their steps. Whether Parliament is either a representative body or an efficient one is questionable, but I value it because it criticises and talks, and because its chatter gets widely reported.

So Two Cheers for Democracy: one because it admits variety and two because it permits criticism. Two cheers are quite enough: there is no occasion to give three. Only Love the Beloved Republic deserves that.

What about Force, though? While we are trying to be sensitive and advanced and affectionate and tolerant, an unpleasant question pops up: does not all society rest upon force? If a government cannot count upon the police and the army, how can it hope to rule? And if an individual gets knocked on the head or sent to a labour camp, of what significance are his opinions?

This dilemma does not worry me as much as it does some. I realise that all society rests upon force. But all the great creative actions, all the decent human relations, occur during the intervals when force has not managed to come to the front. These intervals are what matter. I want them to be as frequent and as lengthy as possible, and I call them "civilisation." Some people idealise force and pull it into the foreground and worship it, instead of keeping it in the background as long as possible. I think they make a mistake, and I think that their opposites, the mystics, err even more when they declare that force does not exist. I believe that it exists, and that one of our jobs is to prevent it from getting out of its box. It gets out sooner or later, and then it destroys us and all the lovely things which we have made. But it is not out all the time, for the fortunate reason that the strong are so stupid. Consider their conduct for a moment in the Niebelung's Ring. The giants there have the guns, or in other words the gold; but they do nothing with it, they do not realise that they are all-powerful, with the result that the catastrophe is delayed and the castle of Walhalla, insecure but glorious, fronts the storms. Fafnir, coiled round his hoard, grumbles and grunts; we can hear him under Europe today; the leaves of the wood already tremble, and the Bird calls its warnings uselessly. Fafnir will destroy us, but by a blessed dispensation he is stupid and slow, and creation goes on just outside the poisonous blast of his breath. The Nietzschean would hurry the monster up, the mystic would say he did not exist, but Wotan, wiser than either, hastens to create warriors before doom declares itself. The Valkyries are symbols not only of courage but of intelligence; they represent the human spirit snatching its opportunity while the going is good, and one of them even finds time to love. Brünnhilde's last song hymns the recurrence of love, and since it is the privilege of art to exaggerate, she goes even further, and proclaims the love which is eternally triumphant and feeds upon freedom, and lives.

So that is what I feel about force and violence. It is, alas! the ultimate reality on this earth, but it does not always get to the front. Some people call its absences "decadence"; I call them "civilisation" and find in such interludes the chief justification for the human experiment. I look the other way until fate strikes me. Whether this is due to courage or to cowardice in my own case I cannot be sure. But I know that if men had not looked the other way in the past, nothing of any value would survive. The people I respect most behave as if they were immortal and as if society was eternal. Both assumptions are false: both of them must be accepted as true if we are to go on eating and working and loving, and are to keep open a few breathing holes for the human spirit. No millennium seems likely to descend upon humanity; no better and stronger League of Nations will be instituted; no form of Christianity and no alternative to Christianity will bring peace to the world or integrity to the individual; no "change of heart" will occur. And yet we need not despair, indeed, we cannot despair; the evidence of history shows us that men have always insisted on behaving creatively under the shadow of the sword; that they have done their artistic and scientific and domestic stuff for the sake of doing it, and that we had better follow their example under the shadow of the aeroplanes. Others, with more vision or courage than myself, see the salvation of humanity ahead, and will dismiss my conception of civilisation as paltry, a sort of tip-and-run game. Certainly it is presumptuous to say that we *cannot* improve, and that Man, who has only been in power for a few thousand years, will never learn to make use of his power. All I mean is that, if people continue to kill one another as they do, the world cannot get better than it is, and that since there are more people than formerly, and their means for destroying one another superior, the world may well get worse. What is good in people—and consequently in the world—is their insistence on creation, their belief in friendship and loyalty for their own sakes; and though Violence remains and is, indeed, the major partner in this muddled establishment, I believe that creativeness remains too, and will always assume direction when violence sleeps. So, though I am not an optimist, I cannot agree with Sophocles that it were better never to have been born. And although, like Horace, I see no evidence that each batch of births is superior to the last, I leave the field open for the more complacent view. This is such a difficult moment to live in, one cannot help getting gloomy and also a bit rattled, and perhaps short-sighted.

In search of a refuge, we may perhaps turn to hero-worship. But here we shall get no help, in my opinion. Hero-worship is a dangerous vice, and one of the minor merits of a democracy is that it does not encourage it, or produce that unmanageable type of citizen known as the Great Man. It produces instead different kinds of small men—a much finer achievement. But people who cannot get interested in the variety of life, and cannot make up their own minds, get discontented over this, and they long for a hero to bow down before and to follow blindly. It is significant that a hero is an integral part of the authoritarian stock-in-trade today. An efficiency-regime cannot be run without a few heroes stuck about it to carry off the dullness—much as plums have to be put into a bad pudding to make it palatable. One hero at the top and a smaller one each side of him is a favourite arrangement, and the timid and the bored are comforted by the trinity, and, bowing down, feel exalted and strengthened.

No, I distrust Great Men. They produce a desert of uniformity around them and often a pool of blood too, and I always feel a little man's pleasure when they come a cropper. Every now and then one reads in the newspapers some such statement as: "The coup d'état appears to have failed, and Admiral Toma's whereabouts is at present unknown." Admiral Toma had probably every qualification for being a Great Man—an iron will, personal magnetism, dash, flair, sexlessness—but fate was against him, so he retires to unknown whereabouts instead of parading history with his peers. He fails with a completeness which no artist and no lover can experience, because with them the process of creation is itself an achievement, whereas with him the only possible achievement is success.

I believe in aristocracy, though—if that is the right word, and if a democrat may use it. Not an aristocracy of power, based upon rank and influence, but an aristocracy of the sensitive, the considerate and the plucky. Its members are to be found in all nations and classes, and all through the ages, and there is a secret understanding between them when they meet. They represent the true human tradition, the one permanent victory of our queer race over cruelty and chaos. Thousands of them perish in obscurity, a few are great names. They are sensitive for others as well as for themselves, they are considerate without being fussy, their pluck is not swankiness but the power to endure, and they can take a joke. I give no examples—it is risky to do that—but the reader may as well consider whether this is the type of person he would like to meet and to be, and whether (going farther with me) he would prefer that this type should *not* be an ascetic one. I am against asceticism myself. I am with the old Scotsman who wanted less chastity and more delicacy. I do not feel that my aristocrats are a real aristocracy if they thwart their bodies, since bodies are the instruments through which we register and enjoy the world. Still, I do not insist. This is not a major point. It is clearly possible to be sensitive, considerate and plucky and yet be an ascetic too, if anyone possesses the first three qualities, I will let him in! On they go—an invincible army, yet not a victorious one. The aristocrats, the elect, the chosen, the Best People—all the words that describe them are false, and all attempts to organise them fail. Again and again Authority, seeing their value, has tried to net them and to utilise them as the Egyptian Priesthood or the Christian Church or the Chinese Civil Service or the Group Movement, or some other worthy stunt. But they slip through the net and are gone; when the door is shut, they are no longer in the room; their temple, as one of them remarked, is the Holiness of the Heart's Affection, and their kingdom, though they never possess it, is the wide-open world.

With this type of person knocking about, and constantly crossing one's path if one has eyes to see or hands to feel, the experiment of earthly life cannot be dismissed as a failure. But it may well be hailed as a tragedy, the tragedy being that no device has been found by which these private decencies can be transmitted to public affairs. As soon as people have power they go crooked and sometimes dotty as well, because the possession of power lifts them into a region where normal honesty never pays. For instance, the man who is selling newspapers outside the Houses of Parliament can safely leave his papers to go for a drink and his cap beside them: anyone who takes a paper is sure to drop a copper into the cap. But the men who are inside the Houses of Parliament—they cannot trust one another like that, still less can the Government they compose trust other governments. No caps upon the pavement here, but suspicion, treachery and armaments. The more highly public life is organised the lower does its morality sink; the nations of today behave to each other worse than they ever did in the past, they cheat, rob, bully and bluff, make war without notice, and kill as many women and children as possible; whereas primitive tribes were at all events restrained by taboos. It is a humiliating outlook—though the greater the darkness, the brighter shine the little lights, reassuring one another, signalling: "Well, at all events, I'm still here. I don't like it very much, but how are you?" Unquenchable lights of my aristocracy! Signals of the invincible army! "Come along—anyway, let's have a good time while we can." I think they signal that too.

The Saviour of the future—if ever he comes—will not preach a new Gospel. He will merely utilise my aristocracy, he will make effective the good will and the good temper which are already existing. In other words, he will introduce a new technique. In economics, we are told that if there was a new technique of distribution, there need be no poverty, and people would not starve in one place while crops were being ploughed under in another. A similar change is needed in the sphere of morals and politics. The desire for it is by no means new; it was expressed, for example, in theological terms by Jacopone da Todi over six hundred years ago. "Ordina questo amore, O tu che m'ami," he said; "O thou who lovest me—set this love in order." His prayer was not granted, and I do not myself believe that it ever will be, but here, and not through a change of heart, is our probable route. Not by becoming better, but by ordering and distributing his native goodness, will Man shut up Force into its box, and so gain time to explore the universe and to set his mark upon it worthily. At present he only explores it at odd moments, when Force is looking the other way, and his divine creativeness appears as a trivial by-product, to be scrapped as soon as the drums beat and the bombers hum.

Such a change, claim the orthodox, can only be made by Christianity, and will be made by it in God's good time: man always has failed and always will fail to organize his own goodness, and it is presumptuous of him to try. This claim—solemn as it is—leaves me cold. I cannot believe that Christianity will ever cope with the present world-wide mess, and I think that such influence as it retains in modern society is due to the money behind it, rather than to its spiritual appeal. It was a spiritual force once, but the indwelling spirit will have to be restated if it is to calm the waters again, and probably restated in a non-Christian form. Naturally a lot of people, and people who are not only good but able and intelligent, will disagree here; they will vehemently deny that Christianity has failed, or they will argue that its failure proceeds from the wickedness of men, and really proves its ultimate success.

They have Faith, with a large F. My faith has a very small one, and I only intrude it because these are strenuous and serious days, and one likes to say what one thinks while speech is comparatively free: it may not be free much longer.

The above are the reflections of an individualist and a liberal who has found liberalism crumbling beneath him and at first felt ashamed. Then, looking around, he decided there was no special reason for shame, since other people, whatever they felt, were equally insecure. And as for individualism—there seems no way of getting off this, even if one wanted to. The dictator-hero can grind down his citizens till they are all alike, but he cannot melt them into a single man. That is beyond his power. He can order them to merge, he can incite them to mass-antics, but they are obliged to be born separately, and to die separately, and, owing to these unavoidable termini, will always be running off the totalitarian rails. The memory of birth and the expectation of death always lurk within the human being, making him separate from his fellows and consequently capable of intercourse with them. Naked I came into the world, naked I shall go out of it! And a very good thing too, for it reminds me that I am naked under my shirt, whatever its colour.

## STUDY QUESTIONS

1.  How can Forster believe in both democracy and aristocracy?

2.  If you had not known that Forster was English, what clues would reveal his nationality to you?

3.  What is the predominant tone of "What I Believe"? Does Forster seem more or less formal than Swift? Than Krutch? Does he seem more or less learned than Swift? Than Krutch?

4.  How effective and "natural" are the transitions between paragraphs?

5.  The sentences in the third paragraph are greatly varied in structure. Why is each of the sentences or phrases in that paragraph structured as it is? Would more regular sentence structuring affect Forster's meaning?

# Martin Buber

# BOOKS AND MEN

Martin Buber (1878–1965) was born in Vienna. He studied at the Universities of Vienna, Berlin, and Zurich. Although he is now considered the most important contemporary Jewish theologian and philosopher, he did not become publicly committed to the Zionist movement and Judaism until 1923, at the University of Leipzig. In Germany he edited *Die Welt, Der Jude,* and *Die Kreatur.* His first teaching position, in 1923, was at the University of Frankfurt. Buber left Germany in 1938 for Palestine, where he lived, teaching until his retirement in 1951 at the University of Jerusalem. Among his honorary degrees is one from the University of Aberdeen, Scotland. His books include *I and Thou* (1937), *Between Man and Man* (1947), *Hasidism* (1948), *Images of Good and Evil, The Eclipse of God, Israel and Palestine,* and *Right and Wrong* (1952).

I F I HAD been asked in my early youth whether I preferred to have dealings only with men or only with books, my answer would certainly have been in favour of books. In later years this has become less and less the case. Not that I have had so much better experiences with men than with books; on the contrary, purely delightful books even now come my way more often than purely delightful men. But the many bad experiences with men have nourished the meadow of my life as the noblest book could not do, and the good experiences have made the earth into a garden for me. On the other hand, no book does more than remove me into a paradise of great spirits, where my innermost heart never forgets I cannot dwell long, nor even wish that I could do so. For (I must say this straight out in order to be understood) my innermost heart loves the world more than it loves the spirit. I have not, indeed, cleaved to life in the world as I might have; in my relations with it I fail it again and again; again and again I remain guilty towards it for falling short of what it expects of me, and this is partly, to be sure, because I am so indebted to the

From *Pointing the Way: Collected Essays* by Martin Buber. Copyright © 1957 by Harper & Row. Reprinted by permission of the publishers and Rafael Buber. Translated by Martin S. Friedman.

spirit. I am indebted to the spirit as I am to myself, but I do not, strictly speaking, love it, even as I do not, strictly speaking, love myself. I do not in reality love him who has seized me with his heavenly clutch and holds me fast; rather I love her, the "world," who comes again and again to meet me and extends to me a pair of fingers.

Both have gifts to share. The former showers on me his manna of books; the latter extends to me the brown bread on whose crust I break my teeth, a bread of which I can never have enough: men. Aye, these tousle-heads and good-for-nothings, how I love them! I revere books—those that I really read—too much to be able to love them. But in the most venerable of living men I always find more to love than to revere: I find in him something of this world, that is simply there as the spirit never can be there. The spirit hovers above me powerfully and pours out his exalted gift of speech, books; how glorious, how weird! But she, the human world, needs only to cast a word-less smile, and I cannot live without her. She is mute; all the prattle of men yields no word such as sounds forth constantly out of books. And I listen to it all in order to receive the silence that penetrates to me through it, the silence of the creature. But just the human creature! That creature means a mixture. Books are pure, men are mixed; books are spirit and word, pure spirit and purified word; men are made up of prattle and silence, and their silence is not that of animals but of men. Out of the human silence behind the prattle the spirit whispers to you, the spirit *as soul*. She, she is the beloved.

Here is an infallible test. Imagine yourself in a situation where you are alone, wholly alone on earth, and you are offered one of the two, books or men. I often hear men prizing their solitude, but that is only because there are still men somewhere on earth, even though in the far distance. I knew nothing of books when I came forth from the womb of my mother, and I shall die without books, with another human hand in my own. I do, indeed, close my door at times and surrender myself to a book, but only because I can open the door again and see a human being looking at me.

STUDY QUESTIONS

1. How and why did Buber's love of men and books change as he matured?

2. What does Buber mean by "him who has seized me with his heavenly clutch and holds me fast"?

3. How "infallible" is the test posited in the last paragraph?

4. Buber contrasts books and men; although his essay is titled "Books and

Men," most of it is really a discussion of books *or* men. Do Buber's
sentence patterns reinforce the contrasts?

5.  Who is more positive, convincing, and dogmatic in his concluding
    paragraph: Forster or Buber?

## *Nathaniel Hawthorne*

# YOUNG GOODMAN BROWN

Nathaniel Hawthorne (1804–1864) was born in Salem, Massachusetts.
Among his ancestors was the Judge Hathorne who presided over the Salem
witch trials. He graduated from Bowdoin College, where his classmates in-
cluded Henry Wadsworth Longfellow and Franklin Pierce. His first novel,
*Fanshawe,* was published in 1828. This was followed by *Twice-Told Tales*
(1837), *Mosses from an Old Manse* (1846), *The Scarlet Letter* (1850), *The
House of Seven Gables* (1851), *The Blithedale Romance* and *A Wonder
Book* (1852), *Tanglewood Tales* (1853), and *The Marble Faun* (1860).
Hawthorne served as surveyor at the Boston Custom House and, after the
publication of *The Life of Franklin Pierce* (1852), was named consul to
Liverpool.

YOUNG Goodman Brown came forth at sunset into the
street at Salem village; but put his head back, after crossing the threshold, to exchange a parting kiss with his
young wife. And Faith, as the wife was aptly named, thrust her own pretty
head into the street, letting the wind play with the pink ribbons of her cap
while she called to Goodman Brown.

"Dearest heart," whispered she, softly and rather sadly, when her lips
were close to his ear, "prithee put off your journey until sunrise and sleep in
your own bed tonight. A lone woman is troubled with such dreams and such
thoughts that she's afeard of herself sometimes. Pray tarry with me this
night, dear husband, of all nights in the year."

"My love and my Faith," replied young Goodman Brown, "of all nights
in the year, this one night must I tarry away from thee. My journey, as
thou callest it, forth and back again, must needs be done 'twixt now and sun-

First published 1835.

rise. What, my sweet, pretty wife, dost thou doubt me already, and we but three months married?"

"Then God bless you!" said Faith, with the pink ribbons; "and may you find all well when you come back."

"Amen!" cried Goodman Brown. "Say thy prayers, dear Faith, and go to bed at dusk, and no harm will come to thee."

So they parted; and the young man pursued his way until, being about to turn the corner by the meeting-house, he looked back and saw the head of Faith still peeping after him with a melancholy air, in spite of her pink ribbons.

"Poor little Faith!" thought he, for his heart smote him. "What a wretch am I to leave her on such an errand! She talks of dreams, too. Methought as she spoke there was trouble in her face, as if a dream had warned her what work is to be done tonight. But no, no; 't would kill her to think it. Well, she's a blessed angel on earth; and after this one night I'll cling to her skirts and follow her to heaven."

With this excellent resolve for the future, Goodman Brown felt himself justified in making more haste on his present evil purpose. He had taken a dreary road, darkened by all the gloomiest trees of the forest, which barely stood aside to let the narrow path creep through, and closed immediately behind. It was all as lonely as could be; and there is this peculiarity in such a solitude, that the traveller knows not who may be concealed by the innumerable trunks and the thick boughs overhead; so that with lonely footsteps he may yet be passing through an unseen multitude.

"There may be a devilish Indian behind every tree," said Goodman Brown to himself; and he glanced fearfully behind him as he added, "What if the devil himself should be at my very elbow!"

His head being turned back, he passed a crook of the road, and, looking forward again, beheld the figure of a man, in grave and decent attire, seated at the foot of an old tree. He arose at Goodman Brown's approach and walked onward side by side with him.

"You are late, Goodman Brown," said he. "The clock of the Old South was striking as I came through Boston, and that is full fifteen minutes agone."

"Faith kept me back a while," replied the young man, with a tremor in his voice, caused by the sudden appearance of his companion, though not wholly unexpected.

It was now deep dusk in the forest, and deepest in that part of it where these two were journeying. As nearly as could be discerned, the second traveller was about fifty years old, apparently in the same rank of life as Goodman Brown, and bearing a considerable resemblance to him, though perhaps more in expression than features. Still they might have been taken for father and son. And yet, though the elder person was as simply clad as the younger, and as simple in manner too, he had an indescribable air of one who knew the world, and who would not have felt abashed at the governor's dinner table or in King William's court, were it possible that his affairs should call him thither. But the only thing about him that could be fixed upon as remarkable was his staff, which bore the likeness of a great black snake, so curiously wrought that it might almost be seen to twist and wriggle itself like a living serpent. This, of course, must have been an ocular deception, assisted by the uncertain light.

"Come, Goodman Brown," cried his fellow-traveller, "this is a dull pace for the beginning of a journey. Take my staff, if you are so soon weary."

"Friend," said the other, exchanging his slow pace for a full stop, "having kept covenant by meeting thee here, it is my purpose now to return whence I came. I have scruples touching the matter thou wot'st of."

"Sayest thou so?" replied he of the serpent, smiling apart. "Let us walk on, nevertheless, reasoning as we go; and if I convince thee not thou shalt turn back. We are but a little way in the forest yet."

"Too far! too far!" exclaimed the goodman, unconsciously resuming his walk. "My father never went into the woods on such an errand, nor his father before him. We have been a race of honest men and good Christians since the days of the martyrs; and shall I be the first of the name of Brown that ever took his path and kept—"

"Such company, thou wouldst say," observed the elder person, interpreting his pause. "Well said, Goodman Brown! I have been as well acquainted with your family as with ever a one among the Puritans; and that's no trifle to say. I helped your grandfather, the constable, when he lashed the Quaker woman so smartly through the streets of Salem; and it was I that brought your father a pitch-pine knot, kindled at my own hearth, to set fire to an Indian village, in King Philip's war. They were my good friends, both; and many a pleasant walk have we had along this path, and returned merrily after midnight. I would fain be friends with you for their sake."

"If it be as thou sayest," replied Goodman Brown, "I marvel they never spoke of these matters; or, verily, I marvel not, seeing that the least rumor of the sort would have driven them from New England. We are a people of prayer, and good works to boot, and abide no such wickedness."

"Wickedness or not," said the traveller with the twisted staff, "I have a very general acquaintance here in New England. The deacons of many a church have drunk the communion wine with me; the selectmen of divers towns make me their chairman; and a majority of the Great and General Court are firm supporters of my interest. The governor and I, too—But these are state secrets."

"Can this be so?" cried Goodman Brown, with a stare of amazement at his undisturbed companion. "Howbeit, I have nothing to do with the governor and council; they have their own ways, and are no rule for a simple husbandman like me. But, were I to go on with thee, how should I meet the eye of that good old man, our minister, at Salem village? Oh, his voice would make me tremble both Sabbath day and lecture day."

Thus far the elder traveller had listened with due gravity; but now burst into a fit of irrepressible mirth, shaking himself so violently that his snake-like staff actually seemed to wriggle in sympathy.

"Ha! ha! ha!" shouted he again and again; then composing himself, "Well, go on, Goodman Brown, go on; but, prithee, don't kill me with laughing."

"Well, then, to end the matter at once," said Goodman Brown, considerably nettled, "there is my wife, Faith. It would break her dear little heart; and I'd rather break my own."

"Nay, if that be the case," answered the other, "e'en go thy ways, Goodman Brown. I would not for twenty old women like the one hobbling before us that Faith should come to any harm."

As he spoke he pointed his staff at a female figure on the path, in whom Goodman Brown recognized a very pious and exemplary dame, who had taught him his catechism in youth, and was still his moral and spiritual adviser, jointly with the minister and Deacon Gookin.

"A marvel, truly, that Goody Cloyse should be so far in the wilderness at nightfall," said he. "But with your leave, friend, I shall take a cut through the woods until we have left this Christian woman behind. Being a stranger to you, she might ask whom I was consorting with and whither I was going."

"Be it so," said his fellow-traveller. "Betake you to the woods, and let me keep the path."

Accordingly the young man turned aside, but took care to watch his companion, who advanced softly along the road until he had come within a staff's length of the old dame. She, meanwhile, was making the best of her way, with singular speed for so aged a woman, and mumbling some indistinct words—a prayer, doubtless—as she went. The traveller put forth his staff and touched her withered neck with what seemed the serpent's tail.

"The devil!" screamed the pious old lady.

"Then Goody Cloyse knows her old friend?" observed the traveller, confronting her and leaning on his writhing stick.

"Ah, forsooth, and is it your worship indeed?" cried the good dame. "Yea, truly is it, and in the very image of my old gossip, Goodman Brown, the grandfather of the silly fellow that now is. But—would your worship believe it?—my broomstick hath strangely disappeared, stolen, as I suspect, by that unhanged witch, Goody Cory, and that, too, when I was all anointed with the juice of smallage, and cinquefoil, and wolf's bane—"

"Mingled with fine wheat and the fat of a new-born babe," said the shape of old Goodman Brown.

"Ah, your worship knows the recipe," cried the old lady, cackling aloud.

"So, as I was saying, being all ready for the meeting, and no horse to ride on, I made up my mind to foot it; for they tell me there is a nice young man to be taken into communion tonight. But now your good worship will lend me your arm, and we shall be there in a twinkling."

"That can hardly be," answered her friend. "I may not spare you my arm, Goody Cloyse; but here is my staff, if you will."

So saying, he threw it down at her feet, where, perhaps, it assumed life, being one of the rods which its owner had formerly lent to the Egyptian magi. Of this fact, however, Goodman Brown could not take cognizance. He had cast up his eyes in astonishment, and, looking down again, beheld neither Goody Cloyse nor the serpentine staff, but his fellow-traveller alone, who waited for him as calmly as if nothing had happened.

"That old woman taught me my catechism," said the young man; and there was a world of meaning in this simple comment.

They continued to walk onward, while the elder traveller exhorted his companion to make good speed and persevere in the path, discoursing so aptly that his arguments seemed rather to spring up in the bosom of his auditor than to be suggested by himself. As they went, he plucked a branch of maple to serve for a walking stick, and began to strip it of the twigs and little boughs, which were wet with evening dew. The moment his fingers touched them they became strangely withered and dried up as with a week's sunshine. Thus the pair proceeded, at a good free pace, until suddenly, in a gloomy hollow of the road, Goodman Brown sat himself down on the stump of a tree and refused to go any farther.

"Friend," said he, stubbornly, "my mind is made up. Not another step will I budge on this errand. What if a wretched old woman do choose to go to the devil when I thought she was going to heaven: is that any reason why I should quit my dear Faith and go after her?"

"You will think better of this by and by," said his acquaintance, composedly. "Sit here and rest yourself a while; and when you feel like moving again, there is my staff to help you along."

Without more words, he threw his companion the maple stick, and was as speedily out of sight as if he had vanished into the deepening gloom. The young man sat a few moments by the roadside, applauding himself greatly, and thinking with how clear a conscience he should meet the minister in his morning walk, nor shrink from the eye of good old Deacon Gookin. And what calm sleep would be his that very night, which was to have been spent so wickedly, but so purely and sweetly now, in the arms of Faith! Amidst these pleasant and praiseworthy meditations, Goodman Brown heard the tramp of horses along the road, and deemed it advisable to conceal himself within the verge of the forest, conscious of the guilty purpose that had brought him thither, though now so happily turned from it.

On came the hoof tramps and the voices of the riders, two grave old voices, conversing soberly as they drew near. These mingled sounds appeared to pass along the road, within a few yards of the young man's hiding-place; but, owing doubtless to the depth of the gloom at that particular spot, neither the travellers nor their steeds were visible. Though their figures brushed the small boughs by the wayside, it could not be seen that they intercepted, even for a moment, the faint gleam from the strip of bright sky athwart which they must have passed. Goodman Brown alternately crouched and stood on tiptoe, pulling aside the branches and thrusting forth his head as far as he durst without discerning so much as a shadow. It vexed him the more, because he could have sworn, were such a thing possible, that he recognized the voices of the minister and Deacon Gookin, jogging along quietly, as they were wont to do, when bound to some ordination or ecclesiastical council. While yet within hearing, one of the riders stopped to pluck a switch.

"Of the two, reverend sir," said the voice like the deacon's, "I had rather miss an ordination dinner than tonight's meeting. They tell me that some of our community are to be here from Falmouth and beyond, and others from Connecticut and Rhode Island, besides several of the Indian powwows, who, after their fashion, know almost as much deviltry as the best of us. Moreover, there is a goodly young woman to be taken into communion."

"Mighty well, Deacon Gookin!" replied the solemn old tones of the minister. "Spur up, or we shall be late. Nothing can be done, you know, until I get on the ground."

The hoofs clattered again; and the voices, talking so strangely in the empty air, passed on through the forest, where no church had ever been gathered or solitary Christian prayed. Whither, then, could these holy men be journeying so deep into the heathen wilderness? Young Goodman Brown caught hold of a tree for support, being ready to sink down on the ground, faint and overburdened with the heavy sickness of his heart. He looked up to the sky, doubting whether there really was a heaven above him. Yet there was the blue arch, and the stars brightening in it.

"With heaven above and Faith below, I will yet stand firm against the devil!" cried Goodman Brown.

While he still gazed upward into the deep arch of the firmament and had lifted his hands to pray, a cloud, though no wind was stirring, hurried across the zenith and hid the brightening stars. The blue sky was still visible, except directly overhead, where this black mass of cloud was sweeping swiftly northward. Aloft in the air, as if from the depths of the cloud, came a confused and doubtful sound of voices. Once the listener fancied that he could distinguish the accents of towns-people of his own, men and women, both pious and ungodly, many of whom he had met at the communion table, and had seen others rioting at the tavern. The next moment, so indistinct were the sounds, he doubted whether he had heard aught but the murmur of the old forest, whispering without a wind. Then came a stronger swell of those familiar tones, heard daily in the sunshine at Salem village, but never until now from a cloud of night. There was one voice of a young woman, uttering lamentations, yet with an uncertain sorrow, and entreating for some favor, which, perhaps, it would grieve her to obtain; and all the unseen multitude, both saints and sinners, seemed to encourage her onward.

"Faith!" shouted Goodman Brown, in a voice of agony and desperation; and the echoes of the forest mocked him, crying, "Faith! Faith!" as if bewildered wretches were seeking her all through the wilderness.

The cry of grief, rage, and terror was yet piercing the night, when the unhappy husband held his breath for a response. There was a scream, drowned immediately in a louder murmur of voices, fading into far-off laughter, as the dark cloud swept away, leaving the clear and silent sky above Goodman Brown. But something fluttered lightly down through the air and caught on the branch of a tree. The young man seized it, and beheld a pink ribbon.

"My Faith is gone!" cried he, after one stupefied moment. "There is no good on earth; and sin is but a name. Come, devil; for to thee is this world given."

And, maddened with despair, so that he laughed loud and long, did Goodman Brown grasp his staff and set forth again, at such a rate that he seemed to fly along the forest path rather than to walk or run. The road grew wilder and drearier and more faintly traced, and vanished at length, leaving him in the heart of the dark wilderness, still rushing onward with the instinct that guides mortal man to evil. The whole forest was peopled with frightful sounds—the creaking of the trees, the howling of wild beasts, and the yell of Indians; while sometimes the wind tolled like a distant church bell, and sometimes gave a broad roar around the traveller, as if all Nature were laughing him to scorn. But he was himself the chief horror of the scene, and shrank not from its other horrors.

"Ha! ha! ha!" roared Goodman Brown when the wind laughed at him. "Let us hear which will laugh loudest. Think not to frighten me with your deviltry. Come witch, come wizard, come Indian powwow, come devil himself, and here comes Goodman Brown. You may as well fear him as he fear you."

In truth, all through the haunted forest there could be nothing more frightful than the figure of Goodman Brown. On he flew among the black pines, brandishing his staff with frenzied gestures, now giving vent to an inspiration of horrid blasphemy, and now shouting forth such laughter as set all the echoes of the forest laughing like demons around him. The fiend in his own shape is less hideous than when he rages in the breast of man. Thus sped the demoniac on his course, until, quivering among the trees, he saw a red light before him, as when the felled trunks and branches of a clearing have been set on fire, and throw up their lurid blaze against the sky, at the hour of midnight. He paused, in a lull of the tempest that had driven him onward, and heard the swell of what seemed a hymn, rolling solemnly from a distance with the weight of many voices. He knew the tune; it was a familiar one in the choir of the village meeting-house. The verse died heavily away, and was lengthened by a chorus, not of human voices, but of all the sounds of the benighted wilderness pealing in awful harmony together. Goodman Brown cried out, and his cry was lost to his own ear by its unison with the cry of the desert.

In the interval of silence he stole forward until the light glared full upon his eyes. At one extremity of an open space, hemmed in by the dark wall of the forest, arose a rock, bearing some rude, natural resemblance either to an altar or a pulpit, and surrounded by four blazing pines, their tops aflame, their stems untouched, like candles at an evening meeting. The mass of foliage that had overgrown the summit of the rock was all on fire, blazing high into the night and fitfully illuminating the whole field. Each pendent twig and leafy festoon was in a blaze. As the red light arose and fell, a numerous congregation alternately shone forth, then disappeared in shadow, and again grew, as it were, out of the darkness, peopling the heart of the solitary woods at once.

"A grave and dark-clad company," quoth Goodman Brown.

In truth they were such. Among them, quivering to and fro between gloom and splendor, appeared faces that would be seen next day at the council board of the province, and others which, Sabbath after Sabbath, looked devoutly heavenward, and benignantly over the crowded pews, from the holiest pulpits in the land. Some affirm that the lady of the governor was there. At least there were high dames well known to her, and wives of honored husbands, and widows, a great multitude, and ancient maidens, all of excellent repute, and fair young girls, who trembled lest their mothers should espy them. Either the sudden gleams of light flashing over the obscure field bedazzled Goodman Brown, or he recognized a score of the church members of Salem village famous for their especial sanctity. Good old Deacon Gookin had arrived, and waited at the skirts of that venerable saint, his revered pastor. But, irreverently consorting with these grave, reputable, and pious people, these elders of the church, these chaste dames and dewy virgins, there were men of dissolute lives and women of spotted fame, wretches given over to all mean and filthy vice, and suspected even of horrid crimes. It was strange to see that the good shrank not from the wicked, nor were the sinners abashed by the saints. Scattered also among their pale-faced enemies were the Indian priests, or powwows, who had often scared their native forest with more hideous incantations than any known to English witchcraft.

"But where is Faith?" thought Goodman Brown; and, as hope came into his heart, he trembled.

Another verse of the hymn arose, a slow and mournful strain, such as the pious love, but joined to words which expressed all that our nature can conceive of sin, and darkly hinted at far more. Unfathomable to mere mortals is the lore of fiends. Verse after verse was sung; and still the chorus of the desert swelled between like the deepest tone of a mighty organ; and with the final peal of that dreadful anthem there came a sound, as if the roaring wind, the rushing streams, the howling beasts, and every other voice of the unconcerted wilderness were mingling and according with the voice of guilty man in homage to the prince of all. The four blazing pines threw up a loftier flame, and obscurely discovered shapes and visages of horror on the smoke wreaths above the impious assembly. At the same moment the fire on the rock shot redly forth and formed a glowing arch above its base, where now appeared a figure. With reverence be it spoken, the figure bore no slight similitude, both in garb and manner, to some grave divine of the New England churches.

"Bring forth the converts!" cried a voice that echoed through the field and rolled into the forest.

At the word, Goodman Brown stepped forth from the shadow of the trees and approached the congregation, with whom he felt a loathful brotherhood by the sympathy of all that was wicked in his heart. He could have well-nigh sworn that the shape of his own dead father beckoned him to advance, looking downward from a smoke wreath, while a woman, with dim features of despair, threw out her hand to warn him back. Was it his mother? But he had no power to retreat one step, nor to resist, even in thought, when the minister and good old Deacon Gookin seized his arms and led him to the blazing rock. Thither came also the slender form of a veiled female, led between Goody Cloyse, that pious teacher of the catechism, and Martha Carrier, who had received the devil's promise to be queen of hell. A rampant hag was she. And there stood the proselytes beneath the canopy of fire.

"Welcome, my children," said the dark figure, "to the communion of your race. Ye have found thus young your nature and your destiny. My children, look behind you!"

They turned; and flashing forth, as it were, in a sheet of flame, the fiend worshippers were seen; the smile of welcome gleamed darkly on every visage.

"There," resumed the sable form, "are all whom ye have reverenced from youth. Ye deemed them holier than yourselves, and shrank from your own sin, contrasting it with their lives of righteousness and prayerful aspirations heavenward. Yet here are they all in my worshipping assembly. This night it shall be granted you to know their secret deeds: how hoary-bearded elders

of the church have whispered wanton words to the young maids of their
households; how many a woman, eager for widows' weeds, has given her
husband a drink at bedtime and let him sleep his last sleep in her bosom;
how beardless youths have made haste to inherit their feathers' wealth; and
how fair damsels—blush not, sweet ones—have dug little graves in the
garden, and bidden me, the sole guest to an infant's funeral. By the sympathy of your human hearts for sin ye shall scent out all the places—
whether in church, bedchamber, street, field, or forest—where crime has
been committed, and shall exult to behold the whole earth one stain of guilt,
one mighty blood spot. Far more than this. It shall be yours to penetrate, in
every bosom, the deep mystery of sin, the fountain of all wicked arts, and
which inexhaustibly supplies more evil impulses than human power—than
my power at its utmost—can make manifest in deeds. And now, my children, look upon each other."

They did so; and, by the blaze of the hell-kindled torches, the wretched
man beheld his Faith, and the wife her husband, trembling before that un-
hallowed altar.

"Lo, there ye stand, my children," said the figure, in a deep and solemn
tone, almost sad with its despairing awfulness, as if his once angelic nature
could yet mourn for our miserable race. "Depending upon one another's
hearts, ye had still hoped that virtue were not all a dream. Now are ye unde-
ceived. Evil is the nature of mankind. Evil must be your only happiness.
Welcome again, my children, to the communion of your race."

"Welcome," repeated the fiend worshippers, in one cry of despair and triumph.

And there they stood, the only pair, as it seemed, who were yet hesitating
on the verge of wickedness in this dark world. A basin was hollowed, naturally, in the rock. Did it contain water, reddened by the lurid light? or was it
blood? or, perchance, a liquid flame? Herein did the shape of evil dip his
hand and prepare to lay the mark of baptism upon their foreheads, that they
might be partakers of the mystery of sin, more conscious of the secret guilt
of others, both in deed and thought, than they could now be of their own.
The husband cast one look at his pale wife, and Faith at him. What polluted
wretches would the next glance show them to each other, shuddering alike at
what they disclosed and what they saw!

"Faith! Faith!" cried the husband, "look up to heaven, and resist the
wicked one."

Whether Faith obeyed he knew not. Hardly had he spoken when he found
himself amid calm night and solitude, listening to a roar of the wind which
died heavily away through the forest. He staggered against the rock, and felt
it chill and damp; while a hanging twig, that had been all on fire, besprinkled
his cheek with the coldest dew.

The next morning young Goodman Brown came slowly into the street of

Salem village, staring around him like a bewildered man. The good old minister was taking a walk along the graveyard to get an appetite for breakfast and meditate his sermon, and bestowed a blessing, as he passed, on Goodman Brown. He shrank from the venerable saint as if to avoid an anathema. Old Deacon Gookin was at domestic worship, and the holy words of his prayer were heard through the open window. "What God doth the wizard pray to?" quoth Goodman Brown. Goody Cloyse, that excellent old Christian, stood in the early sunshine at her own lattice, catechizing a little girl who had brought her a pint of morning's milk. Goodman Brown snatched away the child as from the grasp of the fiend himself. Turning the corner by the meeting-house, he spied the head of Faith, with the pink ribbons, gazing anxiously forth, and bursting into such joy at sight of him that she skipped along the street and almost kissed her husband before the whole village. But Goodman Brown looked sternly and sadly into her face, and passed on without a greeting.

Had Goodman Brown fallen asleep in the forest and only dreamed a wild dream of a witch-meeting?

Be it so if you will; but, alas! it was a dream of evil omen for young Goodman Brown. A stern, a sad, a darkly meditative, a distrustful, if not a desperate man did he become from the night of that fearful dream. On the Sabbath day, when the congregation were singing a holy psalm, he could not listen because an anthem of sin rushed loudly upon his ear and drowned all the blessed strain. When the minister spoke from the pulpit with power and fervid eloquence, and, with his hand on the open Bible, of the sacred truths of our religion, and of saint-like lives and triumphant deaths, and of future bliss or misery unutterable, then did Goodman Brown turn pale, dreading lest the roof should thunder down upon the gray blasphemer and his hearers. Often, waking suddenly at midnight, he shrank from the bosom of Faith; and at morning or eventide, when the family knelt down at prayer, he scowled and muttered to himself, and gazed sternly at his wife, and turned away. And when he had lived long, and was borne to his grave a hoary corpse, followed by Faith, an aged woman, and children and grandchildren, a goodly procession, besides neighbors not a few, they carved no hopeful verse upon his tombstone, for his dying hour was gloom.

## STUDY QUESTIONS

1. What is an allegory? A parable? Is "Young Goodman Brown" either allegory or parable?

2. Why does Hawthorne repeatedly focus attention on Faith's pink ribbons?

3.  What is the significance of Young Goodman Brown's "excellent resolve for the future"?

4.  Does Young Goodman Brown see the minister and Deacon Gookin riding through the forest?

5.  In what instances are reality and appearance called into question?

6.  Why does the narrator call Young Goodman Brown the "chief horror of the scene"?

## Nathaniel Hawthorne

# THE MINISTER'S BLACK VEIL—A Parable[1]

Nathaniel Hawthorne (1804–1864) was born in Salem, Massachusetts. Among his ancestors was the Judge Hathorne who presided over the Salem witch trials. He graduated from Bowdoin College, where his classmates included Henry Wadsworth Longfellow and Franklin Pierce. His first novel, *Fanshawe,* was published in 1828. This was followed by *Twice-Told Tales* (1837), *Mosses from an Old Manse* (1846), *The Scarlet Letter* (1850), *The House of Seven Gables* (1851), *The Blithdale Romance* and *A Wonder Book* (1852), *Tanglewood Tales* (1853), and *The Marble Faun* (1860). Hawthorne served as surveyor at Boston Custom House and, after the publication of *The Life of Franklin Pierce* (1852), was named consul to Liverpool.

THE SEXTON stood in the porch of Milford meetinghouse, pulling lustily at the bell rope. The old people of the village came stooping along the street. Children with bright faces tripped merrily beside their parents, or mimicked a graver gait in the

First published 1836.

[1] Another clergyman in New England, Mr. Joseph Moody, of York, Maine, who died about eighty years since, made himself remarkable by the same eccentricity that is here related of the Reverend Mr. Hooper. In his case, however, the symbol had a different import. In early life he had accidentally killed a beloved friend; and from that day till the hour of his own death, he hid his face from men.

conscious dignity of their Sunday clothes. Spruce bachelors looked sidelong at the pretty maidens, and fancied that the Sabbath sunshine made them prettier than on weekdays. When the throng had mostly streamed into the porch, the sexton began to toll the bell, keeping his eye on the Reverend Mr. Hooper's door. The first glimpse of the clergyman's figure was the signal for the bell to cease its summons.

"But what has good Parson Hooper got upon his face?" cried the sexton in astonishment.

All within hearing immediately turned about and beheld the semblance of Mr. Hooper pacing slowly in his meditative way towards the meeting-house. With one accord they started, expressing more wonder than if some strange minister were coming to dust the cushions of Mr. Hooper's pulpit.

"Are you sure it is our parson?" inquired Goodman Gray of the sexton.

"Of a certainty it is good Mr. Hooper," replied the sexton. "He was to have exchanged pulpits with Parson Shute, of Westbury; but Parson Shute sent to excuse himself yesterday, being to preach a funeral sermon."

The cause of so much amazement may appear sufficiently slight. Mr. Hooper, a gentlemanly person of about thirty, though still a bachelor, was dressed with due clerical neatness, as if a careful wife had starched his band and brushed the weekly dust from his Sunday's garb. There was but one thing remarkable in his appearance. Swathed about his forehead and hanging down over his face so low as to be shaken by his breath, Mr. Hooper had on a black veil. On a nearer view it seemed to consist of two folds of crape, which entirely concealed his features except the mouth and chin, but probably did not intercept his sight farther than to give a darkened aspect to all living and inanimate things. With this gloomy shade before him, good Mr. Hooper walked onward at a slow and quiet pace, stooping somewhat and looking on the ground, as is customary with abstracted men, yet nodding kindly to those of his parishioners who still waited on the meetinghouse steps. But so wonder-struck were they that his greeting hardly met with a return.

"I can't really feel as if good Mr. Hooper's face was behind that piece of crape," said the sexton.

"I don't like it," muttered an old woman, as she hobbled into the meeting-house. "He has changed himself into something awful only by hiding his face."

"Our parson has gone mad!" cried Goodman Gray, following him across the threshold.

A rumor of some unaccountable phenomenon had preceded Mr. Hooper into the meetinghouse, and set all the congregation astir. Few could refrain from twisting their heads towards the door; many stood upright and turned directly about; while several little boys clambered upon the seats, and came down again with a terrible racket. There was a general bustle, a rustling of the women's gowns and shuffling of the men's feet, greatly at variance with that hushed repose which should attend the entrance of the minister. But Mr. Hooper appeared not to notice the perturbation of his people. He entered with an almost noiseless step, bent his head mildly to the pews on each side, and bowed as he passed his oldest parishioner, a white-haired great-grandsire, who occupied an armchair in the center of the aisle. It was strange to observe how slowly this venerable man became conscious of something singular in the appearance of his pastor. He seemed not fully to partake of the prevailing wonder till Mr. Hooper had ascended the stairs and showed himself in the pulpit face to face with his congregation, except for the black veil. That mysterious emblem was never once withdrawn. It shook with his measured breath as he gave out the psalm; it threw its obscurity between him and the holy page as he read the Scriptures; and while he prayed, the veil lay heavily on his uplifted countenance. Did he seek to hide it from the dread Being whom he was addressing?

Such was the effect of this simple piece of crape that more than one woman of delicate nerves was forced to leave the meetinghouse. Yet perhaps the pale-faced congregation was almost as fearful a sight to the minister as his black veil to them.

Mr. Hooper had the reputation of a good preacher, but not an energetic one: he strove to win his people heavenward by mild, persuasive influences, rather than to drive them thither by the thunders of the Word. The sermon which he now delivered was marked by the same characteristics of style and manner as the general series of his pulpit oratory. But there was something either in the sentiment of the discourse itself, or in the imagination of the auditors, which made it greatly the most powerful effort that they had ever heard from their pastor's lips. It was tinged rather more darkly than usual with the gentle gloom of Mr. Hooper's temperament. The subject had reference to secret sin, and those sad mysteries which we hide from our nearest and dearest and would fain conceal from our own consciousness, even forgetting that the Omniscient can detect them. A subtle power was breathed into his words. Each member of the congregation, the most innocent girl and the man of hardened breast, felt as if the preacher had crept upon them behind his awful veil, and discovered their hoarded iniquity of deed or thought. Many spread their clasped hands on their bosoms. There was nothing terrible in what Mr. Hooper said, at least, no violence; and yet, with every tremor of his melancholy voice the hearers quaked. An unsought pathos came hand in hand with awe. So sensible were the audience of some unwonted attribute in their minister that they longed for a breath of wind to blow aside the veil, almost believing that a stranger's visage would be discovered, though the form, gesture, and voice were those of Mr. Hooper.

At the close of the service the people hurried out with indecorous confusion, eager to communicate their pent-up amazement, and conscious of lighter spirits the moment they lost sight of the black veil. Some gathered in little circles, huddled closely together, with their mouths all whispering in the center; some went homeward alone, wrapped in silent meditation; some talked loudly, and profaned the Sabbath day with ostentatious laughter. A few shook their sagacious heads, intimating that they could penetrate the mystery; while one or two affirmed that there was no mystery at all, but only that Mr. Hooper's eyes were so weakened by the midnight lamp as to require a shade. After a brief interval, forth came good Mr. Hooper also, in the rear of his flock. Turning his veiled face from one group to another, he paid due reverence to the hoary heads, saluted the middle-aged with kind dignity, as their friend and spiritual guide, greeted the young with mingled authority and love, and laid his hands on the little children's heads to bless them. Such was always his custom on the Sabbath day. Strange and bewildered looks repaid him for his courtesy. None, as on former occasions, aspired to the honor of walking by their pastor's side. Old Squire Saunders, doubtless by an accidental lapse of memory, neglected to invite Mr. Hooper to his table, where the good clergyman had been wont to bless the food almost every Sunday since his settlement. He returned, therefore, to the parsonage, and, at the moment of closing the door, was observed to look back upon the people, all of whom had their eyes fixed upon the minister. A sad smile gleamed faintly from beneath the black veil and flickered about his mouth, glimmering as he disappeared.

"How strange," said a lady, "that a simple black veil, such as any woman might wear on her bonnet, should become such a terrible thing on Mr. Hooper's face!"

"Something must surely be amiss with Mr. Hooper's intellects," observed her husband, the physician of the village. "But the strangest part of the affair is the effect of this vagary, even on a sober-minded man like myself. The black veil, though it covers only our pastor's face, throws its influence over his whole person, and makes him ghostlike from head to foot. Do you not feel it so?"

"Truly do I," replied the lady; "and I would not be alone with him for the world. I wonder he is not afraid to be alone with himself!"

"Men sometimes are so," said her husband.

The afternoon service was attended with similar circumstances. At its conclusion, the bell tolled for the funeral of a young lady. The relatives and friends were assembled in the house, and the more distant acquaintances stood about the door, speaking of the good qualities of the deceased, when their talk was interrupted by the appearance of Mr. Hooper, still covered with his black veil. It was now an appropriate emblem. The clergyman stepped into the room where the corpse was laid, and bent over the coffin to take a last farewell of his deceased parishioner. As he stooped, the veil hung straight down from his forehead, so that, if her eyelids had not been closed forever, the dead maiden might have seen his face. Could Mr. Hooper be fearful of her glance, that he so hastily caught back the black veil? A person who watched the interview between the dead and living scrupled not to affirm that, at the instant when the clergyman's features were disclosed, the corpse had slightly shuddered, rustling the shroud and muslin cap, though the countenance retained the composure of death. A superstitious old woman was the only witness of this prodigy. From the coffin Mr. Hooper passed into the chamber of the mourners, and thence to the head of the staircase, to make the funeral prayer. It was a tender and heart-dissolving prayer, full of sorrow, yet so imbued with celestial hopes that the music of a heavenly harp, swept by the fingers of the dead, seemed faintly to be heard among the saddest accents of the minister. The people trembled, though they but darkly understood him, when he prayed that they, and himself, and all of mortal race, might be ready, as he trusted this young maiden had been, for the dreadful hour that should snatch the veil from their faces. The bearers went heavily forth, and the mourners followed, saddening all the street, with the dead before them and Mr. Hooper in the black veil behind.

"Why do you look back?" said one in the procession to his partner.

"I had a fancy," replied she, "that the minister and the maiden's spirit were walking hand in hand."

"And so had I at the same moment," said the other.

That night the handsomest couple in Milford village were to be joined in wedlock. Though reckoned a melancholy man, Mr. Hooper had a placid cheerfulness for such occasions which often excited a sympathetic smile where livelier merriment would have been thrown away. There was no quality of his disposition which made him more beloved than this. The company at the wedding awaited his arrival with impatience, trusting that the strange awe which had gathered over him throughout the day would now be dispelled. But such was not the result. When Mr. Hooper came, the first thing that their eyes rested on was the same horrible black veil, which had added deeper gloom to the funeral and could portend nothing but evil to the wedding. Such was its immediate effect on the guests that a cloud seemed to have rolled duskily from beneath the black crape and dimmed the light of the candles. The bridal pair stood up before the minister. But the bride's cold fingers quivered in the tremulous hand of the bridegroom, and her deathlike paleness caused a whisper that the maiden who had been buried a few hours before was come from her grave to be married. If ever another wedding were so dismal, it was that famous one where they tolled the wedding knell. After performing the ceremony, Mr. Hooper raised a glass of wine to his lips, wishing happiness to the new-married couple in a strain of mild pleasantry that ought to have brightened the features of the guests like a cheerful gleam from the hearth. At that instant, catching a glimpse of his figure in the looking glass, the black veil involved his own spirit in the horror with which it overwhelmed all others. His frame shuddered—his lips grew white—he spilled the untasted wine upon the carpet—and rushed forth into the darkness. For the earth, too, had on her black veil.

The next day the whole village of Milford talked of little else than Parson Hooper's black veil. That, and the mystery concealed behind it, supplied a topic for discussion between acquaintances meeting in the street, and good women gossiping at their open windows. It was the first item of news that the tavernkeeper told to his guests. The children babbled of it on their way to school. One imitative little imp covered his face with an old black handkerchief, thereby so affrighting his playmates that the panic seized himself, and he well-nigh lost his wits by his own waggery.

It was remarkable that, of all the busybodies and impertinent people in the parish, not one ventured to put the plain question to Mr. Hooper, wherefore he did this thing. Hitherto, whenever there appeared the slightest call for such interference, he had never lacked advisers, nor shown himself averse to be guided by their judgment. If he erred at all, it was by so painful a degree of self-distrust that even the mildest censure would lead him to consider an indifferent action as a crime. Yet, though so well acquainted with this amiable weakness, no individual among his parishioners chose to make the black veil a subject of friendly remonstrance. There was a feeling of dread, neither plainly confessed nor carefully concealed, which caused each to shift the responsibility upon another, till at length it was found expedient to send a deputation of the church, in order to deal with Mr. Hooper about the mystery before it should grow into a scandal. Never did an embassy so ill discharge its duties. The minister received them with friendly courtesy, but became silent after they were seated, leaving to his visitors the whole burden of introducing their important business. The topic, it might be supposed, was obvious enough. There was the black veil swathed round Mr. Hooper's forehead and concealing every feature above his placid mouth, on which at times they could perceive the glimmering of a melancholy smile. But that piece of crape, to their imagination, seemed to hang down before his heart, the symbol of a fearful secret between him and them. Were the veil but cast aside they might speak freely of it, but not till then. Thus they sat a considerable time, speechless, confused, and shrinking uneasily from Mr. Hooper's eye, which they felt to be fixed upon them with an invisible glance. Finally, the deputies returned abashed to their constituents, pronouncing the matter too weighty to be handled, except by a council of the churches, if indeed it might not require a general synod.

But there was one person in the village unappalled by the awe with which the black veil had impressed all beside herself. When the deputies returned without an explanation, or even venturing to demand one, she, with the calm energy of her character, determined to chase away the strange cloud that appeared to be settling round Mr. Hooper, every moment more darkly than before. As his plighted wife, it should be her privilege to know what the black veil concealed. At the minister's first visit, therefore, she entered upon the subject with a direct simplicity which made the task easier both for him and her. After he had seated himself, she fixed her eyes steadfastly upon the veil, but could discern nothing of the dreadful gloom that had so overawed the multitude: it was but a double fold of crape, hanging down from his forehead to his mouth, and slightly stirring with his breath.

"No," said she, aloud and smiling, "there is nothing terrible in this piece of crape, except that it hides a face which I am always glad to look upon. Come, good sir, let the sun shine from behind the cloud. First lay aside your black veil, then tell me why you put it on."

Mr. Hooper's smile glimmered faintly.

"There is an hour to come," said he, "when all of us shall cast aside our veils. Take it not amiss, beloved friend, if I wear this piece of crape till then."

"Your words are a mystery too," returned the young lady. "Take away the veil from them at least."

"Elizabeth, I will," said he, "so far as my vow may suffer me. Know, then, this veil is a type and a symbol, and I am bound to wear it ever, both in light and darkness, in solitude and before the gaze of multitudes, and as with strangers, so with my familiar friends. No mortal eye will see it withdrawn. This dismal shade must separate me from the world; even you, Elizabeth, can never come behind it!"

"What grievous affliction hath befallen you," she earnestly inquired, "that you should thus darken your eyes forever?"

"If it be a sign of mourning," replied Mr. Hooper, "I, perhaps, like most other mortals, have sorrows dark enough to be typified by a black veil."

"But what if the world will not believe that it is the type of an innocent sorrow?" urged Elizabeth. "Beloved and respected as you are, there may be whispers that you hide your face under the consciousness of secret sin. For the sake of your holy office, do away this scandal!"

The color rose into her cheeks as she intimated the nature of the rumors that were already abroad in the village. But Mr. Hooper's mildness did not forsake him. He even smiled again—that same sad smile, which always appeared like a faint glimmering of light proceeding from the obsurity beneath the veil.

"If I hide my face for sorrow, there is cause enough," he merely replied; "and if I cover it for secret sin, what mortal might not do the same?"

And with this gentle but unconquerable obstinacy did he resist all her entreaties. At length Elizabeth sat silent. For a few moments she appeared lost in thought, considering, probably, what new methods might be tried to withdraw her lover from so dark a fantasy, which, if it had no other meaning, was perhaps a symptom of mental disease. Though of a firmer character than his own, the tears rolled down her cheeks. But in an instant, as it were, a new feeling took the place of sorrow: her eyes were fixed insensibly on the black veil, when, like a sudden twilight in the air, its terrors fell around her. She arose and stood trembling before him.

"And do you feel it then at last?" said he mournfully.

She made no reply, but covered her eyes with her hand, and turned to leave the room. He rushed forward and caught her arm.

"Have patience with me, Elizabeth!" cried he passionately. "Do not desert me, though this veil must be between us here on earth. Be mine, and hereafter there shall be no veil over my face, no darkness between our souls! It is but a mortal veil—it is not for eternity! Oh! you know not how lonely I am, and how frightened, to be alone behind my black veil. Do not leave me in this miserable obscurity forever!"

"Lift the veil but once and look me in the face," said she.

"Never! It cannot be!" replied Mr. Hooper.

"Then, farewell!" said Elizabeth.

She withdrew her arm from his grasp and slowly departed, pausing at the door to give one long, shuddering gaze, that seemed almost to penetrate the mystery of the black veil. But even amid his grief Mr. Hooper smiled to think that only a material emblem had separated him from happiness, though the horrors which it shadowed forth must be drawn darkly between the fondest of lovers.

From that time no attempts were made to remove Mr. Hooper's black veil, or, by a direct appeal, to discover the secret which it was supposed to hide. By persons who claimed a superiority to popular prejudice it was reckoned merely an eccentric whim, such as often mingles with the sober actions of men otherwise rational, and tinges them all with its own semblance of insanity. But with the multitude good Mr. Hooper was irreparably a bugbear. He could not walk the streets with any peace of mind, so conscious was he that the gentle and timid would turn aside to avoid him, and that others would make it a point of hardihood to throw themselves in his way. The impertinence of the latter class compelled him to give up his customary walk at sunset to the burial ground; for when he leaned pensively over the gate, there would always be faces behind the gravestones peeping at his black veil. A fable went the rounds that the stare of the dead people drove him thence. It grieved him to the very depth of his kind heart to observe how the children fled from his approach, breaking up their merriest sports while his melancholy figure was yet afar off. Their instinctive dread caused him to feel more strongly than aught else that a preternatural horror was interwoven with the threads of the black crape. In truth, his own antipathy to the veil was known to be so great that he never willingly passed before a mirror, nor stooped to drink at a still fountain, lest in its peaceful bosom he should be affrighted by himself. This was what gave plausibility to the whispers that Mr. Hooper's conscience tortured him for some great crime too horrible to be entirely concealed, or otherwise than so obscurely intimated. Thus, from beneath the black veil, there rolled a cloud into the sunshine, an ambiguity of sin or sorrow, which enveloped the poor minister, so that love or sympathy could never reach him. It was said that ghost and fiend consorted with him there. With self-shudderings and outward terrors he walked continually in its shadow, groping darkly within his own soul or gazing through a medium that saddened the whole world. Even the lawless wind, it was believed, respected his dreadful secret and never blew aside the veil. But still good Mr. Hooper sadly smiled at the pale visages of the worldly throng as he passed by.

Among all its bad influences, the black veil had the one desirable effect of making its wearer a very efficient clergyman. By the aid of his mysterious emblem—for there was no other apparent cause—he became a man of awful power over souls that were in agony for sin. His converts always regarded him with a dread peculiar to themselves, affirming, though but figuratively that, before he brought them to celestial light, they had been with him behind the black veil. Its gloom, indeed, enabled him to sympathize with all dark affections. Dying sinners cried aloud for Mr. Hooper, and would not yield their breath till he appeared; though ever, as he stooped to whisper consolation, they shuddered at the veiled face so near their own. Such were the terrors of the black veil, even when Death had bared his visage! Strangers came long distances to attend service at his church, with the mere idle purpose of gazing at his figure, because it was forbidden them to behold his face. But many were made to quake ere they departed! Once, during Governor Belcher's administration, Mr. Hooper was appointed to preach the election sermon. Covered with his black veil, he stood before the chief magistrate, the council, and the representatives, and wrought so deep an impression that the legislative measures of that year were characterized by all the gloom and piety of our earliest ancestral sway.

In this manner Mr. Hooper spent a long life, irreproachable in outward act, yet shrouded in dismal suspicions; kind and loving, though unloved and dimly feared; a man apart from men, shunned in their health and joy, but ever summoned to their aid in mortal anguish. As years wore on, shedding their snows above his sable veil, he acquired a name throughout the New England churches, and they called him Father Hooper. Nearly all his parishioners who were of mature age when he was settled had been borne away by many a funeral: he had one congregation in the church, and a more crowded one in the churchyard; and having wrought so late into the evening, and done his work so well, it was now good Father Hooper's turn to rest.

Several persons were visible by the shaded candlelight in the death chamber of the old clergyman. Natural connections he had none. But there was the decorously grave though unmoved physician, seeking only to mitigate the last pangs of the patient whom he could not save. There were the deacons and other eminently pious members of his church. There, also, was the Reverend Mr. Clark, of Westbury, a young and zealous divine, who had ridden in haste to pray by the bedside of the expiring minister. There was the nurse, no hired handmaiden of death, but one whose calm affection had endured thus long in secrecy, in solitude, amid the chill of age, and would not perish, even at the dying hour. Who, but Elizabeth! And there lay the hoary head of good Father Hooper upon the death pillow, with the black veil still swathed about his brow and reaching down over his face, so that each more difficult gasp of his faint breath caused it to stir. All through life that piece of crape had hung between him and the world: it had separated him from cheerful brotherhood and woman's love, and kept him in that saddest of all prisons, his own heart; and still it lay upon his face, as if to deepen the gloom of his darksome chamber, and shade him from the sunshine of eternity.

For some time previous his mind had been confused, wavering doubtfully between the past and the present, and hovering forward, as it were, at intervals, into the indistinctness of the world to come. There had been feverish turns, which tossed him from side to side, and wore away what little strength he had. But in his most convulsive struggles, and in the wildest vagaries of his intellect, when no other thought retained its sober influence, he still showed an awful solicitude lest the black veil should slip aside. Even if his bewildered soul could have forgotten, there was a faithful woman at his pillow, who, with averted eyes, would have covered that aged face, which she had last beheld in the comeliness of manhood. At length the death-stricken old man lay quietly in the torpor of mental and bodily exhaustion, with an imperceptible pulse, and breath that grew fainter and fainter, except when a long, deep, and irregular inspiration seemed to prelude the flight of his spirit.

The minister of Westbury approached the bedside.

"Venerable Father Hooper," said he, "the moment of your release is at hand. Are you ready for the lifting of the veil that shuts in time from eternity?"

Father Hooper at first replied merely by a feeble motion of his head; then, apprehensive, perhaps, that his meaning might be doubtful, he exerted himself to speak.

"Yea," said he, in faint accents, "my soul hath a patient weariness until that veil be lifted."

"And is it fitting," resumed the Reverend Mr. Clark, "that a man so given to prayer, of such a blameless example, holy in deed and thought, so far as mortal judgment may pronounce; is it fitting that a father in the church should leave a shadow on his memory, that may seem to blacken a life so pure? I pray you, my venerable brother, let not this thing be! Suffer us to be gladdened by your triumphant aspect, as you go to your reward. Before the veil of eternity be lifted, let me cast aside this black veil from your face!"

And thus speaking, the Reverend Mr. Clark bent forward to reveal the mystery of so many years. But exerting a sudden energy that made all the beholders stand aghast, Father Hooper snatched both his hands from beneath the bedclothes, and pressed them strongly on the black veil, resolute to struggle if the minister of Westbury would contend with a dying man.

"Never!" cried the veiled clergyman. "On earth, never!"

"Dark old man!" exclaimed the affrighted minister, "with what horrible crime upon your soul are you now passing to the judgment?"

Father Hooper's breath heaved; it rattled in his throat; but, with a mighty effort, grasping forward with his hands, he caught hold of life, and held it back till he should speak. He even raised himself in bed; and there he sat, shivering with the arms of death around him, while the black veil hung down, awful, at that last moment, in the gathered terrors of a lifetime. And yet the faint, sad smile, so often there, now seemed to glimmer from its obscurity, and linger on Father Hooper's lips.

"Why do you tremble at me alone?" cried he, turning his veiled face round the circle of pale spectators. "Tremble also at each other! Have men avoided me, and women shown no pity, and children screamed and fled, only for my black veil? What but the mystery which it obscurely typifies has made this piece of crape so awful? When the friend shows his inmost heart to his friend; the lover to his best beloved; when man does not vainly shrink from the eye of his Creator, loathsomely treasuring up the secret of his sin; then deem me a monster, for the symbol beneath which I have lived, and die! I look around me, and, lo! on every visage a black veil!"

While his auditors shrank from one another in mutual affright, Father Hooper fell back upon his pillow, a veiled corpse, with a faint smile lingering on the lips. Still veiled, they laid him in his coffin, and a veiled corpse they bore him to the grave. The grass of many years has sprung up and withered on that grave, the burial stone is moss-grown, and good Mr. Hooper's face is dust; but awful is still the thought that it moldered beneath the black veil!

STUDY QUESTIONS

1. Hawthorne himself labeled "The Minister's Black Veil" "a parable." What moral lesson can be drawn from his tale? Does Hawthorne's footnote help clarify his intent?

2. In his review of Hawthorne's *Twice-Told Tales,* Edgar Allan Poe called the reader's attention to the episode of the dead girl. What relationship does this episode bear to the rest of the tale?

3. Why does Mr. Hooper smile at Elizabeth's anguished farewell? Why does he smile on his death-bed?

4. How does the attitude of the parishioners toward Mr. Hooper and his veil change with the passage of time?

5. What similarities are there in the last paragraphs of "Young Goodman Brown" and "The Minister's Black Veil"?

*Thomas E. Connolly*

# HAWTHORNE'S "YOUNG GOODMAN BROWN": AN ATTACK ON PURITANIC CALVINISM

Thomas E. Connolly (1918–      ) was born in New York. He received an S.B. (1939) from Fordham University and an A.M. (1947) and a Ph.D. (1951) from the University of Chicago. He has taught at the University of Idaho and Creighton University, and is currently at the State University of Buffalo, New York. In addition to his contributions to scholarly journals, he has published three books about James Joyce.

IT IS SURPRISING, in a way, to discover how few of the many critics who have discussed "Young Goodman Brown" agree on any aspect of the work except that it is an excellent short story. D. M. McKeithan says that its theme is "sin and its blighting effects." [1] Richard H. Fogle observes, "Hawthorne the artist refuses to limit himself to a single and doctrinaire conclusion, proceeding instead by indi-

Reprinted from *American Literature*, XXVIII (1956), by permission of the Duke University Press and Thomas E. Connolly.

[1] D. M. McKeithan, "Hawthorne's 'Young Goodman Brown': An Interpretation," *Modern Language Notes*, LXVII (February, 1952), 94.

88                                                    The Individual

rection," [2] implying, presumably, that it is inartistic to say something
which can be clearly understood by the readers. Gordon and Tate assert,
"Hawthorne is dealing with his favorite theme: the unhappiness which the
human heart suffers as a result of its innate depravity." [3] Austin Warren
says, "His point is the devastating effect of moral scepticism." [4] Almost all
critics agree, however, that Young Goodman Brown lost his faith. Their
conclusions are based, perhaps, upon the statement, "My Faith is gone!"
made by Brown when he recognizes his wife's voice and ribbon. I should like
to examine the story once more to show that Young Goodman Brown did
not lose his faith at all. In fact, not only did he retain his faith, but during his
horrible experience he actually discovered the full and frightening significance of his faith.

Mrs. Leavis comes closest to the truth in her discussion of this story in the
Sewanee Review in which she says: "Hawthorne has imaginatively recre-
ated for the reader that Calvinist sense of sin, that theory which did in actuality shape the early social and spiritual history of New England." [5] But
Mrs. Leavis seems to miss the critical implications of the story, for she goes
on to say: "But in Hawthorne, by a wonderful feat of transmutation, it has
no religious significance, it is a psychological state that is explored. Young
Goodman Brown's Faith is not faith in Christ but faith in human beings, and
losing it he is doomed to isolation forever." [6] Those who persist in reading
this story as a study of the effects of sin on Brown come roughly to this conclusion: "Goodman Brown became evil as a result of sin and thought he saw
evil *where none existed*." [7] Hawthorne's message is far more depressing and
horrifying than this. The story is obviously an individual tragedy, and those
who treat it as such are right, of course; but, far beyond the personal plane,
it has universal implications.

Young Goodman Brown, as a staunch Calvinist, is seen at the beginning
of this allegory to be quite confident that he is going to heaven. The errand
on which he is going is presented mysteriously and is usually interpreted to
be a deliberate quest of sin. This may or may not be true; what is important
is that he is going out to meet the devil by prearrangement. We are told by
the narrator that his purpose in going is evil. When the devil meets him, he
refers to the "beginning of a journey." Brown admits that he "kept covenant" by meeting the devil and hints at the evil purpose of the meeting.

[2] Richard H. Fogle, "Ambiguity and Clarity in Hawthorne's 'Young Goodman
Brown,' " *New England Quarterly*, XVIII (December, 1945), 453.
[3] Caroline Gordon and Allen Tate (eds.), *The House of Fiction* (New York, 1950), p.
38.
[4] Austin Warren, *Nathaniel Hawthorne* (New York, 1934), p. 362.
[5] Q. D. Leavis, "Hawthorne as Poet," *Sewanee Review*, LIX (Spring 1951), 197–
198.
[6] *Ibid.*
[7] McKeithan, *op. cit.*, p. 95. Italics mine.

Though his family has been Christian for generations, the point is made early in the story that Young Goodman Brown has been married to his Faith for only three months. Either the allegory breaks down at this point or the marriage to Faith must be looked upon as the moment of conversion to grace in which he became fairly sure of his election to heaven. That Goodman Brown is convinced he is of the elect is made clear at the beginning: ". . . and after this one night I'll cling to her skirts and follow her to heaven." In other words, at the start of his adventure, Young Goodman Brown is certain that his faith will help man get to heaven. It is in this concept that his disillusionment will come. The irony of this illusion is brought out when he explains to the devil the reason for his tardiness: "Faith kept me back awhile." That is what he thinks! By the time he gets to the meeting place he finds that his Faith is already there. Goodman Brown's disillusionment in his belief begins quickly after meeting the devil. He has asserted proudly that his ancestors "have been a race of honest men and good Christians since the days of the martyrs," and the devil turns his own words on him smartly:

Well said, Goodman Brown! I have been as well acquainted with your family as with ever a one among the Puritans; and that's no trifle to say. I helped your grandfather, the constable, when he lashed the Quaker woman so smartly through the streets of Salem; and it was I that brought your father a pitch-pine knot, kindled at my own hearth, to set fire to an Indian village, in King Philip's war. They were my good friends, both; and many a pleasant walk have we had along this path, and returned merrily after midnight. I would fain be friends with you for their sake.

Goodman Brown manages to shrug off this identification of his parental and grandparental Puritanism with the devil, but the reader should not overlook the sharp tone of criticism in Hawthorne's presentation of this speech.

When the devil presents his next argument, Brown is a little more shaken. The devil has shown him that Goody Cloyse is of his company and Brown responds: "What if a wretched old woman do choose to go to the devil when I thought she was going to heaven: is that any reason why I should quit my dear Faith and go after her?" He still believes at this point that his faith will lead him to heaven. The devil's reply, "You will think better of this by and by," is enigmatic when taken by itself, but a little earlier the narrator had made a comment which throws a great deal of light on this remark by the devil. When he recognized Goody Cloyse, Brown said, "That old woman taught me my catechism," and the narrator added, "and there was a world of meaning in this simple comment." The reader at this point should be fairly well aware of Hawthorne's criticism of Calvinism. The only way there can be a "world of meaning" in Brown's statement is that her catechism teaches the way to the devil and not the way to heaven.

From this point on Brown is rapidly convinced that his original conception about his faith is wrong. Deacon Gookin and the "good old minister," in league with Satan, finally lead the way to his recognition that this faith is diabolic rather than divine. Hawthorne points up this fact by a bit of allegorical symbolism. Immediately after he recognizes the voices of the deacon and the minister, we are told by the narrator that "Young Goodman Brown caught hold of a tree for support, being ready to sink down on the ground, faint and overburdened with the heavy sickness of his heart. He looked up to the sky, doubting whether there really was a heaven above him. Yet there was a blue arch, and the stars brightened in it." Here the doubt has begun to gnaw, but the stars are symbols of the faint hope which he is still able to cherish, and he is able to say: "With heaven above and Faith below, I will yet stand firm against the devil." But immediately a symbolic cloud hides the symbolic stars: "While he still gazed upward into the deep arch of the firmament and had lifted his hands to pray, a cloud, though no wind was stirring, hurried across the zenith and hid the brightening stars." And it is out of this black cloud of doubt that the voice of his faith reaches him and the pink ribbon of his Faith falls.[8] It might be worthwhile to discuss Faith's pink ribbons here, for Hawthorne certainly took great pains to call them to our attention. The ribbons seem to be symbolic of his initial illusion about the true significance of his faith, his belief that his faith will lead him to heaven. The pink ribbons on a Puritan lady's cap, signs of youth, joy, and happiness, are actually entirely out of keeping with the severity of the rest of her dress which, if not somber black, is at least gray. When the ribbon falls from his cloud of doubt, Goodman Brown cries in agony, "My Faith is gone!" and it is gone in the sense that it now means not what it once meant. He is quick to apply the logical, ultimate conclusion of Goody Cloyse's catechizing: "Come, devil; for to thee is this world given."

Lest the reader miss the ultimate implication of the doctrine of predestination, Hawthorne has the devil preach a sermon at his communion service: "Welcome, my children . . . to the communion of your race. Ye have found thus young your nature and your destiny." Calvinism teaches that man is innately depraved and that he can do nothing to merit salvation. He is saved only by the whim of God who selects some, through no deserts of their own, for heaven while the great mass of mankind is destined for hell. The devil concludes his sermon: "Evil is the nature of mankind. Evil must be your only happiness. Welcome again, my children, to the communion of your race." It is not at all insignificant that the word *race* is used several

[8] F. O. Matthiessen made entirely too much of the wrong thing of this ribbon. Had Young Goodman Brown returned to Salem Village clutching the ribbon, there might be some point in what Matthiessen says (*American Renaissance,* New York, 1941, pp. 282–284). As it is, the ribbon presents no more of a problem than do the burning trees turned suddenly cold again.

times in this passage, for it was used earlier by Goodman Brown when he said, "We have been a race of honest men and good Christians. . . ." After this sermon by the devil, Young Goodman Brown makes one last effort to retain the illusion that faith will lead him to heaven; he calls out: "Faith! Faith! . . . look up to heaven, and resist the wicked one." But we are fairly sure that he is unsuccessful, for we are immediately told: "Whether Faith obeyed he knew not."

Young Goodman Brown did not lose his faith (we are even told that his Faith survived him); he learned its full and terrible significance. This story is Hawthorne's criticism of the teachings of Puritanic-Calvinism. His implication is that the doctrine of the elect and damned is not a faith which carries man heavenward on its skirts, as Brown once believed, but, instead, condemns him to hell—bad and good alike indiscriminately—and for all intents and purposes so few escape as to make one man's chance of salvation almost disappear. It is this awakening to the full meaning of his faith which causes Young Goodman Brown to look upon his minister as a blasphemer when he teaches "the sacred truths of our religion, and of saint-like lives and triumphant deaths, and of future bliss or misery unutterable," for he has learned that according to the truths of his faith there is probably nothing but "misery unutterable" in store for him and all his congregation; it is this awakening which causes him to turn away from prayer; it is this awakening which makes appropriate the fact that "they carved no hopeful verse upon his tombstone."

Though much is made of the influence of Puritanism on the writings of Hawthorne, he must also be seen to be a critic of the teachings of Puritanism. Between the position of Vernon L. Parrington,[9] who saw Hawthorne as retaining "much of the older Calvinistic view of life and human destiny," and that of Régis Michaud,[10] who saw him as "an anti-puritan and prophet heralding the Freudian gospel," lies the truth about Hawthorne.

## STUDY QUESTIONS

1.  Connolly quotes Richard H. Fogle and then interprets Fogle's statement. Is Connolly's interpretation of Fogle a just one?

2.  What is the thesis of Connolly's essay? Is this purpose stated explicitly or implicitly?

3.  Connolly feels that the narrator's comment on Young Goodman Brown's remark about Goody Cloyse reveals Hawthorne's criticism of Calvinism.

[9] *Main Currents in American Thought* (New York, 1927), II, 443.
[10] "How Nathaniel Hawthorne Exorcised Hester Prynne," *The American Novel Today* (Boston, 1928), pp. 25–46.

Can you interpret Brown's remark in another way? The narrator's comment?

4. What does Connolly think Faith's ribbons symbolize?

5. Does Connolly's last paragraph suggest that his purpose was twofold: to interpret Hawthorne's short story for the reader, and to interpret Hawthorne *himself* for the reader? Is the last paragraph gratuitous?

*Robert W. Cochran*

# HAWTHORNE'S CHOICE: THE VEIL OR THE JAUNDICED EYE

Robert W. Cochran (1926–      ) was born in Williamsport, Pennsylvania. He received his A.B. (1948) from Indiana University, and his M.A. (1949) and Ph.D. (1957) from the University of Michigan. He is currently Associate Professor of English at the University of Vermont. Cochran contributes regularly to *College English*.

I N HIS STORIES "Young Goodman Brown" and "The Minister's Black Veil," Hawthorne presents the opposite extremes of reaction to mankind within a single alternative view of man's nature. Both young Goodman Brown and the Reverend Mr. Hooper view men as sinners. Yet Brown ends his life in darkness, disillusionment, and despair; whereas Mr. Hooper achieves a steady acceptance of life through relative enlightenment, a total recognition of sin and sorrow, and a firm belief in a traditional afterlife.

Such an interpretation of "The Minister's Black Veil" is at sharp variance with the consensus view that Hooper, like Brown, lives out his days and enters the grave the victim of a dark obsession. In his admirably balanced reading of "The Minister's Black Veil," R. H. Fogle interprets the tale as

Robert W. Cochran, "Reply," *College English*, XXIV (1962). Reprinted by permission of the National Council of Teachers of English and Robert W. Cochran.

mirroring the ambiguity of life in a parallel ambiguity of meaning.[1] But the veil can be more definitely identified, without the oversimplification of which Mr. Hooper's parishioners are guilty and without arriving at what Fogle terms "a single dogmatic conclusion."

The Reverend Mr. Hooper is regularly said to indulge in a special form of self-pity, masochistic at base: Hooper is characterized by Fogle as having an "infatuated love of mystification." The best that may be said of Hooper, in keeping with the generally accepted interpretation of his actions, is to be found in a question Fogle raises:

. . . is it possible that we can go further afield and determine that the message of the veil *is* representative and universal: that the failure to recognize it is simply the last and most chilling proof of man's imprisonment within himself?

Considering the implications of his question with respect to Hawthorne's problem of achieving artistic unity, Fogle concludes:

. . . in order to present forcibly the tragic isolation of one man, Hawthorne is obliged to consider society as a solid group arrayed against his hero, ignoring for the time being the fact that this hero is Everyman.

But, to pursue the direction of Fogle's question yet a step further, Hawthorne's hero is not Everyman: Hooper's experience is not typical, for that which he glimpses is the outer limit of earthly wisdom. The vision he gains is granted to few, though the perception is of a truth which is at the very heart of the nature of all mortal existence.

Ironically, from this new point of view Rev. Hooper achieves a far more penetrating equivalent of that "steady view of life, the *aurea mediocritas*" which Fogle assigns only to Hooper's sweetheart, Elizabeth, and which Fogle believes to be Hawthorne's conception of the "highest good."

## II

By considering the two stories and their protagonists together, it is possible to reject not only Fogle's interpretation of "The Minister's Black Veil," but Thomas E. Connolly's interpretation of "Young Goodman Brown" as well. "Young Goodman Brown" is not, as Connolly says it is, a specific attack on Puritanic Calvinism.[2] In Hawthorne's tales and romances, the Puritan New England setting in time and place is illustrative, not restrictive. The

[1] R. H. Fogle, " 'An Ambiguity of Sin or Sorrow,' " *The New England Quarterly*, 21 (September 1948), 342–349.

[2] Thomas E. Connolly, "Hawthorne's 'Young Goodman Brown': An Attack on Puritanic Calvinism," *American Literature*, 28 (November 1956), 370–375.

diametrically opposed perspectives on man to which the main characters of these two stories come represent a universal difference in approach to the reading of the human condition.

Just as surely as Aylmer, Dr. Rappaccini, or Ethan Brand, Young Goodman Brown is guilty of the Unpardonable Sin of Pride. In fact, Young Goodman Brown's mistake is essentially the same as that which Hawthorne laments in Aylmer, in the concluding sentence of "The Birthmark." In his impatience with human imperfection, Brown loses his Faith in mankind; the milk of human kindness dries up within him. Connolly's argument that "Young Goodman Brown did not lose his faith (we are even told that his Faith survived him)" is certainly based on a too strictly theological interpretation. Hawthorne explicitly states that Faith survives Brown to symbolize the very general religious belief that Faith is always available to the man capable of embracing her. This belief in the availability of Faith to the human heart which remains open to invite her in is familiar to any reader who knows conventional Christianity: invitations to Christ to "enter in" are central to traditional Christian worship.

That Hawthorne uses the term "Goodman" in Brown's name to indicate that Brown is a member of the race which includes Goody Cloyse, Deacon Gookin, and his own father and grandfather is generally recognized (one could go much farther in citing evidence from the story suggesting a breadth of applicability, to include all strata and all generations of Salem society and, by extension, of all human society). But the deeper irony—that Brown is but a youth—is curiously overlooked. That Brown is young suggests that his journey into the forest is not simply premeditated and prearranged, but that it is inevitable. Brown's is therefore a typical human journey—out of innocence and into experience. To borrow from William Blake, Brown is pictured in this story at the moment when he leaves the realm of pink ribbons and the gentle lamb to enter into the disquieting and mysterious realm where the tiger burns bright in the forests of the night.

To this extent, Young Goodman Brown is representative of all mankind; we all have a rendezvous with the Devil. Only the form which the Prince of Darkness takes varies in individual cases. Brown's journey is inevitable, but the results of his journey are not. That Brown is young is significant; that he is called "Goodman" is ironic but primarily tragic, in the sense that it helps the reader to identify with Brown not only the other characters in the story, but himself as well. But that Brown is "but three months married" to Faith is especially meaningful. Brown is representative of all who are innocent and undeveloped. Had he been wed to his Faith longer, had he put his Faith and himself to the test by degrees, he might have won through in his struggle with despair. But he did not because he could not. If the reader condemns Brown, he, like Brown, has become self-righteous. Or, if the reader believes, conversely, that Young Goodman Brown is representative of all mankind and that there is no escape from despair once evil is encountered, he, like Brown, delivers himself into the hands of the Devil, in the terms of the story.

## III

The Reverend Mr. Hooper does not make Brown's mistake. He does not view his fellow creatures with a jaundiced eye. Father Hooper sees the same truth about human nature that Young Goodman Brown sees, but he does not fall prey to Evil by obsessively viewing man as hopelessly sinful and disqualified from Salvation.

Unlike Goodman Brown, Father Hooper profits from his vision: he becomes more understanding of human frailty than he was before he learned his lesson and donned the veil. This increased compassion and pity is the product of Mr. Hooper's sharpened awareness that the black veil figuratively covers all faces, including even the Earth's face. Thus Hooper's isolation is different from other men's only in degree—in intensity—and not in kind.

Hawthorne called "The Minister's Black Veil" a "parable," and one purpose of a parable is to clarify. The parable of the veil clarifies not simply by mirroring the ambiguity of life in a parallel ambiguity of meaning which Fogle has so ably demonstrated, but also by identifying the source of life's ambiguity. In the story, the veil is frequently identified as an emblem of mortality, of human imperfection. It is therefore comparable to the small hand on Georgiana's cheek in "The Birthmark"; for it is similarly a mark visited by Nature on all human beings, although seldom in so concrete a form.

After he has put on the veil, Father Hooper becomes a man apart, in that for him the secret of sin lies in its mysterious depths and not in a sense of particular shame or guilt. He is awed by Sin, rather than fearful of any single manifestation or consequence of sin. One important result of his vision of the truth about the human condition is of course his heightened sense of isolation. Even Elizabeth, the woman he truly loves, is cut off from him. But no two humans can be completely wed, as Hooper is made to realize very sharply when he sees his own reflection in a mirror, just after he has officiated at the wedding ceremony. His spiritual chill upon glimpsing the outside of the veil, presumably coupled with a keen sense that no earthly marriage can be the wedding of two isolated spirits—the perfect union which romantic young couples dimly hope for—indicates the price Reverend Hooper must pay for his vision.

Still, that vision even as it isolates and chills also provides Reverend Hooper with the ultimate in earthly wisdom; for, having recognized the fearful truth of human isolation, Hooper does not withdraw from the human race. The reality of man's innate depravity blinds Goodman Brown to man's innate goodness. Hooper, on the other hand, sees man's mixed nature precisely because he faces at every moment that same reality embodied in the veil.

As Fogle observes, "In one respect, however, the veil makes Mr. Hooper a more efficient clergyman, for 'it enabled him to sympathize with all dark affections.' " From the moment of his vision of the truth, Mr. Hooper becomes a more effective instrument of God, if indeed he does not become the very voice of God:

Mr. Hooper had the reputation of a good preacher, but not an energetic one: he strove to win his people heavenward by mild, persuasive influences, rather than to drive them thither by the thunders of the Word. The sermon which he now delivered was marked by the same characteristics of style and manner as the general series of his pulpit oratory. But there was something, either in the sentiment of the discourse itself, or in the imagination of the auditors, which made it greatly the most powerful effort that they had ever heard from their pastor's lips. It was tinged, rather more darkly than usual, with the gentle gloom of Mr. Hooper's temperament.

The subject had reference to secret sin, and those sad mysteries which we hide from our nearest and dearest, and would fain conceal from our own consciousness, even forgetting that the Omniscient can detect them. A subtle power was breathed into his words. Each member of the congregation, the most innocent girl, and the man of hardened breast, felt as if the preacher had crept upon them, behind his awful veil, and discovered their hoarded iniquity of deed or thought. Many spread their clasped hands on their bosoms. There was nothing terrible in what Mr. Hooper said, at least, no violence; and yet, with every tremor of his melancholy voice, the hearers quaked. An unsought pathos came hand in hand with awe. So sensible were the audience of some unwonted attribute in their minister, that they longed for a breath of wind to blow aside the veil, almost believing that a stranger's visage would be discovered, though the form, gesture, and voice were those of Mr. Hooper.

Furthermore, from this point in the story forward, those who will not—indeed, cannot bring themselves to—admit their sins, even to themselves, shun Hooper's presence or defensively "throw themselves in his way." But those who recognize their own sins call for the one minister who has "qualified" himself by previous words and actions, and Mr. Hooper does not fail them. At the same time that the veil isolates Father Hooper from meaningful human relationships, then, it increases his communicative power as a minister. Paradoxically, Mr. Hooper is not so isolated or so misunderstood as the villagers' oversimplified interpretations of why he wears the veil would lead us to suppose.

The Reverend Mr. Hooper has been permitted to cross over beyond the veil of mystery to achieve the ultimate in human knowledge. By reason of his intellect and his years of dedication to God and devotion to duty, he has been vouchsafed a unique comprehension of what mortality means. The danger to Hooper, as any careful reader of Hawthorne will know, is that, being only in part spirit and in part frail flesh, he may exult in his superior knowledge and fall victim to the sin of Pride. That he does not become self-righteous or contemptuous in his dealings with his fellows is, of course, painstakingly established by Hawthorne.

The veil, then, serves two large functions: First, it captures the imagination of men, not merely during Mr. Hooper's lifetime, but also after his physical death:

Still veiled, they laid him in his coffin, and a veiled corpse they bore him to the grave. The grass of many years has sprung up and withered on that grave, the burial stone is moss-grown, and good Mr. Hooper's face is dust; but awful is still the thought that it mouldered beneath the Black Veil!

And equally important, the veil is a constant reminder to Hooper of his fellowship with man and of his obligation to God. Hooper's sorrow is his steady and painful awareness that all men are sinners and that all men, himself most particularly, are isolated in this life. Hooper's reward is his conviction that " '. . . . hereafter there shall be no veil over my face, no darkness between our souls! It is but a mortal veil—it is not for eternity!' " For all the horror he feels whenever he sees his reflection in a mirror or a fountain, Mr. Hooper's sad smiles and his "gentle, but unconquerable obstinacy" whenever he is begged to remove the veil show the minister to be a man of comparative serenity and of great steadfastness. Hooper's refusal to remove the veil demonstrates that he is wed to it in this life. The veil represents harsh reality, and Hooper understands that so long as he exists in the mortal condition, his spirit is bound to the veil.

Thus, "The Minister's Black Veil" is central to Hawthorne's view of life: in life there is little cause for joy and much cause for gloom; yet wisdom lies not in submitting to despair but in developing a quiet, hopeful patience— in the promise of a traditional Christian afterlife.

How different in effect is Mr. Hooper's comprehension that all men are sinners from Young Goodman Brown's destructive discovery. After his physical death, Mr. Hooper achieves even earthly immortality, in that he inspires feelings of awe in those who survive him. It is not too much to suggest that in contrast Young Goodman Brown, on whose tombstone "no hopeful verse" was carved, lies in an absolutely desolate grave, like Hooper's untended in fact, but unlike Hooper's in that it is not kept green in memory.

Unquestionably, Hawthorne himself felt the pull toward Young Goodman Brown's view of man. His publication of "The Minister's Black Veil" and other parables of life may be interpreted as Hawthorne's public displaying of a black veil over his own face. Hawthorne's works are, therefore, both a measure of his own need for a reminder that he was a member of the human race and a signal of his success in avoiding the Unpardonable Sin.

### STUDY QUESTIONS

1.  What does Cochran mean when he says that Hawthorne's Puritan New England setting is "illustrative, not restrictive"?

2.  Why does Cochran feel that Young Goodman Brown's youth is significant?

3.  Does Cochran's discussion of "The Minister's Black Veil" lend credence to his interpretation of "Young Goodman Brown"?

4.  According to Cochran, what is Hawthorne's view of life?

5.  In what way do Cochran and Connolly reach similar conclusions in their interpretation of the story?

*Thomas E. Connolly*

# HOW YOUNG GOODMAN BROWN BECAME OLD BADMAN BROWN

$\mathcal{M}$R. COCHRAN'S thought-provoking essay on Hawthorne's two short stories, "Hawthorne's Choice: Veil or Jaundiced Eye" (*CE*, February 1962), prompted me to review my own thoughts on "Young Goodman Brown" (*AL*, November 1956). Unfortunately, I was not moved to renounce my position, but, like a hardened sinner confirmed in my sin, I reject the new way to light and cling to the old

Thomas E. Connolly, "How Young Goodman Brown Became Old Badman Brown," *College English*, XXIV (1962). Reprinted by permission of the National Council of Teachers of English and Thomas E. Connolly.

habits. Mr. Cochran unconsciously contributed to the hardening of my heart by a few comments. First, he referred to my theological interpretation as being "too theological." This is very much like saying, "His artistic interpretation is too artistic"; or "His political interpretation is too political." Second, the placement of the adverb *explicitly* in this sentence in his article confirmed me in my Calvinistic awareness of sin in this world: "Hawthorne explicitly states that Faith survives Brown to symbolize the very general religious belief that Faith is always available to the man capable of embracing her." The casual reader might feel from this sentence that it was Hawthorne who had made that symbolic interpretation. I went back to the short story and could find Hawthorne saying nothing of the kind.

Third, Mr. Cochran emphasizes that the protagonist Brown is young. I answer that he is young at the beginning of the story but old at the end.

I went back, as I say, and reconsidered my theological interpretation of the story and decided to cling to it, but, as a concession to Mr. Cochran, I decided to broaden the base of it and to parallel the theological (spiritual) with a sexual (naturalistic) interpretation. With all this concentration on sin, I asked myself, just what sin did Young Goodman Brown contemplate (not, I suggest, commit)? The only sin that begs for recognition is that of sexual infidelity. But the sting in the newly married Young Goodman Brown's temptation to have one last fling is that he realizes (from Faith's warning to him as he marches off to his tryst in the forest) that marital infidelity is a game at which two can play. The first note is struck by Faith as she begs her husband, ". . . prithee, put off your journey until sunrise and sleep in your own bed tonight. . . ." His reply is significant: "What, my sweet, pretty wife, dost thou doubt me already, and we but three months married?" Faith immediately responds with a grim warning: "Then God bless you! and may you find all well when you come back."

As he goes off to the tryst, Brown's conscience gives him a slight marital and theological twinge: "Well, she's a blessed angel on earth; and after this one night I'll cling to her skirts and follow her to heaven." The disillusionment comes as he realizes that, while he is on his way to his sin, his wife may very well be on her way to hers: "Moreover, there is a goodly young woman to be taken into communion."

Finally, turning back from what he thought would be a theologically (he is of the Elect and therefore not vulnerable) and maritally (he is married to a blessed angel) safe last fling, Young Goodman Brown is shocked to discover that his faith-Faith is not what he thought it-her to be (a doctrine that smugly places him in the Elect whatever he does, or a wife that is beyond the temptations of the flesh) and spends his life alternating from attraction to and revulsion from faith-Faith: often, awakening at midnight, he shrank from the bosom of Faith," and "Children and grandchildren, a goodly procession," followed him to his grave.

# Robert W. Cochran

# REPLY

Fɪʀsᴛ, any theological interpretation which is strictly theological, restrictively theological is "too" theological. I
am not immediately suspicious of art or artistic interpretation; but with politics as with theology, I consider any unreconstructed political position "too political."

Second, the statement is explicit, the symbolism implicit.

Third, Mr. Connolly's casual reader might suppose from one of Mr. Connolly's sentences that Hawthorne refers to Brown as "old" and not as
"young," as "Badman" and not as "Goodman" toward the end of the story.
On the contrary, Hawthorne writes "young Goodman Brown" and "Goodman Brown" even in his final paragraph.

Fourth, I caution Mr. Connolly not to harden in his "broadened" interpretation, based as it is on an attempt to identify the sin which Young Goodman Brown contemplated. I remind Mr. Connolly of Edgar Allan Poe's
similarly oversimplified interpretation of why Reverend Hooper donned the
black veil.

In conclusion, I feel that Brown's belief that his Faith was "a blessed
angel on earth" is not only hopelessly naive, but hopelessly demanding. The
wife Faith cannot be angelic, for she is "on earth." But Brown makes impossible demands on his wife and on all the other townspeople as well. Thus he
remains young and foolish to his death. A "good man" he has never been;
and an intimate, meaningful relationship in his "own bed" and in "the
bosom of Faith," he has never had, his "goodly procession" of children and
grandchildren notwithstanding. (The purpose of reference to succeeding as
well as preceding generations is to place Brown in the human continuum.)

Robert W. Cochran, "Hawthorne's Choice: The Veil or The Jaundiced Eye," *College
English*, XXIII (1962). Reprinted with the permission of the National Council of
Teachers of English and Robert W. Cochran.

## STUDY  QUESTIONS

1.  How  does  Connolly  answer  Cochran's  criticism  that  his  interpretation
    of  "Young  Goodman  Brown"  is  "too  theological"?

2.  Is  Connolly's  point  about  the  adverb  *explicitly*  well  taken?

3.  Does  Connolly's  decision  "to  broaden  the  base"  of  his  argument  make
    that  argument  more  convincing?

4.  Comment  on  the  difference  of  opinion  between  Connolly  and  Cochran
    on  the  words  *young*  and  *Goodman.*

5.  How  significant  is  Cochran's  seemingly  parenthetical  last  sentence?


*Harry  Golden*

# FOR  TWO  CENTS  PLAIN

Harry  Golden  (1902–      )  was  born  in  New  York  City.  He  attended  The
City  College  of  New  York  from  1919  to  1922,  and  was  named  Doctor  of
Letters  by  Belmont  Abbey  College  in  1962.  He  lives  in  Charlotte,  North
Carolina,  where  he  has  edited  the  *Carolina  Israelite*  since  1942.  His  books
include  *Only  in  America*  (1958),  *For  2¢  Plain*  (1959),  *Enjoy!  Enjoy!*  and
*Carl  Sandburg*  (1961),  *You're  Entitle*  (1962),  *Forgotten  Pioneer*  (1963),
*Mr.  Kennedy  and  the  Negroes*  (1964),  *So  What  Else  Is  New?*  and  *A  Little
Girl  Is  Dead*  (1965),  *Ess,  Ess,  Mein  Kindt*  (1966),  *The  Best  of  Harry
Golden*  (1967),  and  *Right  Time*  (1969).


THE  RABBINICAL  students  in  Europe  and  in  America  had  a
regular  schedule  of  "eating  days."  Mondays  he  ate  with
family  A;  Tuesdays  with  B;  and  so  forth.  On  the  Lower
East  Side  this  system  still  lingered  to  some  extent,  but  it  usually  involved  a

young boy who had immigrated without a family. His fellow-townsmen set up his seven eating days. Usually this was a very religious boy who would not take a chance to eat "out" or could not yet afford to buy his meals. Some of the hosts on these eating days used the fellow to check up on the melamed (Hebrew teacher). The melamed came at half past three and taught the children for a half-hour—for a twenty-five-cent fee. Learning the prayers was entirely by rote. There was no explanation or translation of the Hebrew into English or Yiddish. Once in a while the mother would ask the eating-days fellow to come a half-hour earlier. The boy came with his usual appetite, but soon learned the reason for the early appointment. The mother wanted him to test the children to see if the melamed was doing all right. The boy always gave the melamed a clean bill of health.

Sometimes the eating-days boy ate too much and in poor households this was quite a problem. But in most homes the mother saw to it that he kept packing it away, and in addition always had something wrapped up for him to take back to his room—for later. Many households had these strangers at their tables, but only the very religious boys remained, those who expected to continue their religious studies.

The others were soon gone. America was too great and too wonderful; there were too many things to see and do, and even a hot dog at a pushcart was an adventure, to say nothing of the wonderful Max's Busy Bee.

The streets were crowded with vendors with all sorts of delightful and exotic tidbits and nasherei (delicacies).

Across the border (the Bowery) was the Italian hot-dog man. The hot plate (a coal fire) was mounted on his pushcart, and behind the stove was a barrel of lemonade to which he added chunks of ice every few hours. The hot dog, roll, mustard, and relish was three cents; the drink, two cents; and it was all a memorable experience.

A few years ago I saw a fellow with a similar cart near the Battery on Lower Broadway and I made a mad dash for him. The whole operation was now fifteen cents, but it wasn't anywhere near as wonderful as it was when I was twelve years old.

In the late fall and winter came the fellow with the haiseh arbus (hot chickpeas). He started to make his rounds a few minutes before noon as the children were leaving the schools for lunch. You sat in the classroom and everything was quiet and dignified, and all of a sudden you heard those loud blasts —"Haiseh arbus," "Haiseh, haiseh" (hot, hot)—and you knew it was time to go. Sometimes he was a little early and the teacher had to close the window. The price was one penny for a portion which the man served in a rolled-up piece of newspaper, like the English working people buy their fish and chips. There were also fellows with roasted sweet potatoes; two cents each, and three cents for an extra large one. These people used a galvanized tin contraption on wheels which looked exactly like a bedroom dresser with three drawers. In the bottom drawer were the potatoes he was roasting, while in the upper drawers were the two different sizes ready to serve. On the bottom of everything, of course, was the coal-burning fire. He had a small bag of coal attached to the front of the stove and every once in a while he shook up the fire.

My uncle Berger once operated one of those sweet-potato pushcarts with the stove on the bottom, and years later he always said that he began life in America as an engineer. He boasted of this after he had made a million dollars operating the Hotel Normandie on Broadway and 38th Street during World War I.

An interesting fellow was the peddler with a red fez, a "Turk," who sold an exotic sweet drink. He carried a huge bronze water container strapped to his back. This beautiful container had a long curved spout which came over his left shoulder. Attached to his belt, in front, was a small pail of warm water to rinse his two glasses. The drink was one penny. You held the glass, and he leaned toward you as the liquid came forth.

Nuts were very popular. There were pushcarts loaded down with "polly seeds." I have forgotten the authentic name for this nut but the East Side literally bathed in the stuff. "Polly seed" because it was the favorite food of parrots—"Polly want a cracker?"

Indian nuts, little round brown nuts. The father of one of the kids on the block sold Indian nuts, of all things. On his pushcart he had a huge glass bowl the size of an army soup vat, and it was filled with Indian nuts. I had daydreams of taking my shoes off and jumping up and down in that vat of Indian nuts, like the French girls make champagne.

This was the era when people walked a great deal. Shoeshine parlors were all over the place. On Sunday mornings you went out to get a shine and did not mind waiting in line for it either. "We are going for a walk next Saturday night." Sounds silly today, but it was an event, and make no mistake. And on every corner there were pushcarts selling fruit in season. Apples, pears, peaches, and above all, grapes. A common sight was a boy and girl eating grapes. The boy held the stem aloft as each of them pulled at the bunch and walked along the street. The grapes were sold by weight per bunch; the other fruits were sold individually, of course. And "in season" there was the man or the woman with "hot corn." I did not hear the term "corn-on-the-cob" till quite a few years later. We knew it only as "hot corn." The vendor had boiled the ears at home and usually carried the large vat to a convenient street corner, or he put the vat on a baby carriage and wheeled it around the neighborhood. A lot of women were in this hot-corn business. The hot corn was a nickel, and there was plenty of bargaining. "Throw it back, give me that one, the one over there." We kids waited around until the lady was all sold out, except the ones which had been thrown back, and often we paid no more than a penny. There are two moments when it is best to buy from a peddler, a "first" and the "close-out."

Confections of all sorts were sold, many of them famous in the Orient and eastern Europe. Fellows sold candy known as "rah-hott," which sounds Turkish or Arabic. It was beautiful to look at and there were two or three different tastes with each bite. Halvah, of course, was the real big seller, and the memory of this has lingered to this day. No delicatessen store today is without halvah, although I shall not do them the injustice of comparing the East Side halvah and the stuff they sell today. But at least you are getting a whiff of it, which is worth anything you pay. I had a Gentile friend here who had been courting a widow for years without any success and I gave him a box of chocolate-covered halvah to take to her, and the next time I saw the guy he was dancing in the streets of Charlotte. We used to eat it between slices of rye bread, "a halvah sonavich," and it was out of this world. There was another candy called "buckser" (St. John's bread), imported from Palestine. It had a long, hard, curved shell and inside a very black seed with an interesting taste which is hard to describe.

There were pushcarts loaded down with barrels of dill pickles and pickled tomatoes, which we called "sour tomatoes." Working people, men and women on the way home from the needle factories, stopped off to buy a sour tomato as a sort of appetizer for their evening meal, or perhaps to take the edge off the appetite. These tidbits sold for two and three cents each, and you served yourself. You put your hand into the vinegar barrel and pulled one out. Years later a relative of mine asked me to accompany him to a lawyer's office to "talk for him." I met him on the old East Side and we decided to walk out of the district and into Lower Broadway.

Suddenly I noticed that he was no longer at my side. I looked back and there he was biting into one sour tomato and holding a fresh one in the other hand, all ready to go. I had become a fancy guy by then and he was afraid he would embarrass me, but my mouth was watering, Broadway and all.

And then there were the permanent vendors—the soda-water stands. On nearly every corner a soda-water stand. These were the size and shape of the average newsstand you see in most of the big cities today. There was a soda fountain behind a narrow counter, and a rack for factory-made American candy, which was becoming increasingly popular, especially the Hershey bar. The fellow also sold cigarettes. No woman was ever seen smoking a cigarette in those days. The brands were Mecca, Hassan, Helmar, Sweet Caporal (which are still sold), Egyptian Deities, Moguls, Schinasi, Fifth Avenue, and Afternoons.

My father smoked Afternoons. Half the cigarette was a hard mouthpiece, or what the advertising boys today call a filter. I bought many a box of Afternoons and they were seven cents for ten cigarettes. I also bought whiskey. There was no inhibition about it and no sense of guilt. We had no drunks down there, and a kid could buy a bottle of whiskey for his father the same as he could buy a loaf of bread. I read the label many times on the way home, "Pennsylvania Rye Whiskey; we guarantee that this whiskey has been aged in the wood twenty years before bottling; signed, Park and Tilford." Cost, $1.80 for an imperial quart. No fancy "fifth-shmifth" business.

The fellow with the stand had a small marble counter on which he served his drinks and made change for candy and cigarettes. Along the counter were jars of preserves—cherry, raspberry, mulberry—for his mixed drinks. He also had a machine to make malted milks. How the immigrants took to the malted milk!

Like the other folks, my mother pronounced it "ah molta." But, of course, the big seller was seltzer (carbonated water), either plain or with syrup. A small glass of seltzer cost a penny—"Give me a small plain." That meant no syrup. And for the large glass you said, "Give me for two cents plain." For an extra penny he ladled out a spoonful of one of his syrups and mixed it with the seltzer. Here, too, there was plenty of bargaining. A fellow said, "Give me for two cents plain," and as the man was filling the glass with seltzer the customer said, casuallike, "Put a little on the top." This meant syrup, of course, and yet it did not mean the extra penny. You did not say, "Give me a raspberry soda." It was all in the way you said it, nonchalantly and in a sort of deprecating tone, "Put a little on the top." It meant that you were saving the fellow the trouble of even stirring the glass. Well, the man had already filled the glass with seltzer and what could he do with it unless you paid for it? So he "put a little on the top" but not the next time if he could help it. Often he would take the two cents first and give you a glass of plain. "I know my customers," he'd say. The man who had the stand on our corner was an elderly gent, "Benny," and once when I was playing around his counter, one of his jars fell down and the syrup got all over me. Every time I came near Benny's stand after that he took extra precautions; "Go way hard luck," he always said to me. Benny wore a coat he had brought from Europe and it reached down to his ankles. He would take a handful of that coat, feel it a while, and tell you whether it was going to rain the next day. People came from blocks around to get a weather forecast from Benny and his coat. He rarely missed.

And so you can hardly blame the young boy, the eating-days boy, when he quit the table of those home-cooked meals and went down into this world of pleasures and joys.

STUDY QUESTIONS

1. There is, of course, no question of the Jewish family's desire to help an eating-day fellow. But, what advantage did they take of him?

2. What is the thesis sentence of Golden's essay?

3. In the discussion of street vendors, are there any vendors who do not logically belong in this essay by virtue of the wares they peddle? What is the organizing principle for the two paragraphs on page 104 beginning, "And then there were the permanent vendors—the soda-water stands." and "My father smoked Afternoons"? Do these paragraphs have topic sentences?

4. Golden uses parentheses rather freely. Why does he use them when he does?

5. How does the audience for whom Golden wrote, and the medium in which this essay appeared explain the tone and style of "For Two Cents Plain"?

*Charles Lamb*

# DREAM-CHILDREN

Charles Lamb (1775–1834) was born in London and attended Christ's Hospital School. He began his public career as a clerk in the South Sea House, and worked a total of thirty-three years for The East India Company. Unlike the other major Romantics (Wordsworth, Coleridge, and Keats were his close friends), he preferred the city to the country, did not admire Shelley, and remained quietly conservative. Walter Pater compared Lamb's life to "an old Greek tragedy": Lamb's sister, Mary, stabbed their mother to death and remained in Lamb's care for those periods when she was released from the insane asylum to which she was committed. Lamb published *Rosamund Gray,* a novel, in 1798 and *John Woodvil,* a play, in 1802; however, his fame rests on *Essays of Elia* (1823), *More Essays of Elia* (1833), his dramatic criticism, and his *Tales from Shakespeare* (1807), of which his sister was coauthor.

CHILDREN love to listen to stories about their elders when *they* were children; to stretch their imagination to the conception of a traditionary great-uncle, or grandame whom they never saw. It was in this spirit that my little ones crept about me

First published 1822.

the other evening to hear about their great-grandmother Field who lived in a great house in Norfolk (a hundred times bigger than that in which they and papa lived) which had been the scene—so at least it was generally believed in that part of the country—of the tragic incidents which they had lately become familiar with from the ballad of *The Children in the Wood.* Certain it is that the whole story of the children and their cruel uncle was to be seen fairly carved out in wood upon the chimney-piece of the great hall, the whole story down to the Robin Redbreasts, till a foolish rich person pulled it down to set up a marble one of modern invention in its stead, with no story upon it. Here Alice put out one of her dear mother's looks, too tender to be called upbraiding. Then I went on to say how religious and how good their great-grandmother Field was, how beloved and respected by every body, though she was not indeed the mistress of this great house, but had only the charge of it (and yet in some respects she might be said to be the mistress of it too) committed to her by the owner, who preferred living in a newer and more fashionable mansion which he had purchased somewhere in the adjoining county; but still she lived in it in a manner as if it had been her own, and kept up the dignity of the great house in a sort while she lived, which afterwards came to decay, and was nearly pulled down, and all its old ornaments stripped and carried away to the owner's other house, where they were set up, and looked as awkward as if some one were to carry away the old tombs they had seen lately at the Abbey, and stick them up in Lady C.'s tawdry gilt drawing-room. Here John smiled, as much as to say, "that would be foolish indeed." And then I told how, when she came to die, her funeral was attended by a concourse of all the poor, and some of the gentry too, of the neighborhood for many miles round, to show their respect for her memory, because she had been such a good and religious woman; so good indeed that she knew all the Psaltery, by heart, ay, and a great part of the Testament besides. Here little Alice spread her hands. Then I told what a tall, upright, graceful person their great-grandmother Field once was; and how in her youth she was esteemed the best dancer—here Alice's little right foot played an involuntary movement, till, upon my looking grave, it desisted— the best dancer, I was saying, in the county, till a cruel disease, called a cancer, came, and bowed her down with pain; but it could never bend her good spirits, or make them stoop, but they were still upright, because she was so good and religious. Then I told how she was used to sleep by herself in a lone chamber of the great lone house; and how she believed that an apparition of two infants was to be seen at midnight gliding up and down the great staircase near where she slept, but she said "those innocents would do her no harm"; and how frightened I used to be, though in those days I had my maid to sleep with me, because I was never half so good or religious as she—and yet I never saw the infants. Here John expanded all his eyebrows and tried to look courageous. Then I told how good she was to all her grandchildren, having us to the great-house in the holydays, where I in par-

ticular used to spend many hours by myself, in gazing upon the old busts of
the Twelve Cæsars, that had been Emperors of Rome, till the old marble
heads would seem to live again, or I to be turned into marble with them; how
I never could be tired with roaming about that huge mansion, with its vast
empty rooms, with their worn-out hangings, fluttering tapestry, and carved
oaken panels, with the gilding almost rubbed out—sometimes in the spacious old-fashioned gardens, which I had almost to myself, unless when now
and then a solitary gardening man would cross me—and how the nectar-
ines and peaches hung upon the walls, without my ever offering to pluck
them, because they were forbidden fruit, unless now and then,—and because I had more pleasure in strolling about among the old melancholy-
looking yew trees, or the firs, and picking up the red berries, and the fir
apples, which were good for nothing but to look at—or in lying about upon
the fresh grass, with all the fine garden smells around me—or basking in
the orangery, till I could almost fancy myself ripening too along with the
oranges and the limes in that grateful warmth—or in watching the dace
that darted to and fro in the fishpond, at the bottom of the garden, with here
and there a great sulky pike hanging midway down the water in silent state,
as if it mocked at their impertinent friskings,—I had more pleasure in
these busy-idle diversions than in all the sweet flavors of peaches, nectar-
ines, oranges, and such like common baits of children. Here John slyly deposited back upon the plate a bunch of grapes, which, not unobserved by
Alice, he had meditated dividing with her, and both seemed willing to relin-
quish them for the present as irrelevant. Then in somewhat a more heightened tone, I told how, though their great-grandmother Field loved all her
grand-children, yet in an especial manner she might be said to love their
uncle, John L——, because he was so handsome and spirited a youth, and a
king to the rest of us; and, instead of moping about in solitary corners, like
some of us, he would mount the most mettlesome horse he could get, when
but an imp no bigger than themselves, and make it carry him half over the
county in a morning, and join the hunters when there were any out—and
yet he loved the old great house and gardens too, but had too much spirit to
be always pent up within their boundaries—and how their uncle grew up to
man's estate as brave as he was handsome, to the admiration of every body,
but of their great-grandmother Field especially; and how he used to carry
me upon his back when I was a lame-footed boy—for he was a good bit
older than me—many a mile when I could not walk for pain;—and how in
after life he became lame-footed too, and I did not always (I fear) make al-
lowances enough for him when he was impatient, and in pain, nor remember
sufficiently how considerate he had been to me when I was lame-footed; and
how when he died, though he had not been dead an hour, it seemed as if he
had died a great while ago, such a distance there is betwixt life and death;
and how I bore his death as I thought pretty well first, but afterwards it

haunted and haunted me; and though I did not cry or take it to heart as some do, and as I think he would have done if I had died, yet I missed him all day long, and knew not till then how much I had loved him. I missed his kindness, and I missed his crossness, and wished him to be alive again, to be quarrelling with him (for we quarrelled sometimes) rather than not have him again, and was as uneasy without him, as he their poor uncle must have been when the doctor took off his limb. Here the children fell a-crying, and asked if their little mourning which they had on was not for uncle John, and they looked up, and prayed me not to go on about their uncle, but to tell them some stories about their pretty dead mother. Then I told how for seven long years, in hope sometimes, sometimes in despair, yet persisting ever, I courted the fair Alice W——n; and, as much as children could understand, I explained to them what coyness, and difficulty, and denial meant in maidens —when suddenly, turning to Alice, the soul of the first Alice looked out at her eyes with such a reality of re-presentment, that I became in doubt which of them stood there before me, or whose that bright hair was; and while I stood gazing, both the children gradually grew fainter to my view, receding, and still receding till nothing at last but two mournful features were seen in the uttermost distance, which, without speech, strangely impressed upon me the effects of speech: "We are not of Alice, nor of thee, nor are we children at all. The children of Alice called Bartrum father. We are nothing; less than nothing, and dreams. We are only what might have been, and must wait upon the tedious shores of Lethe millions of ages before we have existence, and a name"——and immediately awaking, I found myself quietly seated in my bachelor arm-chair, where I had fallen asleep, with the faithful Bridget unchanged by my side—but John L. (or James Elia) was gone forever.

## STUDY QUESTIONS

1. Lamb's friends customarily described him as "gentlehearted." Does this essay demonstrate the accuracy of the description?

2. What devices does Lamb use to individualize the children?

3. At what point does Lamb realize that his "little ones" are only dream-children?

4. Why does Lamb use such extremely long sentences? What effect is achieved by them? Why do so many of the sentences begin with *then?*

5. "Dream-Children" is one-paragraph long. Obviously, Lamb could have constructed his essay in a more traditional manner, with paragraphs of more traditional length. Why, then, did he choose the one-paragraph structure?

*Graham Greene*

# THE REVOLVER IN THE CORNER CUPBOARD

Graham Greene (1904–      ) was born in Berkhamstead, England, and educated at Balliol College, Oxford. He holds an honorary Litt.D. from Cambridge University. Although a well-known playwright, essayist, and short-story writer, he is most famous for his novels and "entertainments." These include *Babbling April* (1925), *It's a Battlefield* (1934), *A Gun for Sale* (1936), *Brighton Rock* (1938), *The Power and the Glory* (1940), *The Ministry of Fear* (1943), *The Heart of the Matter* (1948), *The Third Man* (1950), *The End of the Affair* (1951), *The Quiet American* (1955), *Our Man in Havana* (1958), *A Burnt-out Case* (1961), and *The Comedians* (1966). His *Collected Essays* were published in 1969.

$I$ CAN remember very clearly the afternoon I found the revolver in the brown deal corner cupboard in the bedroom which I shared with my elder brother. It was the early autumn of 1922. I was seventeen and terribly bored and in love with my sister's governess—one of those miserable, hopeless, romantic loves of adolescence that set in many minds the idea that love and despair are inextricable and that successful love hardly deserves the name. At that age one may fall irrevocably in love with failure, and success of any kind loses half its savour before it is experienced. Such a love is surrendered once and for all to the singer at the pavement's edge, the bankrupt, the old school friend who wants to touch you for a dollar. Perhaps in many so conditioned it is the love for God that mainly survives, because in his eyes they can imagine themselves remaining always drab, seedy, unsuccessful, and therefore worthy of notice.

The revolver was a small genteel object with six chambers like a tiny egg stand, and there was a cardboard box of bullets. It has only recently oc-

curred to me that they may have been blanks; I always assumed them to be
live ammunition, and I never mentioned the discovery to my brother because I had realized the moment I saw the revolver the use I intended to
make of it. (I don't to this day know why he possessed it; certainly he had no
licence, and he was only three years older than myself. A large family is as
departmental as a Ministry.)

My brother was away—probably climbing in the Lake District—and
until he returned the revolver was to all intents mine. I knew what to do with
it because I had been reading a book (the name Ossendowski comes to mind
as the possible author) describing how the White Russian officers, condemned to inaction in South Russia at the tail-end of the counter-
revolutionary war, used to invent hazards with which to escape boredom.
One man would slip a charge into a revolver and turn the chambers at random, and his companion would put the revolver to his head and pull the
trigger. The chance, of course, was six to one in favour of life.

How easily one forgets emotions. If I were dealing now with an imaginary
character, I would feel it necessary for verisimilitude to make him hesitate,
put the revolver back into the cupboard, return to it again after an interval,
reluctantly and fearfully, when the burden of boredom became too great.
But in fact I think there was no hesitation at all, for the next I can remember
is crossing Berkhamstead Common, gashed here and there between the
gorse bushes with the stray trenches of the first Great War, towards the
Ashridge beeches. Perhaps before I had made the discovery, boredom had
already reached an intolerable depth.

I think the boredom was far deeper than the love. It had always been a
feature of childhood: it would set in on the second day of the school holidays. The first day was all happiness, and, after the horrible confinement
and publicity of school, seemed to consist of light, space and silence. But a
prison conditions its inhabitants. I never wanted to return to it (and finally
expressed my rebellion by the simple act of running away), but yet I was so
conditioned that freedom bored me unutterably.

The psycho-analysis that followed my act of rebellion had fixed the boredom as hypo fixes the image on the negative. I emerged from those delightful months in London spent at my analyst's house—perhaps the happiest
months of my life—correctly orientated, able to take a proper extrovert
interest in my fellows (the jargon rises to the lips), but wrung dry. For years,
it seems to me, I could take no aesthetic interest in any visual thing at all:
staring at a sight that others assured me was beautiful, I would feel nothing.
I was fixed in my boredom. (Writing this I come on a remark of Rilke:
"Psycho-analysis is too fundamental a help for me, it helps you once and for
all, it clears you up, and to find myself finally cleared up one day might be
even more helpless than this chaos.")

Now with the revolver in my pocket I was beginning to emerge. I had stumbled on the perfect cure. I was going to escape in one way or another, and because escape was inseparably connected with the Common in my mind, it was there that I went.

The wilderness of gorse, old trenches, abandoned butts was the unchanging backcloth of most of the adventures of childhood. It was to the Common I had decamped for my act of rebellion some years before, with the intention, expressed in a letter left after breakfast on the heavy black sideboard, that there I would stay, day and night, until either I had starved or my parents had given in; when I pictured war it was always in terms of this Common, and myself leading a guerilla campaign in the ragged waste, for no one, I was persuaded, knew its paths so intimately (how humiliating that in my own domestic campaign I was ambushed by my elder sister after a few hours).

Beyond the Common lay a wide grass ride known for some reason as Cold Harbour to which I would occasionally with some fear take a horse, and beyond this again stretched Ashridge Park, the smooth olive skin of beech trees and the thick last year's quagmire of leaves, dark like old pennies. Deliberately I chose my ground, I believe without any real fear—perhaps because I was uncertain myself whether I was play-acting; perhaps because so many acts which my elders would have regarded as neurotic, but which I still consider to have been under the circumstances highly reasonable, lay in the background of this more dangerous venture.

There had been, for example, perhaps five or six years before, the disappointing morning in the dark room by the linen cupboard on the eve of term when I had patiently drunk a quantity of hypo under the impression that it was poisonous: on another occasion the blue glass bottle of hay fever lotion which as it contained a small quantity of cocaine had probably been good for my mood: the bunch of deadly nightshade that I had eaten with only a slight narcotic effect: the twenty aspirins I had taken before swimming in the empty out-of-term school baths (I can still remember the curious sensation of swimming through wool): these acts may have removed all sense of strangeness as I slipped a bullet into a chamber and, holding the revolver behind my back, spun the chambers round.

Had I romantic thoughts about the governess? Undoubtedly I must have had, but I think that at the most they simply eased the medicine down. Boredom, aridity, those were the main emotions. Unhappy love has, I suppose, sometimes driven boys to suicide, but this was not suicide, whatever a coroner's jury might have said of it: it was a gamble with six chances to one against an inquest. The romantic flavour—the autumn scene, the small heavy compact shape lying in the fingers—that perhaps was a tribute to adolescent love, but the discovery that it was possible to enjoy again the visible world by risking its total loss was one I was bound to make sooner or later.

I put the muzzle of the revolver in my right ear and pulled the trigger. There was a minute click, and looking down at the chamber I could see that the charge had moved into place. I was out by one. I remember an extraordinary sense of jubilation. It was as if a light had been turned on. My heart was knocking in its cage, and I felt that life contained an infinite number of possibilities. It was like a young man's first successful experience of sex— as if in that Ashridge glade one had passed a test of manhood. I went home and put the revolver back in the corner cupboard.

The odd thing about this experience was that it was repeated several times. At fairly long intervals I found myself craving for the drug. I took the revolver with me when I went up to Oxford and I would walk out from Headington towards Elsfield down what is now a wide arterial road, smooth and shiny like the walls of a public lavatory. Then it was a sodden unfrequented country lane. The revolver would be whipped behind my back, the chambers twisted, the muzzle quickly and surreptitiously inserted beneath the black and ugly winter tree, the trigger pulled.

Slowly the effect of the drug wore off—I lost the sense of jubilation, I began to gain from the experience only the crude kick of excitement. It was like the difference between love and lust. And as the quality of the experience deteriorated so my sense of responsibility grew and worried me. I wrote a very bad piece of free verse (free because it was easier in that way to express my meaning without literary equivocation) describing how, in order to give a fictitious sense of danger, I would "press the trigger of a revolver I already know to be empty." This piece of verse I would leave permanently on my desk, so that if I lost my gamble, there would be incontrovertible evidence of an accident, and my parents, I thought, would be less troubled than by an apparent suicide—or than by the rather bizarre truth.

But it was back at Berkhamstead that I paid a permanent farewell to the drug. As I took my fifth dose it occurred to me that I wasn't even excited: I was beginning to pull the trigger about as casually as I might take an aspirin tablet. I decided to give the revolver—which was six-chambered—a sixth and last chance. Twirling the chambers round, I put the muzzle to my ear for the last time and heard the familiar empty click as the chambers revolved. I was through with the drug, and walking back over the Common, down the new road by the ruined castle, past the private entrance to the gritty old railway station—reserved for the use of Lord Brownlow—my mind was already busy on other plans. One campaign was over, but the war against boredom had got to go on.

I put the revolver back in the corner cupboard, and going downstairs I lied gently and convincingly to my parents that a friend had invited me to join him in Paris.

STUDY QUESTIONS

1. Was Greene deliberately and repeatedly attempting suicide? Had he attempted suicide before?

2. How did the governess contribute to Greene's state of mind? Was she the main reason for it?

3. Earlier, why had Greene run away from school?

4. Why did he eventually stop playing his dangerous, solitary game?

5. What is the point of the lie he tells his parents?

6. Why is the first-person point-of-view particularly effective in this essay? Besides the obvious changes of pronouns and tenses, what changes would a third-person point-of-view have necessitated?

*George Orwell*     When telling experience set sense time, places

# A HANGING

George Orwell (1903–1950) was the pen name of Eric Blair, who was born in Bengal, India. He graduated from Eton College, served with the Indian Imperial Police in Burma from 1922 to 1927, and then returned to England to begin his career as a writer. His works include *Burmese Days* (1934), *Homage to Catalonia* (1936), *Dickens, Dali, and Others* (1946), and *Shooting an Elephant* (1950). His fame, however, is primarily the result of *Animal Farm* (1946) and *1984* (1949), the former one of the most famous modern satires and the latter a classic novel of social protest. His *Collected Essays* were published in 1969.

IT WAS in Burma, a sodden morning of the rains. A sickly light, (like yellow tinfoil,) was slanting over the high walls into the jail yard. We were waiting outside the condemned cells, a row of sheds fronted with double bars, like small animal cages. Each cell measured about ten feet by ten and was quite bare within except for a plank bed and a pot for drinking water. In some of them brown, silent men were squatting at the inner bars, with their blankets draped round them. These were the condemned men, due to be hanged within the next week or two.

One prisoner had been brought out of his cell. He was a Hindu, a puny wisp of a man, with a shaven head and vague liquid eyes. He had a thick, sprouting moustache, absurdly too big for his body, rather like the moustache of a comic man on the films. Six tall Indian warders were guarding him and getting him ready for the gallows. Two of them stood by with rifles and fixed bayonets, while the others handcuffed him, passed a chain through his handcuffs and fixed it to their belts, and lashed his arms tight to his sides. They crowded very close about him, with their hands always on him in a careful, caressing grip, as though all the while feeling him to make sure he was there. It was like men handling a fish which is still alive and may jump back into the water. But he stood quite unresisting, yielding his arms limply to the ropes, as though he hardly noticed what was happening.

Eight o'clock struck and a bugle call, desolately thin in the wet air, floated from the distant barracks. The superintendent of the jail, who was standing apart from the rest of us, moodily prodding the gravel with his stick, raised his head at the sound. He was an army doctor, with a grey toothbrush moustache and a gruff voice. "For God's sake hurry up, Francis," he said irritably. "The man ought to have been dead by this time. Aren't you ready yet?"

Francis, the head jailer, a fat Dravidian in a white drill suit and gold spectacles, waved his black hand. "Yes sir, yes sir," he bubbled. "All iss satisfactorily prepared. The hangman iss waiting. We shall proceed."

"Well, quick march, then. The prisoners can't get their breakfast till this job's over."

We set out for the gallows. Two warders marched on either side of the prisoner, with their rifles at the slope; two others marched close against him, gripping him by arm and shoulder, as though at once pushing and supporting him. The rest of us, magistrates and the like, followed behind. Suddenly, when we had gone ten yards, the procession stopped short without any order or warning. A dreadful thing had happened—a dog, come goodness knows whence, had appeared in the yard. It came bounding among us with a loud volley of barks and leapt round us wagging its whole body, wild with glee at finding so many human beings together. It was a large woolly dog, half Airedale, half pariah. For a moment it pranced round us, and then, before anyone could stop it, it had made a dash for the prisoner, and jumping up tried to lick his face. Everybody stood aghast, too taken aback even to grab the dog.

"Who let that bloody brute in here?" said the superintendent angrily. "Catch it, someone!"

A warder detached from the escort, charged clumsily after the dog, but it danced and gambolled just out of his reach, taking everything as part of the game. A young Eurasian jailer picked up a handful of gravel and tried to stone the dog away, but it dodged the stones and came after us again. Its yaps echoed from the jail walls. The prisoner, in the grasp of the two wardens, looked on incuriously, as though this was another formality of the hanging. It was several minutes before someone managed to catch the dog. Then we put my handkerchief through its collar and moved off once more, with the dog still straining and whimpering.

It was about forty yards to the gallows. I watched the bare brown back of the prisoner marching in front of me. He walked clumsily with his bound arms, but quite steadily, with that bobbing gait of the Indian who never straightens his knees. At each step his muscles slid neatly into place, the lock of hair on his scalp danced up and down, his feet printed themselves on the wet gravel. And once, in spite of the men who gripped him by each shoulder, he stepped lightly aside to avoid a puddle on the path.

It is curious, but till that moment I had never realized what it means to destroy a healthy, conscious man. When I saw the prisoner step aside to avoid the puddle I saw the mystery, the unspeakable wrongness, of cutting a life short when it is in full tide. This man was not dying, he was alive just as we are alive. All the organs of his body were working—bowels digesting food, skin renewing itself, nails growing, tissues forming—all toiling away in solemn foolery. His nails would still be growing when he stood on the drop, when he was falling through the air with a tenth-of-a-second to live. His eyes saw the yellow gravel and the grey walls, and his brain still remembered, foresaw, reasoned—even about puddles. He and we were a party of men walking together, seeing, hearing, feeling, understanding the same world; and in two minutes, with a sudden snap, one of us would be gone— one mind less, one world less.

The gallows stood in a small yard, separate from the main grounds of the prison, and overgrown with tall prickly weeds. It was a brick erection like three sides of a shed, with planking on top, and above that two beams and a crossbar with the rope dangling. The hangman, a grey-haired convict in the white uniform of the prison, was waiting beside his machine. He greeted us with a servile crouch as we entered. At a word from Francis the two warders, gripping the prisoner more closely than ever, half led, half pushed him to the gallows and helped him clumsily up the ladder. Then the hangman climbed up and fixed the rope round the prisoner's neck.

We stood waiting, five yards away. The warders had formed in a rough circle round the gallows. And then, when the noose was fixed, the prisoner began crying to his god. It was a high, reiterated cry of "Ram! Ram! Ram! Ram!" not urgent and fearful like a prayer or cry for help, but steady, rhythmical, almost like the tolling of a bell. The dog answered the sound with a whine. The hangman, still standing on the gallows, produced a small cotton bag like a flour bag and drew it down over the prisoner's face. But the sound, muffled by the cloth, still persisted, over and over again: "Ram! Ram! Ram! Ram! Ram!"

The hangman climbed down and stood ready, holding the lever. Minutes seemed to pass. The steady, muffled crying from the prisoner went on and on, "Ram! Ram! Ram!" never faltering for an instant. The superintendent, his head on his chest, was slowly poking the ground with his stick; perhaps he was counting the cries, allowing the prisoner a fixed number—fifty, perhaps, or a hundred. Everyone had changed colour. The Indians had gone grey like bad coffee, and one or two of the bayonets were wavering. We looked at the lashed, hooded man on the drop, and listened to his cries— each cry another second of life; the same thought was in all our minds: oh, kill him quickly, get it over, stop that abominable noise!

Suddenly the superintendent made up his mind. Throwing up his head he made a swift motion with his stick. "Chalo!" he shouted almost fiercely.

There was a clanking noise, and then dead silence. The prisoner had vanished, and the rope was twisting on itself. I let go of the dog, and it galloped immediately to the back of the gallows; but when it got there it stopped short, barked, and then retreated into a corner of the yard, where it stood among the weeds, looking timorously out at us. We went round the gallows to inspect the prisoner's body. He was dangling with his toes pointed straight downwards, very slowly revolving, as dead as a stone.

The superintendent reached out with his stick and poked the bare brown body; it oscillated slightly. *"He's* all right," said the superintendent. He backed out from under the gallows, and blew out a deep breath. The moody look had gone out of his face quite suddenly. He glanced at his wrist-watch. "Eight minutes past eight. Well, that's all for this morning, thank God."

The warders unfixed bayonets and marched away. The dog, sobered and conscious of having misbehaved itself, slipped after them. We walked out of the gallows yard, past the condemned cells with their waiting prisoners, into the big central yard of the prison. The convicts, under the command of warders armed with lathis, were already receiving their breakfast. They squatted in long rows, each man holding a tin pannikin, while two warders with buckets marched round ladling out rice; it seemed quite a homely, jolly scene, after the hanging. An enormous relief had come upon us now that the job was done. One felt an impulse to sing, to break into a run, to snigger. All at once everyone began chattering gaily.

The Eurasian boy walking beside me nodded towards the way we had come, with a knowing smile: "Do you know, sir, our friend (he meant the dead man) when he heard his appeal had been dismissed, he pissed on the floor of his cell. From fright. Kindly take one of my cigarettes, sir. Do you not admire my new silver case, sir? From the boxwallah, two rupees eight annas. Classy European style."

Several people laughed—at what, nobody seemed certain.

Francis was walking by the superintendent, talking garrulously: "Well, sir, all hass passed off with the utmost satisfactoriness. It was all finished— flick! like that. It iss not always so—oah, no! I have known cases where the doctor wass obliged to go beneath the gallows and pull the prissoner's legs to ensure decease. Most disagreeable!"

"Wriggling about, eh? That's bad," said the superintendent.

"Ach, sir, it iss worse when they become refractory! One man, I recall, clung to the bars of hiss cage when we went to take him out. You will scarcely credit, sir, that it took six warders to dislodge him, three pulling at each leg. We reasoned with him, 'My dear fellow,' we said, 'think of all the pain and trouble you are causing to us!' But no, he would not listen! Ach, he wass very troublesome!"

I found that I was laughing quite loudly. Everyone was laughing. Even the superintendent grinned in a tolerant way. "You'd better all come out and have a drink," he said quite genially. "I've got a bottle of whisky in the car. We could do with it."

We went through the big double gates of the prison into the road. "Pulling at his legs!" exclaimed a Burmese magistrate suddenly, and burst into a loud chuckling. We all began laughing again. At that moment Francis' anecdote seemed extraordinarily funny. We all had a drink together, native and European alike, quite amicably. The dead man was a hundred yards away.

## STUDY QUESTIONS

1. Why is the superintendent irritated by the delay in the hanging?

2. How does the incident with the dog contribute to the effectiveness of "A Hanging"?

3. Why does the prisoner's stepping aside to avoid a puddle bring Orwell to a full realization of the scene before him?

4. Why do the men feel an impulse to sing, to break into a run, to snigger after the hanging? Why does Orwell end his essay with, "The dead man was a hundred yards away"?

5. What is the tone of the essay? How does the narrator's attitude toward the hanging help determine the response elicited from the reader?

# Modern Social Problems

"Some Must Watch"

# Norman Mailer

# LOOKING FOR THE MEAT AND POTATOES—THOUGHTS ON BLACK POWER

Norman Mailer (1925–     ), after graduation from Harvard University and service in World War II, became a literary celebrity with the publication of his bestseller *The Naked and the Dead* in 1948. His other publications include *Barbary Shore* (1951), *The Deer Park* (1955), *The White Negro* (1958), *Advertisement of Myself* (1959), *The Presidential Papers* (1963), *An American Dream* (1965), *Cannibals and Christians* (1966), *Why Are We In Viet Nam* (1967), and *The Armies of the Night* (1968). Mailer's stories and articles are in great demand by the leading magazines and in recent years he has devoted much of his writing to the cause of Black Power and the radical movements in politics.

"You don't even know who you are," Reginald had said. "You don't even know, the white devil has hidden it from you, that you are of a race of people of ancient civilizations, and riches in gold and kings. You don't even know your true family name, you wouldn't recognize your true language if you heard it. You have been cut off by the devil white man from all true knowledge of your own kind. You have been a victim of the evil of the devil white man ever since he murdered and raped and stole you from your native land in the seeds of your forefathers. . . ."

THE AUTOBIOGRAPHY OF MALCOLM X

I~N NOT TOO MANY YEARS, we will travel to the moon, and on the trip, the language will be familiar. We have not had our education for nothing—all those sanitized hours of orientation via high school, commercials, corporations and mass media have given us one expectation: no matter how beautiful, insane, dangerous, sacrilegious, explosive, holy or damned a new venture may be, count on it, fellow Americans, the language will be familiar. Are you going in for a serious operation, voting on the political future of the country, buying insurance, discussing nuclear disarmament or taking a trip to the moon? You can depend on the one great American certainty—the public vocabulary of the discussion will suggest the same relation to the resources of the English language that a loaf of big-bakery bread in plastic bag and wax bears to the secret heart of wheat and butter and eggs and yeast.

Your trip to the moon will not deal needlessly with the vibrations of the heavens (now that man dares to enter eschatology) nor the metaphysical rifts in the philosophical firmament; no poets will pluck a stringed instrument to conjure with the pale shades of the white lady as you move along toward the lunar space. Rather, a voice will emerge from the loudspeaker, "This is your pilot. On our starboard bow at four o'clock directly below, you can pick out a little doojigger of land down there like a vermiform appendix, and that, as we say good-bye to the Pacific Coast, is Baja California. The spot of light at the nub, that little bitty illumination like the probe bulb in a systoscope or comparable medical instrument is Ensenada, which the guidebooks call a jewelred resort."

Good-bye to earth, hello the moon! We will skip the technological dividend in the navigator's voice as he delivers us to that space station which will probably look like a breeding between a modern convention hall and the computer room at CBS. Plus the packaged air in the space suits when the tourists, after two days of acclimation in air-sealed moon motels, take their first reconnoiter outside in the white moon dust while their good American bowels accommodate to relative weightlessness.

All right, bright fellow, the reader now may say—what does all this have to do with Black Power? And the author, while adept at dancing in the interstices of a metaphor, is going to come back nonetheless straight and fast with this remark—our American mass-media language is not any more equipped to get into a discussion of Black Power than it is ready to serve as interpreter en route to the moon. The American language has become a conveyer belt to carry each new American generation into its ordained position in the American scene, which is to say the corporate technological world. It can deal with external descriptions of everything which enters or leaves a man, it can measure the movements of that man, it can predict until such moment as it is wrong what the man will do next, but it cannot give a spiritual preparation for our trip to the moon any more than it can talk to us about death, or the inner experiences of real sex, real danger, real dread. Or Black Power.

If the preface has not been amusing, cease at once to read, for what follows will be worse: the technological American is programmed to live with answers, which is why his trip to the moon will be needlessly God-awful; the subject of Black Power opens nothing but questions, precisely those unendurable questions which speak of premature awakenings and the hour of the wolf. But let us start with something comfortable, something we all know, and may encounter with relaxation, for the matter is familiar:

. . . think of that black slave man filled with fear and dread, hearing the screams of his wife, his mother, his daughter being *taken*—in the barn, the kitchen, in the bushes! . . . *Think* of hearing wives, mothers, daughters, being *raped!* And you were too filled with *fear* of the rapist to do anything about it! . . . Turn around and look at each other, brothers and sisters, and *think* of this! You and me, polluted all these colors—and this devil has the arrogance and the gall to think we, his victims, should *love* him!

THE AUTOBIOGRAPHY OF MALCOLM X

"Okay," you say, "I know that, I know that already. I didn't do it. My great-grandfather didn't even do it. He was a crazy Swede. He never even saw a black skin. And now for Crysake, the girls in Sweden are crazy about Floyd Patterson. I don't care, I say more power to him. All right," goes the dialogue of this splendid American now holding up a hand, "all right, I know about collective responsibility. If some Scotch-Irish planter wanted to tomcat in the magnolias, then I'll agree it's easier for me than for the victim to discern subtle differences between one kind of WASP and another, I'll buy my part of the ancestral curse for that Scotch-Irish stud's particular night of pleasure, maybe I'm guilty of something myself, but there are limits, man. All right, we never gave the Negro a fair chance, and now we want to, we're willing to put up with a reasonable amount of disadvantage, in fact, discomfort, outright inequality and inefficiency. I'll hire Negroes who are not as equipped in the productive scheme of things as whites; that doesn't mean we have to pay iota for iota on every endless misdemeanor of the past and suffer a vomit bag of bad manners to boot. Look, every student of revolution can tell you that the danger comes from giving the oppressed their first liberties. A poor man who wins a crazy bet always squanders it. The point, buddy, is that the present must forgive the past, there must be forgiveness for old sins, or else progress is impossible." And there is the key to the first door: progress depends upon anesthetizing the past. What if, says Black Power, we are not interested in progress, not your progress with packaged food for soul food, smog for air, hypodermics for roots, air conditioning for breeze— what if we think we have gotten strong by living without progress and your social engineering, what if we think that an insult to the blood is never to be forgotten because it keeps your life alive and reminds you to meditate before you urinate. Who are you to say that spooks don't live behind the left ear and ha'nts behind the right? Whitey, you smoke so much you can't smell, taste, or kiss—your breath is too bad. If you don't have a gun, I can poke you and run—you'll never catch me. I'm alive 'cause I keep alive the curse you put in my blood. Primitive people don't forget. If they do, they turn out no better than the civilized and the sick. Who are you, Whitey, to tell me to drop my curse, and join your line of traffic going to work? I'd rather keep myself in shape and work out the curse, natural style. There's always white women, ahem! Unless we decide they're too full of your devil's disease, hypocritical pus-filled old white blood, and so we stay black with black, and repay the curse by drawing blood. That's the life-giving way to repay a curse."

"Why must you talk this way?" says the splendid American. "Can't you see that there are whites and whites, whites I do not begin to control? They wish to destroy you. They agree with your values. They are primitive whites. They think in blood for blood. In a war, they will kill you, and they will kill me."

"Well, daddy, I'm just putting you on. Didn't you ever hear of the here-after? That's where it will all work out, there where us Blacks are the angels and honkies is the flunky. Now, let me take you by the tail, white cat, long enough to see that I want some more of these handouts, see, these homey horse balls and government aid."

The splendid American has just been left in the mire of a put-on and throwaway. How is he to know if this is spring mud or the muck of the worst Negro Hades?

The native's relaxation takes precisely the form of a muscular orgy in which the most acute aggressivity and the most impelling violence are canalised, trans-formed and conjured away. . . . At certain times on certain days, men and women come together at a given place, and there, under the solemn eye of the tribe, fling themselves into a seemingly unorganized pantomime, which is in real-ity extremely systematic, in which by various means—shakes of the head, bend-ing of the spinal column, throwing of the whole body backwards—may be de-ciphered as in an open book the huge effort of a community to exorcise itself, to liberate itself . . . in reality your purpose in coming together is to allow the ac-cumulated libido, the hampered aggressivity to dissolve as in a volcanic eruption. Symbolical killings, fantastic rites, imaginary mass murders—all must be brought out. The evil humours are undammed, and flow away with a din as of molten lava. . . .

FRANTZ FANON—THE WRETCHED OF THE EARTH

Here is the lesson learned by the struggles of present-day colonial coun-tries to obtain their independence: a war of liberation converts the energies of criminality, assassination, religious orgy, voodoo and the dance into the determined artful phalanxes of bold guerrilla armies. A sense of brotherhood comes to replace the hitherto murderous clan relations of the natives. Once, that propensity to murder each other had proved effective in keeping the peace—for the settler. Now, these violent sentiments turn against the whites who constrain them. Just as the natives upon a time made good ser-vants and workers for the whites, while reserving the worst of their characters for each other, now they looked to serve each other, to cleanse the furies of their exploited lives in open rude defiance against the authority.

This is the conventional explanation offered by any revolutionary spokesman for the Third World—that new world which may or may not emerge triumphant in Latin America, Asia and Africa. It is a powerful argument, an uplifting argument, it stirs the blood of anyone who has ever had a revolutionary passion, for the faith of the revolutionary (if he is revolutionary enough to have faith) is that the repressed blood of mankind is ultimately good and noble blood. Its goodness may be glimpsed in the emotions of its release. If a sense of brotherhood animates the inner life of guerrilla armies, then it does not matter how violent they are to their foe. That violence safeguards the sanctity of their new family relations.

If this is the holy paradigm of the colonial revolutionary, its beauty has been confirmed in places, denied in others. While the struggles of the NLF and the North Vietnamese finally proved impressive even to the most gung ho Marine officers in Southeast Asia, the horrors of the war in Biafra go far toward proving the opposite. The suspicion remains that beneath the rhetoric of revolution, another war, quite separate from a revolutionary war, is also being waged, and the forces of revolution in the world are as divided by this concealed war as the civilized powers who would restrain them. It is as if one war goes on between the privileged and the oppressed to determine how the productive wealth of civilization will be divided; the other war, the seed contained within this first war, derives from a notion that the wealth of civilization is not wealth but a corporate productive poisoning of the wellsprings, avatars and conduits of nature; the power of civilization is therefore equal to the destruction of life itself. It is, of course, a perspective open to the wealthy as well as to the poor—not every mill owner who kills the fish in his local rivers with the wastes from his factory is opposed to protecting our wilderness preserve, not at all, some even serve on the State Conservation Committee. And our First Lady would try to keep billboards from defacing those new highways which amputate the ecology through which they pass. Of course, her husband helped to build those highways. But then the rich, unless altogether elegant, are inevitably comic. It is in the worldwide militancy of the underprivileged, undernourished and exploited that the potential horror of this future war (concealed beneath the present war) will make itself most evident. For the armies of the impoverished, unknown to themselves, are already divided. Once victorious over the wealthy West— if ever!—they could only have a new war. It would take place between those forces on their side who are programmatic, scientific, more or less Socialist, and near maniac in their desire to bring technological culture at the fastest possible rate into every backward land, and those more traditional and/or primitive forces in the revolution of the Third World who reject not only the exploitation of the Western world but reject the West as well, in toto, as a philosophy, a culture, a technique, as a way indeed of even attempting to solve the problems of man himself.

Of these colonial forces, black, brown and yellow, which look to overthrow the economic and social tyrannies of the white man, there is no force in Africa, Asia, or Latin America which we need think of as being any more essentially colonial in stance than the American Negro. Consider these remarks in *The Wretched of the Earth* about the situation of colonials:

"The colonial world is a world cut in two. The dividing line, the frontiers are shown by barracks and police stations." (Of this, it may be said that Harlem is as separate from New York as East Berlin from West Berlin.)

". . . if, in fact, my life is worth as much as the settler's, his glance no longer shrivels me up nor freezes me, and his voice no longer turns me into stone. I am no longer on tenterhooks in his presence; in fact, I don't give a damn for him. Not only does his presence no longer trouble me, but I am already preparing such efficient ambushes for him that soon there will be no way out but that of flight." (Now, whites flee the subways in New York.)

". . . there is no colonial power today which is capable of adopting the only form of contest which has a chance of succeeding, namely, the prolonged establishment of large forces of occupation." (How many divisions of paratroops would it take to occupy Chicago's South Side?)

The American Negro is of course not synonymous with Black Power. For every Black militant, there are ten Negroes who live quietly beside him in the slums, resigned for the most part to the lessons, the action and the treadmill of the slums. As many again have chosen to integrate. They live now like Negroid Whites in mixed neighborhoods, suburbs, factories, obtaining their partial peace within the white dream. But no American Negro is contemptuous of Black Power. Like the accusing finger in the dream, it is the rarest nerve in their head, the frightening pulse in their heart, equal in emotional weight to that passion which many a noble nun sought to conquer on a cold stone floor. Black Power obviously derives from a heritage of anger which makes the American Negro one man finally with the African, the Algerian and even the Vietcong—he would become schizophrenic if he tried to suppress his fury over the mutilations of the past.

The confrontation of Black Power with American life gives us then not only an opportunity to comprehend some of the forces and some of the style of that war now smoldering between the global rich and the global poor, between the culture of the past and the intuitions of the future, but—since Black Power has more intimate, everyday knowledge of what it is like to live in an advanced technological society than any other guerrilla force on earth —the division of attitudes within Black Power has more to tell us about the shape of future wars and revolutions than any other militant force in the world. Technological man in his terminal diseases, dying of air he can no longer breathe, of packaged food he can just about digest, of plastic clothing

his skin can hardly bear and of static before which his spirit has near ex-
pired, stands at one end of revolutionary ambition—at the other is an in-
choate glimpse of a world now visited only by the primitive and the drug-
ridden, a world where technology shatters before magic and electronic communication is surpassed by the psychic telegraphy of animal mood.

Most of the literature of Black Power is interested entirely, or so it would
seem, in immediate political objectives of the most concrete sort. Back in
1923, Marcus Garvey, father of the Back-to-Africa movement, might have
written, "When Europe was inhabited by a race of cannibals, a race of savages, naked men, heathens and pagans, Africa was peopled with a race of
cultured black men, who were masters in art, science and literature, men
who were cultured and refined; men who, it was said, were like the gods,"
but the present leaders of Black Power are concerned with political mandate
and economic clout right here. Floyd McKissick of CORE the Black Power
Movement seeks to win power in a half-dozen ways. These are:

1. The growth of Black *political* power.
2. The building of Black *economic* power.
3. The improvement of the *self-image* of Black people.
4. The development of Black *leadership*.
5. The attainment of *Federal law enforcement*.
6. The mobilization of Black *consumer power*.

These demands present nothing exceptional. On their face, they are not
so different from manifestos by the NAACP or planks by the Democratic
party. A debater with the skill of William F. Buckley or Richard Nixon
could stay afloat for hours on the life-saving claim that there is nothing in
these six points antithetical to conservatives. Indeed, there is not. Not on the
face. For example, here is Adam Clayton Powell, a politician most respected by Black Power militants, on some of these points. Political power:
"Where we are 20% of the voters, we should command 20% of the jobs,
judgeships, commissionerships, and all political appointments." Economic
power: "Rather than a race primarily of consumers and stock boys, we must
become a race of producers and stockbrokers." Leadership: "Black communities . . . must neither tolerate nor accept outside leadership—black
or white." Federal law enforcement: "The battle against segregation in
America's public school systems must become a national effort, instead of
the present regional skirmish that now exists." Even consumer protest
groups to stand watch on the quality of goods sold in a slum neighborhood
are hardly revolutionary, more an implementation of good conservative
buying practices. *Consumers Digest* is not yet at the barricades.

Indeed, which American institution of power is ready to argue with these
six points? They are so rational! The power of the technological society is
shared by the corporations, the military, the mass media, the trade unions

and the Government. It is to the interest of each to have a society which is *rational,* even as a machine is rational. When a machine breaks down, the cause can be discovered; in fact, the cause must be capable of being discovered or we are not dealing with a machine. So the pleasure of working with machines is that malfunctions are correctable; satisfaction is guaranteed by the application of work, knowledge and reason. Hence, any race problem is anathema to power groups in the technological society, because the subject of race is irrational. At the very least, race problems seem to have the property of repelling reason. Still, the tendency of modern society to shape men for function in society like parts of a machine grows more powerful all the time. So we have the paradox of a conservative capitalistic democracy, profoundly entrenched in racial prejudice (and hitherto profoundly attracted to racial exploitation) now transformed into the most developed technological society in the world. The old prejudices of the men who wield power have become therefore inefficient before the needs of the social machine—so inefficient, in fact, that prejudiced as many of them still are, they consider it a measure of their responsibility to shed prejudice. (We must by now move outside the center of power before we can even find Gen. Curtis LeMay.)

So the question may well be posed: if the demands formally presented by Black Power advocates like McKissick and Powell are thus rational, and indeed finally fit the requirements of the technological society, why then does Black Power inspire so much fear, distrust, terror, horror and even outright revulsion among the best liberal descendants of the beautiful old Eleanor Roosevelt bag and portmanteau? And the answer is that an intellectual shell game has been played up to here. We have not covered McKissick's six points, only five. The sixth (point number three) was "The improvement of the *self-image* of Black people." It is here that sheer Black hell busts loose. A technological society can deal comfortably with people who are mature, integrated, goal-oriented, flexible, responsive, groupresponsive, etc., etc.—the word we cannot leave out is white or whiteoriented. The technological society is not able to deal with the self-image of separate peoples and races if the development of their self-image produces personalities of an explosive individuality. We do not substitute sticks of dynamite for the teeth of a gear and assume we still have an automotive transmission.

McKissick covers his third point, of course: "Negro history, art, music and other aspects of Black culture . . . make Black people aware of their contributions to the American heritage and to world civilization." Powell bastes the goose with orotundities of rhetorical gravy: "We must give our children a sense of pride in being black. The glory of our past and the dignity of our present must lead the way to the power of our future." Amen. We have been conducted around the point.

Perhaps the clue is that political Right and political Left are meaningless terms when applied conventionally to Black Power. If we are to use them at all (and it is a matter of real convenience), then we might call the more or less rational, programmatic and recognizably political arm of Black Power, presented by McKissick and Powell, as the Right Wing, since their program can conceivably be attached to the programs of the technological society, whether Democrat or Republican. The straight-out political demands of this kind of Black Power not only can be integrated (at least on paper) into the needs of the technological society, but must be, because—we would repeat —an exploited class creates disruption and therefore irrationality in a social machine; efforts to solve exploitation and disruption become mandatory for the power groups. If this last sentence sounds vaguely Marxist in cadence, the accident is near. What characterizes technological societies is that they tend to become more and more like one another. So America and the Soviet will yet have interchangeable parts, or at least be no more different than a four-door Ford from a two-door Chevrolet. It may thus be noticed that what we are calling the Right Wing of Black Power—the technological wing—is in the conventional sense interested in moving to the left. Indeed, after the Blacks attain equality—so goes the unspoken assumption —America will be able to progress toward a rational society of racial participation, etc., etc. What then is the Left Wing of Black Power? Say, let us go back to Africa, back to Garvey.

We must understand that we are *replacing* a dying culture, and we must be prepared to do this, and be absolutely conscious of what we are replacing it with. We are sons and daughters of the most ancient societies on this planet. . . . No movement shaped or contained by Western culture will ever benefit Black people. Black power must be the actual force and beauty and wisdom of Blackness . . . reordering the world.

                                                                          LE ROI JONES

Are you ready to enter the vision of the Black Left? It is profoundly anti-technological. Jump into it all at once. Here are a few remarks by Ron Karenga:

"The fact that we are Black is our ultimate reality. We were Black before we were born.

"The white boy is engaged in the worship of technology; we must not sell our souls for money and machines. We must free ourselves culturally before we proceed politically.

"Revolution to us is the creation of an alternative . . . we are not here to be taught by the world, but to teach the world."

We have left the splendid American far behind. He is a straight-punching all-out truth-sayer; he believes in speaking his mind; but if LeRoi Jones— insults, absolute rejection and consummate bad-mouthing—is not too much for him, then Karenga will be his finish. Karenga obviously believes that in the root is the answer to where the last growth went wrong—so he believes in the wisdom of the blood, and blood-wisdom went out for the splendid American after reading *Lady Chatterley's Lover* in sophomore year. Life is hard enough to see straight without founding your philosophy on a metaphor.

Nonetheless the mystique of Black Power remains. Any mystique which has men ready to die for it is never without political force. The Left Wing of Black Power speaks across the void to the most powerful conservative passions—for any real conservatism is founded on regard for the animal, the oak and the field; it has instinctive detestation of science, of the creation-by-machine. Conservatism is a body of traditions which once served as the philosophical home of society. If the traditions are now withered in the hum of electronics; if the traditions have become almost hopelessly inadequate to meet the computed moves of the technological society; if conservatism has become the grumbling of the epicure at bad food, bad air, bad manners; if conservatism lost the future because it enjoyed the greed of its privileged position to that point where the exploited depths stirred in righteous rage; if the conservatives and their traditions failed because they violated the balance of society, exploited the poor too savagely and searched for justice not nearly enough; if finally the balance between property rights and the rights of men gave at last too much to the land and too little to the living blood, still conservatism and tradition had one last Herculean strength: they were of the marrow, they partook of primitive wisdom. The tradition had been founded on some half-remembered sense of primitive perception, and so was close to life and the sense of life. Tradition had appropriated the graceful movements with which primitive strangers and friends might meet in the depth of a mood, all animal in their awareness: lo! the stranger bows before the intense presence of the monarch or the chief, and the movement is later engraved upon a code of ceremony. So tradition was once a key to the primitive life still breathing within us, a key too large, idiosyncratic and unmanageable for the quick shuttles of the electronic. Standing before technology, tradition began to die, and air turned to smog. But the black man, living a life on the fringe of technological society, exploited by it, poisoned by it, half-rejected by it, gulping prison air in the fluorescent nightmare of shabby garish electric ghettos, uprooted centuries ago from his native Africa, his instincts living ergo like nerves in the limbo of an amputated limb, had thereby an experience unique to modern man—he was forced to live at one and the same time in the old primitive jungle of the slums, and the hygienic surrealistic landscape of the technological society. And as he began to arise from his exploitation, he discovered that the culture which had saved him owed more to the wit and telepathy of the jungle than the value and programs of the West. His dance had taught him more than writs and torts, his music was sweeter than Shakespeare or Bach (since music had never been a luxury to him but a need), prison had given him a culture deeper than libraries in the grove, and violence had produced an economy of personal relations as negotiable as money. The American Black had survived—of all the peoples of the Western World, he was the only one in the near seven decades of the twentieth century to have undergone the cruel weeding of real survival. So it was possible his manhood had improved while the manhood of others was being leached. He had at any rate a vision. It was that he was black, beautiful and secretly superior—he had therefore the potentiality to conceive and create a new culture (perchance a new civilization), richer, wiser, deeper, more beautiful and profound than any he had seen. (And conceivably more demanding, more torrential, more tyrannical.) But he would not know until he had power for himself. He would not know if he could provide a wiser science, subtler schooling, deeper medicine, richer victual and deeper view of creation until he had the power. So while some (the ones the Blacks called Negroes) looked to integrate into the super-suburbs of technology land (and find, was their hope, a little peace for the kids), so others dreamed of a future world which their primitive lore and sophisticated attainments might now bring. And because they were proud and loved their vision, they were warriors as well, and had a mystique which saw the cooking of food as good or bad for the soul. And taste gave the hint. That was the Left of Black Power, a movement as mysterious, dedicated, instinctive and conceivably bewitched as a gathering of Templars for the next Crusade. Soon their public fury might fall upon the fact that civilization was a trap, and therefore their wrath might be double, for they had been employed to build civilization, had received none of its gains, and yet, being allowed to enter now, now, this late, could be doomed with the rest. What a thought!

When the *canaille roturière* took the liberty of beheading the high *noblesse*, it was done less, perhaps, to inherit their goods than to inherit their ancestors.

                                                                          **HEINRICH HEINE**

But I am a white American, more or less, and writing for an audience of Americans, white and Negro in the main. So the splendid American would remind me that my thoughts are romantic projections, hypotheses unverifiable by any discipline, no more legitimate for discussion than melody. What, he might ask, would you do with the concrete problem before us. . . .

You mean: not jobs, not schools, not votes, not production, not consumption. . . .

No, he said hoarsely, law and order.

Well, the man who sings the melody is not normally consulted for the by-laws of the Arranger's Union.

Crap and craparoola, said the splendid American, what it all comes down to is: how do you keep the peace?

I do not know. If they try to keep it by force—we will not have to wait so very long before there are Vietnams in our own cities. A race which arrives at a vision must test that vision by deeds.

Then what would you do?

If I were king?

We are a republic and will never support a king.

Ah, if I were a man who had a simple audience with Richard Milhous Nixon, I would try to say, "Remember when all else has failed, that honest hatred searches for responsibility. I would look to encourage not merely new funding for businessmen who are Black, but Black schools with their own teachers and their own texts, Black solutions to Black housing where the opportunity might be given to rebuild one's own slum room by room, personal idiosyncrasy next to mad neighbor's style, floor by floor, not block by block; I would try to recognize that an area of a city where whites fear to go at night belongs by all existential—which is to say natural—law to the Blacks, and would respect the fact, and so would encourage Black local self-government as in a separate city with a Black sanitation department run by themselves, a Black fire department, a funding for a Black concert hall, and most of all a Black police force responsible only to this city within our city and Black courts of justice for their own. There will be no peace short of the point where the Black man can measure his new superiorities and inferiorities against our own."

You are absolutely right but for one detail, said the splendid American. What will you do when they complain about the smog *our* factories push into *their* air?

Oh, I said, the Blacks are so evil their factories will push worse air back. And thus we went on arguing into the night. Yes, the times are that atrocious you can hardly catch your breath. "Confronted by outstanding merit in another, there is no way of saving one's ego except by love."

Goethe is not the worst way to say goodnight.

## STUDY QUESTIONS

1. Mailer starts his essay dealing with language. What is the connection between his observations about language and the rest of the essay?

2. What is the rhetorical strategy of the opening sentence of paragraph seven?

3. What support does Mailer offer for his claim that the American Negro is more essentially colonial in stance than any other colonial force?

4.  According to Mailer, what are the goals and aspirations of the Black Power Left Wing?

5.  As a white man writing about Black Power, how does Mailer lend authority to his essay?

6.  According to Mailer, how can "honest hatred" lead to means that will help keep the peace?

7.  How does the concluding quotation from Goethe relate to the essay?

*James Baldwin*

# UNNAMEABLE OBJECTS, UNSPEAKABLE CRIMES

James Baldwin (1924–     ) has established a reputation as one of America's outstanding contemporary writers. Born and raised in Harlem, Baldwin received a Eugene F. Saxton Fellowship in 1945 that enabled him to devote his time to writing. He has written three novels: *Go Tell It on the Mountain* (1953), *Giovanni's Room* (1956), and *Another Country* (1962). His collections of essays are *Notes of a Native Son* (1955), *Nobody Knows My Name* (1960), *The Fire Next Time* (1963), *Fifty Famous Stories Retold* (1967), and *Tell Me How Long the Train's Been Gone* (1968). Active in civil rights activities, he has lectured in numerous colleges and universities. He is a member of the national advisory board of the Congress of Racial Equality. He has won Rosenthal, Guggenheim, and National Institute of Arts and Letters awards.

I HAVE OFTEN wondered, and it is not a pleasant wonder, just what white Americans talk about with one another.

I wonder this because they do not, after all, seem to find very much to say to *me*, and I concluded long ago that they found the color

Reprinted from *The White Problem in America*. First published in *Ebony*, as "White Man's Guilt." With permission of the publishers and Robert Lantz, Literary Agent.

of my skin inhibitory. This color seems to operate as a most disagreeable mirror, and a great deal of one's energy is expended in reassuring white Americans that they do not see what *they* see. This is utterly futile, of course, since *they do* see what *they* see. And what they see is an appallingly oppressive and bloody history, known all over the world. What they see is a disastrous, continuing, present, condition which menaces them, and for which they bear an inescapable responsibility. But since, in the main, they appear to lack the energy to change this condition, they would rather not be reminded of it. Does this mean that, in their conversations with one another, they merely make reassuring sounds? It scarcely seems possible, and yet, on the other hand, it seems all too likely.

Whatever they bring to one another, it is certainly not *freedom from guilt.*

The guilt remains, more deeply rooted, more securely lodged, than the oldest of old trees; and it can be unutterably exhausting to deal with people who, with a really dazzling ingenuity, a tireless agility, are perpetually defending themselves against charges which one has not made.

One does not have to make them. The record is there for all to read. It resounds all over the world. It might as well be written in the sky.

One wishes that Americans, white Americans, would read, for their own sakes, this record, and stop defending themselves against it. Only then will they be enabled to change their lives. The fact that Americans, white Americans, have not yet been able to do this—to face their history, to change their lives—hideously menaces this country. Indeed, it menaces the entire world.

For history, as nearly no one seems to know, is not merely something to be read. And it does not refer merely, or even principally, to the past. On the contrary, the great force of history comes from the fact that we carry it within us, are unconsciously controlled by it in many ways, and history is literally *present* in all that we do. It could scarcely be otherwise, since it is to history that we owe our frames of reference, our identities, and our aspirations.

And it is with great pain and terror that one begins to realize this. In great pain and terror, one begins to assess the history which has placed one where one is, and formed one's point of view. In great pain and terror, because, thereafter, one enters into battle with that historical creation, oneself, and attempts to re-create oneself according to a principle more humane and more liberating; one begins the attempt to achieve a level of personal maturity and freedom which robs history of its tyrannical power, and also changes history.

But, obviously, I am speaking as an historical creation which has had bitterly to contest its history, to wrestle with it and finally accept it, in order to bring myself out of it. My point of view is certainly formed by my history, and it is probable that only a creature despised by history finds history a questionable matter. On the other hand, people who imagine that history flatters them (as it does, indeed, since they wrote it) are impaled on their history like a butterfly on a pin and become incapable of seeing or changing themselves or the world.

This is the place in which, it seems to me, most white Americans find themselves. They are dimly, or vividly, aware that the history they have fed themselves is mainly a lie, but they do not know how to release themselves from it, and they suffer enormously from the resulting personal incoherence. This incoherence is heard nowhere more plainly than in those stammering, terrified dialogues white Americans sometimes entertain with that black conscience, the black man in America.

The nature of this stammering can be reduced to a plea: Do not blame *me*. I was not there. I did not do it. My history has nothing to do with Europe or the slave trade. Anyway, it was *your* chiefs who sold *you* to *me*. I was not present on the middle passage. I am not responsible for the textile mills of Manchester, or the cotton fields of Mississippi. Besides, consider how the English, too, suffered in those mills and in those awful cities! I, also, despise the governors of Southern states and the sheriffs of Southern counties; and I also want your child to have a decent education and rise as high as his capabilities will permit. I have nothing against you, *nothing!* What have *you* got against *me? What do you want?*

But, on the same day, in another gathering, and in the most private chamber of his heart always, he, the white man, remains proud of that history for which he does not wish to pay, and from which, materially, he has profited so much. On that same day, in another gathering, and in the most private chamber of the black man's heart always, he finds himself facing the terrible roster of the lost: the dead, black junkie; the defeated, black father; the unutterably weary, black mother; the unutterably ruined black girl. And one begins to suspect an awful thing: that people believe that they *deserve* their history and that when they operate on this belief, they perish. But they can scarcely avoid believing that they deserve it—one's short time on this earth is very mysterious and very dark and hard. I have known many black men and women and black boys and girls, who really believed that it was better to be white than black, whose lives were ruined or ended by this belief; and I myself carried the seeds of this destruction within me for a long time.

Now, if I, as a black man, profoundly believe that I deserve my history and deserve to be treated as I am, then I must also, fatally, believe that white people deserve their history and deserve the power and the glory which their testimony and the evidence of my own senses assure me that they have. And if black people fall into this trap, the trap of believing that they deserve their fate, white people fall into the yet more stunning and intricate trap of believing that they deserve *their* fate, and their comparative safety; and that black people, therefore, need only do as white people have done to rise to where white people now are. But this simply cannot be said, not only for reasons of politeness or charity, but also because white people carry in them a carefully muffled fear that black people long to do to others what has been done to them. Moreover, the history of white people has led them to a fearful, baffling place where they have begun to lose touch with reality—to lose touch, that is, with themselves—and where they certainly are not happy. They do not know how this came about; they do not dare examine how this came about. On the one hand, they can scarcely dare to open a dialogue which must, if it is honest, become a personal confession—a cry for help and healing, which is really, I think, the basis of all dialogues—and, on the other hand, the black man can scarcely dare to open a dialogue which must, if it is honest, become a personal confession which, fatally, contains an accusation. And yet, if we cannot do this, each of us will perish in those traps in which we have been struggling for so long.

The American situation is very peculiar, and it may be without precedent in the world. No curtain under heaven is heavier than that curtain of guilt and lies behind which Americans hide: it may prove to be yet more deadly to the lives of human beings than that iron curtain of which we speak so much —and know so little. The American curtain is color. We have used this word, this concept, to justify unspeakable crimes, not only in the past, but in the present. One can measure very neatly the white American's distance from his conscience—from himself—by observing the distance between himself and black people. One has only to ask oneself who established this distance. Who is this distance designed to protect? And from what is this distance designed to protect him?

I have seen this very vividly, for example, in the eyes of Southern law enforcement officers barring, let us say, the door to the courthouse. There they stand, comrades all, invested with the authority of the community, with helmets, with sticks, with guns, with cattle prods. Facing them are unarmed black people—or, more precisely, they are faced by a group of unarmed people arbitrarily called black, whose color really ranges from the Russian steppes to the Golden Horn, to Zanzibar. In a moment, because he can resolve the situation in no other way, this sheriff, this deputy, this honored American citizen, must begin to club these people down. Some of these people may be related to him by blood; they are assuredly related to the black Mammy of his memory, and the black playmates of his childhood. And for a moment, therefore, he seems nearly to be pleading with the people facing him not to force him to commit yet another crime and not to make yet deeper that ocean of blood in which his conscience is drenched, in which his manhood is perishing. The people do not go away, of course; once a people arise, they never go away, a fact which should be included in the Marine handbook; and the club rises, the blood comes down, and our crimes and our bitterness and our anguish are compounded. Or, one sees it in the eyes of rookie cops in Harlem, who are really among the most terrified people in the world, and who must pretend to themselves that the black mother, the black junkie, the black father, the black child are of a different human species than themselves. They can only deal with their lives and their duties by hiding behind the color curtain. This curtain, indeed, eventually becomes their principal justification for the lives they lead.

But it is not only on this level that one sees the extent of our disaster. Not so very long ago, I found myself in Montgomery, with many, many thousands, marching to the Capitol. Much has been written about this march—for example, the Confederate flag was flying from the Capitol dome; the Federalized National Guard, assigned to protect the marchers, wore Confederate flags on their jackets; if the late Mrs. Viola Liuzzo was avoiding the patrols on that deadly stretch of road that night, she had far sharper eyesight than mine, for I did not see any. Well, there we were, marching to that mansion from which authority had fled. All along that road—I pray that my countrymen will hear me—old, black men and women, who have endured an unspeakable oppression for so long, waved and cheered and sang and wept. They could not march, but they had done something else: they had brought us to the place where we could march. How many of us, after all, were brought up on the white folks leavings, and how mighty a price those old men and women paid to bring those leavings home to us!

We reached the white section of town. There the businessmen stood, on balconies, jeering; there stood their maids, in back doors, silent, not daring to wave, but nodding. I watched a black, or rather, a beige-colored woman, standing in the street, watching us thoughtfully; she looked as though she probably held a clerical job in one of those buildings; proof, no doubt, to the jeering white businessmen that the South was making progress. This woman decided to join us, for when we reached the Capitol, I noticed that she was there. But, while we were still marching, through the white part of town, the watching, the waiting, the frightened part of town, we lifted our small American flags, and we faced those eyes—which could not face ours—and we sang. I was next to Harry Belafonte. From upstairs office windows, white American secretaries were leaning out of windows, jeering and mocking, and using the ancient Roman sentence of death: thumbs down. Then they saw Harry, who is my very dear friend and a beautiful cat, and who is also, in this most desperately schizophrenic of republics, a major, a reigning matinée idol. One does not need to be a student of Freud to understand what buried forces create a matinée idol, or what he represents to that public which batters down doors to watch him (one need only watch the rise and fall of American politicians. This is a sinister observation. And I mean it very seriously). The secretaries were legally white—it was on that basis that they lived their lives, from this principle that they took, collectively, their values; which is, as I have tried to indicate, an interesting spiritual condition. But they were also young. In that ghastly town, they were certainly lonely. They could only, after all, look forward to an alliance, by and by, with one of the jeering businessmen; their boyfriends could only look forward to becoming one of them. And they were also female, a word, which, in the context of the color curtain, has suffered the same fate as the word, "male": it has become practically obscene. When the girls saw Harry Belafonte, a collision occurred in them so visible as to be at once hilarious and unutterably sad. At one moment, the thumbs were down, they were barricaded within their skins, at the next moment, those downturned thumbs flew to their mouths, their finger pointed, their faces changed, and exactly like bobbysoxers, they oohed, and aahed and moaned. God knows what was happening in the minds and hearts of those girls. Perhaps they would like to be free.

The white man's guilt, which he pretends is due to the fact that the world is a place of many colors, has nothing to do with color. If one attempts to reduce his dilemma to its essence, it really does not have much to do with his crimes, except in the sense that he has locked himself into a place where he is doomed to continue repeating them. The great, unadmitted crime is what he has done to himself. A man is a man, a woman is a woman, and a child is a child. To deny these facts is to open the doors on a chaos deeper and deadlier, and, within the space of a man's lifetime, more timeless, more eternal, than the medieval vision of Hell. And we have arrived at this unspeakable blasphemy in order to acquire things, in order to make money. We cannot endure the things we acquire—the only reason we continually acquire them, like junkies on a hundred dollar a day habit—and our money exists mainly on paper. God help us on that day when the population demands to know what is behind the paper. But, beyond all this, it is terrifying to consider the precise nature of the things we buy with the flesh we sell.

In Henry James' novel *The Ambassadors* published not long before World War I, and not long before his death, he recounts the story of a middle-aged New Englander, assigned by his middle-aged bride-to-be—a widow—the task of rescuing from the flesh-pots of Paris her only son. She wants him to come home to take over the direction of the family factory. In the event, it is the middle-aged New Englander—*The Ambassador*—who is seduced, not so much by Paris, as by a new and less utilitarian view of life. He counsels the young man to "live. Live all you can. It is a mistake not to." Which I translate as meaning "Trust life, and it will teach you, in joy and sorrow, all you need to know." Jazz musicians know this. Those old men and women who waved and sang and wept as we marched in Montgomery know this. White Americans, in the main, do not know this. They are still trapped in that factory to which, in Henry James' novel, the son returns. We never know what this factory produces, for James never tells us. He only conveys

to us that the factory, at an unbelievable human expense, produces unnameable objects.

### STUDY QUESTIONS

1.  What is Baldwin's thesis, and how does he develop it?

2.  In what way does his view of history relate to his thesis?

3.  How does the "curtain of guilt" affect the white man?

4.  Baldwin speaks with a prose voice of authority. In what ways does he
    establish and maintain this voice?

5.  How does the concluding paragraph relate to the rest of the essay? What
    is Baldwin's strategy here?

*Ebony*

# WHAT WHITES CAN LEARN FROM NEGROES

TROUBLE don't last always, says an old Negro spiritual, but
according to screaming newspaper headlines, convulsed
TV commentators and a frayed-nerved public, Old Man
Trouble has pitched his teepee square in the middle of the twentieth century
and settled down for a record run.

The whole world is on edge. Nations are bickering with nations. Races
are pitted against races. Everybody seems beset by fears, overwrought by
frustrations. They are jittery about the war in Viet Nam that had no beginning and the war that has no ending in the Dominican Republic and the cold

Reprinted from *The White Problem in America*. First published in *Ebony*, August 1965. With permission of the publishers.

war that occasionally gets mighty warm. They are hearing noises that do not exist, seeing objects that are not there.

In times like these, white people seeking a panacea for their problems might well take a lesson from the Negro on how to live in a troubled world. The Negro is an expert. He has known nothing but trouble all of his life. His grievances are multiple for he has all of the white man's fears and doubts plus the additional burden of being black. Yet the Negro can still smile, for the progress that he has made up from slavery to his present status—short of first class citizenship though it is—is one of the most remarkable advancements in the history of mankind. In the process he has learned to turn his liabilities into assets, to adjust to that over which he has no control and to have faith in his ability to overcome all of the other obstacles between himself and full equality.

## The Philosophy of "If"

The way to tell a Negro from a white man when physical appearances failed, swore the old time armchair anthropologists, was to engage the suspect in conversation. Query him about his ambitions, his future plans, his next step. If he said he "hoped" to become a lawyer or a merchant, that he "wanted" to buy a car, spend his vacation in Canada, then that man was white. But if he prefaced his desire by the phrase: "If I live and nothing happens," he was colored. This homely philosophy with the built-in disaster clause allowed the Negro to take his setbacks and misfortunes in stride. It was this philosophy, born of heart-breaking experiences, which kept his insanity and suicide rates below those of his fair-skinned brothers. But today's Negro has added a positive dimension to a probable clause. If he lives, he will *make* something happen.

The white man stakes his all on a business venture or a political campaign. He will even put his life's savings in schemes that can pay off only with a hoped-for boom, and bet his last five dollars on a long-shot nag. If he loses he will have an opportunity to recoup and start all over again, but all too often, he is found below an open window or his last will and testament is contained in a brief note on the railing of a bridge.

The Negro, whose existence is riddled with reverses and disappointments, has learned not to put all of his eggs in one shopping bag or his complete trust in one man. He knows that if he fails, there is no second chance. For him there are no short cuts to success. Only through his own supreme efforts can he attain his cherished goal. When bad luck overtook him, he used to console himself with the adage that "everything happens for the best." Today, he does not wait for things to happen, and the best may not be good enough. Instead of taking his troubles to the window or the water, he is more likely to try them in the courts or dramatize them in the streets.

The Negro is particularly adept at making the best of a bad situation, not because of any inherent powers that he may have, but because he has had an abundance of practice and more bad situations than the white man. More put upon and less protected than any other ethnic group in our society except the Indian, he has been under the strain of racial tensions all of his life; has always been handicapped by patterns of prejudice and walls of discrimination. The Negro in America is kept so busy trying to live under the same flag as the Ku Klux Klan, the White Citizens Councils and other hate-Negro, hate-minority organizations, that he has little time to worry about communism in China or India's population explosion.

A nuclear bomb which he may never see is not nearly as imminent as an electric cattle prod he has felt. Wars in distant lands in which he too must fight, are not as personal as demonstrations in Chicago or boycotts in Birmingham. Although some white citizens would rather cloud the image of this country abroad than practice democracy here at home, the Negro remains loyal to America. He fights for it and he dies for it and he hopes fervently that it will soon be at peace, for he needs all his war-spent energies to earn his daily bread and a little butter. Now that his right to the ballot has been reaffirmed, he needs his war-spent strength to make things happen: to lead registration drives in the South and to discourage voter apathy in the North, to exercise his right to live where his money and desires dictate, to obtain better education for his children, to fit himself for a better job so that he can improve his standard of living. He knows that these things are now possible, but wishing alone will not make them so.

In the South and to some extent in the North, the Negro's very existence once depended upon his ability to get along with white people. The psychology of fear employed by race supremacists to frighten him into 100 years of submission is no longer applicable. His is the faith that overcomes, the courage that marches around bigots and laughs at the Klan. His is an example of faith and courage that other men might follow.

Trapped in a white-dominated world, the black man has learned to live with trouble. To yesterday's motto "don't get mad, get smart," he has added "do something!" If white men are to have peace of mind they must also stop getting mad and getting nervous and do something. For one thing, they must learn to live with men who are black and red and yellow and brown. They, too, must learn to become bedfellows with fear and frustration, to turn liabilities into assets, adjust to that which cannot be helped and change those things that are morally wrong.

To master the art of doing with and doing without is essential to all men. With very little of this world's goods the Negro has been able to an unbelievable degree to survive—even thrive—under oppressions, uncertainties and inconveniences. He has worn hand-me-down clothing, lived in second-class housing, worked at low-paying jobs. But those conditions were morally

wrong and he found a way to change them. In doing so, he has transferred
his disappointments into hopes and hopes into actions and actions into improvements which, if continued, will bring him the full equality and ultimate happiness all men seek.

If white people would profit by the Negro's ability to overcome, they can
begin by cultivating his sense of humor. His public posture may be that of
the angry young man, but his capacity to laugh at his troubles, even though
he does so in the privacy of his race, is his means of releasing pent-up emotions. White people who would have peace of mind, must ease their guilty
consciences. Like the Negro, they must put their trust in God and their
shoulder to the wheel. Faith alone will not move mountains.

If the black man can make it by adding new dimensions to old adages,
surely white men can follow his example. No people can have peace always
nor can their prosperity continue unbroken. All of this country's citizens
have worked hard and sacrificed much to make America the great nation
that it is today. Surely those who by virtue of color have inherited the bulk of
her many benefits can, like the Negro, learn to endure her limitations.

## STUDY QUESTIONS

1.  How does the author use comparison and contrast to develop his thesis?

2.  What does the author mean by the philosophy of "if"?

3.  According to the essay, how does the Negro's sense of humor serve him?

4.  Do you regard the author's advice as practical? Is the white man prepared
    to follow such course of action as the author recommends?

5.  Is the author's strategy to appeal to the reader's reason or his emotions?

*William Faulkner*

# ON FEAR: DEEP SOUTH
# IN LABOR: MISSISSIPPI

William Faulkner (1897–1962), winner of the Nobel Prize for Literature in 1950 and regarded as one of the leading novelists of this century, was born in New Albany, Mississippi. He attended the University of Mississippi, but did not graduate. During World War I he trained with the Royal Canadian Air Force, but the war ended before he went overseas. He is the author of more than twenty novels and several collections of short stories. His best-known works are *The Sound and the Fury* (1929), *Light in August* (1932), *Absalom, Absalom!* (1936), and *Go Down Moses* (1942).

*I*MMEDIATELY after the Supreme Court decision abolishing segregation in schools, the talk began in Mississippi of ways and means to increase taxes to raise the standard of the Negro schools to match the white ones. I wrote the following letter to the open forum page of our most widely-read Memphis paper:

We Mississippians already know that our present schools are not good enough. Our young men and women themselves prove that to us every year by the fact that, when the best of them want the best of education which they are entitled to and competent for, not only in the humanities but in the professions and crafts— law and medicine and engineering—too, they must go out of the state to get it. And quite often, too often, they dont come back.

So our present schools are not even good enough for white people; our present State reservoir of education is not of high enough quality to assuage the thirst of even our white young men and women. In which case, how can it possibly assuage the thirst and need of the Negro, who obviously is thirstier, needs it worse, else the Federal Government would not have had to pass a law compelling Mississippi (among others of course) to make the best of our education available to him.

That is, our present schools are not even good enough for white people. So what do we do? make them good enough, improve them to the best possible? No. We beat the bushes, rake and scrape to raise additional taxes to establish another system at best only equal to that one which is already not good enough, which therefore wont be good enough for Negroes either; we will have two identical systems neither of which are good enough for anybody.

A few days after my letter was printed in the paper, I received by post the carbon copy of a letter addressed to the same forum page of the Memphis paper. It read as follows: "When Weeping Willie Faulkner splashes his tears about the inadequacy of Mississippi schools . . . we question his gumption in these respects" etc. From there it went on to cite certain facts of which all Southerners are justly proud: that the seedstock of education in our land was preserved through the evil times following the Civil War when our land was a defeated and occupied country, by dedicated teachers who got little in return for their dedication. Then, after a brief sneer at the quality of my writing and the profit motive which was the obvious reason why I was a writer, he closed by saying: "I suggest that Weeping Willie dry his tears and work up a little thirst for knowledge about the basic economy of his state."

Later, after this letter was printed in the Memphis paper in its turn, I received from the writer of it a letter addressed to him by a correspondent in another small Mississippi town, consisting in general of a sneer at the Nobel Prize which was awarded me, and commending the Weeping Willie writer for his promptness in taking to task anyone traitorous enough to hold education more important than the color of the educatee's skin. Attached to it was the Weeping Willie writer's reply. It said in effect: "In my opinion Faulkner is the most capable commentator on Southern facts of life to date. . . . If we could insult him into acquiring an insight into the basic economy of our region, he could (sic) do us a hell of a lot of good in our fight against integration."

My answer was that I didn't believe that insult is a very sound method of teaching anybody anything, of persuading anyone to think or act as the insulter believes they should. I repeated that what we needed in Mississippi was the best possible schools, to make the best possible use of the men and women we produced, regardless of what color they were. And even if we could not have a school system which would do that, at least let us have one which would make no distinction among pupils except that of simple ability, since our principal and perhaps desperate need in America today was that all Americans at least should be on the side of America; that if all Americans were on the same side, we would not need to fear that other nations and ideologies would doubt us when we talked of human freedom.

But this is beside the point. The point is, what is behind this. The tragedy is not the impasse, but what is behind the impasse—the impasse of the two apparently irreconcilable facts which we are faced with in the South: the one being the decree of our national government that there be absolute equality in education among all citizens, the other being the white people in the South who say that white and Negro pupils shall never sit in the same classroom. Only apparently irreconcilable, because they must be reconciled since the only alternative to change is death. In fact, there are people in the South, Southerners born, who not only believe they can be reconciled but who love our land—not love white people specifically nor love Negroes specifically, but our land, our country: our climate and geography, the qualities in our people, white and Negro too, for honesty and fairness, the splendors in our traditions, the glories in our past—enough to try to reconcile them, even at the cost of displeasing both sides: the contempt of the Northern radicals who believe we dont do enough, the contumely and threats of our own Southern reactionaries who are convinced that anything we do is already too much.

The tragedy is, the reason behind the fact, the fear behind the fact that some of the white people in the South—people who otherwise are rational, cultured, gentle, generous and kindly—will—must—fight against every inch which the Negro gains in social betterment; the fear behind the desperation which could drive rational and successful men (my correspondent, the Weeping Willie one, is a banker, perhaps president of a—perhaps the— bank in another small Mississippi town like my own) to grasp at such straws for weapons as contumely and threat and insult to change the views or anyway the voice which dares to suggest that betterment of the Negro's condition does not necessarily presage the doom of the white race. Nor is the tragedy the fear so much as the tawdry quality of the fear—fear not of the Negro as an individual Negro nor even as a race, but as an economic class or stratum or factor, since what the Negro threatens is not the Southern white man's social system but the Southern white man's economic system—that economic system which the white man knows and dares not admit to himself is established on an obsolescence—the artificial inequality of man—and so is itself already obsolete and hence doomed. He knows that only three hundred years ago the Negro's naked grandfather was eating rotten elephant or hippo meat in an African rain-forest, yet in only three hundred years the Negro produced Dr. Ralph Bunche and George Washington Carver and Booker T. Washington. The white man knows that only ninety years ago not one percent of the Negro race could own a deed to land, let alone read that deed; yet in only ninety years, although his only contact with a county courthouse is the window through which he pays the taxes for which he has no representation, he can own his land and farm it with inferior stock and worn-out tools and gear—equipment which any white man would starve with—and raise children and feed and clothe them and send them to what schools are available and even now and then send them North where they can have equal scholastic opportunity, and end his life holding his head up because he owes no man, with even enough over to pay for his coffin and funeral. That's what the white man in the South is afraid of: that the Negro, who has done so much with no chance, might do so much more with an equal one that he might take the white man's economy away from him, the Negro now the banker or the merchant or the planter and the white man the share-cropper or the tenant. That's why the Negro can gain our country's highest decoration for valor beyond all call of duty for saving or defending or preserving white lives on foreign battle-fields yet the Southern white man dares not let that Negro's children learn their abc's in the same classroom with the children of the white lives he saved or defended.

Now the Supreme Court has defined exactly what it meant by what it said: that by "equality" it meant, simply, equality, without qualifying or conditional adjectives: not "separate but equal" nor "equally separate," but simply, equal; and now the Mississippi voices are talking of something which does not even exist anymore.

In the first half of the nineteenth century, before slavery was abolished by law in the United States, Thomas Jefferson and Abraham Lincoln both held that the Negro was not yet competent for equality.

That was more than ninety years ago now, and nobody can say whether their opinions would be different now or not.

But assume that they would not have changed their belief, and that that opinion is right. Assume that the Negro is still not competent for equality, which is something which neither he nor the white man knows until we try it.

But we do know that, with the support of the Federal Government, the Negro is going to gain the right to try and see if he is fit or not for equality. And if the Southern white man cannot trust him with something as mild as equality, what is the Southern white man going to do when he has power— the power of his own fifteen millions of unanimity backed by the Federal Government—when the only check on that power will be that Federal Government which is already the Negro's ally?

In 1849, Senator John C. Calhoun made his address in favor of secession if the Wilmot Proviso was ever adopted. On Oct. 12th of that year, Senator Jefferson Davis wrote a public letter to the South, saying: "The generation which avoids its responsibility on this subject sows the wind and leaves the whirlwind as a harvest to its children. Let us get together and build manufactures, enter upon industrial pursuits, and prepare for our own self-sustenance."

At that time the Constitution guaranteed the Negro as property along with all other property, and Senator Calhoun and Senator Davis had the then undisputed validity of States' Rights to back their position. Now the Constitution guarantees the Negro equal right to equality, and the states' rights which the Mississippi voices are talking about do not exist anymore.

We—Mississippi—sold our states' rights back to the Federal Government when we accepted the first cotton price-support subsidy twenty years ago. Our economy is not agricultural any longer. Our economy is the Federal Government. We no longer farm in Mississippi cotton-fields. We farm now in Washington corridors and Congressional committee-rooms.

We—the South—didn't heed Senator Davis's words then. But we had better do it now. If we are to watch our native land wrecked and ruined twice in less than a hundred years over the Negro question, let us be sure this time that we know where we are going afterward.

There are many voices in Mississippi. There is that of one of our United States senators, who, although he is not speaking for the United States Senate and what he advocates does not quite match the oath he took when he entered into his high office several years ago, at least has made no attempt to hide his identity and his condition. And there is the voice of one of our circuit judges, who, although he is not now speaking from the Bench and what he advocates also stands a little awry to his oath that before the law all men are equal and the weak shall be succored and defended, makes no attempt either to conceal his identity and condition. And there are the voices of the ordinary citizens who, although they do not claim to speak specifically for the white Citizens' Councils and the NAACP, do not try to hide their sentiments and their convictions; not to mention those of the schoolmen— teachers and professors and pupils—though, since most Mississippi schools are State-owned or -supported, they dont always dare to sign their names to the open letters.

There are all the voices in fact, except one. That one voice which would adumbrate them all to silence, being the superior of all since it is the living articulation of the glory and the sovereignty of God and the hope and aspiration of man. The Church, which is the strongest unified force in our Southern life since all Southerners are not white and are not democrats, but all Southerners are religious and all religions serve the same single God, no matter by what name He is called. Where is that voice now, the only reference to which I have seen was in an open forum letter to our Memphis paper which said that to his (the writer's) knowledge, none of the people who begged leave to doubt that one segment of the human race was forever doomed to be inferior to all the other segments just because the Old Testament five thousand years ago said it was, were communicants of any church.

Where is that voice now, which should have propounded perhaps two but certainly one of these still-unanswered questions?

1. The Constitution of the U.S. says: Before the law, there shall be no artificial inequality—race, creed or money— among citizens of the United States.

2.   Morality says: Do unto others as you would have others do unto you.

3.   Christianity says: I am the only distinction among men since whosoever believeth in Me, shall never die.

Where is this voice now, in our time of trouble and indecision? Is it trying by its silence to tell us that it has no validity and wants none outside the sanctuary behind its symbolical spire?

If the facts as stated in the *Look* magazine account of the Till affair are correct, this remains: two adults, armed, in the dark, kidnap a fourteen-year-old boy and take him away to frighten him. Instead of which, the fourteen-year-old boy not only refuses to be frightened, but, unarmed, alone, in the dark, so frightens the two armed adults that they must destroy him.

What are we Mississippians afraid of? Why do we have so low an opinion of ourselves that we are afraid of people who by all our standards are our inferiors?—economically: i.e., they have so much less than we have that they must work for us not on their terms but on ours; educationally: i.e., their schools are so much worse than ours that the Federal Government has to threaten to intervene to give them equal conditions; politically: i.e., they have no recourse in law for protection from nor restitution for injustice and violence.

Why do we have so low an opinion of our blood and traditions as to fear that, as soon as the Negro enters our house by the front door, he will propose marriage to our daughter and she will immediately accept him?

Our ancestors were not afraid like this—our grandfathers who fought at First and Second Manassas and Sharpsburg and Shiloh and Franklin and Chickamauga and Chancellorsville and the Wilderness; let alone those who survived that and had the additional and even greater courage and endurance to resist and survive Reconstruction, and so preserved to us something of our present heritage. Why are we, descendants of that blood and inheritors of that courage, afraid? What are we afraid of? What has happened to us in only a hundred years?

For the sake of argument, let us agree that all white Southerners (all white Americans maybe) curse the day when the first Briton or Yankee sailed the first shipload of manacled Negroes across the Middle Passage and auctioned them into American slavery. Because that doesn't matter now. To live anywhere in the world today and be against equality because of race or color, is like living in Alaska and being against snow. We have already got snow. And as with the Alaskan, merely to live in armistice with it is not enough. Like the Alaskan, we had better use it.

Suddenly about five years ago and with no warning to myself, I adopted the habit of travel. Since then I have seen (a little of some, a little more of others) the Far and Middle East, North Africa, Europe and Scandinavia. The countries I saw were not communist (then) of course, but they were more: they were not even communist-inclined, where it seemed to me they should have been. And I wondered why. Then suddenly I said to myself with a kind of amazement: It's because of America. These people still believe in the American dream; they do not know yet that something happened to it. They believe in us and are willing to trust and follow us not because of our material power: Russia has that: but because of the idea of individual human freedom and liberty and equality on which our nation was founded, which our founding fathers postulated the word "America" to mean.

And, five years later, the countries which are still free of communism are still free simply because of that: that belief in individual liberty and equality and freedom which is the one idea powerful enough to stalemate the idea of communism. And we can thank our gods for that since we have no other weapon to fight communism with; in diplomacy we are children to communist diplomats, and production in a free country can always suffer because under monolithic government all production can go to the aggrandisement of the State. But then, we dont need anything more since that simple belief of man that he can be free is the strongest force on earth and all we need to do is use it.

Because it makes a glib and simple picture, we like to think of the world situation today as a precarious and explosive balance of two irreconcilable ideologies confronting each other: which precarious balance, once it totters, will drag the whole universe into the abyss along with it. That's not so. Only one of the opposed forces is an ideology. The other one is that simple fact of Man: that simple belief of individual man that he can and should and will be free. And if we who are still free want to continue so, all of us who are still free had better confederate and confederate fast with all others who still have a choice to be free—confederate not as black people nor white people nor blue or pink or green people, but as people who still are free, with all other people who are still free; confederate together and stick together too, if we want a world or even a part of a world in which individual man can be free, to continue to endure.

And we had better take in with us as many as we can get of the nonwhite peoples of the earth who are not completely free yet but who want and intend to be, before that other force which is opposed to individual freedom, befools and gets them. Time was when the nonwhite man was content to— anyway, did—accept his instinct for freedom as an unrealisable dream. But not anymore; the white man himself taught him different with that phase of his—the white man's—own culture which took the form of colonial expansion and exploitation based and morally condoned on the premise of inequality not because of individual incompetence but of mass race or color. As a result of which, in only ten years we have watched the nonwhite peoples expel, by bloody violence when necessary, the white man from all the portions of the Middle East and Asia which he once dominated, into which vacuum has already begun to move that other and inimical power which people who believe in freedom are at war with—that power which says to the nonwhite man: "We dont offer you freedom because there is no such thing as freedom; your white overlords whom you have just thrown out have already proved that to you. But we offer you equality, at least equality in slavedom; if you are to be slaves, at least you can be slaves to your own color and race and religion."

We, the western white man who does believe that there exists an individual freedom above and beyond this mere equality of slavedom, must teach the nonwhite peoples this while there is yet a little time left. We, America, who are the strongest national force opposing communism and monolithicism, must teach all other peoples, white and nonwhite, slave or (for a little while yet) still free. We, America, have the best opportunity to do this because we can begin here, at home; we will not need to send costly freedom task-forces into alien and inimical nonwhite places already convinced that there is no such thing as freedom and liberty and equality and peace for nonwhite people too, or we would practise it at home. Because our nonwhite minority is already on our side; we dont need to sell the Negro on America and freedom because he is already sold; even when ignorant from inferior or no education, even despite the record of his history of inequality, he still believes in our concepts of freedom and democracy.

That is what America has done for them in only three hundred years. Not done *to* them: done *for* them because to our shame we have made little effort so far to teach them to be Americans, let alone to use their capacities and capabilities to make us a stronger and more unified America;—the people who only three hundred years ago lived beside one of the largest bodies of inland water on earth and never thought of sail, who yearly had to move by whole villages and tribes from famine and pestilence and enemies without once thinking of wheel, yet in three hundred years have become skilled artisans and craftsmen capable of holding their own in a culture of technocracy; the people who only three hundred years ago were eating the carrion in the tropical jungles yet in only three hundred years have produced the Phi Beta Kappas and the Doctor Bunches and the Carvers and the Booker Washingtons and the poets and musicians; who have yet to produce a Fuchs or Rosenberg or Gold or Burgess or McLean or Hiss, and where for every Robeson there are a thousand white ones.

The Bunches and Washingtons and Carvers and the musicians and the poets who were not just good men and women but good teachers too, teaching him—the Negro—by precept and example what a lot of our white people have not learned yet: that to gain equality, one must deserve it, and to deserve equality, one must understand what it is: that there is no such thing as equality *per se,* but only equality *to:* equal right and opportunity to make the best one can of one's life within one's capacity and capability, without fear of injustice or oppression or violence. If we had given him this equality ninety or fifty or even ten years ago, there would have been no Supreme Court ruling about segregation in 1954.

But we didn't. We dared not; it is our southern white man's shame that in our present economy the Negro must not have economic equality; our double shame that we fear that giving him more social equality will jeopardise his present economic status; our triple shame that even then, to justify our stand, we must becloud the issue with the bugaboo of miscegenation; what a commentary that the one remaining place on earth where the white man can flee and have his uncorrupted blood protected and defended by law, is in Africa—Africa: the source and origin of the threat whose present presence in America will have driven the white man to flee it.

Soon now all of us—not just Southerners nor even just Americans, but all people who are still free and want to remain so—are going to have to make a choice, lest the next (and last) confrontation we face will be, not communists against anti-communists, but simply the remaining handful of white people against the massed myriads of all the people on earth who are not white. We will have to choose not between color nor race nor religion nor between East and West either, but simply between being slaves and being free. And we will have to choose completely and for good; the time is already past now when we can choose a little of each, a little of both. We can choose a state of slavedom, and if we are powerful enough to be among the top two or three or ten, we can have a certain amount of license—until someone more powerful rises and has us machine-gunned against a cellar wall. But we cannot choose freedom established on a hierarchy of degrees of freedom, on a caste system of equality like military rank. We must be free not because we claim freedom, but because we practise it; our freedom must be buttressed by a homogeny equally and unchallengeably free, no matter what color they are, so that all the other inimical forces everywhere— systems political or religious or racial or national—will not just respect us because we practise freedom, they will fear us because we do.

[*Harper's,* June 1956; the text printed here has been taken from Faulkner's revised typescript.]

## STUDY QUESTIONS

1. Compare Faulkner's concept of the white man's fear with Baldwin's concept of the white man's guilt.

2. What line of reasoning does Faulkner follow in developing his thesis?

3. What are Faulkner's views on the position the church has taken on the civil rights issues?

4. On the basis of what Faulkner says in this essay, do you believe he would agree with the *Ebony* essay? Explain.

5. What appears to be Faulkner's attitude toward his subject? Note specific details that express his attitude.

6. Faulkner begins his essay with a personal anecdote. What is his strategy in this? Is it effective?

*Flannery O'Connor*

# EVERYTHING THAT RISES MUST CONVERGE

Flannery O'Connor (1925–1960) was a promising writer whose tragic death cut short what undoubtedly was destined to be a brilliant career. She was born in Savannah, Georgia, and all of her stories and novels deal with her native South. The limited literary legacy she left behind demonstrates her rare perception and skill. She wrote about healing preachers, Civil War veterans, Bible salesmen, decadent families, conniving widows, and numerous other picturesque and grotesque types. Her first novel *Wise Blood* was published in 1952; *A Good Man Is Hard to Find* appeared in 1955, *The Violent Bear It Away* in 1960, and *Everything That Rises Must Converge* in 1956. In 1959, the year before her death, she was awarded a Ford Foundation fellowship in creative writing.

HER DOCTOR had told Julian's mother that she must lose twenty pounds on account of her blood pressure, so on Wednesday nights Julian had to take her downtown on the bus for a reducing class at the Y. The reducing class was designed for working girls over fifty, who weighed from 165 to 200 pounds. His mother was one of the slimmer ones, but she said ladies did not tell their age or weight. She would not ride the buses by herself at night since they had been integrated, and because the reducing class was one of her few pleasures, necessary for her health, and *free,* she said Julian could at least put himself out to take her, considering all she did for him. Julian did not like to consider all she did for him, but every Wednesday night he braced himself and took her.

She was almost ready to go, standing before the hall mirror, putting on her hat, while he, his hands behind him, appeared pinned to the door frame, waiting like Saint Sebastian for the arrows to begin piercing him. The hat was new and had cost her seven dollars and a half. She kept saying, "Maybe I shouldn't have paid that for it. No, I shouldn't have. I'll take it off and return it tomorrow. I shouldn't have bought it."

Julian raised his eyes to heaven. "Yes, you should have bought it," he said. "Put it on and let's go." It was a hideous hat. A purple velvet flap came down on one side of it and stood up on the other; the rest of it was green and looked like a cushion with the stuffing out. He decided it was less comical than jaunty and pathetic. Everything that gave her pleasure was small and depressed him.

She lifted the hat one more time and set it down slowly on top of her head. Two wings of gray hair protruded on either side of her florid face, but her eyes, sky-blue, were as innocent and untouched by experience as they must have been when she was ten. Were it not that she was a widow who had struggled fiercely to feed and clothe and put him through school and who was supporting him still, "until he got on his feet," she might have been a little girl that he had to take to town.

"It's all right, it's all right," he said. "Let's go." He opened the door himself and started down the walk to get her going. The sky was a dying violet and the houses stood out darkly against it, bulbous liver-colored monstrosities of a uniform ugliness though no two were alike. Since this had been a fashionable neighborhood forty years ago, his mother persisted in thinking they did well to have an apartment in it. Each house had a narrow collar of dirt around it in which sat, usually, a grubby child. Julian walked with his hands in his pockets, his head down and thrust forward and his eyes glazed with the determination to make himself completely numb during the time he would be sacrificed to her pleasure.

The door closed and he turned to find the dumpy figure, surmounted by the atrocious hat, coming toward him. "Well," she said, "you only live once and paying a little more for it, I at least won't meet myself coming and going."

"Some day I'll start making money," Julian said gloomily—he knew he never would—"and you can have one of those jokes whenever you take the fit." But first they would move. He visualized a place where the nearest neighbors would be three miles away on either side.

"I think you're doing fine," she said, drawing on her gloves. "You've only been out of school a year. Rome wasn't built in a day."

She was one of the few members of the Y reducing class who arrived in hat and gloves and who had a son who had been to college. "It takes time," she said, "and the world is in such a mess. This hat looked better on me than any of the others, though when she brought it out I said, 'Take that thing back. I wouldn't have it on my head,' and she said, 'Now wait till you see it on,' and when she put it on me, I said, 'We-ull,' and she said, 'If you ask me, that hat does something for you and you do something for the hat, and besides,' she said, 'with that hat, you won't meet yourself coming and going.'"

Julian thought he could have stood his lot better if she had been selfish, if she had been an old hag who drank and screamed at him. He walked along, saturated in depression, as if in the midst of his martyrdom he had lost his faith. Catching sight of his long, hopeless, irritated face, she stopped suddenly with a grief-stricken look, and pulled back on his arm. "Wait on me," she said. "I'm going back to the house and take this thing off and tomorrow I'm going to return it. I was out of my head. I can pay the gas bill with that seven-fifty."

He caught her arm in a vicious grip. "You are not going to take it back," he said. "I like it."

"Well," she said, "I don't think I ought . . ."

"Shut up and enjoy it," he muttered, more depressed than ever.

"With the world in the mess it's in," she said, "it's a wonder we can enjoy anything. I tell you, the bottom rail is on the top."

Julian sighed.

"Of course," she said, "if you know who you are, you can go anywhere." She said this every time he took her to the reducing class. "Most of them in it are not our kind of people," she said, "but I can be gracious to anybody. I know who I am."

"They don't give a damn for your graciousness," Julian said savagely. "Knowing who you are is good for one generation only. You haven't the foggiest idea where you stand now or who you are."

She stopped and allowed her eyes to flash at him. "I most certainly do know who I am," she said, "and if you don't know who you are, I'm ashamed of you."

"Oh hell," Julian said.

"Your great-grandfather was a former governor of this state," she said. "Your grandfather was a prosperous landowner. Your grandmother was a Godhigh."

"Will you look around you," he said tensely, "and see where you are now?" and he swept his arm jerkily out to indicate the neighborhood, which the growing darkness at least made less dingy.

"You remain what you are," she said. "Your great-grandfather had a plantation and two hundred slaves."

"There are no more slaves," he said irritably.

"They were better off when they were," she said. He groaned to see that she was off on that topic. She rolled onto it every few days like a train on an open track. He knew every stop, every junction, every swamp along the way, and knew the exact point at which her conclusion would roll majestically into the station: "It's ridiculous. It's simply not realistic. They should rise, yes, but on their own side of the fence."

"Let's skip it," Julian said.

"The ones I feel sorry for," she said, "are the ones that are half white. They're tragic."

"Will you skip it?"

"Suppose we were half white. We would certainly have mixed feelings."

"I have mixed feelings now," he groaned.

"Well let's talk about something pleasant," she said. "I remember going to Grandpa's when I was a little girl. Then the house had double stairways that went up to what was really the second floor—all the cooking was done on the first. I used to like to stay down in the kitchen on account of the way the walls smelled. I would sit with my nose pressed against the plaster and take deep breaths. Actually the place belonged to the Godhighs but your grandfather Chestny paid the mortgage and saved it for them. They were in reduced circumstances," she said, "but reduced or not, they never forgot who they were."

"Doubtless that decayed mansion reminded them," Julian muttered. He never spoke of it without contempt or thought of it without longing. He had seen it once when he was a child before it had been sold. The double stairways had rotted and been torn down. Negroes were living in it. But it remained in his mind as his mother had known it. It appeared in his dreams regularly. He would stand on the wide porch, listening to the rustle of oak leaves, then wander through the high-ceilinged hall into the parlor that opened onto it and gaze at the worn rugs and faded draperies. It occurred to him that it was he, not she, who could have appreciated it. He preferred its threadbare elegance to anything he could name and it was because of it that all the neighborhoods they had lived in had been a torment to him—whereas she had hardly known the difference. She called her insensitivity "being adjustable."

"And I remember the old darky who was my nurse, Caroline. There was no better person in the world. I've always had a great respect for my colored friends," she said. "I'd do anything in the world for them and they'd . . ."

"Will you for God's sake get off that subject?" Julian said. When he got on a bus by himself, he made it a point to sit down beside a Negro, in reparation as it were for his mother's sins.

"You're mighty touchy tonight," she said. "Do you feel all right?"

"Yes I feel all right," he said. "Now lay off."

She pursed her lips. "Well, you certainly are in a vile humor," she observed. "I just won't speak to you at all."

They had reached the bus stop. There was no bus in sight and Julian, his hands still jammed in his pockets and his head thrust forward, scowled down the empty street. The frustration of having to wait on the bus as well as ride on it began to creep up his neck like a hot hand. The presence of his mother was borne in upon him as she gave a pained sigh. He looked at her bleakly. She was holding herself very erect under the preposterous hat, wearing it like a banner of her imaginary dignity. There was in him an evil urge to break her spirit. He suddenly unloosened his tie and pulled it off and put it in his pocket.

She stiffened. "Why must you look like *that* when you take me to town?" she said. "Why must you deliberately embarrass me?"

"If you'll never learn where you are," he said, "you can at least learn where I am."

"You look like a—thug," she said.

"Then I must be one," he murmured.

"I'll just go home," she said. "I will not bother you. If you can't do a little thing like that for me . . ."

Rolling his eyes upward, he put his tie back on. "Restored to my class," he muttered. He thrust his face toward her and hissed, "True culture is in the mind, the *mind,*" he said, and tapped his head, "the mind."

"It's in the heart," she said, "and in how you do things and how you do things is because of who you *are.*"

"Nobody in the damn bus cares who you are."

"I care who I am," she said icily.

The lighted bus appeared on top of the next hill and as it approached, they moved out into the street to meet it. He put his hand under her elbow and hoisted her up on the creaking step. She entered with a little smile, as if she were going into a drawing room where everyone had been waiting for her. While he put in the tokens, she sat down on one of the broad front seats for three which faced the aisle. A thin woman with protruding teeth and long yellow hair was sitting on the end of it. His mother moved up beside her and left room for Julian beside herself. He sat down and looked at the floor across the aisle where a pair of thin feet in red and white canvas sandals were planted.

His mother immediately began a general conversation meant to attract anyone who felt like talking. "Can it get any hotter?" she said and removed from her purse a folding fan, black with a Japanese scene on it, which she began to flutter before her.

"I reckon it might could," the woman with the protruding teeth said, "but I know for a fact my apartment couldn't get no hotter."

"It must get the afternoon sun," his mother said. She sat forward and looked up and down the bus. It was half filled. Everybody was white. "I see we have the bus to ourselves," she said. Julian cringed.

"For a change," said the woman across the aisle, the owner of the red and white canvas sandals. "I come on one the other day and they were thick as fleas—up front and all through."

"The world is in a mess everywhere," his mother said. "I don't know how we've let it get in this fix."

"What gets my goat is all those boys from good families stealing automobile tires," the woman with the protruding teeth said. "I told my boy, I said you may not be rich but you been raised right and if I ever catch you in any such mess, they can send you on to the reformatory. Be exactly where you belong."

"Training tells," his mother said. "Is your boy in high school?"

"Ninth grade," the woman said.

"My son just finished college last year. He wants to write but he's selling typewriters until he gets started," his mother said.

The woman leaned forward and peered at Julian. He threw her such a malevolent look that she subsided against the seat. On the floor across the aisle there was an abandoned newspaper. He got up and got it and opened it out in front of him. His mother discreetly continued the conversation in a lower tone but the woman across the aisle said in a loud voice, "Well that's nice. Selling typewriters is close to writing. He can go right from one to the other."

"I tell him," his mother said, "that Rome wasn't built in a day."

Behind the newspaper Julian was withdrawing into the inner compartment of his mind where he spent most of his time. This was a kind of mental bubble in which he established himself when he could not bear to be a part of what was going on around him. From it he could see out and judge but in it he was safe from any kind of penetration from without. It was the only place where he felt free of the general idiocy of his fellows. His mother had never entered it but from it he could see her with absolute clarity.

The old lady was clever enough and he thought that if she had started from any of the right premises, more might have been expected of her. She lived according to the laws of her own fantasy world, outside of which he had never seen her set foot. The law of it was to sacrifice herself for him after she had first created the necessity to do so by making a mess of things. If he had permitted her sacrifices, it was only because her lack of foresight had made them necessary. All of her life had been a struggle to act like a

Chestny without the Chestny goods, and to give him everything she thought a Chestny ought to have; but since, said she, it was fun to struggle, why complain? And when you had won, as she had won, what fun to look back on the hard times! He could not forgive her that she had enjoyed the struggle and that she thought *she* had won.

What she meant when she said she had won was that she had brought him up successfully and had sent him to college and that he had turned out so well—good looking (her teeth had gone unfilled so that his could be straightened), intelligent (he realized he was too intelligent to be a success), and with a future ahead of him (there was of course no future ahead of him). She excused his gloominess on the grounds that he was still growing up and his radical ideas on his lack of practical experience. She said he didn't yet know a thing about "life," that he hadn't even entered the real world— when already he was as disenchanted with it as a man of fifty.

The further irony of all this was that in spite of her, he had turned out so well. In spite of going to only a third-rate college, he had, on his own initiative, come out with a first-rate education; in spite of growing up dominated by a small mind, he had ended up with a large one; in spite of all her foolish views, he was free of prejudice and unafraid to face facts. Most miraculous of all, instead of being blinded by love for her as she was for him, he had cut himself emotionally free of her and could see her with complete objectivity. He was not dominated by his mother.

The bus stopped with a sudden jerk and shook him from his meditation. A woman from the back lurched forward with little steps and barely escaped falling in his newspaper as she righted herself. She got off and a large Negro got on. Julian kept his paper lowered to watch. It gave him a certain satisfaction to see injustice in daily operation. It confirmed his view that with a few exceptions there was no one worth knowing within a radius of three hundred miles. The Negro was well dressed and carried a briefcase. He looked around and then sat down on the other end of the seat where the woman with the red and white canvas sandals was sitting. He immediately unfolded a newspaper and obscured himself behind it. Julian's mother's elbow at once prodded insistently into his ribs. "Now you see why I won't ride on these buses by myself," she whispered.

The woman with the red and white canvas sandals had risen at the same time the Negro sat down and had gone further back in the bus and taken the seat of the woman who had got off. His mother leaned forward and cast her an approving look.

Julian rose, crossed the aisle, and sat down in the place of the woman with the canvas sandals. From this position, he looked serenely across at his mother. Her face had turned an angry red. He stared at her, making his eyes the eyes of a stranger. He felt his tension suddenly lift as if he had openly declared war on her.

He would have liked to get in conversation with the Negro and to talk with him about art or politics or any subject that would be above the comprehension of those around them, but the man remained entrenched behind his paper. He was either ignoring the change of seating or had never noticed it. There was no way for Julian to convey his sympathy.

His mother kept her eyes fixed reproachfully on his face. The woman with the protruding teeth was looking at him avidly as if he were a type of monster new to her.

"Do you have a light?" he asked the Negro.

Without looking away from his paper, the man reached in his pocket and handed him a packet of matches.

"Thanks," Julian said. For a moment he held the matches foolishly. A NO SMOKING sign looked down upon him from over the door. This alone would not have deterred him; he had no cigarettes. He had quit smoking some months before because he could not afford it. "Sorry," he muttered and handed back the matches. The Negro lowered the paper and gave him an annoyed look. He took the matches and raised the paper again.

His mother continued to gaze at him but she did not take advantage of his momentary discomfort. Her eyes retained their battered look. Her face seemed to be unnaturally red, as if her blood pressure had risen. Julian allowed no glimmer of sympathy to show on his face. Having got the advantage, he wanted desperately to keep it and carry it through. He would have liked to teach her a lesson that would last her a while, but there seemed no way to continue the point. The Negro refused to come out from behind his paper.

Julian folded his arms and looked stolidly before him, facing her but as if he did not see her, as if he had ceased to recognize her existence. He visualized a scene in which, the bus having reached their stop, he would remain in his seat and when she said, "Aren't you going to get off?" he would look at her as at a stranger who had rashly addressed him. The corner they got off on was usually deserted, but it was well lighted and it would not hurt her to walk by herself the four blocks to the Y. He decided to wait until the time came and then decide whether or not he would let her get off by herself. He would have to be at the Y at ten to bring her back, but he could leave her wondering if he was going to show up. There was no reason for her to think she could always depend on him.

He retired again into the high-ceilinged room sparsely settled with large pieces of antique furniture. His soul expanded momentarily but then he became aware of his mother across from him and the vision shriveled. He studied her coldly. Her feet in little pumps dangled like a child's and did not quite reach the floor. She was training on him and exaggerated look of reproach. He felt completely detached from her. At that moment he could with pleasure have slapped her as he would have slapped a particularly obnoxious child in his charge.

He began to imagine various unlikely ways by which he could teach her a lesson. He might make friends with some distinguished Negro professor or lawyer and bring him home to spend the evening. He would be entirely justified but her blood pressure would rise to 300. He could not push her to the extent of making her have a stroke, and moreover, he had never been successful at making any Negro friends. He had tried to strike up an acquaintance on the bus with some of the better types, with ones that looked like professors or ministers or lawyers. One morning he had sat down next to a distinguished-looking dark brown man who had answered his questions with a sonorous solemnity but who had turned out to be an undertaker. Another day he had sat down beside a cigar-smoking Negro with a diamond ring on his finger, but after a few stilted pleasantries, the Negro had rung the buzzer and risen, slipping two lottery tickets into Julian's hand as he climbed over him to leave.

He imagined his mother lying desperately ill and his being able to secure only a Negro doctor for her. He toyed with that idea for a few minutes and then dropped it for a momentary vision of himself participating as a sympathizer in a sit-in demonstration. This was possible but he did not linger with it. Instead, he approached the ultimate horror. He brought home a beautiful suspiciously Negroid woman. Prepare yourself, he said. There is nothing you can do about it. This is the woman I've chosen. She's intelligent, dignified, even good, and she's suffered and she hasn't thought it *fun*. Now persecute us, go ahead and persecute us. Drive her out of here, but remember, you're driving me too. His eyes were narrowed and through the indignation he had generated, he saw his mother across the aisle, purple-faced, shrunken to the dwarf-like proportions of her moral nature, sitting like a mummy beneath the ridiculous banner of her hat.

He was tilted out of his fantasy again as the bus stopped. The door opened with a sucking hiss and out of the dark a large, gaily dressed, sullen-looking colored woman got on with a little boy. The child, who might have been four, had on a short plaid suit and a Tyrolean hat with a blue feather in it. Julian hoped that he would sit down beside him and that the woman would push in beside his mother. He could think of no better arrangement.

As she waited for her tokens, the woman was surveying the seating possibilities—he hoped with the idea of sitting where she was least wanted. There was something familiar-looking about her but Julian could not place what it was. She was a giant of a woman. Her face was set not only to meet opposition but to seek it out. The downward tilt of her large lower lip was like a warning sign: DON'T TAMPER WITH ME. Her bulging figure was encased in a green crepe dress and her feet overflowed in red shoes. She had on a hideous hat. A purple velvet flap came down on one side of it and stood up on the other; the rest of it was green and looked like a cushion with the stuffing out. She carried a mammoth red pocketbook that bulged throughout as if it were stuffed with rocks.

To Julian's disappointment, the little boy climbed up on the empty seat beside his mother. His mother lumped all children, black and white, into the common category, "cute," and she thought little Negroes were on the whole cuter than little white children. She smiled at the little boy as he climbed on the seat.

Meanwhile the woman was bearing down upon the empty seat beside Julian. To his annoyance, she squeezed herself into it. He saw his mother's face change as the woman settled herself next to him and he realized with satisfaction that this was more objectionable to her than it was to him. Her face seemed almost gray and there was a look of dull recognition in her eyes, as if suddenly she had sickened at some awful confrontation. Julian saw that it was because she and the woman had, in a sense, swapped sons. Though his mother would not realize the symbolic significance of this, she would feel it. His amusement showed plainly on his face.

The woman next to him muttered something unintelligible to herself. He was conscious of a kind of bristling next to him, a muted growling like that of an angry cat. He could not see anything but the red pocketbook upright on the bulging green thighs. He visualized the woman as she had stood waiting for her tokens—the ponderous figure, rising from the red shoes upward over the solid hips, the mammoth bosom, the haughty face, to the green and purple hat.

His eyes widened.

The vision of the two hats, identical, broke upon him with the radiance of a brilliant sunrise. His face was suddenly lit with joy. He could not believe that Fate had thrust upon his mother such a lesson. He gave a loud chuckle so that she would look at him and see that he saw. She turned her eyes on him slowly. The blue in them seemed to have turned a bruised purple. For a moment he had an uncomfortable sense of her innocence, but it lasted only a second before principle rescued him. Justice entitled him to laugh. His grin hardened until it said to her as plainly as if he were saying aloud: Your punishment exactly fits your pettiness. This should teach you a permanent lesson.

Her eyes shifted to the woman. She seemed unable to bear looking at him and to find the woman preferable. He became conscious again of the bristling presence at his side. The woman was rumbling like a volcano about to become active. His mother's mouth began to twitch slightly at one corner. With a sinking heart, he saw incipient signs of recovery on her face and realized that this was going to strike her suddenly as funny and was going to be no lesson at all. She kept her eyes on the woman and an amused smile came over her face as if the woman were a monkey that had stolen her hat. The little Negro was looking up at her with large fascinated eyes. He had been trying to attract her attention for some time.

"Carver!" the woman said suddenly. "Come heah!"

When he saw that the spotlight was on him at last, Carver drew his feet up and turned himself toward Julian's mother and giggled.

"Carver!" the woman said. "You heah me? Come heah!"

Carver slid down from the seat but remained squatting with his back against the base of it, his head turned slyly around toward Julian's mother, who was smiling at him. The woman reached a hand across the aisle and snatched him to her. He righted himself and hung backwards on her knees, grinning at Julian's mother. "Isn't he cute?" Julian's mother said to the woman with the protruding teeth.

"I reckon he is," the woman said without conviction.

The Negress yanked him upright but he eased out of her grip and shot across the aisle and scrambled, giggling wildly, onto the seat beside his love.

"I think he likes me," Julian's mother said, and smiled at the woman. It was the smile she used when she was being particularly gracious to an inferior. Julian saw everything lost. The lesson had rolled off her like rain on a roof.

The woman stood up and yanked the little boy off the seat as if she were snatching him from contagion. Julian could feel the rage in her at having no weapon like his mother's smile. She gave the child a sharp slap across his leg. He howled once and then thrust his head into her stomach and kicked his feet against her shins. "Be-have," she said vehemently.

The bus stopped and the Negro who had been reading the newspaper got off. The woman moved over and set the little boy down with a thump between herself and Julian. She held him firmly by the knee. In a moment he put his hands in front of his face and peeped at Julian's mother through his fingers.

"I see yooooooooo!" she said and put her hand in front of her face and peeped at him.

The woman slapped his hand down. "Quit yo' foolishness," she said, "before I knock the living Jesus out of you!"

Julian was thankful that the next stop was theirs. He reached up and pulled the cord. The woman reached up and pulled it at the same time. Oh my God, he thought. He had the terrible intuition that when they got off the bus together, his mother would open her purse and give the little boy a nickel. The gesture would be as natural to her as breathing. The bus stopped and the woman got up and lunged to the front, dragging the child, who wished to stay on, after her. Julian and his mother got up and followed. As they neared the door, Julian tried to relieve her of her pocketbook.

"No," she murmured, "I want to give the little boy a nickel."

"No!" Julian hissed. "No!"

She smiled down at the child and opened her bag. The bus door opened and the woman picked him up by the arm and descended with him, hanging at her hip. Once in the street she set him down and shook him.

Julian's mother had to close her purse while she got down the bus step but as soon as her feet were on the ground, she opened it again and began to rummage inside. "I can't find but a penny," she whispered, "but it looks like a new one."

"Don't do it!" Julian said fiercely between his teeth. There was a street-light on the corner and she hurried to get under it so that she could better see into her pocketbook. The woman was heading off rapidly down the street with the child still hanging backward on her hand.

"Oh little boy!" Julian's mother called and took a few quick steps and caught up with them just beyond the lamppost. "Here's a bright new penny for you," and she held out the coin, which shone bronze in the dim light.

The huge woman turned and for a moment stood, her shoulders lifted and her face frozen with frustrated rage, and stared at Julian's mother. Then all at once she seemed to explode like a piece of machinery that had been given one ounce of pressure too much. Julian saw the black fist swing out with the red pocketbook. He shut his eyes and cringed as he heard the woman shout, "He don't take nobody's pennies!" When he opened his eyes, the woman was disappearing down the street with the little boy staring wide-eyed over her shoulder. Julian's mother was sitting on the sidewalk.

"I told you not to do that," Julian said angrily. "I told you not to do that!"

He stood over her for a minute, gritting his teeth. Her legs were stretched out in front of her and her hat was on her lap. He squatted down and looked her in the face. It was totally expressionless. "You got exactly what you deserved," he said. "Now get up."

He picked up her pocketbook and put what had fallen out back in it. He picked the hat up off her lap. The penny caught his eye on the sidewalk and he picked that up and let it drop before her eyes into the purse. Then he stood up and leaned over and held his hands out to pull her up. She remained immobile. He sighed. Rising above them on either side were black apartment buildings, marked with irregular rectangles of light. At the end of the block a man came out of a door and walked off in the opposite direction. "All right," he said, "suppose somebody happens by and wants to know why you're sitting on the sidewalk?"

She took the hand and, breathing hard, pulled heavily up on it and then stood for a moment, swaying slightly as if the spots of light in the darkness were circling around her. Her eyes, shadowed and confused, finally settled on his face. He did not try to conceal his irritation. "I hope this teaches you a lesson," he said. She leaned forward and her eyes raked his face. She seemed trying to determine his identity. Then, as if she found nothing familiar about him, she started off with a headlong movement in the wrong direction.

"Aren't you going on to the Y?" he asked.

"Home," she muttered.

"Well, are we walking?"

For answer she kept going. Julian followed along, his hands behind him. He saw no reason to let the lesson she had had go without backing it up with an explanation of its meaning. She might as well be made to understand what had happened to her. "Don't think that was just an uppity Negro woman," he said. "That was the whole colored race which will no longer take your condescending pennies. That was your black double. She can wear the same hat as you, and to be sure," he added gratuitously (because he thought it was funny), "it looked better on her than it did on you. What all this means," he said, "is that the old world is gone. The old manners are obsolete and your graciousness is not worth a damn." He thought bitterly of the house that had been lost for him. "You aren't who you think you are," he said.

She continued to plow ahead, paying no attention to him. Her hair had come undone on one side. She dropped her pocketbook and took no notice. He stooped and picked it up and handed it to her but she did not take it.

"You needn't act as if the world had come to an end," he said, "because it hasn't. From now on you've got to live in a new world and face a few realities for a change. Buck up," he said, "it won't kill you."

She was breathing fast.

"Let's wait on the bus," he said.

"Home," she said thickly.

"I hate to see you behave like this," he said. "Just like a child. I should be able to expect more of you." He decided to stop where he was and make her stop and wait for a bus. "I'm not going any farther," he said, stopping. "We're going on the bus."

She continued to go on as if she had not heard him. He took a few steps and caught her arm and stopped her. He looked into her face and caught his breath. He was looking into a face he had never seen before. "Tell Grandpa to come get me," she said.

He stared, stricken.

"Tell Caroline to come get me," she said.

Stunned, he let her go and she lurched forward again, walking as if one leg were shorter than the other. A tide of darkness seemed to be sweeping her from him. "Mother!" he cried. "Darling, sweetheart, wait!" Crumpling, she fell to the pavement. He dashed forward and fell at her side, crying, "Mamma, Mamma!" He turned her over. Her face was fiercely distorted. One eye, large and staring, moved slightly to the left as if it had become unmoored. The other remained fixed on him, raked his face again, found nothing and closed.

"Wait here, wait here!" he cried and jumped up and began to run for help toward a cluster of lights he saw in the distance ahead of him. "Help, help!" he shouted, but his voice was thin, scarcely a thread of sound. The lights drifted farther away the faster he ran and his feet moved numbly as if they carried him nowhere. The tide of darkness seemed to sweep him back to her, postponing from moment to moment his entry into the world of guilt and sorrow.

### STUDY QUESTIONS

1. It has been noted that Flannery O'Connor's stories show how people live practically sealed off against one another. Does that observation apply to this story? If so, in what way?

2. What is the basic conflict between Julian and his mother? Does he have any inner conflicts?

3. We are told in the story that Julian receives "a certain satisfaction to see injustices in daily operation." What does this tell us about him?

4. Compare and contrast Julian's and his mother's feelings and behavior toward Negroes.

5. What is significant about Julian's claim that culture is a matter of the mind?

6. What is the basis for the idea that Julian has no future ahead of him?

*William Styron*

# IT IS DONE
## (Part IV, *The Confessions of Nat Turner*)

William Styron (1925–      ), well-known author, is a native of the Tidewater region of Virginia, the area where Nat Turner's revolt took place. Styron earned his college degree at Duke University. He has been honored by the American Academy of Arts and Letters and by the National Institute of Arts and Literature. Before writing *The Confessions of Nat Turner* (1967), he had published three novels: *Lie Down in Darkness* (1951), *The*

*Long March* (1953), and *Set This House On Fire* (1960). In addition he has
published numerous short stories and articles.

### Surely I come quickly . . .

Cloudless sunlight suggesting neither hour nor season
glows down upon me, wraps me with a cradle's warmth
as I drift toward the river's estuary; the little boat rocks gently in our benign
descent together toward the sea. On the unpeopled banks the woods are silent, silent as snowfall. No birds call; in windless attitudes of meditation the
crowd of green trees along the river shore stands drooping and still. This low
country seems untouched by humanity, by past or future time. Beneath me
where I recline I feel the boat's sluggish windward drift, glimpse rushing
past eddies of foam, branches, leaves, clumps of grass all borne on the serene unhurried flood to the place where the river meets the sea. Faintly now
I hear the oceanic roar, mark the sweep of sunlit water far-near, glinting
with whitecaps, the ragged shoulder of a beach where sea and river join in a
tumultuous embrace of swirling waters. But nothing disturbs me, I drowse
in the arms of a steadfast and illimitable peace. Salt stings my nostrils. The
breakers roll to shore, the lordly tide swells back beneath a cobalt sky arch-
ing eastward toward Africa. An unhurried booming fills me not with fear
but only with repose and slumbrous anticipation—serenity as ageless as
those rocks, in garlands of weeping seaweed, thrown up by the groaning
waves.

Now as I approach the edge of land I look up for one last time to study the
white building standing on its promontory high above the shore. Again I
cannot tell what it is or what it means. Stark white, glittering, pure as ala-
baster, it rests on the precipice unravaged by weather or wind, neither temple nor monument nor sarcophagus but relic of the ages—of all past and all
futurity—white inscrutable paradigm of a mystery beyond utterance or
even wonder. The sun bathes its tranquil marble sides, its doorless façade,
the arches that sweep around it, revealing no entry anywhere, no window;
inside, it would be as dark as the darkest tomb. Yet I cannot dwell on that
place too long, for again as always I know that to try to explore the mystery
would be only to throw open portals on even deeper mysteries, on and on
everlastingly, into the remotest corridors of thought and time. So I turn
away. I cast my eyes toward the ocean once more, watch the blue waves and
glitter of spume-borne light approaching, listen to the breaking surf move
near as I pass, slowly, in contemplation of a great mystery, out toward the
sea . . .

I come awake with a start, feeling the cedar plank cold beneath my back,
the leg irons colder still—like encircling bands of ice. It is full dark, I can

see nothing. I rise up on my elbows, letting the dream dwindle away from my mind, fade out—this one last time, and forever—from recollection. The chains at my feet chink in the morning's black silence. It is bitterly cold but the wind has died and I no longer shiver so; I draw the remnant of my ragged shirt close around my chest. Then I tap with my knuckles against the wall separating me from Hark. He sleeps deeply, his breath a jagged sigh as it rattles through his wound. *Tap-tap*. Silence. *Tap-tap* again, louder. Hark awakes. "Dat you, Nat?"

"It's me," I reply, "we go soon."

He is quiet for a moment. Then he says, yawning: "I knows it. Lawd, I wish dey would git on wid it. What time it is you reckon, Nat?"

"I don't know," I say, "they must be a couple hours more."

I hear the heavy thump of his feet and the sound of his chain-links clinking together, then the noise of a bucket scraping across the floor. Hark chuckles faintly. "Lawd me, Nat," he says. "Wisht I could move about. Hit hard enough to pee lyin' down in de daytime, at night I cain't hit dat bucket in no way." I hear a noisy spatter and splash and Hark's laughter again, low in his throat, rich, amused at himself. "Ain't nothin' mo' useless dan a twofifty-pound nigger dat cain't hardly move. Did you know, Nat, dey gwine hang me all roped up in a *chair?* Leastwise, dat's what dat man Gray done said. Dat sho' is *some* way to go."

I make no reply, the sound of flowing water ceases, and Hark's voice too falls still. Somewhere far off in the town a dog howls on and on without lull or respite, a continuous harsh lonely cry from the bowels of the dark morning, touching me with dread. *Lord,* I whisper to myself in anguish, *Lord?* And I clench my eyelids together in a sudden spasm, hoping to find some vision, some word or sign in the profounder darkness of my own mind, but there is still no answer. I will go without Him, I think, I will go without Him because He has abandoned me without any last sign at all. Was what I done wrong in His sight? And if what I done was wrong is there no redemption?

"Dat God durned dog," I hear Hark say. "Lissen at him, Nat. Dat sho de sign of somepn, awright. Lawd, dat dog done barked right on th'ough my dreams jes' now. Dreamed I was back home at Barnett's long long time ago when I was jes' a little ole thing 'bout knee-high to a duck. An' me an' my sister Jamie was gwine fishin' together down in de swamp. And we was walkin' along underneath dem wild cherry trees, jes' as happy as we could be, talkin' about all dem fish we was gwine catch. On'y dey dis yere dog a-barkin' at us an followin' us th'ough the woods. An' Jamie she done kep' sayin', 'Hark, how come dat dog make all dat holler?' An' I say back to Jamie, 'Don' bothah 'bout no dog, don' pay dat ole dog no nem'mine.' Den you done knock on de wall, Nat, and now here dat *same* dog a-barkin' way off in de road, and here *I* is, an' dis mornin' dey gwine hang me."

*Then behold I come quickly* . . .

I drowse off dreamless for a time, then I wake abruptly to see that morning approaches with the faintest tinge of pale frosty light, stealing through the barred window and touching the cedar walls with a glow barely visible, like ashes strewn upon a dying fire. Way off in the lowlands across the river, somewhere among the fields and frosty meadows, I hear the sad old blast of a horn as it rouses up the Negroes for work. Nearer there is a tinkle and a rustle, barely heard; the town stirs. A single horse passes *cloppetyclop* over the wooden bridge, and far away in the distance a cock crows, then another, and they cease suddenly; for a moment all is still and sleeping. Hark again slumbers, the air whistles from his wounded chest. I rise and make my way to the end of the chain, shuffling in a sideways motion toward the window. Then I lean forward against the freezing sill, and stand motionless in the still-encompassing dark. Against the rim of the heavens, high above the river and the towering wall of cypress and pine, dawn begins to rise in light of the softest blue. I raise my eyes upward. There alone amidst the blue, steadfast, unmoving, fiery marvel of brightness, shines the morning star. Never has that star seemed so radiant, and I stand gazing at it and do not move though the chill of the damp floor imprisons my feet in piercing ice-bound pain.

*Surely I come quickly* . . .

I wait for minutes at the window, looking out at the new day which is still dark. Behind me I hear a noise in the tiny corridor, hear Kitchen's keys jangling, and see against the walls a lantern's ruddy orange glow. Footsteps scrape on the floor with a gritty sound. I turn about slowly and find that it is Gray. But this time he does not enter the cell, merely stands outside the door as he peers in, then beckons me with his finger. With clumsy trouble I move across the floor, chain dragging between my feet. In the lantern light I see that he is clasping something in his hand; when I draw closer to the door I can tell that it is a Bible. For once Gray seems quiet, subdued.

"I brung you what you asked for, Reverend," he says in a soft voice. So composed does he seem, so tranquil, so gentle are his tones, that I almost take him for another man. "I done it against the will of the court. It's my doing, my risk. But you've been pretty fair and square with me, all in all. You can have this solace if you want it."

He hands the Bible to me through the bars of the door. For a long moment we gaze at each other in the flickering light and I have a strange sensation which passes almost as quickly as it comes, that never have I seen this man in my life. I say nothing to him in answer. At last he reaches through the bars and grasps my hand; as he does so I know by some strange and tentative feeling in his hasty grip that this is the first black hand he has ever shaken, no doubt the last.

"Good-bye, Reverend," he says.

"Good-bye, Mr. Gray," I reply.

Then he is gone, the lantern flame fades and dies out, and the cell again is filled with darkness. I turn and place the Bible down gently on the cedar plank. I know that I would not open it now even if I had the light to read it by. Yet its presence warms the cell and for the first time since I have been in jail, for the first time since I gazed into his irksome face, I feel a wrench of pity for Gray and for his mortal years to come. Again I move to the window, inhaling deeply the wintry morning air. It tastes of smoke, of burning apple wood, and I am flooded with swift shifting memories, too sweet to bear, of all distant childhood, of old time past. I lean against the sill of the window, and gaze up at the morning star. *Surely I come quickly* . . .

*Then behold I come quickly* . . .

And as I think of her, the desire swells within me and I am stirred by a longing so great that like those memories of time past and long-ago voices, flowing waters, rushing winds, it seems more than my heart can abide. *Beloved, let us love one another: for love is of God; and everyone that loveth is born of God, and knoweth God.* Her voice is close, familiar, real, and for an instant I mistake the wind against my ear, a gentle gust, for her breath, and I turn to seek her in the darkness. And now beyond my fear, beyond my dread and emptiness, I feel the warmth flow into my loins and my legs tingle with desire. I tremble and I search for her face in my mind, seek her young body, yearning for her suddenly with a rage that racks me with a craving beyond pain; with tender stroking motions I pour out my love within her; pulsing flood; she arches against me, cries out, and the twain—black and white— are one. I faint slowly. My head falls toward the window, my breath comes hard. I recall a meadow, June, the voice a whisper: *Is it not true, Nat? Did He not say, I am the root and the offspring of David, and the bright and morning star?*

*Surely I come quickly* . . .

Footsteps outside the door jar me from my reverie, I hear white men's voices. Again a lantern casts a bloom of light through the cell, but the half-dozen men go past with thumping boots and stop at Hark's door. I hear jingling keys and a bolt slides back with a thud. I turn and see the outline of two men pushing the chair past my door. Its legs bump and clatter on the plank floor, there is a heavy jolt as its arms strike against the doorjamb of Hark's cell. "Raise up," I hear one of the men say to Hark. "Raise yore ass up, we got to rope you in." There is silence, then a creaking sound. I hear Hark begin to moan in pain. "Easy dar!" he cries out, gasping. *Easy!*

"Move his legs," I hear one of the white men order another.

"Grab him by the arms," says someone else.

Hark's voice becomes a wail of hurt and wild distress. The sound of bumping and shoving fills the air.

*"Easy!"* Hark cries out, sobbing.

"Push him down!" says a voice.

I find myself hammering at the walls. *"Don't hurt him!"* I rage. "Don't hurt him, you white sons of bitches! You've done hurt him enough! All his life! Now God damn you don't hurt him no more!"

Silence descends as the men cease talking. In a long drawn-out breath Hark's wail dies away. Now I hear a hurried sound of snapping ropes as they tie him into the chair. Then the white men whisper and grunt while they strain beneath the weight of their burden and lift Hark out into the hallway. Shadows leap up and quiver in the lantern's brassy radiance. The white men shuffle in furious labor, gasping with the effort. Hark's bound and seated shape, like the silhouette of some marvelous black potentate borne in stately procession toward his throne, passes slowly by my door. I reach out as if to touch him, feel nothing, clutch only a handful of air.

"Dis yere some way to go," I hear Hark say. "Good-bye, ole Nat!" he calls.

"Good-bye, Hark," I whisper, "good-bye, good-bye."

"Hit gwine be all right, Nat," he cries out to me, the voice fading. "Ev'y-thin' gwine be all right! Dis yere ain't nothin', Nat, nothin' atall! Good-bye, ole Nat, good-bye!"

*Good-bye, Hark, good-bye.*

The edge of dawn pales, brightens; stars wink away like dying sparks as the night fades and dusty sunrise begins to streak the far sky. Yet steadfast the morning star rides in the heavens radiant and pure, set like crystal amid the still waters of eternity. Morning blooms softly upon the rutted streets of Jerusalem; the howling dog and the crowing roosters at last are silent. Somewhere behind me in the jail I hear a murmuration of voices; I sense a presence at my back, I feel the approach of gigantic, unrelenting footfalls. I turn and retrieve the Bible from the cedar plank and for one last time take my station by the window, breathing deeply in the apple-sweet air. My breath is smoke, I shudder in the cold newborn beauty of the world. The footsteps draw near, suddenly cease. There is a rattle of bolts and keys. A voice says: "Nat!" And when I do not answer, the same voice calls out: "Come!"

*We'll love one another,* she seems to be entreating me, very close now, *we'll love one another by the light of heaven above.* I feel the nearness of flowing waters, tumultuous waves, rushing winds. The voice calls again: "Come!"

*Yes,* I think just before I turn to greet him, *I would have done it all again. I would have destroyed them all. Yet I would have spared one. I would have spared her that showed me Him whose presence I had not fathomed or maybe never even known. Great God, how early it is! Until now I had almost forgotten His name.*

"Come!" the voice booms, but commanding me now: *Come, My son!* I turn in surrender.

Surely I come quickly. Amen.

Even so, come, Lord Jesus.

Oh how bright and fair the morning star . . .

The bodies of those executed, with one exception, were buried in a decent and becoming manner. That of Nat Turner was delivered to the doctors, who skinned it and made grease of the flesh. Mr. R. S. Barham's father owned a money purse made of his hide. His skeleton was for many years in the possession of Dr. Massenberg, but has since been misplaced.

—Drewry, *The Southampton Insurrection*

\*      \*      \*

*And he said unto me, It is done.*
*I am Alpha and Omega, the beginning and*
*the end. I will give unto him that is*
*athirst of the fountain of the water*
*of life freely. He that overcometh shall inherit*
*all things; and I will be his God and*
*he shall be my son.*

## STUDY QUESTIONS

1.  What poetic qualities do you find in the language of Nat's dreams and reveries?

2.  What can we surmise about Nat's character and personality from this selection? Note what he thinks, dreams, says, and does; note also the tone he employs in relating these.

3.  What is the rhetorical effect of the repetitive "Then behold I come quickly" and "Surely I come quickly"?

4.  What is the significance of the howling dog Nat hears in the distance?

5.  Does this selection present a creditable portrayal of a condemned man in his final hours of life?

C. Vann Woodward

# CONFESSIONS OF A REBEL: 1831

C. Vann Woodward (1908–      ) is an eminent historian who has received numerous honors and awards for his work in Southern history. He earned his undergraduate degree at Emory University, his M.A. at Columbia University and Oxford University, and his Ph.D. at the University of North Carolina. He has taught history at the University of Florida, the University of Virginia, Scripps College, Johns Hopkins University, Harvard University, the University of Chicago, Louisiana State University and the University of London. He was the Harnsworth Professor of American History at Oxford University and the Stirling Professor at Yale University. He has been accorded honors by the National Institute of Arts and Letters, the Social Science Research Council, and the American Council of Learned Societies. Among his books are the following: *Tom Watkins: Agrarian Rebel* (1938), *The Battle For Leyte Gulf* (1947), *Origins of the New South* (1951), *Reunion and Reaction* (1951), *The Burden of Southern History* (1960), and *The Comparative Approach to American History* (1960).

IN THE ANNALS of American slavery two figures stand out with unrivaled prominence among the very few who resorted to armed rebellion—John Brown and Nat Turner, one white and one black. The historical importance of their roles is roughly comparable and there is as much reason for enduring curiosity about the one as about the other. Of the two, Turner's rebellion was far more bloody, both in the lives it took and in the reprisals it evoked. As a threat to the security of a slave based society, Turner's conspiracy was more momentous than Brown's. John Brown's Raid never had the remotest chance of success.

Yet there is a remarkable disparity in the amount that is known and in what has been written about the two men and their deeds. On John Brown there exists a vast library, forty-odd biographies, massive monographs, scores of poems, plays, and works of fiction. This is partly explained by the

Reprinted by Permission of *The New Republic,* © 1967, Harrison-Blaine of New Jersey, Inc.

relative abundance of source materials. Brown left extensive (though misleading) accounts of himself and a large mass of correspondence. He was
acquainted with some of the most prominent writers of his day. A few intellectuals were personally involved and many were passionately interested in
his conspiracy and left their own records. Two congressional hearings and a
mountain of archival material multiply the sources.

In striking contrast, the sources on Nat Turner and the scholarly as well
as creative writing about him are minuscule. Since there were no white participants in the rebellion and the life of no white witness of the massacres
was spared by the rebels, the information about the conspiracy boils down
largely to twenty-odd pages of Turner's "Confessions" in the stilted prose of
the Virginia lawyer to whom he dictated them in prison. Mainly on this and
on a pedestrian monograph or two rests all we know of the only slave rebellion of consequence in the largest slave society in the 19th-century world.

If there were ever a free hand for a novelist, this was it. Yet the obstacles
were formidable. There were no models. The only major American novelist
to treat a slave rebellion was Melville, and *Benito Cereno* is viewed entirely
through the eyes of the white man. Nat's story would have to be seen from
behind the black mask. That was the boldest decision William Styron made.
There was little to go on beyond the author's imagination. What history tells
us about slavery is mainly the white man's experience, not the black man's
—what it was like to *have* slaves, not what it was like to *be* slaves. No one
has more than an ill-informed guess about why the greatest slave republic
in the New World had by far the fewest rebellions; why smaller and allegedly more benevolent slave societies bred vast insurrections, blood baths involving many thousands of slaves that lasted scores of years, and America
had one that recruited seventy-five and petered out in three days; why servility and submission were the rule and Sambo the stereotype and heritage
of American slavery. And most of all, what explains the terrible enigma of
Nat Turner, the other-worldly young carpenter of obscure origins and apocalyptic visions who at the age of thirty-one took the road to Jerusalem, Va.,
martyrdom, and immortality.

To complicate the enigma, the rebellion took place not in the brutal Delta
cotton fields or the Louisiana sugar cane, but in mellowed, impoverished
tidewater Virginia, where even Nat Turner thought there was "still an ebb
and flow of human sympathy—no matter how strained and imperfect—
between slave and master." And Nat himself was a product of benevolent, if
unusual, paternalism at its best—fondly educated, trained in a craft, and
promised liberation. The picture of Nat's life and motivation the novelist
constructs is, but for a few scraps of evidence, without historical underpin-
nings, but most historians would agree, I think, not inconsistent with anything historians know. It is informed by a respect for history, a sure feeling
for the period, and a deep and precise sense of place and time.

Nat was the child of a house servant and grew up in the big house, familiar with "the chink of silver and china" as well as his "black Negro world" of the kitchen, but not with the toil of field and mill. His mistress taught him to read and gave him a Bible, of which he learned great parts by heart and knew better than the white preachers of the parish. He discovered his intelligence and his ability to charm, grew accustomed to love from all sides, and never encountered harshness or brutality. "I became in short a pet, the darling, the little black jewel of Turner's Mill. Pampered, fondled, nudged, pinched, I was the household's spoiled child." Toward his master, Samuel Turner, he felt a regard "very close to the feeling one should bear only toward the Divinity." Between them were "strong ties of emotion," in fact, "a kind of love." The master responded by giving encouragement, careful training, flattering responsibilities, and three years before Nat came of age, the intoxicating promise of freedom. Toward the field hands beyond the big house perimeter little Nat felt a contemptuous disdain, regarding them as "a lower order of people—a ragtag mob, coarse, raucous, clownish, uncouth." He identified completely with his master and looking back later realized that had this life continued he would have achieved in old age "a kind of purse-lipped dignity, known as Uncle Nat, well loved and adoring in return, a palsied stroker of the silken pates of little white grandchildren." But that life came to an end when Samuel Turner went bankrupt and moved to Alabama when Nat was twenty. Before leaving Virginia he placed Nat in the care of a poverty-ravaged, fanatical Baptist preacher under legal obligation to free his charge in a stated time. Instead, after giving Nat a year's taste of how degrading slavery could be, the preacher sold him for $460 to an illiterate brute named Moore, from whom he eventually passed into the hands of his last owner, Travis. Among the many harsh lessons these experiences taught Nat was "how greatly various were the moral attributes of white men who possessed slaves, how different each owner might be by way of severity or benevolence." They ranged "from the saintly," such as his first owner, "to a few who were unconditionally monstrous." Nat never fell into the hands of the last type, and his owner at the time of the rebellion generally behaved "like every slave's ideal master." Whatever accounts for Nat's rebellion, it was not the irrepressible rage of the intolerably oppressed. Instead, he observed, "the more tolerable and human white people became in their dealings with me, the keener was my passion to destroy them."

Nat was twenty and on the threshold of freedom before he suddenly realized what slavery was, "the *true* world in which a Negro moves and breathes. It was like being plunged into freezing water." A year later came his betrayal, the final shattering of the dream of freedom, and his submission to a master he knew to be his moral inferior, stupid, brutal, swinish. For

nearly ten years his disciplined defense was to become "a paragon of rectitude, of alacrity, of lively industriousness, of sweet equanimity and uncom-
plaining obedience," the ideal slave. He had learned never to look a white
man in the eye, how to smell danger, how like a dog "to interpret the *tone* of
what is being said," how to assume "that posture of respect and deference it
is wise for any Negro to assume" in the presence of a strange white man, and
how to "merge faceless and nameless with the common swarm." He learned
how, when necessary, to shuffle and scrape and adopt the egregious, gluey
cornfield accents and postures of niggerness.

He became a discriminating connoisseur of Sambo types, those given to
"wallowing in the dust at the slightest provocation, midriffs clutched in idiot
laughter," those who "endear themselves to all, white and black, through
droll interminable tales about ha'nts and witches and conjures," and at the
other extreme those who "reverse this procedure entirely and in *their* niggerness are able to outdo many white people in presenting to the world a
grotesque swagger," a posture suited to the black driver or the tyrannical
kitchen mammy and butler, who were skilled in keeping "safely this side of
insolence." For his own part, Nat "decided upon humility, a soft voice, and
houndlike obedience." Yet he was always conscious of "the weird unnatu-
ralness of this adopted role," always counseling himself "to patience, patience, *patience* to the end," biding his time.

As he watched the potential recruits for his divine mission of vengeance
and liberation he often despaired. His black brothers, "half drowned from
birth in a kind of murky mindlessness," drifted before him "mouths agape
or with sloppy uncomprehending smiles, shuffling their feet." They would
suddenly seem to him "as meaningless and as stupid as a barnful of mules,"
and he would "hate them one and all." But this hatred would alternate with
"a kind of wild, desperate love for them." The ambivalence came out in his
feelings about Hark (originally named Hercules) whom he intended to make
one of his lieutenants. Hark had "the face of an African chieftain," a godlike
frame and strength, and a mortal grievance against his master for selling his
wife and child. "Yet the very sight of white skin cowed him, humbled him to
the most servile abasement." He drove Nat to incoherent rage when in the
presence of any white he unconsciously became "the unspeakable bootlick-
ing Sambo, all giggles and smirks and oily, sniveling servility." Hark's defense was that he was overcome by "dat black-assed feelin'," and Nat admitted to himself that the expression perfectly expressed "the numbness and
dread which dwells in every Negro's heart."

Nat labored desperately to quell this fear in his recruits and to instill
pride and confidence and blind faith in their leader. He clung to his faith
that in every Sambo was a Nat Turner, that while "most Negroes are hopelessly docile, many of them are filled with fury," and that servility was "but a

form of self-preservation." In the more desperate of them he counted upon the common postulate that "nigger life ain't worth pig shit"—they had nothing to lose.

It is one mark of William Styron's genius that he deliberately threw away the Christ symbol, which would have been irresistible to many novelists. For Nat was strictly Old Testament, the stuff of Ezekiel, Daniel, Isaiah, and Jeremiah, the blood-stained righteousness of his somber Hebrew heroes, Joshua and David. He thought and spoke in the rhetoric of the Prophets and the Psalms and scriptural poetry weaves in and out of his ruminations. He fasted and prayed in the wilderness and waited for a sign. And the sign came: "Then swiftly in the very midst of the rent in the clouds I saw a black angel clothed in black armor with black wings outspread from east to west; gigantic, hovering, he spoke in a thunderous voice louder than anything I had ever heard: *'Fear God and give glory to Him for the Hour of His judgment is come. . .'.*"

Against the hour of the bloodbath Nat had steeled himself in apocalyptic hatred, "hatred so pure and obdurate that no sympathy, no human warmth, no flicker of compassion can make the faintest nick or scratch upon the stony surface of its being." He had achieved this exaltation, he thought, by "knowing the white man at close hand," by becoming "knowledgeable about the white man's wiles, his duplicity, his greediness, and his ultimate depravity," and most of all by "having submitted to his wanton and arrogant kindness." Then when the moment came and the dread axe was poised over his master's head, Nat's hand palsied and the blow missed. Again and again between violent seizures of vomitting he tried to kill and failed. Initiative fell to a demented black monster maddened by a master's brutality. The only life Nat was able to take, among the score slaughtered, was that of the one white person he still loved, a simple-hearted and sympathetic girl.

This is the most profound fictional treatment of slavery in our literature. It is, of course, the work of a skilled and experienced novelist with other achievements to attest his qualifications. It is doubtful, however, if the rare combination of talents essential to this formidable undertaking, a flawless command of dialect, a native instinct for the subtleties and ambivalences of race in the South, and a profound and unerring sense of place—Styron's native place as it was Nat Turner's—could well have been found anywhere else.

Charles V. Hamilton

# OUR NAT TURNER AND WILLIAM STYRON'S CREATION

Charles V. Hamilton is Professor of Political Science at Columbia University. He was formerly head of the Political Science Departments at Roosevelt University, in Chicago, and at Lincoln University, in Pennsylvania. He is the co-author of *Black-Power*.

WILLIAM STYRON classifies his story, *The Confessions of Nat Turner*, as "a meditation on history." It is important for us, then, to view it in this sense and to see precisely what this means in terms of white America's ability or inability to come to terms with the black man in this country. This book is a best seller because it raises and treats all the problems of black people versus whites—the assertive black male, the white woman bugaboo, violence, freedom—and the ultimate treatment reinforces what white America wants to believe about black America. The treatment, in other words, turns out right for whites.

Black youth (and some not so youthful) today who are challenging the values and practices of this society, especially in regard to race, find Styron's book a prime example of the obstacles to overcome. Black youth on college campuses I visit across this country, who form black student associations and who insist on a redefinition of historical and educational legitimacy, can never and should never accept the portrayal (or is the word "betrayal"?) of Nat Turner as set forth by Styron. Granted, Styron is entitled to his literary license, but black people today cannot afford the luxury of having their leaders manipulated and toyed with. Nat Turner struck a blow for freedom; Nat Turner was a revolutionary who did *not* fail, but rather one who furthered the idea and cause of freedom precisely because he chose to act for freedom. Black people today must not permit themselves to be divested of

Reprinted from *William Styron's Nat Turner: Ten Black Writers Respond*. First appeared in Saturday Review (June 22, 1968), under the title "Nat Turner Reconsidered: The Fiction and the Reality." With permission of the author.

their historical revolutionary leaders. And it is incumbent upon blacks to make this clear to the Styrons and to all who read his book and are soothed.

We will not permit Styron's "meditation" to leave unchallenged an image of Nat Turner as a fanatical black man who dreams of going to bed with white women, who holds nothing but contempt for his fellow blacks, and who understands, somewhat, the basic human desire to be free but still believes in the basic humanity of some slaveholders.

We will not permit Styron to picture unchallenged Nat Turner as a leader who did not understand that the military defeat should not be confused with the ideological victory: i.e., a blow for freedom. The rebellion of 1831, led by Nat Turner, is important today for blacks to understand and whites to accept precisely because its lesson is that there will be leaders who *will* rise up—against all odds—to strike blows for freedom against an oppressive, inhumane system. And there can be no refuge in the thought that Turner felt himself divinely inspired or waited for signs from heaven, etc. The important thing is that the desire for human freedom resides in the black breast as well as in any other. No amount of explicating about the harshness of slavery or the gentleness of slavery, about the docility of the masses of slaves, etc., can keep that desire from exploding. Man—black or white or yellow or red—moves to maximize his freedom: *That* is the lesson of Nat Turner that Styron did not deal with.

Styron's literary mind can wander about homosexuality and the like, and his vast readership can have their stereotypes strengthened by an image of a black preacher who is irrational and weak (unable to kill, excepting some white woman he loves) and uncertain. But black people should reject this; and white people should not delude themselves.

Let us see how Styron's "meditation on history" fits perfectly with traditional, widely acclaimed historical accounts of the event and the institution of slavery. And in doing this, we will see how his book feeds the distortions of white America. I will cite two major historical texts, sources used widely in colleges and high schools. First—simply to observe the uses of history —note how Professor Thomas A. Bailey in his *The American Pageant: A History of the Republic* describes the American Revolution:

> The revolutionists were blessed with outstanding leadership. Washington was a giant among men; Benjamin Franklin was a master among diplomats, . . . The Americans, in addition, enjoyed the moral advantage that came from what they regarded as a just cause. . . . The brutal truth is that only a select minority of the American colonials attached themselves to the cause of independence with a spirit of selfless devotion. These were the dedicated souls who bore the burden of battle and the risks of defeat; these were the freedom-loving patriots who deserved the gratitude and approbation of generations yet unborn. Seldom have so few done so much for so many.

Now let us see how this same objective, white American scholar deals with Nat Turner:

Fanatical Nat Turner, a semi-educated Negro preacher who had visions, organized a conspiracy which resulted in the butchering of about sixty white Virginians, mostly women and children. The outburst was speedily crushed, but an understandable wave of hysteria swept over the South.

(When I taught at a southern Negro college, a black history professor once told me: "Oh, I always use Bailey's *American Pageant*. It is simple and clear and my students like it and find it easy to read.") To my knowledge, Professor Bailey, then on the faculty at Stanford University, is not noted for racist views.

One other source is useful: *The American Republic* (Vol. I, to 1865) by Richard Hofstadter, William Miller, and Daniel Aaron. Note their treatment of slavery:

The kindliest slaveholder, either as a buyer or seller, was sometimes forced to break up Negro families. In short, the slaveholder was frequently victimized by the system.

But there is a brighter side of the picture. Even some of the anti-slavery men acknowledged that ordinarily the slaves were adequately housed, clothed, and fed. The slave's diet of pork, cornmeal, molasses, and greens was coarse and monotonous, and the slave quarters were unhygienic by modern standards. But many poor-white farmers lived no better. Slaves worked no longer than many northern agricultural and industrial laborers and, in areas where the "task" system was employed, a slave might complete his assigned chores by early afternoon and spend the rest of the day as he chose. Progressive planters encouraged their slaves to cultivate truck gardens and keep pigs and chickens for their use or to sell. Incentive payments, holidays, and entertainments alleviated the drudgery on some plantations, and where the work became too exacting the slaves developed their own slow-down techniques. House-servants found life much easier than field hands, and some gifted slaves were rewarded with positions of trust and responsibility. It seems true enough that many white southerners treated their slaves affectionately and that many slaves responded to this treatment with loyalty and devotion.

Styron's novel is in this historical tradition. He does not assign to Nat Turner a basic revolutionary desire to overcome oppression. In fact, Styron clearly asserts that Turner and his followers needed specific traumatic acts to galvanize them into action being whipped unmercifully, being sold by a "decent" owner to a tyrant, having one's wife and children taken. On the other hand, Styron joins that school of thought which believes that the kinder you treat the subjects, the more likely they are to rebel. This is related to the current notion of growing black militancy resulting from rising expectations. Some of us black Americans view human bondage as bad per se, and we believe that Nat Turner, with his basically revolutionary temperament, had to strike out against that bondage. He was the real freedom-lover, the true freedom-fighter.

Styron dwells on the reason the slaves would kill those masters who were kinder to them—like Travis. This, indeed, should be a message. The focus is on the fact that they were "masters," not that they were kinder than other masters. And so the white liberal today tries to remove himself from the racism of the system, without understanding that he is part of the racist system, and those of us who are real live victims of that system cannot afford irrelevant distinctions. The white liberal feels that good intentions are sufficient to relieve him of responsibility. He is sadly mistaken. To him, the problem is abstract, academic. To us, it is real, tangible.

Styron imputes irony to the fact that "almost the only white man in the county who owned a truly illustrious reputation for cruelty to Negroes escaped the blade of [our] retribution." The implication being, of course, that all the violence still did not get the "right" ones, that the "good" whites suffered. And, thus, further evidence of failure. Nonsense! Then and now. The Nathaniel Francises in Styron's story exist precisely because of the support —covert or overt—of the "good white folk." No sensitive black man today confuses this point—even if Styron does.

It is perfectly clear why Styron's book would be a hit on the American market: it confirms white America's racist feelings. Here was an ungrateful slave, taught to read by his master, who repaid that "gift" by murder. (See what happens when you try to be a little kind to them.) Here was the fanatical black leader who held profound contempt for his own people and who led them into a senseless bloodbath destined to fail, all the while dreaming of copulating with "Miss Anne." (They are really incapable of sticking together or of being leaders. All they really want is to have sexual intercourse with our women.) Here was the visionary who frequently doubted himself and his venture. (They are little children who really must be led and brought along slowly—for their own sake.) And, of course, here was the final act of nobility on the part of the Great White Father—Gray, the attorney—who extends the hand of forgiveness through the bars. (We must be patient and understanding with these little savages. We must show them that we are big enough to forgive.)

If this is Styron's (and white America's) "meditation on history," let the record show that this is meditation mired in misinterpretation, and that this is history many black people reject.

Nat Turner is our hero, unequivocally understood. He is a man who had profound respect and love for his fellow blacks and who respected black womanhood and held utter contempt for those white slavemasters who violated the purity and beauty of our black women. Nat Turner *was a success* because he perpetuated the *idea* of freedom—freedom at all cost. He will not be denied his place in the revolutionary annals of black people by white people who—through the guise of art or otherwise—feel a conscious or subconscious need to belittle him. If white America feels a need to relieve its conscience, to soften *its* confession, let it be clear that it will not be done, unchallenged, at the expense of our black brothers—past or present. That day is done.

### STUDY QUESTIONS

1. On what grounds do Hamilton and Woodward ("Confessions of a Rebel: 1831") judge *The Confessions of Nat Turner?*

2. What are the principal differences in their opinions of the book?

3. Of the two reviews, which one appears to be the more authoritative?

4. Hamilton contends that Styron's book "confirms white America's racist feelings," and he notes some of them. Is there any evidence of such feelings in the selection "It is Done"?

## Eric Sevareid

# THE WORLD STILL MOVES OUR WAY

Eric Sevareid (1912–     ) is well-known to the American public for his work in broadcasting and reporting. He received his college degree from the University of Minnesota and started his career in journalism as a copy boy with the *Minneapolis Journal.* After working as a reporter for various other papers he became Paris editor of the *New York Herald-Tribune.* During World War II he was a foreign correspondent for the Columbia Broadcasting Company. His books include *Not So Wild A Dream* (1946), *In One*

*Ear* (1952), *Small Sounds in the Night* (1956), *Candidates* (1960), and *This Is Eric Sevareid* (1964). At present he is correspondent for Columbia Broadcasting Company and is a regular contributor to various magazines.

THERE ARE THOSE WHO SAY the dream is dead or dying, poisoned by self-interest, rotted by surfeit and indifference, maimed by violence. The great aspiration is ended, they tell us, and America is now only another crowded nation, not even able to maintain order; a Power, but not a society, not a culture. We have gone, almost directly, they would have us believe, from primitiveness to decadence, a far poorer record than that of Rome.

The fireworks of this July 4—which may well illuminate the scene, again, of whole urban blocks consumed by flames, from the Molotov cocktail, not the holiday sparkler—will give further force to this cry of the Cassandras.

But the cry is as old as the nation. It was sounded in Jefferson's time, when the states seemed ready to drift apart; in Lincoln's time, when they split apart; in Roosevelt's time, when, by the millions, husbands shuffled in soup lines; in Truman's time, when the Russians and Chinese were supposedly reordering the earth and Communist traitors were supposedly infesting the Government.

But this is not It—this is not our Armageddon, not the great day of judgment on America. For America is change, and the changes have come, often enough, in convulsive spasms. This country is the vast experimental laboratory in human relations for the twentieth century; it is, in a sense, defining and creating the twentieth century for much of the world.

Unless it is seen in this light, America cannot be understood at all. If many of our contemporary intellectuals, especially those communing with one another in New York City, almost a separate nation in spirit, do not understand it, this is partly because they do not understand themselves. As they attest in innumerable books, they do not know who they are. It may be news to them that the over-whelming majority of Americans *do* know who they are, do *not* feel alienated from their country or their generation.

This is not a "sick society." It is a deeply unsettled and bewildered society, and the reason is not merely the extraordinary changes in this last generation but the speed of these changes. It is the *rate* of change that is new. The life of Americans today resembles that of, say, Grant's time, less than life in Grant's time resembled life in ancient China. The nation is not over-populated, but the population has shifted out of balance. In the last 20 years alone, 18 million people, including, of course, the Negroes, have moved into the urban centers. This second industrial-scientific revolution has jammed us together, polluted much of our air and waters, smeared ugliness over much of our countryside, obliged us to work within greater economic units and increased the tensions of daily living.

Two other revolutions have been taking place in concert with the new industrial-scientific revolution. One is the communications revolution, which brings every social evil, every human tragedy and conflict immediately and intimately within everyone's ken. The other is the educational revolution, which adds millions every year to the ranks of those moved to add their investigation, articulation or actions to the processes of problem-solving and problem-creating.

We are not becoming less democratic but more democratic. It is not our individual freedom that is in jeopardy, in the first instance, but our public order. It could be argued that we are moving away from representative government in the direction, at least, of direct democracy, by no means an unmixed blessing. For the immediate future, the problem is not only the indifference or "apathy" of the much-abused middle class or any other group. It is also the problem of too many untrained cooks in the kitchen.

Many current phenomena to the contrary notwithstanding, Americans are the most natural workers-together in the world. We say we live by the system of individual enterprise, while we are the supreme cooperative society. Totalitarian countries say they are cooperative societies, while their regimes must coerce their people to work. It is absurd to believe that the races of men who turned an empty, forbidding continent into the most efficient engine of production and distribution ever seen, who created the first *mass* democracy with essential order and essential freedom will not solve the problems of crowding, poverty, pollution and ugliness. The solutions will create new problems, after which there will be new solutions, then new problems, and so our life will go on. Time is life. Were human problems ever totally solved, change would come to a stop, and we would begin to die.

American cynics and Cassandras see neither their own history nor the rest of the world with clarity. Violence? We have *always* had a high tolerance level for violence. Abraham Lincoln worried about what he called "the increasing disregard for law which pervades the country; the growing disposition to substitute the wild and furious passions, in lieu of the sober judgment of courts; and the worse than savage mobs, for the executive ministers of justice."

It is even to be doubted that crime is more prevalent than it was in the nineteenth century. Historian Arthur Schlesinger, Jr., reminds us that a century ago, every tenth person in New York City had a police record.

Alienated and irreverent youth? To a degree, youth is always alienated and to a degree ought to be. More than 2,000 years ago, Plato wrote that in a democracy, the father "accustoms himself to become like his child and to fear his sons. . . . The schoolmaster fears and flatters his pupils . . . the young act like their seniors, and compete with them in speech and action, while the old men condescend to the young. . . ." This happens because democratic life carries the in-built impulse to wish to please and accommodate to others.

The alarm over drug-taking is also exaggerated. There is far less use of dangerous drugs today than a half century ago, before narcotics control, when about one American in every four hundred was an addict of some harmful drug, ten times the present rate.

Americans, of course, are not spiritually geared to the past but to the future. It is a reflection of what John Steinbeck, speaking of the onpushing, haggard "Okies" in the dust-bowl years, called the "terrible faith," that we are constantly seized with concern for our children more than for ourselves. Yet it is not possible to see our society in perspective without these backward glances to what we once were, with the consequent realization that we are using different scales of measuring well-being today.

At the turn of the century, a newborn could expect to live about to the age of 50; today, the expectancy is about 70. Once, a mother had sound reason to fear giving birth; today, death in childbirth is regarded as intolerable. Once, a full high school education was the best achievement of a minority; today, it is the barest minimum for decent employment and self-respect. Once, the timber and mining barons stripped away the forests and topsoil wholesale; today, these companies are confronted by their communities at every other move.

One could cite hundreds of similar examples of how our standards of expectancy have risen, as they should, along with our standard of life. The truth is that we Americans are perfectionists, which simply means that we were not, are not and never will be satisfied either with the quantities or the qualities in our life.

By the year 2000, we will look back upon these present years not only as one of America's periodic convulsions but as a rather backward period. By then, the typical American family will have an income of around $20,000 a year or more; the typical American adult will have had at least two years of college, with far broader intellectual and aesthetic horizons. By then, the old urban centers will have been rebuilt, and many millions will live in satellite "new cities," part-urban, part-rural. The incurable diseases like cancer and arthritis will be under far better control.

The present explosion in books, theater, music and art will have transformed tastes and comprehension to an enormous degree. And already, according to the Englishman C. P. Snow, something like 80 percent of the advanced study of science in the Western world is going on in the United States of America. This is the heart reason for the "brain drain" from abroad to the U.S., not merely the higher pay. The facilities, the action, the creative excitement are increasingly here. None of this guarantees a single new Shakespeare, Rembrandt, Beethoven or Einstein, because genius is not developed (though even this may occur one day through selective breeding and cell transplant).

What it does guarantee is a great lifting of the massive center, of the "ordinary" people. This is the premise and the point about America—ours is the first organized dedication to *massive* improvement, to the development of a *mass* culture, the first attempt to educate *everyone* to the limit of his capacities. We have known for a long time that this can be done only through the chemistry of individual freedom. Soviet Russia is just now beginning to discover this for itself. I am unable to understand the thrust of the sufferings and strivings of Western man over the last thousand years save in terms of this kind of achievement.

The popular passion of Americans is not politics, baseball, money or material things. It is education. Education is now our biggest industry, involving more people even than national defense. The percentage of children in kindergarten has doubled in a rather short period; the percentage of youth in college climbs steeply upward. Today, even a Negro boy in the South has a better statistical chance of getting into college than an English youth. And there are about 44 million full- and part-time *adult* students pursuing some kind of formalized learning on their own!

Intelligent foreigners nearly everywhere understand the mountainous meaning of all this for the world as well as for America. They know that much of the world will be transformed in the American image, culturally if not politically. They know that struggle is really all over—it is the Western way of living and doing, our way and the way of Europe combined, that the world wants. It is North America and West Europe that make up the "in" world; Russia and China are still the outsiders trying to enter.

Communism already appears irrelevant, essentially passé. The more the Communist regimes educate their people, the more complex their life will become. They will struggle with the complexities the Western world confronts already, and they will discover that authoritarian direction from the top cannot cope with them. Only the essentially liberal society can manage twentieth-century life, even in practical terms. They will learn, as we have always known, that the effective, the lasting revolution lies in the West, particularly in America.

Why, then, are we in such a state of uproar in this year of Our Lord, and why is much of the world upset about the America of today? Because, as a philosopher once said, "nothing that is vast enters into the life of mortals without a curse," and America is struggling to rid itself of one old curse and one new one. The old curse is the Negro slavery Europeans fastened upon this land long ago, which continues in a hundred psychological, social and economic, if not legal, forms. The Negro Passion of today is a revolution within the continuing American revolution, and the one absolute certainty about it is that it is going to succeed, however long and distracting the agony for everyone. It will succeed not only because it has justice with it (justice has been suppressed before) but because there is a deep evangelical streak in the American people, a true collective conscience, and it has been aroused.

Racism exists in almost all societies on this globe, virulently so, incidentally, in Black Africa. It may be that race prejudice—the psychologists' "stranger hatred"—is an instinct tracing from our animal origins, and therefore ineradicable. Yet man is the only animal *aware* of his instincts; the only animal, therefore, capable of controlling, if not eliminating, his instincts. New law, enforced, compels new behavior. Behavior repeated daily comes to seem normal, and attitudes change. Illusions tend to vanish. The idea that a difference in skin color is an essential difference is an illusion. I am struck by an observation of McGeorge Bundy of the Ford Foundation. He said discrimination will end, partly because this college generation regards racial equality as natural, whereas the older generation regards it only as logical.

The twentieth-century war over racial injustice is now in its virulent stage. The nineteenth-century war in its virulent stage lasted four years. This one will last much longer because it is fought on a thousand narrow fronts, like guerrilla war, and because no grand climacteric is possible. But it is not going to "tear this country apart" or "burn America down" or anything of the sort. A tiny percentage of extremists among only 12 percent of the American population can do much, but they cannot do that.

The new curse has come with America's new military power. A form of Parkinson's Law operates here. The greater the power, the more the men who associate with it, extol it and find needs, real or sophistical, for its use. The use of available, flexible force becomes easier than hard thought; and the worst aspect of the curse is the gradual, almost unconscious identification of power with virtue. John Adams said, "Power always thinks it has a great soul and vast views beyond the comprehension of the weak. . . ."

We have fallen into this trap with the Vietnam intervention. For the first time, we have misused our power on a massive scale. But it does not mean that we are a "fascist" or aggressive people, any more than the racial mess means that we are a hating or oppressive people. Vietnam is not typical; it is a mistake, now recognized as such by most serious thinkers in this country. If millions of people in Europe (every province of which is soaked in blood) stand aghast at what we have done and reproach us bitterly, one unarticulated reason is that they *expect* the United States to act with humaneness and common sense. They do not shout advice to Russia and China, whatever their misdeeds, for the same reason that the crowd in the bullring does not shout advice to the bull but to the bullfighter.

The reassuring thing is not merely that we will get out of this trap and undo the damage as best we can but that we will do so because our own people demand it, not because the enemy is too strong, not because of foreign criticism. We could, if we would, lay North Vietnam totally waste. The American conscience will not permit it. We may not win a military victory in Vietnam, but we will win a victory in our own soul.

No—the humaneness of the American people is still here. The new problems have piled up too rapidly for our brains and our institutions to cope with at anything like the same rate, but the will for justice is as strong as ever—stronger, in my own belief, because thought and expression are freer today than ever before. This is why the Negro revolution has come now—not because conditions of life became worse, save for some, but because of a climate of free expression. In just such periods of great intellectual freedom have nearly all revolutions been generated.

It is a remarkable fact that great numbers of very ordinary people in distant lands understand all this about America better than some of our own intellectuals. If, by some magic, all barriers to emigration and immigration around the world were lifted tomorrow, by far the single biggest human caravan would start moving in one direction—our way.

One day recently, I asked a Cuban refugee why most Cubans like himself wanted to come to the United States rather than go to Latin Ameican countries with the same language and the same general culture. Was it just the thought of greater economic opportunity?

"No," he said, "many of us would have an easier time, economically, in a Latin country. It's just that we feel better here. We can feel like a human being. There seems to be something universal about this country."

This is living testimony, not abstract argument, from men who know the meaning of America in their bones and marrow. Of course, it is the truth. Of course, the dream lives on.

Let those who wish compare America with Rome. Rome lasted around a thousand years.


## STUDY QUESTIONS

1. Describe Sevareid's method of presentation and note the advantages of such an approach.

2. What types of arguments does he use? Are there any that may be challenged as invalid or unconvincing?

3. According to Sevareid, how will America handle its old curse and its new curse?

4. What is the basic characteristic of the American people that informs Sevareid's optimism for the future of the country?

*Jonathan Swift*

# A MODEST PROPOSAL

Jonathan Swift (1667–1745) is one of England's greatest prose writers. He was born in Dublin, Ireland, and was educated there at Trinity College. The fact that he took orders in the Church of England did not prevent him from becoming one of the Tory propagandists. However, Queen Anne disapproved of *A Tale of a Tub* (1704), and Swift was given the deanery of St. Patrick's, Dublin, instead of the English preferment he wanted. Among his now-classic works are *The Battle of the Books* (1704), *Gulliver's Travels* (1726), *A Modest Proposal* (1729), and *The Journal to Stella* (1766).

IT IS A melancholly Object to those, who walk through this great Town or travel in the Country, when they see the Streets, the Roads and Cabbin-doors crowded with Beggers of the Female Sex, followed by three, four, or six Children, all in Rags, and importuning every Passenger for an Alms. These Mothers instead of being able to work for their honest livelyhood, are forced to employ all their time in Stroling to beg Sustenance for their helpless Infants, who, as they grow up, either turn Thieves for want of Work, or leave their dear Native Country, to fight for the Pretender in Spain, or sell themselves to the Barbadoes.

I think it is agreed by all Parties, that this prodigious number of Children in the Arms, or on the Backs, or at the Heels of their Mothers, and frequently of their Fathers, is in the present deplorable state of the Kingdom, a very great additional grievance; and therefore whoever could find out a fair, cheap and easy method of making these Children sound and useful Members of the Common-wealth, would deserve so well of the publick, as to have his Statue set up for a Preserver of the Nation.

But my Intention is very far from being confined to provide only for the Children of professed Beggers, it is of a much greater Extent, and shall take in the whole Number of Infants at a certain Age, who are born of Parents in

First published in 1729.

effect as little able to support them, as those who demand our Charity in the Streets.

As to my own part, having turned my Thoughts, for many Years, upon this important Subject, and maturely weighed the several Schemes of other Projectors, I have always found them grossly mistaken in their computation. It is true, a Child just dropt from its Dam, may be supported by her Milk, for a Solar Year with little other Nourishment, at most not above the Value of two Shillings, which the Mother may certainly get, or the Value in Scraps, by her lawful Occupation of Begging; and it is exactly at one Year Old that I propose to provide for them in such a manner, as, instead of being a Charge upon their Parents, or the Parish, or wanting Food and Raiment for the rest of their Lives, they shall, on the Contrary, contribute to the Feeding and partly to the Cloathing of many Thousands.

There is likewise another great Advantage in my Scheme, that it will prevent those voluntary Abortions, and that horrid practice of Women murdering their Bastard Children, alas! too frequent among us, Sacrificing the poor innocent Babes, I doubt, more to avoid the Expense than the Shame, which would move Tears and Pity in the most Savage and inhuman breast.

The number of Souls in this Kingdom being usually reckoned one Million and a half, Of these I calculate there may be about two hundred thousand Couples whose Wives are Breeders; from which number I substract thirty Thousand Couples, who are able to maintain their own Children, although I apprehend there cannot be so many, under the present Distresses of the Kingdom; but this being granted, there will remain an hundred and seventy thousand Breeders. I again Substract fifty Thousand, for those Women who miscarry, or whose Children die by accident, or disease within the Year. There only remain an hundred and twenty thousand Children of poor Parents annually born: The question therefore is, How this number shall be reared, and provided for? which, as I have already said, under the present Situation of Affairs, is utterly impossible by all the Methods hitherto proposed; for we can neither employ them in Handicraft or Agriculture; we neither build Houses, (I mean in the Country) nor cultivate Land: They can very seldom pick up a Livelihood by Stealing till they arrive at six years Old; except where they are of towardly parts; although, I confess, they learn the Rudiments much earlier; during which time they can however be properly looked upon only as Probationers; as I have been informed by a principal Gentleman in the County of Cavan, who protested to me, that he never knew above one or two Instances under the Age of six, even in a part of the Kingdom so renowned for the quickest proficiency in that Art.

I am assured by our Merchants, that a Boy or a Girl before twelve years Old, is no saleable Commodity, and even when they come to this Age, they will not yield above three Pounds, or three Pounds and half a Crown at most, on the Exchange; which cannot turn to Account either to the Parents or Kingdom, the Charge of Nutriment and Rags having been at least four times that Value.

I shall now therefore humbly propose my own Thoughts, which I hope will not be liable to the least Objection.

I have been assured by a very knowing American of my acquaintance in London, that a young healthy Child well Nursed is at a year Old a most delicious nourishing and wholesome Food, whether Stewed, Roasted, Baked, or Boiled; and I make no doubt that it will equally serve in a Fricasie, or a Ragout.

I do therefore humbly offer it to publick consideration, that of the Hundred and twenty thousand Children, already computed, twenty thousand may be reserved for Breed, whereof only one fourth part to be Males; which is more than we allow to Sheep, black Cattle, or Swine, and my Reason is, that these Children are seldom the Fruits of Marriage, a Circumstance not much regarded by our Savages, therefore, one Male will be sufficient to serve four Females. That the remaining Hundred thousand may at a year Old be offered in Sale to the Persons of Quality and Fortune, through the Kingdom, always advising the Mother to let them Suck plentifully in the last Month, so as to render them Plump, and Fat for a good Table. A Child will make two Dishes at an Entertainment for Friends, and when the Family dines alone, the fore or hind Quarter will make a reasonable Dish, and seasoned with a little Pepper or Salt will be very good Boiled on the fourth Day, especially in Winter.

I have reckoned upon a Medium, that a Child just born will weigh 12 pounds, and in a solar Year, if tolerably nursed, encreaseth to 28 Pounds.

I grant this food will be somewhat dear, and therefore very proper for Landlords, who, as they have already devoured most of the Parents seem to have the best Title to the Children.

Infant's flesh will be in Season throughout the Year, but more plentiful in March, and a little before and after; for we are told by a grave Author an eminent French Physician, that Fish being a prolifick Dyet, there are more Children born in Roman Catholick Countries about nine Months after Lent, than at any other Season; therefore reckoning a Year after Lent, the Markets will be more glutted than usual, because the Number of Popish Infants, is at least three to one in this Kingdom, and therefore it will have one other Collateral advantage, by lessening the Number of Papists among us.

I have already computed the Charge of nursing a Begger's Child (in which List I reckon all Cottagers, Labourers, and four fifths of the Farmers) to be about two Shillings per Annum, Rags included; and I believe no Gentleman would repine to give Ten Shillings for the Carcass of a good fat Child, which, as I have said will make four Dishes of excellent Nutritive Meat, when he hath only some particular Friend, or his own Family to dine with him. Thus the Squire will learn to be a good Landlord, and grow popular among his Tenants, the Mother will have Eight Shillings neat Profit, and be fit for Work till she produces another Child.

Those who are more thrifty (as I must confess the Times require) may flay the Carcass; the Skin of which, Artificially dressed, will make admirable Gloves for Ladies, and Summer Boots for fine Gentlemen.

As to our City of Dublin, Shambles may be appointed for this purpose, in the most convenient parts of it, and Butchers we may be assured will not be wanting; although I rather recommend buying the Children alive, and dressing them hot from the Knife, as we do roasting Pigs.

A very worthy Person, a true Lover of his Country, and whose Virtues I highly esteem, was lately pleased, in discoursing on this matter, to offer a refinement upon my Scheme. He said, that many Gentlemen of this Kingdom, having of late destroyed their Deer, he conceived that the Want of Venison might be well supply'd by the Bodies of young Lads and Maidens, not exceeding fourteen Years of Age, nor under twelve; so great a Number of both Sexes in every Country being now ready to Starve, for want of Work and Service: And these to be disposed of by their Parents if alive, or otherwise by their nearest Relations. But with due deference to so excellent a Friend, and so deserving a Patriot, I cannot be altogether in his Sentiments; for as to the Males, my American acquaintance assured me from frequent Experience, that their Flesh was generally Tough and Lean, like that of our Schoolboys, by continual exercise, and their Taste disagreeable, and to fatten them would not answer the Charge. Then as to the Females, it would, I think with humble Submission, be a Loss to the Publick, because they soon would become Breeders themselves: And besides it is not improbable that some scrupulous People might be apt to Censure such a Practice, (although indeed very unjustly) as a little bordering upon Cruelty, which, I confess, hath always been with me the strongest Objection against any Project, how well soever intended.

But in order to justify my Friend, he confessed, that this expedient was put into his Head by the famous Sallmanaazor, a Native of the Island Formosa, who came from thence to London, above twenty Years ago, and in Conversation told my Friend, that in his Country when any young Person happened to be put to Death, the Executioner sold the Carcass to Persons of Quality, as a prime Dainty, and that, in his Time, the Body of a plump Girl of fifteen, who was crucified for an attempt to poison the Emperor, was sold to his Imperial Majesty's prime Minister of State, and other great Mandarins of the Court, in Joints from the Gibbet, at four hundred Crowns. Neither indeed can I deny, that if the same Use were made of several plump young Girls in this Town, who, without one single Groat to their Fortunes, cannot stir abroad without a Chair, and appear at a Play-house, and Assemblies in Foreign fineries, which they never will pay for; the Kingdom would not be the worse.

Some Persons of a desponding Spirit are in great concern about that vast Number of poor People, who are Aged, Diseased, or Maimed, and I have been desired to imploy my Thoughts what Course may be taken, to ease the Nation of so grevious an Incumbrance. But I am not in the least Pain upon that matter, because it is very well known, that they are every Day dying, and rotting, by cold and famine, and filth, and vermin, as fast as can be reasonably expected. And as to the younger Labourers, they are now in almost as hopeful a Condition. They cannot get Work, and consequently pine away for want of Nourishment, to a degree, that if at any Time they are accidentally hired to common Labour, they have not Strength to perform it, and thus the Country and themselves are happily delivered from the Evils to come.

I have too long digressed, and therefore shall return to my Subject. I think the Advantages by the Proposal which I have made are obvious and many, as well as of the highest Importance.

For *First,* as I have already observed, it would greatly lessen the Number of Papists, with whom we are Yearly over-run, being the principal Breeders of the Nation, as well as our most dangerous Enemies, and who stay at home on purpose with a Design to deliver the Kingdom to the Pretender, hoping to take their Advantage by the Absence of so many good Protestants, who have chosen rather to leave their Country, than stay at home, and pay Tithes against their conscience, to an Episcopal Curate.

*Secondly,* The poorer Tenants will have something valuable of their own which by Law may be made lyable to Distress, and help to pay their Landlord's Rent, their Corn and Cattle being already seized, and Money a Thing unknown.

*Thirdly,* Whereas the Maintenance of an hundred thousand Children, from two Years old, and upwards, cannot be computed at less than Ten Shillings a Piece per Annum, the Nation's Stock will be thereby increased fifty thousand Pounds per Annum, beside the Profit of a new Dish, introduced to the Tables of all Gentlemen of Fortune in the Kingdom, who have any Refinement in Taste, and the Money will circulate among our Selves, the Goods being entirely of our own Growth and Manufacture.

*Fourthly,* The constant Breeders besides the gain of eight Shillings Sterling per Annum, by the Sale of their Children, will be rid of the Charge of maintaining them after the first Year.

*Fifthly,* This Food would likewise bring great Custom to Taverns, where the Vintners will certainly be so prudent as to procure the best Receipts for dressing it to Perfection; and consequently have their Houses frequented by all the fine Gentlemen, who justly value themselves upon their Knowledge in good Eating; and a skilful Cook, who understands how to oblige his Guests, will contrive to make it as expensive as they please.

*Sixthly,* This would be a great Inducement to Marriage, which all wise

Nations have either encouraged by Rewards, or enforced by Laws and Penalties. It would encrease the Care and Tenderness of Mothers towards their Children, when they were sure of a Settlement for Life, to the poor Babes, provided in some Sort by the Publick, to their annual Profit instead of Expence; we should soon see an honest Emulation among the married Women, which of them could bring the fattest Child to the Market. Men would become as fond of their Wives, during the Time of their Pregnancy, as they are now of their Mares in Foal, their Cows in Calf, or Sows when they are ready to farrow, nor offer to beat or kick them (as is too frequent a Practice) for fear of a Miscarriage.

Many other Advantages might be enumerated. For Instance, the Addition of some thousand Carcasses in our Exportation of Barrel'd Beef: The Propagation of Swine's Flesh, and Improvement in the Art of making good Bacon, so much wanted among us by the great Destruction of Pigs, too frequent at our Tables, which are no way comparable in Taste, or Magnificence to a well grown, fat yearling Child, which roasted whole will make a considerable Figure at a Lord Mayor's Feast, or any other Publick Entertainment. But this, and many others, I omit, being studious of Brevity.

Supposing that one thousand Families in this City, would be constant Customers for Infant's Flesh, besides others who might have it at merry Meetings, particularly at Weddings and Christenings, I compute that Dublin would take off Annually about twenty thousand Carcasses, and the rest of the Kingdom (where probably they will be sold somewhat cheaper) the remaining eighty Thousand.

I can think of no one Objection, that will possibly be raised against this Proposal, unless it should be urged, that the Number of People will be thereby much lessened in the Kingdom. This I freely own, and 'twas indeed one principal Design in offering it to the World. I desire the Reader will observe, that I calculate my Remedy for this one individual Kingdom of Ireland, and for no Other that ever was, is, or, I think, ever can be upon Earth. Therefore let no man talk to me of other Expedients: Of taxing our Absentees at five Shillings a Pound: Of using neither Cloaths, nor Household Furniture, except what is of our own Growth and Manufacture: Of utterly rejecting the Materials and Instruments that promote Foreign Luxury: Of curing the Expensiveness of Pride, Vanity, Idleness, and Gaming in our Women: Of introducing a Vein of Parcimony, Prudence and Temperance: Of learning to love our Country, wherein we differ even from Laplanders, and the Inhabitants of Topinamboo: Of quitting our Animosities, and Factions, nor act any longer like the Jews, who were murdering one another at the very Moment their City was taken: Of being a little cautious not to sell our Country and Consciences for nothing: Of teaching Landlords to have at least one Degree of Mercy towards their Tenants. Lastly, Of putting a Spirit of Honesty, Industry, and Skill into our Shop-keepers, who, if a Resolution could now be taken to buy only our Native Goods, would immediately unite to cheat and exact upon us in the Price, the Measure, and the Goodness, nor could ever yet be brought to make one fair Proposal of just Dealing, though often and earnestly invited to it.

Therefore I repeat, let no Man talk to me of these and the like Expedients, till he hath at least some Glimpse of Hope, that there will ever be some hearty and sincere Attempt to put them in Practice.

But as to my self, having been wearied out for many Years with offering vain, idle, visionary Thoughts, and at length utterly despairing of Success, I fortunately fell upon this Proposal, which as it is wholly new, so it hath something Solid and Real, of no Expence and little Trouble, full in our own Power, and whereby we can incur no Danger in disobliging England. For this kind of Commodity will not bear Exportation, the Flesh being of too tender a Consistence, to admit a long Continuance in Salt, although perhaps I cou'd name a Country, which wou'd be glad to eat up our whole Nation without it.

After all, I am not so violently bent upon my own Opinion, as to reject any Offer, proposed by wise Men, which shall be found equally Innocent, Cheap, Easy, and Effectual. But before something of that Kind shall be advanced in Contradiction to my Scheme, and offering a better, I desire the Author or Authors, will be pleased maturely to consider two Points. *First,* As Things now stand, how they will be able to find Food and Raiment for a hundred Thousand useless Mouths and Backs. And *Secondly,* There being a round Million of Creatures in Human Figure, throughout this Kingdom, whose whole Subsistence put into a common Stock, would leave them in Debt two Millions of Pounds Sterling, adding those, who are Beggers by Profession, to the Bulk of Farmers, Cottagers and Labourers, with their Wives and Children, who are Beggers in Effect; I desire those Politicians, who dislike my Overture, and may perhaps be so bold to attempt an Answer, that they will first ask the Parents of these Mortals, Whether they would not at this Day think it a great Happiness to have been sold for Food at a Year Old, in the manner I prescribe, and thereby have avoided such a perpetual Scene of Misfortunes, as they have since gone through, by the Oppression of Landlords, the Impossibility of paying Rent without Money or Trade, the Want of common Sustenance, with neither House nor Cloaths to cover them from the Inclemencies of the Weather, and the most inevitable Prospect of intailing the like, or greater Miseries, upon their Breed for ever.

I profess in the Sincerity of my Heart, that I have not the least Personal Interest in endeavouring to promote this Necessary Work, having no other Motive than the Publick Good of my Country, by advancing our Trade, providing for infants, relieving the Poor, and giving some Pleasure to the Rich. I have no Children, by which I can propose to get a single Penny; the youngest being nine Years Old, and my Wife past Child-bearing.

## STUDY QUESTIONS

1. Before he reveals his proposal, Swift devotes the first part of his essay to describing the advantages of his proposal. What is his strategy in this?

2. At what point does the reader realize that Swift is not to be taken literally in his proposal?

3. How does Swift give his proposal the appearance of authenticity?

4. Swift follows a logical outline in presenting his proposal. What is the general framework of the outline?

5. Swift makes a number of topical references and allusions that the reader will recognize only if he is familiar with the historical setting and context of the proposal. But why do you think he used "a very knowing American of my acquaintance" for one of his authorities?

*Sir Julian Huxley*

# THE CROWDED WORLD

Sir Julian Huxley (1887–    ) is a British scientist and writer who has a distinguished reputation both in America and his own country. He has been a professor of zoology at King's College, University of London, and general director of UNESCO. He has been biology editor of the *Encyclopaedia Britannica,* and is the author of many scholarly articles and books. He was knighted for his many contributions and services to science.

POPULATION has at last made the grade and emerged as a World Problem. Unfortunately, most of those who speak or write about the problem persist in thinking of it in terms of a race between human numbers and world resources, especially of food—a kind of competition between production and reproduction. The

Reprinted by permission of A. D. Peters & Co.

neo-Malthusians, supported by progressive opinion in the Western World and by leading figures in most Asian countries, produce volumes of alarming statistics about the world population explosion and the urgent need for birth-control, while the anti-Malthusians, supported by the two ideological blocks of Catholicism and Communism, produce equal volumes of hopeful statistics, or perhaps one should say of wishful estimates, purporting to show how the problem can be solved by science, by the exploitation of the Amazon or the Arctic, by better distribution, or even by shipping our surplus population to other planets.

Certainly, the statistics are important. The major fact emerging from them is that there really *is* a population explosion. During the millennia of man's early history, world population increased steadily but very slowly, so that by the end of the seventeenth century it had barely topped the half-billion mark. But then, as a result of the great explorations during and after the Renaissance, and still more of the rise of natural science and technology at the end of the seventeenth century, the process was stepped up, so that by the beginning of the present century world population stood at about 1½ billion, and its compound interest rate of increase had itself increased from under ½ of 1 per cent in 1650 to nearly 1 per cent (and we all know what big results can flow from even a small increase in compound interest rates).

But the real explosion is a twentieth-century phenomenon, due primarily to the spectacular developments in medicine and hygiene, which have drastically cut down death-rates without any corresponding reduction in birth-rates—death-control without birth-control. The compound interest rate of increase meanwhile crept, or rather leapt, up and up, from under 1 per cent in 1900 to 1½ per cent at mid-century, and nearly 1¾ per cent today; and it will certainly go on increasing for some decades more. This means that the *rate* of human doubling has itself been doubled within the past 80 years. World population has more than doubled since 1900 to reach about 2¾ billion today; and it will certainly reach well over 5½ billion, probably 6 billion, and possibly nearly 7 billion by the year 2000.

Coming down to details, Britons will be jolted by the fact that the net increase of world population amounts to about 150,000 every 24 hours, or the equivalent of a good-sized New Town every day—Hemel Hempstead yesterday, Harlow today, Crawley tomorrow, and so on through the weeks and months; while Americans will be startled out of any complacency they may have possessed by the fact that this is the equivalent of 10 baseball teams, complete with coach, every minute of every day and night. Such facts make the idea of interplanetary disposal of the earth's surplus population merely ridiculous.

It is also salutary to be reminded that the number of human beings alive in A.D. 1999—within the lifetime of many now living—will be about double that of those alive today; that some populations, like that of Barbados, are growing at a rate of over 3 per cent compound interest per annum, which means doubling in less than 20 years; that in an underdeveloped but already densely populated country like India, successful industrialization will be impossible unless the birth-rate is cut to about half within the next 30 or 40 years, for otherwise the capital and the trained man- and woman-power needed to give the country a stable industrial economy will be swallowed up in feeding, housing, educating, and servicing the excess population; that religious opposition to population-control is strongest and most effective in regions like Latin America, where population-increase is most rampant; that there is no provision for international study and research on population-control as there is on atomic energy, on the world's arid zones, on brain function, or on oceanography; that there is already an alarming (and increasing) shortage of available water-supplies, high-grade mineral resources, and educational facilities, even in industrially advanced countries like the U.S.A.; that the annual increase of Communist China's population is 13 million, more than the equivalent of a new Sweden and a new Denmark every year; or that the World Health Organization has twice been prevented by Roman Catholic pressure from even considering population-density as a factor in the world's health.

But in the broad view the most important thing about the population explosion is that it is making everyone—or rather everyone capable of serious thought—think seriously about the future of our human species on our human planet.

The Middle Ages were brought to an end by a major revolution in thought and belief, which stimulated the growth of science and the secularization of life at the expense of significance in art and religion, generated the industrial-technological revolution, with its stress on economics and quantitative production at the expense of significance in quality, human values and fulfilment, and culminated in what we are pleased to call the Atomic Age, with two World Wars behind it, the threat of annihilation before it, and an ideological split at its core.

Actually our modern age merits the adjective atomistic rather than atomic. Further, it will soon become very unmodern. For we are on the threshold of another major revolution, involving a new pattern of thought and a new approach to human destiny and its practical problems. It will usher in a new phase of human history, which I like to call the Evolutionary Age, because it envisages man as both product and agent of the evolutionary process on this planet.

The new approach is beginning to take effect in two rather distinct fields, of ecology and ideology, and is generating two parallel but linked currents of thought and action, that may be called the Ecological Revolution and the Humanist Revolution.

The population explosion is giving a powerful impetus to both these revolutionary currents. Ecology is the science of relational adjustment—the balanced relations of living organisms with their environment and with each other. It started botanically in a rather modest way as a study of plant communities in different habitats; went on to the fruitful idea of the ecological succession of different plant communities in a given habitat, leading up to an optimum climax community—mixed forest in the humid tropics, rich grassland on the prairies; was extended to take in animal communities, and so to the illuminating concepts of food-chains and adaptive niches; and finally, though rather grudgingly, was still further enlarged to include human as well as biological ecology.

The population explosion has brought us up against a number of tough ecological facts. Man is at last pressing hard on his spatial environment— there is little leeway left for his colonization of new areas of the world's surface. He is pressing hard on his resources, notably nonrenewable but also renewable resources. As Professor Harrison Brown has so frighteningly made clear in his book, *The Challenge of Man's Future,* ever-increasing consumption by an ever-increasing number of human beings will lead in a very few generations to the exhaustion of all easily exploitable fossil fuels and high-grade mineral ores, to the taking up of all first-rate agricultural land, and so to the invasion of more and more second-rate marginal land for agriculture. In fact, we are well on our way to ruining our material habitat. But we are beginning to ruin our own spiritual and mental habitat also. Not content with destroying or squandering our resources of material things, we are beginning to destroy the resources of true enjoyment—spiritual, aesthetic, intellectual, emotional. We are spreading great masses of human habitation over the face of the land, neither cities nor suburbs nor towns nor villages, just a vast mass of urban sprawl or subtopia. And to escape from this, people are spilling out farther and farther into the wilder parts and so destroying them. And we are making our cities so big as to be monstrous, so big that they are becoming impossible to live in. Just as there is a maximum possible size for an efficient land animal—you can't have a land animal more than about twice as large as an elephant—so there is a maximum possible efficient size for a city. London, New York, and Tokyo have already got beyond that size.

In spite of all that science and technology can do, world food-production is not keeping up with world population, and the gap between the haves and the have-nots of this world is widening instead of being narrowed.

Meanwhile everywhere, though especially in the so-called Free Enterprise areas of the world, economic practice (and sometimes economic theory) is concerned not primarily with increased production, still less with a truly balanced economy, but with exploitation of resources in the interests of maximized and indiscriminate consumption, even if this involves present waste and future shortage.

Clearly this self-defeating, self-destroying process must be stopped. The population explosion has helped to take our economic blinkers off and has shown us the gross and increasing imbalance between the world's human population and its material resources. Unless we quickly set about achieving some sort of balance between reproduction and production, we shall be dooming our grandchildren and all their descendants, through thousands upon thousands of monotonous generations, to an extremely unpleasant and unsatisfactory existence, overworked and undernourished, overcrowded and unfulfilled.

To stop the process means planned conservation in place of reckless exploitation, regulation and control of human numbers, as well as of industrial and technological enterprise, in place of uninhibited expansion. And this means an ecological approach. Ecology will become the basic science of the new age, with physics and chemistry and technology as its hand-maidens, not its masters. The aim will be to achieve a balanced relation between man and nature, an equilibrium between human needs and world resources.

The Humanist Revolution, on the other hand, is destined to supersede the current pattern of ideas and beliefs about nature (including human nature) and man's place and role in it, with a new vision of reality more in harmony with man's present knowledge and circumstances. This new pattern of ideas can be called humanist, since it is focused on man as a product of natural evolution, not on the vast inanimate cosmos, nor on a God or gods, nor on some unchanging spiritual Absolute. For humanism in this sense, man's duty and destiny is to be the spearhead and creative agent of the overall evolutionary process on this planet.

The explosive growth of scientific and historical knowledge in the past hundred years, especially about biological and human evolution, coupled with the rise of rationalist criticism of established theologies and ancient philosophies, had cleared the ground for this revolution in thought and executed some of the necessary demolition work. But now the population explosion poses the world with the fundamental question of human destiny —*What are people for?* Surely people do not exist just to provide bomb fodder for an atomic bonfire, or religion-fodder for rival churches, or cannon-fodder for rival nations, or disease-fodder for rival parasites, or labour-fodder for rival economic systems, or ideology-fodder for rival political systems, or even consumer-fodder for profit-making systems. It cannot be their aim just to eat, drink and be merry, and to hell with posterity. Nor merely to prepare for some rather shadowy afterlife. It cannot be their destiny to exist in ever larger megalopolitan sprawls, cut off from contact with nature and from the sense of human community and condemned to increasing frustration, noise, mechanical routine, traffic congestion and endless commuting; nor to live out their undernourished lives in some squalid Asian or African village.

When we try to think in more general terms it is clear that the dominant aim of human destiny cannot be anything so banal as just maximum quantity, whether of human beings, machines, works of art, consumer goods, political power, or anything else. Man's dominant aim must be increase in quality—quality of human personality, of achievement, of works of art and craftsmanship, of inner experience, of quality of life and living in general.

"Fulfilment" is probably the embracing word: more fulfilment and less frustration for more human beings. We want more varied and fuller achievement in human societies, as against drabness and shrinkage. We want more variety as against monotony. We want more enjoyment and less suffering. We want more beauty and less ugliness. We want more adventure and disciplined freedom, as against routine and slavishness. We want more knowledge, more interest, more wonder, as against ignorance and apathy.

We want more sense of participation in something enduring and worth while, some embracing project, as against a competitive rat-race, whether with the Russians or our neighbours on the next street. In the most general terms, we want more transcendence of self in the fruitful development of personality: and we want more human dignity not only as against human degradation, but as against more self-imprisonment in the human ego or more escapism. But the inordinate growth of human numbers bars the way to any such desirable revolution, and produces increasing frustration instead of greater fulfilment.

There are many urgent special problems which the population explosion is raising—how to provide the increasing numbers of human beings with their basic quotas of food and shelter, raw materials and energy, health and education, with opportunities for adventure and meditation, for contact with nature and with art, for useful work and fruitful leisure; how to prevent frustration exploding into violence or subsiding into apathy; how to avoid unplanned chaos on the one hand and over-organized authoritarianism on the other.

Behind them all, the long-term general problem remains. Before the human species can settle down to any constructive planning of his future on earth (which, let us remember, is likely to be many times longer than his past, to be reckoned in hundreds of millions of years instead of the hundreds of thousands of his prehistory or the mere millennia of History), it must clear the world's decks for action. If man is not to become the planet's cancer instead of its partner and guide, the threatening plethora of the unborn must be forever banished from the scene.

Above all we need a world population policy—not at some unspecified date in the future, but now. The time has now come to think seriously about population policy. We want every country to have a population policy, just as it has an economic policy or a foreign policy. We want the United Nations to have a population policy. We want all the international agencies of the U.N. to have a population policy.

When I say a population policy, I don't mean that anybody is going to tell every woman how many children she may have, any more than a country which has an economic policy will say how much money an individual businessman is allowed to make and exactly how he should do it. It means that you recognize population as a major problem of national life, that you have a general aim in regard to it, and that you try to devise methods for realizing this aim. And if you have an international population policy, again it doesn't mean dictating to backward countries, or anything of that sort; it means not depriving them of the right (which I should assert is a fundamental human right) to scientific information on birth-control, and it means help in regulating and controlling their increase and planning their families.

Its first aim must be to cut down the present excessive rate of increase to manageable proportions: once this is done we can think about planning for an optimum size of world population—which will almost certainly prove to be less than its present total. Meanwhile we, the people of all nations, through the U.N. and its Agencies, through our own national policies and institutions, and through private Foundations, can help those courageous countries which have already launched a population policy of their own, or want to do so, by freely giving advice and assistance and by promoting research on the largest scale.

When it comes to United Nations agencies, one of the great scandals of the present century is that owing to pressure, mainly from Roman Catholic countries, the World Health Organization has not been allowed even to consider the effects of population density on health. It is essential and urgent that this should be reversed.

There is great frustration in the minds of medical men all over the world, especially those interested in international affairs, who, at the cost of much devoted labour, have succeeded in giving people information on how to control or avoid disease. Malaria in Ceylon is a striking example. As a result of all this wonderful scientific effort and goodwill, population has exploded, and new diseases, new frustrations, new miseries are arising. Meanwhile medical men are not allowed to try to cope with these new troubles on an international scale—and indeed sometimes not even on a national scale. It is an astonishing and depressing fact that even in the advanced and civilized U.S.A. there are two States in which the giving of birth-control information on medical grounds even by non-Catholic doctors to non-Catholic patients, is illegal.

In conclusion I would simply like to go back to where I started and repeat that we must look at the whole question of population increase not merely as an immediate problem to be dealt with *ad hoc*. We must look at it in the light of the new vision of human destiny which human science and learning has revealed to us. We must look at it in the light of the glorious possibilities that are still latent in man, not merely in the light of the obvious fact that the world could be made a little better than it is. We must also look at it in the light of the appalling possibilities for evil and misery that still hang over the future of evolving man.

This vision of the possibilities of wonder and more fruitful fulfilment on the one hand as against frustration and increasing misery and regimentation on the other is the twentieth-century equivalent of the traditional Christian view of salvation as against damnation. I would indeed say that this new point of view that we are reaching, the vision of evolutionary humanism, is essentially a religious one, and that we can and should devote ourselves with truly religious devotion to the cause of ensuring greater fulfilment for the human race in its future destiny. And this involves a furious and concerted attack on the problem of population; for the control of population is, I am quite certain, a prerequisite for any radical improvement in the human lot.

We do indeed need a World Population Policy. We have learnt how to control the forces of outer nature. If we fail to control the forces of our own reproduction, the human race will be sunk in a flood of struggling people, and we, its present representatives, will be conniving at its future disaster.

STUDY QUESTIONS

1. Huxley contends that the population problem is more than a "race between numbers and world resources." What does he regard to be the more important problem?

2. How does Huxley use comparison and contrast to develop his thesis?

3. He sees a relationship between the decrease of man's material resources and his resources of true enjoyment. What is this relationship?

4. He claims that the population explosion has caused man to ask, "What are people for?" What is Huxley's answer to this question? Would you say that most people agree?

5. Does Huxley appeal to our reason or to our emotions?

6. What is the effect of the repetitive sentence structure in the paragraph beginning " 'Fulfilment' is probably the embracing word"?

*Arthur Schopenhauer*

# ON NOISE

Arthur Schopenhauer (1788–1860) was a German philosopher who became well known for his fine prose style and his pessimism. During his lifetime he had a large following who were attracted to his atheistic philosophy and his concept of blind will as the ultimate reality. His main work is *The World as Will and Idea* (1819), but his essays have been widely read, especially his bitter discussion "On Women."

K<small>ANT</small> WROTE a treatise on *The Vital Powers.* I should prefer to write a dirge for them. The superabundant display of vitality, which takes the form of knocking, hammering, and tumbling things about, has proved a daily torment to me all my life long. There are people, it is true—nay, a great many people—who smile at such things, because they are not sensitive to noise; but they are just the very people who are also not sensitive to argument, or thought, or poetry, or art, in a word, to any kind of intellectual influence. The reason of it is that the tissue of their brains is of a very rough and coarse quality. On the other hand, noise is a torture to intellectual people. In the biographies of almost all great writers, or wherever else their personal utterances are recorded, I find complaints about it; in the case of Kant, for instance, Goethe, Lichtenberg, Jean Paul; and if it should happen that any writer has omitted to express himself on the matter, it is only for want of an opportunity.

This aversion to noise I should explain as follows: If you cut up a large diamond into little bits, it will entirely lose the value it had as a whole; and an army divided up into small bodies of soldiers, loses all its strength. So a great intellect sinks to the level of an ordinary one, as soon as it is interrupted and disturbed, its attention distracted and drawn off from the matter in hand; for its superiority depends upon its power of concentration—of bringing all its strength to bear upon one theme, in the same way as a con-

From *The Pessimist's Handbook,* by Arthur Schopenhauer translated by T. Bailey Saunders. By permission of George Allen & Unwin, Ltd., London.

cave mirror collects into one point all the rays of light that strike upon it. Noisy interruption is a hindrance to this concentration. That is why distinguished minds have always shown such an extreme dislike to disturbance in any form, as something that breaks in upon and distracts their thoughts. Above all have they been averse to that violent interruption that comes from noise. Ordinary people are not much put out by anything of the sort. The most sensible and intelligent of all nations in Europe lays down the rule, *Never Interrupt!* as the eleventh commandment. Noise is the most impertinent of all forms of interruption. It is not only an interruption, but also a disruption of thought. Of course, where there is nothing to interrupt, noise will not be so particularly painful. Occasionally it happens that some slight but constant noise continues to bother and distract me for a time before I become distinctly conscious of it. All I feel is a steady increase in the labor of thinking—just as though I were trying to walk with a weight on my foot. At last I find out what it is.

Let me now, however, pass from genus to species. The most inexcusable and disgraceful of all noises is the cracking of whips—a truly infernal thing when it is done in the narrow resounding streets of a town. I denounce it as making a peaceful life impossible; it puts an end to all quiet thought. That this cracking of whips should be allowed at all seems to me to show in the clearest way how senseless and thoughtless is the nature of mankind. No one with anything like an idea in his head can avoid a feeling of actual pain at this sudden, sharp crack, which paralyzes the brain, rends the thread of reflection, and murders thought. Every time this noise is made, it must disturb a hundred people who are applying their minds to business of some sort, no matter how trivial it may be; while on the thinker its effect is woeful and disastrous, cutting his thoughts asunder, much as the executioner's axe severs the head from the body. No sound, be it ever so shrill, cuts so sharply into the brain as this cursed cracking of whips; you feel the sting of the lash right inside your head; and it affects the brain in the same way as touch affects a sensitive plant, and for the same length of time.

With all due respect for the most holy doctrine of utility, I really cannot see why a fellow who is taking away a wagon-load of gravel or dung should thereby obtain the right to kill in the bud the thoughts which may happen to be springing up in ten thousand heads—the number he will disturb one after another in half an hour's drive through the town. Hammering, the barking of dogs, and the crying of children are horrible to hear; but your only genuine assassin of thought is the crack of a whip; it exists for the purpose of destroying every pleasant moment of quiet thought that any one may now and then enjoy. If the driver had no other way of urging on his horse than by making this most abominable of all noises, it would be excusable; but quite the contrary is the case. This cursed cracking of whips is not only unnecessary, but even useless. Its aim is to produce an effect upon the intel-

ligence of the horse; but through the constant abuse of it, the animal becomes habituated to the sound, which falls upon blunted feelings and produces no effect at all. The horse does not go any faster for it. You have a
remarkable example of this in the ceaseless cracking of his whip on the part
of a cab-driver, while he is proceeding at a slow pace on the lookout for a
fare. If he were to give his horse the slightest touch with the whip, it would
have much more effect. Supposing, however, that it were absolutely necessary to crack the whip in order to keep the horse constantly in mind of its
presence, it would be enough to make the hundredth part of the noise. For it
is a well-known fact that, in regard to sight and hearing, animals are sensitive to even the faintest indications; they are alive to things that we can
scarcely perceive. The most surprising instances of this are furnished by
trained dogs and canary birds.

It is obvious, therefore, that here we have to do with an act of pure wan-
tonness; nay, with an impudent defiance offered to those members of the
community who work with their heads by those who work with their hands.
That such infamy should be tolerated in a town is a piece of barbarity and
iniquity, all the more as it could easily be remedied by a police-notice to the
effect that every lash shall have a knot at the end of it. There can be no harm
in drawing the attention of the mob to the fact that the classes above them
work with their heads, for any kind of headwork is mortal anguish to the
man in the street. A fellow who rides through the narrow alleys of a populous town with unemployed post-horses or cart-horses, and keeps on cracking a whip several yards long with all his might, deserves there and then to
stand down and receive five really good blows with a stick.

All the philanthropists in the world, and all the legislators, meeting to
advocate and decree the total abolition of corporal punishment, will never
persuade me to the contrary! There is something even more disgraceful than
what I have just mentioned. Often enough you may see a carter walking
along the street, quite alone, without any horses, and still cracking away in-
cessantly; so accustomed has the wretch become to it in consequence of the
unwarrantable toleration of this practice. A man's body and the needs of his
body are now everywhere treated with a tender indulgence. Is the thinking
mind then, to be the only thing that is never to obtain the slightest measure
of consideration or protection, to say nothing of respect? Carters, porters,
messengers—these are the beasts of burden amongst mankind; by all
means let them be treated justly, fairly, indulgently, and with forethought;
but they must not be permitted to stand in the way of the higher endeavors of
humanity by wantonly making a noise. How many great and splendid
thoughts, I should like to know, have been lost to the world by the crack of a
whip? If I had the upper hand, I should soon produce in the heads of these
people an indissoluble association of ideas between cracking a whip and getting a whipping.

Let us hope that the more intelligent and refined among the nations will make a beginning in this matter, and then that the Germans may take example by it and follow suit.[1] Meanwhile, I may quote what Thomas Hood says of them: [2] *For a musical nation, they are the most noisy I ever met with.* That they are so is due to the fact, not that they are more fond of making a noise than other people—they would deny it if you asked them—but that their senses are obtuse; consequently, when they hear a noise, it does not affect them much. It does not disturb them in reading or thinking, simply because they do not think; they only smoke, which is their substitute for thought. The general toleration of unnecessary noise—the slamming of doors, for instance, a very unmannerly and ill-bred thing—is direct evidence that the prevailing habit of mind is dullness and lack of thought. In Germany it seems as though care were taken that no one should ever think for mere noise—to mention one form of it, the way in which drumming goes on for no purpose at all.

Finally, as regards the literature of the subject treated of in this chapter, I have only one work to recommend, but it is a good one. I refer to a poetical epistle in *terzo rimo* by the famous painter Bronzino, entitled *De' Romori: a Messer Luca Martini.* It gives a detailed description of the torture to which people are put by the various noises of a small Italian town. Written in a tragicomic style, it is very amusing. The epistle may be found in *Opere burlesche del Berni, Aretino ed altri,* Vol. II., p. 258, apparently published in Utrecht in 1771.

## STUDY QUESTIONS

1. Schopenhauer follows a fairly basic outline in this essay. Describe it, and note how he begins with something general (noise) and then narrows it down to something specific.

2. Do you find any humor in this essay? If so, what is the source of the humor?

3. Does Schopenhauer appear to be simply cranky, or does he convince you that he has a legitimate complaint? Explain.

4. If Schopenhauer were living today, what noises would annoy him?

[1] According to a notice issued by the Society for the Protection of Animals in Munich, the superfluous whipping and the cracking of whips were, in December, 1858, positively forbidden in Nuremberg.

[2] In *Up the Rhine.*

# Section Three

# Science

## "Brave New World"

# Ashley Montagu

# INTRODUCING ANTHROPOLOGY

Ashley Montagu (1905–     ) was born in England and became a United States citizen in 1940. An anthropologist and social biologist, he was educated at the Universities of London and Florence, and received his Ph.D. from Columbia University in 1937. He has taught at New York University, Rutgers-The State University, and the New School for Social Research. Since 1930 he has served as a legal expert on scientific problems related to race and, in 1949, helped draft the UNESCO statement on race. Among his books are *Coming into Being Among Australian Aborigines* (1937), *Man's Most Dangerous Myth: The Fallacy of Race* (1942), *The Natural Superiority of Women* (1953), *Life Before Birth* (1964), *The Idea of Race* (1965), and *Man and His First Two Million Years: A Brief Introduction to Anthropology* (1969).

ANTHROPOLOGY is the science of man. That's a pretty broad definition. Let's try to draw a line around it so that we can really grasp what the science is concerned with. The word "anthropology" is derived from two Greek words, the one *anthropos* meaning "man," and the other *logos* meaning "ordered knowledge." So anthropology is the ordered knowledge of man. The fact is that anything relating to man is grist to the anthropologist's mill. Anthropology is divided into two great divisions: (1) cultural anthropology, and (2) physical anthropology.

## Cultural Anthropology

Cultural anthropology is concerned with the study of man's cultures. By "culture" the anthropologist understands what may be called the man-made part of the environment: the pots and pans, the laws and institutions, the art, religion, philosophy. Whatever a particular group of people living together as a functioning population have learned to do as human beings, their way of life, in short, is to be regarded as culture. The cultural anthropologist studies different cultures and compares them with one another in order to learn how it is that people come to do what they do in so many different ways, and also to learn, wherever possible, the relationships of one culture to another. He tries to find those common elements in all cultures which can be summarized in terms of generalizations or laws which are true of all cultures. Where there are differences, he tries to find the causes of these differences.

The cultural anthropologist is interested in all the forms that human social behavior assumes in organized societies. He cannot remain contented with the mere description of these forms, for he desires to understand how they have come into being, and so the cultural anthropologist must often be quite as good a psychologist as he is anything else. Fundamentally what he is really interested in is the nature of human nature. Today there is quite a flourishing school of anthropologists known as the personality-in-culture school. These cultural anthropologists, such as Margaret Mead, Clyde Kluckhohn, John Honigmann, Francis Hsu, and many others, are interested in tracing the relationship of the cultures in which human beings are socialized, that is, brought up, to the kind of personalities they develop.

Other cultural anthropologists are interested as specialists in studying such aspects of the cultures of different peoples as their legal institutions, social organization, religion, mythology, language, and their material culture such as their art, pottery, basketry, implements, and the like. Some cultural anthropologists take whole tribes for their special study and spend from many months to many years attempting to study every aspect of their culture.

Traditionally the cultural anthropologist has studied the so-called "primitive peoples" of this earth, and the major part of the anthropologist's attention still continues to be devoted to the cultures of such peoples, but in more recent years anthropologists have been turning their attention to the study of the technologically more advanced peoples of the earth. Today we have good anthropological studies not only of the Australian aborigines and the Congo pygmies, but also of the Japanese, the Chinese, the Germans, the Americans, the English, the Norwegians, and many others.

Formerly the study of modern societies was left to the sociologist (sociology = the study of society). Today the methods of the cultural anthropologist have greatly influenced those of the sociologist, but the difference between the two disciplines remains: the sociologist studies modern societies in great detail; the anthropologist brings to the study of modern societies a method which is at once wider and deeper than that of the sociologist.

Today there are specialists who are known as *applied* anthropologists. These are essentially cultural anthropologists who bring their special methods to bear principally upon the problems of industry. They go into a plant and study the relationships between the workers and their employers, between the worker and his work, and they advise on the methods of improving these relationships.

There are cultural anthropologists who work in hospitals in collaboration with psychiatrists. They study the relationships within the hospital between patient and doctor, administration and staff, and they conduct collaborative studies of whole districts in order to throw light upon the genesis of mental illness and its possible prevention.

The collaboration between anthropologists and psychiatrists in the study of the cultures of different societies has been very fruitful indeed, and holds much promise for the future.

Another branch of cultural anthropology is *archaeology* (often unkindly called the moldier part of anthropology). Archaeology is the science which studies cultures that no longer exist, basing its findings on the study of cultural products and subsistence remains recovered by excavation and similar means. If anthropologists are "the glamour boys" of the social sciences, archaeologists are "the glamour boys" of anthropology. All of which means that their specialty can be a very exciting one indeed, even though it generally entails a great deal of hard work, with far too much sand in one's hair, one's boots, and one's dried-out sandwiches. What the archaeologist is interested in doing is not merely to disinter an extinct culture, but to trace its relationships to other cultures. In this way archaeologists have been able to solve many problems which would otherwise have remained puzzling and to link up cultures which in their present form hardly seem related.

Anthropological archaeologists are to be distinguished from classical archaeologists; the latter are interested in the extinct cultures of classical antiquity, such as those of Greece, Rome, Crete, Persia, and Palestine.

## Physical Anthropology

Just as the cultural anthropologist is interested in studying man as a cultural being, so the physical anthropologist is interested in the comparative study of man as a physical being. The physical anthropologist studies the origin and evolution of man's physical characters and the diversity of forms which those physical characters may take. He tries to discover the means by which the likenesses and the differences between groups of human beings have been produced. He tries to discover how man, in his various physical shapes, got to be the way he is now.

There are all sorts of specialists in physical anthropology. There are those who study man's origin and evolution; these are called paleoanthropologists (paleo = old). They study the extinct remains of man and everything related to them. Then there are those who study the comparative anatomy of the primates, the classificatory group to which man in common with the apes and monkeys belongs. Here the primatologist, as he is called, is interested in discovering possible physical relationships between the large variety of types that constitute this group.

There are physical anthropologists who study growth and development. There are those who study physiology, and those who study the blood groups and blood types. There are those that study the so-called "races" of man, and there are a few who study all these subjects in the attempt to unify what they know into a consistent body of knowledge.

There are also applied physical anthropologists. These are largely concerned with the measurement of man, anatomically and physiologically, in order to determine, for example, standards for clothes, equipment in the armed forces, seats for railroad cars, hat sizes for men, shoe sizes for women, and the like.

There are also some constitutional physical anthropologists. These attempt to study the possible relationships between body-form and disease, body-form and personality, and even body-form and race.

## Anthropology and Humanity

The anthropologist is first and foremost interested in human beings, no matter what the shape of their heads, the color of their skin, or the form of their noses. As a scientist he is interested in the facts about human beings, and as an anthropologist he knows that the facts are vastly more interesting than the fancies, the false beliefs, and the downright distortions of the facts, which some misguided persons seem always to have found it necessary to perpetrate. Humanity has a wonderfully interesting history, and it is the principal function of the anthropologist to reveal that history to the student as simply and as clearly as possible. This is what we shall now attempt to do in the following pages.

In concluding this introduction to anthropology I should like to quote the words of a great anthropologist, Thomas Henry Huxley (1825–95), writing in 1889 to a young man who later became a distinguished physical anthropologist at Cambridge University (Alfred Cort Haddon, 1855–1940). They are as true today as when they were written. Wrote Huxley: "I know of no department of natural science more likely to reward a man who goes into it thoroughly than anthropology. There is an immense deal to be done in the science pure and simple, and it is one of those branches of inquiry which brings one into contact with the great problems of humanity in every direction."

STUDY QUESTIONS

1.  What are the main structural divisions of this essay? What part do defini-
    tions play in marking the points of division?

2.  What does Montagu mean when he says: "Let's try to draw a line around
    it. . . ."?

3.  How do you suppose a sociologist would react to Montagu's comment that
    anthropology has a method which is "wider and deeper" than that of
    sociology? Does Montagu provide any evidence for this statement?

4.  Can you account for the departure from a badly objective prose style
    in the paragraph about anthropological archeologists ("All of which . . .
    sandwiches.")?

5.  What does Montagu accomplish by quoting Thomas Henry Huxley in the last
    paragraph? Could this be considered a kind of name dropping?

*John James Audubon*

# THE WILD TURKEY

John James Audubon (1780?–1851) was born in New Orleans and educated in France. In 1803 he inherited the Audubon estate near Philadelphia, where he performed the first bird-banding experiments in America.
From 1808–1820 he lived in Henderson, Kentucky, continuing his ornithological studies. A curious combination of scientist and artist, Audubon
went to Great Britain in 1826 to find a publisher for his drawings of birds.
*The Birds of America* was published between 1827 and 1838; *Ornithological Biographies,* the accompanying text, followed between 1831 and 1839.
The Audubon Society, dedicated to the preservation and study of wildlife in
America, was named for him.

From *Ornithological Biography,* 1831.

𝒯HE GREAT size and beauty of the Wild Turkey, its value
as a delicate and highly prized article of food, and the
circumstance of its being the origin of the domestic race
now generally dispersed over both continents, render it one of the most interesting of the birds indigenous to the United States of America.

The unsettled parts of the States of Ohio, Kentucky, Illinois, and Indiana,
an immense extent of country to the north-west of these districts, upon the
Mississippi and Missouri, and the vast regions drained by these rivers from
their confluence to Louisiana, including the wooded parts of Arkansas,
Tennessee, and Alabama, are the most abundantly supplied with this magnificent bird. It is less plentiful in Georgia and the Carolinas, becomes still
scarcer in Virginia and Pennsylvania, and is now very rarely seen to the
eastward of the last mentioned States. In the course of my rambles through
Long Island, the State of New York, and the country around the Lakes, I did
not meet with a single individual, although I was informed that some exist in
those parts. Turkeys are still to be found along the whole line of the Alle-
gheny Mountains, where they have become so wary as to be approached
only with extreme difficulty. While, in the Great Pine Forest, in 1829, I
found a single feather that had been dropped from the tail of a female, but
saw no bird of the kind. Farther eastward, I do not think they are now to be
found. I shall describe the manners of this bird as observed in the countries
where it is most abundant, and having resided for many years in Kentucky
and Louisiana, may be understood as referring chiefly to them.

The Turkey is irregularly migratory, as well as irregularly gregarious.
With reference to the first of these circumstances, I have to state, that whenever the *mast* [1] of one portion of the country happens greatly to exceed that
of another, the Turkeys are insensibly led toward that spot, by gradually
meeting in their haunts with more fruit the nearer they advance towards the
place where it is most plentiful. In this manner flock follows after flock, until
one district is entirely deserted, while another is, as it were, overflowed by
them. But as these migrations are irregular, and extend over a vast expanse
of country, it is necessary that I should describe the manner in which they
take place.

About the beginning of October, when scarcely any of the seeds and fruits
have yet fallen from the trees, these birds assemble in flocks, and gradually
move towards the rich bottom lands of the Ohio and Mississippi. The males,
or, as they are more commonly called, the *gobblers,* associate in parties of
from ten to a hundred, and search for food apart from the females; while the
latter are seen either advancing singly, each with its brood of young, then
about two-thirds grown, or in connexion with other families, forming parties

[1] In America, the term *mast* is not confined to the fruit of the beech, but is used as a
general name for all kinds of forest fruits, including even grapes and berries.

often amounting to seventy or eighty individuals, all intent on shunning the old cocks, which, even when the young birds have attained this size, will fight with, and often destroy them by repeated blows on the head. Old and young, however, all move in the same course, and on foot, unless their progress be interrupted by a river, or the hunter's dog force them to take wing. When they come upon a river, they betake themselves to the highest eminences, and there often remain a whole day, or sometimes two, as if for the purpose of consultation. During this time, the males are heard *gobbling,* calling, and making much ado, and are seen strutting about, as if to raise their courage to a pitch befitting the emergency. Even the females and young assume something of the same pompous demeanour, spread out their tails, and run round each other, *purring* loudly, and performing extravagant leaps. At length, when the weather appears settled, and all around is quiet, the whole party mounts to the tops of the highest trees, whence, at a signal, consisting of a single *cluck,* given by a leader, the flock takes flight for the opposite shore. The old and fat birds easily get over, even should the river be a mile in breadth; but the younger and less robust frequently fall into the water,—not to be drowned, however, as might be imagined. They bring their wings close to their body, spread out their tail as a support, stretch forward their neck, and, striking out their legs with great vigour, proceed rapidly towards the shore; on approaching which, should they find it too steep for landing, they cease their exertions for a few moments, float down the stream until they come to an accessible part, and by a violent effort generally extricate themselves from the water. It is remarkable, that immediately after thus crossing a large stream, they ramble about for some time, as if bewildered. In this state, they fall an easy prey to the hunter.

When the Turkeys arrive in parts where the mast is abundant, they separate into smaller flocks, composed of birds of all ages and both sexes, promiscuously mingled, and devour all before them. This happens about the middle of November. So gentle do they sometimes become after these long journeys, that they have been seen to approach the farmhouses, associate with the domestic fowls, and enter the stables and corncribs in quest of food. In this way, roaming about the forests, and feeding chiefly on mast, they pass the autumn and part of the winter.

As early as the middle of February, they begin to experience the impulse of propagation. The females separate, and fly from the males. The latter strenuously pursue, and begin to gobble or to utter the notes of exultation. The sexes roost apart, but at no great distance from each other. When a female utters a call-note, all the gobblers within hearing return the sound, rolling note after note with as much rapidity as if they intended to emit the last and the first together, not with spread tail, as when fluttering round the females on the ground, or practising on the branches of the trees on which they have roosted for the night, but much in the manner of the domestic turkey, when an unusual or unexpected noise elicits its singular hubbub. If the call of the female comes from the ground, all the males immediately fly towards the spot, and the moment they reach it, whether the hen be in sight or not, spread out and erect their tail, draw the head back on the shoulders, depress their wings with a quivering motion, and strut pompously about, emitting at the same time a succession of puffs from the lungs, and stopping now and then to listen and look. But whether they spy the female or not, they continue to puff and strut, moving with as much celerity as their ideas of ceremony seem to admit. While thus occupied, the males often encounter each other, in which case desperate battles take place, ending in bloodshed, and often in the loss of many lives, the weaker falling under the repeated blows inflicted upon their head by the stronger.

I have often been much diverted, while watching two males in fierce conflict, by seeing them move alternately backwards and forwards, as either had obtained a better hold, their wings drooping, their tails partly raised, their body-feathers ruffled, and their heads covered with blood. If, as they thus struggle, and gasp for breath, one of them should lose his hold, his chance is over, for the other, still holding fast, hits him violently with spurs and wings, and in a few minutes brings him to the ground. The moment he is dead, the conqueror treads him under foot, but, what is strange, not with hatred, but with all the motions which he employs in caressing the female.

When the male has discovered and made up to the female (whether such a combat has previously taken place or not), if she be more than one year old, she also struts and gobbles, turns round him as he continues strutting, suddenly opens her wings, throws herself towards him, as if to put a stop to his idle delay, lays herself down, and receives his dilatory caresses. If the cock meet a young hen, he alters his mode of procedure. He struts in a different manner, less pompously and more energetically, moves with rapidity, sometimes rises from the ground, taking a short flight around the hen, as is the manner of some Pigeons, the Red-breasted Thrush, and many other birds, and on alighting, runs with all his might, at the same time rubbing his tail and wings along the ground, for the space of perhaps ten yards. He then draws near the timorous female, allays her fears by purring, and when she at length assents, caresses her.

When a male and a female have thus come together, I believe the connexion continues for that season, although the former by no means confines his attentions to one female, as I have seen a cock caress several hens, when he happened to fall in with them in the same place, for the first time. After this the hens follow their favourite cock, roosting in his immediate neighbourhood, if not on the same tree, until they begin to lay, when they separate themselves, in order to save their eggs from the male, who would break them all, for the purpose of protracting his sexual enjoyments. The females then carefully avoid him, excepting during a short period each day. After this the males become clumsy and slovenly, if one may say so, cease to fight each other, give up gobbling or calling so frequently, and assume so careless a habit, that the hens are obliged to make all the advances themselves. They *yelp* loudly and almost continually for the cocks, run up to them, caress them, and employ various means to rekindle their expiring ardour.

Turkey-cocks when at roost sometimes strut and gobble, but I have more generally seen them spread out and raise their tail, and emit the pulmonic puff, lowering their tail and other feathers immediately after. During clear nights, or when there is moonshine, they perform this action at intervals of a few minutes, for hours together, without moving from the same spot, and indeed sometimes without rising on their legs, especially towards the end of the love-season. The males now become greatly emaciated, and cease to gobble, their *breast-sponge* becoming flat. They then separate from the hens, and one might suppose that they had entirely deserted their neighbourhood. At such seasons I have found them lying by the side of a log, in some retired part of the dense woods and cane thickets, and often permitting one to approach within a few feet. They are then unable to fly, but run swiftly, and to a great distance. A slow-turkey-hound has led me miles before I could flush the same bird. Chases of this kind I did not undertake for the purpose of killing the bird, it being then unfit for eating, and covered with ticks, but with the view of rendering myself acquainted with its habits. They thus retire to recover flesh and strength, by purging with particular species of grass, and using less exercise. As soon as their condition is improved, the cocks come together again, and recommence their rambles. Let us now return to the females.

About the middle of April, when the season is dry, the hens begin to look out for a place in which to deposit their eggs. This place requires to be as much as possible concealed from the eye of the Crow, as that bird often watches the Turkey when going to her nest, and, waiting in the neighbourhood until she has left it, removes and eats the eggs. The nest, which consists of a few withered leaves, is placed on the ground, in a hollow scooped out, by the side of a log, or in the fallen top of a dry leafy tree, under a thicket of sumach or briars, or a few feet within the edge of a cane-brake, but always in a dry place. The eggs, which are of a dull cream colour, sprinkled with red dots, sometimes amount to twenty, although the more usual number is from ten to fifteen. When depositing her eggs, the female always approaches the nest with extreme caution, scarcely ever taking the same course twice; and when about to leave them, covers them carefully with leaves, so that it is very difficult for a person who may have seen the bird to discover the nest. Indeed, few Turkeys' nests are found, unless the female has been suddenly started from them, or a cunning Lynx, Fox, or Crow has sucked the eggs and left their shells scattered about.

Turkey hens not unfrequently prefer islands for depositing their eggs and rearing their young, probably because such places are less frequented by hunters, and because the great masses of drifted timber which usually accumulate at their heads, may protect and save them in cases of great emergency. When I have found these birds in such situations, and with young, I have always observed that a single discharge of a gun made them run immediately to the pile of drifted wood, and conceal themselves in it. I have often walked over these masses, which are frequently from ten to twenty feet in height, in search of the game which I knew to be concealed in them.

When an enemy passes within sight of a female, while laying or sitting, she never moves, unless she knows that she has been discovered, but crouches lower until he has passed. I have frequently approached within five or six paces of a nest, of which I was previously aware, on assuming an air of carelessness, and whistling or talking to myself, the female remaining undisturbed; whereas if I went cautiously towards it, she would never suffer me to approach within twenty paces, but would run off, with her tail spread on one side, to a distance of twenty or thirty yards, when assuming a stately gait, she would walk about deliberately, uttering every now and then a cluck. They seldom abandon their nest, when it has been discovered by men; but, I believe, never go near it again, when a snake or other animal has sucked any of the eggs. If the eggs have been destroyed or carried off, the female soon yelps again for a male; but, in general, she rears only a single brood each season. Several hens sometimes associate together, I believe for their mutual safety, deposit their eggs in the same nest, and rear their broods together. I once found three sitting on forty-two eggs. In such cases, the common nest is always watched by one of the females, so that no Crow, Raven, or perhaps even Pole-cat, dares approach it.

The mother will not leave her eggs, when near hatching, under any circumstances, while life remains. She will even allow an enclosure to be made around her, and thus suffer imprisonment, rather than abandon them. I once witnessed the hatching of a brood of Turkeys, which I watched for the purpose of securing them together with the parent. I concealed myself on the ground within a very few feet, and saw her raise herself half the length of her legs, look anxiously upon the eggs, cluck with a sound peculiar to the mother on such occasions, carefully remove each half-empty shell, and with her bill caress and dry the young birds, that already stood tottering and attempting to make their way out of the nest. Yes, I have seen this, and have left mother and young to better care than mine could have proved,—to the care of their Creator and mine. I have seen them all emerge from the shell, and, in a few moments after, tumble, roll, and push each other forward, with astonishing and inscrutable instinct.

Before leaving the nest with her young brood, the mother shakes herself in a violent manner, picks and adjusts the feathers about her belly, and assumes quite a different aspect. She alternately inclines her eyes obliquely upwards and sideways, stretching out her neck, to discover hawks or other enemies, spreads her wings a little as she walks, and softly clucks to keep her innocent offspring close to her. They move slowly along, and as the hatching generally takes place in the afternoon, they frequently return to the nest to spend the first night there. After this, they remove to some distance, keeping on the highest undulated grounds, the mother dreading rainy weather, which is extremely dangerous to the young, in this tender state, when they are only covered by a kind of soft hairy down, of surprising delicacy. In very rainy seasons, Turkeys are scarce, for if once completely wetted, the young seldom recover. To prevent the disastrous effects of rainy weather, the mother, like a skilful physician, plucks the buds of the spice-wood bush, and gives them to her young.

In about a fortnight, the young birds, which had previously rested on the ground, leave it and fly, at night, to some very large low branch, where they place themselves under the deeply curved wings of their kind and careful parent, dividing themselves for that purpose into two nearly equal parties. After this, they leave the woods during the day, and approach the natural glades or prairies, in search of strawberries, and subsequently of dew-berries, blackberries and grasshoppers, thus obtaining abundant food, and enjoying the beneficial influence of the sun's rays. They roll themselves in deserted ants' nests, to clear their growing feathers of the loose scales, and prevent ticks and other vermin from attacking them, these insects being un-able to bear the odour of the earth in which ants have been.

The young Turkeys now advance rapidly in growth, and in the month of August are able to secure themselves from unexpected attacks of Wolves, Foxes, Lynxes, and even Cougars, by rising quickly from the ground, by the help of their powerful legs, and reaching with ease the highest branches of the tallest trees. The young cocks shew the tuft on the breast about this time, and begin to gobble and strut, while the young hens purr and leap, in the manner which I have already described.

The old cocks have also assembled by this time, and it is probable that all the Turkeys now leave the extreme north-western districts, to remove to the Wabash, Illinois, Black River, and the neighbourhood of Lake Erie.

STUDY QUESTIONS

1. How effective an introduction is Audubon's first paragraph? Is the punctuation in his introduction in any way unconventional?

2. In the second paragraph, why does Audubon insist on stating the extent of his observations? Does this qualification make his observations scientifically less valid? Why or why not?

3.   What sentence serves as the structural center of the essay, by dividing it into two parts? Where does each of these parts begin?

4.   How does Audubon keep the reader aware of the precarious existence which these game birds lead?

5.   Does Audubon *interpret* anything he sees?

6.   Does he reveal his own personality in this essay?

# *Walter Van Tilburg Clark*

# HOOK

Walter Van Tilburg Clark (1901–      ) is a highly regarded writer and teacher of creative writing, whose stories and novels about the West have helped rescue Western fiction from the popularizers of the Western "myth." His *The Ox-Bow Incident* (1940) is considered a classic Western novel. Among his other well-known works are *The City of Trembling Leaves* (1945), *The Track of the Cat* (1949), and *The Watchful Gods and Other Stories* (1950). He has been in great demand as a teacher of writers. He was Writer in Residence at the University of Nevada, Visiting Lecturer at the Universities of Iowa, Utah, Wyoming, California, Washington, Oregon, and Stanford University and Reed College. In 1945 he won the O'Henry Memorial Award for *The Wind and the Snow of Winter*.

Hook, the hawks' child, was hatched in a dry spring among the oaks, beside the seasonal river, and was struck from the nest early. In the drouth his single-willed parents had to extend their hunting ground by more than twice, for the ground creatures upon which they fed died and dried by the hundreds. The range became too great for them to wish to return and feed Hook, and when they had lost interest in each other they drove Hook down into the sand and brush and went back to solitary courses over the bleaching hills.

Unable to fly yet, Hook crept over the ground, challenging all large movements with recoiled head, erected, rudimentary wings, and the small rasp of his clattering beak. It was during this time of abysmal ignorance and continual fear that his eyes took on the first quality of a hawk, that of being wide, alert and challenging. He dwelt, because of his helplessness, among the rattling brush which grew between the oaks and the river. Even in his thickets and near the water, the white sun was the dominant presence. Except in the dawn, when the land wind stirred, or in the late afternoon, when the sea wind became strong enough to penetrate the half-mile inland to this turn in the river, the sun was the major force, and everything was dry and motionless under it. The brush, small plants and trees alike husbanded the little moisture at their hearts; the moving creatures waited for dark, when sometimes the sea fog came over and made a fine, soundless rain which relieved them.

The two spacious sounds of his life environed Hook at this time. One was the great rustle of the slopes of yellowed wild wheat, with over it the chattering rustle of the leaves of the California oaks, already as harsh and individually tremulous as in autumn. The other was the distant whisper of the foaming edge of the Pacific, punctuated by the hollow shoring of the waves. But these Hook did not yet hear, for he was attuned by fear and hunger to the small, spasmodic rustlings of live things. Dry, shrunken, and nearly starved, and with his plumage delayed, he snatched at beetles, dragging in the sand to catch them. When swifter and stronger birds and animals did not reach them first, which was seldom, he ate the small, silver fish left in the mud by the failing river. He watched, with nearly chattering beak, the quick, thin lizards pause, very alert, and raise and lower themselves, but could not catch them because he had to raise his wings to move rapidly, which startled them.

Only one sight and sound not of his world of microscopic necessity was forced upon Hook. That was the flight of the big gulls from the beaches, which sometimes, in quealing play, came spinning back over the foothills and the river bed. For some inherited reason, the big, shipbodied birds did not frighten Hook, but angered him. Small and chewed-looking, with his wide, already yellowing eyes glaring up at them, he would stand in an open place on the sand in the sun and spread his shaping wings and clatter his bill like shaken dice. Hook was furious about the swift, easy passage of gulls.

His first opportunity to leave off living like a ground owl came accidentally. He was standing in the late afternoon in the red light under the thicket, his eyes half-filmed with drowse and the stupefaction of starvation, when suddenly something beside him moved, and he struck, and killed a field mouse driven out of the wheat by thirst. It was a poor mouse, shriveled and lice ridden, but in striking, Hook had tasted blood, which raised nest memories and restored his nature. With started neck plumage and shining eyes, he tore and fed. When the mouse was devoured, Hook had entered hoarse adolescence. He began to seek with a conscious appetite, and to move more readily out of shelter. Impelled by the blood appetite, so glorious after his long preservation upon the flaky and bitter stuff of bugs, he ventured even into the wheat in the open sun beyond the oaks, and discovered the small trails and holes among the roots. With his belly often partially filled with flesh, he grew rapidly in strength and will. His eyes were taking on their final change, their yellow growing deeper and more opaque, their stare more constant, their challenge less desperate. Once during this transformation, he surprised a ground squirrel, and although he was ripped and wingbitten and could not hold his prey, he was not dismayed by the conflict, but exalted. Even while the wing was still drooping and the pinions not grown back, he was excited by other ground squirrels and pursued them futilely, and was angered by their dusty escapes. He realized that his world was a great arena for killing, and felt the magnificence of it.

The two major events of Hook's young life occurred in the same day. A little after dawn he made the customary essay and succeeded in flight. A little before sunset, he made his first sustained flight of over two hundred yards, and at its termination struck and slew a great buck squirrel whose thrashing and terrified gnawing and squealing gave him a wild delight. When he had gorged on the strong meat, Hook stood upright, and in his eyes was the stare of the hawk, never flagging in intensity but never swelling beyond containment. After that the stare had only to grow more deeply challenging and more sternly controlled as his range and deadliness increased. There was no change in kind. Hook had mastered the first of the three hungers which are fused into the single, flaming will of a hawk, and he had experienced the second.

The third and consummating hunger did not awaken in Hook until the following spring, when the exultation of space had grown slow and steady in him, so that he swept freely with the wind over the miles of coastal foothills, circling, and ever in sight of the sea, and used without struggle the warm currents lifting from the slopes, and no longer desired to scream at the range of his vision, but intently sailed above his shadow swiftly climbing to meet him on the hillsides, sinking away and rippling across the brush-grown canyons.

That spring the rains were long, and Hook sat for hours, hunched and angry under their pelting, glaring into the fogs of the river valley, and killed only small, drenched things flooded up from their tunnels. But when the rains had dissipated, and there were sun and sea wind again, the game ran plentiful, the hills were thick and shining green, and the new river flooded about the boulders where battered turtles climbed up to shrink and sleep. Hook then was scorched by the third hunger. Ranging farther, often forgetting to kill and eat, he sailed for days with growing rage, and woke at night clattering on his dead tree limb, and struck and struck and struck at the porous wood of the trunk, tearing it away. After days, in the draft of a coastal canyon miles below his own hills, he came upon the acrid taint he did not know but had expected, and sailing down it, felt his neck plumes rise and his wings quiver so that he swerved unsteadily. He saw the unmated female perched upon the tall and jagged stump of a tree that had been shorn by storm, and he stooped, as if upon game. But she was older than he, and wary of the gripe of his importunity, and banked off screaming, and he screamed also at the intolerable delay.

At the head of the canyon, the screaming pursuit was crossed by another male with a great wing-spread, and the light golden in the fringe of his plumage. But his more skillful opening played him false against the ferocity of the twice-balked Hook. His rising maneuver for position was cut short by Hook's wild, upward swoop, and at the blow he raked desperately and tumbled off to the side. Dropping, Hook struck him again, struggled to clutch, but only raked and could not hold, and, diving, struck once more in passage, and then beat up, yelling triumph, and saw the crippled antagonist side-slip away, half-tumble once, as the ripped wing failed to balance, then steady and glide obliquely into the cover of brush on the canyon side. Beating hard and stationary in the wind above the bush that covered his competitor, Hook waited an instant, but when the bush was still, screamed again, and let himself go off with the current, reseeking, infuriated by the burn of his own wounds, the thin choke-thread of the acrid taint.

On a hilltop projection of stone two miles inland, he struck her down, gripping her rustling body with his talons, beating her wings down with his wings, belting her head when she whimpered or thrashed, and at last clutching her neck with his hook and, when her coy struggles had given way to stillness, succeeded.

In the early summer, Hook drove the three young ones from their nest, and went back to lone circling above his own range. He was complete.

## II

Throughout that summer and the cool, growthless weather of the winter, when the gales blew in the river canyon and the ocean piled upon the shore, Hook was master of the sky and the hills of his range. His flight became a lovely and certain thing, so that he played with the treacherous currents of the air with a delicate ease surpassing that of the gulls. He could sail for hours, searching the blanched grasses below him with telescopic eyes, gaining height against the wind, descending in mile-long, gently declining swoops when he curved and rode back, and never beating either wing. At the swift passage of his shadow within their vision, gophers, ground squirrels and rabbits froze, or plunged gibbering into their tunnels beneath matted turf. Now, when he struck, he killed easily in one hard-knuckled blow. Occasionally, in sport, he soared up over the river and drove the heavy and weaponless gulls downstream again, until they would no longer venture inland.

There was nothing which Hook feared now, and his spirit was wholly belligerent, swift and sharp, like his gaze. Only the mixed smells and incomprehensible activities of the people at the Japanese farmer's home, inland of the coastwise highway and south of the bridge across Hook's river, troubled him. The smells were strong, unsatisfactory and never clear, and the people, though they behaved foolishly, constantly running in and out of their built-up holes, were large, and appeared capable, with fearless eyes looking up at him, so that he instinctively swerved aside from them. He cruised over their yard, their gardens, and their bean fields, but he would not alight close to their buildings.

But this one area of doubt did not interfere with his life. He ignored it, save to look upon it curiously as he crossed, his afternoon shadow sliding in an instant over the chicken-and-crate-cluttered yard, up the side of the unpainted barn, and then out again smoothly, just faintly, liquidly rippling over the furrows and then over the stubble of the grazing slopes. When the season was dry, and the dead earth blew on the fields, he extended his range to satisfy his great hunger, and again narrowed it when the fields were once more alive with the minute movements he could not only see but anticipate.

Four times that year he was challenged by other hawks blowing up from behind the coastal hills to scud down his slopes, but two of these he slew in mid-air, and saw hurtle down to thump on the ground and lie still while he circled, and a third, whose wing he tore, he followed closely to earth and beat to death in the grass, making the crimson jet out from its breast and neck into the pale wheat. The fourth was a strong flier and experienced fighter, and theirs was a long, running battle, with brief, rising flurries of striking and screaming, from which down and plumage soared off.

Here, for the first time, Hook felt doubts, and at moments wanted to drop away from the scoring, burning talons and the twisted hammer strokes of the strong beak, drop away shrieking, and take cover and be still. In the end, when Hook, having outmaneuvered his enemy and come above him, wholly in control, and going with the wind, tilted and plunged for the death rap, the other, in desperation, threw over on his back and struck up. Talons locked, beaks raking, they dived earthward. The earth grew and spread under them amazingly, and they were not fifty feet above it when Hook, feeling himself turning toward the underside, tore free and beat up again on heavy, wrenched wings. The other, stroking swiftly, and so close to down that he lost wing plumes to a bush, righted himself and planed up, but flew on lumberingly between the hills and did not return. Hook screamed the triumph, and made a brief pretense of pursuit, but was glad to return, slow and victorious, to his dead tree.

In all these encounters Hook was injured, but experienced only the fighter's pride and exultation from the sting of wounds received in successful combat. And in each of them he learned new skill. Each time the wounds healed quickly, and left him a more dangerous bird.

In the next spring, when the rains and the night chants of the little frogs were past, the third hunger returned upon Hook with a new violence. In this quest, he came into the taint of a young hen. Others too were drawn by the unnerving perfume, but only one of them, the same with which Hook had fought his great battle, was a worthy competitor. This hunter drove off two, while two others, game but neophytes, were glad enough that Hook's impatience would not permit him to follow and kill. Then the battle between the two champions fled inland, and was a tactical marvel, but Hook lodged the neck-breaking blow, and struck again as they dropped past the treetops. The blood had already begun to pool on the gray, fallen foliage as Hook flapped up between branches, too spent to cry his victory. Yet his hunger would not let him rest until, late in the second day, he drove the female to ground among the laurels of a strange river canyon.

When the two fledglings of this second brood had been driven from the nest, and Hook had returned to his own range, he was not only complete, but supreme. He slept without concealment on his bare limb, and did not open his eyes when, in the night, the heavy-billed cranes coughed in the shallows below him.

### III

The turning point of Hook's career came that autumn, when the brush in the canyons rustled dryly and the hills, mowed close by the cattle, smoked under the wind as if burning. One midafternoon, when the black clouds were torn on the rim of the sea and the surf flowered white and high on the rocks, raining in over the low cliffs, Hook rode the wind diagonally across the river mouth. His great eyes, focused for small things, stirring in the dust and leaves, overlooked so large and slow a movement as that of the Japanese farmer rising from the brush and lifting the two black eyes of his shotgun. Too late Hook saw and, startled, swerved, but wrongly. The surf muffled the reports, and nearly without sound, Hook felt the minute whips of the first shot, and the astounding, breath-taking blow of the second.

Beating his good wing, tasting the blood that quickly swelled into his beak, he tumbled off with the wind and struck into the thickets on the far side of the river mouth. The branches tore him. Wild with rage, he thrust up and clattered his beak, challenging, but when he had fallen over twice, he knew that the trailing wing would not carry, and then heard the boots of the hunter among the stones in the river bed and, seeing him loom at the edge of the bushes, crept back among the thickest brush and was still. When he saw the boots stand before him, he reared back, lifting his good wing and cocking his head for the serpent-like blow, his beak open but soundless, his great eyes hard and very shining. The boots passed on. The Japanese farmer, who believed that he had lost chickens, and who had cunningly observed Hook's flight for many afternoons, until he could plot it, did not greatly want a dead hawk.

When Hook could hear nothing but the surf and the wind in the thicket, he let the sickness and shock overcome him. The fine film of the inner lid dropped over his big eyes. His heart beat frantically, so that it made the plumage of his shot-aching breast throb. His own blood throttled his breathing. But these things were nothing compared to the lightning of pain in his left shoulder, where the shot had bunched, shattering the airy bones so the pinions trailed on the ground and could not be lifted. Yet, when a sparrow lit in the bush over him, Hook's eyes flew open again, hard and challenging, his good wing was lifted and his beak strained open. The startled sparrow darted piping out over the river.

Throughout that night, while the long clouds blew across the stars and the wind shook the bushes about him, and throughout the next day, while the clouds still blew and massed until there was no gleam of sunlight on the sand bar, Hook remained stationary, enduring his sickness. In the second evening, the rains began. First there was a long, running patter of drops upon the beach and over the dry trees and bushes. At dusk there came a heavier squall, which did not die entirely, but slacked off to a continual, spaced splashing of big drops, and then returned with the front of the storm. In long, misty curtains, gust by gust, the rain swept over the sea, beating down its heaving, and coursed up the beach. The little jets of dust ceased to rise about the drops in the fields, and the mud began to gleam. Among the boulders of the river bed, darkling pools grew slowly.

Still Hook stood behind his tree from the wind, only gentle drops reaching him, falling from the upper branches and then again from the brush. His eyes remained closed, and he could still taste his own blood in his mouth, though it had ceased to come up freshly. Out beyond him, he heard the storm changing. As rain conquered the sea, the heave of the surf became a hushed sound, often lost in the crying of the wind. Then gradually, as the night turned toward morning, the wind also was broken by the rain. The crying became fainter, the rain settled toward steadiness, and the creep of the waves could be heard again, quiet and regular upon the beach.

At dawn there was no wind and no sun, but everywhere the roaring of the vertical, relentless rain. Hook then crept among the rapid drippings of the bushes, dragging his torn sail, seeking better shelter. He stopped often and stood with the shutters of film drawn over his eyes. At midmorning he found a little cave under a ledge at the base of the sea cliff. Here, lost without branches and leaves about him, he settled to await improvement.

When, at midday of the third day, the rain stopped altogether, and the sky opened before a small, fresh wind, letting light through to glitter upon a tremulous sea, Hook was so weak that his good wing trailed also to prop him upright, and his open eyes were lusterless. But his wounds were hardened, and he felt the return of hunger. Beyond his shelter, he heard the gulls flying in great numbers and crying their joy at the cleared air. He could even hear, from the fringe of the river, the ecstatic and unstinted bubblings and chirpings of the small birds. The grassland, he felt, would be full of the stirring anew of the close-bound life, the undrowned insects clicking as they dried out, the snakes slithering down, heads half erect, into the grasses where the mice, gophers and ground squirrels ran and stopped and chewed and licked themselves smoother and drier.

With the aid of his hunger, and on the crutches of his wings, Hook came down to stand in the sun beside his cave, whence he could watch the beach. Before him, in ellipses on tilting planes, the gulls flew. The surf was rearing again, and beginning to shelve and hiss on the sand. Through the white foam-writing it left, the long-billed pipers twinkled in bevies, escaping each wave, then racing down after it to plunge their fine drills into the minute double holes there the sand crabs bubbled. In the third row of breakers two seals lifted sleek, streaming heads and barked, and over them, trailing his spider legs, a great crane flew south. Among the stones at the foot of the cliff, small red and green crabs made a little, continuous rattling and knocking. The cliff swallows glittered and twanged on aerial forays.

The afternoon began auspiciously for Hook also. One of the two gulls which came squabbling above him dropped a freshly caught fish to the sand. Quickly Hook was upon it. Gripping it, he raised his good wing and cocked his head with open beak at the many gulls which had circled and come down at once toward the fall of the fish. The gulls sheered off, cursing raucously. Left alone on the sand, Hook devoured the fish and, after resting in the sun, withdrew again to his shelter.

## IV

In the succeeding days, between rains, he foraged on the beach. He learned to kill and crack the small green crabs. Along the edge of the river mouth, he found the drowned bodies of mice and squirrels and even sparrows. Twice he managed to drive feeding gulls from their catch, charging upon them with buffeting wing and clattering beak. He grew stronger slowly, but the shot sail continued to drag. Often, at the choking thought of soaring and striking and the good, hot-blood kill, he strove to take off, but only the one wing came up, winnowing with a hiss, and drove him over onto his side in the sand. After these futile trials, he would rage and clatter. But gradually he learned to believe that he could not fly, that his life must now be that of the discharged nestling again. Denied the joy of space, without which the joy of loneliness was lost, the joy of battle and killing, the blood lust, became his whole concentration. It was his hope, as he charged feeding gulls, that they would turn and offer battle, but they never did. The sandpipers, at his approach, fled peeping, or, like a quiver of arrows shot together, streamed out over the surf in a long curve. Once, pent beyond bearing, he disgraced himself by shrieking challenge at the businesslike heron which flew south every evening at the same time. The heron did not even turn his head, but flapped and glided on.

Hook's shame and anger became such that he stood awake at night. Hunger kept him awake also, for these little leavings of the gulls could not sustain his great body in its renewed violence. He became aware that the gulls slept at night in flocks on the sand, each with one leg tucked under him. He discovered also that the curlews and the pipers, often mingling, likewise slept, on the higher remnant of the bar. A sensation of evil delight filled him in the consideration of protracted striking among them.

There was only half of a sick moon in a sky of running but far-separated clouds on the night when he managed to stalk into the center of the sleeping gulls. This was light enough, but so great was his vengeful pleasure that there broke from him a shrill scream of challenge as he first struck. Without the power of flight behind it, the blow was not murderous, and this newly discovered impotence made Hook crazy, so that he screamed again and again as he struck and tore at the felled gull. He slew the one, but was twice knocked over by its heavy flounderings, and all the others rose above him, weaving and screaming, protesting in the thin moonlight. Wakened by their clamor, the wading birds also took wing, startled and plaintive. When the beach was quiet again, the flocks had settled elsewhere, beyond his pitiful range, and he was left alone beside the single kill. It was a disappointing victory. He fed with lowering spirit.

Thereafter, he stalked silently. At sunset he would watch where the gulls settled along the miles of beach, and after dark he would come like a sharp shadow among them, and drive with his hook on all sides of him, till the beatings of a poorly struck victim sent the flock up. Then he would turn vindictively upon the fallen and finish them. In his best night, he killed five from one flock. But he ate only a little from one, for the vigor resulting from occasional repletion strengthened only his ire, which became so great at such a time that food revolted him. It was not the joyous, swift, controlled hunting anger of a sane hawk, but something quite different, which made him dizzy if it continued too long, and left him unsatisfied with any kill.

Then one day, when he had very nearly struck a gull while driving it from a gasping yellowfin, the gull's wing rapped against him as it broke for its running start, and, the trailing wing failing to support him, he was knocked over. He flurried awkwardly in the sand to regain his feet, but his mastery of the beach was ended. Seeing him, in clear sunlight, struggling after the chance blow, the gulls returned about him in a flashing cloud, circling and pecking on the wing. Hook's plumage showed quick little jets of irregularity here and there. He reared back, clattering and erecting the good wing, spreading the great, rusty tail for balance. His eyes shone with a little of the old pleasure. But it died, for he could reach none of them. He was forced to turn and dance awkwardly on the sand, trying to clash bills with each tormentor. They banked up quealing and returned, weaving about him in concentric and overlapping circles. His scream was lost in their clamor, and he appeared merely to be hopping clumsily with his mouth open. Again he fell sideways. Before he could right himself, he was bowled over, and a second time, and lay on his side, twisting his neck to reach them and clappering in blind fury, and was struck three times by three successive gulls, shrieking their flock triumph.

Finally he managed to roll to his breast, and to crouch with his good wing spread wide and the other stretched nearly as far, so that he extended like a gigantic moth, only his snake head, with its now silent scimitar, erect. One great eye blazed under its level brow, but where the other had been was a shallow hole from which thin blood trickled to his russet gap.

In this crouch, by short stages, stopping repeatedly to turn and drive the gulls up, Hook dragged into the river canyon and under the stiff cover of the bitter-leafed laurel. There the gulls left him, soaring up with great clatter of their valor. Till nearly sunset Hook, broken spirited and enduring his hardening eye socket, heard them celebrating over the waves.

When his will was somewhat replenished, and his empty eye socket had stopped the twitching and vague aching which had forced him often to roll ignominiously to rub it in the dust, Hook ventured from the protective lacings of his thicket. He knew fear again, and the challenge of his remaining eye was once more strident, as in adolescence. He dared not return to the beaches, and with a new, weak hunger, the home hunger, enticing him, made his way by short hunting journeys back to the wild wheat slopes and the crisp oaks. There was in Hook an unwonted sensation now, that of the ever-neighboring possibility of death. This sensation was beginning, after his period as a mad bird on the beach, to solidify him into his last stage of life. When, during his slow homeward passage, the gulls wafted inland over him, watching the earth with curious, miserish eyes, he did not cower, but neither did he challenge, either by opened beak or by raised shoulder. He merely watched carefully, learning his first lessons in observing the world with one eye.

At first the familiar surroundings of the bend in the river and the tree with the dead limb to which he could not ascend, aggravated his humiliation, but in time, forced to live cunningly and half-starved, he lost much of his savage pride. At the first flight of a strange hawk over his realm, he was wild at his helplessness, and kept twisting his head like an owl, or spinning in the grass like a small and feathered dervish, to keep the hateful beauty of the wind-rider in sight. But in the succeeding weeks, as one after another coasted his beat, his resentment declined, and when one of the raiders, a haughty year-ling, sighted his upstaring eye, and plunged and struck him dreadfully, and failed to kill him only because he dragged under a thicket in time, the second of his great hungers was gone. He had no longer the true lust to kill, no joy of battle, but only the poor desire to fill his belly.

Then truly he lived in the wheat and the brush like a ground owl, ridden with ground lice, dusty or muddy, ever half-starved, forced to sit for hours by small holes for petty and unsatisfying kills. Only once during the final months before his end did he make a kill where the breath of danger recalled his valor, and then the danger was such as a hawk with wings and eyes would scorn. Waiting beside a gopher hole, surrounded by the high, yellow grass, he saw the head emerge, and struck, and was amazed that there writhed in his clutch the neck and dusty coffin-skull of a rattlesnake. Holding his grip, Hook saw the great, thick body slither up after, the tip an erect, strident blur, and writhe on the dirt of the gopher's mound. The weight of the snake pushed Hook about, and once threw him down, and the rising and falling whine of the rattles made the moment terrible, but the vaulted mouth, gap-ing from the closeness of Hook's grip, so that the pale, envenomed sabers stood out free, could not reach him. When Hook replaced the grip of his beak with the grip of his talons, and was free to strike again and again at the base of the head, the struggle was over. Hook tore and fed on the fine, wat-ery flesh, and left the tattered armor and the long, jointed bone for the marching ants.

When the heavy rains returned, he ate well during the period of the first escapes from flooded burrows, and then well enough, in a vulture's way, on the drowned creatures. But as the rains lingered, and the burrows hung full of water, and there were no insects in the grass and no small birds sleeping in the thickets, he was constantly hungry, and finally unbearably hungry. His sodden and ground-broken plumage stood out raggedly about him, so that he looked fat, even bloated, but underneath it his skin clung to his bones. Save for his great talons and clappers, and the rain in his down, he would have been like a handful of air. He often stood for a long time under some bush or ledge, heedless of the drip, his one eye filmed over, his mind neither asleep or awake, but between. The gurgle and swirl of the brimming river, and the sound of chunks of the bank cut away to splash and dissolve in the already muddy flood, became familiar to him, and yet a torment, as if that great, ceaselessly working power of water ridiculed his frailty, within which only the faintest spark of valor still glimmered. The last two nights before the rain ended, he huddled under the floor of the bridge on the coastal highway, and heard the palpitant thunder of motors swell and roar over him. The trucks shook the bridge so that Hook, even in his famished lassitude, would sometimes open his one great eye wide and startled.

## V

After the rains, when things became full again, bursting with growth and sound, the trees swelling, the thickets full of song and chatter, the fields, turning green in the sun, alive with rustling passages, and the moonlit nights strained with the song of the peepers all up and down the river and in the pools in the fields, Hook had to bear the return of the one hunger left him. At times this made him so wild that he forgot himself and screamed challenge from the open ground. The fretfulness of it spoiled his hunting, which was not entirely a matter of patience. Once he was in despair, and lashed himself through the grass and thickets, trying to rise when that virgin scent drifted for a few moments above the current of his own river. Then, breathless, his beak agape, he saw the strong suitor ride swiftly down on the wind over him, and heard afar the screaming fuss of the harsh wooing in the alders. For that moment even the battle heart beat in him again. The rim of his good eye was scarlet, and a little bead of new blood stood in the socket of the other. With beak and talon, he ripped at a fallen log, and made loam and leaves fly from about it.

But the season of love passed over to the nesting season, and Hook's love hunger, unused, shriveled in him with the others, and there remained in him only one stern quality befitting a hawk, and that the negative one, the remnant, the will to endure. He resumed his patient, plotted hunting, now along a field of the Japanese farmer, but ever within reach of the river thickets.

Growing tough and dry again as the summer advanced, inured to the family of the farmer, whom he saw daily, stooping and scraping with sticks in the ugly, open rows of their fields, where no lovely grass rustled and no life stirred save the shameless gulls, which walked at the heels of the workers, gobbling the worms and grubs they turned up, Hook became nearly content with his shard of life. The only longing or resentment to pierce him was that which he suffered occasionally when forced to hide at the edge of the mile-long bean field from the wafted cruising and the restive, down-bent gaze of one of his own kind. For the rest, he was without flame, a snappish, dust-colored creature, fading into the grasses he trailed through, and suited to his petty ways.

At the end of that summer, for the second time in his four years, Hook underwent a drouth. The equinoctial period passed without a rain. The laurel and the rabbit-brush dropped dry leaves. The foliage of the oaks shriveled and curled. Even the night fogs in the river canyon failed. The farmer's red cattle on the hillside lowed constantly, and could not feed on the dusty stubble. Grass fires broke out along the highways, and ate fast in the wind, filling the hollows with the smell of smoke, and died in the dirt of the shorn hills. The river made no sound. Scum grew on its vestigial pools, and turtles died and stank among the rocks. The dust rode before the wind, and ascended and flowered to nothing between the hills, and every sunset was red with the dust in the air. The people in the farmer's house quarreled, and even struck one another. Birds were silent, and only the hawks flew much. The animals lay breathing hard for very long spells, and ran and crept jerkily. Their flanks were fallen in, and their eyes were red.

At first Hook gorged at the fringe of the grass fires on the multitudes of tiny things that came running and squeaking. But thereafter there were the blackened strips on the hills, and little more in the thin, crackling grass. He found mice and rats, gophers and ground-squirrels, and even rabbits, dead in the stubble and under the thickets, but so dry and fleshless that only a faint smell rose from them, even on the sunny days. He starved on them. By early December he had wearily stalked the length of the eastern foothills, hunting at night to escape the voracity of his own kind, resting often upon his wings. The queer trail of his short steps and great horned toes zigzagged in the dust and was erased by the wind at dawn. He was nearly dead, and could make no sound through the horn funnels of his clappers.

Then one night the dry wind brought him, with the familiar, lifeless dust, another familiar scent, troublesome, mingled and unclear. In his vision-dominated brain he remembered the swift circle of his flight a year past, crossing in one segment, his shadow beneath him, a yard cluttered with crates and chickens, a gray barn and then again the plowed land and the stubble. Traveling faster than he had for days, impatient of his shrunken sweep, Hook came down to the farm. In the dark wisps of cloud blown among the stars over him, but no moon, he stood outside the wire of the chicken run. The scent of fat and blooded birds reached him from the shelter, and also within the enclosure was water. At the breath of the water, Hook's gorge contracted, and his tongue quivered and clove in its groove of horn. But there was the wire. He stalked its perimeter and found no opening. He beat it with his good wing, and felt it cut but not give. He wrenched at it with his beak in many places, but could not tear it. Finally, in a fury which drove the thin blood through him, he leaped repeatedly against it, beating and clawing. He was thrown back from the last leap as from the first, but in it he had risen so high as to clutch with his beak at the top wire. While he lay on his breast on the ground, the significance of this came upon him.

Again he leapt, clawed up the wire, and, as he would have fallen, made even the dead wing bear a little. He grasped the top and tumbled within. There again he rested flat, searching the dark with quick-turning head.

There was no sound or motion but the throb of his own body. First he drank at the chill metal trough hung for the chickens. The water was cold, and loosened his tongue and his tight throat, but it also made him drunk and dizzy, so that he had to rest again, his claws spread wide to brace him. Then he walked stiffly, to stalk down the scent. He trailed it up the runway. Then there was the stuffy, body-warm air, acrid with droppings, full of soft rustlings as his talons clicked on the board floor. The thick, white shapes showed faintly in the darkness. Hook struck quickly, driving a hen to the floor with one blow, its neck broken and stretched out stringily. He leaped the still pulsing body, and tore it. The rich, streaming blood was overpowering to his dried senses, his starved, leathery body. After a few swallows, the flesh choked him. In his rage, he struck down another hen. The urge to kill took him again, as in those nights on the beach. He could let nothing go. Balked of feeding, he was compelled to slaughter. Clattering, he struck again and again. The henhouse was suddenly filled with the squawking and helpless rushing and buffeting of the terrified, brainless fowls.

Hook reveled in mastery. Here was game big enough to offer weight against a strike, and yet unable to soar away from his blows. Turning in the midst of the turmoil, cannily, his fury caught at the perfect pitch, he struck unceasingly. When the hens finally discovered the outlet, and streamed into the yard, to run around the fence, beating and squawking, Hook followed them, scraping down the incline, clumsy and joyous. In the yard, the cock, a bird as large as he, and much heavier, found him out and gave valiant battle. In the dark, and both earthbound, there was little skill, but blow upon blow, and only chance parry. The still squawking hens pressed into one corner of the yard. While the duel went on, a dog, excited by the sustained scuffling, began to bark. He continued to bark, running back and forth along the fence on one side. A light flashed on in an uncurtained window of the farmhouse, and streamed whitely over the crates littering the ground.

Enthralled by his old battle joy, Hook knew only the burly cock before him. Now, in the farthest reach of the window light, they could see each other dimly. The Japanese farmer, with his gun and lantern, was already at the gate when the finish came. The great cock leapt to jab with his spurs and, toppling forward with extended neck as he fell, was struck and extinguished. Blood had loosened Hook's throat. Shrilly he cried his triumph. It was a thin and exhausted cry, but within him as good as when he shrilled in mid-air over the plummeting descent of a fine foe in his best spring.

The light from the lantern partially blinded Hook. He first turned and ran directly from it, into the corner where the hens were huddled. They fled apart before his charge. He essayed the fence, and on the second try, in his desperation, was out. But in the open dust, the dog was on him, circling, dashing in, snapping. The farmer, who at first had not fired because of the chickens, now did not fire because of the dog, and, when he saw that the hawk was unable to fly, relinquished the sport to the dog, holding the lantern up in order to see better. The light showed his own flat, broad, dark face as sunken also, the cheekbones very prominent, and showed the torn-off sleeves of his shirt and the holes in the knees of his overalls. His wife, in a stained wrapper, and barefooted, heavy black hair hanging around a young, passionless face, joined him hesitantly, but watched, fascinated and a little horrified. His son joined them too, encouraging the dog, but quickly grew silent. Courageous and cruel death, however it may afterward sicken the one who has watched it, is impossible to look away from.

In the circle of the light, Hook turned to keep the dog in front of him. His one eye gleamed with malevolence. The dog was an Airedale, and large. Each time he pounced, Hook stood ground, raising his good wing, the pinions newly torn by the fence, opening his beak soundlessly, and, at the closest approach, hissed furiously, and at once struck. Hit and ripped twice by the whetted horn, the dog recoiled more quickly from several subsequent jumps and, infuriated by his own cowardice, began to bark wildly. Hook maneuvered to watch him, keeping his head turned to avoid losing the foe on the blind side. When the dog paused, safely away, Hook watched him quietly, wing partially lowered, beak closed, but at the first move again lifted the wing and gaped. The dog whined, and the man spoke to him encouragingly. The awful sound of his voice made Hook for an instant twist his head to stare up at the immense figures behind the light. The dog again sallied, barking, and Hook's head spun back. His wing was bitten this time, and with a furious sideblow, he caught the dog's nose. The dog dropped him with a yelp, and then, smarting, came on more warily, as Hook propped himself up from the ground again between his wings. Hook's artificial strength was waning, but his heart still stood to the battle, sustained by a fear of such dimension as he had never known before, but only anticipated when the arrogant young hawk had driven him to cover. The dog, unable to find any point at which the merciless, unwinking eye was not watching him, the parted beak waiting, paused and whimpered again.

"Oh, kill the poor thing," the woman begged.

The man, though, encouraged the dog again, saying, "Sick him; sick him."

The dog rushed bodily. Unable to avoid him, Hook was bowled down, snapping and raking. He left long slashes, as from the blade of a knife, on the dog's flank, but before he could right himself and assume guard again, was caught by the good wing and dragged, clattering, and seeking to make a good stroke from his back. The man followed them to keep the light on them, and the boy went with him, wetting his lips with his tongue and keeping his fists closed tightly. The woman remained behind, but could not help watching the diminished conclusion.

In the little, palely shining arena, the dog repeated his successful maneuver three times, growling but not barking, and when Hook thrashed up from the third blow, both wings were trailing, and dark, shining streams crept on his black-fretted breast from the shoulders. The great eye flashed more furiously than it ever had in victorious battle, and the beak still gaped, but there was no more clatter. He faltered when turning to keep front; the broken wings played him false even as props. He could not rise to use his talons.

The man had tired of holding the lantern up, and put it down to rub his arm. In the low, horizontal light, the dog charged again, this time throwing the weight of his forepaws against Hook's shoulder, so that Hook was crushed as he struck. With his talons up, Hook raked at the dog's belly, but the dog conceived the finish, and furiously worried the feathered bulk. Hook's neck went limp, and between his gaping clappers came only a faint chittering, as from some small kill of his own in the grasses.

In this last conflict, however, there had been some minutes of the supreme fire of the hawk whose three hungers are perfectly fused in the one will; enough to burn off a year of shame.

Between the great sails the light body lay caved and perfectly still. The dog, smarting from his cuts, came to the master and was praised. The woman, joining them slowly, looked at the great wingspread, her husband raising the lantern that she might see it better.

"Oh, the brave bird," she said.

### STUDY QUESTIONS

1. Audubon's "Wild Turkey" is an excellent piece of expository prose. Clark's "Hook" is a short story. What obvious differences can you point out?

2. Clark's story is divided into five sections. What major development of plot occurs in each of these sections?

3. How are Sections I and IV related?

4. When does Clark provide the first suggestion of Hook's approaching confrontation with the gulls? With the Japanese farmer?

5. In Section III, why does the farmer permit the hawk to live?

6. How do the reactions of the farmer and his wife to Hook's battle with the dog differ?

Loren C. Eiseley

# THE BIRD AND THE MACHINE

Loren Eiseley (1907–    ) was born in Lincoln, Nebraska. He received his B.A. (1933) from the University of Nebraska, and his M.A. (1935) and Ph.D. (1937) from the University of Pennsylvania. He taught at the University of Kansas and Oberlin College before returning, in 1947, to the University of Pennsylvania where he is now University Professor in anthropology and history of science and head of the Department of the History and Philosophy of Science. A Guggenheim fellow, he has published widely in both popular periodicals and learned journals. *Darwin's Century* was given the Phi Beta Kappa science award in 1959, and *The Firmament of Time* (1960) received the John Burroughs medal and the Lecomte de Nouy award. His other books include *The Immense Journey* (1951), *Francis Bacon and the Modern Temper* (1952), and *Galapagos: The Flow of Wilderness* (1968).

I SUPPOSE THEIR little bones have years ago been lost among the stones and winds of those high glacial pastures. I suppose their feathers blew eventually into the piles of tumbleweed beneath the straggling cattle fences and rotted there in the mountain snows, along with dead steers and all the other things that drift to an end in the corners of the wire. I do not quite know why I should be thinking of birds over the *New York Times* at breakfast, particularly the birds of my youth half a continent away. It is a funny thing what the brain will do with memories and how it will treasure them and finally bring them into odd juxtapositions with other things, as though it wanted to make a design, or get some meaning out of them, whether you want it or not, or even see it.

It used to seem marvelous to me, but I read now that there are machines that can do these things in a small way, machines that can crawl about like animals, and that it may not be long now until they do more things—maybe even make themselves—I saw that piece in the *Times* just now. And then they will, maybe—well, who knows—but you read about it more and more with no one making any protest, and already they can add better than we and reach up and hear things through the dark and finger the guns over the night sky.

This is the new world that I read about at breakfast. This is the world that confronts me in my biological books and journals, until there are times when I sit quietly in my chair and try to hear the little purr of the cogs in my head and the tubes flaring and dying as the messages go through them and the circuits snap shut or open. This is the great age, make no mistake about it; the robot has been born somewhat appropriately along with the atom bomb, and the brain they say now is just another type of more complicated feedback system. The engineers have its basic principles worked out; it's mechanical, you know; nothing to get superstitious about; and man can always improve on nature once he gets the idea. Well, he's got it all right and that's why, I guess, that I sit here in my chair, with the article crunched in my hand, remembering those two birds and that blue mountain sunlight. There is another magazine article on my desk that reads "Machines Are Getting Smarter Every Day." I don't deny it, but I'll still stick with the birds. It's life I believe in, not machines.

Maybe you don't believe there is any difference. A skeleton is all joints and pulleys, I'll admit. And when man was in his simpler stages of machine building in the eighteenth century, he quickly saw the resemblances. "What," wrote Hobbes, "is the heart but a spring, and the nerves but so many strings, and the joints but so many wheels, giving motion to the whole body?" Tinkering about in their shops it was inevitable in the end that men would see the world as a huge machine "subdivided into an infinite number of lesser machines."

The idea took on with a vengeance. Little automatons toured the country —dolls controlled by clockwork. Clocks described as little worlds were taken on tours by their designers. They were made up of moving figures, shifting scenes and other remarkable devices. The life of the cell was unknown. Man, whether he was conceived as possessing a soul or not, moved and jerked about like these tiny puppets. A human being thought of himself in terms of his own tools and implements. He had been fashioned like the puppets he produced and was only a more clever model made by a greater designer.

Then in the nineteenth century, the cell was discovered, and the single machine in its turn was found to be the product of millions of infinitesimal machines—the cells. Now, finally, the cell itself dissolves away into an abstract chemical machine—and that into some intangible, inexpressible flow of energy. The secret seems to lurk all about, the wheels get smaller and smaller, and they turn more rapidly, but when you try to seize it the life is gone—and so, by popular definition, some would say that life was never there in the first place. The wheels and the cogs are the secret and we can make them better in time—machines that will run faster and more accurately than real mice to real cheese.

I have no doubt it can be done, though a mouse harvesting seeds on an autumn thistle is to me a fine sight and more complicated, I think, in his multiform activity, than a machine "mouse" running a maze. Also, I like to think of the possible shape of the future brooding in mice, just as it brooded once in a rather ordinary mousy insectivore who became a man. It leaves a nice fine indeterminate sense of wonder that even an electronic brain hasn't got, because you know perfectly well that if the electronic brain changes, it will be because of something man has done to it. But what man will do to himself he doesn't really know. A certain scale of time and a ghostly intangible thing called change are ticking in him. Powers and potentialities like the oak in the seed, or a red and awful ruin. Either way, it's impressive; and the mouse has it, too. Or those birds, I'll never forget those birds—yet before I measured their significance, I learned the lesson of time first of all. I was young then and left alone in a great desert—part of an expedition that had scattered its men over several hundred miles in order to carry on research more effectively. I learned there that time is a series of planes existing superficially in the same universe. The tempo is a human illusion, a subjective clock ticking in our own kind of protoplasm.

As the long months passed, I began to live on the slower planes and to observe more readily what passed for life there. I sauntered, I passed more and more slowly up and down the canyons in the dry baking heat of midsummer. I slumbered for long hours in the shade of huge brown boulders that had gathered in tilted companies out on the flats. I had forgotten the world of men and the world had forgotten me. Now and then I found a skull in the canyons, and these justified my remaining there. I took a serene cold interest in these discoveries. I had come, like many a naturalist before me, to view life with a wary and subdued attention. I had grown to take pleasure in the divested bone.

I sat once on a high ridge that fell away before me into a waste of sand dunes. I sat through hours of a long afternoon. Finally, as I glanced beside my boot an indistinct configuration caught my eye. It was a coiled rattlesnake, a big one. How long he had sat with me I do not know. I had not frightened him. We were both locked in the sleepwalking tempo of the earlier world, baking in the same high air and sunshine. Perhaps he had been there when I came. He slept on as I left, his coils, so ill discerned by me, dissolving once more among the stones and gravel from which I had barely made him out.

Another time I got on a higher ridge, among some tough little windwarped pines half covered over with sand in a basin-like depression that

caught everything carried by the air up to those heights. There were a few
thin bones of birds, some cracked shells of indeterminable age, and the
knotty fingers of pine roots bulged out of shape from their long and agoniz-
ing grasp upon the crevices of the rock. I lay under the pines in the sparse
shade and went to sleep once more.

It grew cold finally, for autumn was in the air by then, and the few things
that lived thereabouts were sinking down into an even chillier scale of time.
In the moments between sleeping and waking I saw the roots about me and
slowly, slowly, a foot in what seemed many centuries, I moved my sleep-
stiffened hands over the scaling bark and lifted my numbed face after the
vanishing sun. I was a great awkward thing of knots and aching limbs,
trapped up there in some long, patient endurance that involved the necessity
of putting living fingers into rock and by slow, aching expansion bursting
those rocks asunder. I suppose, so thin and slow was the time of my pulse by
then, that I might have stayed on to drift still deeper into the lower cadences
of the frost, or the crystalline life that glistens pebbles, or shines in a snow-
flake, or dreams in the meteoric iron between the worlds.

It was a dim descent, but time was present in it. Somewhere far down in
that scale the notion struck me that one might come the other way. Not many
months thereafter I joined some colleagues heading higher into a remote
windy tableland where huge bones were reputed to protrude like boulders
from the turf. I had drowsed with reptiles and moved with the century-long
pulse of trees; now, lethargically, I was climbing back up some invisible
ladder of quickening hours. There had been talk of birds in connection with
my duties. Birds are intense, fast-living creatures—reptiles, I suppose one
might say, that have escaped out of the heavy sleep of time, transformed
fairy creatures dancing over sunlit meadows. It is a youthful fancy, no
doubt, but because of something that happened up there among the escarp-
ments of that range, it remains with me a lifelong impression. I can never
bear to see a bird imprisoned.

We came into that valley through the trailing mists of a spring night. It
was a place that looked as though it might never have known the foot of
man, but our scouts had been ahead of us and we knew all about the abandoned cabin of stone that lay far up on one hillside. It had been built in the
land rush of the last century and then lost to the cattlemen again as the marginal soils failed to take to the plow.

There were spots like this all over that country. Lost graves marked by
unlettered stones and old corroding rim-fire cartridge cases lying where
somebody had made a stand among the boulders that rimmed the valley.
They are all that remain of the range wars; the men are under the stones
now. I could see our cavalcade winding in and out through the mist below
us: torches, the reflection of the truck lights on our collecting tins, and the
far-off bumping of a loose dinosaur thigh bone in the bottom of a trailer. I

stood on a rock a moment looking down and thinking what it cost in money and equipment to capture the past.

We had, in addition, instructions to lay hands on the present. The word had come through to get them alive—birds, reptiles, anything. A zoo somewhere abroad needed restocking. It was one of those reciprocal matters in which science involves itself. Maybe our museum needed a stray ostrich egg and this was the payoff. Anyhow, my job was to help capture some birds and that was why I was there before the trucks.

The cabin had not been occupied for years. We intended to clean it out and live in it, but there were holes in the roof and the birds had come in and were roosting in the rafters. You could depend on it in a place like this where everything blew away, and even a bird needed some place out of the weather and away from coyotes. A cabin going back to nature in a wild place draws them till they come in, listening at the eaves, I imagine, pecking softly among the shingles till they find a hole and then suddenly the place is theirs and man is forgotten.

Sometimes of late years I find myself thinking the most beautiful sight in the world might be the birds taking over New York after the last man has run away to the hills. I will never live to see it, of course, but I know just how it will sound because I've lived up high and I know the sort of watch birds keep on us. I've listened to sparrows tapping tentatively on the outside of air conditioners when they thought no one was listening, and I know how other birds test the vibrations that come up to them through the television aerials.

"Is he gone?" they ask, and the vibrations come up from below, "Not yet, not yet."

Well, to come back, I got the door open softly and I had the spotlight all ready to turn on and blind whatever birds there were so they couldn't see to get out through the roof. I had a short piece of ladder to put against the far wall where there was a shelf on which I expected to make the biggest haul. I had all the information I needed just like any skilled assassin. I pushed the door open, the hinges squeaking only a little. A bird or two stirred—I could hear them—but nothing flew and there was a faint starlight through the holes in the roof.

I padded across the floor, got the ladder up and the light ready, and slithered up the ladder till my head and arms were over the shelf. Everything was dark as pitch except for the starlight at the little place back of the shelf near the eaves. With the light to blind them, they'd never make it. I had them. I reached my arm carefully over in order to be ready to seize whatever was there and I put the flash on the edge of the shelf where it would stand by itself when I turned it on. That way I'd be able to use both hands.

Everything worked perfectly except for one detail—I didn't know what kind of birds were there. I never thought about it at all, and it wouldn't have mattered if I had. My orders were to get something interesting. I snapped on the flash and sure enough there was a great beating and feathers flying, but instead of my having them, they, or rather he, had me. He had my hand, that is, and for a small hawk not much bigger than my fist he was doing all right. I heard him give one short metallic cry when the light went on and my hand descended on the bird beside him; after that he was busy with his claws and his beak was sunk in my thumb. In the struggle I knocked the lamp over on the shelf, and his mate got her sight back and whisked neatly through the hole in the roof and off among the stars outside. It all happened in fifteen seconds and you might think I would have fallen down the ladder, but no, I had a professional assassin's reputation to keep up, and the bird, of course, made the mistake of thinking the hand was the enemy and not the eyes behind it. He chewed my thumb up pretty effectively and lacerated my hand with his claws, but in the end I got him, having two hands to work with.

He was a sparrow hawk and a fine young male in the prime of life. I was sorry not to catch the pair of them, but as I dripped blood and folded his wings carefully, holding him by the back so that he couldn't strike again, I had to admit the two of them might have been more than I could have handled under the circumstances. The little fellow had saved his mate by diverting me, and that was that. He was born to it, and made no outcry now, resting in my hand hopelessly, but peering toward me in the shadows behind the lamp with a fierce, almost indifferent glance. He neither gave nor expected mercy and something out of the high air passed from him to me, stirring a faint embarrassment.

I quit looking into that eye and managed to get my huge carcass with its fist full of prey back down the ladder. I put the bird in a box too small to allow him to injure himself by struggle and walked out to welcome the arriving trucks. It had been a long day, and camp still to make in the darkness. In the morning that bird would be just another episode. He would go back with the bones in the truck to a small cage in a city where he would spend the rest of his life. And a good thing, too. I sucked my aching thumb and spat out some blood. An assassin has to get used to these things. I had a professional reputation to keep up.

In the morning, with the change that comes on suddenly in that high country, the mist that had hovered below us in the valley was gone. The sky was a deep blue, and one could see for miles over the high outcroppings of stone. I was up early and brought the box in which the little hawk was imprisoned out onto the grass where I was building a cage. A wind as cool as a mountain spring ran over the grass and stirred my hair. It was a fine day to be alive. I looked up and all around and at the hole in the cabin roof out of which the other little hawk had fled. There was no sign of her anywhere that I could see.

"Probably in the next county by now," I thought cynically, but before beginning work I decided I'd have a look at my last night's capture.

Secretively, I looked again all around the camp and up and down and opened the box. I got him right out in my hand with his wings folded properly and I was careful not to startle him. He lay limp in my grasp and I could feel his heart pound under the feathers but he only looked beyond me and up.

I saw him look that last look away beyond me into a sky so full of light that I could not follow his gaze. The little breeze flowed over me again, and nearby a mountain aspen shook all its tiny leaves. I suppose I must have had an idea then of what I was going to do, but I never let it come up into consciousness. I just reached over and laid the hawk on the grass.

He lay there a long minute without hope, unmoving, his eyes still fixed on that blue vault above him. It must have been that he was already so far away in heart that he never felt the release from my hand. He never even stood. He just lay with his breast against the grass.

In the next second after that long minute he was gone. Like a flicker of light, he had vanished with my eyes full on him, but without actually seeing even a premonitory wing beat. He was gone straight into that towering emptiness of light and crystal that my eyes could scarcely bear to penetrate. For another long moment there was silence. I could not see. The light was too intense. Then from far up somewhere a cry came ringing down.

I was young then and had seen little of the world, but when I heard that cry my heart turned over. It was not the cry of the hawk I had captured; for, by shifting my position against the sun, I was now seeing further up. Straight out of the sun's eye, where she must have been soaring restlessly above us for untold hours, hurtled his mate. And from far up, ringing from peak to peak of the summits over us, came a cry of such unutterable and ecstatic joy that it sounds down across the years and tingles among the cups on my quiet breakfast table.

I saw them both now. He was rising fast to meet her. They met in a great soaring gyre that turned to a whirling circle and a dance of wings. Once more, just once, their two voices, joined in a harsh wild medley of question and response, struck and echoed against the pinnacles of the valley. Then they were gone forever somewhere into those upper regions beyond the eyes of men.

I am older now, and sleep less, and I have seen most of what there is to see and am not very much impressed any more, I suppose, by anything. "What Next in the Attributes of Machines?" my morning headline runs. "It Might Be the Power to Reproduce Themselves."

I lay the paper down and across my mind a phrase floats insinuatingly: "It does not seem that there is anything in the construction, constituents, or behavior of the human being which it is essentially impossible for science to duplicate and synthesize. On the other hand . . . ."

All over the city the cogs in the hard, bright mechanisms have begun to turn. Figures move through computers, names are spelled out, a thoughtful machine selects the fingerprints of a wanted criminal from an array of thousands. In the laboratory an electronic mouse runs swiftly through a maze toward the cheese it can neither taste nor enjoy. On the second run it does better than a living mouse.

"On the other hand . . ." Ah, my mind takes up, on the other hand the machine does not bleed, ache, hang for hours in the empty sky in a torment of hope to learn the fate of another machine, nor does it cry out with joy nor dance in the air with the fierce passion of a bird. Far off, over a distance greater than space, that remote cry from the heart of heaven makes a faint buzzing among my breakfast dishes and passes on and away.

## STUDY QUESTIONS

1. If any one sentence can be called the thesis sentence of this essay, which sentence is it? How effective is the transition between this sentence and the paragraph following it?

2. The introduction to this essay is set off from the body of the essay by extra spacing. Why isn't the conclusion similarly set off?

3. This essay is entitled "The Bird and the Machine." Does the essay compare birds and machines? Contrast them? Both compare and contrast them? What is the relationship of the episode of the bird to the thesis sentence?

4. What is your reaction to the conversation between the sparrows and the vibrations? Is Eiseley there too "cute"?

5. Why is Eiseley slightly embarrassed by the bird's glance? Why does he say, "I quit looking into that eye . . ." instead of "those eyes"?

*Joseph Wood Krutch*

# HE WAS THERE BEFORE CORONADO

Joseph Wood Krutch (1893–      ) was born in Knoxville, Tennessee. He received his B.A. (1915) from the University of Tennessee and his M.A. (1916) and Ph.D. (1932) from Columbia University. He has taught English, journalism, and drama at Columbia; lectured at the New School for Research; served as drama critic for the *Nation;* and acted as president of the New York Drama Critics Circle. Krutch now lives in Tucson, Arizona, and is a trustee of the Arizona–Sonora Desert Museum. He has edited the works of William Congreve, Eugene O'Neill, Marcel Proust, and Thomas Gray; and written critical studies of Restoration comedy, and of Samuel Johnson, Edgar Allan Poe, and Henry David Thoreau. Other books include *The Modern Temper* (1929), *The Desert Year* (1952), *The Measure of Man* (1954), *Grand Canyon* (1958), and the revised *Baja California, and the Geography of Hope* (1969).

A̲CCORDING to an ancient and anonymous jocosity the bravest man who ever lived must have been the first to eat an oyster—alive.

A soberer judgment might want to make a case for that equally forgotten hero of paleolithic times who first domesticated fire. It must have been one of the first of his home-building achievements, but no wolf destined to turn into a dog and no buffalo destined to become a cow can possibly have seemed one-tenth so dangerous as devouring flame. Early man, like every other animal, must have long been accustomed to flee from it in abject terror. We shall never know what Prometheus first dared snatch a bit from some forest fire or some erupting volcano. But when he put it down in the middle of the domestic circle he must have said, "This I can tame and use."

Long before even his day, courage of some sort must have been a characteristic of living things and even the tamer of fire was not the first hero. Perhaps the first and greatest of all was whatever little blob of jelly—not yet either plant or animal but a little of both—first consented to take on the responsibility of being alive at all. And surely the second greatest was that plant or animal which first dared leave the water where, ever since the very dawn of creation, every other organism before it had been born and died. Men are talking now about journeys to the moon or to Mars, but neither is more unsuited to human life than the bare earth was to the first creatures who risked it.

For millions of years only the submerged areas of the earth had been habitable. It was in water that the first hypothetical one-celled creatures, too insubstantial to leave fossil remains, must have been generated. None ventured out of it during millions of years while stony skeletons were evolved and became the earliest sure evidence of life in some of the oldest rocks. In water also stayed all the wormlike and squidlike and shrimplike creatures which represented, in their day, the highest development of life. Meanwhile, during the major part of the earth's history, during considerably more than half the time since life began, all dry land was desert to a degree almost inconceivable—without soil of any kind, as bare as the moon, and subject to no changes except those produced by geological forces. Volcanoes flowed and mountains heaved. Rain falling on an earth without any plant cover to protect it washed cruel gullies as remorselessly as they are cut in the most unqualified "bad lands" of today. Had any creature of that time been capable of thought, life in any medium other than water would have seemed as fantastic as life without an atmosphere would seem to us.

Then at some time, geologists say it was probably something like three hundred million years ago, the first living thing dared to expose itself temporarily to the deadly air. If it was an animal, as some think most probable, then it must have rushed back (or perhaps ducked back) before the gills through which it breathed could dry out. It could hardly have done much more during many thousands of years after the first bold venture, because it could not actually live beyond easy reach of water until its whole anatomy and physiology had undergone fundamental changes. But patience is a quality which the universe seems never to have lacked (until man came along) and it was always the animal which broke most rashly with all previous tradition, which presently became the most highly developed and the most competent—as well as the least patient.

So far as I am concerned I see no reason to apologize for calling that animal a "hero" or for referring to his "courage." Such terms can have no real meaning except in connection with something which is alive and when we talk about "the suffering earth" or the "nobility" of a mountain range we are merely using a figure of speech. But it is hard to say just where reality begins or to decide just which animal or even which plant is still too simple to be capable of something genuinely analogous to daring and courage. If these virtues are real in man, then they are real because they began to be so as soon as there was anything in the universe which could defy law and habit by risking something which had never been done before.

Few of us are so committed to a merely mechanical behaviorism that we would refuse to call brave and adventurous the first human pioneers who came to live in the American West. So in their own way were the plants and animals who had preceded them there. And so, *a fortiori,* were those far back in time who first dared learn how to adapt themselves to that desert which all dry land then was. If daring to do what our intelligence recognizes as dangerous constitutes "courage," then the animal who similarly rejects the imperatives of its instinct is exhibiting a virtue at least analogous, and so, in some still dimmer fashion, is the simplest creature, animal or even vegetable, which refuses to obey its long established reflexes. The whole course of evolution is directed by just such courageous acts. It must have its countless unremembered heroes who created diversity by daring to do what no member of its species had ever done before.

Most scientists, I am well aware, would object strenuously to any such line of reasoning. But then many scientists are firmly convinced that in man himself there is also no such thing as either daring or courage as distinguished from a reflex, congenital or conditioned. And perhaps that conclusion is inevitable if you begin by denying their reality to all creatures "lower" than man. If every other animal is a machine then why shouldn't human beings be machines also. And if to speak of the "courage" of some very lowly creature is to indulge in exaggeration, it is at least an exaggeration opposite and corrective to a more usual one.

Is it possible, one may ask, to guess at the identity of the first great pioneer and radical who came to dry land? Or is it, like the song the Sirens sang, "beyond all conjecture?" Does he have a name and can we honor him by saying, "but for you and your enterprise I might still be a fish?" At least our own direct amphibious ancestors came to land only because that pioneer's descendants were there to be eaten!

Well, if the paleontologists are right—and their evidence seems pretty good—we can answer this question. As a matter of fact, I met only the day before yesterday one of the almost unchanged relatives of the first air-breathing creatures, and he did not seem especially proud. He crawled on eight legs out from under a board in my storeroom and I confess that, though I do not do such things lightly, I put my foot upon him. Before he was crushed into nothing he was about two inches long and pale straw in color. He carried two pinchers before him and over his back he carried a long tail with a sting at its end. He was, in short, one of the least popular of desert dwellers—a scorpion.

Finding out about one's ancestors, especially correlative ones, is often a risky business and perhaps most people would rather not know how much

all of us are indebted to this rather unattractive creature. But so far as geologists can tell from the fossils they study and date, the first animal actually
capable of breathing air was not only a member of the scorpion kind but
amazingly like the one we step on when we find him.

To even the most uninstructed eye a scorpion fossilized during the Silurian
or Devonian epoch—say something like three hundred million years ago
—is unmistakably a scorpion. If one of them were to come to life again and
crawl out of his stone sarcophagus into your desert patio, you would not be
particularly surprised by his appearance unless you happened to be a biologist especially devoted to the study of that group of animals called arachnids
to which the scorpion belongs. There are several species now common
hereabout—some, like the victim of my brutality, only two inches long and
some several times that length. A three hundred million year old specimen
would look to the casual eye like merely a sort one had not happened to see
before and not much more different from the familiar kinds than they are
from one another.

In the highly improbable event that a living dinosaur should be found in
some African or South American hiding place, it would create quite a stir in
even the popular press and any big-game hunter would count it a high distinction to shoot one. Yet anyone who happens to live in one of the many
parts of the earth where scorpions abound can have the privilege of stepping
upon a creature who has been going about his business (such as it is) far
longer than any dinosaur went about dinosaur business. As a matter of fact,
scorpions put in their appearance more years before the first dinosaur than
have slipped away since the last known dinosaur decided that he and his
kind had had their day.

The horseshoe crab and the gingko tree are sometimes called "living fossils," and the epithet has more recently been applied to that strange fish
known as Latimeria which was taken not many years ago off the coast of
Africa in spite of the fact that it, as well as all its immediate relatives, was
supposed to have become extinct a very long time ago. Yet no sort of fish is
much older than the scorpion, and the horseshoe crab is not as nearly like
any very ancient form as the scorpion in my storeroom is like his Silurian
ancestor. He may not be much to look at, but the least we can do is to regard
him in the spirit of the naturalist Sutherland when he contemplated the living members of a tribe somewhat less ancient than the scorpions: "If the test
of nobility is antiquity of family, then the cockroach that hides behind the
kitchen sink is the true aristocrat. He does not date back merely to the three
brothers who came over in 1640 or to William the Conqueror. Wherever
there have been great epoch-making movements of people he has been with
them heart and soul. . . . Since ever a ship turned a foamy furrow in the
sea he has been a passenger, not a paying one certainly but still a passenger.
But man himself is but a creature of the last twenty minutes or so compared

with the cockroach, for, from its crevice by the kitchen sink, it can point its antennae to the coal in the hod and say: 'When that was being made my family was already well established.' " Scorpions have never been as closely associated with man as the cockroach, but they may not consider that anything to be ashamed of and on the score of antiquity they have a right to snub the cockroaches as upstarts, relatively speaking at least.

It may seem odd that they have hung on so long while changing so little. It may seem even odder that they shall be found in deserts despite the fact that they are so similar to the scorpions which had recently left the water. But they do not insist upon its being dry and some species will even tolerate a certain amount of cold. Though there are none in New England or in the Great Lakes region, they are found in the Alps and on our continent as far north as southern Canada. On the whole, however, they prefer warm climates and they have been in the Southwest for a long, long time. Tracks almost precisely like those made by a living species have been found in the Coconino sandstone which was laid down in Permian times or not more than a million or a million and a half years after scorpions took the first drastic step out of the water.

Most people today underestimate the intelligence and awareness of most creatures other than man because recent official science has often encouraged them to do so. But the scorpion is probably even dumber than he looks. At first sight you would have no reason to suppose that his senses were much less keen or his awareness much less dim than those of any common insect. But they are. By comparison even a beetle, to say nothing of a bee, an ant or a fly, is a miracle of alertness and competence. The life which I extinguished when I stepped on my specimen was about as dim as we can imagine life to be. The scorpion's brain stopped growing not long after he left the water and braininess had not got very far by then.

Neither his habits nor his character are very engaging even as such things go. The young—miniature replicas of their parents—are born alive and like the young of the wolf spider they clamber about on their mother's back until they are old enough to take care of themselves. But maternal solicitude is probably a rather large term to use in connection with the mother's tolerance, and at least until mating time comes around, scorpions do not seem to do anything very interesting. They skulk under bits of wood or stone and they sometimes choose to hide in shoes incautiously left in their neighborhood. I have never seen a scorpion outside captivity do anything more interesting than to nibble rather languidly at the body of a moth who had come to my light.

In fact, watching scorpions closely even in captivity does not provide much excitement most of the time. If two or three are kept together one sometimes absentmindedly eats a companion but the cannibalism, which is usual, is probably nothing very deliberate. The poor things not only have a

very rudimentary brain but also eyesight which is probably just keen enough
to distinguish the dark corners where they hide from the bright light they
avoid and too dim even to make them aware of movement. Probably they do
not actually perceive anything they do not touch.

As one observer has put it, if you see two together then they are either
making love or one of them is being eaten. Even anatomically the most interesting thing about scorpions is their curious way of breathing. Insects
have, of course, no lungs. They have merely ramifying tubes open to the
outside which permit the penetration of air into the body cavity. But scorpions, being even older than the insect tribe, have what are called book
lungs—curious purselike organs which no insect possesses, though spiders,
more nearly related to scorpions than to insects, often have both the insect's
tubes or tracheae and the scorpion's book lungs. No doubt book lungs,
which are a sort of air-breathing gills, were invented close to the water's
edge.

So far as I know no detailed account of the mating habits of the Arizona
species has ever been published, but in a creature which varies so little they
are probably the same as those described in Henri Fabre's classic account of
the kind which live in Provence and also, more recently, of a Philippine
species. Male and female stand face to face with their tails raised and their
stings touching. The male takes his partner by the claw and then backs
away, leading her with him. This holding of hands in a sort of dance may last
for more than an hour, after which the couple disappears under a stone or
into some other recess, the male walking backward as he conducts his partner. This sounds almost romantic and it probably does involve a sort of
courtship. But the holding of hands is also probably necessary because creatures which are deaf and almost blind can't afford to lose one another once
happy accident has brought them together. And though human lovers have
been known on occasion to call one another "good enough to eat," we are
likely to be shocked when the female scorpion takes this extravagant metaphor literally, as she frequently does.

Even the scorpion's venom is said to be of some very ancient kind quite
different from that of the serpent. And for once a creature commonly regarded as dangerous really is so to some slight extent. The largest kind are
relatively innocuous and capable of giving, as I have been informed by a
friend who knows from direct experience, nothing worse than a wasp sting.
But two Arizona species, neither more than about two inches long, can be
deadly to small children and may give even an adult several painful days in
bed. Records kept at the Arizona State University over a period of thirty-six
years ending in 1965 charge them with causing seventy-five fatalities during
that time, or more than three times as many as rattlesnakes can be blamed
for.[1] Naturalists get rather tired of insisting that few animals are dangerous
at all and very few indeed anything like so dangerous as we like to imagine

[1] These statistics have been updated by the editors with the permission of the author.

them, and it is almost a relief for them to be able to say: Scorpions really do sting, some species really are deadly to small children, and even adults should beware of them.

Even so, we tend to exaggerate their dangerousness both because we always do exaggerate such dangers and also perhaps because in the scorpion we recognize something terrifyingly ancient. Nevertheless, even the so-called deadly sort are deadly only to the very young or the very feeble and I myself have seen a healthy adult who had been stung by one ready to go back to his work after keeping fingers in ice water for an hour. By comparison with the automobile, they have very little effect upon the life expectancy of any inhabitant of the desert country. And though men have doubtless been killing them on sight at least since the earliest stone age, men must have found them impressive also, because Scorpio was put among the zodiacal constellations a very long time ago. And it is appropriate that this constellation, inconspicuous in the north, becomes very prominent in the summer sky above the desert.

So much, then, for this creature which, only a few pages back, I insisted upon endowing with "daring" and with "courage" because it ventured upon the land some three hundred millions of years ago. Judged even by the acuteness of its senses, much less by its intelligence, it belongs very low indeed in the hierarchy of life. What a long, long way it was from, say, the scorpion's eye—too primitive almost to deserve the name—to the eye of even so primitive an insect as the praying mantis. Yet the fact remains that between the scorpion and man himself the distance is not nearly so great as it is between the scorpion and anything which does not live at all. The difference between seeing, no matter how dimly, and not seeing at all is greater than the difference between the scorpion's vision and ours. It is easier to imagine how, given time enough, a scorpion could become a man than it is to imagine how sea water and mineral substances could have become a scorpion. Primitive as his eye is, it is indubitably an eye. Its owner can see with it—however dimly. And seeing itself is a process beyond comprehension. It involves awareness of some sort. Perhaps the difference between the scorpion's courage and what is possible for us is no greater than that between his eyesight and ours. Yet who would refuse to use the word "seeing" to describe what even a scorpion can do? Why should we not assume that his courage and ours are no less essentially, though remotely, the same?

Granting all this it is, however, still possible to wonder why this once so adventurous creature became so soon a very paragon of conservatism. As the first air-breather he may very well have been the remote ancestor of all the insects who were to proceed from originality to originality until they became capable of achievements which even man cannot wholly grasp. But this prototype of the insect himself continues to crawl upon the desert and to poison human beings with his ancient venom millions of years after almost all the other creatures which were even his near contemporaries gave up their effort to survive in their original forms. Like the horseshoe crab and the gingko tree, he should have become extinct eons ago. But he has changed even less than they and become one of the most striking examples not of evolution but of a refusal to evolve. Some of the irrational distaste and fear which the sight of him inspires in most people is partly the result of their dim half-realization that he comes down from a past too remote not to suggest unimaginable horrors. He is a living reminder of "the dark and backward abysm of time" and, like the earliest myths of the human race, he suggests the monstrous beginnings of instinct and mind and emotion. He is altogether too much like some bad dream and we would rather not be reminded of it.

As to the mystery of why he is still here, we shall have to be content to put him down as a left-over without knowing precisely how he managed to achieve that humble status. A long time ago he wandered into the desert pretty much what he is now and found that he could survive there, partly no doubt because his demands are modest and he can satisfy them without exposing himself very much. He eats insects which are plentiful and he can do without water as well as without food for long periods. Like the members of certain very old human families he has little to be proud of except the achievements of his remote ancestors, and if he were capable of pride he might, like them, grow prouder just in proportion as he comes to be more and more remote in time from them and their virtues. Like such people, he also makes us wonder what became of all the greatness which was once in his race. Did the scorpion use up all the daring of his tribe in his one great exploit all those millions of years ago? Did he squander it all at once like the wits at the Mermaid Tavern, each of whom seemed resolved to:

> *Put his whole wit in one jest*
> *And live a fool the rest of his dull life?*

It is a pleasant fancy but one had better not put it into words when there are any paleontologists about. We honor the scorpion for his early achievement but it has to be admitted that he doesn't seem to have done much to be proud of in recent years.

### STUDY QUESTIONS

1.  Who was Coronado?

2.  What is the reason for the two breaks in Krutch's text?

3.  How does Krutch answer the objection to which he calls the reader's attention in the eighth paragraph?

4.  What evidence does Krutch provide to dispel our fears of the scorpion's dangerousness?

5.  In the last two paragraphs, Krutch suggests that he has been more fanciful than scientific. Are there any other paragraphs in which his fancy seems to get the best of him?

6.  Despite Krutch's "pleasant fancy" and sometimes bantering tone, we never doubt the truthfulness of what he tells us about the scorpion. Why? How does his lucid, informal style help us to accept him as an authority on scorpions?

*Stephen Vincent Benét*

# WE AREN'T SUPERSTITIOUS

> Stephen Vincent Benét (1898–1943) was born in Bethlehem, Pennsylvania, and was the younger brother of William Rose Benét. Among his classmates at Yale, where he received an M.A., were Archibald MacLeish, Philip Barry, and Thornton Wilder. *Heavens and Earth,* a book of poems, was published in 1920, but Benét achieved real fame with two short stories —"Johnny Pye and the Fool Killer" and "The Devil and Daniel Webster." With support from a Guggenheim Fellowship, he wrote *John Brown's Body* (1928), the distinctly American classic that won a Pulitzer Prize. Benét did propagandist work during World War II. His use of American history and folklore made him both a critical and popular success during his own lifetime, but his reputation has now diminished.

USUALLY, our little superstitious rituals and propitiations don't hurt our daily lives. Usually. And then, on occasion, a superstition—a belief—flares into crowd-madness and kills and kills again before it has run its course. As it did in Salem Village, in 1692.

That story is worth retelling, as a very typical example of what wild belief and crowd hysteria can do to an average community. For Salem Village, in 1691, was no different in any way, from any one of a dozen little New England hamlets. It didn't expect celebrity or notoriety and its citizens were the average people of their day and age. There was the main road and the parsonage and the meeting house, the block house, the Ingersoll house where travelers put up for the night, the eight or nine other houses that made up the village. Beyond, lay the outlying farms with their hard working farmers—a few miles away lay Salem Town itself—fifteen miles away, the overgrown village that was Boston. King Philip's War had been over for some fourteen years and the Colony recovering from the shock of it—there were still individual slayings by Indians but the real power of the Indian was very largely broken. Men might look forward, with hope, to peace and thriving for a time.

And, as for the men and women of Salem Village—they were tough and knotty stock, if you like, not widely lettered, not particularly tolerant, especially in religion—but no different from their neighbors at Andover and Topsfield or in Boston itself. There were sensible men and stupid men among them, model housewives and slatterns, trouble makers and more peaceable folk. The names were the Puritan names that we are accustomed to reverence—Mercy and Abigail and Deborah, Nathaniel and Samuel and John. They lived a life of hard work and long winters, drank rum on occasion, took their religion with that mixture of grimness and enthusiasm that marked the Puritan, and intended, under God's providence, to beat wilderness and Indian, and wax and increase in the land. They were a great deal more human, crotchety and colorful than the schoolbook pictures of dour-faced men in steeple-crowned hats would suggest. In fact, if you want to find out how human they were, you have only to read Judge Sewall's diary. He was one of the judges at the Salem witch trials—and heartily sorry for it, later. But his Pepysian account of his own unsuccessful courtship of Madam Winthrop, and how he brought her gloves and sweets, is in the purest vein of unconscious farce.

And yet, to this ordinary community in the early Spring of 1692, came a madness that was to shake all Massachusetts before its fever was burned out. We are wiser, now. We do not believe in witches. But if, say, three cases of Asiatic cholera were discovered in your own hometown, and certified as such by the local board of health—and if your local newspaper promptly ran a boxed warning to all citizens on the front page—you would have some faint idea of how the average Salem Villager felt, when the "afflicted children" denounced their first victims.

For witchcraft, to almost all the New Englanders of 1692, was as definite, diagnosable and dangerous an evil as bubonic plague. It had its symptoms, its prognosis and its appalling results. Belief in it was as firmly fixed in most people's minds as belief in the germ theory of disease is in ours. Cotton Mather was one of the most able and promising young ministers of his day. But when, in 1688, in Boston, an eleven-year-old girl named Martha Goodwin accused an unhappy Irish Catholic laundress of bewitching her, Cotton Mather believed the eleven-year-old girl. In fact, he took the precocious brat into his own house, to study her symptoms and cure them by fasting and prayer, and wrote and published an elaborate, scientific account of his treatment of the case—which doubtless played its own part in preparing men's minds for the Salem madness.

True, there had been only some twenty witch trials in New England up to the Salem affair—compared to the hundreds and thousands of hangings, burnings, duckings, drownings, that had gone on in Europe and the British Isles during the last few centuries. But people believed in witches—why should they not? They were in the Bible—even the Bible itself said, "Thou shalt not suffer a witch to live." They were in every old wives' tale that was whispered about the winter fires. And, in 1692, they were in Salem Village.

Three years before, Salem Village had got a new minister—the Reverend Samuel Parris, ex-merchant in the West Indies. He seems to have been a self-willed, self-important man with a great sense of his own and the church's dignity, and, no sooner were he and his family well settled in the parsonage, than a dispute began as to whether the parsonage property belonged to him or to the congregation. But there was nothing unusual about that—Salem Village was a rather troublesome parish and two, at least, of the three previous ministers had had salary and other difficulties with the good folk of Salem. The quarrel dragged on like the old boundary dispute between Salem and Topsfield, creating faction and hard feeling, a typically New England affair. But there were boundary disputes elsewhere and other congregations divided in mind about their ministers.

But the most important thing about Samuel Parris was neither his self-importance nor his attempt to get hold of the parsonage property. It was the fact that he brought with him to Salem Village, two West Indian servants— a man known as John Indian and a woman named Tituba. And when he bought those two or their services in the West Indies, he was buying a rope that was to hang nineteen men and women of New England—so odd are the links in the circumstantial chain.

Perhaps the nine-year-old Elizabeth Parris, the daughter of the parsonage, boasted to her new friends of the odd stories Tituba told and the queer things she could do. Perhaps Tituba herself let the report of her magic powers be spread about the village. She must have been as odd and imagination-stirring a figure as a parrot or a tame monkey in the small New England town. And the winters were long and white—and any diversion a godsend.

In any case, during the winter of 1691–92, a group of girls and women began to meet nightly at the parsonage, with Tituba and her fortune-telling as the chief attraction. Elizabeth Parris, at nine, was the youngest—then came Abigail Williams, eleven and Ann Putnam, twelve. The rest were older—Mercy Lewis, Mary Wolcott and Elizabeth Hubbard were seventeen, Elizabeth Booth and Susan Sheldon, eighteen, and Mary Warren and Sarah Churchill, twenty. Three were servants—Mercy Lewis had been employed by the Reverend George Burroughs, a previous minister of Salem Village, and now worked for the Putnams—Mary Warren was a maid at the John Procters', Sarah Churchill at the George Jacobs'. All, except for Elizabeth Parris, were adolescent or just leaving adolescence.

The elder women included a pair of gossipy, superstitious busybodies—Mrs. Pope and Mrs. Bibber—and young Ann Putnam's mother, Ann Putnam, Senior, who deserves a sentence to herself.

For the Putnams were a powerful family in the neighborhood and Ann Putnam, married at seventeen and now only thirty, is described as handsome, arrogant, temperamental and high-strung. She was also one of those people who can cherish a grudge and revenge it.

The circle met—the circle continued to meet—no doubt with the usual giggling, whispering and gossip. From mere fortune-telling it proceeded to other and more serious matters—table-rapping, perhaps, and a little West Indian voodoo—weird stories told by Tituba and weird things shown, while the wind blew outside and the big shadows flickered on the wall. Adolescent girls, credulous servants, superstitious old women—and the two enigmatic figures of Tituba, the West Indian, and Ann Putnam, Sr.

But soon the members of the circle began to show hysterical symptoms. They crawled under tables and chairs, they made strange sounds, they shook and trembled with nightmare fears. The thing became a village celebrity—and more. Something strange and out of nature was happening—who had ever seen normal young girls behave like these young girls? And no one—certainly not the Reverend Samuel Parris—even suggested that a mixed diet of fortune-telling, ghost stories and voodoo is hardly the thing for impressionable minds during a long New England winter. Hysteria was possession by an evil spirit; pathological lying, the Devil putting words into one's mouth. No one suggested that even Cotton Mather's remedy of fasting and prayer would be a good deal better for such cases than widespread publicity. Instead the Reverend Samuel became very busy. Grave ministers were called in to look at the afflicted children. A Dr. Gregg gave his opinion. It was almost too terrible to believe, and yet what else could be believed? Witchcraft!

Meanwhile, one may suppose, the "afflicted children," like most hysterical subjects, enjoyed the awed stares, the horrified looks, the respectful questions that greeted them, with girlish zest. They had been unimportant girls of a little hamlet—now they were, in every sense of the word, spot news. And any reporter knows what that does to certain kinds of people. They continued to writhe and demonstrate—and be the center of attention. There was only one catch about it. If they were really bewitched— somebody must be doing the bewitching—

On the 29th of February, 1692, in the midst of an appropriate storm of thunder-and-lightning, three women, Sarah Good, Sarah Osburn and Tituba, were arrested on the deadly charge of bewitching the children.

The next day, March 1, two Magistrates, Justice Hathorne and Justice Corwin, arrived with appropriate pomp and ceremony. The first hearing was held in the crowded meetinghouse of the Village—and all Salem swarmed to it, as crowds in our time have swarmed to other sleepy little villages, suddenly notorious.

The children—or the children and Tituba—had picked their first victims well. Sarah Good and Sarah Osburn were old women of no particular standing in the community. Sarah Good had been a beggar and a slattern— her husband testified, according to report and with a smugness that makes one long to kick him, that she "either was a witch or would be one very quickly," ending "I may say, with tears, that she is an enemy to all good." As for Sarah Osburn, she had married a redemptioner servant after the death of her former husband and probably lost caste in consequence. Also, she had been bedridden for some time and therefore not as regular in her church attendance as a good Christian should be.

We can imagine that meetinghouse—and the country crowd within it— on that chill March day. At one end was the majesty of the law—and the "afflicted children" where all might see them and observe. Dressed in their best, very likely, and with solicitous relatives near at hand. Do you see Mercy Lewis? Do you see Ann Putnam? And then the whole crowd turned to one vast, horrified eye. For there was the accused—the old woman—the witch!

The justices—grim Justice Hathorne in particular—had, evidently, arrived with their minds made up. For the first question addressed to Sarah Good was, bluntly:

"What evil spirit have you familiarity with?"

"None," said the piping old voice. But everybody in the village knew worthless Sarah Good. And the eye of the audience went from her to the deadly row of "afflicted children" and back again.

"Have you made no contracts with the devil?" proceeded the Justice.

"No."

The Justice went to the root of the matter at once.

"Why do you hurt these children?"

A rustle must have gone through the meetinghouse at that. Aye, that's it—the Justice speaks shrewdly—hark to the Justice! Aye, but look, too! Look at the children! Poor things, poor things!

"I do not hurt them. I scorn it," said Sarah Good, defiantly. But the Justice had her, now—he was not to be brushed aside.

"Who then do you employ to do it?"

"I employ nobody."

"What creature do you employ then?" For all witches had familiars.

"No creature, but I am falsely accused." But the sweat must have been on the old woman's palms by now.

The Justice considered. There was another point—minor but illuminating.

"Why did you go away muttering from Mr. Parris, his house?"

"I did not mutter but I thanked him for what he gave my child."

The Justice returned to the main charge, like any prosecuting attorney. "Have you made no contract with the devil?"

"No."

It was time for Exhibit A. The Justice turned to the children. Was Sarah Good one of the persons who tormented them? Yes, yes!—and a horrified murmur running through the crowd. And then, before the awe-stricken eyes of all, they began to be tormented. They writhed, they grew stiff, they contorted, they were stricken moaning or speechless. Yet, when they were brought to Sarah Good and allowed to touch her, they grew quite quiet and calm. For, as everyone knew, a witch's physical body was like an electric conductor—it reabsorbed, on touch, the malefic force discharged by witchcraft into the bodies of the tormented. Everybody could see what happened —and everybody saw. When the meetinghouse was quiet, the Justice spoke again.

"Sarah Good, do you not see now what you have done? Why do you not tell us the truth? Why do you torment these poor children?"

And with these words, Sarah Good was already hanged. For all that she could say was, "I do not torment them." And yet everyone had seen her, with their own eyes.

The questions went on—she fumbled in her answers—muttered a bit of prayer. Why did she mutter? And didn't you see how hard it was for her to pronounce the name of God? Pressed and desperate, she finally said that if anyone tormented the children, it must be Sarah Osburn—she knew herself guiltless. The pitiful fable did not save her. To Boston Jail.

Sarah Osburn's examination followed the same course—the same prosecutor's first question—the same useless denial—the same epileptic feats of the "afflicted children"—the same end. It was also brought out that Sarah Osburn had said that "she was more like to be bewitched than to be a witch"—very dangerous that!—and that she had once had a nightmare about "a thing all black like an Indian that pinched her in the neck."

Then Tituba was examined and gave them their fill of marvels, prodigies and horrors.

The West Indian woman, a slave in a strange land, was fighting for her life and she did it shrewdly and desperately. She admitted, repentantly, that she had tormented the children. But she had been forced to do so. By whom? By Goody Good and Goody Osburn and two other witches whom she hadn't yet been able to recognize. Her voodoo knowledge aided her—she filled the open ears of Justices and crowd with tales of hairy familiars and black dogs, red cats and black cats and yellow birds, the phantasm of a woman with legs and wings. And everybody could see that she spoke the truth. For, when she was first brought in, the children were tormented at her presence, but as soon as she had confessed and turned King's evidence, she was tormented herself, and fearfully. To Boston Jail with her—but she had saved her neck.

The hearing was over—the men and women of Salem and its outlying farms went broodingly or excitedly back to their homes to discuss the fearful workings of God's providence. Here and there a common-sense voice murmured a doubt or two—Sarah Good and Sarah Osburn were no great losses to the community—but still, to convict two old women of heinous crime on the testimony of greensick girls and a West Indian slave! But, on the whole, the villagers of Salem felt relieved. The cause of the plague had been found —it would be stamped out and the afflicted children recover. The Justices, no doubt, congratulated themselves on their prompt and intelligent action. The "afflicted children" slept, after a tiring day—they were not quite so used to such performances as they were to become.

As for the accused women, they went to Boston Jail—to be chained there, while waiting trial and gallows. There is an item of, "To chains for Sarah Good and Sarah Osburn, 14 shillings," in the jailor's record. Only, Sarah Osburn was not to go to the gallows—she died in jail instead, some five and a half weeks later, at a recorded expense to the Colony of one pound, three shillings and five-pence for her keep. And Tituba stayed snugly in prison till the madness collapsed—and was then sold by the Colony to defray the expenses of her imprisonment. One wonders who bought her and whether she ever got back to the West Indies. But, with that, her enigmatic figure disappears from the scene.

Meanwhile, on an outlying farm, Giles Corey, a turbulent, salty old fellow of 81, began to argue the case with his wife, Martha. He believed, fanatically, in the "afflicted children." She did not, and said so—even going so far as to say that the magistrates were blinded and she could open their eyes. It was one of those marital disputes that occur between strong-willed people. And it was to bring Martha Corey to the gallows and Giles Corey to an even stranger doom.

Yet now there was a lull, through which people whispered.

As for what went on in the minds of "the afflicted children," during that lull, we may not say. But this much is evident. They had seen and felt their power. The hearing had been the greatest and most exciting event of their narrow lives. And it was so easy to do—they grew more and more ingenious with each rehearsal. You twisted your body and groaned—and grown people were afraid.

Add to this, the three girl-servants, with the usual servants' grudges against present or former masters. Add to this, that high-strung, dominant woman, Ann Putnam, Sr., who could hold a grudge and remember it. Such a grudge as there might be against the Towne sisters, for instance—they were all married women of the highest standing, particularly Rebecca Nurse. But they'd taken the Topsfield side in that boundary dispute with Salem. So suppose—just suppose—that one of them were found out to be a witch? And hadn't Tituba deposed that there were other women, besides Good and Osburn, who made her torment the children?

On March 19, Martha Corey and Rebecca Nurse were arrested on the charge of witchcraft. On March 21, they were examined and committed. And, with that, the real reign of terror began.

For if Martha Corey, notably religious and Godfearing, and Rebecca Nurse, saintly and thoughtful, could be witches, no one in Salem or New England was safe from the charge. The examinations were brutally unfair —the "children" yet bolder and more daring. They would interrupt questions now to shout that "a black man" was whispering in the prisoner's ear —if the accused stood still, they were tormented, if she moved her hands, they suffered even greater agonies. Their self-confidence became monstrous—there was no trick too fantastic for them to try. When Deodat Lawson, a former minister of Salem and a well-educated and intelligent man, came to Ingersoll's on March 19, he first saw Mary Wolcott who "as she stood by the door was bitten, so that she cried out of her wrist, and, looking at it, we saw apparently the marks of teeth, both upper and lower set, on each side of her wrist." It would not have deceived a child—but Mary Wolcott was one of the "afflicted children" and her words and self-bitings were as gospel. He then went to the parsonage, where Abigail Williams, another afflicted child, put on a very effective vaudeville-act indeed, throwing firebrands around the house, crying "Whish, whish, whish!" and saying that she was being tormented by Rebecca Nurse who was trying to make her sign the Devil's book.

After that, there was, obviously, nothing for the Reverend Lawson to do but to preach a thunderous sermon on the horrors of witchcraft— interrupted by demonstrations and cries from "the afflicted"—and thus do his little bit toward driving the madness on. For by now, Salem Village, as a community, was no longer sane.

Let us get the rest of it over quickly. The Salem witches ceased to be

Salem's affair—they became a matter affecting the whole colony. Sir William Phips, the new governor, appointed a special court of Oyer and Terminer to try the cases. And the hangings began.

On January 1, 1692, no one, except possibly the "Circle children" had heard of Salem witches. On June 10, Bridget Bishop was hanged. She had not been one of the first accused, but she was the first to suffer. She had been married three times, kept a roadhouse on the road to Beverley where people drank rum and played shovelboard, and dressed, distinctively for the period, in a "black cap and black hat and red paragon bodice broidered and looped with diverse colors." But those seem to have been her chief offences. When questioned, she said "I never saw the Devil in my life."

All through the summer, the accusations, the arrest, the trials came thick and fast till the jails were crowded. Nor were those now accused friendless old beldames like Sarah Good. They included Captain John Alden (son of Miles Standish's friend) who saved himself by breaking jail, and the wealthy and prominent Englishes who saved themselves by flight. The most disgraceful scenes occurred at the trial of the saintly Rebecca Nurse. Thirty-nine citizens of Salem were brave enough to sign a petition for her and the jury brought in a verdict of "not guilty." The mob in the sweating courtroom immediately began to cry out and the presiding judge as much as told the jury to reverse their verdict. They did so, to the mob's delight. Then the Governor pardoned her. And "certain gentlemen of Salem"—and perhaps the mob—persuaded him into reversing his pardon. She was hanged on Gallows Hill on July 19 with Sarah Good, Sarah Wilds, Elizabeth How and Susanna Martin.

Susanna Martin's only witchcraft seems to have been that she was an unusually tidy woman and had once walked a muddy road without getting her dress bedraggled. No, I am quoting from testimony, not inventing. As for Elizabeth How, a neighbor testified, "I have been acquainted with Goodwife How as a naybor for nine or ten years and I never saw any harm in her but found her just in her dealings and faithful to her promises . . . I never heard her revile any person but she always pitied them and said, 'I pray God forgive them now'," But the children cried, "I am stuck with a pin. I am pinched," when they saw her—and she hanged.

It took a little more to hang the Reverend George Burroughs. He had been Salem Village's second minister—then gone on to a parish in Maine. And the cloth had great sanctity. But Ann Putnam and Mercy Lewis managed to doom him between them—with the able assistance of the rest of the troupe. Mr. Burroughs was unfortunate enough to be a man of unusual physical strength—anyone who could lift a gun by putting four fingers in its barrel, must do so by magic arts. Also, he had been married three times. So when the ghosts of his first two wives, dressed in winding-sheets, appeared in a sort of magic-lantern show to Ann Putnam and cried out that Mr. Burroughs had murdered them—the cloth could not save him then. Perhaps one of the most pathetic documents connected with the trials is the later petition of his orphaned children. It begins, "We were left a parcel of small children, helpless—"

Here and there, in the records, gleams a flash of frantic common sense. Susanna Martin laughs when Ann Putnam and her daughter go into convulsions at her appearance. When asked why, she says, "Well I may, at such folly. I never hurt this woman or her child in my life." John Procter, the prosperous farmer who employed Mary Warren, said sensibly, before his arrest, "If these girls are left alone, we will all be devils and witches. They ought all to be sent to the whipping-post." He was right enough about it— but his servant helped hang him. White-haired old George Jacobs, leaning on his two sticks, cried out, "You tax me for a wizard, you might as well tax me for a buzzard!" Nevertheless, he hanged. A member of the Nurse family testifies, "Being in court this 29th June, 1692, I saw Goodwife Bibber pull pins out of her clothes and hold them between her fingers and clasp her hands around her knee and then she cried out and said Goodwife Nurse pinched her." But such depositions did not save Rebecca Nurse or her sister, Mary Easty.

Judge, jury and colony preferred to believe the writhings of the children, the stammerings of those whose sows had died inexplicably, the testimony of such as Bernard Peach who swore that Susanna Martin had flown in through his window, bent his body into the shape of a "whoope" and sat upon him for an hour and a half.

One hanging on June 10, five on July 19, five on August 19, eight on September 22, including Mary Easty and Martha Corey. And of these the Reverend Noyes remarked, with unction, "What a sad thing it is to see eight firebrands of hell hanging there!" But for stubborn Giles Corey a different fate was reserved.

The old man had begun by believing in the whole hocus-pocus. He had quarreled with his wife about it. He had seen her arrested as a witch, insulted by the magistrates, condemned to die. Two of his sons-in-law had testified against her—he himself had been closely questioned as to her actions and had made the deposition of a badgered and simple man. Yes, she prayed a good deal—sometimes he couldn't hear what she said—that sort of thing. The memory must have risen to haunt him when she was condemned. Now, he himself was in danger.

Well, he could die as his wife would. But there was the property—his goods, his prospering lands. By law, the goods and property of those convicted of witchcraft were confiscated by the State and the name attainted. With a curious, grim heroism, Giles Corey drew up a will leaving that property to the two sons-in-law who had not joined in the prevailing madness. And then at his trial, he said "I will not plead. If I deny, I am condemned already in courts where ghosts appear as witnesses and swear men's lives away."

A curious, grim heroism? It was so. For those who refused to plead either guilty or not guilty in such a suit were liable to the old English punishment called *peine forte et dure*. It consisted in heaping weights or stones upon the unhappy victim till he accepted a plea—or until his chest was crushed. And exactly that happened to old Giles Corey. They heaped the stones upon him until they killed him—and two days before his wife was hanged, he died. But his property went to the two loyal sons-in-law, without confiscation— and his name was not attainted. So died Giles Corey, New England to the bone.

And then, suddenly and fantastically as the madness had come, it was gone.

Not without other victims. At Andover, for instance, the wife of a citizen had fallen unaccountably ill. The first thought had been to call in two of the "afflicted children" as experts on witchcraft. As a result, something like fifty people were arrested and several hanged. But, after the hangings of September 22, the special court of Oyer and Terminer did not meet again— though the jails were crowded with accused and condemned.

The "afflicted children," at long last, had gone too far. They had accused the Governor's lady. They had accused Mrs. Hall, the wife of the minister at Beverley and a woman known throughout the colony for her virtues. And there comes a point when driven men and women revolt against blood and horror. It was that which ended Robespierre's terror—it was that which ended the terror of the "afflicted children." The thing had become a *reductio ad absurdum*. If it went on, logically, no one but the "afflicted children" and their protégées would be left alive.

So the madness died. In January, 1693, the Superior Court brought twenty-one to trial and condemned three. But no one was executed. In May, 1693, a proclamation emptied the jails.

So it ended. And Cotton Mather published *Wonders of the Invisible World* to prove it had all been true and Robert Calef, of Boston, promptly replied with *More Wonders of the Invisible World,* confuting and attacking Cotton Mather. And, in 1706, Ann Putnam made public confession that she had been deluded by the Devil in testifying as she had. She had testified in every case but one. And in 1711, the colony of Massachusetts paid 50 pounds to the heirs of George Burroughs, 21 pounds to the heirs of Giles Corey—578 pounds in all to the heirs of various victims. An expensive business for the colony, on the whole.

What happened to the survivors? Well, the Reverend Samuel Parris quit Salem Village to go into business in Boston and died at Sudbury in 1720. And Ann Putnam died in 1716 and from the stock of the Putnams sprang Israel Putnam, the Revolutionary hero. And from the stock of the "witches," the Nurses and the others, sprang excellent and distinguished people of service to State and nation. And hanging Judge Hathorne's descendant was Nathaniel Hawthorne. And Cotton Mather remained a brilliant minister, but his ambitions, on the whole, did not prosper as he thought they should. While as for the sanctimonious Dr. Noyes who spoke so unctuously of the "eight firebrands of hell," according to legend, he got his just deserts. For the legend goes that Sarah Good cursed him, saying, "I am no witch and because you say I am, God will give you blood to drink"—and he is supposed to have died of a hemorrhage of the throat. But Mercy Lewis and the rest of the "afflicted children" did not die so. They went on and lived their lives.

And I have not even spoken of the fifty-five who actually confessed to being witches—or the solemn examination of a five-year-old child for witchcraft—or of how two of the Carrier boys were hung up by the heels to make them testify against their mother—or of the time when Benjamin Hutchinson and Eleazer Putnam went stabbing with their rapiers at invisible cats and were solemnly assured they had slain three witches, equally invisible.

We have no reason to hold Salem up to obloquy. It was a town, like another, and a strange madness took hold of it. But it is no stranger thing to hang a man for witchcraft than to hang him for the shape of his nose or the color of his skin. We are not superstitious, no. Well, let us be a little sure we are not. For persecution follows superstition and intolerance as fire follows the fuse. And, once we light that fire, we cannot foresee where it will end or what it will consume—any more than they could in Salem, two hundred and forty-five years ago.

STUDY QUESTIONS

1. Why does Benét feel that this historical narrative has relevance in a twentieth-century society? Do you agree?

2. Why did the "afflicted" children pretend they were bewitched? What does Benét mean when he says that the children "had picked their victims well"?

3. How did Giles Cory triumph over his judges?

4. Does the last paragraph seem an integral part of the essay? Why?

5. What words, sentences, paragraphs most clearly reveal Benét's attempt to sway the reader's emotions and even his judgment?

*Newsweek*

# THE NEW MEDICINE AND ITS WEAPONS

C ALL HIM Harry Wilson, a 46-year-old sales executive. He had just strolled out of a restaurant with his wife when he felt a sudden crushing pressure on his chest and slumped to the sidewalk, the victim of a heart attack.

A clot had formed in an artery of his heart, part of the heart muscle was no longer pumping blood, blood pressure had fallen and his skin was already cold. In a matter of minutes an ambulance was rushing him to the hospital—and the beginning of a month-long battle to save his life.

The oldest of human emotions would be exposed in that time: a man struck down in his prime, a wife alone, children wondering if they would ever see their father again. But these fears would be met by the newest creations of human ingenuity. There is, of course, no "right" time to have a coronary, but for Wilson and literally thousands of others who fall victim to heart attacks, liver disorders, kidney failures and other killer diseases, something extra is now working to sustain their lives today. Doctors and nurses bring not only their traditional skills and time-tested drugs to the battle but also an extraordinary array of life-saving mechanical and electronic aids that didn't exist a few years ago.

Some items represent fallout from military research, the space program and even the atomic bomb; still others are the products of new alliances between industrial giants and hospitals. Lockheed and the Mayo Clinic, for example, are collaborating on a new computerized system of hospital care; North American Aviation is working on an emphysema belt that makes the breath of life easier for men and women suffering lung damage. In some modern operating rooms where the New Medicine is practiced, the technicians manning the machines and monitors often outnumber the doctors.

*Alarm:* In hospitals from Newport News, Va., to Mountain View, Calif., heart patients like Wilson are taken to coronary intensive-care units where electrodes similar to those used by the Gemini astronauts are placed on their chest and legs so that technicians can monitor their electrocardiogram, pulse and blood pressure around the clock. Three hours after Wilson was admitted, an alarm flashed on the central control desk—his heart had stopped beating. Within seconds, a nurse had wheeled a cart to the bedside. Called the Max (for Maximum Care), the cart was equipped with everything needed for cardiac resuscitation. Quickly a doctor placed two plunger-like electrodes on Wilson's chest and gave him a 100-watt shock that started his heart going again.

Sometimes coronaries are followed by a pulmonary embolism—a clot lodged in a blood vessel in the lung. As soon as he coughed blood—a telltale sign—Wilson was wheeled to the nuclear-medicine lab and given an injection of radioactive albumin particles. When the particles passed through the tiny capillaries in the lung, a scanner outside the chest picked up the radiation and printed out a picture of the lung in black dots. A wedge-shaped blank in the scan pinpointed the portion of the lung not receiving blood, confirming the doctors' diagnosis. Wilson was given anticoagulant drugs.

The physicians also checked for clots with a thermograph. This distant relative of the U.S. Army's sniperscope and of space satellite detectors measures the heat given off in the form of infra-red radiations by various parts of the body. Variations in the intensity of the infra-red appear as "hot" and "cold" spots on film. The area of a clot—with its seriously diminished blood supply—is cold, and shows up much darker than the normal areas on the thermograph.

Four weeks after the attack that struck him down, Wilson, 20 pounds lighter and the drug digitalis in his pocket, walked out of the hospital. But he wasn't beyond the ministrations of the New Medicine yet. The heart attack had damaged the nerve center—or pacemaker—that controls the regularity of the heartbeat; he could suffer from heart block culminating in heart failure. To prevent this, surgeons supplied him with an artificial pacemaker made possible by advances in miniaturized computer parts.

The pacemaker comes in several models. Wilson's is a 2½-inch plastic, battery-powered generator installed under the skin high on the chest. It is connected to the heart with a plastic-coated wire threaded through a vein under the collarbone and into the right pumping chamber, or ventricle. Over a three-year period, the generator releases minibursts of electricity to keep the heart beating at a steady rate. When the generator wears out, it can be easily replaced during a relatively simple chest operation. A two-speed model comes with a magnetized actuator shaped like a ball-point pen. "If the wearer wants to increase his heart rate in order to play a set of tennis or run to catch a train," explains James Nelson of GE's X-ray department in Milwaukee, "he simply passes the pen over the spot on his body where the battery is implanted to speed the impulse."

*Innovations:* Nothing, it seems, is so far out that it can't be applied in the New Medicine. A NASA metal alloy, originally used for bearings, is being tested for artificial hip and elbow joints. An accelerometer intended to measure the impact of micrometeorites against spacecraft has been converted into a means of measuring minute muscle tremors in diagnosing neurologic disease. And the lunar walker, developed for unmanned exploration of the moon's surface, has been adapted as a walking wheelchair to allow paraplegics to climb stairs by manipulating manual or chin-strap controls.

So much is happening in the field of biomedical engineering that a group of doctors and manufacturers recently formed the Association for Advancement of Medical Instrumentation as a clearinghouse for information. "The big firms are loaded with technicians who can help us solve our problems," says Harvard's Dr. John P. Merrill, a pioneer in the use of the artificial kidney and kidney transplants. Merrill visualizes the day when artificial kidneys and other hardware will be subjected to government tests by some sort of Federal Spare Parts Administration similar to the way medications are policed by the Food and Drug Administration.

The Federal government's involvement in the biomedical field is already large. In the fiscal year ending in June, expenditures for applied research are estimated at $832 million. And only last week, the U.S. Public Health Service awarded more than $2.5 million—the largest grant since passage of the 1946 Hill-Burton program for hospital construction—to the University of Southern California to develop an automated system for diagnosis, continuous monitoring and treatment of the critically ill.

But the New Medicine still leaves many old problems unsolved. Gadgetry and special-care untis add to the already soaring costs of medical care. A heart-lung machine costs $15,000 and the average open-heart operation may cost $3,000. A cobalt unit for deep cancer therapy can run as high as $95,000 and the charge for each treatment may be $15 or $20. The cost of the hardware is only part of the price the patient must pay, of course. For each new device, a technician with the skills to run it must be found—and medical technologists of all kinds are in short supply. And sometimes the shortage of skilled hands spells disaster. Just three months ago, three patients at Hennepin County General Hospital in Minneapolis died of salt and mineral depletion while being "run" on the hospital's artificial kidney machine because of an improper mixture of the solution used in the machine.

*Personal Touch:* Moreover, the huge radiotherapy units, glowing oscilloscopes and snake-like catheters characteristic of the New Medicine can have a frightening effect on patients. "You can put in all the machinery you want," says a doctor at the National Institutes of Health, "but the patient wants some attention from a person, not a machine."

Sometimes, too, physicians become bedazzled and overly dependent on the machine gadgetry of their surroundings. One NIH official recalls a brain surgeon who balked at proceeding with a relatively routine operation when an electrical defect occurred in one of the operating-room monitors. After his initial dismay, he was persuaded to go on without the monitor. "I think there is a tyranny of technology," says Dr. Irving S. Cooper of New York's St. Barnabas Hospital. "The machine is not the message."

Still, an estimated 12,000 persons are living useful lives today wearing implanted heart pacemakers. Hundreds have been saved by artificial heart valves made of metal and plastic. And rapidly, even these experimental methods of treatment are being supplanted by more ingenious techniques. Some of the newest weapons of the New Medicine:

## Gas Endarterectomy

Heart attacks kill about 525,000 Americans annually. They occur because fatty deposits of atherosclerosis clog the coronary arteries feeding the heart muscle. Although surgeons have learned how to remove or clear obstructed blood vessels elsewhere in the body, few have successfully operated on the delicate coronaries. Recently, Doctors Philip Sawyer, Martin Kaplitt and Sol Sobel of the State University of New York Downstate Medical Center in Brooklyn have developed a way of clearing the coronaries with injections of carbon dioxide.

The procedure, called a gas endarterectomy, imitates the destructive pattern of the disease known as dissecting aneurysm. The surgeons insert a fine hypodermic needle attached to a carbon-dioxide cylinder into the wall of the artery. A few jets of the gas tear the lining away from the artery wall, at the same time loosening the fatty core of atherosclerosis. A small incision is then made in the artery and another burst of gas frees the deposit completely. Then the surgeons simply remove the core with forceps.

## The Laser Knife

The laser started out as a possible death ray; its military uses are still untested, but its role as a tool of surgery is being demonstrated daily. Lasers produce bursts of light millions of times brighter than sunlight when electrical energy strikes a gas such as argon and makes it emit light which is amplified and reflected repeatedly. The result is light of one pure wave length instead of the usual jumble of waves from the whole spectrum. This "coherent" light can be focused in a narrow beam with enough heat to cut through diamonds and the precision to raise a blister on a single red blood cell.

To date, lasers have been used most successfully in medicine to repair small tears and defects in the retina, the lining at the back of the eye. Through a focusing scope, the ophthalmologist aims the laser at the defect and fires a brief burst of energy. The beam passes harmlessly through the lens of the eye, but it burns the layer of blood vessels behind the retina. This layer, called the choroid, oozes a thick substance that hardens, gluing the retina to the back of the eye. Hundreds of cases have been treated satisfactorily by laser at New York's Columbia-Presbyterian Medical Center.

Lasers have been used to destroy skin cancers. And since laser light tends to be absorbed more readily by dark tissue than by light tissue, lasers are being tried experimentally in the destruction of malignant melanoma, a darkly pigmented and usually lethal form of cancer. In some cases the beam has destroyed individual growths, usually on the skin, but no one has yet reported any complete cures. Some researchers fear the use of lasers in cancer surgery because the beams may splatter cancer cells from the tumor and hasten spread of the disease to other parts of the body.

### Cryosurgery

The most promising of the new surgical methods is cryosurgery, destruction of tissue by freezing. The technique was pioneered by Dr. Irving Cooper, director of neurosurgery at St. Barnabas, to relieve the rigidity and uncontrollable tremors of Parkinson's disease by freezing a tiny cluster of nerve cells inside the brain. The patient is given a local anesthetic and a dime-size hole is cut in his skull. Guided by a series of Polaroid X-rays, Cooper inserts a probe the size of a crochet needle into the thalamus, about 2½ inches deep in the brain. He then circulated liquid nitrogen at temperatures ranging from—94 to—58 degrees Fahrenheit through the probe, controlling the temperature at the uninsulated tip by the rate of flow. The rest of the probe is vacuum-insulated, Thermos-bottle fashion, to avoid damage to normal tissue as it rests in the brain.

A ball of frozen tissue gradually forms around the tip and, since the patient is conscious, Cooper can gauge the effect by observing his hand movements. The procedure is safe, because if the ice ball grows too large and the patient shows signs of paralysis, he has 30 seconds to raise the probe temperature and avert permanent damage.

Cryosurgery is being tested increasingly in other types of surgery. Cooper, for example, has frozen brain tumors that are too deep in the brain to be removed by conventional methods. After destruction by freezing, the dead tumor breaks down and is removed by the blood stream. "It looks very promising," Cooper notes, "but I don't want to shout about it yet." At Buffalo VA hospital, Dr. Andrew Gage has frozen bone tumors by wrapping a freezing coil around the bone shaft. The dead bone forms a structure around which new bone forms, Gage reports. Dr. Maurice J. Gonder, also of Buffalo VA, and his associate Dr. Ward A. Soanes have found the cryosurgical probe a good way to remove the prostate gland with relatively little pain and blood loss. And Dr. William G. Cahan of New York's Memorial Hospital has used cryosurgery to remove tonsils, to stop abnormal uterine bleeding (by destroying the lining of the uterus) and to control bleeding and relieve pain from large incurable tumors. Cryosurgery, Cahan notes, "bids well for becoming the most versatile modality in medicine."

## Treatment Under Pressure

Hyperbaric oxygen chambers look like huge submarines moored improbably to hospital basement floors. The resemblance is apt; patients undergoing open-heart surgery in the chambers are given pure oxygen to breathe while the chamber pressure is raised to about three times normal atmospheric pressure. This saturates their blood and body tissues with up to fifteen times the normal concentration of oxygen—giving the surgeon more time to operate.

Chicago's Lutheran General Hospital has three chambers ranging in size from 23 feet to 41 feet long; one contains a fully equipped operating room, another, a six-bed intensive-care unit, and the third is used for research and isolation of patients with severe infections. Together they cost more than $1.1 million to install. In addition to heart surgery, hyperbaric therapy has proved its worth in the treatment of tetanus and gas gangrene, because the bacteria causing these diseases are killed by oxygen in heavy concentration.

Some researchers have found that hyperbaric oxygen treatments improve a stroke victim's chances of recovery by compensating for the impaired blood supply to the brain; the chambers have also averted the need for amputation in patients with injuries or atherosclerotic deposits that cut off circulation to the arms or legs. Finally, they are widely used in operations to repair heart defects in infants, whose circulatory systems are often too tiny to be hooked to the tubes of a heart-lung machine.

A novel variation of high-pressure therapy has been devised by Doctors W. James Gardner and John Storer of Cleveland's Huron Road Hospital. They adapted the principle of the flyer's G-suit to treat shock and abdominal bleeding. In shock, blood pressure drops, causing blood to drain from the brain and lungs to pool in the abdomen. When shock patients are placed in the inflatable plastic suit, the pressure forces blood back into the upper part of the body. The suit also can reduce internal hemorrhage by closing the bleeding vessels. Gardner and Storer have also developed a plastic G-splint that works on the same pressure principle. The inflated splint holds an injured arm or leg on a cushion of air and protects it from infection at the same time.

## Super-Clean Care

Control of infection remains one of the biggest problems in U.S. hospitals, especially for patients with severe burns or cancer patients receiving drugs that suppress their ability to produce antibodies against disease. The space program's experience with "White Rooms" made dustfree by elaborate controls demonstrates what can be done to create a super-clean area. The medical version is the "life island," a transparent plastic canopy that completely engulfs the patient's bed. A filtered ventilating unit at the foot of the bed provides fresh air nearly 100 per cent free of bacteria and dust particles. Before being placed in the life island, the patient showers with hexachlorophene solution twice a day for three days and takes antibiotics to rid his body of bacteria.

*Sterile Food:* The patient's meals come from cans and are passed through an ultraviolet-treated portal on prewrapped, sterilized plates; even his razor and toothbrush are sterilized. Doctors and nurses tend the patient through plastic sleeves constructed in the canopy wall. At the National Institutes of Health in Bethesda, Md., an electronic stethoscope is being used to take readings of the patient's chest sounds from a distance. Among the life island's most promising uses: patients may be able to take higher doses of cancer-killing drugs without threat of infection.

NIH is now planning entire clean rooms built around the laminar-flow principle. Conceived initially for dust-free aerospace processes such as satellite assembly and checkout, laminar flow protects the patient with a curtain of air. In one laminar-flow room, air is filtered into the end where the patient's bed is located and is expelled at the other. Visitors entering at the exit end are, in effect, standing downstream and unable to contaminate the patient.

## Ultrasonic Treatment

To relieve bronchial and lung congestion in infants with such disorders as pneumonia and cystic fibrosis, an inherited disease that clogs the lungs with mucus, physicians at Chicago's Children's Memorial Hospital have devised an ultrasonic nebulizer adapted by Dr. David Allen from a paint sprayer. A decongestant fog to break up the mucus is brewed in a container with a quartz crystal in the bottom. When the crystal is set in vibration at ultrasound frequencies, the water breaks up into fine particles that are then pumped into a plastic canopy over the child's bed. The size of the particles is controlled by changing the crystal frequency. Since the distance the mist will travel down into the baby's chest is determined by particle size—the smallest go farthest—physicians can aim treatment at any level—from the windpipe to the lungs. For most infections, a child spends all day in the fog tent for three or four days; Allen is convinced that the ultrasonic fog therapy shortens time in the hospital.

## Atomic Attack

Radiation therapy and drugs are standard treatment for adult forms of leukemia, but both can damage normal tissue while combating the cancer. Researchers have recently begun experiments with extracorporeal blood irradiators. The irradiator at the Brookhaven National Laboratory, Upton, N.Y., is a 5-foot-high steel dome containing a core of cobalt 60, a potent source of gamma rays. The leukemia patient is attached to the irradiator by means of plastic tubes permanently placed in an artery and a vein in the forearm; the tubes are joined together when not in use. During irradiation, in effect, all the patient's blood is shipped outside his body for treatment. As his blood flows into the device, the cancerous white cells are exposed to the radio-cobalt source, while his body is shielded by lead and steel shielding (the red cells are less vulnerable to radiation). Two patients are treated at a time, lying in beds on either side of the irradiation unit.

At Boston's Massachusetts General Hospital, Dr. Benjamin Barnes has tested a way of irradiating a 48-year-old leukemia patient's blood with an irradiator worn on the wrist. Plastic tubes in the blood vessels in his arm conduct blood through a plastic capsule that is about an inch long and contains a small cylinder of strontium 90. This radioactive isotope produces beta rays which pass no further than the walls of the capsule. During a month of treatment, Barnes reports, the patient's lymphocytes (the white cells involved in one form of leukemia) dropped from a count of 40,000 to 1,000. Treatment was stopped because the effect of further loss of lymphocytes might be dangerous. Barnes reports that his patient seems "substantially" improved after wrist-irradiator treatment.

## Max Care

At least a third of the patients rushed to hospitals after heart attacks die despite the best medical care. Usually the cause of death is a disturbance in the electrical system that regulates the heartbeat; the ventricles, or pumping chambers, may fibrillate—flutter uncontrollably—and fail to pump blood properly. Or the heart may stop beating entirely. Coronary-care units rapidly being established in a growing number of hospitals are beginning to reduce the death toll from arrhythmias.

In a typical unit, the patient is monitored continuously by electrocardiographs, blood-pressure and pulse recorders at his bed and at a central control console. At the first sign of serious abnormality in the heart rhythm, an alarm sounds at the control desk and at key stations throughout the hospital. While the patient is given oxygen, his heartbeat may be returned to normal by plunger-like electrodes that deliver a shock through the chest wall. In some units, "demand pacemakers" are attached to the patient's chest and back to restore automatically normal heart rate if it should slow down or speed up.

For hospitals that don't have separate coronary-care units, Dr. Joel J. Nobel of Philadelphia's Graduate Pain Research Foundation and biomedical engineer Richard M. Rauch designed the Max emergency cart. A rolling operating table, the cart is equipped with defibrillator, mechanical cardiac-massage pump, oxygen mask, EKG oscilloscope and blood-pressure recorder, drugs and surgical instruments.

Coronary intensive care, some experts believe, can cut heart-attack deaths in the U.S. by 50,000 a year. At Philadelphia's Presbyterian Medical Center, the survival rate of patients admitted after coronaries has increased by a third. But most cardiologists agree that the record could be even better if serious arrhythmias could be prevented from occurring in the first place. Of the 130 patients admitted to the coronary unit at Boston's Peter Bent Brigham Hospital during the first year of operation none has died from serious arrhythmias, mainly because the staff was trained to look for early-warning changes in the EKG and gave the patients drugs to prevent trouble.

## Artificial Kidneys

The artificial kidney, the first mechanical substitute for a human organ, has been used since the 1940s to help patients with infections, shock or some types of high blood pressure get over the crisis of kidney failure. But in the last seven years, doctors have started using artificial kidneys to sustain the lives of patients afflicted with renal disease. The patients, wearing permanently attached plastic tubes in their arms or legs, report to the hospital once or twice a week for dialysis—having their blood cleansed of accumulated wastes.

The Washington VA hospital has one of the most modern kidney centers, capable of handling ten patients at a time. The fluid that removes poisons from the patient's blood is mixed automatically and delivered from a central storage tank to five bedside units, each serving two patients. The center can treat up to 25 patients a week.

Unfortunately, there are still not enough artificial kidneys to go around. Approximately 700 patients are receiving treatment in hospitals or in their homes, yet at least 5,000 Americans develop a form of renal disease each year that could be treated by chronic dialysis—if machines were available. One of the main reasons for the kidney gap is cost. Some kidneys cost $3,-000; just changing coils costs $25 per treatment. For the hospital, staffing a kidney machine may cost $10,000 to $25,000 a year per patient, while the cost for a dialysis in special home units may range from $5,000 to $15,000. Recently, Dr. Willem Kloff, who developed the first artificial kidney more than two decades ago, has ingeniously fashioned a cheaper artificial kidney unit out of an old washing machine. The whole rig cost $350, and each dialysis costs $16.

## Scanning the Body

The use of radioactive isotopes to trace diseases throughout the body was one of the most dramatic postwar developments in medical diagnosis. Radioactive iodine, one of the oldest diagnostic isotopes, travels to the thyroid gland; a radio-sensitive scanner records radiation from the isotope and prints a map of the gland. A light area on the map might be a cancer. Radioactive gold collects in the liver, acting as a way of detecting a malignancy or the scar tissue of cirrhosis. More sensitive scanners and isotopes that produce better pictures while exposing the patient to less radiation are rapidly becoming available.

One of the best scanners is the "gamma camera," developed at the University of California's Donner Lab. Gamma rays emitted from an isotope create faint flashes of light on a crystal that are then amplified by phototubes. A computer relays the flashes to a picture tube where they can be recorded on Polaroid film as a series of white dots, showing the distribution of the isotope in the patient's body. After administration of technetium, for example, a patient can be examined for a brain tumor in three minutes, as compared with up to one hour for older scanning equipment. The camera also can provide a rapid series of Polaroid shots to trace the flow of blood to reveal, for example, where a stroke has occluded the blood supply to the brain.

Ultrasound, working on the same principle as naval sonar, is another important diagnostic tool. Ultrasonic scanners emit sound waves, measure the time they take to echo from tissues inside the body and record the "contacts" on an oscilloscope. An ultrasonic probe attached to a tweezer device has been used to locate and remove a tiny metal fragment inside the eye. Sound waves can also locate brain tumors by showing that the midline membrane separating the two halves of the cerebrum has been squeezed to one side. And they can measure the size of a baby's head inside the womb, helping the obstetrician decide whether a Caesarean section is necessary without X-rays —a radiation hazard to mother or child.

## A Spare Heart

The grand achievement in medical technology within the next few years will be the artificial heart. The National Heart Institute is spending $7 million this year to support artificial-heart research; some experts believe the goal could be reached by 1970. Just last year, Dr. Michael E. DeBakey of

Houston's Baylor University College of Medicine and Dr. Adrian Kantrowitz of the State University of New York Downstate Medical Center in Brooklyn were able to implant partial replacements for the heart in critically ill patients.

Both devices are made of plastic and synthetic fabric. They are actually air-driven pumps to take over part of the work of the left ventricle—the heart's main pumping chamber. One of DeBakey's patients, a 37-year-old woman with rheumatic heart disease, recovered after a ten-day boost from the pump.

The DeBakey auxiliary heart, designed with the aid of Rice University engineers, is a plastic globe about the size of a grapefruit containing a double lining of plastic fabric. It is installed on the left side of the chest, the top half protruding above the ribs. The Kantrowitz auxiliary ventricle is a curved Dacron tube containing a flexible rubber lining and was designed by an Avco-Everett Research Laboratory team led by physicist Arthur Kantrowitz, the surgeon's brother. The device is placed entirely inside the chest.

Kantrowitz points out that the left ventricle is the first to fail in serious heart disease, and that a perfected ventricle booster would adequately serve 98 per cent of heart patients. As for a completely artificial heart, the Brooklyn surgeon says: "I want to leave that to the next generation."

*Priority:* The Cleveland Clinic's Willem Kolff has constructed several models intended to replace the heart—and they are startlingly like the real thing and have four chambers. The hearts are made of silicone or natural rubber, have a synthetic valve system and a right ventricle to pump blood to the lungs, as well as a left one to send blood to the body. Air-driven from outside the body, like the DeBakey and Kantrowitz ventricles, one of Kolff's hearts kept a calf alive for two days until blood clots formed.

Kolff must solve the clotting problem and perfect the valves that open and close the chambers before it is ready for use in people. Moreover, sensitive controls are needed for regulating blood flow in and out of the heart. With the aid of NASA's Lewis Research Center, Kolff and his colleagues are experimenting with a mechanical control system that would simulate the pumping pattern of the natural heart and help the artificial heart's four chambers work in harmony. "Naturally," says Kolff, "I believe that the artificial heart is the major priority for the immediate future."

What about the more distant future? The era of collaboration between doctor and engineer is just getting under way. Other parts of the body will be constructed. Researchers at Western Reserve and the Case Institute are working on computerized artificial arms. Researchers at Baylor are trying to devise synthetic skin to cover burns. And many technologists speak seriously of an artificial liver, stomach, intestine and pancreas, made of exotic plastics, metals and ingenuity. Indeed, miniaturized computers might even make possible a synthetic brain. "We cannot duplicate God's work," says one member of Kolff's team, "but we can come very close."

## STUDY QUESTIONS

1. According to *Newsweek*, the newest weapons against illness and disease are the result of alliances between medicine and what two unlikely sources?

2. What old problems has the "New Medicine" left unsolved?

3. What does *Newsweek* predict will be medicine's "grand achievement"? What artificial organ has already proven successful?

4. The *Newsweek* article is replete with technical jargon. Can you define *cryosurgery, the life island, Max,* and *the laminar-flow principle* after a single reading?

5. Do the divisions and their headings clarify either the structure or informational content of the essay?

*Rachel Carson*

# THE OBLIGATION TO ENDURE

Rachel Carson (1907–1964) was born in Springdale, Pennsylvania and attended Pennsylvania College for Women and Johns Hopkins University. She was awarded honorary doctorates by Oberlin College, the Drexel Institute of Technology, and Smith College. She received the George Westinghouse AAAS Science Writing Award (1950), a Guggenheim Fellowship (1951), the John Burroughs Medal (1952), and the Page-One Award (1952). Her books include *Under the Sea Wind* (1941), *The Sea Around Us* (1951), *The Edge of the Sea* (1956), and *Silent Spring* (1962). *Silent Spring* became one of the most controversial books of the past decade.

$T$HE HISTORY of life on earth has been a history of interac-
tion between living things and their surroundings. To a
large extent, the physical form and the habits of the
earth's vegetation and its animal life have been molded by the environment.
Considering the whole span of earthly time, the opposite effect, in which life
actually modifies its surroundings, has been relatively slight. Only within
the moment of time represented by the present century has one species—
man—acquired significant power to alter the nature of his world.

During the past quarter century this power has not only increased to one
of disturbing magnitude but it has changed in character. The most alarming
of all man's assaults upon the environment is the contamination of air,
earth, rivers, and sea with dangerous and even lethal materials. This pollution is for the most part irrecoverable; the chain of evil it initiates not only in
the world that must support life but in living tissues is for the most part irreversible. In this now universal contamination of the environment, chemicals
are the sinister and little-recognized partners of radiation in changing the
very nature of the world—the very nature of its life. Strontium 90, released
through nuclear explosions into the air, comes to earth in rain or drifts down
as fallout, lodges in soil, enters into the grass or corn or wheat grown there,
and in time takes up its abode in the bones of a human being, there to remain
until his death. Similarly, chemicals sprayed on croplands or forests or gardens lie long in soil, entering into living organisms, passing from one to another in a chain of poisoning and death. Or they pass mysteriously by underground streams until they emerge and, through the alchemy of air and sunlight, combine into new forms that kill vegetation, sicken cattle, and work
unknown harm on those who drink from once pure wells. As Albert
Schweitzer has said, "Man can hardly even recognize the devils of his own
creation."

It took hundreds of millions of years to produce the life that now inhabits
the earth—eons of time in which that developing and evolving and diversi-
fying life reached a state of adjustment and balance with its surroundings.
The environment, rigorously shaping and directing the life it supported,
contained elements that were hostile as well as supporting. Certain rocks
gave out dangerous radiation; even within the light of the sun, from which
all life draws its energy, there were short-wave radiations with power to injure. Given time—time not in years but in millennia—life adjusts, and a
balance has been reached. For time is the essential ingredient; but in the
modern world there is no time.

The rapidity of change and the speed with which new situations are created follow the impetuous and heedless pace of man rather than the deliberate pace of nature. Radiation is no longer merely the background radiation
of rocks, the bombardment of cosmic rays, the ultraviolet of the sun that
have existed before there was any life on earth; radiation is now the unnatu-

ral creation of man's tampering with the atom. The chemicals to which life is asked to make its adjustment are no longer merely the calcium and silica and copper and all the rest of the minerals washed out of the rocks and carried in rivers to the sea; they are the synthetic creations of man's inventive mind, brewed in his laboratories, and having no counterparts in nature.

To adjust to these chemicals would require time on the scale that is nature's; it would require not merely the years of a man's life but the life of generations. And even this, were it by some miracle possible, would be futile, for the new chemicals come from our laboratories in an endless stream; almost five hundred annually find their way into actual use in the United States alone. The figure is staggering and its implications are not easily grasped—500 new chemicals to which the bodies of men and animals are required somehow to adapt each year, chemicals totally outside the limits of biologic experience.

Among them are many that are used in man's war against nature. Since the mid-1940's over 200 basic chemicals have been created for use in killing insects, weeds, rodents, and other organisms described in the modern vernacular as "pests"; and they are sold under several thousand different brand names.

These sprays, dusts, and aerosols are now applied almost universally to farms, gardens, forests, and homes—nonselective chemicals that have the power to kill every insect, the "good" and the "bad," to still the song of birds and the leaping of fish in the streams, to coat the leaves with a deadly film, and to linger on in soil—all this though the intended target may be only a few weeds or insects. Can anyone believe it is possible to lay down such a barrage of poisons on the surface of the earth without making it unfit for all life? They should not be called "insecticides," but "biocides."

The whole process of spraying seems caught up in an endless spiral. Since DDT was released for civilian use, a process of escalation has been going on in which ever more toxic materials must be found. This has happened because insects, in a triumphant vindication of Darwin's principle of the survival of the fittest, have evolved super races immune to the particular insecticide used, hence a deadlier one has always to be developed—and then a deadlier one than that. It has happened also because, for reasons to be described later, destructive insects often undergo a "flareback," or resurgence, after spraying, in numbers greater than before. Thus the chemical war is never won, and all life is caught in its violent crossfire.

Along with the possibility of the extinction of mankind by nuclear war, the central problem of our age has therefore become the contamination of man's total environment with such substances of incredible potential for harm—substances that accumulate in the tissues of plants and animals and even penetrate the germ cells to shatter or alter the very material of heredity upon which the shape of the future depends.

Some would-be architects of our future look toward a time when it will be possible to alter the human germ plasm by design. But we may easily be doing so now by inadvertence, for many chemicals, like radiation, bring about gene mutations. It is ironic to think that man might determine his own future by something so seemingly trivial as the choice of an insect spray.

All this has been risked—for what? Future historians may well be amazed by our distorted sense of proportion. How could intelligent beings seek to control a few unwanted species by a method that contaminated environment and brought the threat of disease and death even to their own kind? Yet this is precisely what we have done. We have done it, moreover, for reasons that collapse the moment we examine them. We are told that the enormous and expanding use of pesticides is necessary to maintain farm production. Yet is our real problem not one of *overproduction?* Our farms, despite measures to remove acreages from production and to pay farmers *not* to produce, have yielded such a staggering excess of crops that the American taxpayer in 1962 is paying out more than one billion dollars a year as the total carrying cost of the surplus-food storage program. And is the situation helped when one branch of the Agriculture Department tries to reduce production while another states, as it did in 1958, "It is believed generally that reduction of crop acreages under provisions of the Soil Bank will stimulate interest in use of chemicals to obtain maximum production on the land retained in crops."

All this is not to say there is no insect problem and no need of control. I am saying, rather, that control must be geared to realities, not to mythical situations, and that the methods employed must be such that they do not destroy us along with the insects.

The problem whose attempted solution has brought such a train of disaster in its wake is an accompaniment of our modern way of life. Long before the age of man, insects inhabited the earth—a group of extraordinarily varied and adaptable beings. Over the course of time since man's advent, a small percentage of the more than half a million species of insects have come into conflict with human welfare in two principal ways: as competitors for the food supply and as carriers of human disease.

Disease-carrying insects become important where human beings are crowded together, especially under conditions where sanitation is poor, as in time of natural disaster or war or in situations of extreme poverty and deprivation. Then control of some sort becomes necessary. It is a sobering fact, however, as we shall presently see, that the method of massive chemical control has had only limited success, and also threatens to worsen the very conditions it is intended to curb.

Under primitive agricultural conditions the farmer had few insect problems. These arose with the intensification of agriculture—the devotion of immense acreages to a single crop. Such a system set the stage for explosive increases in specific insect populations. Single-crop farming does not take advantage of the principles by which nature works; it is agriculture as an engineer might conceive it to be. Nature has introduced great variety into the landscape, but man has displayed a passion for simplifying it. Thus he undoes the built-in checks and balances by which nature holds the species within bounds. One important natural check is a limit on the amount of suitable habitat for each species. Obviously then, an insect that lives on wheat can build up its population to much higher levels on a farm devoted to wheat than on one in which wheat is intermingled with other crops to which the insect is not adapted.

The same thing happens in other situations. A generation or more ago, the towns of large areas of the United States lined their streets with the noble elm tree. Now the beauty they hopefully created is threatened with complete destruction as disease sweeps through the elms, carried by a beetle that would have only limited chance to build up large populations and to spread from tree to tree if the elms were only occasional trees in a richly diversified planting.

Another factor in the modern insect problem is one that must be viewed against a background of geologic and human history: the spreading of thousands of different kinds of organisms from their native homes to invade new territories. This worldwide migration has been studied and graphically described by the British ecologist Charles Elton in his recent book *The Ecology of Invasions*. During the Cretaceous Period, some hundred million years ago, flooding seas cut many land bridges between continents and living things found themselves confined in what Elton calls "colossal separate nature reserves." There, isolated from others of their kind, they developed many new species. When some of the land masses were joined again, about 15 million years ago, these species began to move out into new territories— a movement that is not only still in progress but is now receiving considerable assistance from man.

The importation of plants is the primary agent in the modern spread of species, for animals have almost invariably gone along with the plants, quarantine being a comparatively recent and not completely effective innovation. The United States Office of Plant Introduction alone has introduced almost 200,000 species and varieties of plants from all over the world. Nearly half of the 180 or so major insect enemies of plants in the United States are accidental imports from abroad, and most of them have come as hitchhikers on plants.

In new territory, out of reach of the restraining hand of the natural enemies that kept down its numbers in its native land, an invading plant or animal is able to become enormously abundant. Thus it is no accident that our most troublesome insects are introduced species.

These invasions, both the naturally occurring and those dependent on human assistance, are likely to continue indefinitely. Quarantine and massive chemical campaigns are only extremely expensive ways of buying time. We are faced, according to Dr. Elton, "with a life-and-death need not just to find new technological means of suppressing this plant or that animal"; instead we need the basic knowledge of animal populations and their relations to their surroundings that will "promote an even balance and damp down the explosive power of outbreaks and new invasions."

Much of the necessary knowledge is now available but we do not use it. We train ecologists in our universities and even employ them in our governmental agencies but we seldom take their advice. We allow the chemical death rain to fall as though there were no alternative, whereas in fact there are many, and our ingenuity could soon discover many more if given opportunity.

Have we fallen into a mesmerized state that makes us accept as inevitable that which is inferior or detrimental, as though having lost the will or the vision to demand that which is good? Such thinking, in the words of the ecologist Paul Shepard, "idealizes life with only its head out of water, inches above the limits of toleration of the corruption of its own environment . . . Why should we tolerate a diet of weak poisons, a home in insipid surroundings, a circle of acquaintances who are not quite our enemies, the noise of motors with just enough relief to prevent insanity? Who would want to live in a world which is just not quite fatal?"

Yet such a world is pressed upon us. The crusade to create a chemically sterile, insect-free world seems to have engendered a fanatic zeal on the part of many specialists and most of the so-called control agencies. On every hand there is evidence that those engaged in spraying operations exercise a ruthless power. "The regulatory entomologists . . . function as prosecutor, judge and jury, tax assessor and collector and sheriff to enforce their own orders," said Connecticut entomologist Neely Turner. The most flagrant abuses go unchecked in both state and federal agencies.

It is not my contention that chemical insecticides must never be used. I do content that we have put poisonous and biologically potent chemicals indiscriminately into the hands of persons largely or wholly ignorant of their potentials for harm. We have subjected enormous numbers of people to contact with these poisons, without their consent and often without their knowledge. If the Bill of Rights contains no guarantee that a citizen shall be secure against lethal poisons distributed either by private individuals or by public officials, it is surely only because our forefathers, despite their considerable wisdom and foresight, could conceive of no such problem.

I contend, furthermore, that we have allowed these chemicals to be used with little or no advance investigation of their effect on soil, water, wildlife, and man himself. Future generations are unlikely to condone our lack of prudent concern for the integrity of the natural world that supports all life.

There is still very limited awareness of the nature of the threat. This is an era of specialists, each of whom sees his own problem and is unaware of or intolerant of the larger frame into which it fits. It is also an era dominated by industry, in which the right to make a dollar at whatever cost is seldom challenged. When the public protests, confronted with some obvious evidence of damaging results of pesticide applications, it is fed little tranquilizing pills of half truth. We urgently need an end to these false assurances, to the sugar coating of unpalatable facts. It is the public that is being asked to assume the risks that the insect controllers calculate. The public must decide whether it wishes to continue on the present road, and it can do so only when in full possession of the facts. In the words of Jean Rostand, "the obligation to endure gives us the right to know."

## STUDY QUESTIONS

1.  What does Rachel Carson feel is the central problem of our age?

2.  According to Miss Carson, how has the history of man's relationship to his environment changed in the twentieth century?

3.  How has the chemical contamination of man's environment upset the balance of nature?

4.  In what way is man's experimenting with the atom "unnatural"?

5.  How has Darwin's principle of the survival of the fittest escalated the production of toxic materials?

6.  What two factors have increased the effectiveness of insect invasions?

*Loren C. Eiseley*

# USING A PLAGUE TO
# FIGHT A PLAGUE

Loren Eiseley (1907–      ) was born in Lincoln, Nebraska. He received his B.A. (1933) from the University of Nebraska, and his M.A. (1935) and Ph.D. (1937) from the University of Pennsylvania. He taught at the University of Kansas and Oberlin College before returning, in 1947, to the University of Pennsylvania where he is now University Professor in anthropology and history of science and head of the Department of the History and Philosophy of Science. A Guggenheim fellow, he has published widely in both popular periodicals and learned journals. *Darwin's Century* was given the Phi Beta Kappa science award in 1959, and *The Firmament of Time* (1960) received the John Burroughs medal and the Lecomte de Nouy award. His other books include *The Immense Journey* (1951), *Francis Bacon and the Modern Temper* (1952), and *Galapagos: The Flow of Wilderness* (1968).

$A$ FEW DAYS ago I stood amidst the marshes of a well-known wildlife refuge. As I studied a group of herons through my glasses, there floated by the margin of my vision the soapy, unsightly froth of a detergent discharged into the slough's backwaters from some source upstream. Here nature, at first glance, seemed green and uncontaminated. As I left, however, I could not help wondering how long it would be before seeping industrial wastes destroyed the water-life on which those birds subsisted—how long it would be before poisonous and vacant mudflats had replaced the chirping frogs and waving cattails I loved to visit. I thought also of a sparkling stream in the Middle West in which, as a small boy, I used to catch sunfish, but which today is a muddy, lifeless treacle filled with oil from a nearby pumping station. No living thing now haunts its polluted waters.

These two episodes out of my own experience are trifling, however, compared with that virulent facet of man's activities treated in Rachel Carson's latest book. It is a devastating, heavily documented, relentless attack upon human carelessness, greed, and irresponsibility—an irresponsibility that has let loose upon man and the countryside a flood of dangerous chemicals in a situation which, as Miss Carson states, is without parallel in medical history. "No one," she adds, "yet knows what the ultimate consequences may be."

*Silent Spring* is her account of those floods of insecticides and well-intentioned protective devices which have indiscriminately slaughtered our wildlife of both forest and stream. Such ill-considered activities break the necessary food chains of nature and destroy the livelihood of creatures not even directly affected by the pesticides. The water run-off from agricultural and forested areas carries to our major rivers and to the seas chemicals which may then impregnate the food we eat. We have no assurance that we are not introducing into nature heavy concentrates of non-natural substances whose effects are potentially as dangerous as those that came to light in the dramatic medical episode that shocked the public in recent weeks. I refer, of course, to the foetal monsters produced by the sleep drug Thalidomide. Imperfect though the present legal controls in the field of direct medical experiment may be, they are less inadequate than in the domain of agricultural chemistry, where aerial spraying is cascading a rain of poison over field and farmland.

D'Arcy Thompson, the great British biologist of the late nineteenth century, commented astutely in 1897 that the increasing tempo of human cultural evolution produces a kind of evolution of chance itself—an increasing dissonance and complexity of change beyond what one finds in the world before man came. Though this evolution of chance arises within the human domain, it does not long remain confined to it. Instead, the erratic and growingly unpredictable fantasies created in the human mind invade nature itself. Tremendous agricultural productivity is correlated with the insatiable demands of ever-growing populations. Wastes in the air and wastes polluting the continental arteries increasingly disrupt the nature that we have taken for granted since the first simple hunters wandered out of the snowy winter of the Ice Age and learned to live in cities.

Man's sanitary engineering, in western civilization, never amounted to much until the middle phase of the industrial revolution and the discovery of the relation of bacteria to disease. Now it is apparent that man must learn to handle more wisely the products of his own aspiring chemistry. He is faced with the prospect of learning to be a creative god in nature without, at the same time, destroying his surroundings and himself through thoughtless indifference to the old green world out of which he has so recently emerged and to which (though he forgets) he is as indissolubly bound in his own way as the herons that stalked before my field glasses.

Essentially there are two ways of approaching the control of noxious insects: a natural and a chemical means. I am deliberately confining my remarks here, not to the effect of man's accidental industrial wastes upon his environment—a subject worthy of attention in itself—but to his deliberate and largely post-World War II use of peculiar carbon compounds in crop dusting and other forms of insect control. DDT is an excellent and spectacular example. With the passage of time the chemical industries have pressed more and more such substances upon the receptive public. Extensive research has been carried on in this field, frequently with results, at first glance, of an impressive character. That there may be other results, less favorable when viewed over a longer time span, is not always so well publicized.

The reason that Rachel Carson has chosen the more conservative biological approach to the problem of insect control lies in the following facts: Ill or uncontrolled spraying with deadly chemicals destroys beneficial as well as undesirable forms of life; furthermore, the poisonous residues may and do find their way into human food. Secondly, because insect generations are short and their numbers large, they rapidly become immune to the poisons that originally decimated them. By contrast, birds and the higher mammals, including man, cannot rapidly develop this selective immunity. They are eventually threatened not only by tougher and more formidable insect disease-carriers, but also by progressively dangerous chemicals devised against the mounting numbers of insects that refuse to succumb but whose natural enemies—the birds and fish—are being slaughtered in growing numbers by these same chemicals. The normal balance of life is thus increasingly disrupted. Man is whetting the cutting edge of natural selection, but its edge is turned against himself and his allies in the animal world.

In case after case, Miss Carson succeeds in documenting her thesis with complete adequacy. It is not pleasant to learn of the casual spraying of the landscape with chemicals capable of mutagenic effects and regarded by some authorities as representing as great a menace as high levels of radiation. Nor is it reassuring to read that the hydrocarbons have an affinity for mammalian germ cells. At present there is no law on the statute books that requires manufacturers to demonstrate the genetic effects, as distinguished from the toxicity, of their concoctions. Nor is there any way of controlling what the average uninformed farmer may do with his insecticides. An equally ill-educated and impatient public wants its weeds, gnats, and mosquitoes eliminated in one fell blow. It is not sophisticated enough to trouble over the looming demise of our beautiful national bird, the bald eagle, nor to connect the return of many supposedly eliminated pests with the fact that the newer generation may be able to flourish in a sack of DDT and thus be twice as formidable.

The biological controls which Miss Carson favors, along with other informed biologists, are not just more careful and discreet use of pesticides, but also such clever natural manipulations as the release of sterilized screw worm flies, causing a greater reduction in the population of this parasite than any insecticide would have achieved. Successful experiments such as this depend upon precise knowledge of the life history of an organism. They strike directly at the heart of the problem. They do not leave poisonous residues or resistant life-strains, nor do they result in the mass killing that frequently destroys valuable food chains on which even man is in the long run dependent.

All of these facts Rachel Carson has set forth sensibly in the quiet, rational prose for which she is famous. If her present book does not possess the beauty of *The Sea Around Us,* it is because she has courageously chosen, at the height of her powers, to educate us upon a sad, an unpleasant, an unbeautiful topic, and one of our own making. *Silent Spring* should be read by every American who does not want it to be the epitaph of a world not very far beyond us in time.

## STUDY QUESTIONS

1.  What episodes from his own experience does Eiseley use in support of Miss Carson's thesis?

2.  What two basic means of approaching the control of noxious insects are open to men?

3.  According to Eiseley, what facts led Miss Carson to choose the more conservative of these two approaches?

*William J. Darby*

# SILENCE, MISS CARSON

William J. Darby (1913–      ) was born in Galloway, Arkansas, and received his B.S. (1936) and M.D. (1937) from the University of Arkansas and his M.S. (1941) and Ph.D. (1942) from the University of Michigan. He is now head of the Department of Biochemistry and director of the Division of Nutrition, School of Medicine, at Vanderbilt University. He has served with the National Research Council and the World Health Organization. Darby is coauthor of *Nutrition and Diet in Health and Disease* and codiscoverer of vitamin M and the activity of pteroylglutamic acid in sprue.

$S$*ilent Spring* starts with a bit of dramatic description of a situation which the author then acknowledges does not actually exist. It then orients the reader to its subject matter by stating that "only within . . . the present century has man . . . acquired significant power to alter the nature of his world." It identifies as irrecoverable and "for the most part irreversible" the effects of "this now universal contamination of the environment (in which) chemicals are the sinister and little recognized partners of radiation in changing the very nature of the world, the very nature of life itself." Man has, according to Miss Carson, now upset that ideal state of "adjustment and balance" of life on this planet through "synthetic creations of man's inventive mind, brewed in his laboratory, and having no counterpart in nature." These products, the reader is told, are "staggering in number," have "power to kill," have "incredible potential for harm," represent a "train of disaster," result in a "chemical death rain," and are being used with "little or no advance investigation of their effect on soil, water, wildlife, and man himself." She further warns the reader that all of these sinister chemicals will not only extinguish plant life, wild life, aquatic life, and man, but they will produce cancer, leukemia, sterility, and cellular mutations.

A review of *Silent Spring* by Rachel Carson. Reprinted from *Chemical and Engineering News*, Vol. 40, October 1, 1962, pp. 60–63. Copyright 1962 by The American Chemical Society and reprinted by permission.

There are 297 pages devoted to reiteration of these views. There then follows a 55-page "list of principal sources" designed to impress the reader
with the extent of the support for Miss Carson's views. This list uses an ex-
tender and is artificially colored and flavored. Its apparent bulk is made one
third greater through devoting a line of type to identify each page on which a
source bears, and by repeating in full the title of each source in relation to
recurrent pages. Its bulk will appeal to those readers who are as uncritical as
the author, or to those who find the flavor of her product to their taste. These
consumers will include the organic gardeners, the antifluoride leaguers, the
worshipers of "natural foods," those who cling to the philosophy of a vital
principle, and pseudo-scientists and faddists.

The flavor of this product is indicated in part by the source list. She refers
frequently to testimony given at 1950, 1951, and 1952 Congressional hearings, seldom to later years, and to the opinions of Morton S. Siskind and
W. C. Hueper.

The author ignores the sound appraisals of such responsible, broadly
knowledgeable scientists as the President of the National Academy of Sciences, the members of the President's Scientific Advisory Committee, the
Presidents of the Rockefeller Foundation and Nutrition Foundation, the
several committees of the National Academy of Sciences-National Research
Council (including the Food and Nutrition Board, the Agricultural Board,
the Food Protection Committee) who have long given thoughtful study to
these questions, and the special advisory committees appointed by the governors of California and Wisconsin. The latter committees were chaired by
two distinguished scientist-presidents of universities, Dr. Emil Mrak and
the late Dr. Conrad A. Elvehjem.

All of these groups of scientists have recognized the essentiality of use of
agricultural chemicals to produce the food required by the expanding world
population and to sustain an acceptable standard of living and health. They
have recognized the safety of proper use of agricultural chemicals and, indeed, the benefits to the consumer which accrue from their proper use in
food and agricultural production.

Miss Carson's book adds no new factual material not already known to
such serious scientists as those concerned with these developments, nor does
it include information essential for the reader to interpret the knowledge. It
does confuse the information and so mix it with her opinions that the uninitiated reader is unable to sort fact from fancy. In view of the mature, responsible attention which this whole subject receives from able, qualified scientific groups such as those identified in the foregoing (and whom Miss Carson
chooses to ignore); in view of her scientific qualifications in contrast to those
of our distinguished scientific leaders and statesmen, this book should be
ignored.

Logically, it should be possible to terminate this review here. Unfortunately, however, this book will have wide circulation on one of the standard subscription lists. It is doubtful that many readers can bear to wade through its high-pitched sequences of anxieties. It is likely to be perused uncritically, to be regarded by the layman as authoritative (which it is not), and to arouse in him manifestations of anxieties and psychoneuroses exhibited by some of the subjects cited by the author in the chapter "The Human Price." Indeed, the author's efforts at appraising psychologic evidence concerning the effects of substances reveal a remarkable lack of competence as a psychiatrist, even as great a lack in the area of toxicology or even knowledge of existing regulatory controls. The obvious effect of all of this on the reader will be to aggravate unjustifiably his own neurotic anxiety.

Her thesis is revealed by the dedicatory quotations: "Man has lost the capacity to foresee and to forestall. He will end by destroying the earth." (Albert Schweitzer) "Our approach to nature is to beat it into submission. We would stand a better chance of survival if we accommodated ourselves to this planet and viewed it appreciatively instead of skeptically and dictatorially." (E. B. White)

Such a passive attitude as the latter coupled with such pessimistic (and to this reviewer, unacceptable) philosophy as the former, means the end of all human progress, reversion to a passive social state devoid of technology, scientific medicine, agriculture, sanitation, or education. It means disease, epidemics, starvation, misery, and suffering incomparable and intolerable to modern man. Indeed, social, educational, and scientific development is prefaced on the conviction that man's lot will be and is being improved by greater understanding of and thereby increased ability to control or mold those forces responsible for man's suffering, misery, and deprivation.

The author's motivation is not quite so evident, but the emotional call to write the book is revealed by her acknowledgment that "In a letter written in January 1958, Olga Owens Huckins told me of her own bitter experience of a small world made lifeless, and so brought my attention sharply back to a problem with which I had long been concerned. I then realized *I must write this book*" (italics are the reviewer's).

So impelled, Miss Carson has effectively used several literary devices to present her thesis and make it appear to be a widely held scientific one. She "name-drops" by quoting or referring to renowned scientists out of context. A statement divorced from its original meaning is then approximated to an opinion of the author or else to a question posed by her with an implied answer. The reader is led to conclude thereby that the authority mentioned is in accord with the author's position. Nobel prize winners are recognized as especially useful names for such a purpose.

Another device used is that of confusion of the reader with (to him) unintelligible scientific jargon or irrelevant discussions of cellular processes.

Miss Carson's failure to distinguish between the occupational and residue hazards is common to almost all popular writers on this subject. The occupational hazard associated with the manufacture and application of agricultural chemicals is similar to that of other work and can, should be, and is being reduced. That accidents have occurred is well known, but this is no more reason to ban useful chemicals than is the lamentable occurrence of preventable automobile or airplane accidents reason to ban these modern modes of transportation. Despite all of the implications of harm from residues on foods, Miss Carson has not produced one single example of injury resulting to man from these residues.

Miss Carson is infatuated with biologic control and the balance of nature. Despite her statement that the really effective control of insects is that applied by nature, one must observe that the very ineffectiveness of such control is the raison d'être of chemical pesticides.

She commits the scientifically indefensible fallacy of considering that any substance which in any quantity is toxic must per se be a poison. By such a definition almost everything—water, salt, sugar, amino acids, minerals, vitamins A or D, etc.—is a poison. She gives the reader a mistaken concept of tolerances. Tolerances are not ill-defined levels of maximum quantities which can be ingested without acute harm. They are minimum amounts of a substance which should exist when the chemical has been employed in good and proper beneficial practice. They are based on extensive use data and toxicologic testing in animals and frequently metabolic studies in man. They include a very wide margin of safety, usually being set at 100 times the *minimum* amount of the substance which induces any physiologic effect in the most sensitive of at least two species of animals for lifetime or two- to four-year periods.

The benefit of use of chemicals, charges Miss Carson, is for the producer. She ignores the requirement under the Miller bill that a chemical must be *effective,* which means benefit to the consumer. She fails to recognize that "the consumer" includes the producer, farmer, wholesaler, retailer, equipment manufacturer, their families, and even the scientists who evaluate the chemicals. The toxicologists in industry, in the Food and Drug Administration, in our universities and research institutes have, as consumers, equal stake in protecting the nation's health as does Miss Carson—and I believe, are better qualified to assume this protection.

Her ignorance or bias on some of the considerations throws doubt on her competence to judge policy. For example, she indicates that it is neither wise nor responsible to use pesticides in the control of insect-borne diseases. The July–August 1962 *World Health* (WHO publication) reports that a malaria eradication program in Mexico has since 1957 reduced the malaria area from 978,185 sq. km. with 18 million inhabitants to 224,500 sq. km. with 1.5 million inhabitants. "In most areas the simple technique of indoor spraying of houses proved effective . . ."; where bedbugs were resistant to

DDT, an insecticide mixture was successfully used. "As a result of the campaign, the Mexican Government is expanding its agricultural programme, distributing land, and undertaking irrigation and hydroelectric schemes." It is most doubtful that Miss Carson really is ignorant of these and other facts which any objective appraisal of this subject demands. Instead, it seems that a call to write a book has completely outweighed any semblance of scientific objectivity.

The public may be misled by this book. If it stimulates the public to press for unwise and ill-conceived restrictions on the production, use, or development of new chemicals, it will be the consumer who suffers. If, on the other hand, it inspires some users to read and heed labels more carefully, it may aid in the large educational effort in which industry, government, colleges, and many other groups are engaged (despite Miss Carson's implication that they are not.)

The responsible scientist should read this book to understand the ignorance of those writing on the subject and the educational task which lies ahead.

## STUDY QUESTIONS

1.  What does Darby seek to accomplish by the numerous quotations in the first paragraph? *lay case about to attack before reader*

2.  What objections does he raise to Miss Carson's bibliography? *Source list reharsh self?*

3.  What significance does Darby find in Miss Carson's reference to testimony given in 1950–1952 Congressional hearings? Is this significance explicit or implicit? *Views feel outdated*

4.  What effect does Darby feel *Silent Spring* will have on the layman? *believe her, want action*

5.  How does Darby explain Miss Carson's having ignored the statistics he presents? *ignored them, just wanted to write a book*

*Bertrand Russell*

# THE SCIENCE TO SAVE
# US FROM SCIENCE

Bertrand Russell (1872–     ) was born in Trelleck, England. The English
lord was educated at Trinity College, Cambridge. Few contemporary philosophers have been as widely praised and as loudly damned as has Russell.
His books include *Philosophical Essays* (1910), *Mysticism and Logic*
(1918), *What I Believe* (1925), *An Outline of Philosophy* (1927), *Which
Way to Peace?* (1936), *Unpopular Essays* (1950), *Why I Am Not a Christian* (1957), *Has Man a Future?* (1961), and *War Crimes in Vietnam* (1967).
Two volumes of his remarkable autobiography have been published.
Among the almost countless honors and awards which have been bestowed
on Russell are the Nobel Prize for Literature (1950) and the UNESCO
Kalinga Prize (1951).

SINCE THE beginning of the seventeenth century scientific
discovery and invention have advanced at a continually
increasing rate. This fact has made the last three hundred
and fifty years profoundly different from all previous ages. The gulf separating man from his past has widened from generation to generation, and
finally from decade to decade. A reflective person, meditating on the extinction of trilobites, dinosaurs and mammoths, is driven to ask himself some
very disquieting questions. Can our species endure so rapid a change? Can
the habits which insured survival in a comparatively stable past still suffice
amid the kaleidoscopic scenery of our time? And, if not, will it be possible to
change ancient patterns of behavior as quickly as the inventors change our
material environment? No one knows the answer, but it is possible to survey
probabilities, and to form some hypotheses as to the alternative directions
that human development may take.

The first question is: Will scientific advance continue to grow more and
more rapid, or will it reach a maximum speed and then begin to slow down?

The discovery of scientific method required genius, but its utilization requires only talent. An intelligent young scientist, if he gets a job giving access to a good laboratory, can be pretty certain of finding out something of interest, and may stumble upon some new fact of immense importance. Science, which was still a rebellious force in the early seventeenth century, is now integrated with the life of the community by the support of governments and universities. And as its importance becomes more evident, the number of people employed in scientific research continually increases. It would seem to follow that, so long as social and economic conditions do not become adverse, we may expect the rate of scientific advance to be maintained, and even increased, until some new limiting factor intervenes.

It might be suggested that, in time, the amount of knowledge needed before a new discovery could be made would become so great as to absorb all the best years of a scientist's life, so that by the time he reached the frontier of knowledge he would be senile. I suppose this may happen some day, but that day is certainly very distant. In the first place, methods of teaching improve. Plato thought that students in his academy would have to spend ten years learning what was then known of mathematics; nowadays any mathematically minded schoolboy learns much more mathematics in a year.

In the second place, with increasing specialization, it is possible to reach the frontier of knowledge along a narrow path, involving much less labor than a broad highway. In the third place, the frontier is not a circle but an irregular contour, in some places not far from the center. Mendel's epoch-making discovery required little previous knowledge; what it needed was a life of elegant leisure spent in a garden. Radio-activity was discovered by the fact that some specimens of pitchblende were unexpectedly found to have photographed themselves in the dark. I do not think, therefore, that purely intellectual reasons will slow up scientific advances for a very long time to come.

There is another reason for expecting scientific advance to continue, and that is that it increasingly attracts the best brains. Leonardo da Vinci was equally pre-eminent in art and science, but it was from art that he derived his greatest fame. A man of similar endowments living at the present day would almost certainly hold some post which would require his giving all his time to science; if his politics were orthodox, he would probably be engaged in devising the hydrogen bomb, which our age would consider more useful than his pictures. The artist, alas, has not the status that he once had. Renaissance princes might compete for Michelangelo; modern states compete for nuclear physicists.

There are considerations of quite a different sort which might lead to an expectation of scientific retrogression. It may be held that science itself generates explosive forces which will, sooner or later, make it impossible to preserve the kind of society in which science can flourish. This is a large and different question, to which no confident answer can be given. It is a very important question, which deserves to be examined. Let us therefore see what is to be said about it.

Industrialism, which is in the main a product of science, has provided a certain way of life and a certain outlook on the world. In America and Britain, the oldest industrial countries, this outlook and this way of life have come gradually, and the population has been able to adjust itself to them without any violent breach of continuity. These countries, accordingly, did not develop dangerous psychological stresses. Those who preferred the old ways could remain on the land, while the more adventurous could migrate to the new centers of industry. There they found pioneers who were compatriots, who shared in the main the general outlook of their neighbors. The only protests came from men like Carlyle and Ruskin, whom everybody at once praised and disregarded.

It was a very different matter when industrialism and science, as well-developed systems, burst violently upon countries hitherto ignorant of both, especially since they came as something foreign, demanding imitation of enemies and disruption of ancient national habits. In varying degrees this shock has been endured by Germany, Russia, Japan, India and the natives of Africa. Everywhere it has caused and is causing upheavals of one sort or another, of which as yet no one can foresee the end.

The earliest important result of the impact of industrialism on Germans was the Communist Manifesto. We think of this now as the Bible of one of the two powerful groups into which the world is divided, but it is worth while to think back to its origin in 1848. It then shows itself as an expression of admiring horror by two young university students from a pleasant and peaceful cathedral city, brought roughly and without intellectual preparation into the hurly-burly of Manchester competition.

Germany, before Bismarck had "educated it," was a deeply religious country, with a quiet, exceptional sense of public duty. Competition, which the British regarded as essential to efficiency, and which Darwin elevated to an almost cosmic dignity, shocked the Germans, to whom service to the state seemed the obviously right moral ideal. It was therefore natural that they should fit industrialism into a framework of nationalism or socialism. The Nazis combined both. The somewhat insane and frantic character of German industrialism and the policies it inspired is due to its foreign origin and its sudden advent.

Marx's doctrine was suited to countries where industrialism was new. The German Social Democrats abandoned his dogmas when their country became industrially adult. But by that time Russia was where Germany had been in 1848, and it was natural that Marxism should find a new home. Stalin, with great skill, has combined the new revolutionary creed with the traditional belief in "Holy Russia" and the "Little Father." This is as yet the most notable example of the arrival of science in an environment that is not ripe for it. China bids fair to follow suit.

Japan, like Germany, combined modern technique with worship of the state. Educated Japanese abandoned as much of their ancient way of life as was necessary in order to secure industrial and military efficiency. Sudden change produced collective hysteria, leading to insane visions of world power unrestrained by traditional pieties.

These various forms of madness—communism, nazism, Japanese imperialism—are the natural result of the impact of science on nations with a strong pre-scientific culture. The effects in Asia are still at an early stage. The effects upon the native races of Africa have hardly begun. It is therefore unlikely that the world will recover sanity in the near future.

The future of science—nay more, the future of mankind—depends upon whether it will be possible to restrain these various collective hysterias until the populations concerned have had time to adjust themselves to the new scientific environment. If such adjustment proves impossible, civilized society will disappear, and science will be only a dim memory. In the Dark Ages science was not distinguished from sorcery, and it is not impossible that a new Dark Ages may revive this point of view.

The danger is not remote; it threatens within the next few years. But I am not now concerned with such immediate issues. I am concerned with the wider question: Can a society based, as ours is, on science and scientific technique, have the sort of stability that many societies had in the past, or is it bound to develop explosive forces that will destroy it? This question takes us beyond the sphere of science into that of ethics and moral codes and the imaginative understanding of mass psychology. This last is a matter which political theorists have quite unduly neglected.

Let us begin with moral codes. I will illustrate the problem by a somewhat trivial illustration. There are those who think it wicked to smoke tobacco, but they are mostly people untouched by science. Those whose outlook has been strongly influenced by science usually take the view that smoking is neither a vice nor a virtue. But when I visited a Nobel works, where rivers of nitro-glycerine flowed like water, I had to leave all matches at the entrance, and it was obvious that to smoke inside the works would be an act of appalling wickedness.

This instance illustrates two points: first, that a scientific outlook tends to make some parts of traditional moral codes appear superstitious and irrational; second, that by creating a new environment science creates new duties, which may happen to coincide with those that have been discarded. A world containing hydrogen bombs is like one containing rivers of nitro-glycerine; actions elsewhere harmless may become dangerous in the highest degree. We need therefore, in a scientific world, a somewhat different moral code from the one inherited from the past. But to give to a new moral code sufficient compulsive force to restrain actions formerly considered harmless is not easy, and cannot possibly be achieved in a day.

As regards ethics, what is important is to realize the new dangers and to consider what ethical outlook will do most to diminish them. The most important new facts are that the world is more unified than it used to be, and that communities at war with each other have more power of inflicting mutual disaster than at any former time. The question of power has a new importance. Science has enormously increased human power, but has not increased it without limit. The increase of power brings an increase of responsibility; it brings also a danger of arrogant self-assertion, which can only be averted by continuing to remember that man is not omnipotent.

The most influential sciences, hitherto, have been physics and chemistry; biology is just beginning to rival them. But before very long psychology and especially mass psychology, will be recognized as the most important of all sciences from the standpoint of human welfare. It is obvious that populations have dominant moods, which change from time to time according to their circumstances. Each mood has a corresponding ethic. Nelson inculcated these ethical principles on midshipmen: to tell the truth, to shoot straight, and to hate a Frenchman as you would the devil. This last was chiefly because the English were angry with France for intervening on the side of America. Shakespeare's Henry V says:

> If it be a sin to covet honor,
> I am the most offending soul alive.

This is the ethical sentiment that goes with aggressive imperialism: "honor" is proportional to the number of harmless people you slaughter. A great many sins may be excused under the name of "patriotism." On the other hand complete powerlessness suggests humility and submission as the greatest virtues; hence the vogue of stoicism in the Roman Empire and of Methodism among the English poor in the early nineteenth century. When, however, there is a chance of successful revolt, fierce vindictive justice suddenly becomes the dominant ethical principle.

In the past, the only recognized way of inculcating moral precepts has been by preaching. But this method has very definite limitations: it is notorious that, on the average, sons of clergy are not morally superior to other people. When science has mastered this field, quite different methods will be adopted. It will be known what circumstances generate what moods, and what moods incline men to what ethical systems. Governments will then decide what sort of morality their subjects are to have and their subjects will adopt what the Government favors, but will do so under the impression that they are exercising free will. This may sound unduly cynical, but that is only because we are not yet accustomed to applying science to the human mind.

Science has powers for evil, not only physically, but mentally: the hydrogen bomb can kill the body, and government propaganda (as in Russia) can kill the mind.

In view of the terrifying power that science is conferring on governments, it is necessary that those who control governments should have enlightened and intelligent ideals, since otherwise they can lead mankind to disaster.

I call an ideal "intelligent" when it is possible to approximate to it by pursuing it. This is by no means sufficient as an ethical criterion, but it is a test by which many aims can be condemned. It cannot be supposed that Hitler desired the fate which he brought upon his country and himself, and yet it was pretty certain that this would be the result of his arrogance. Therefore the ideal of "Deutschland ueber Alles" can be condemned as unintelligent. (I do not mean to suggest that this is its only defect.) Spain, France, Germany and Russia have successively sought world dominion: three of them have endured defeat in consequence, but their fate has not inspired wisdom.

Whether science—and indeed civilization in general—can long survive depends upon psychology, that is to say, it depends upon what human beings desire. The human beings concerned are rulers in totalitarian countries, and the mass of men and women in democracies. Political passions determine political conduct much more directly than is often supposed. If men desire victory more than cooperation, they will think victory possible.

But if hatred so dominates them that they are more anxious to see their enemies killed than to keep their own children alive, they will discover all kinds of "noble" reasons in favor of war. If they resent inferiority or wish to preserve superiority, they will have the sentiments that promote the class war. If they are bored beyond a point, they will welcome excitement even of a painful kind.

Such sentiments, when widespread, determine the policies and decisions of nations. Science can, if rulers so desire, create sentiments which will avert disaster and facilitate cooperation. At present there are powerful rulers who have no such wish. But the possibility exists, and science can be just as potent for good as for evil. It is not science, however, which will determine how science is used.

Science, by itself, cannot supply us with an ethic. It can show us how to achieve a given end, and it may show us that some ends cannot be achieved. But among ends that can be achieved our choice must be decided by other than purely scientific considerations. If a man were to say, "I hate the human race, and I think it would be a good thing if it were exterminated," we could say, "Well, my dear sir, let us begin the process with you." But this is hardly argument, and no amount of science could prove such a man mistaken.

But all who are not lunatics are agreed about certain things: That it is better to be alive than dead, better to be adequately fed than starved, better to be free than a slave. Many people desire those things only for themselves and their friends; they are quite content that their enemies should suffer. These people can be refuted by science: Mankind has become so much one family that we cannot insure our own prosperity except by insuring that of everyone else. If you wish to be happy yourself, you must resign yourself to seeing others also happy.

Whether science can continue, and whether, while it continues, it can do more good than harm, depends upon the capacity of mankind to learn this simple lesson. Perhaps it is necessary that all should learn it, but it must be learned by all who have great power, and among those some still have a long way to go.

## STUDY QUESTIONS

1. What two questions serve as the structural basis for Russell's essay? Are Russell's answers to these questions as tentative as he suggests they will be in the first paragraph?

2. How have the function and status of the scientist changed with the passage of time? Of the artist?

3. According to Russell, of what have political theorists been neglectful?

4. Russell calls psychology—mass psychology—a science. Do you agree? Why or why not?

5. What moral imperative must men of science learn?

6. What word could be substituted for *intelligent,* as Russell uses it when discussing ideals?

Philip Wylie

# SCIENCE HAS SPOILED MY SUPPER

Philip Wylie (1902–      ) was born in Beverly, Massachusetts. He was a
student at Princeton from 1920 to 1923, and received an honorary Litt. D.
from the University of Miami, Florida. Wylie has been on the *New Yorker*
staff, written screenplays for Paramount and Metro-Goldwyn-Mayer, and
contributed to the *Saturday Evening Post, Redbook, Reader's Digest,* and
*Look.* He is the recipient of a Freedom Foundation medal (1953). His
books include *Heavy Laden* (1928), *Gladiator* (1930), *Generation of Vipers*
(1942), *An Essay in Morals* (1947), *The Answer* (1956), *The Innocent Ambassadors* (1957), *Autumn Romance* (1968), and *Magical Animal* (1969).
*Generation of Vipers* includes the famous discussion of "Moms."

I AM A FAN for Science. My education is scientific and I
have, in one field, contributed a monograph to a scientific
journal. Science, to my mind, is applied honesty, the one
reliable means we have to find out truth. That is why, when error is committed in the name of Science, I feel the way a man would if his favorite
uncle had taken to drink.

Over the years, I have come to feel that way about what science has done
to food. I agree that America can set as good a table as any nation in the
world. I agree that our food is nutritious and that the diet of most of us is
well-balanced. What America eats is handsomely packaged; it is usually
clean and pure; it is excellently preserved. The only trouble with it is this:
year by year it grows less good to eat. It appeals increasingly to the eye. But
who eats with his eyes? Almost everything used to taste better when I was a
kid. For quite a long time I thought that observation was merely another
index of advancing age. But some years ago I married a girl whose mother is
an expert cook of the kind called "old-fashioned." This gifted woman's
daughter (my wife) was taught her mother's venerable skills. The mother
lives in the country and still plants an old-fashioned garden. She still buys
dairy products from the neighbors and, in so far as possible, she uses the

same materials her mother and grandmother did—to prepare meals that are superior. They are just as good, in this Year of Grace, as I recall them from my courtship. After eating for a while at the table of my mother-in-law, it is sad to go back to eating with my friends—even the alleged "good cooks" among them. And it is a gruesome experience to have meals at the best big-city restaurants.

Take cheese, for instance. Here and there, in big cities, small stores and delicatessens specialize in cheese. At such places, one can buy at least some of the first-rate cheeses that we used to eat—such as those we had with pie and in macaroni. The latter were sharp but not too sharp. They were a little crumbly. We called them American cheeses, or even rat cheese; actually, they were Cheddars. Long ago, this cheese began to be supplanted by a material called "cheese foods." Some cheese foods and "processed" cheese are fairly edible; but not one comes within miles of the old kinds—for flavor.

A grocer used to be very fussy about his cheese. Cheddar was made and sold by hundreds of little factories. Representatives of the factories had particular customers, and cheese was prepared by hand to suit the grocers, who knew precisely what their patrons wanted in rat cheese, pie cheese, American and other cheeses. Some liked them sharper; some liked them yellower; some liked anise seeds in cheese, or caraway.

What happened? Science—or what is called science—stepped in. The old-fashioned cheeses didn't ship well enough. They crumbled, became moldy, dried out. "Scientific" tests disclosed that a great majority of the people will buy a less-good-tasting cheese if that's all they can get. "Scientific marketing" then took effect. Its motto is "Give the people the least quality they'll stand for." In food, as in many other things, the "scientific marketers" regard quality as secondary so long as they can sell most persons anyhow; what they are after is "durability" or "shippability."

It is not possible to make the very best cheese in vast quantities at a low average cost. "Scientific sampling" got in its statistically nasty work. It was found that the largest number of people will buy something that is bland and rather tasteless. Those who prefer a product of a pronounced and individualistic flavor have a variety of preferences. Nobody is altogether pleased by bland foodstuff, in other words; but nobody is very violently put off. The result is that a "reason" has been found for turning out zillions of packages of something that will "do" for nearly all and isn't even imagined to be superlatively good by a single soul!

Economics entered. It is possible to turn out in quantity a bland, impersonal, practically imperishable substance more or less resembling, say, cheese—at lower cost than cheese. Chain groceries shut out the independent stores and "standardization" became a principal means of cutting costs.

Imitations also came into the cheese business. There are American dupli-
cations of most of the celebrated European cheeses, mass-produced and
cheaper by far than the imports. They would cause European food-lovers to
gag or guffaw—but generally the imitations are all that's available in the
supermarkets. People buy them and eat them.

Perhaps you don't like cheese—so the fact that decent cheese is hardly
ever served in America any more, or used in cooking, doesn't matter to you.
Well, take bread. There has been (and still is) something of a hullabaloo
about bread. In fact, in the last few years, a few big bakeries have taken to
making a fairly good imitation of real bread. It costs much more than what is
nowadays called bread, but it is edible. Most persons, however, now eat as
"bread" a substance so full of chemicals and so barren of cereals that it approaches a synthetic.

Most bakers are interested mainly in how a loaf of bread looks. They are
concerned with how little stuff they can put in it—to get how much money.
They are deeply interested in using chemicals that will keep bread from
molding, make it seem "fresh" for the longest possible time, and so render it
marketable and shippable. They have been at this monkeyshine for a generation. Today a loaf of "bread" looks deceptively real; but it is made from
heaven knows what and it resembles, as food, a solidified bubble bath. Some
months ago I bought a loaf of the stuff and, experimentally, began pressing
it together, like an accordion. With a little effort, I squeezed the whole loaf
to a length of about one inch!

Yesterday, at the home of my mother-in-law, I ate with country-churned
butter and home-canned wild strawberry jam several slices of actual bread,
the same thing we used to have every day at home. People who have eaten
actual bread will know what I mean. They will know that the material commonly called bread is not even related to real bread, except in name.

## II

For years, I couldn't figure out what had happened to vegetables. I knew,
of course, that most vegetables, to be enjoyed in their full deliciousness,
must be picked fresh and cooked at once. I knew that vegetables cannot be
overcooked and remain even edible, in the best sense. They cannot stand on
the stove. That set of facts makes it impossible, of course, for any American
restaurant—or, indeed, any city-dweller separated from supply by more
than a few hours—to have decent fresh vegetables. The Parisians managed
by getting their vegetables picked at dawn and rushed in farmers' carts to
market, where no middleman or marketman delays produce on its way to
the pot.

Our vegetables, however, come to us through a long chain of command.
There are merchants of several sorts—wholesalers before the retailers,

commission men, and so on—with the result that what were once edible products become, in transit, mere wilted leaves and withered tubers.

Homes and restaurants do what they can with this stuff—which my mother-in-law would discard on the spot. I have long thought that the famed blindfold test for cigarettes should be applied to city vegetables. For I am sure that if you puréed them and ate them blindfolded, you couldn't tell the beans from the peas, the turnips from the squash, the Brussels sprouts from the broccoli.

It is only lately that I have found how much science has had to do with this reduction of noble victuals to pottage. Here the science of genetics is involved. Agronomists and the like have taken to breeding all sorts of vegetables and fruits—changing their original nature. This sounds wonderful and often is insane. For the scientists have not as a rule taken any interest whatsoever in the taste of the things they've tampered with!

What they've done is to develop "improved" strains of things for every purpose but eating. They work out, say, peas that will ripen all at once. The farmer can then harvest his peas and thresh them and be done with them. It is extremely profitable because it is efficient. What matter if such peas taste like boiled paper wads?

Geneticists have gone crazy over such "opportunities." They've developed string beans that are straight instead of curved, and all one length. This makes them easier to pack in cans, even if, when eating them, you can't tell them from tender string. Ripening time and identity of size and shape are, nowadays, more important in carrots than the fact that they taste like carrots. Personally, I don't care if they hybridize onions till they are big as your head and come up through the snow; but, in doing so, they are producing onions that only vaguely and feebly remind you of onions. We are getting some varieties, in fact, that have less flavor than the water off last week's leeks. Yet, if people don't eat onions because they taste like onions, what in the name of Luther Burbank do they eat them for?

The women's magazines are about one third dedicated to clothes, one third to mild comment on sex, and the other third to recipes and pictures of handsome salads, desserts, and main courses. "Institutes" exist to experiment and tell housewives how to cook attractive meals and how to turn leftovers into works of art. The food thus pictured looks like famous paintings of still life. The only trouble is it's tasteless. It leaves appetite unquenched and merely serves to stave off famine.

I wonder if this blandness of our diet doesn't explain why so many of us are overweight and even dangerously so. When things had flavor, we knew what we were eating all the while—and it satisfied us. A teaspoonful of my mother-in-law's wild strawberry jam will not just provide a gastronome's ecstasy: it will entirely satisfy your jam desire. But, of the average tinned or glass-packed strawberry jam, you need half a cupful to get the idea of what you're eating. A slice of my mother-in-law's apple pie will satiate you far better than a whole bakery pie.

That thought is worthy of investigation—of genuine scientific investigation. It is merely a hypothesis, so far, and my own. But people—and their ancestors—have been eating according to flavor for upwards of a billion years. The need to satisfy the sense of taste may be innate and important. When food is merely a pretty cascade of viands, with the texture of boiled cardboard and the flavor of library paste, it may be the instinct of *genus homo* to go on eating in the unconscious hope of finally satisfying the ageless craving of the frustrated taste buds. In the days when good-tasting food was the rule in the American home, obesity wasn't such a national curse.

How can you feel you've eaten if you haven't tasted, and fully enjoyed tasting? Why (since science is ever so ready to answer the beck and call of mankind) don't people who want to reduce merely give up eating and get the nourishment they must have in measured doses shot into their arms at hospitals? One ready answer to that question suggests that my theory of overeating is sound: people like to taste! In eating, they try to satisfy that like.

The scientific war against deliciousness has been stepped up enormously in the last decade. Some infernal genius found a way to make biscuit batter keep. Housewives began to buy this premixed stuff. It saved work, of course. But any normally intelligent person can learn, in a short period, how to prepare superb baking powder biscuits. I can make better biscuits, myself, than can be made from patent batters. Yet soon after this fiasco became an American staple, it was discovered that a half-baked substitute for all sorts of breads, pastries, rolls, and the like could be mass-manufactured, frozen—and sold for polishing off in the home oven. None of these two-stage creations is as good as even a fair sample of the thing it imitates. A man of taste, who had eaten one of my wife's cinnamon buns, might use the premixed sort to throw at starlings—but not to eat! Cake mixes, too, come ready-prepared—like cement and not much better-tasting compared with true cake.

It is, however, "deep-freezing" that has really rung down the curtain on American cookery. Nothing is improved by the process. I have yet to taste a deep-frozen victual that measures up, in flavor, to the fresh, unfrosted original. And most foods, cooked or uncooked, are destroyed in the deep freeze for all people of sense and sensibility. Vegetables with crisp and crackling texture emerge as mush, slippery and stringy as hair nets simmered in Vaseline. The essential oils that make peas peas—and cabbage cabbage—must undergo fission and fusion in freezers. Anyhow, they vanish. Some meats turn to leather. Others to wood pulp. Everything, pretty much, tastes like the mosses of tundra, dug up in midwinter. Even the appearance changes, oftentimes. Handsome comestibles you put down in the summer come out looking very much like the corpses of woolly mammoths recovered from the last Ice Age.

Of course, all this scientific "food handling" tends to save money. It certainly preserves food longer. It reduces work at home. But these facts, and especially the last, imply that the first purpose of living is to avoid work—at home, anyhow.

Without thinking, we are making an important confession about ourselves as a nation. We are abandoning quality—even, to some extent, the quality of people. The "best" is becoming too good for us. We are suckling ourselves on machine-made mediocrity. It is bad for our souls, our minds, and our digestion. It is the way our wiser and calmer forebears fed, not people, but hogs: as much as possible and as fast as possible, with no standard of quality.

The Germans say, *"Mann ist was er isst—Man is what he eats."* If this be true, the people of the U.S.A. are well on their way to becoming a faceless mob of mediocrities, or robots. And if we apply to other attributes the criteria we apply these days to appetite, that is what would happen! We would not want bright children any more; we'd merely want them to look bright—and get through school fast. We wouldn't be interested in beautiful women —just a good paint job. And we'd be opposed to the most precious quality of man: his individuality, his differentness from the mob.

There are some people—sociologists and psychologists among them—who say that is exactly what we Americans are doing, are becoming. Mass man, they say, is on the increase. Conformity, standardization, similarity—all on a cheap and vulgar level—are replacing the great American ideas of colorful liberty and dignified individualism. If this is so, the process may well begin, like most human behavior, in the home—in those homes where a good meal has been replaced by something-to-eat-in-a-hurry. By something not very good to eat, prepared by a mother without very much to do, for a family that doesn't feel it amounts to much anyhow.

I call, here, for rebellion.

## STUDY QUESTIONS

1. How does Wylie define *science?*

2. Why does he put quotation marks around "scientific" tests, "scientific marketing," and "scientific sampling"?

3. To what does Wylie attribute the changes in cheese and bread? The "improvements" in vegetables? The deep-freezing of a variety of foods?

4. With what connotation does Wylie use "pottage"?

5. What hypothesis does Wylie advance to explain overweight Americans?

# H. G. Wells

# THE LORD OF THE DYNAMOS

H. G. Wells (1866–1946) was born in Bromley, England, and was an apprentice draper before going to the University of London. Greatly influenced by Thomas Henry Huxley, he first wrote articles and then books on science. Among his numerous books are science-fiction classics—*The Time Machine* (1895), *The Invisible Man* (1897), and *The War of the Worlds* (1898); and novels of contemporary life—*Kipps* (1905), *Tono-Bungay* (1909), *The History of Mr. Polly* (1910), and *Mr. Britling Sees It Through* (1916). An original member of the Fabian Society, his interest in social problems found a vent in *A Modern Utopia* (1905) and *The Shape of Things To Come* (1933). *His Outline of History* (1920) has been widely criticized.

THE CHIEF ATTENDANT of the three dynamos that buzzed and rattled at Camberwell, and kept the electric railway going, came out of Yorkshire, and his name was James Holroyd. He was a practical electrician, but fond of whiskey, a heavy red-haired brute with irregular teeth. He doubted the existence of the deity, but accepted Carnot's cycle, and he had read Shakespeare and found him weak in chemistry. His helper came out of the mysterious East, and his name was Azuma-zi. But Holroyd called him Pooh-bah. Holroyd liked the nigger help because he would stand kicking—a habit with Holroyd—and did not pry into the machinery and try to learn the ways of it. Certain odd possibilities of the negro mind brought into abrupt contact with the crown of our civilisation Holroyd never fully realised, though just at the end he got some inkling of them.

To define Azuma-zi was beyond ethnology. He was, perhaps, more negroid than anything else, though his hair was curly rather than frizzy, and his nose had a bridge. Moreover, his skin was brown rather than black, and the whites of his eyes were yellow. His broad cheek-bones and narrow chin gave his face something of the viperine V. His head, too, was broad behind, and low and narrow at the forehead, as if his brain had been twisted round in the reverse way to a European's. He was short of stature and still shorter of English. In conversation he made numerous odd noises of no known marketable value, and his infrequent words were carved and wrought into heraldic grotesqueness. Holroyd tried to elucidate his religious beliefs, and—especially after whiskey—lectured to him against superstition and missionaries. Azuma-zi, however, shirked the discussion of his gods, even though he was kicked for it.

Azuma-zi had come, clad in white but insufficient raiment, out of the stoke-hole of the *Lord Clive,* from the Straits Settlements, and beyond, into London. He had heard even in his youth of the greatness and riches of London, where all the women are white and fair, and even the beggars in the streets are white; and he had arrived, with newly earned gold coins in his pocket, to worship at the shrine of civilisation. The day of his landing was a dismal one; the sky was dun, and a wind-worried drizzle filtered down to the greasy streets, but he plunged boldly into the delights of Shadwell, and was presently cast up, shattered in health, civilised in costume, penniless, and, except in matters of the direst necessity, practically a dumb animal, to toil for James Holroyd and to be bullied by him in the dynamo shed at Camberwell. And to James Holroyd bullying was a labour of love.

There were three dynamos with their engines at Camberwell. The two that have been there since the beginning are small machines; the larger one was new. The smaller machines made a reasonable noise; their straps hummed over the drums, every now and then the brushes buzzed and fizzled, and the air churned steadily, whoo! whoo! whoo! between their poles. One was loose in its foundations and kept the shed vibrating. But the big dynamo drowned these little noises altogether with the sustained drone of its iron core, which somehow set part of the ironwork humming. The place made the visitor's head reel with the throb, throb, throb of the engines, the rotation of the big wheels, the spinning ball-valves, the occasional spittings of the steam, and over all the deep, unceasing, surging note of the big dynamo. This last noise was from an engineering point of view a defect; but Azuma-zi accounted it unto the monster for mightiness and pride.

If it were possible we would have the noises of that shed always about the reader as he reads, we would tell all our story to such an accompaniment. It was a steady stream of din, from which the ear picked out first one thread and then another; there was the intermittent snorting, panting, and seething of the steam-engines, the suck and thud of their pistons, the dull beat on the air as the spokes of the great driving-wheels came round, a note the leather straps made as they ran tighter and looser, and a fretful tumult from the dynamos; and, over all, sometimes inaudible, as the ear tired of it, and then creeping back upon the senses again, was this trombone note of the big machine. The floor never felt steady and quiet beneath one's feet, but quivered and jarred. It was a confusing, unsteady place, and enough to send anyone's thoughts jerking into odd zigzags. And for three months, while the big strike of the engineers was in progress, Holroyd, who was a blackleg, and Azuma-zi, who was a mere black, were never out of the stir and eddy of it, but slept and fed in the little wooden shanty between the shed and the gates.

Holroyd delivered a theological lecture on the text of his big machine soon after Azuma-zi came. He had to shout to be heard in the din. "Look at that," said Holroyd; "where's your 'eathen idol to match 'im?" And Azuma-zi looked. For a moment Holroyd was inaudible, and then Azuma-zi heard: "Kill a hundred men. Twelve per cent on the ordinary shares," said Holroyd, "and that's something like a Gord!"

Holroyd was proud of his big dynamo, and expatiated upon its size and power to Azuma-zi until heaven knows what odd currents of thought that, and the incessant whirling and shindy, set up within the curly, black cranium. He would explain in the most graphic manner the dozen or so ways in which a man might be killed by it, and once he gave Azuma-zi a shock as a sample of its quality. After that, in the breathing-times of his labour—it was heavy labour, being not only his own but most of Holroyd's—Azuma-zi would sit and watch the big machine. Now and then the brushes would sparkle and spit blue flashes, at which Holroyd would swear, but all the rest was as smooth and rhythmic as breathing. The band ran shouting over the shaft, and ever behind one as one watched was the complacent thud of the piston. So it lived all day in this big airy shed, with him and Holroyd to wait upon it; not prisoned up and slaving to drive a ship as the other engines he knew—mere captive devils of the British Solomon—had been, but a machine enthroned. Those two smaller dynamos, Azuma-zi by force of contrast despised; the large one he privately christened the Lord of the Dynamos. They were fretful and irregular, but the big dynamo was steady. How great it was! How serene and easy in its working! Greater and calmer even than the Buddhas he had seen at Rangoon, and yet not motionless, but living! The great black coils spun, spun, spun, the rings ran round under the brushes, and the deep note of its coil steadied the whole. It affected Azuma-zi queerly.

Azuma-zi was not fond of labour. He would sit about and watch the Lord of the Dynamos while Holroyd went away to persuade the yard porter to get whiskey, although his proper place was not in the dynamo shed but behind the engines, and, moreover, if Holroyd caught him skulking he got hit for it with a rod of stout copper wire. He would go and stand close to the colossus and look up at the great leather band running overhead. There was a black patch on the band that came round, and it pleased him somehow among all the clatter to watch this return again and again. Odd thoughts spun with the

whirl of it. Scientific people tell us that savages give souls to rocks and trees
—and a machine is a thousand times more alive than a rock or a tree. And
Azuma-zi was practically a savage still; the veneer of civilisation lay no
deeper than his slop suit, his bruises and the coal grime on his face and
hands. His father before him had worshipped a meteoric stone; kindred
blood, it may be, had splashed the broad wheels of Juggernaut.

He took every opportunity Holroyd gave him of touching and handling
the great dynamo that was fascinating him. He polished and cleaned it until
the metal parts were blinding in the sun. He felt a mysterious sense of service in doing this. He would go up to it and touch its spinning coils gently.
The gods he had worshipped were all far away. The people in London hid
their gods.

At last his dim feelings grew more distinct, and took shape in thoughts
and acts. When he came into the roaring shed one morning he salaamed to
the Lord of the Dynamos; and then, when Holroyd was away, he went and
whispered to the thundering machine that he was its servant, and prayed it
to have pity on him and save him from Holroyd. As he did so a rare gleam of
light came in through the open archway of the throbbing machine-shed, and
the Lord of the Dynamos, as he whirled and roared, was radiant with pale
gold. Then Azuma-zi knew that his service was acceptable to his Lord. After
that he did not feel so lonely as he had done, and he had indeed been very
much alone in London. And even when his work time was over, which was
rare, he loitered about the shed.

Then, the next time Holroyd maltreated him, Azuma-zi went presently to
the Lord of the Dynamos and whispered, "Thou seest, O my Lord!" and the
angry whirr of the machinery seemed to answer him. Thereafter it appeared
to him that whenever Holroyd came into the shed a different note came into
the sounds of the great dynamo. "My Lord bides his time," said Azuma-zi to
himself. "The iniquity of the fool is not yet ripe." And he waited and
watched for the day of reckoning. One day there was evidence of short cir-
cuiting, and Holroyd, making an unwary examination—it was in the afternoon—got a rather severe shock. Azuma-zi from behind the engine saw
him jump off and curse at the peccant coil.

"He is warned," said Azuma-zi to himself. "Surely my Lord is very patient."

Holroyd had at first initiated his "nigger" into such elementary concep-
tions of the dynamo's working as would enable him to take temporary
charge of the shed in his absence. But when he noticed the manner in which
Azuma-zi hung about the monster, he became suspicious. He dimly per-
ceived his assistant was "up to something," and connecting him with the
anointing of the coils with oil that had rotted the varnish in one place, he
issued an edict, shouted above the confusion of the machinery, "Don't 'ee go

nigh that big dynamo any more, Pooh-bah, or a'll take thy skin off!" Besides, if it pleased Azuma-zi to be near the big machine, it was plain sense and decency to keep him away from it.

Azuma-zi obeyed at the time, but later he was caught bowing before the Lord of the Dynamos. At which Holroyd twisted his arm and kicked him as he turned to go away. As Azuma-zi presently stood behind the engine and glared at the back of the hated Holroyd, the noises of the machinery took a new rhythm, and sounded like four words in his native tongue.

It is hard to say exactly what madness is. I fancy Azuma-zi was mad. The incessant din and whirl of the dynamo shed may have churned up his little store of knowledge and big store of superstitious fancy, at last, into something akin to frenzy. At any rate, when the idea of making Holroyd a sacrifice to the Dynamo Fetich was thus suggested to him, it filled him with a strange tumult of exultant emotion.

That night the two men and their black shadows were alone in the shed together. The shed was lit with one big arc light that winked and flickered purple. The shadows lay black behind the dynamos, the ball governors of the engines whirled from light to darkness, and their pistons beat loud and steady. The world outside seen through the open end of the shed seemed incredibly dim and remote. It seemed absolutely silent, too, since the riot of the machinery drowned every external sound. Far away was the black fence of the yard with grey, shadowy houses behind, and above was the deep blue sky and the pale little stars. Azuma-zi suddenly walked across the centre of the shed above which the leather bands were running, and went into the shadow by the big dynamo. Holroyd heard a click, and the spin of the armature changed.

"What are you dewin' with that switch?" he bawled in surprise. "Ha'n't I told you—"

Then he saw the set expression of Azuma-zi's eyes as the Asiatic came out of the shadow towards him.

In another moment the two men were grappling fiercely in front of the great dynamo.

"You coffee-headed fool!" gasped Holroyd, with a brown hand at his throat. "Keep off those contact rings." In another moment he was tripped and reeling back upon the Lord of the Dynamos. He instinctively loosened his grip upon his antagonist to save himself from the machine.

The messenger, sent in furious haste from the station to find out what had happened in the dynamo shed, met Azuma-zi at the porter's lodge by the gate. Azuma-zi tried to explain something, but the messenger could make nothing of the black's incoherent English, and hurried on to the shed. The machines were all noisily at work, and nothing seemed to be disarranged. There was, however, a queer smell of singed hair. Then he saw an odd-looking, crumpled mass clinging to the front of the big dynamo, and, approaching, recognised the distorted remains of Holroyd.

The man stared and hesitated a moment. Then he saw the face and shut his eyes convulsively. He turned on his heel before he opened them, so that he should not see Holroyd again, and went out of the shed to get advice and help.

When Azuma-zi saw Holroyd die in the grip of the Great Dynamo he had been a little scared about the consequences of his act. Yet he felt strangely elated and knew that the favour of the Lord Dynamo was upon him. His plan was already settled when he met the man coming from the station, and the scientific manager who speedily arrived on the scene jumped at the obvious conclusion of suicide. This expert scarcely noticed Azuma-zi except to ask a few questions. Did he see Holroyd kill himself? Azuma-zi explained he had been out of sight at the engine furnace until he heard a difference in the noise from the dynamo. It was not a difficult examination, being untinctured by suspicion.

The distorted remains of Holroyd, which the electrician removed from the machine, were hastily covered by the porter with a coffee-stained tablecloth. Somebody, by a happy inspiration, fetched a medical man. The expert was chiefly anxious to get the machine at work again, for seven or eight trains had stopped midway in the stuffy tunnels of the electric railway. Azuma-zi, answering or misunderstanding the questions of the people who had by authority or impudence come into the shed, was presently sent back to the stoke-hole by the scientific manager. Of course a crowd collected outside the gates of the yard,—a crowd, for no known reason, always hovers for a day or two near the scene of a sudden death in London; two or three reporters percolated somehow into the engine-shed, and one even got to Azuma-zi; but the scientific expert cleared them out again, being himself an amateur journalist.

Presently the body was carried away, and public interest departed with it. Azuma-zi remained very quietly at his furnace, seeing over and over again in the coals a figure that wriggled violently and became still. An hour after the murder, to any one coming into the shed it would have looked exactly as if nothing remarkable had ever happened there. Peeping presently from his engine-room the black saw the Lord Dynamo spin and whirl beside his little brothers, the driving wheels were beating round, and the steam in the pistons went thud, thud, exactly as it had been earlier in the evening. After all, from the mechanical point of view, it had been a most insignificant incident—the mere temporary deflection of a current. But now the slender form and slender shadow of the scientific manager replaced the sturdy outline of Holroyd travelling up and down the lane of light upon the vibrating floor under the straps between the engines and the dynamos.

"Have I not served my Lord?" said Azuma-zi, inaudibly, from his shadow, and the note of the great dynamo rang out full and clear. As he looked at the big, whirling mechanism the strange fascination of it that had been a little in abeyance since Holroyd's death resumed its sway.

Never had Azuma-zi seen a man killed so swiftly and pitilessly. The big, humming machine had slain its victim without wavering for a second from its steady beating. It was indeed a mighty god.

The unconscious scientific manager stood with his back to him, scribbling on a piece of paper. His shadow lay at the foot of the monster.

"Was the Lord Dynamo still hungry? His servant was ready."

Azuma-zi made a stealthy step forward, then stopped. The scientific manager suddenly stopped writing, and walked down the shed to the end-most of the dynamos, and began to examine the brushes.

Azuma-zi hesitated, and then slipped across noiselessly into the shadow by the switch. There he waited. Presently the manager's footsteps could be heard returning. He stopped in his old position, unconscious of the stoker crouching ten feet away from him. Then the big dynamo suddenly fizzled, and in another moment Azuma-zi had sprung out of the darkness upon him.

First, the scientific manager was gripped round the body and swung towards the big dynamo, then, kicking with his knee and forcing his antagonist's head down with his hands, he loosened the grip on his waist and swung round away from the machine. Then the black grasped him again, putting a curly head against his chest, and they swayed and panted as it seemed for an age or so. Then the scientific manager was impelled to catch a black ear in his teeth and bite furiously. The black yelled hideously.

They rolled over on the floor, and the black, who had apparently slipped from the vise of the teeth or parted with some ear—the scientific manager wondered which at the time—tried to throttle him. The scientific manager was making some ineffectual efforts to claw something with his hands and to kick, when the welcome sound of quick footsteps sounded on the floor. The next moment Azuma-zi had left him and darted towards the big dynamo. There was a splutter amid the roar.

The officer of the company, who had entered, stood staring as Azuma-zi caught the naked terminals in his hands, gave one horrible convulsion, and then hung motionless from the machine, his face violently distorted.

"I'm jolly glad you came in when you did," said the scientific manager, still sitting on the floor.

He looked at the still quivering figure. "It is not a nice death to die, apparently—but it is quick."

The official was still staring at the body. He was a man of slow apprehension.

There was a pause.

The scientific manager got up on his feet rather awkwardly. He ran his fingers along his collar thoughtfully, and moved his head to and fro several times.

"Poor Holroyd! I see now." Then almost mechanically he went towards the switch in the shadow and turned the current into the railway circuit again. As he did so the singed body loosened its grip upon the machine and fell forward on its face. The cone of the dynamo roared out loud and clear, and the armature beat the air.

So ended prematurely the Worship of the Dynamo Deity, perhaps the most shortlived of all religions. Yet withal it could boast a Martyrdom and a Human Sacrifice.

## STUDY QUESTIONS

1. Three or four characters have obvious functions in the story. The narrator himself is a character to a certain extent. What function does he serve?

2. At what point in "The Lord of the Dynamos" does Wells begin to prepare the reader for the conflict that will end in Holroyd's death?

3. How is Azuma-zi's new god superior to the gods he formerly worshipped? How does Holroyd add to Azuma-zi's idolization of the dynamo?

4. Is there any evidence from which to conclude that Azuma-zi was mad?

5. What does the reaction of the "civilized" men to Holroyd's death contribute to the over-all effect of the story?

# Section Four

# Language

"The Soul of Wit"

# George Orwell

# POLITICS AND THE ENGLISH LANGUAGE

George Orwell (1903–1950) was the pen name of Eric Blair, who was born in Bengal, India. He graduated from Eton College, served with the Indian Imperial Police in Burma from 1922 to 1927, and then returned to England to begin his career as a writer. His works include *Burmese Days* (1934), *Homage to Catalonia* (1936), *Dickens, Dali, and Others* (1946), and *Shooting an Elephant* (1950). His fame, however, is primarily the result of *Animal Farm* (1946) and *1984* (1949), the former one of the most famous modern satires and the latter a classic novel of social protest. His *Collected Essays* were published in 1969.

𝓜OST PEOPLE who bother with the matter at all would admit that the English language is in a bad way, but it is generally assumed that we cannot by conscious action do anything about it. Our civilization is decadent and our language—so the argument runs—must inevitably share in the general collapse. It follows that any struggle against the abuse of language is a sentimental archaism, like preferring candles to electric light or hansom cabs to aeroplanes. Underneath this lies the half-conscious belief that language is a natural growth and not an instrument which we shape for our own purposes.

Now, it is clear that the decline of a language must ultimately have political and economic causes: it is not due simply to the bad influence of this or that individual writer. But an effect can become a cause, reinforcing the original cause and producing the same effect in an intensified form, and so on indefinitely. A man may take to drink because he feels himself to be a failure, and then fail all the more completely because he drinks. It is rather the same thing that is happening to the English language. It becomes ugly and inaccurate because our thoughts are foolish, but the slovenliness of our language makes it easier for us to have foolish thoughts. The point is that the process is reversible. Modern English, especially written English, is full of bad habits which spread by imitation and which can be avoided if one is willing to take the necessary trouble. If one gets rid of these habits one can think more clearly, and to think clearly is a necessary first step towards political regeneration: so that the fight against bad English is not frivolous and is not the exclusive concern of professional writers. I will come back to this presently, and I hope that by that time the meaning of what I have said here will have become clearer. Meanwhile, here are five specimens of the English language as it is now habitually written.

These five passages have not been picked out because they are especially bad—I could have quoted far worse if I had chosen—but because they illustrate various of the mental vices from which we now suffer. They are a little below the average, but are fairly representative samples. I number them so that I can refer back to them when necessary:

"(1) I am not, indeed, sure whether it is not true to say that the Milton who once seemed not unlike a seventeenth-century Shelley had not become, out of an experience ever more bitter in each year, more alien [*sic*] to the founder of that Jesuit sect which nothing could induce him to tolerate."

Professor Harold Laski<br>(Essay in Freedom of Expression).

"(2) Above all, we cannot play ducks and drakes with a native battery of idioms which prescribes such egregious collocations of vocables as the Basic *put up with* for *tolerate* or *put at a loss* for *bewilder*."

Professor Lancelot Hogben (Interglossa).

"(3) On the one side we have the free personality: by definition it is not neurotic, for it has neither conflict nor dream. Its desires, such as they are, are transparent, for they are just what institutional approval keeps in the forefront of consciousness; another institutional pattern would alter their number and intensity; there is little in them that is natural, irreducible, or culturally dangerous. But *on the other side,* the social bond itself is nothing but the mutual reflection of these self-secure integrities. Recall the definition of love. Is not this the very picture of a small academic? Where is there a place in this hall of mirrors for either personality or fraternity?"

Essay on psychology in Politics (New York).

"(4) All the 'best people' from the gentlemen's clubs, and all the frantic fascist captains, united in common hatred of Socialism and bestial horror of the rising tide of the mass revolutionary movement, have turned to acts of provocation, to foul incendiarism, to medieval legends of poisoned wells, to legalize their own destruction of proletarian organizations, and rouse the agitated petty-bourgeoisie to chauvinistic fervour on behalf of the fight against the revolutionary way out of the crisis."

Communist pamphlet.

"(5) If a new spirit *is* to be infused into this old country, there is one thorny and contentious reform which must be tackled, and that is the humanization and galvanization of the B.B.C. Timidity here will bespeak cancer and atrophy of the soul. The heart of Britain may be sound and of strong beat, for instance, but the British lion's roar at present is like that of Bottom in Shakespeare's *Midsummer Night's Dream*—as gentle as any sucking dove. A virile new Britain cannot continue indefinitely to be traduced in the eyes or rather ears, of the world by the effete languors of Langham Place, brazenly masquerading as 'standard English.' When the Voice of Britain is heard at nine o'clock, better far and infinitely less ludicrous to hear aitches honestly dropped than the present priggish, inflated, inhibited, schoolma'amish arch braying of blameless bashful mewing maidens!"

Letter in *Tribune*.

Each of these passages has faults of its own, but, quite apart from avoidable ugliness, two qualities are common to all of them. The first is staleness of imagery: the other is lack of precision. The writer either has a meaning and cannot express it, or he inadvertently says something else, or he is almost indifferent as to whether his words mean anything or not. This mixture of vagueness and sheer incompetence is the most marked characteristic of modern English prose, and especially of any kind of political writing. As soon as certain topics are raised, the concrete melts into the abstract and no one seems able to think of turns of speech that are not hackneyed: prose consists less and less of *words* chosen for the sake of their meaning, and more and more of *phrases* tacked together like the sections of a prefabricated hen-house. I list below, with notes and examples, various of the tricks by means of which the work of prose-construction is habitually dodged:

*Dying Metaphors.*   A newly invented metaphor assists thought by evoking a visual image, while on the other hand a metaphor which is technically "dead" (e.g. *iron resolution*) has in effect reverted to being an ordinary word and can generally be used without loss of vividness. But in between these two classes there is a huge dump of worn-out metaphors which have lost all evocative power and are merely used because they save people the trouble of inventing phrases for themselves. Examples are: *Ring the changes on, take up the cudgels for, toe the line, ride roughshod over, stand shoulder to shoulder with, play into the hands of, no axe to grind, grist to the mill, fishing in troubled waters, on the order of the day, Achilles' heel, swan song, hotbed.* Many of these are used without knowledge of their meaning (what is a "rift," for instance?), and incompatible metaphors are frequently mixed, a sure sign that the writer is not interested in what he is saying. Some metaphors now current have been twisted out of their original meaning without those who use them even being aware of the fact. For example, *toe the line* is sometimes written *tow the line*. Another example is *the hammer and the anvil*, now always used with the implication that the anvil gets the worst of it. In real life it is always the anvil that breaks the hammer, never the other way about: a writer who stopped to think what he was saying would be aware of this, and would avoid perverting the original phrase.

*Operators* or *Verbal False Limbs*.   These save the trouble of picking out appropriate verbs and nouns, and at the same time pad each sentence with extra syllables which give it an appearance of symmetry. Characteristic phrases are: *render inoperative, militate against, make contact with, be subjected to, give rise to, give grounds for, have the effect of, play a leading part (role) in, make itself felt, take effect, exhibit a tendency to, serve the purpose of, etc., etc.* The keynote is the elimination of simple verbs. Instead of being a single word, such as *break, stop, spoil, mend, kill,* a verb becomes a *phrase*, made up of a noun or adjective tacked on to some general-purposes verb such as *prove, serve, form, play, render*. In addition, the passive voice is wherever possible used in preference to the active, and noun constructions are used instead of gerunds (*by examination of* instead of *by examining*). The range of verbs is further cut down by means of the *-ize* and *de-* formation, and the banal statements are given an appearance of profundity by means of the *not un-* formation. Simple conjunctions and prepositions are replaced by such phrases as *with respect to, having regard to, the fact that, by dint of, in view of, in the interests of, on the hypothesis that;* and the ends of sentences are saved from anticlimax by such resounding commonplaces as *greatly to be desired, cannot be left out of account, a development to be expected in the near future, deserving of serious consideration, brought to a satisfactory conclusion,* and so on and so forth.

*Pretentious Diction*.   Words like *phenomenon, element, individual* (as noun), *objective, categorical, effective, virtual, basic, primary, promote, constitute, exhibit, exploit, utilize, eliminate, liquidate,* are used to dress up simple statements and give an air of scientific impartiality to biased judgments. Adjectives like *epoch-making, epic, historic, unforgettable, triumphant, age-old, inevitable, inexorable, veritable,* are used to dignify the sordid processes of international politics, while writing that aims at glorifying war usually takes on an archaic colour, its characteristic words being: *realm, throne, chariot, mailed fist, trident, sword, shield, buckler, banner, jackboot, clarion*. Foreign words and expressions such as *cul de sac, ancien régime, deus ex machina, mutatis mutandis, status quo, gleichschaltung, weltanschauung,* are used to give an air of culture and elegance. Except for the useful abbreviations *i.e., e.g.,* and *etc.,* there is no real need for any of the hundreds of foreign phrases now current in English. Bad writers, and especially scientific, political and sociological writers, are nearly always haunted by the notion that Latin or Greek words are grander than Saxon ones, and unnecessary words like *expedite, ameliorate, predict, extraneous, deracinated, clandestine, subaqueous* and hundreds of others constantly gain ground from their Anglo-Saxon opposite numbers.[1] The jargon peculiar to Marxist writing (*hyena, hangman, cannibal, petty bourgeois, these gentry, lacquey, flunkey, mad dog, White Guard,* etc.) consists largely of words and phrases translated from Russian, German or French; but the normal way of coining a new word is to use a Latin or Greek root with the appropriate affix and, where necessary, the -ize formation. It is often easier to make up words of this kind (*deregionalize, impermissible, extramarital, nonfragmentatory* and so forth) than to think up the English words that will cover one's meaning. The result, in general, is an increase in slovenliness and vagueness.

*Meaningless Words.* In certain kinds of writing, particularly in art criticism and literary criticism, it is normal to come across long passages which are almost completely lacking in meaning.[2] Words like *romantic, plastic, values, human, dead, sentimental, natural, vitality,* as used in art criticism, are strictly meaningless in the sense that they not only do not point to any discoverable object, but are hardly ever expected to do so by the reader. When one critic writes, "The outstanding feature of Mr. X's work is its living quality," while another writes, "The immediately striking thing about Mr. X's work is its peculiar deadness," the reader accepts this as a simple difference of opinion. If words like *black* and *white* were involved, instead of the jargon words *dead* and *living,* he would see at once that language was being used in an improper way. Many political words are similarly abused. The word *Fascism* has now no meaning except in so far as it signifies "something not desirable." The words *democracy, socialism, freedom, patriotic, realistic, justice,* have each of them several different meanings which cannot

[1] An interesting illustration of this is the way in which the English flower names which were in use till very recently are being ousted by Greek ones, *snapdragon* becoming *antirrhinum, forget-me-not* becoming *myosotis,* etc. It is hard to see any practical reason for this change of fashion: it is probably due to an instinctive turning-away from the more homely word and a vague feeling that the Greek word is scientific.

[2] Example: "Comfort's catholicity of perception and image, strangely Whitmanesque in range, almost the exact opposite in aesthetic compulsion, continues to evoke that trembling atmospheric accumulative hinting at a cruel, an inexorably serene timelessness . . . Wrey Gardiner scores by aiming at simple bull's-eyes with precision. Only they are not so simple, and through this contented sadness runs more than the surface bitter-sweet of resignation." (*Poetry Quarterly.*)

be reconciled with one another. In the case of a word like *democracy,* not only is there no agreed definition, but the attempt to make one is resisted from all sides. It is almost universally felt that when we call a country democratic we are praising it: consequently the defenders of every kind of régime claim that it is a democracy, and fear that they might have to stop using the word if it were tied down to any one meaning. Words of this kind are often used in a consciously dishonest way. That is, the person who uses them has his own private definition, but allows his hearer to think he means something quite different. Statements like *Marshal Pétain was a true patriot, The Soviet Press is the freest in the world, The Catholic Church is opposed to persecution,* are almost always made with intent to deceive. Other words used in variable meanings, in most cases more or less dishonestly, are: *class, totalitarian, science, progressive, reactionary, bourgeois, equality.*

Now that I have made this catalogue of swindles and perversions, let me give another example of the kind of writing that they lead to. This time it must of its nature be an imaginary one. I am going to translate a passage of good English into modern English of the worst sort. Here is a well-known verse from *Ecclesiastes:*

"I returned and saw under the sun, that the race is not to the swift, nor the battle to the strong, neither yet bread to the wise, nor yet riches to men of understanding, nor yet favour to men of skill; but time and chance happeneth to them all."

Here it is in modern English:

"Objective considerations of contemporary phenomena compels the conclusion that success or failure in competitive activities exhibits no tendency to be commensurate with innate capacity, but that a considerable element of the unpredictable must invariably be taken into account."

This is a parody, but not a very gross one. Exhibit (3), above, for instance, contains several patches of the same kind of English. It will be seen that I have not made a full translation. The beginning and ending of the sentence follow the original meaning fairly closely, but in the middle the concrete illustrations—race, battle, bread—dissolve into the vague phrase "success or failure in competitive activities." This had to be so, because no modern writer of the kind I am discussing—no one capable of using phrases like "objective consideration of contemporary phenomena"—would ever tabulate his thoughts in that precise and detailed way. The whole tendency of modern prose is away from concreteness. Now analyse these two sentences a little more closely. The first contains forty-nine words but only sixty syllables, and all its words are those of everyday life. The second contains thirty-eight words of ninety syllables: eighteen of its words are from Latin roots, and one from Greek. The first sentence contains six vivid images, and only one phrase ("time and chance") that could be called vague. The second contains not a single fresh, arresting phrase, and in spite of its ninety syllables it gives only a shortened version of the meaning contained in the first. Yet without a doubt it is the second kind of sentence that is gaining ground in modern English. I do not want to exaggerate. This kind of writing is not yet universal, and outcrops of simplicity will occur here and there in the worst-written page. Still, if you or I were told to write a few lines on the uncertainty of human fortunes, we should probably come much nearer to my imaginary sentence than to the one from *Ecclesiastes.*

As I have tried to show, modern writing at its worst does not consist in picking out words for the sake of their meaning and inventing images in order to make the meaning clearer. It consists in gumming together long strips of words which have already been set in order by someone else, and making the results presentable by sheer humbug. The attraction of this way of writing is that it is easy. It is easier—even quicker, once you have the habit—to say *In my opinion it is a not unjustifiable assumption that* than to say *I think.* If you use ready-made phrases, you not only don't have to hunt about for words; you also don't have to bother with the rhythms of your sentences, since these phrases are generally so arranged as to be more or less euphonious. When you are composing in a hurry—when you are dictating to a stenographer, for instance, or making a public speech—it is natural to fall into a pretentious, Latinized style. Tags like *a consideration which we should do well to bear in mind* or *a conclusion to which all of us would readily assent* will save many a sentence from coming down with a bump. By using stale metaphors, similes and idioms, you save much mental effort, at the cost of leaving your meaning vague, not only for your reader but for yourself. This is the significance of mixed metaphors. The sole aim of a metaphor is to call up a visual image. When these images clash—as in *The Fascist octopus has sung its swan song, the jackboot is thrown into the melting pot*—it can be taken as certain that the writer is not seeing a mental image of the objects he is naming; in other words he is not really thinking. Look again at the examples I gave at the beginning of this essay. Professor Laski (1) uses five negatives in fifty-three words. One of these is superfluous, making nonsense of the whole passage, and in addition there is the slip *alien* for akin, making further nonsense, and several avoidable pieces of clumsiness which increase the general vagueness. Professor Hogben (2) plays ducks and drakes with a battery which is able to write prescriptions, and, while disapproving of the everyday phrase *put up with,* is unwilling to look *egregious* up in the dictionary and see what it means. (3), if one takes an uncharitable attitude towards it, is simply meaningless: probably one could work out its intended meaning by reading the whole of the article in which it occurs. In (4), the writer knows more or less what he wants to say, but an accumulation of stale phrases chokes him like tea leaves blocking a sink. In (5), words and meaning have almost parted company. People who write in this manner usually have a general emotional meaning—they dislike one

thing and want to express solidarity with another—but they are not interested in the detail of what they are saying. A scrupulous writer, in every
sentence that he writes, will ask himself at least four questions, thus: What
am I trying to say? What words will express it? What image or idiom will
make it clearer? Is this image fresh enough to have an effect? And he will
probably ask himself two more: Could I put it more shortly? Have I said
anything that is avoidably ugly? But you are not obliged to go to all this
trouble. You can shirk it by simply throwing your mind open and letting the
ready-made phrases come crowding in. They will construct your sentences
for you—even think your thoughts for you, to a certain extent—and at
need they will perform the important service of partially concealing your
meaning even from yourself. It is at this point that the special connection
between politics and the debasement of language becomes clear.

In our time it is broadly true that political writing is bad writing. Where it
is not true, it will generally be found that the writer is some kind of rebel,
expressing his private opinions and not a "party line." Orthodoxy, of whatever colour, seems to demand a lifeless, imitative style. The political dialects to be found in pamphlets, leading articles, manifestos, White Papers and
the speeches of under-secretaries do, of course, vary from party to party, but
they are all alike in that one almost never finds in them a fresh, vivid, home-
made turn of speech. When one watches some tired hack on the platform
mechanically repeating the familiar phrases—*bestial atrocities, iron heel,
bloodstained tyranny, free peoples of the world, stand shoulder to shoulder*
—one often has a curious feeling that one is not watching a live human
being but some kind of dummy: a feeling which suddenly becomes stronger
at moments when the light catches the speaker's spectacles and turns them
into blank discs which seem to have no eyes behind them. And this is not
altogether fanciful. A speaker who uses that kind of phraseology has gone
some distance towards turning himself into a machine. The appropriate
noises are coming out of his larynx, but his brain is not involved as it would
be if he were choosing his words for himself. If the speech he is making is
one that he is accustomed to make over and over again, he may be almost
unconscious of what he is saying, as one is when one utters the responses in
church. And this reduced state of consciousness, if not indispensable, is at
any rate favourable to political conformity.

In our time, political speech and writing are largely the defence of the
indefensible. Things like the continuance of British rule in India, the Russian purges and deportations, the dropping of the atom bombs on Japan, can
indeed be defended, but only by arguments which are too brutal for most
people to face, and which do not square with the professed aims of political
parties. Thus political language has to consist largely of euphemism,
question-begging and sheer cloudy vagueness. Defenceless villages are
bombarded from the air, the inhabitants driven out into the countryside, the

cattle machine-gunned, the huts set on fire with incendiary bullets: this is called *pacification*. Millions of peasants are robbed of their farms and sent trudging along the roads with no more than they can carry: this is called *transfer of population* or *rectification of frontiers*. People are imprisoned for years without trial, or shot in the back of the neck or sent to die of scurvy in Arctic lumber camps: this is called *elimination of unreliable elements*. Such phraseology is needed if one wants to name things without calling up mental pictures of them. Consider for instance some comfortable English professor defending Russian totalitarianism. He cannot say outright, "I believe in killing off your opponents when you can get good results by doing so." Probably, therefore, he will say something like this:

"While freely conceding that the Soviet régime exhibits certain features which the humanitarian may be inclined to deplore, we must, I think, agree that a certain curtailment of the right to political opposition is an unavoidable concomitant of transitional periods, and that the rigours which the Russian people have been called upon to undergo have been amply justified in the sphere of concrete achievement."

The inflated style is itself a kind of euphemism. A mass of Latin words falls upon the facts like soft snow, blurring the outlines and covering up all the details. The great enemy of clear language is insincerity. When there is a gap between one's real and one's declared aims, one turns as it were instinctively to long words and exhausted idioms, like a cuttlefish squirting out ink. In our age there is no such thing as "keeping out of politics." All issues are political issues, and politics itself is a mass of lies, evasions, folly, hatred and schizophrenia. When the general atmosphere is bad, language must suffer. I should expect to find—this is a guess which I have not sufficient knowledge to verify—that the German, Russian and Italian languages have all deteriorated in the last ten or fifteen years, as a result of dictatorship.

But if thought corrupts language, language can also corrupt thought. A bad usage can spread by tradition and imitation, even among people who should and do know better. The debased language that I have been discussing is in some ways very convenient. Phrases like *a not unjustifiable assumption, leaves much to be desired, would serve no good purpose, a consideration which we should do well to bear in mind,* are a continuous temptation, a packet of aspirins always at one's elbow. Look back through this essay, and for certain you will find that I have again and again committed the very faults I am protesting against. By this morning's post I have received a pamphlet dealing with conditions in Germany. The author tells me that he "felt impelled" to write it. I open it at random, and here is almost the first sentence that I see: "(The Allies) have an opportunity not only of achieving a radical transformation of Germany's social and political structure in such a way as to avoid a nationalistic reaction in Germany itself, but at the same time of laying the foundations of a co-operative and unified

Europe." You see, he "feels impelled" to write—feels, presumably, that he has something new to say—and yet his words, like cavalry horses answering the bugle, group themselves automatically into the familiar dreary pattern. This invasion of one's mind by ready-made phrases (*lay the foundations, achieve a radical transformation*) can only be prevented if one is constantly on guard against them, and every such phrase anaesthetizes a portion of one's brain.

I said earlier that the decadence of our language is probably curable. Those who deny this would argue, if they produced an argument at all, that language merely reflects existing social conditions, and that we cannot influence its development by any direct tinkering with words and constructions. So far as the general tone or spirit of a language goes, this may be true, but it is not true in detail. Silly words and expressions have often disappeared, not through any evolutionary process but owing to the conscious action of a minority. Two recent examples were *explore every avenue* and *leave no stone unturned,* which were killed by the jeers of a few journalists. There is a long list of flyblown metaphors which could similarly be got rid of if enough people would interest themselves in the job; and it should also be possible to laugh the *not un-* formation out of existence,[3] to reduce the amount of Latin and Greek in the average sentence, to drive out foreign phrases and strayed scientific words, and, in general, to make pretentiousness unfashionable. But all these are minor points. The defence of the English language implies more than this, and perhaps it is best to start by saying what it does *not* imply.

To begin with it has nothing to do with archaism, with the salvaging of obsolete words and turns of speech, or with the setting up of a "standard English" which must never be departed from. On the contrary, it is especially concerned with the scrapping of every word or idiom which has outworn its usefulness. It has nothing to do with correct grammar and syntax, which are of no importance so long as one makes one's meaning clear, or with the avoidance of Americanisms, or with having what is called a "good prose style." On the other hand it is not concerned with fake simplicity and the attempt to make written English colloquial. Nor does it even imply in every case preferring the Saxon word to the Latin one, though it does imply using the fewest and shortest words that will cover one's meaning. What is above all needed is to let the meaning choose the word, and not the other way about. In prose, the worst thing one can do with words is to surrender to them. When you think of a concrete object, you think wordlessly, and then, if you want to describe the thing you have been visualizing you probably hunt about till you find the exact words that seem to fit. When you think of something abstract you are more inclined to use words from the start, and

[3] One can cure oneself of the *not un-* formation by memorizing this sentence: *A not unblack dog was chasing a not unsmall rabbit across a not ungreen field.*

unless you make a conscious effort to prevent it, the existing dialect will come rushing in and do the job for you, at the expense of blurring or even changing your meaning. Probably it is better to put off using words as long as possible and get one's meaning as clear as one can through pictures or sensations. Afterwards one can choose—not simply *accept*—the phrases that will best cover the meaning, and then switch round and decide what impression one's words are likely to make on another person. This last effort of the mind cuts out all stale or mixed images, all prefabricated phrases, needless repetitions, and humbug and vagueness generally. But one can often be in doubt about the effect of a word or a phrase, and one needs rules that one can rely on when instinct fails. I think the following rules will cover most cases:

    (i)   Never use a metaphor, simile or other figure of speech which you are used to seeing in print.

    (ii)   Never use a long word where a short one will do.

    (iii)   If it is possible to cut a word out, always cut it out.

    (iv)   Never use the passive where you can use the active.

    (v)   Never use a foreign phrase, a scientific word or a jargon word if you can think of an everyday English equivalent.

    (vi)   Break any of these rules sooner than say anything outright barbarous.

These rules sound elementary, and so they are, but they demand a deep change of attitude in anyone who has grown used to writing in the style now fashionable. One could keep all of them and still write bad English, but one could not write the kind of stuff that I quoted in those five specimens at the beginning of this article.

I have not here been considering the literary use of language, but merely language as an instrument for expressing and not for concealing or preventing thought. Stuart Chase and others have come near to claiming that all abstract words are meaningless, and have used this as a pretext for advocating a kind of political quietism. Since you don't know what Fascism is, how can you struggle against Fascism? One need not swallow such absurdities as this, but one ought to recognize that the present political chaos is connected with the decay of language, and that one can probably bring about some improvement by starting at the verbal end. If you simplify your English, you are freed from the worst follies of orthodoxy. You cannot speak any of the necessary dialects, and when you make a stupid remark its stupidity will be obvious, even to yourself. Political language—and with variations this is true of all political parties, from Conservatives to Anarchists—is designed to make lies sound truthful and murder respectable, and to give an appearance of solidity to pure wind. One cannot change this all in a moment, but one can at least change one's own habits, and from time to time one can

even, if one jeers loudly enough, send some worn-out and useless phrase—
some *jackboot, Achilles' heel, hotbed, melting pot, acid test, veritable inferno* or other lump of verbal refuse—into the dustbin where it belongs.

## STUDY QUESTIONS

1.  What do each of the five examples illustrate that Orwell finds objection-
    able?

2.  What is a dying metaphor? Can you add examples to those Orwell gives?

3.  According to Orwell, what is the connection between politics and the de-
    basement of language?

4.  In what ways does language corrupt thought, and thought corrupt lan-
    guage?

5.  Compare MacDonald's view ("The Decline and Fall of English," p. 326)
    on the debasement of English with Orwell's.

*Dwight MacDonald*

# THE DECLINE AND FALL OF ENGLISH

Dwight MacDonald (1906–    ) was born in New York City. He received his undergraduate degree from Yale University in 1928. He became
a critic, political commentator, and reviewer, and has been a regular contributor to numerous magazines and journals. He has been editor of *Fortune* magazine and *Partisan Review*. He founded and edited the magazine
*Politics*. Among his books are *Memoirs of a Revolutionist* (1957), *Henry
Wallace, the Man and the Myth* (1948), and *Parodies: An Anthology from
Chaucer to Beerbohm and After* (1960), which he edited.

Now THAT English has become the most widely used common language in the world, the great lingua franca of
our time, it is ironical that signs of disintegration are ap-

First published in *Life* International, © 1962 Time, Inc. Reprinted in *Against the
American Grain: Essays in Mass Culture,* by Dwight MacDonald (Random House).

pearing in its chief home, the U.S.A. It is as though Alexander the Great, encamped on the Indus, had received news of an insurrection back in Macedon.

In *Words and Idioms* (1925) the late Logan Pearsall Smith wrote:

More and more, too, this standard speech, and the respect for its usages, is being extended, and there is not the slightest danger at the present day that its authority or dominance will be questioned or disregarded. The danger lies rather in the other direction—that in our scrupulous and almost superstitious respect for correct English we may forget that other and freer forms of spoken English have also their value. . . . The duty of [ the educated classes] is, under normal conditions, one of conservatism, of opposition to the popular tendencies. But when the forces of conservatism become too strong, they may do well to relax their rigour and lean more to the democratic side.

Mr. Smith, an American living in England, was a connoisseur of English whose *Trivia* is still readable because of its style. But he was a bad prophet. In 1957 another authority, Sir Ernest Gowers, addressing the English Association in London, felt obliged to strike rather a different note:

Strange things are happening in the English language. The revolt against the old grammarians seems to be producing a school of thought who hold that grammar is obsolete and it does not matter how we write so long as we can make ourselves understood. It cannot be denied that if we had to choose between the two, it would be better to be ungrammatical than unintelligible. But we do not have to choose between the two. We can rid ourselves of those grammarians' fetishes which make it more difficult to be intelligible without throwing the baby away with the bath water.

The democratic ignoramus (who may have a Ph.D.) is now to be feared more than the authoritarian pedant. For the forces of tradition and conservation in the use of English have been weakened, and the forces of disintegration strengthened, to a degree which Logan Pearsall Smith could not have anticipated a mere thirty-five years ago.

It is not a question of the language changing. All languages change and often for the better—as the de-sexualization of English nouns and the de-inflection of English verbs and adjectives. I don't know which "grammarians' fetishes" Sir Ernest had in mind, but my own list would include: "It's me" (the man who says "It's I" is a prig); the split infinitive (often much neater, as "to thoroughly examine"); prepositions at the end of sentences (which H. W. Fowler in *Modern English Usage* sees as "an important element in the flexibility of the language"); the who-whom bother (I have my own opinion of the receptionist who says "Whom do you wish to see?"); and all the nonsense about "shall" v. "will" and "can" v. "may."

Such finicky "refinements," analogous to the extended little finger in drinking tea, have nothing to do with the problem of good English. What is to the point is that the language is being massacred, particularly by us Americans. When the comedian Phil Silvers says "I feel nauseous" when he means "nauseated," or the television commentator David Susskind speaks of "a peripatetic rush" when he means "precipitate," or the Consumers Commercial Corporation begins a sales letter: "As a good customer of ours, we want to be sure you know that . . . ," or models in ads request each other to "Scotch me lightly" or to "cigarette me" (not to mention "to host" and "to gift")—when these little contretemps occur, one shrugs and lights a Winston, which tastes good like a cigarette should. But then one reads the opening of a feature article in the respected New York *Herald Tribune:* "Bernard Goldfine's troubles keep multiplying. Aside from the prospect of spending more time in prison, his family already is fighting . . . over the estate." Or, in a recent issue of *Dissent,* a highbrow quarterly, such locutions as "Mr. Jadhav's angry retort to my remarks about Rommanohar Lohia and his Socialist party are regrettable. . . ." Or, in a *New York Times* review: "Oddly enough, of all the great plays that the great Eugene O'Neill wrote, only nine talking films (according to our reckoning) have been made of them."

The *Times* is especially disturbing because of its justified prestige as a newspaper. Its critical departments tirelessly chip away at the structure of English prose. The *Times Book Review,* the most influential critical organ in America as far as sales go, is a veritable lead mine of bad English. As, recently:

Though random samplings disclose the daily Buchwald column to be considerably less of a gastronomic delight than his year-end ragouts, still . . . the pay-dirt to raw-ore ratio runs high, and his humor remains a green isle in the rising tide of dullness.

And the rot extends much higher than journalism. Those who should be the guardians of the language, namely the members of our learned professions, have developed a new vocabulary which is as barbarously specialized as the beatniks' lingo and which has had as disastrous an effect on English. "The concept of sociocultural levels is a heuristic means of analyzing developmental sequences and internal structures. The approach seeks hierarchies both of organization and of sequence—the autonomous nuclear family, extended families of various types superimposed upon the nuclear family, or a multicommunity state unifying hitherto independent settlements." So states a recent article in *Daedalus,* the official organ of the American Academy of Arts and Sciences, a prestigious review which any aspiring academic would be proud to be printed in. American universities are factories of bad prose. On a single page of the February 4, 1962, *New York Times Book Review* two college presidents masquerading as critics commit grammatical howlers that should not be forgiven a fifth-grader. "The worst effect of this composite approach," writes Dr. Edward D. Eddy, Jr., president of Chatham College, "is to instill in the college graduate the notion that somehow he or she must be different than others because a degree was granted." Dr. Eddy's degree hasn't made him different "than" others. Dr. Francis H. Horn, president of the University of Rhode Island, swings into action lower down the same page: "An eminent mathematician with more than thirty years experience as teacher and administrator, his voice must be heard and his observations receive serious consideration. . . ." Now, class . . .

Even when the writer is professionally engaged in the study of English, the result, while grammatical, is often deplorable. Thus Professor Albert H. Marckwardt, a scholar of repute, can find no better words to end his recent work on *American English* than:

It is our responsibility to realize whither the language is tending, and the duty of our schools and teachers to promulgate healthy linguistic attitudes. If this is done, we may be certain that some individuals can and will attain greatness in the use of the language, which in turn will make of it a more flexible and sensitive medium for the rest of us. In this sense, a new era lies before all the English-speaking people.

Physician, heal thyself.

As for Dr. Marckwardt's coming "new era" to be promoted by "healthy linguistic attitudes," these concepts strike a chill into anyone who has been following what some of our learned men have been doing to English of late. The revisions of the King James Bible are a case in point, as is the third edition of the unabridged Merriam-Webster dictionary. This last, as I have noted earlier, is one of the many unfortunate effects of that new method of language study called Structural Linguistics.[1]

The origins of Structural Linguistics go back to the end of the last century when the Danish scholar Otto Jespersen put forward a theory that change in language is not only natural but good, and when the Oxford English Dictionary began publishing its thirteen volumes. Up to then the prevailing view of English was that it was a logical structure based on Latin and that any departure from the rules deduced from this assumption meant deterioration and vulgarization. The difficulty was that English, like all living

---

[1] A distinction is sometimes made between Structural Linguistics and Descriptive Linguistics, the former term being used for the purely scientific methods developed by such scholars as Chomsky, Lees, and Harris, and the latter for the application of these methods to teaching and lexicography. It is useful (and fair) to distinguish the scholars from the vulgarizers, but this terminology is not common, so I have followed the usual practice and used Structural Linguistics to cover both the doctrine and its practical application.

languages, was in fact in a constant state of change, and that the changes were usually away from the grammarians' and purists' notions of what English really *was*. By the end of the nineteenth century, there seemed to be two languages: English as she was spoke and English as the grammarians insisted she should be spoke (and wrote)—a real language versus a Platonic archetype that was as mystical and hard to grasp as the Holy Ghost. The importance of the Oxford English Dictionary, which began to appear in 1884 and published its last volume in 1928, was that it followed the changes in the meaning of each word by giving examples of usage from the Anglo-Saxon period on. There was no doubt about it, the language had constantly changed.

Structural Linguistics is an American invention and its impact has been felt mostly in America. I am incompetent to judge its technical claims but my impression is that it is—scientifically—greatly superior to the approach of the old grammarians. The trouble is that, like some other scientific advances—one thinks of Freud—it has been applied to areas which, because they involve qualitative judgments, simply cannot be reduced to the objective, quantitative terms of science. Such areas are the teaching of English and the making of dictionaries.

The basic principles of Structural Linguistics are defined as follows in *The English Language Arts,* a book published in 1952 by the Commission on the English Curriculum of the National Council of Teachers of English:

1. Language changes constantly.
2. Change is normal.
3. Spoken language is the language.
4. Correctness rests upon usage.
5. All usage is relative.

At first glance, these principles seem unexceptionable, indeed almost truisms. But a closer look reveals that the last three are half-truths, the most dangerous of formulations; half a truth is *not* better than no truth at all.

It may be natural for the Structural Linguists, who have devoted most of their attention to primitive languages, to assume that the "real" language is the spoken one and not the written one, but this has not always been true: many of the words coined from Latin and Greek in the Elizabethan period, words we still use, were introduced by scholars or poets in their writings. Today, what with far greater literacy and the proliferation of printed matter, the written word would seem to be even more important than in the past.

"Correctness rests upon usage" is more nearly true, but the Structural Linguists underestimate the influence of purists, grammarians and schoolmarms. It is true that Swift, an arch-conservative, objected to such eighteenth century neologisms as *mob, bully, sham, bubble* and *banter,* all of which have since become standard English. But he also objected, and suc-

cessfully, to contractions like *disturb'd*, to *phiz* for *face, hyp* for *hypochon-*
*driac,* and *pozz* for *positive.* The purists have won at least two major victories: they have made the double negative, often used by Shakespeare and a
perfectly legitimate means of emphasis, a stigma of illiteracy, and they have
crusaded so effectively against *ain't* that, though Webster's Third alleges
differently, it can't be used any more even as a contraction of *am not* without
danger of cultural excommunication. One may deplore these victories, as I
do, but we cannot deny they have take place, as the Structural Linguists
sometimes seem to do.

"All usage is relative" is either a truism (different classes and localities
speak differently) or else misleading. "The contemporary linguist does not
employ the terms 'good English' and 'bad English' except in a purely relative sense," *The English Language Arts* explains. "He recognizes the fact
that language is governed by the situation in which it occurs." But this principle leads to an undemocratic freezing of status, since "irregardless" and
"he knowed" are standard usage in certain circles, and those not the richest
or best educated. So the Horatio Alger of today, bemused by teachers well
grounded in Structural Linguistics, will keep on massacring the king's English because his fellow newsboys do ("language is governed by the situation
in which it occurs") and the philanthropic merchant will be so appalled by
Horatio's double negatives that he will not give him The Job. In their *Modern American Grammar and Usage* (1956), J. N. Hook and E. G. Mathews,
writing in the orthodox canon, observe apropos of what they delicately call
"sub-standard English"; "We must re-emphasize that this language is not
wrong; it is merely not in harmony with the usages generally found in
books . . . or heard in the conversations of those persons with a strong
consciousness of language." They then give an example of substandard English: "Bein's he uz a'ready late, he done decide not to pay her no mind." If
this is not wrong, it seems hardly worth the bother to teach English at all.

One of the far-out books in the canon is a 1960 paperback called *Linguistics and Your Language,* by Robert A. Hall, Jr., professor of linguistics at
Cornell. Browsing through Professor Hall's book is an unsettling experience. "A dictionary or grammar is not as good an authority for your own
speech as the way you yourself speak," he observes. Thus: *"Hisn, hern* and
so forth are often heard from illiterate people, perhaps more often than from
people who know how to read and write; but there is no necessary connection." (I do like "perhaps more often" and "no necessary connection.")
Then Dr. Hall goes all the way: " 'Correct' spelling, that is, obedience to the
rules of English spelling as grammarians and dictionary-makers set them
up, has come to be a major shibboleth in our society. . . . Consequently,
anyone who goes through our schooling system has to waste years of his life
in acquiring a wasteful and, in the long run, damaging set of spelling habits,
thus ultimately unfitting himself to understand the nature of language." En-

glish spelling is indeed maddeningly illogical, but we're stuck with it. For one thing, if spelling is to be "relativized" according to "the situation in which it occurs," it would be impossible to look up a word in the dictionary, which would be all right with Dr. Hall, who believes that the free, democratic and linguistically structured citizen should not bow to authority. Logically, Dr. Gove should agree with him, but in fact Dr. Gove edited Webster's Third. And logically, Dr. Hall should not submit to shibboleths of "correct" spelling imposed on us by authoritarian grammarians, but in fact he does; every word in his book is "correctly" spelled.

One of Dr. Hall's special fields is pidgin English and one gets the impression he thinks it just about as good as any other kind—after all, it *communicates,* doesn't it? Me writem big fella book along say teacher man no savvy more nobody other fella.

Dr. Hall is a member of the academic establishment, which brings up the question of how effectively Americans are being taught to use their language. Last year the National Council of Teachers of English published a disturbing report: *The National Interest and the Teaching of English.* Its main findings were: some four million U.S. school children have "reading disabilities"; 150,000 students failed college entrance tests in English in 1960; two-thirds of America's colleges have to provide remedial work in English. The same note was sounded in another recent report, by the Council for Basic Education. This report estimates that 35 per cent of all U.S. students are seriously retarded in reading. It blames mostly the "whole-word" or "look-say" method of reading instruction which has become standard in American public schools, by which the child is taught to recognize only whole words instead of to build up words by learning his alphabet and its sounds (the "phonic" system which was traditional until the 'thirties). The child learns not his ABC's but his AT-BAT-CAT's. This device enables the successful pupils to recognize 1,342 words by the end of the third grade. The report claims that the old-fashioned phonic method would produce twice as big a vocabulary by the end of the *first* grade.

There is also the comparison of Soviet and American school programs recently made by Dr. Arthur S. Trace: *What Ivan Knows That Johnny Doesn't.* Dr. Trace confined himself to demonstrating the inferiority of our textbooks and curricula in reading, history, literature, foreign languages and geography—we already know how superior Soviet schools are in physics and mathematics. His findings about reading are to the point here. Ivan in the *first* grade uses a primer that has 2,000 words, which is just 500 more than Johnny gets in his *fourth*-grade readers. Ivan reads Tolstoy in the first grade; Johnny reads Mary Louise Friebele, whose works include *A Good, Big Fire, The Blue and Yellow Boats,* and *A Funny Sled.* By the fourth grade, Ivan is coping with a vocabulary of 10,000 words, which is more than five times as many as Johnny has learned in school (though, of course, he is at liberty to pick up as many extracurricular words as he likes; our educationists have not so far discovered a way to prevent children getting wised up outside the classroom, such as supplementing Mary Louise Friebele with a little Dickens read by flashlight under the bedclothes). This result is achieved, according to Dr. Trace, by another Rube Goldbergian device called "vocabulary control" which actually is designed to *reduce* the number of new words that a school child will encounter. The theory is that too many new words may have a traumatic effect.

As might be expected, the illiteracy of the young is even worse when it comes to writing. The University of Pittsburgh recently tested 450,000 high-school students and found that only one out of a hundred was able to produce a five-minute theme without faults in English. In my own slight experience teaching English—three months at Northwestern University several years ago—I was struck by the contrast between the fluency of my students when they spoke in class and the difficulty most of them had in producing a grammatical and correctly spelled composition. The only explanation I could think of was that they had learned to speak outside the classroom—and to write inside it.

The jeremiads of the National Council of Teachers of English seem to be written from the moon. They offer no criticism of the things outside observers think are responsible for student illiteracy: the "look-say" method of teaching reading, infantile textbooks, and "vocabulary control." For these are part of official doctrine and it would be unthinkable that the illiteracy the Council deplores might be caused by the educational techniques the Council approves. The Council has quite a lot to say about Structural Linguistics, and all favorable. If only, one gathers, more teachers were indoctrinated with this approach, what wonders would follow.

The English scholar I. A. Richards, who, with C. K. Ogden, wrote *The Meaning of Meaning* and later invented Basic English, delivered himself of some thoughts and emotions on this topic in 1955:

There are vast areas of so-called "purely descriptive" linguistics which are a grim danger at present to the conduct of language, to education, to standards of intelligence. . . . The appeal to mere *usage* . . . is a case in point. Every useful feature of language was *not in use* once upon a time. Every degradation of language too starts somewhere. Behind usage is the question of efficiency. Inefficient language features are not OK, however widespread their use. Of course, to the linguistic botanist it is important to preserve all varieties until they have been collected and described. But that is not the point of view of the over-all study of language, its services and its powers. That over-all view is, I am insisting, inescapably NORMATIVE. It is concerned . . . with the maintenance and improvement of the use of language.

The word "normative," which implies there is a norm or standard, produces the same reactions in a Structural Linguist as "integration" does in a Southern White Supremacist. Dr. Richards instanced as an example of the degradation of English the growing interchangeability of *disinterested* and *uninterested,* which Webster's Third gives as synonyms. The Structural Linguist position on these words was explained in a recent article in *College Composition and Communication* by Dr. Robert J. Geist. Dr. Geist could see no reason for making a fuss: "I think it can safely be stated that a word means what a speaker intends it to mean and what a hearer interprets it to mean." That there might be some discrepancy between what a speaker intends and what a hearer interprets, and that language is efficient only insofar as it reduces this discrepancy—these truisms didn't occur to Dr. Geist at the moment of writing the foregoing sentence. But he seems to have vaguely sensed later on that something was wrong; at least he does add a parenthesis: "(I use *disinterested* to mean *impartial* only.)" Like other permissive linguists, he doesn't dare to practice what he preaches.

The whole matter of the development of English is more complicated than it is thought to be by either the old-school grammarians or the Structural Linguists. In the early period of the language, when it was in a state of chronic (and creative) flux, nobody bothered much about correctness. Even spelling was not taken seriously—our greatest writer spelled his name Shakespeare, Shakspere, or Shakspeare as the spirit moved him. It was not until 1721 that the first real dictionary appeared, when Nathaniel Bailey had the novel idea of trying to include *all* the words. Up to then, there had only been lists of "hard words." Such lists were welcomed because of the enormous accretion of new words, mostly invented from Greek or Latin roots, in the Elizabethan and Jacobean periods. Conservatives denounced these as "inkhorn terms"—i.e., used only in writing to show one's learning —and so many of them were. But most have survived. A contemporary rhetorician composed a parody "inkhorn" letter; while many have perished (*revolute, obtestate, fatigate, splendidious*), most are still current (*affability, ingenious, fertile, contemplate, clemency, verbosity*). By 1650, the language was settling down, the new words were largely accepted, and even spelling was beginning to be standardized. "Some people if they but spy a hard word are as much amazed as if they met with a hobgoblin," Edward Phillips wrote contemptuously in his *New World of Words* (1658).

But usage was not really fixed until the eighteenth century when the literate public expanded suddenly—between 1700 and 1800 the publication of new books quadrupled—because of the rise of the bourgeoisie and the beginning of the industrial revolution. The new-rich classes wanted to show they were cultured gentlemen and so offered a market for dictionaries and grammars, which played the same social role as the books of etiquette which first became popular then. (In Soviet Russia a similar sudden rise in literacy similarly connected with industrialization has produced similar effects—*kulturny* is a potent word there, applied to everything from diction to using a handkerchief to blow one's nose.) In the eighteenth century the literary atmosphere was favorable to the language's becoming standardized. The creative surge of 1550–1650 had ebbed and now, from Pope to Johnson, there followed an Augustan age of classic consolidation. Swift was an impassioned conservative who hoped to "fix the language." But he was not alone in fearing that, if change went on unchecked, in a few generations his own works "shall hardly be understood without an interpreter." He tried to revive Dryden's proposal for an English Academy—on the model of the French Academy founded by Cardinal Richelieu in the preceding century —which would have for its object, in the words of the French Academy's statute: "to give definite rules to our language, and to render it pure, eloquent and capable of treating the arts and sciences [and] to establish a certain usage of words." Nothing came of this project, despite impressive intellectual backing. Even Dr. Johnson, hardly a permissive type, opposed it in the preface to his dictionary (1755) as hostile to "the spirit of English liberty." Johnson also advanced a more pragmatic criticism: "Those who have been persuaded to think well of my design require that it should fix our language and put a stop to those alterations which time and chance have hitherto been suffered to make in it without opposition. With this consequence I will confess that I flattered myself for a while; but now begin to fear that I have indulged expectations which neither reason nor experience can justify." He pointed out that there is "no example of a nation that has preserved their words and phrases from mutability"—later purists must have shuddered at the confusion of plural and singular—and noted that "the French language has visibly changed under the inspection of the academy." The grammarians of the eighteenth and nineteenth centuries, lacking Johnson's common sense, objected to change per se because their model of a proper language, Latin, had not changed for 1,500 years. But it had not changed because it was a dead language for precisely that period; the Latin that continued to live, monks' Latin, changed until it became a patois related to Latin as pidgin English is related to English.

On the other hand, while no permanent deep freeze is possible in a language, the fact is that English has been to some extent "fixed" in the last two centuries. (Johnson's dictionary was an important factor in the fixing.) The forces that tended this way in the eighteenth century became much stronger in the nineteenth when there was more literacy, more social mobility, and more industrialization—there seems to be some relation between the requirements of a rationalized industrial society and the standardization of language. More and more people came into the cultural market place—

ambitious workingmen who wanted to "better" themselves, *nouveaux riches* who wanted to be considered gentlemen. The upper classes hitherto had used English with the easy negligence of proprietors who can do as they like with their own, but now the rich were not so secure in their ownership. Now began the long dominance of the grammarians and the schoolmarms. The economic base was exposed by Bernard Shaw: "People know very well that certain sorts of speech cut off a person forever from getting more than three or four pounds a week all their life long—sorts of speech which make them entirely impossible to certain professions." The ambitious working-man who uses Webster's Third as a guide will be in for some rude shocks when he says "I ain't" to the personnel director.

Or he may not be. The personnel manager may say "ain't" to *him*. Perhaps the most ominous sign of the decay of English in the United States, the vanishing of the very notion of standards under the pressure of the vulgarians and the academicians, is the recent decision of the Sherwin Cody School of English to drop its traditional advertising punch line: "DO *you* MAKE THESE MISTAKES IN ENGLISH?" For forty years this has been a classic of correspondence-school advertising, on a par with "THEY LAUGHED WHEN I SAT DOWN AT THE PIANO." Now it is obsolete. "The key fact is," an executive of the school has explained, "people don't want to speak good English any more. The correspondence course used to be popular among people who wanted to advance themselves and speak better. Now no one cares about grammatical errors." And indeed the horrible examples that the school's ads used to cite—"Leave them lay," "Between you and I"— would be swallowed without a wink by any good Structural Linguist.

English is not just a convenient means of communicating, as the Structural Linguists seem to think. The language of a people, like its art and literature and music and architecture, is a record of its past that has much to say to the present. If this connection is broken, then a people gets into the condition of a psychotic who has lost contact with his past. Superseding the King James Version of the Bible with a translation in the modern idiom is like updating Shakespeare—"The problem of existence or nonexistence confronts us." Language is a specially important part of a people's past, or culture, because everybody is exposed to it and has to learn to use it. The evolution of words is a capsule history of the race, as one can verify by reading a few pages of the Oxford English Dictionary. There is always a struggle between tradition and novelty. If the society is too permissive, novelty has it too easy and the result is language that has lost contact with its past and that is, usually, ineffective as communication because it is vague and formless— in beatnik slang "man" and "like" have degenerated to mere interruptions, more stammer than grammar.

Language does indeed change, but there must be some brakes and it is the function of teachers, writers and lexicographers to apply them.[2] It is their job to make it tough for new words and usages to get into circulation so that the ones that survive will be the fittest. *Mob* made it despite Swift, but *pozz* didn't; the point is not that Swift was right or wrong but that he had a sense of the language, which he used as well as any writer has, and that he cared enough about it to raise the question. Today the best English is written and spoken in London—the contrast is painful between the letters-to-the-editor departments of the London *Times* and the *New York Times*—because there an educated class still values the tradition of the language. For English, like other languages, is an aesthetic as well as a practical means of communication. It is compounded of tradition and beauty and style and experience and not simply of what happens when two individuals meet in a barroom, or a classroom. "We must write for the people in the language of kings," Bertolt Brecht once said. Americans seem to be reversing his maxim.

## STUDY QUESTIONS

1.  MacDonald contends that the English language is being "massacred," and cites examples to support his contention. What does he find objectionable in each of the examples?

2.  What are the shortcomings he finds in the structural linguistics approach to language study? How does he support his views?

3.  What is MacDonald's position on the older, traditional approach to language?

4.  How does he regard change in language?

[2] Everybody, including myself, now sneers at the "schoolmarms," and they do have some ghastly mistakes on their conscience. But at least they accepted responsibility and at least they understood their pupils needed prescription as well as description. And the worst mistake they made, as my friend Dean Moody Prior, of Northwestern University, has recently pointed out to me, was to humbly transmit to their students the theories about language that were dominant in the scholarly circles of their day. I can see the linguists of the year 2,000 (who will by then have developed some vast new theory, perhaps based on the Jungian racial unconscious) sneering at the "schoolmarms" of the sixties with their myopic and dogmatic adherence to outworn notions, i.e., Structural Linguistics. And I can see the schoolmarms again taking the rap (*slang*) rather than the eminent scholars whose theories they accepted with a faith as incautious as it was touchingly modest. When does a teacher become a schoolmarm? When the Authorities he or she relies on are considered outdated by the new Authorities. Up to then, he or she is a member in good standing of the National Council of Teachers of English and a useful member of society.

5.  According to MacDonald, what is the teacher's responsibility?

6.  Would MacDonald be more inclined to agree with Follett's views ("Sabotage in Springfield," p. 355) or with Evans' ("But What's a Dictionary For?" p. 364)? Explain.

# H. L. Mencken

# HELL AND ITS OUTSKIRTS

Henry Louis Mencken (1880–1956), editor, critic, columnist, and scholar, was born in Baltimore, Maryland. For many years he was editor and columnist for the *Baltimore Sun,* and then later literary critic and editor of *Smart Set* magazine. He gained a reputation as a master of wit and invective. The American public, particularly the middle class, became his special target. He helped to found *The American Mercury,* a magazine devoted to satire and comment on American life, politics, and customs. He is well known among students of the English language for his scholarly *The American Language* (1919) and its two supplements. Titles of his other books are *The Philosophy of Friedrich Nietzsche* (1908), *In Defense of Women* (1918), *Prejudices* (in six series, 1919–1927), *Treatise on the Gods* (1930), *Treatise on Right and Wrong* (1934), and *A Mencken Chrestomathy* (1949).

> *It doesn't matter what they preach,*
> *Of high or low degree:*
> *The old Hell of the Bible*
> *Is Hell enough for me.*
>
> *'Twas preached by Paul and Peter;*
> *They spread it wide and free;*
> *'Twas Hell for old John Bunyan*
> *And it's Hell enough for me.*

THE AUTHOR of these elegiac strophes, Frank Lebby Stanton, has been moldering in the red clay of Georgia for a long, long while, but what he wrote went straight to the hearts of the American people, and there it still glows warmly. Hell remains the very essence not only of their dogmatic theology but also of their every-day invective. They employ it casually more than any other *Kulturvolk,* and perhaps more than all others put together. They have enriched it with a vast store of combinations, variations, licks, breaks, and riffs. They have made it roar and howl, and they have made it coo and twitter. It helps to lift them when supersonic waves of ecstasy rush through their lymphatic systems, and it soothes them when they roll in the barbed wire of despair. To find its match, you must go to the Buddhist *Om mani padma Hum,* meaning any-thing you please, or the Moslem *al-hamdu lil'lah,* meaning the same, or the ancient Mesopotamian Word from the Abyss, *Muazagagu-abzu.* Even so, *hell* is far ahead, for, compared to it, all these ejaculations have a pale and pansy cast, as does *hell* itself in nearly every other language; e.g., *enfer* in French, *inferno* in Spanish, *helvede* in Danish, *jigoku* in Japanese, and *Hölle* in German. So long ago as 1880, in the appendix on "The Awful Ger-man Language" to "A Tramp Abroad," Mark Twain derided *Hölle* as "chipper, frivolous and unimpressive" and marveled that anyone invited to go there could "rise to the dignity of feeling insulted." He had never heard, apparently, of the even more flaccid Finnish *manala,* which in These States would be the name of an infant food or perhaps of a female infant among the Bible-searchers of the Dust Bowl.

*Hell* is one of the most ancient and honorable terms in English, and ety-mologists in their dusty cells have traced it to the first half of the ninth cen-tury. It is thus appreciably older than either *home* or *mother* and nearly five centuries older than its great rival, *damn.* But it was not until Shakespeare's time that it began to appear in the numerous blistering phrases that now glorify it—e.g., *go to hell, to hell with, hell to pay, hell is loose, hellcat,* and so on—and even then it rose only to be knocked down, for Shakespeare's time also saw the beginnings of the Puritan murrain, and once the bluenoses were in power they put down all strong language with a brutal hand. At the Restoration, of course, it was reliberated, but only in a spavined state. The Cavaliers, male and female, were great swearers, but their oaths were nearly all cautious and cushioned. Such examples as *gadzooks, zounds, 'sdeath, 'sblood, by'r Lady, a plague on't, rat me, split my windpipe, marry,* and *burn me* are heard in America today, when they are heard at all, only among can-didates in theology and Boy Scouts. The English, indeed, have never recov-ered from the blight of Puritanism, and their swearing strikes all other civi-lized peoples as puny. They are constantly working up a pother over such forms as *bloody,* which to the rest of the world are quite innocuous. *Good gracious,* which appeared in Oliver Goldsmith's "Good Natur'd Man" in 1768, seems to have been regarded in that day as pretty pungent, and *mercy,* which preceded it by some years, was frowned upon as blasphemous. "Our armies," says Uncle Toby in *Tristram Shandy,* "swore terribly in Flanders," but at home such virtuosity was rare, even among the military. In the wars of our own time, the swearing of the English has provoked the contempt of both their allies and their enemies. In both World War I and World War II, they depended mainly upon a couple of four-letter words that are obscene but not profane, and what they made of them showed little ingenuity or imagination. The American military borrowed these terms in a spirit probably more derisory than admiring, and dropped them the instant they were restored to Mom.

But as the brethren of the Motherland lost their Elizabethan talent for wicked words it was transferred to these shores. Even the Puritans of New England, once they settled down, took to cussing out one another in a violent manner, and thousands of them were sent to the stocks or whipping post for it by their baffled magistrates. The heroes of the Revolution not only swore in all the orthodox forms but also invented a new expletive, *tarnation,* which survived until the Mexican War. As Dr. Louise Pound has demonstrated with great learning, both *tarnation* and *darn* were derived from *eternal* and the former preceded the latter in refined use. George Washington himself cut loose with *hell* and *damn* whenever the imbecilities of his brass went too far. But it was the great movement into the West following the War of 1812 that really laid the foundations of American profanity and got *hell* firmly on its legs. Such striking forms as *to raise hell, to hell around, hell-bent for election, to be hell on, to play hell with, what the hell, heller, merry hell, hellish, hellcat, hell on wheels, hell and high water, from hell to breakfast, a hoot in hell, the hell of it, hell's a-poppin', the hell you say, hell with the lid off,* and *the hinges of hell* were then invented by the gallant fellows, many of them fugitives from Eastern sheriffs, who legged it across the great plains to die for humanity at the hands of Indians, buffalo, catamounts, rattlesnakes, bucking broncos, and vigilance committees. For nearly two generations nine-tenths of the new terms in America, whether profane or not, came from the region beyond Wheeling, West Virginia, and were commonly called West-ernisms. It was not until after the Civil War that the newspaper wits of the East began to contribute to the store, and not until after World War I that concocting such things became the monopoly of Hollywood press agents, radio mountebanks, and Broadway columnists.

The great upsurge of *hell* that rose to a climax in the Mexican War era naturally upset the contemporary wowsers, and they busied themselves launching euphemistic surrogates. Some of these seem to have been imported from the British Isles, along with Dundreary whiskers, soda water, and bathing; for example, *by heck,* which originated there as a substitute for *by Hector,* itself a substitute for *by God,* but was already obsolete at home by the time it appeared in America. Here it not only flourished among the prissy in its prototypical form but also moved over into the domain of *hell* and gave birth to *a heck of a, to raise heck, to run like heck, colder than heck, to play heck with, to beat heck, what the heck,* and *go to heck.* Other deputies for *hell* were invented on American soil, notably *thunder and blazes. Go to thunder* in the sense of *go to hell* is traced by the "Dictionary of American English" to 1848 and marked an Americanism, and at about the same time *thunderation* began to be used for *damnation.* But soon *thunderation* was used in place of *hell,* as in *what the thunderation.* It is possible that German immigration helped to spread it in its various forms, for a favorite German expletive in those days was *Donnerwetter;* i.e., thundery weather. But this is only a guess, and, like all other learned men, I am suspicious of guessing.

After the Civil War there was another great upsurge of wowserism, culminating in the organization of the Comstock Society in 1873 [1] and of the Woman's Christian Temperance Union the year following. Neither organization devoted itself specifically to profanity, but the moral indignation that radiated from both of them soon began to afflect it, and by 1880 it was being denounced violently in thousands of far-flung evangelical pulpits. In this work, the leader was the Reverend Sam Jones, who had been converted and ordained a Methodist clergyman in 1872. Sam roared against cussing as he roared against boozing, but the Devil fetched him by seducing him into using stronger and stronger language himself, and toward the end of his life I more than once heard him let go with objurgations that would have cheered a bouncer clearing out a Sailor's Bethel. Even the Catholics, who ordinarily never mistake the word for the deed, joined the crusade, and in 1882 they were reviving the Holy Name Society, which had been organized back in 1274 and then forgotten. This combined assault had some effect; indeed, it probably had much more effect than it has been given credit for. At all events, the lush profanity of the Civil War era began to shrink and pale, and such unearthly oaths as *Jesus Christ and John Jacob Astor, by the high heels of St. Patrick,* and *by the double-barreled jumping Jiminetty* began to vanish from the American repertory. *God damn* kept going downhill throughout my youth in the eighties and nineties, and by the time I came of age I seldom used it. Many new euphemisms took the places of the forthright oaths of an earlier day, and one of them, *hully gee,* quickly became so innocuous that when Edward W. Townsend introduced it into "Chimmie Fadden," in 1895, it fell almost as flat as the four-letter words with which the lady novelists now pepper their pages.

But *hell* and *damn* somehow survived this massacre—maybe because the new euphemisms left a man choking and gasping when the steam really rose in his gauges, or maybe because some amateur canon lawyer discovered that in their naked state, uncoupled to sacred names, they are not officially

[1] Its legal name was The New York Society for the Suppression of Vice. In 1947 that name was changed to the Society to Maintain Public Decency. Old Anthony Comstock was snatched up to Heaven in 1915 and succeeded by John S. Sumner.

blasphemous. Whatever the reason, American profanity was saved, and to this day it revolves around them and recruits itself from their substance. *Damn* is plainly the feebler of the two, despite its crashing effect when used by a master. *Hell* is enormously more effective, if only because it is more protean. For one phrase embodying the former there are at least forty embodying the latter, and many of them are susceptible to elegant and ingenious permutations. It is impossible for *damn* to bust loose, or to freeze over; it is impossible to knock it out of anyone, or to give it to anyone, or to beat it, or to raise it, or to think of a snowball or a bat in it, or to link it to high water, or to be *damn*-bent for election, or to plunge from *damn*-to-breakfast, or to *damn* around, or to get the *damn* out of any place, or to pull its lid off, or to think of it as having hubs or hinges. There is no such thing as a *damn*-hound, a *damn*cat, a *damn*hole, or a *damn*ion. Nothing is as black as *damn,* as busy as *damn,* as hot (or cold) as *damn,* or as deep, crazy, dumb, clever, cockeyed, crooked, touchy, dead, drunk, nervous, dull, expensive, scared, funny, hungry, lonely, mad, mean, poor, real, rotten, rough, serious, sick, smart, or sore as *damn. Damn* is a simple verb and its only child is a simple adjective, but *hell* ranges over all the keys of the grammatical scale and enters into combinations as avidly as oxygen.

There was a time when men learned in the tongues turned trembling backs upon such terms, but in recent years they have shown a libido for studying them, and the result is a rising literature. One of the earliest of the new monographs upon the subject—and still one of the best—was published in *American Speech* in August, 1931, by Dr. L. W. Merryweather. Probing scientifically, he discovered a great deal about *hell* that no one had ever noticed before. It can be slung about, he found, through nearly all the parts of speech. It can be used to represent almost every shade of meaning from yes to no, so that *hell of a time* may mean both the seraphic felicity of a police sergeant in a brewery and the extreme discomfort of a felon in the electric chair. A thing may be either *hotter than hell* or *colder than hell.* A *hellcat* may be either a woman so violent that her husband jumps overboard or nothing worse than a college cheerleader. *What in hell* is a mere expression of friendly interest, but *who the hell says so* is a challenge to fight. Merryweather threw out the suggestion that the upsurge and proliferation of *hell* in the Old West may have been due to Mormon influence. The Saints, he said, were very pious fellows and avoided the vain use of sacred names, but they were also logicians and hence concluded that the use of terms of precisely opposite connotation might be allowable, and even praise-worthy. At all events, they began to swear *by hell* and to call ordinary Christians *hellions* and *sons of hell,* and these terms were quickly borrowed by the miners, trappers, highwaymen, and others who invaded their Zion, and out of them flowed some of the most esteemed terms in *hell* of today. Whether Merryweather was right here I do not presume to say, but in another of his conclusions he undoubtedly slipped, as even savants sometimes do. "Today," he said, *"hell* fills so large a place in the American vulgate that it will probably be worn out in a few years more, and will become obsolescent." We all know now that nothing of the sort has happened. *Hell,* in fact, is flourishing as never before. I have many hundreds of examples of its use in my archives, and new ones are being added almost every day.

A large number of swell ones were assembled into a monograph by another scholar, Dr. Bartlett Jere Whiting, published in *Harvard Studies and Notes in Philology and Literature,* Vol. XX, 1938. Whiting, a sequestered philologian interested chiefly in Old and Middle England, sought his material not in the market place but in books—mostly novels of the 1920–37 period. But even within this narrow and somewhat dephlogisticated field he found enough phrases based on *hell* to fill twenty-four pages of the austere journal in which he wrote. I have space for only a few examples: *holy hell, fifteen kinds of hell, to batter hell into, assorted hell, the seven hinges of hell, thicker than fiddlers in hell, four naked bats out of hell, like a shot out of hell, the chance of a celluloid collar in hell, three hurrahs in hell, hell's own luck, hell up Sixth Street, hell on toast, from hell to Harvard, hell gone from nowhere, like a hangman from hell, hell's half acre, hell-for-leather,* and *what the red* (or *bloody*) *hell.* Whiting duly noted *hell of a business, hurry, jam, job, life, mess, place, note, row, time,* and *way* but overlooked George Ade's *hell of a Baptist.* He added some euphemisms for *hell*—for example, *billy-be-damned, billy-ho,* and *blazes*—but he had to admit that these "makeshifts and conscience-easers," as he called them, were all pretty feeble.

Robert Southey, more than a century ago, investigated the names of the principal devils of Hell, and not only printed a list of them in one of his books but also suggested that some might be useful as cuss words; e.g., *Lacahabarrutu, Buzache, Knockadawe, Baa,* and *Ju.* There were, however, no takers for his suggestion and he got no further with the subject. In Harlem, according to Zora Neale Hurston, the dark geographers have discovered that there is a hotter Hell lying somewhat south of the familiar Christian resort, and have given it the name of *Beluthahatchie.* So far, not much has been learned about its amperage, sociology, or public improvements, but its temperature has been fixed tentatively somewhere between that of a blast furnace and that of the sun. These Afro-American explorers also believe that their spectroscopes have found three suburbs of Hell proper, by name *Diddy-wah-diddy, Ginny Gall,* and *West Hell.* Unhappily, not much is known about them, though several ghosts returned to earth report that *Diddy-wah-diddy* is a sort of Long Island, given over mainly to eating houses and night clubs, and that *West Hell* lies beyond the railroad tracks and is somewhat tacky.

## Study Questions

1.  According to Mencken, what is the early history of the word *hell?* What is the effect of his noting that it is older than either *home* or *mother?*

2.  What evidence does he cite for the growth of the use of *hell* in this country?

3.  Look up the meaning of the word *wowser*. What, according to Mencken, did the wowsers have to do with the history of the word *hell* in this country?

4.  To Mencken, *hell* is much stronger and more effective than *damn*. How does he support his opinion? Do you agree?

5.  Can you add any phrases based on *hell* to the list Mencken gives as collected by Dr. Whiting? What is the status of *hell* and phrases based on it today?

6.  Examine Mencken's diction. It has been called vigorous. Can you cite his use of particular words that justify this? How does he use certain words to make judgments?

## *Wallace E. Stegner*

# "GOOD-BYE TO ALL T--T"

Wallace Stegner is a well-known writer and teacher of writers at Stanford University, where he heads a creative writing program. He earned his undergraduate degree at the University of Utah and his M.A. and Ph.D. degrees at the University of Iowa. He has taught at Augustana College, the Universities of Utah and Wisconsin, and Harvard University. He was awarded Guggenheim Fellowships in 1950, 1952, and 1959, and has won the O'Henry First Prize for Short Stories. His books include *The Woman on the Wall* (1950), *The Preacher and the Slave* (1950), *Beyond the Hun-*

*dredth Meridian* (1954), *The City of the Living* (1956), *A Shooting Star* (1961), *Wolf Willow* (1962), *The Gathering of Zion* (1964) and *All the Little Live Things* (1967). He has also written numerous articles and short stories.

NOT EVERYONE who laments what contemporary novelists have done to the sex act objects to the act itself, or to its mention. Some want it valued higher than fiction seems to value it; they want the word "climax" to retain some of its literary meaning. Likewise, not everyone who has come to doubt the contemporary freedom of language objects to strong language in itself. Some of us object precisely because we value it.

I acknowledge that I have used four-letter words familiarly all my life, and have put them into books with some sense that I was insisting on the proper freedom of the artist. I have applauded the extinction of those d----d emasculations of the Genteel Tradition and the intrusion into serious fiction of honest words with honest meanings and emphasis. I have wished, with D. H. Lawrence, for the courage to say shit before a lady, and have sometimes had my wish.

Words are not obscene: naming things is a legitimate verbal act. And "frank" does not mean "vulgar," any more than "improper" means "dirty." What vulgar does mean is "common"; what improper means is "unsuitable." Under the right circumstances, any word is proper. But when any sort of word, especially a word hitherto taboo and therefore noticeable, is scattered across a page like chocolate chips through a tollhouse cookie, a real impropriety occurs. The sin is not the use of an "obscene" word; it is the use of a loaded word in the wrong place or in the wrong quantity. It is the sin of false emphasis, which is not a moral but a literary lapse, related to sentimentality. It is the sin of advertisers who so plaster a highway with neon signs that you can't find the bar or liquor store you're looking for. Like any excess, it quickly becomes comic.

If I habitually say shit before a lady, what do I say before a flat tire at the rush hour in Times Square or on the San Francisco Bay Bridge? What do I say before a revelation of the inequity of the universe? And what if the lady takes the bit in her teeth and says shit before *me?*

I have been a teacher of writing for many years and have watched this problem since it was no bigger than a man's hand. It used to be that with some Howellsian notion of the young-girl audience one tried to protect tender female members of a mixed class from the coarse language of males trying to show off. Some years ago Frank O'Connor and I agreed on a system. Since we had no intention whatever of restricting students' choice of subject or language, and no desire to expurgate or bowdlerize while reading their stuff aloud for discussion, but at the same time had to deal with these young girls of an age our daughters might have been, we announced that any stuff so strong that it would embarrass us to read it aloud could be read by its own author.

It was no deterrent at all, but an invitation, and not only to coarse males. For clinical sexual observation, for full acceptance of the natural functions, for discrimination in the selection of graffiti, for boldness in the use of words that it should take courage to say before a lady, give me a sophomore girl every time. Her strength is as the strength of ten, for she assumes that if one shocker out of her pretty mouth is piquant, fifty will be literature. And so do a lot of her literary idols.

Some acts, like some words, were never meant to be casual. That is why houses contain bedrooms and bathrooms. Profanity and so-called obscenities are literary resources, verbal ways of rendering strong emotion. They are not meant to occur every ten seconds, any more than—Norman Mailer to the contrary notwithstanding—orgasms are.

So I am not going to say shit before any more ladies. I am going to hunt words that have not lost their sting, and it may be I shall have to go back to gentility to find them. Pleasant though it is to know that finally a writer can make use of any word that fits his occasion, I am going to investigate the possibilities latent in restraint.

I remember my uncle, a farmer who had used four-letter words ten to the sentence ever since he learned to talk. One day he came too near the circular saw and cut half his fingers off. While we stared in horror, he stood watching the bright arterial blood pump from his ruined hand. Then he spoke, and he did not speak loud. "Aw, the dickens," he said.

I think he understood, better than some sophomore girls and better than some novelists, the nature of emphasis.


## STUDY QUESTIONS

1. According to Stegner, the sin of false emphasis is related to sentimentality. Explain.

2. What are the premises of the argument in the third paragraph. Is this a valid argument?

3. What is the objection to "those d----d" emasculations of the Genteel Tradition"?

4. Why do writers today have license to use words that were formerly taboo?

5. Does Stegner give any consideration to taste in the use of certain words?

*Mark Twain*

# BUCK FANSHAW'S FUNERAL

Mark Twain, pen name for Samuel Langhorne Clemens (1835–1910), internationally known humorist and satirist, was born in Florida, Missouri, and spent his boyhood in Hannibal, Missouri. In his youth and early manhood he worked at a variety of occupations—journeyman printer, steamboat pilot, newspaper reporter, prospector, free-lance writer, and lecturer. His experiences gave him a lifetime of material for his writings. In his own time he enjoyed an international reputation as a wit and social commentator. In his later years he became bitterly cynical, but by most Americans he is remembered as the author of *Tom Sawyer* (1876) and *The Adventures of Huckleberry Finn* (1884).

SOMEBODY has said that in order to know a community, one must observe the style of its funerals and know what manner of men they bury with most ceremony. I cannot say which class we buried with most éclat in our "flush times," the distinguished public benefactor or the distinguished rough—possibly the two chief grades or grand divisions of society honored their illustrious dead about equally; and hence, no doubt, the philosopher I have quoted from would have needed to see two representative funerals in Virginia before forming his estimate of the people.

There was a grand time over Buck Fanshaw when he died. He was a representative citizen. He had "killed his man"—not in his own quarrel, it is true, but in defense of a stranger unfairly beset by numbers. He had kept a sumptuous saloon. He had been the proprietor of a dashing helpmeet whom he could have discarded without the formality of a divorce. He had held a high position in the fire department and been a very Warwick in politics. When he died there was great lamentation throughout the town, but especially in the vast bottom-stratum of society.

On the inquest it was shown that Buck Fanshaw, in the delirium of a wast-

Chapter VI in *Roughing It* by Mark Twain. Reprinted by permission of Harper & Row, publishers.

ing typhoid fever, had taken arsenic, shot himself through the body, cut his throat, and jumped out of a four-story window and broken his neck—and after due deliberation, the jury, sad and tearful, but with intelligence unblinded by its sorrow, brought in a verdict of death "by the visitation of God." What could the world do without juries?

Prodigious preparations were made for the funeral. All the vehicles in town were hired, all the saloons put in mourning, all the municipal and fire-company flags hung at half-mast, and all the firemen ordered to muster in uniform and bring their machines duly draped in black. Now—let us remark in parentheses—as all the peoples of the earth had representative adventurers in the Silverland, and as each adventurer had brought the slang of his nation or his locality with him, the combination made the slang of Nevada the richest and the most infinitely varied and copious that had ever existed anywhere in the world, perhaps, except in the mines of California in the "early days." Slang was the language of Nevada. It was hard to preach a sermon without it, and be understood. Such phrases as "You bet!" "Oh, no, I reckon not!" "No Irish need apply," and a hundred others, became so common as to fall from the lips of a speaker unconsciously—and very often when they did not touch the subject under discussion and consequently failed to mean anything.

After Buck Fanshaw's inquest, a meeting of the short-haired brotherhood was held, for nothing can be done on the Pacific coast without a public meeting and an expression of sentiment. Regretful resolutions were passed and various committees appointed; among others, a committee of one was deputed to call on the minister, a fragile, gentle, spiritual new fledgling from an Eastern theological seminary, and as yet unacquainted with the ways of the mines. The committeeman, "Scotty" Briggs, made his visit; and in after days it was worth something to hear the minister tell about it. Scotty was a stalwart rough, whose customary suit, when on weighty official business, like committee work, was a fire-helmet, flaming red flannel shirt, patent-leather belt with spanner and revolver attached, coat hung over arm, and pants stuffed into boot-tops. He formed something of a contrast to the pale theological student. It is fair to say of Scotty, however, in passing, that he had a warm heart, and a strong love for his friends, and never entered into a quarrel when he could reasonably keep out of it. Indeed, it was commonly said that whenever one of Scotty's fights was investigated, it always turned out that it had originally been no affair of his, but that out of native good-heartedness he had dropped in of his own accord to help the man who was getting the worst of it. He and Buck Fanshaw were bosom friends, for years, and had often taken adventurous "pot-luck" together. On one occasion, they had thrown off their coats and taken the weaker side in a fight among strangers, and after gaining a hard-earned victory, turned and found that the men they were helping had deserted early, and not only that, but had stolen their coats and made off with them. But to return to Scotty's visit to the minister. He was on a sorrowful mission, now, and his face was the picture of woe. Being admitted to the presence he sat down before the clergyman, placed his fire-hat on an unfinished manuscript sermon under the minister's nose, took from it a red silk handkerchief, wiped his brow and heaved a sigh of dismal impressiveness, explanatory of his business. He choked, and even shed tears; but with an effort he mastered his voice and said in lugubrious tones:

"Are you the duck that runs the gospel-mill next door?"

"Am I the—pardon me, I believe I do not understand?"

With another sigh and a half-sob, Scotty rejoined:

"Why you see we are in a bit of trouble, and the boys thought maybe you would give us a lift, if we'd tackle you—that is, if I've got the rights of it and you are the head clerk of the doxology-works next door."

"I am the shepherd in charge of the flock whose fold is next door."

"The which?"

"The spiritual adviser of the little company of believers whose sanctuary adjoins these premises."

Scotty scratched his head, reflected a moment, and then said:

"You ruther hold over me, pard. I reckon I can't call that hand. Ante and pass the buck."

"How? I beg pardon. What did I understand you to say?"

"Well, you've ruther got the bulge on me. Or maybe we've both got the bulge, somehow. You don't smoke me and I don't smoke you. You see, one of the boys has passed in his checks, and we want to give him a good send-off, and so the thing I'm on now is to roust out somebody to jerk a little chin-music for us and waltz him through handsome."

"My friend, I seem to grow more and more bewildered. Your observations are wholly incomprehensible to me. Cannot you simplify them in some way? At first I thought perhaps I understood you, but I grope now. Would it not expedite matters if you restricted yourself to categorical statements of fact unencumbered with obstructing accumulations of metaphor and allegory?"

Another pause, and more reflection. Then, said Scotty:

"I'll have to pass, I judge."

"How?"

"You've raised me out, pard."

"I still fail to catch your meaning."

"Why, that last lead of yourn is too many for me—that's the idea. I can't neither trump nor follow suit."

The clergyman sank back in his chair perplexed. Scotty leaned his head on his hand and gave himself up to thought. Presently his face came up, sorrowful but confident.

"I've got it now, so's you can savvy," he said. "What we want is a gospel-sharp. See?"

"A what?"

"Gospel-sharp. Parson."

"Oh! Why did you not say so before? I am a clergyman—a parson."

"Now you talk! You see my blind and straddle it like a man. Put it there!"—extending a brawny paw, which closed over the minister's small hand and gave it a shake indicative of fraternal sympathy and fervent gratification.

"Now we're all right, pard. Let's start fresh. Don't you mind my snuffling a little—becuz we're in a power of trouble. You see, one of the boys has gone up the flume—"

"Gone where?"

"Up the flume—throwed up the sponge, you understand."

"Thrown up the sponge?"

"Yes—kicked the bucket—"

"Ah—has departed to that mysterious country from whose bourne no traveler returns."

"Return! I reckon not. Why, pard, he's *dead!*"

"Yes, I understand."

"Oh, you do? Well I thought maybe you might be getting tangled some more. Yes, you see he's dead again—"

*"Again!* Why, has he ever been dead before?"

"Dead before? No! Do you reckon a man has got as many lives as a cat? But you bet you he's awful dead now, poor old boy, and I wish I'd never seen this day. I don't want no better friend than Buck Fanshaw. I knowed him by the back; and when I know a man and like him, I freeze to him—you hear *me*. Take him all round, pard, there never was a bullier man in the mines. No man ever knowed Buck Fanshaw to go back on a friend. But it's all up, you know, it's all up. It ain't no use. They've scooped him."

"Scooped him?"

"Yes—death has. Well, well, well, we've got to give him up. Yes, indeed. It's a kind of a hard world, after all, *ain't* it? But pard, he was a rustler! You ought to seen him get started once. He was a bully boy with a glass eye! Just spit in his face and give him room according to his strength, and it was just beautiful to see him peel and go in. He was the worst son a thief that ever drawed breath. Pard, he was *on* it! He was on it bigger than an Injun!"

"On it? On what?"

"On the shoot. On the shoulder. On the fight, you understand. *He* didn't give a continental for *any*body. *Beg* your pardon, friend, for coming so near saying a cuss-word—but you see I'm on an awful strain, in this palaver, on account of having to cramp down and draw everything so mild. But we've got to give him up. There ain't any getting around that, I don't reckon. Now if we can get you to help plant him—"

"Preach the funeral discourse? Assist at the obsequies?"

"Obs'quies is good. Yes. That's it—that's our little game. We are going to get the thing up regardless, you know. He was always nifty himself, and so you bet you his funeral ain't going to be no slouch—solid-silver door-plate on his coffin, six plumes on the hearse, and a nigger on the box in a biled shirt and a plug hat—how's that for high? And we'll take care of *you,* pard. We'll fix you all right. There'll be a kerridge for you; and whatever you want, you just 'scape out and we'll 'tend to it. We've got a shebang fixed up for you to stand behind, in No. 1's house, and don't you be afraid. Just go in and toot your horn, if you don't sell a clam. Put Buck through as bully as you can, pard, for anybody that knowed him will tell you that he was one of the whitest men that was ever in the mines. You can't draw it too strong. He never could stand it to see things going wrong. He's done more to make this town quiet and peaceable than any man in it. I've seen him lick four Greasers in eleven minutes, myself. If a thing wanted regulating, *he* warn't a man to go browsing around after somebody to do it, but he would prance in and regulate it himself. He warn't a Catholic. Scasely. He was down on 'em. His word was, 'No Irish need apply!' But it didn't make no difference about that when it came down to what a man's rights was—and so, when some roughs jumped the Catholic boneyard and started in to stake out town lots in it he *went* for 'em! And he *cleaned* 'em, too! I was there, pard, and I seen it myself."

"That was very well indeed—at least the impulse was—whether the act was strictly defensible or not. Had deceased any religious convictions? That is to say, did he feel a dependence upon, or acknowledge allegiance to a higher power?"

More reflection.

"I reckon you've stumped me again, pard. Could you say it over once more, and say it slow?"

"Well, to simplify it somewhat, was he, or rather had he ever been connected with any organization sequestered from secular concerns and devoted to self-sacrifice in the interests of morality?"

"All down but nine—set 'em up on the other alley, pard."

"What did I understand you to say?"

"Why, you're most too many for me, you know. When you get in with your left I hunt grass every time. Every time you draw, you fill; but I don't seem to have any luck. Let's have a new deal."

"How? Begin again?"

"That's it."

"Very well. Was he a good man, and—"

"There—I see that; don't put up another chip till I look at my hand. A good man, says you? Pard, it ain't no name for it. He was the best man that ever—pard, you would have doted on that man. He could lam any galoot of his inches in America. It was him that put down the riot last election before it got a start; and everybody said he was the only man that could have done it. He waltzed in with a spanner in one hand and a trumpet in the other, and sent fourteen men home on a shutter in less than three minutes. He had that riot all broke up and prevented nice before anybody ever got a chance to strike a blow. He was always for peace, and he would *have* peace—he could not stand disturbances. Pard, he was a great loss to this town. It would please the boys if you could chip in something like that and do him justice. Here once when the Micks got to throwing stones through the Methodis' Sunday-school windows, Buck Fanshaw, all of his own notion, shut up his saloon and took a couple of six-shooters and mounted guard over the Sunday-school. Says he, 'No Irish need apply!' And they didn't. He was the bulliest man in the mountains, pard! He could run faster, jump higher, hit harder, and hold more tanglefoot whisky without spilling it than any man in seventeen counties. Put that in, pard—it'll please the boys more than anything you could say. And you can say, pard, that he never shook his mother."

"Never shook his mother?"

"That's it—any of the boys will tell you so."

"Well, but why *should* he shake her?"

"That's what *I* say—but some people does."

"Not people of any repute?"

"Well, some that averages pretty so-so."

"In my opinion the man that would offer personal violence to his own mother, ought to—"

"Cheese it, pard; you've banked your ball clean outside the string. What I was a drivin' at, was, that he never *throwed off* on his mother—don't you see? No indeedy. He give her a house to live in, and town lots, and plenty of money; and he looked after her and took care of her all the time; and when she was down with the smallpox I'm d—d if he didn't set up nights and nuss her himself! *Beg* your pardon for saying it, but it hopped out too quick for yours truly. You've treated me like a gentleman, pard, and I ain't the man to hurt your feelings intentional. I think you're white. I think you're a square man, pard. I like you, and I'll lick any man that don't. I'll lick him tell he can't tell himself from a last year's corpse! Put it *there!*" [Another fraternal handshake—and exit.]

The obsequies were all that "the boys" could desire. Such a marvel of funeral pomp had never been seen in Virginia. The plumed hearse, the dirge-breathing brass-bands, the closed marts of business, the flags drooping at half-mast, the long, plodding procession of uniformed secret societies, military battalions and fire companies, draped engines, carriages of officials, and citizens in vehicles and on foot, attracted multitudes of spectators to the sidewalks, roofs, and windows; and for years afterward, the degree of grandeur attained by any civic display in Virginia was determined by comparison with Buck Fanshaw's funeral.

Scotty Briggs, as a pall-bearer and a mourner, occupied a prominent place at the funeral, and when the sermon was finished and the last sentence of the prayer for the dead man's soul ascended, he responded, in a low voice, but with feeling:

"AMEN. No Irish need apply."

As the bulk of the response was without apparent relevancy, it was probably nothing more than a humble tribute to the memory of the friend that was gone; for, as Scotty had once said, it was "his word."

Scotty Briggs, in after days, achieved the distinction of becoming the only convert to religion that was ever gathered from the Virginia roughs; and it transpired that the man who had it in him to espouse the quarrel of the weak out of inborn nobility of spirit was no mean timber whereof to construct a Christian. The making him one did not warp his generosity or diminish his courage; on the contrary it gave intelligent direction to the one and a broader field to the other. If his Sunday-school class progressed faster than the other classes, was it matter for wonder? I think not. He talked to his pioneer small-fry in a language they understood! It was my large privilege, a month before he died, to hear him tell the beautiful story of Joseph and his brethren to his class "without looking at the book." I leave it to the reader to fancy what it was like, as it fell, riddled with slang, from the lips of that grave, earnest teacher, and was listened to by his little learners with a consuming interest that showed that they were as unconscious as he was that any violence was being done to the sacred proprieties!

STUDY QUESTIONS

1. In addition to Scotty's and the minister's language, we have the language of the author, who introduces the story and concludes it. Compare his manner of speech with that of the other two.

2. Make note of the many different expressions Scotty and the minister use for death and funeral. Can you add to these?

3. Some of Scotty's expressions are current today. What are some of them?

*Max Beerbohm*

# HOW SHALL I WORD IT?

Max Beerbohm (1872–1956), well-known critic and satirist, was born in London. He received his A.B. degree from Merton College, Oxford. After gaining an early reputation for his satirical essays in the famous *Yellow Book,* he succeeded George Bernard Shaw as drama critic of the *Saturday Review.* In addition to countless essays published in magazines, he wrote *The Happy Hypocrite* (1897), *More* (1899), *Yet Again* (1907), *And Even Now* (1920), *A Variety of Things* (1928), *Mainly on the Air* (1946), and *Around Theatres* (1953). He was knighted in 1939.

IT WOULD SEEM that I am one of those travellers for whom the railway bookstall does not cater. Whenever I start on a journey, I find that my choice lies between well-printed books which I have no wish to read, and well-written books which I could not read without permanent injury to my eyesight. The keeper of the bookstall, seeing me gaze vaguely along his shelves, suggests that I should take *Fen Country Fanny* or else *The Track of Blood* and have done with it. Not wishing to hurt his feelings, I refuse these works on the plea that I have read them. Whereon he, divining despite me that I am a superior person, says "Here is a nice little handy edition of More's *Utopia*" or "Carlyle's *French Revolution*" and again I make some excuse. What pleasure could I get from trying to cope with a masterpiece printed in diminutive grey-ish type on a semi-transparent little grey-ish page? I relieve the bookstall of nothing but a newspaper or two.

The other day, however, my eye and fancy were caught by a book entitled *How Shall I Word It?* and sub-entitled *A Complete Letter Writer for Men and Women.* I had never read one of these manuals, but had often heard that there was a great and constant "demand" for them. So I demanded this one. It is no great fun in itself. The writer is no fool. He has evidently a natural

talent for writing letters. His style is, for the most part, discreet and easy. If
you were a young man writing "to Father of Girl he wishes to Marry" or
"thanking Fiancée for Present" or "reproaching Fiancée for being a Flirt,"
or if you were a mother "asking Governess her Qualifications" or "replying
to Undesirable Invitation for her Child," or indeed if you were in any other
one of the crises which this book is designed to alleviate, you might copy out
and post the specially-provided letter without making yourself ridiculous in
the eyes of its receiver—unless, of course, he or she also possessed a copy
of the book. But—well, can you conceive any one copying out and posting
one of these letters, or even taking it as the basis for composition? You cannot. That shows how little you know of your fellow-creatures. Not you nor I
can plumb the abyss at the bottom of which such humility is possible. Nevertheless, as we know by that great and constant "demand," there the abyss is,
and there multitudes are at the bottom of it. Let's peer down . . . No, all is
darkness. But faintly, if we listen hard, is borne up to us a sound of the
scratching of innumerable pens—pens whose wielders are all trying, as the
author of this handbook urges them, to "be original, fresh, and interesting"
by dint of more or less strict adherence to sample.

Giddily you draw back from the edge of the abyss. Come!—here is a
thought to steady you. The mysterious great masses of helpless folk for
whom *How Shall I Word It?* is written are sound at heart, delicate in feeling,
anxious to please, most loth to wound. For it must be presumed that the
author's style of letter-writing is informed as much by a desire to give his
public what it needs, and will pay for, as by his own beautiful nature; and in
the course of all the letters that he dictates you will find not one harsh word,
not one ignoble thought or unkind insinuation. In all of them, though so
many are for the use of persons placed in the most trying circumstances, and
some of them are for persons writhing under a sense of intolerable injury,
sweetness and light do ever reign. Even "yours truly, Jacob Langton," in his
"letter to his Daughter's Mercenary Fiancé," mitigates the sternness of his
tone by the remark that his "task is inexpressibly painful." And he, Mr.
Langton, is the one writer who lets the post go out on his wrath. When Horace Masterton, of Thorpe Road, Putney, receives from Miss Jessica Weir, of
Fir Villa, Blackheath, a letter "declaring her Change of Feelings," does he
upbraid her? No; "it was honest and brave of you to write to me so straight-
forwardly and at the back of my mind I know you have done what is best.
. . . I give you back your freedom only at your desire. God bless you,
dear." Not less admirable is the behaviour, in similar case, of Cecil Grant
(14, Glover Street, Streatham). Suddenly, as a bolt from the blue, comes a
letter from Miss Louie Hawke (Elm View, Deerhurst), breaking off her be-
trothal to him. Haggard, he sits down to his desk; his pen traverses the note-
paper—calling down curses on Louie and on all her sex? No; "one cannot
say good-bye for ever without deep regret to days that have been so full of

happiness. I must thank you sincerely for all your great kindness to me. . . . With every sincere wish for your future happiness," he bestows complete freedom on Miss Hawke. And do not imagine that in the matter of self-control and sympathy, of power to understand all and pardon all, the men are lagged behind by the women. Miss Leila Johnson (The Manse, Carlyle) has observed in Leonard Wace (Dover Street, Saltburn) a certain coldness of demeanour; yet "I do not blame you; it is probably your nature"; and Leila in her sweet forbearance is typical of all the other pained women in these pages: she is but one of a crowd of heroines.

Face to face with all this perfection, the not perfect reader beings to crave some little outburst of wrath, of hatred or malice, from one of these imaginary ladies and gentleman. He longs for—how shall he word it?—a glimpse of some bad motive, of some little lapse from dignity. Often, passing by a pillar-box, I have wished I could unlock it and carry away its contents, to be studied at my leisure. I have always thought such a haul would abound in things fascinating to a student of human nature. One night, not long ago, I took a waxen impression of the lock of the pillar-box nearest to my house, and had a key made. This implement I have as yet lacked either the courage or the opportunity to use. And now I think I shall throw it away. . . . No, I shan't. I refuse, after all, to draw my inference that the bulk of the British public writes always in the manner of this handbook. Even if they all have beautiful natures they must sometimes be sent slightly astray by inferior impulses, just as are you and I.

And, if err they must, surely it were well they should know how to do it correctly and forcibly. I suggest to our author that he should sprinkle his next edition with a few less righteous examples, thereby both purging his book of its monotony and somewhat justifying its subtitle. Like most people who are in the habit of writing things to be printed, I have not the knack of writing really good letters. But let me crudely indicate the sort of thing that our manual needs. . . .

LETTER FROM POOR MAN TO OBTAIN MONEY FROM RICH ONE.

[*The English law is particularly hard on what is called blackmail. It is therefore essential that the applicant should write nothing that might afterwards be twisted to incriminate him.*—ED.]

DEAR SIR,
To-day, as I was turning out a drawer in my attic, I came across a letter which by a curious chance fell into my hands some years ago, and which, in the stress of grave pecuniary embarrassment, had escaped my memory. It is a letter written by yourself to a lady, and the date shows it to have been written shortly after your marriage. It is of a confidential nature, and might, I fear, if it fell into the wrong hands, be cruelly misconstrued. I would wish

you to have the satisfaction of destroying it in person. At first I thought of
sending it on to you by post. But I know how happy you are in your domestic
life; and probably your wife and you, in your perfect mutual trust, are in the
habit of opening each other's letters. Therefore, to avoid risk, I would prefer
to hand the document to you personally. I will not ask you to come to my
attic, where I could not offer you such hospitality as is due to a man of your
wealth and position. You will be so good as to meet me at 3.0 A.M. (sharp) tomorrow (Thursday) beside the tenth lamp-post to the left on the Surrey side
of Waterloo Bridge; at which hour and place we shall not be disturbed.

I am, dear Sir,<br>
Yours respectfully,<br>
JAMES GRIDGE.

### LETTER FROM YOUNG MAN REFUSING TO PAY HIS TAILOR'S BILL.

Mr. Eustace Davenant has received the half-servile, half-insolent screed
which Mr. Yardley has addressed to him. Let Mr. Yardley cease from crawling on his knees and shaking his fist. Neither this posture nor this gesture
can wring one bent farthing from the pockets of Mr. Davenant, who was a
minor at the time when that series of ill-made suits was supplied to him and
will hereafter, as in the past, shout (without prejudice) from the house-tops
that of all the tailors in London Mr. Yardley is at once the most grasping and
the least competent.

### LETTER TO THANK AUTHOR FOR INSCRIBED COPY OF BOOK

DEAR MR EMANUEL FLOWER,

It was kind of you to think of sending me a copy of your new book. It
would have been kinder still to think again and abandon that project. I am a
man of gentle instincts, and do not like to tell you that "A Flight into Ar-
cady" (of which I have skimmed a few pages, thus wasting two or three minutes of my not altogether worthless time) is trash. On the other hand, I am
determined that you shall not be able to go around boasting to your friends,
if you have any, that this work was not condemned, derided, and dismissed
by your sincere well-wisher, WREXFORD CRIPPS.

### LETTER TO MEMBER OF PARLIAMENT UNSEATED AT GENERAL ELECTION

DEAR MR. POBSBY-BURFORD,

Though I am myself an ardent Tory, I cannot but rejoice in the crushing
defeat you have just suffered in West Odgetown. There are moments when
political conviction is overborne by personal sentiment; and this is one of
them. Your loss of the seat that you held is the more striking by reason of the

splendid manner in which the northern and eastern divisions of Odgetown have been wrested from the Liberal Party. The great bulk of the newspaper-reading public will be puzzled by your extinction in the midst of our party's triumph. But then, the great mass of the newspaper-reading public has not met you. I have. You will probably not remember me. You are the sort of man who would not remember anybody who might not be of some definite use to him. Such, at least, was one of the impressions you made on me when I met you last summer at a dinner given by our friends the Pelhams. Among the other things in you that struck me were the blatant pomposity of your manner, your appalling flow of cheap platitudes, and your hoggish lack of ideas. It is such men as you that lower the tone of public life. And I am sure that in writing to you thus I am but expressing what is felt, without distinction of party, by all who sat with you in the late Parliament.

The one person in whose behalf I regret your withdrawal into private life is your wife, whom I had the pleasure of taking in to the aforesaid dinner. It was evident to me that she was a woman whose spirit was well-nigh broken by her conjunction with you. Such remnants of cheerfulness as were in her I attributed to the Parliamentary duties which kept you out of her sight for so very many hours daily. I do not like to think of the fate to which the free and independent electors of West Odgetown have just condemned her. Only, remember this: chattel of yours though she is, and timid and humble, she despises you in her heart.

> I am, dear Mr. Pobsby-Burford,
> Yours very truly,
> HAROLD THISTLAKE.

### LETTER FROM YOUNG LADY IN ANSWER TO INVITATION FROM OLD SCHOOLMISTRESS.

MY DEAR MISS PRICE,

How awfully sweet of you to ask me to stay with you for a few days but how *can* you think I may have forgotten you for of course I think of you so very often and of the three ears I spent at your school because it is such a joy not to be there any longer and if one is at all down it bucks one up derectly to remember that *thats* all over atanyrate and that one has enough food to nurrish one and not that awful monottany of life and not the petty fogging daily tirrany you went in for and I can imagin no greater thrill and luxury in a way than to come and see the whole dismal grind still going on but without me being in it but this would be *rather* beastly of me wouldnt it so please dear Miss Price dont expect me and do excuse mistakes of English Composition and Spelling and etcetra in your affectionate old pupil,

> EMILY THÉRÈSE LYNN-ROYSTON.

ps, I often rite to people telling them where I was edducated and highly reckomending you.

## Letter in Acknowledgement of Wedding Present.

Dear Lady Amblesham,

Who gives quickly, says the old proverb, gives twice. For this reason I have purposely delayed writing to you, lest I should appear to thank you more than once for the small, cheap, hideous present you sent me on the occasion of my recent wedding. Were you a poor woman, that little bowl of ill-imitated Dresden china would convict you of tastelessness merely; were you a blind woman, of nothing but an odious parsimony. As you have normal eyesight and more than normal wealth, your gift to me proclaims you at once a Philistine and a miser (or rather did so proclaim you until, less than ten seconds after I had unpacked it from its wrappings of tissue paper, I took it to the open window and had the satisfaction of seeing it shattered to atoms on the pavement). But stay! I perceive a possible flaw in my argument. Perhaps you were guided in your choice by a definite wish to insult me. I am sure, on reflection, that this was so. *I shall not forget.*

Yours, etc.,
Cynthia Beaumarsh.

PS. My husband asked me to tell you to warn Lord Amblesham to keep out of his way or to assume some disguise so complete that he will not be recognised by him and horsewhipped.

PPS. I am sending copies of this letter to the principal London and provincial newspapers.

## Letter from . . .

But enough! I never thought I should be so strong in this line. I had not foreseen such copiousness and fatal fluency. Never again will I tap these deep dark reservoirs in a character that had always seemed to me, on the whole, so amiable.

## Study Questions

1. In the opening paragraph, what does Beerbohm indirectly tell us about himself?

2. What is Beerbohm's criticism of the models in the letter-writing manual? What does he see as the rhetorical strategy in these letters?

3. Examine each of the letters he writes and determine his rhetorical strategy.

*Philip B. Gove*

# PREFACE TO WEBSTER'S THIRD NEW INTERNATIONAL DICTIONARY

Philip B. Gove (1902–      ) is editor in chief of the controversial *Webster's Third New International Dictionary*. He received his B.A. from Dartmouth College, his A.M. from Harvard, and his Ph.D. from Columbia. After teaching for several years at Rice University and New York University, he joined the staff of the Merriam-Webster Company. He has published widely in the learned journals and is active in professional organizations; he is the author of *The Imaginary Voyage of Prose Fiction* (1941).

WEBSTER'S THIRD NEW INTERNATIONAL DICTIONARY is a completely new work, redesigned, restyled, and reset. Every line of it is new. This latest unabridged Merriam-Webster is the eighth in a series which has its beginning in Noah Webster's *American Dictionary of the English Language,* 1828. On Webster's death in 1843 the unsold copies and publishing rights of his dictionary were acquired by George and Charles Merriam, who in 1847 brought out a revision edited by Noah Webster's son-in-law, Professor Chauncey A. Goodrich of Yale College. The 1847 edition became the first Merriam-Webster unabridged dictionary.* G. & C. Merriam Company now offers WEBSTER'S THIRD NEW INTERNATIONAL DICTIONARY to the English-speaking world as a prime linguistic aid to interpreting the culture and civilization of today, as the first edition served the America of 1828.

* The successors in the Merriam-Webster series are *American Dictionary of the English Language,* popularly known as the *Unabridged,* 1864, edited by Dr. Noah Porter, president of Yale College; *Webster's International Dictionary,* 1890, Noah Porter, editor in chief; *Webster's New International Dictionary,* 1909, Dr. William Torrey Harris, U. S. Commissioner of Education, editor in chief, and F. Sturges Allen, general editor; *Webster's New International Dictionary, Second Edition,* 1934, Dr. William Allan Neilson, president of Smith College, editor in chief, and Dr. Thomas A. Knott, general editor.

As the number of students in school and college jumps to ever-increasing heights, the quantity of printed matter necessary to their education increases too. Not only are more words used more often with these increases; words must be used more economically and more efficiently both in school and out. More and more do people undertaking a new job, practicing a new hobby, or developing a new interest turn to how-to pamphlets, manuals, and books for both elementary instruction and advanced guidance. Where formerly they had time to learn by doing, they now need to begin by reading and understanding what has been recorded. A quick grasp of the meanings of words becomes necessary if one is to be successful. A dictionary opens the way to both formal learning and to the daily self-instruction that modern living requires. It is the key also to the daily newspaper and to a vast number of other periodicals that demand our attention. This edition has been prepared with a constant regard for the needs of the high school and college student, the technician, and the periodical reader, as well as of the scholar and professional. It undertakes to provide for the changes in public interest in all classes of words as manifested by what people want to read, discuss, and study. The dictionary more than ever is the indispensable instrument of understanding and progress.

G. & C. Merriam Company have produced this THIRD NEW INTERNATIONAL at a cost of over $3,500,000. The budgetary and technical planning underlying its production has been directed and coordinated since 1953 by the Company's president, Mr. Gordon J. Gallan. His activity, understanding, and cooperation have contributed indispensably to its editorial completion and have made possible the maintenance of a Merriam-Webster permanent office staff constituted according to need. This staff is in effect a faculty which specializes in different branches of knowledge much as a small college faculty does. Listed among the resident editors are a mathematician, a physicist, a chemist, a botanist, a biologist, a philosopher, a political scientist, a comparative religionist, a classicist, a historian, and a librarian as well as philologists, linguists, etymologists, and phoneticians whose specialty is the English language itself. Their academic affiliations and their degrees can be seen one by one in the "Merriam-Webster Editorial Staff" that follows this preface. Besides the office staff over two hundred other scholars and specialists have served as outside consultants in supplementary reviewing, revising, and submitting new definitions in subjects in which they are authorities. The range and experience of this special knowledge appear in the listing of their names alphabetically after the editorial staff.

In conformity with the principle that a definition, to be adequate, must be written only after an analysis of usage, the definitions in this edition are based chiefly on examples of usage collected since publication of the preceding edition. Members of the editorial staff began in 1936 a systematic reading of books, magazines, newspapers, pamphlets, catalogs, and learned journals. By the time of going to press the collection contained just under 4,500,000 such new examples of recorded usage, to be added to more than 1,665,000 citations already in the files for previous editions. Further, the citations in the indispensable many-volume *Oxford English Dictionary,* the new citations in Sir William Craigie's four-volume *Dictionary of American English* and Mitford M. Mathews' two-volume *Dictionary of Americanisms,* neither of which was available to the editors of the preceding edition, and the uncounted citations in dozens of concordances to the Bible and to works of English and American writers and in numerous books of quotations push the citation background for the definitions in this dictionary to over ten million. This figure does not include freely consulted text matter in the office library of reference books. Nor does it include thousands of textbooks in the private and academic libraries of the editors and consultants, nor books consulted in the Springfield City Library whose librarians have generously given the editorial staff ready and frequent access to its large and valuable word-hoard.

While dictionaries of special subjects, glossaries, indexes, and checklists are collected and examined to verify the existence of special words, no word has been entered in this dictionary merely on the authority of another dictionary, special or general, and no definition in this dictionary has been derived from any other dictionary (except, of course, Merriam-Webster predecessors). Learned and industrial organizations have created numerous committees of nomenclature to collect, define, and standardize the terminology in their fields. Some of the staff editors serve as advisory members of such committees. Nevertheless prescriptive and canonical definitions have not been taken over nor have recommendations been followed unless confirmed by independent investigation of usage borne out by genuine citations.

The primary objective of precise, sharp defining has been met through development of a new dictionary style based upon completely analytical one-phrase definitions throughout the book. Since the headword in a definition is intended to be modified only by structural elements restrictive in some degree and essential to each other, the use of commas either to separate or to group has been severely limited, chiefly to units in apposition or in series. The new defining pattern does not provide for a predication which conveys further expository comment. Instead of encyclopedic treatment at one place of a group of related terms, each term is defined at its own place in the alphabet. Every phrase in lowercase roman type following a heavy black colon and running to the next heavy colon or to a divisional number or letter is a complete definition of one sense of the word to which it is attached. Defining by synonym is carefully avoided by putting all unqualified or undifferentiated terms in small capital letters. Such a term in small capitals should not be considered a definition but a cross-reference to a definition of equivalent meaning that can be substituted for the small capitals.

A large number of verbal illustrations mostly from the mid-twentieth century has been woven into the defining pattern with a view to contributing considerably to the user's interest and understanding by showing a word used in context. The illustration is often a brief combination of words that has actually been used in writing and when this is so the illustration is attributed to its author or source. More than 14,000 different authors are quoted for their use of words or for the structural pattern of their words but not for their opinions or sentiments.

A number of other features are (1) the recognition and separate entry (with part-of-speech label) of verb-plus-adverb compounds (as *run down*) that function like one-word verbs in every way except for having a separable suffix, (2) the recognition (by using the label *n* for noun) that substantive open compounds (as *clothes moth*) belong in the same class as nouns written solid or hyphened, (3) the recognition (by using the label *often attrib*) of nouns that often function as adjectives but otherwise do not behave like the class of adjectives, (4) the indication (by inserting suffix-symbols, as -s or -ES, -ED/-ING/-S or -ES, -ER/-EST) of the inflectional forms of nouns, verbs, adjectives, and adverbs at which the forms are not written out in full, (5) the recognition (by beginning entries with a lowercase letter and by inserting either the label *cap, usu cap, often cap,* or *sometimes cap*) that words vary considerably in capitalization according to circumstances and environment, (6) the recognition (by not using at all the status label *colloquial*) that it is impossible to know whether a word out of context is colloquial or not, and (7) the incorporation of abbreviations alphabetically in the main vocabulary.

In continuation of Merriam-Webster policy the editors of this new edition have held steadfastly to the three cardinal virtues of dictionary making: accuracy, clearness, and comprehensiveness. Whenever these qualities are at odds with each other, accuracy is put first and foremost, for without accuracy there could be no appeal to WEBSTER'S THIRD NEW INTERNATIONAL as an authority. Accuracy in addition to requiring freedom from error and conformity to truth requires a dictionary to state meanings in which words are in fact used, not to give editorial opinion on what their meanings should be.

In the editorial striving for clearness the editors have tried to make the definitions as readable as possible. Even so, the terminology of many subjects contains words that can be adequately and clearly explained only to those who have passed through preliminary stages of initiation, just as a knowledge of algebra is prerequisite for trigonometry. A dictionary demands of its user much understanding and no one person can understand all of it. Therefore there is no limit to the possibilities for clarification. Somewhat paradoxically a user of the dictionary benefits in proportion to his effort and knowledge, and his contribution is an essential part of the process of understanding even though it may involve only a willingness to look up a few additional words.

Comprehensiveness requires maximum coverage with a minimum of compromise. The basic aim is nothing less than coverage of the current vocabulary of standard written and spoken English. At the same time the scientific and technical vocabulary has been considerably expanded to keep pace with progress especially in physical science (as in electronics, nuclear physics, statistics, and soil science), in technology (as in rocketry, communications, automation, and synthetics), in medicine, and in the experimental phases of natural science. Therefore space has been found not only for new terms but also for new uses of old terms, for English like other living languages is in a metabolic process of constant change. The changes affect not only word stock but meaning, syntax, morphology, and pronunciation.

The demands for space have made necessary a fresh judgment on the claims of many parts of the old vocabulary. This dictionary is the result of a highly selective process in which discarding material of insubstantial or evanescent quality has gone hand in hand with adding terms that have obtained a place in the language. It confines itself strictly to generic words and their functions, forms, sounds, and meanings as distinguished from proper names that are not generic. Selection is guided by usefulness, and usefulness is determined by the degree to which terms most likely to be looked for are included. Many obsolete and comparatively useless or obscure words have been omitted. These include in general words that had become obsolete before 1755 unless found in well-known major works of a few major writers.

In definitions of words of many meanings the earliest ascertainable meaning is given first. Meanings ot later derivation are arranged in the order shown to be most probable by dated evidence and semantic development. This arrangement applies alike to all meanings whether standard, technical, scientific, historical, or obsolete. No definitions are grouped alphabetically by subject labels. In fact this edition uses very few subject labels. It depends upon the definition for incorporating necessary subject orientation.

The pronunciation editor is Mr. Edward Artin. This edition shows as far as possible the pronunciations prevailing in general cultivated conversational usage, both informal and formal, throughout the English-speaking world. It does not attempt to dictate what that usage should be. It shows a wide variety of acceptable pronunciations based on a large file of transcriptions made by attentive listening to actual educated speech in all fields and in all parts of the country—the speech of those expecting to be completely understood by their hearers. The facility with which such speech can be checked today by television, radio, and recordings has made it possible to show more representative and more realistic pronunciations than in the past.

To this end the Merriam-Webster pronunciation key has been revised. Many of the symbols of preceding editions have been retained, some with slight alteration, a few substitutions have been made, and some symbols that have outlived their usefulness have been dropped altogether. It is still fundamentally a diacritical key that makes use of many of the conventions of English spelling and is based on the principles that every distinct significant sound should have a distinct symbol to represent it and that no sound should be represented in more than one way. The elimination of symbols for all nonsignificant differences in sound makes it possible for transcriptions to convey to speakers in different parts of the English-speaking world sounds proper to their own speech. The new pronunciation alphabet is designed to represent clearly the standard speech of educated Americans.

It should be clearly understood that in striving to show realistic pronunciations definite limitations are fixed by the very nature of a dictionary. Each word must be isolated and considered apart from its place in connected spoken discourse. It is impracticable to show in a dictionary many kinds of variations—rising or falling pitch, syllabic emphasis or lack of emphasis, contraction or prolongation of sounds—to which the pronunciation of a word is susceptible under the influence of other words temporarily associated with it. Some of these variations are discussed under several headings in "Guide to Pronunciation," which contains also several paragraphs on the subject of correctness in pronunciation.

The etymologist for this edition is Dr. Charles R. Sleeth. In the etymologies the aim has been to retrace step by step the line of transmission by which the words have come down to modern English from the language in which they are first recorded. The present work adheres in this respect to the sound general principles governing the presentation of word histories in previous editions and indeed applies them with a consistency that has not previously been attained. With particular care it traces back to Middle English every word which is recorded in Middle English; also it carefully distinguishes the age of borrowings from French by giving the source language as Old French if the word came into English before 1300, as Middle French if it came into English between 1300 and 1600, and as French only if it came into English in the seventeenth century or later.

The etymologies fall into four general groups based on the origins of English words. Native words (as *hound*) that have been in the language as long as it has existed are traced back first through Middle English to Old English and then to Germanic languages other than English and to Indo-European languages other than Germanic. Old and well-established borrowings (as *chief, add,* and *dialect*) that have been in English since medieval or Renaissance times and come from languages, usually French, Latin, or often indirectly Greek, which belong, like English, to the Indo-European language family are traced back through their immediate source to their ultimate source in as much detail as native words. Many more recent borrowings (as *éclair, anile, hubris, sforzando, lariat, dachshund, smorgasbord, galore, muzhik,* and *karma*) are incorporated into the network of Indo-European etymology more thoroughly than in earlier dictionaries by going beyond the immediate source to either a list of cognates or a cross-reference to another entry. Borrowings (as *bushido, tepee, sheikh, sampan,* and *taboo*) from non-Indo-European languages are traced to the immediate source and analyzed into their parts if in the source language they are compounds or derivatives.

In the modern technical vocabulary of the sciences it is difficult if not impossible to adhere strictly to the principle of tracing step by step the line of transmission of a word, because such vocabulary has expanded rapidly in numerous fields and has been transmitted freely across language boundaries. Very few works of reference give full or systematic information about the language of origin of technical terms in any one field, and consequently it is impossible for the etymological staff of a general dictionary to garner and present such information about the technical terms of all fields. The present work attempts a new solution of this problem by introducing the label ISV (for International Scientific Vocabulary), for use in the etymology of such words when their language of origin is not positively ascertainable but they are known to be current in at least one language other than English. Examples of the use of ISV and further details about it are given in "Explanatory Notes," 7.6. Some ISV words (like *haploid*) have been created by taking a word with a rather general and simple meaning from one of the languages of antiquity, usually Latin or Greek, and conferring upon it a very specific and complicated meaning for the purposes of modern scientific discourse. More typically, however, ISV words are compounds or derivatives, made up of constituents that can be found entered in their own alphabetical position with their own ulterior etymology, again generally involving Latin or Greek. In either case an ISV etymology as given in the present work incorporates the word into the system of Indo-European etymology as well as if the immediate source language were known and stated. At the same time, use of ISV avoids the often untenable implication that the word in question was coined in English, and recognizes that the word as such is a product of the modern world and gets only its raw materials, so to speak, from antiquity.

The scheme of biological classification used has been concerted in consultation between Dr. Mairé Weir Kay, staff biologist, and specialists in the several divisions of taxonomy. It is planned to coordinate in the broadest way with current professional usage and specifically avoids undue reliance on any single school or system. The total taxonomic coverage is far more extensive than this characterization might imply and is designed to include and link with the preferred scheme both historically important though now disused terminology and the more important terms pertinent to divergent schools of professional thought (as in the question of whether the leguminous plants constitute one or several families).

Words that are believed to be trademarks have been investigated in the files of the United States Patent Office. No investigation has been made of common law trademark rights in any word since such investigation is impracticable. Those that have current registrations are shown with an initial capital and are also identified as trademarks. The inclusion of any word in this dictionary is not, however, an expression of the publishers' opinion on whether or not it is subject to proprietary rights. Indeed, no definition in this dictionary is to be regarded as affecting the validity of any trademark.

This dictionary has a vocabulary of over 450,000 words. It would have been easy to make the vocabulary larger although the book, in the format of the preceding edition, could hardly hold any more pages or be any thicker. By itself, the number of entries is, however, not of first importance. The number of words available is always far in excess of and for a one-volume dictionary many times the number that can possibly be included. To make all the changes mentioned only to come out with the same number of pages and the same number of vocabulary entries as in the preceding edition would allow little or no opportunity for new words and new senses. The compactness and legibility of Times Roman, a typeface new to Merriam-Webster dictionaries, have made possible more words to a line and more lines to a column than in the preceding edition, and a larger size page makes a better proportioned book.

The preparation of this edition has absorbed 757 editor-years. This figure does not include the time of typists, photocopiers, and clerical assistants or the time of over 200 consultants. The book appears, like its predecessor, after more than ten years of active full-time preparation. It is hardly necessary to observe that no one editor could harmonize all the diverse and disparate matter by reading and criticizing every line or even determine and keep firm control over editorial policy, nor could an editiorial board of fixed membership. Instead the editor in chief has used his editors one by one and has delegated multiple responsibilities to them individually as occasion required. In this way members of the Merriam-Webster staff have been grouped and regrouped to form hundreds of task forces performing simultaneously thousands of missions. The editor can say with gratitude and relief that the accomplishment is not a one-man dictionary. "What individual," asks Noah Webster in his preface, "is competent to trace to their source, and define in all their various applications, popular, scientific, and technical, sixty or seventy thousand words!"

WEBSTER'S THIRD NEW INTERNATIONAL DICTIONARY is a collaborative effort. Without the cooperation of the scholarly, scientific, and technical world, the specialized guidance of our outside consultants, and the ingenuity of the compositors and printers, G. & C. Merriam Company and its permanent editorial staff could not have brought the work to its successful culmination. Those most deeply involved with overall responsibility deserve special mention here. Three associate editors, Mr. Artin, Dr. Kay, and Dr. Sleeth, have already been named in this preface. Among others who have shared large responsibilities are these associate editors: Miss Anne M. Driscoll, Dr. Philip H. Goepp, Mr. Hubert P. Kelsey, Dr. Howard G. Rhoads, and Dr. H. Bosley Woolf; two assistant editors, Miss Ervina E. Foss and Mrs. Laverne W. King; and the departmental secretary, Mrs. Christine M. Mullen.

It is now fairly clear that before the twentieth century is over every community of the world will have learned how to communicate with all the rest of humanity. In this process of intercommunication the English language has already become the most important language on earth. This new Merriam-Webster unabridged is the record of this language as it is written and spoken. It is offered with confidence that it will supply in full measure that information on the general language which is required for accurate, clear, and comprehensive understanding of the vocabulary of today's society.

Springfield, Mass.
*June* 1, 1961

PHILIP B. GOVE

## STUDY QUESTIONS

1. What is meant by the principle "that a definition, to be adequate, must be written only after an analysis of usage"?

2. Why did the editors elect not to use the status label "colloquial"? See Follett ("Sabotage in Springfield," p. 355) and Evans ("But What's a Dictionary For?" p. 364) on this point.

3. According to the "Preface," what is the basic aim of *Webster's Third?*

4. What are the limitations to showing in a dictionary the realistic pronunciation of words?

5. What are the four general groups of the etymologies in *Webster's Third?*

*Wilson Follett*

# SABOTAGE IN SPRINGFIELD

Wilson Follett (1887–1963) was born in Ahleborough, Massachusetts. He received his A.B. from Harvard in 1909, and had a distinguished career as a writer, critic, and editor. He was a frequent contributor to such publications as *Harper's, Saturday Review, Virginia Quarterly,* and *Bookman.* He translated *Molière, the Man Seen Through the Plays,* by Ramon Fernandez, but he is perhaps best known to scholars of American literature as the editor of the twelve-volume works of Stephen Crane.

OF DICTIONARIES, as of newspapers, it might be said that the bad ones are too bad to exist, the good ones too good not to be better. No dictionary of a living language is perfect or ever can be, if only because the time required for compilation, editing, and issuance is so great that shadows of obsolescence are falling on parts of any such work before it ever gets into the hands of a user. Preparation of *Webster's Third New International Dictionary of the English Language* began intensively in the Springfield establishment of G. & C. Merriam Company in 1936, but the century was nine months into its seventh decade before any outsider could have his first look at what had been accomplished. His first look is, of course, incompetent to acquaint him with the merits of the new work; these no one can fully discover without months or years of everyday use. On the other hand, it costs only minutes to find out that what will rank as the great event of American linguistic history in this decade, and perhaps in this quarter century, is in many crucial particulars a very great calamity.

Why should the probable and possible superiorities of the Third New International be so difficult to assess, the shortcomings so easy? Because the superiorities are special, departmental, and recondite, the shortcomings general and within the common grasp. The new dictionary comes to us with a claim of 100,000 new words or new definitions. These run almost overwhelmingly to scientific and technological terms or meanings that have come into existence since 1934, and especially to words classified as ISV (belonging to the international scientific vocabulary). No one person can possibly use or even comprehend all of them; the coverage in this domain, certainly impressive to the nonspecialist, may or may not command the admiration of specialists. It is said that historians of the graphic arts and of architecture were displeased with the 1934 Webster, both for its omissions and for some definitions of what it included in their fields. Its 1961 successor may have disarmed their reservations; only they can pronounce.

But all of us may without brashness form summary judgments about the treatment of what belongs to all of us—the standard, staple, traditional language of general reading and speaking, the ordinary vocabulary and idioms of novelist, essayist, letter writer, reporter, editorial writer, teacher, student, advertiser; in short, fundamental English. And it is precisely in this province that Webster III has thrust upon us a dismaying assortment of the questionable, the perverse, the unworthy, and the downright outrageous.

Furthermore, what was left out is as legitimate a grievance to the ordinary reader as anything that has been put in. Think—if you can—of an unabridged dictionary from which you cannot learn who Mark Twain was (though *mark twain* is entered as a leadsman's cry), or what were the names of the twelve apostles, or that the Virgin was Mary the mother of Jesus of Nazareth, or what and where the District of Columbia is!

The disappointment and the shock are intensified, of course, because of the unchallenged position earned by the really unabridged immediate predecessor of this strange work. *Webster's New International Dictionary*, Second Edition (1934), consummated under the editorship of William Allan Neilson, at once became the most important reference book in the world to American writers, editors, teachers, students, and general readers—everyone to whom American English was a matter of serious interest. What better could the next revision do than extend the Second Edition in the direction of itself, bring it up to date, and correct its scattering of oversights and errata?

The 1934 dictionary had been, heaven knows, no citadel of conservatism, no last bastion of puristical bigotry. But it had made shrewd reports on the status of individual words; it had taken its clear, beautifully written definitions from fit uses of an enormous vocabulary by judicious users; it had provided accurate, impartial accounts of the endless guerrilla war between grammarian and antigrammarian and so given every consultant the means to work out his own decisions. Who could wish the forthcoming revision any better fortune than a comparable success in applying the same standards to whatever new matter the new age imposed?

Instead, we have seen a century and a third of illustrious history largely jettisoned; we have seen a novel dictionary formula improvised, in great part out of snap judgments and the sort of theoretical improvement that in practice impairs; and we have seen the gates propped wide open in enthusiastic hospitality to miscellaneous confusions and corruptions. In fine, the anxiously awaited work that was to have crowned cisatlantic linguistic scholarship with a particular glory turns out to be a scandal and a disaster. Worse yet, it plumes itself on its faults and parades assiduously cultivated sins as virtues without precedent.

Examination cannot proceed far without revealing that Webster III, behind its front of passionless objectivity, is in truth a fighting document. And the enemy it is out to destroy is every obstinate vestige of linguistic punctilio, every surviving influence that makes for the upholding of standards, every criterion for distinguishing between better usages and worse. In other words, it has gone over bodily to the school that construes traditions as enslaving, the rudimentary principles of syntax as crippling, and taste as irrelevant. This revolution leaves it in the anomalous position of loudly glorifying its own ancestry—which is indeed glorious—while tacitly sabotaging the principles and ideals that brought the preceding Merriam-Webster to its unchallengeable preeminence. The Third New International is at once a resounding tribute of lip service to the Second and a wholesale repudiation of it—a sweeping act of apology, contrition, and reform.

The right-about-face is, of course, particularly evident in the vocabulary approved. Within a few days of publication the new dictionary was inevitably notorious for its unreserved acceptance as standard of *wise up, get hep* (it uses the second as a definition of the first), *ants in one's pants, one for the book; hugeous, nixie, passel, hepped up* (with *hepcat* and *hepster*), *anyplace, someplace,* and so forth. These and a swarm of their kind it admits to full canonical standing by the suppression of such qualifying status labels as *colloquial, slang, cant, facetious,* and *substandard.* The classification *colloquial* it abolishes outright: "it is impossible to know whether a word out of context is colloquial or not." Of *slang* it makes a chary occasional use despite a similar reservation: "No word is invariably slang, and many standard words can be given slang connotations or used so inappropriately as to become slang." *Cornball* is ranked as slang, *corny* is not.

The overall effect signifies a large-scale abrogation of one major responsibility of the lexicographer. He renounces it on the curious ground that helpful discriminations are so far beyond his professional competence that he is obliged to leave them to those who, professing no competence at all, have vainly turned to him for guidance. If some George Ade of the future, aspiring to execute a fable in slang, were to test his attempt by the status labels in Webster III, he would quickly discover with chagrin that he had expressed himself almost without exception in officially applauded English. With but slight exaggeration we can say that if an expression can be shown to have been used in print by some jaded reporter, some candidate for office or his speech writer, some potboiling minor novelist, it is well enough credentialed for the full blessing of the new lexicography.

This extreme tolerance of crude neologisms and of shabby diction generally, however, is but one comparatively trifling aspect of the campaign against punctilio. We begin to sound its deeper implications when we plunge into the definitions and the copious examples that illustrate and support them. Under the distributive pronoun *each* we find, side by side: "(each of them is to pay his own fine) (each of them are to pay their own fine)." Where could anyone look for a neater, more succinct way to outlaw the dusty dogma that a pronoun should always agree in number with its antecedent? Here is the same maneuver again under another distributive, *everybody:* "usu. referred to by the third person singular (everybody is bringing his own lunch) but sometimes by a plural personal pronoun (everybody had made up their minds). "Or try *whom* and *whomever:* "(a . . . recruit whom he hoped would prove to be a crack salesman) (people . . . whom you never thought would sympathize) . . . (I go out to talk to whomever it is) . . . (he attacked whomever disagreed with him)." It is, then, all right to put the subject of a finite verb in the accusative case—"esp. after a preposition or a verb of which it might mistakenly be considered the object."

Shall we look into what our dictionary does with a handful of the more common solecisms, such as a publisher might introduce into a cooked-up test for would-be copy editors? Begin with *center around* (or *about*). It seems obvious that expressions derived from Euclidean geometry should make Euclidean sense. A center is a point; it is what things are around, not what is around them; they center *in* or *on* or *at* the point. The Second Edition defined the Great White Way as "That part of Broadway . . . centering about Times Square"—patently an oversight. Is it the same oversight that produces, in the Third: *"heresy . . . 3:* a group or school of thought centering around a particular heresy"? We look up *center* itself, and, lo: "(a story to tell, centered around the political development of a great state) . . . (more scholarship than usual was centered around the main problems)," followed by several equivalent specimens.

Here is *due to.* First we come on irreproachable definitions, irreproachably illustrated, of *due* noun and *due* adjective, and we think we are out of the woods. Alas, they are followed by the manufacture of a composite preposition, *due to,* got up solely to extenuate such abominations as "the event was canceled due to inclement weather." An adjective can modify a verb, then. And here is a glance at that peculiarly incriminating redundancy of the slipshod writer, *equally as:* "equally opposed to Communism as to Fascism." The intolerable *hardly than* or *scarcely than* construction is in full favor: "hardly had the birds dropped than she jumped into the water and retrieved them." The sequence *different than* has the double approbation of editorial use and a citation: conjunctive *unlike* means "in a manner that is different than," and a passage under *different* reads "vastly different in size than it was twenty-five years ago." Adjectival *unlike* and conjunctive *unlike* both get illustrations that implicitly commend the unanchored and grammarless modifier: "so many fine men were outside the charmed circle that, unlike most colleges, there was no disgrace in not being a club man"; "unlike in the gasoline engine, fuel does not enter the cylinder with air on the intake stroke."

This small scattering should not end without some notice of that darling of the advanced libertarians, *like* as a conjunction, first in the meaning of *as,* secondly (and more horribly) in that of *as if.* Now, it is well known to the linguistic historian that *like* was so used for a long time before and after Langland. But it is as well known that the language rather completely sloughed off this usage; that it has long been no more than a regional colloquialism, a rarely seen aberration among competent writers, or an artificially cultivated irritant among defiant ones. The *Saturday Evening Post,* in which *like* for *as* is probably more frequent than in any other painstakingly edited magazine, has seldom if ever printed that construction except in reproducing the speech or tracing the thoughts of characters to whom it might be considered natural. The arguments for *like* have been merely defensive and permissive. Not for centuries has there been any real pressure of authority on a writer to use *like* as a conjunction—until our Third New International Dictionary decided to exert its leverage.

How it is exerted will appear in the following: "(impromptu programs where they ask questions much like I do on the air) . . . (looks like they can raise better tobacco) (looks like he will get the job) (wore his clothes like he was . . . afraid of getting dirt on them) (was like he'd come back from a long trip) (acted like she felt sick) . . . (sounded like the motor had stopped) . . . (the violin now sounds like an old masterpiece should) (did it like he told me to) . . . (wanted a doll like she saw in the store window) . . . (anomalies like just had occurred)."

By the processes represented in the foregoing and countless others for which there is no room here, the latest Webster whittles away at one after another of the traditionary controls until there is little or nothing left of them. The controls, to be sure, have often enough been overvalued and overdone by pedants and purists, by martinets and bigots; but more often, and much more importantly, they have worked as aids toward dignified, workmanlike, and cogent uses of the wonderful language that is our inheritance. To erode and undermine them is to convert the language into a confusion of unchanneled, incalculable williwaws, a capricious wind blowing whithersoever it listeth. And that, if we are to judge by the total effect of the pages under scrutiny—2720 of them and nearly 8000 columns of vocabulary, all compact, set in Times Roman—is exactly what is wanted by the patient and dedicated saboteurs in Springfield. They, if they keep their ears to the ground, will hear many echoes of the despairing cry already wrung from one editorial assistant on a distinguished magazine that still puts its faith in standards: "Why have a Dictionary at all if anything goes?"

The definitions are reinforced, it will have been conveyed, with copious citations from printed sources. These citations occupy a great fraction of the total space. They largely account for the reduction in the number of entries (from 600,000 to 450,000) and for the elimination of the Gazetteer, the Biographical Dictionary, and the condensed key to pronunciation and symbols that ran across the bottoms of facing pages—all very material deprivations. Some 14,000 authors, we are told, are represented in the illustrative quotations—"mostly from the mid-twentieth century."

Can some thousands of authors truly worth space in a dictionary ever be found in any one brief period? Such a concentration can hardly fail to be, for the purposes of a dictionary, egregiously overweighted with the contemporary and the transient. Any very short period, such as a generation, is a period of transition in the history of English, and any great mass of examples drawn primarily from it will be disproportionately focused on transitional and ephemeral elements. To say that recording English *as we find it today* is precisely the purpose of a new dictionary is not much of a retort. For the bulk of the language that we use has come down to us with but minor, glacially slow changes from time out of mind, and a worthy record of it must stand on a much broader base than the fashions of yesterday.

It is, then, a mercy that among the thousands of scraps from recent authors, many of them still producing, we can also find hundreds from Shakespeare, the English Bible, Fielding, Dickens, Hawthorne, Melville, Henry James, Mark Twain, and so on. But the great preponderance of latter-day prose, little of it worth repeating and a good deal of it hardly worth printing in the first place, is likely to curtail by years the useful life of the Third New International.

So much is by the way. When we come to the definitions proper we face something new, startling, and formidable in lexicography. The definitions, all of them conformed to a predetermined rhetorical pattern, may be products of a theory—Gestaltist, perhaps?—of how the receiving mind works. The pattern, in the editor's general preface, is described as follows: "The primary objective of precise, sharp defining has been met through development of a new dictionary style based upon completely analytical one-phrase definitions throughout the book. Since the head-word in a definition is intended to be modified only by structural elements restrictive in some degree and essential to each other, the use of commas either to separate or to group has been severely limited, chiefly to elements in apposition or in series. The new defining pattern does not provide for a predication which conveys further expository comment."

This doctrine of the strictly unitary definition is of course formulated and applied in the interest of a logical integrity and a simplification never before consistently attained by lexical definitions. What it produces, when applied with the rigor here insisted on, is in the first place some of the oddest prose ever concocted by pundits. A typical specimen, from the definition of the simplest possible term: *"rabbit punch . . . :* a short chopping blow delivered to the back of the neck or the base of the skull with the edge of the hand opposite the thumb that is illegal in boxing." When the idea, being not quite so simple, requires the one-phrase statement of several components, the definition usually turns out to be a great unmanageable and unpunctuated blob of words strung out beyond the retentive powers of most minds that would need the definition at all. Both theory and result will emerge clearly enough from a pair of specimens, the first dealing with a familiar everyday noun, the second with a mildly technical one:

*groan* . . . *1:* a deep usu. inarticulate and involuntary often strangled sound typically abruptly begun and ended and usu. indicative of pain or grief or tension or desire or sometimes disapproval or annoyance.
*kymograph* . . . *1:* a recording device including an electric motor or clockwork that drives a usu. slowly revolving drum which carries a roll of plain or smoked paper and also having an arrangement for tracing on the paper by means of a stylus a graphic record of motion or pressure (as of the organs of speech, blood pressure, or respiration) often in relation to particular intervals of time.

About these typical definitions as prose, there is much that any good reader might well say. What must be said is that the grim suppression of commas is a mere crotchet. It takes time to read such definitions anyway; commas in the right places would speed rather than slow the reading and would clarify rather than obscure the sense, so that the unitary effect—largely imaginary at best—would be more helped than hurt. In practice, the one-phrase design without further expository predication lacks all the asserted advantages over a competently written definition of the free conventional sort; it is merely much more difficult to write, often impossible to write well, and tougher to take in. Compare the corresponding definitions from the Second Edition:

*groan* . . . A low, moaning sound; usually, a deep, mournful sound uttered in pain or great distress; sometimes, an expression of strong disapprobation; as, the remark was received with *groans.*
*kymograph* . . . *a* An automatic apparatus consisting of a motor revolving a drum covered with smoked paper, on which curves of pressure, etc., may be traced.

Everyone professionally concerned with the details of printed English can be grateful to the new Webster for linking the parts of various expressions that have been either hyphenated compounds or separate words—*highlight, highbrow* and *lowbrow, overall, wisecrack, lowercase* and *uppercase,* and so on. Some of the unions now recognized were long overdue; many editors have already got them written into codes of house usage. But outside this small province the new work is a copy editor's despair, a propounder of endless riddles.

What, for example, are we to make of the common abbreviations *i.e.* and *e.g.?* The first is entered in the vocabulary as *ie* (no periods, no space), the second as *e g* (space, no periods). In the preliminary list, "Abbreviations Used in This Dictionary," both are given the customary periods. (Oddly, the list translates its *i.e.* into "that is," but merely expands *e.g.* into "exempli gratia.") Is one to follow the vocabulary or the list? What point has the seeming inconsistency?

And what about capitalization? All vocabulary entries are in lowercase except for such abbreviations as ARW (air raid warden), MAB (medical advisory board), and PX (post exchange). Words possibly inviting capitalization are followed by such injunctions as *cap, usu cap, sometimes not cap, usu cap 1st A, usu cap A&B.* (One of the small idiosyncrasies is that "usu.," the most frequent abbreviation, is given a period when roman, denied it when italic.) From *america,* adjective—all proper nouns are excluded—to *american yew* there are over 175 consecutive entries that require such injunctions; would it not have been simpler and more economical to capitalize the entries? A flat *"cap,"* of course, means "always capitalized." But how often is "usually," and when is "sometimes"? We get dictionaries expressly that they may settle such problems for us. This dictionary seems to make a virtue of leaving them in flux, with the explanation that many matters are subjective and that the individual must decide them for himself—a curious abrogation of authority in a work extolled as "more useful and authoritative than any previous dictionary."

The rock-bottom practical truth is that the lexicographer cannot abrogate his authority if he wants to. He may think of himself as a detached scientist reporting the facts of language, declining to recommend use of anything or abstention from anything; but the myriad consultants of his work are not going to see him so. He helps create, not a book of fads and fancies and private opinions, but a Dictionary of the English Language. It comes to every reader under auspices that say, not "Take it or leave it," but rather something like this: "Here in 8000 columns is a definitive report of what a synod of the most trustworthy American experts consider the English language to be in the seventh decade of the twentieth century. This is your language; take it and use it. And if you use it in conformity with the principles and practices here exemplified, your use will be the most accurate attainable by any American of this era." The fact that the compilers disclaim authority and piously refrain from judgments is meaningless: the work itself, by virtue of its inclusions and exclusions, its mere existence, is a whole universe of judgments, received by millions as the Word from on high.

And there we have the reason why it is so important for the dictionary maker to keep his discriminations sharp, why it is so damaging if he lets them get out of working order. Suppose he enters a new definition for no better reason than that some careless, lazy, or uninformed scribbler has jumped to an absurd conclusion about what a word means or has been too harrassed to run down the word he really wanted. This new definition is going to persuade tens of thousands that, say, *cohort,* a word of multitude, means one associate or crony "(he and three alleged housebreaking cohorts were arraigned on attempted burglary charges)" or that the vogue word *ambivalence,* which denotes simultaneous love and hatred of someone or something, means "continual oscillation between one thing and its opposite (novels . . . vitiated by an ambivalence between satire and sentimentalism)." To what is the definer contributing if not to subversion and decay? To the swallower of the definition it never occurs that he can have drunk corruption from a well that he has every reason to trust as the ultimate in purity. Multiply him by the number of people simultaneously influenced, and the resulting figure by the years through which the influence continues, and a great deal of that product by the influences that will be disseminated through speech and writing and teaching and you begin to apprehend the scope of the really enormous disaster that can and will be wrought by the lexicographer's abandonment of his responsibility.

## STUDY QUESTIONS

1. What does Follett believe to be the responsibility of the lexicographer? Compare his view with that expressed in the "Preface" to *Webster's Third New International Dictionary.*

2. What are his chief objections to *Webster's Third?*

3. In what respects does he judge *Webster's New International Dictionary,* Second Edition (1934), to be a superior dictionary?

4. What does Follett say about the citations that reinforce the definitions? Why does he feel that a great number of citations from contemporary prose will curtail the useful life of the dictionary?

5. How would you describe Follett's tone in this review? What particular words and expressions reflect his tone?

## Bergen Evans

# BUT WHAT'S A DICTIONARY FOR?

Bergen Evans (1902–      ) was born in Franklin, Ohio. He received his
A.B. from Miami University (Ohio) and his A.M. and Ph.D. from Harvard
University. He was a Rhodes Scholar and received his B.Litt. from Oxford
University. He has taught at Miami University, and is now professor of
English at Northwestern University. He is author of *The Natural History of
Nonsense* (1946) and *Comfortable Words* (1962) and is coauthor of *A Dic-
tionary of Contemporary American Usage* (1957). He is the recipient of the
George Foster Peabody Award for excellence in radio and television
broadcasting.

THE STORM of abuse in the popular press that greeted the
appearance of *Webster's Third New International Dictionary* is a curious phenomenon. Never has a scholarly
work of this stature been attacked with such unbridled fury and contempt.
An article in the *Atlantic* viewed it as a "disappointment," a "shock," a
"calamity," "a scandal and a disaster." *The New York Times,* in a special
editorial, felt that the work would "accelerate the deterioration" of the language and sternly accused the editors of betraying a public trust. The *Journal* of the American Bar Association saw the publication as "deplorable," "a
flagrant example of lexicographic irresponsibility," "a serious blow to the
cause of good English." *Life* called it "a non-word deluge," "monstrous,"
"abominable," and "a cause for dismay." They doubted that "Lincoln could
have modelled his Gettysburg Address" on it—a concept of how things get
written that throws very little light on Lincoln but a great deal on *Life*.

What underlies all this sound and fury? Is the claim of the G. & C. Merriam Company, probably the world's greatest dictionary maker, that the
preparation of the work cost $3.5 million, that it required the efforts of three
hundred scholars over a period of twenty-seven years, working on the largest collection of citations ever assembled in any language—is all this a
fraud, a hoax?

Reprinted with permission of the author. First published in *The Atlantic Monthly,*
May 1962.

So monstrous a discrepancy in evaluation requires us to examine basic principles. Just what's a dictionary for? What does it propose to do? What does the common reader go to a dictionary to find? What has the purchaser of a dictionary a right to expect for his money?

Before we look at basic principles, it is necessary to interpose two brief statements. The first of these is that a dictionary is concerned with words. Some have tables of weights and measures on the flyleaves. Some list historical events, and some, home remedies. And there's nothing wrong with their so doing. But the great increase in our vocabulary in the past three decades compels all dictionaries to make more efficient use of their space. And if something must be eliminated, it is sensible to throw out these extraneous things and stick to words.

Yet wild wails arose. The *Saturday Review* lamented that one can no longer find the goddess Astarte under a separate heading—though they point out that a genus of mollusks named after the goddess is included! They seemed to feel that out of sheer perversity the editors of the dictionary stooped to mollusks while ignoring goddesses and that, in some way, this typifies modern lexicography. Mr. Wilson Follett, folletizing (his mental processes demand some special designation) in the *Atlantic,* cried out in horror that one is not even able to learn from the Third International "that the Virgin was Mary the mother of Jesus!"

The second brief statement is that there has been even more progress in the making of dictionaries in the past thirty years than there has been in the making of automobiles. The difference, for example, between the much-touted Second International (1934) and the much-clouted Third International (1961) is not like the difference between yearly models but like the difference between the horse and buggy and the automobile. Between the appearance of these two editions a whole new science related to the making of dictionaries, the science of descriptive linguistics, has come into being.

Modern linguistics gets its charter from Leonard Bloomfield's *Language* (1933). Bloomfield, for thirteen years professor of Germanic philology at the University of Chicago and for nine years professor of linguistics at Yale, was one of those inseminating scholars who can't be relegated to any department and don't dream of accepting established categories and procedures just because they're established. He was as much an anthropologist as a linguist, and his concepts of language were shaped not by Strunk's *Elements of Style* but by his knowledge of Cree Indian dialects.

The broad general findings of the new science are:

1. All languages are systems of human conventions, not systems of natural laws. The first—and essential—step in the study of any language is observing and setting down precisely what happens when native speakers speak it.

2. Each language is unique in its pronunciation, grammar, and vocabu-

lary. It cannot be described in terms of logic or of some theoretical, ideal language. It cannot be described in terms of any other language or even in terms of its own past.

3. All languages are dynamic rather than static, and hence a "rule" in any language can only be a statement of contemporary practice. Change is constant—and normal.

4. "Correctness" can rest only upon usage, for the simple reason that there is nothing else for it to rest on. And all usage is relative.

From these propositions it follows that a dictionary is good only insofar as it is a comprehensive and accurate description of current usage. And to be comprehensive it must include some indication of social and regional associations.

New dictionaries are needed because English has changed more in the past two generations than at any other time in its history. It has had to adapt to extraordinary cultural and technological changes, two world wars, unparalleled changes in transportation and communication, and unprecedented movements of populations.

More subtly, but pervasively, it has changed under the influence of mass education and the growth of democracy. As written English is used by increasing millions and for more reasons than ever before, the language has become more utilitarian and more informal. Every publication in America today includes pages that would appear, to the purist of forty years ago, unbuttoned gibberish. Not that they are; they simply show that you can't hold the language of one generation up as a model for the next.

It's not that you mustn't. You *can't*. For example, in the issue in which *Life* stated editorially that it would follow the Second International, there were over forty words, constructions, and meanings which are in the Third International but not in the Second. The issue of *The New York Times* which hailed the Second International as the authority to which it would adhere and the Third International as a scandal and a betrayal which it would reject used one hundred and fifty-three separate words, phrases, and constructions which are listed in the Third International but not in the Second and nineteen others which are condemned in the Second. Many of them are used many times, more than three hundred such uses in all. The Washington *Post,* in an editorial captioned "Keep Your Old Webster's," says, in the first sentence, "don't throw it away," and in the second, "hang on to it." But the old Webster's labels *don't* "colloquial" and doesn't include "hang on to," in this sense, at all.

In short, all of these publications are written in the language that the Third International describes, even the very editorials which scorn it. And this is no coincidence, because the Third International isn't setting up any new standards at all; it is simply describing what *Life,* the Washington *Post,* and the *The New York Times* are doing. Much of the dictionary's material comes from these very publications, the *Times,* in particular, furnishing more of its illustrative quotations than any other newspaper.

And the papers have no choice. No journal or periodical could sell a single issue today if it restricted itself to the American language of twenty-eight years ago. It couldn't discuss half the things we are interested in, and its style would seem stiff and cumbrous. If the editorials were serious, the public—and the stockholders—have reason to be grateful that the writers on these publications are more literate than the editors.

And so back to our questions: what's a dictionary for, and how, in 1962, can it best do what it ought to do? The demands are simple. The common reader turns to a dictionary for information about the spelling, pronunciation, meaning, and proper use of words. He wants to know what is current and respectable. But he wants—and has a right to—the truth, the full truth. And the full truth about any language, and especially about American English today, is that there are many areas in which certainty is impossible and simplification is misleading.

Even in so settled a matter as spelling, a dictionary cannot always be absolute. *Theater* is correct, but so is *theatre.* And so are *traveled* and *travelled, plow* and *plough, catalog* and *catalogue,* and scores of other variants. The reader may want a single certainty. He may have taken an unyielding position in an argument, he may have wagered in support of his conviction and may demand that the dictionary "settle" the matter. But neither his vanity nor his purse is any concern of the dictionary's; it must record the facts. And the fact here is that there are many words in our language which may be spelled, with equal correctness, in either of two ways.

So with pronunciation. A citizen listening to his radio might notice that James B. Conant, Bernard Baruch, and Dwight D. Eisenhower pronounce *economics* as ECKuhnomiks, while A. Whitney Griswold, Adlai Stevenson, and Herbert Hoover pronounce it EEKuhnomiks. He turns to the dictionary to see which of the two pronunciations is "right" and finds that they are both acceptable.

Has he been betrayed? Has the dictionary abdicated its responsibility? Should it say that one *must* speak like the president of Harvard or like the president of Yale, like the thirty-first President of the United States or like the thirty-fourth? Surely its none of its business to make a choice. Not because of the distinction of these particular speakers; lexicography, like God, is no respecter of persons. But because so wide-spread and conspicuous a use of two pronunciations among people of this elevation shows that there *are* two pronunciations. Their speaking establishes the fact which the dictionary must record.

Among the "enormities" with which *Life* taxes the Third International is its listing of "the common mispronunciation" *heighth*. That it is labeled a "dialectal variant" seems, however, to compound the felony. But one hears the word so pronounced, and if one professes to give a full account of American English in the 1960s, one has to take some cognizance of it. All people do not possess *Life*'s intuitive perception that the word is so "monstrous" that even to list it as a dialect variation is to merit scorn. Among these, by the way, was John Milton, who, in one of the greatest passages in all literature, besought the Holy Spirit to raise him to the "highth" of his great argument. And even the *Oxford English Dictionary* is so benighted as to list it, in full boldface, right alongside of *Height* as a variant that has been in the language since at least 1290.

Now there are still, apparently, millions of Americans who retain, in this as in much else, some of the speech of Milton. This particular pronunciation seems to be receding, but the *American Dialect Dictionary* still records instances of it from almost every state on the Eastern seaboard and notes that it is heard from older people and "occasionally in educated speech," "common with good speakers," "general," "widespread."

Under these circumstances, what is a dictionary to do? Since millions speak the word this way, the pronunciation can't be ignored. Since it has been in use as long as we have any record of English and since it has been used by the greatest writers, it can't be described as substandard or slang. But it is heard now only in certain localities. That makes it a dialectal pronunciation, and an honest dictionary will list it as such. What else can it do? Should it do?

The average purchaser of a dictionary uses it most often, probably, to find out what a word "means." As a reader, he wants to know what an author intended to convey. As a speaker or writer, he wants to know what a word will convey to his auditors. And this, too, is complex, subtle, and forever changing.

An illustration is furnished by an editorial in the Washington *Post* (January 17, 1962). After a ringing appeal to those who "love truth and accuracy" and the usual bombinations about "abdication of authority" and "barbarism," the editorial charges the Third International with "pretentious and obscure verbosity" and specifically instances its definition of "so simple an object as a door."

The definition reads:

a movable piece of firm material or a structure supported usu. along one side and swinging on pivots or hinges, sliding along a groove, rolling up and down, revolving as one of four leaves, or folding like an accordion by means of which an opening may be closed or kept open for passage into or out of a building, room, or other covered enclosure or a car, airplane, elevator, or other vehicle.

Then follows a series of special meanings, each particularly defined and, where necessary, illustrated by a quotation.

Since, aside from roaring and admonishing the "gentlemen from Springfield" that "accuracy and brevity are virtues," the *Post*'s editorial fails to explain what is wrong with the definition, we can only infer from "so simple" a thing that the writer takes the plain, downright, man-in-the-street attitude that a door is a door and any damn fool knows that.

But if so, he has walked into one of lexicography's biggest booby traps: the belief that the obvious is easy to define. Whereas the opposite is true. Anyone can give a fair description of the strange, the new, or the unique. It's the commonplace, the habitual, that challenges definition, for its very commonness compels us to define it in uncommon terms. Dr. Johnson was ridiculed on just this score when his dictionary appeared in 1755. For two hundred years his definition of a network as "any thing reticulated or decussated, at equal distances, with interstices between the intersections" has been good for a laugh. But in the merriment one thing is always overlooked: no one has yet come up with a better definition! Subsequent dictionaries defined it as a mesh and then defined a mesh as a network. That's simple, all right.

Anyone who attempts sincerely to state what the word *door* means in the United States of America today can't take refuge in a log cabin. There has been an enormous proliferation of closing and demarking devices and structures in the past twenty years, and anyone who tries to thread his way through the many meanings now included under *door* may have to sacrifice brevity to accuracy and even have to employ words that a limited vocabulary may find obscure.

Is the entrance to a tent a door, for instance? And what of the thing that seals the exit of an airplane? Is this a door? Or what of those sheets and jets of air that are now being used, in place of old-fashioned oak and hinges, to screen entrances and exits. Are they doors? And what of those accordion-like things that set off various sections of many modern apartments? The fine print in the lease takes it for granted that they are doors and that spaces demarked by them are rooms—and the rent is computed on the number of rooms.

Was I gypped by the landlord when he called the folding contraption that shuts off my kitchen a door? I go to the Second International, which the editor of the *Post* urges me to use in preference to the Third International. Here I find that a door is

The movable frame or barrier of boards, or other material, usually turning on hinges or pivots or sliding, by which an entranceway into a house or apartment is closed and opened; also, a similar part of a piece of furniture, as in a cabinet or bookcase.

This is only forty-six words, but though it includes the cellar door, it excludes the barn door and the accordion-like thing.

So I go on to the Third International. I see at once that the new definition is longer. But I'm looking for accuracy, and if I must sacrifice brevity to get it, then I must. And, sure enough, in the definition which raised the *Post*'s blood pressure, I find the words "folding like an accordion." The thing *is* a door, and my landlord is using the word in one of its currently accepted meanings.

We don't turn to a work of reference merely for confirmation. We all have words in our vocabularies which we have misunderstood, and to come on the true meaning of one of these words is quite a shock. All our complacency and self-esteem rise to oppose the discovery. But eventually we must accept the humiliation and laugh it off as best we can.

Some, often those who have set themselves up as authorities, stick to their error and charge the dictionary with being in a conspiracy against them. They are sure that their meaning is the only "right" one. And when the dictionary doesn't bear them out they complain about "permissive" attitudes instead of correcting their mistake.

*The New York Times* and the *Saturday Review* both regarded as contemptibly "permissive" the fact that one meaning of one word was illustrated by a quotation from Polly Adler. But a rudimentary knowledge of the development of any language would have told them that the underworld has been a far more active force in shaping and enriching speech than all the synods that have ever convened. Their attitude is like that of the patriot who canceled his subscription to the *Dictionary of American Biography* when he discovered that the very first volume included Benedict Arnold!

The ultimate of "permissiveness," singled out by almost every critic for special scorn, was the inclusion in the Third International of *finalize*. It was this, more than any other one thing, that was given as the reason for sticking to the good old Second International—that "peerless authority on American English," as the *Times* called it. But if it was such an authority, why didn't they look into it? They would have found *finalize* if they had.

And why shouldn't it be there? It exists. It's been recorded for two generations. Millions employ it every day. Two Presidents of the United States—men of widely differing cultural backgrounds—have used it in formal statements. And so has the Secretary-General of the United Nations, a man of unusual linguistic attainment. It isn't permitting the word but omitting it that would break faith with the reader. Because it is exactly the sort of word we want information about.

To list it as substandard would be to imply that it is used solely by the ignorant and the illiterate. But this would be a misrepresentation: President Kennedy and U Thant are highly educated men, and both are articulate and literate. It isn't even a freak form. On the contrary, it is a classic example of a regular process of development in English, a process which has given us such thoroughly accepted words as *generalize, minimize, formalize,* and *verbalize.* Nor can it be dismissed on logical grounds or on the ground that it is a mere duplication of *complete.* It says something that *complete* doesn't say and says it in a way that is significant in the modern bureaucratic world: one usually *completes* something which he has initiated but *finalizes* the work of others.

One is free to dislike the word. I don't like it. But the editor of a dictionary has to examine the evidence for a word's existence and seek it in context to get, as clearly and closely as he can, the exact meaning that it conveys to those who use it. And if it is widely used by well-educated, literate, reputable people, he must list it as a standard word. He is not compiling a volume of his own prejudices.

An individual's use of his native tongue is the surest index to his position within his community. And those who turn to a dictionary expect from it some statement of the current status of a word or a grammatical construction. And it is with the failure to assume this function that modern lexicography has been most fiercely charged. The charge is based on a naïve assumption that simple labels can be attached in all instances. But they can't. Some words are standard in some constructions and not in others. There may be as many shades of status as of meaning, and modern lexicography instead of abdicating this function has fulfilled it to a degree utterly unknown to earlier dictionaries.

Consider the word *fetch,* meaning to "go get and bring to." Until recently a standard word of full dignity ("Fetch me, I pray thee, a little water in a vessel"—I Kings 17:10), it has become slightly tainted. Perhaps the command latent in it is resented as undemocratic. Or maybe its use in training dogs to retrieve has made some people feel that it is an undignified word to apply to human beings. But, whatever the reason, there is a growing uncertainty about its status, and hence it is the sort of word that conscientious people look up in a dictionary.

Will they find it labeled "good" or "bad"? Neither, of course, because either applied indiscriminately would be untrue. The Third International lists nineteen different meanings of the verb *to fetch.* Of these some are labeled "dialectal," some "chiefly dialectal," some "obsolete," one "chiefly Scottish," and two "not in formal use." The primary meaning—"to go after and bring back"—is not labeled and hence can be accepted as standard, accepted with the more assurance because the many shades of labeling show us that the word's status has been carefully considered.

On grammatical questions the Third International tries to be equally exact and thorough. Sometimes a construction is listed without comment, meaning that in the opinion of the editors it is unquestionably respectable. Sometimes a construction carries the comment "used by speakers and writers on all educational levels though disapproved by some grammarians." Or the comment may be "used in substandard speech and formerly also by reputable writers." Or "less often in standard than in substandard speech." Or simply "dial."

And this very accurate reporting is based on evidence which is presented for our examination. One may feel that the evidence is inadequate or that the evaluation of it is erroneous. But surely, in the face of classification so much more elaborate and careful than any known heretofore, one cannot fly into a rage and insist that the dictionary is "out to destroy . . . every vestige of linguistic punctilio . . . every criterion for distinguishing between better usages and worse."

Words, as we have said, are continually shifting their meanings and connotations and hence their status. A word which has dignity, say, in the vocabulary of an older person may go down in other people's estimation. Like *fetch*. The older speaker is not likely to be aware of this and will probably be inclined to ascribe the snickers of the young at his speech to that degeneration of manners which every generation has deplored in its juniors. But a word which is coming up in the scale—like *jazz,* say, or, more recently, *crap*—will strike his ear at once. We are much more aware of offenses given us than of those we give. And if he turns to a dictionary and finds the offending word listed as standard—or even listed, apparently—his response is likely to be an outburst of indignation.

But the dictionary can neither snicker nor fulminate. It records. It will offend many, no doubt, to find the expression *wise up,* meaning to inform or to become informed, listed in the Third International with no restricting label. To my aging ears it still sounds like slang. But the evidence— quotations from the *Kiplinger Washington Letter* and the *Wall Street Journal*—convinces me that it is I who am out of step, lagging behind. If such publications have taken to using *wise up* in serious contexts, with no punctuational indication of irregularity, then it is obviously respectable. And finding it so listed and supported, I can only say that it's nice to be informed and sigh to realize that I am becoming an old fogy. But, of course, I don't have to use it (and I'll be damned if I will! "Let them smile, as I do now, At the old forsaken bough Where I cling").

In part, the trouble is due to the fact that there is no standard for standard. Ideas of what is proper to use in serious, dignified speech and writing are changing—and with breathtaking rapidity. This is one of the major facts of contemporary American English. But it is no more the dictionary's business to oppose this process than to speed it up.

Even in our standard speech some words are more dignified and some more informal than others, and dictionaries have tried to guide us through these uncertainties by marking certain words and constructions as "colloquial," meaning "inappropriate in a formal situation." But this distinction, in the opinion of most scholars, has done more harm than good. It has created the notion that these particular words are inferior, when actually they might be the best possible words in an informal statement. And so—to the rage of many reviewers—the Third International has dropped this label. Not all labels, as angrily charged, but only this one out of a score. And the doing so may have been an error, but it certainly didn't constitute "betrayal" or "abandoning of all distinctions." It was intended to end a certain confusion.

In all the finer shades of meaning, of which the status of a word is only one, the user is on his own, whether he likes it or not. Despite *Life*'s artless assumption about the Gettysburg Address, nothing worth writing is written *from* a dictionary. The dictionary, rather, comes along afterwards and describes what *has been* written.

Words in themselves are not dignified, or silly, or wise, or malicious. But they can be used in dignified, silly, wise, or malicious ways by dignified, silly, wise, or malicious people. *Egghead,* for example, is a perfectly legitimate word, as legitimate as *highbrow* or *long-haired.* But there is something very wrong and very undignified, by civilized standards, in a belligerent dislike for intelligence and education. *Yak* is an amusing word for persistent chatter. Anyone could say, "We were just yakking over a cup of coffee," with no harm to his dignity. But to call a Supreme Court decision *yakking* is to be vulgarly insulting and so, undignified. Again, there's nothing wrong with *confab* when it's appropriate. But when the work of a great research project, employing hundreds of distinguished scholars over several decades and involving the honor of one of the greatest publishing houses in the world, is described as *confabbing* (as *The New York Times* editorially described the preparation of the Third International), the use of this particular word asserts that the lexicographers had merely sat around and talked idly. And the statement becomes undignified—if not, indeed, slanderous.

The lack of dignity in such statements is not in the words, nor in the dictionaries that list them, but in the hostility that deliberately seeks this tone of expression. And in expressing itself the hostility frequently shows that those who are expressing it don't know how to use a dictionary. Most of the reviewers seem unable to read the Third International and unwilling to read the Second.

The *American Bar Association Journal,* for instance, in a typical outburst ("a deplorable abdication of responsibility"), picked out for special scorn the inclusion in the Third International of the word *irregardless.* "As far as the new Webster's is concerned," said the *Journal,* "this meaningless verbal bastard is just as legitimate as any other word in the dictionary." Thirty seconds spent in examining the book they were so roundly condemning would have shown them that in it *irregardless* is labeled "nonstand"—which means "nonstandard," which means "not conforming to the usage generally characteristic of educated native speakers of the language." Is that "just as legitimate as any other word in the dictionary"?

The most disturbing fact of all is that the editors of a dozen of the most influential publications in America today are under the impression that *authoritative* must mean *authoritarian.* Even the "permissive" Third International doesn't recognize this identification—editors' attitudes being not yet, fortunately, those of the American people. But the Fourth International may have to.

The new dictionary may have many faults. Nothing that tries to meet an ever-changing situation over a terrain as vast as contemporary English can hope to be free of them. And much in it is open to honest, and informed, disagreement. There can be linguistic objection to the eradication of proper names. The removal of guides to pronunciation from the foot of every page may not have been worth the valuable space it saved. The new method of defining words of many meanings has disadvantages as well as advantages. And of the half million or more definitions, hundreds, possibly thousands, may seem inadequate or imprecise. To some (of whom I am one) the omission of the label "colloquial" will seem meritorious; to others it will seem a loss.

But one thing is certain: anyone who solemnly announces in the year 1962 that he will be guided in matters of English usage by a dictionary published in 1934 is talking ignorant and pretentious nonsense.

## STUDY QUESTIONS

1. What type of argument does Evans use to answer the critics of *Webster's Third?*

2. According to Evans, what is the responsibility of the lexicographer? Compare his view with Follett's ("Sabotage in Springfield").

3. The title of Evans' essay is a question. What is his answer to this question?

4. Compare Evans' views on the status symbol *colloquial* with Follett's views.

5. What general outline does Evans follow in this essay? Compare his tone with Follett's.

Section Five

# Education

"Unwillingly to School"

*Hugh Kenner*

# DON'T SEND JOHNNY TO COLLEGE

Hugh Kenner (1923–    ) was born in Petersborough, Canada. He received his B.A. and M.A. from the University of Toronto and his Ph.D.
from Yale University. He is professor of English at the University of California, Santa Barbara. Mr. Kenner has received fellowships from the American Council of Learned Societies and the Guggenheim foundation. In
1950 he won the Porter Prize at Yale. He is an outstanding scholar and the
author of numerous articles on contemporary literature. In addition to his
studies on T. S. Eliot and Samuel Beckett, he is the author of *The Poetry of
Ezra Pound, Wyndham Lewis,* and *Dublin's Joyce.* His most recent book is
*Counterfeiters: An Historical Comedy* (1968).

JOHNNY GOES BY the official title of "student." Yet Johnny's
is the face every professor would prefer to see anywhere
but in his classroom, where it blocks with its dreary
smile, or its stoical yawn, the educational process on which we are proud to
spend annually billions of dollars. By his sheer inert numbers he is making
the common pursuit of professors and students—real students—impossible.

No one, least of all his professor, wills Johnny an injustice. Even the dean
of students, whose lot he renders abysmal, finds it impossible not to like him,
though some miraculous multiplication of loafers and fish sends Johnnies in
an endless column trooping past the dean's receptionist, to stammer out
their tale of dragging grades and just not digging the stuff.

Johnnies by the thousand, by the hundred thousand, clutter up every college in the land, where they long ago acquired a numerical majority. If you
have a teenager in your home, thinking of college, the chances are you have
Johnny. On behalf of my 400,000 colleagues in the academic profession, I'd
be grateful if you'd keep him home.

Though Johnny is by definition multitudinous and anonymous, bits of
Johnnyism stick in every teacher's mind. I remember the set neon smile that

greeted me class after class for three whole weeks from a front-row seat just next to the door. The smile's owner and operator—let's call her Jonnie—never said a word, never took a note, never turned a page in her copy of *Gulliver's Travels*. Then, the day after I assigned a paper, the smile was gone, and so was she, apparently for good.

A month later, having heard that I would welcome some explanation, Jonnie turned up in my office, smiling. No, she couldn't do papers at all, not at all. Then what, pray, had brought her to a university, where, as everyone knows, one does papers? Well, she had enrolled on the advice of her psychiatrist. He had said the College Experience would be good therapy. Unwilling to monkey with therapy, I referred her, smile and all, to the dean. I've forgotten what he decided. There are so many Johnnies and Jonnies.

And there is no end to what their mentors and counselors, not to say psychiatrists, expect a university to do. Teach Johnny to behave like a gentleman. Prevent his simultaneous presence with Jonnie in parked cars after 10 P.M. Help him (her) get to know girls (boys). Improve his work habits. Open his mind (he has nothing but prejudices). Shut his mouth (he does nothing but talk). Tighten his morals. Loosen his imagination. Spread beneath his slack chin the incredible banquet of Western Civilization. And discharge him fit to earn a better living, make a better marriage and digest (Lord help him) *The New York Times*.

The parents and mentors who expect all this expect it not of the college but of the College Experience, which is turning, accordingly, into the experience of living in a whole cityful of Johnnies. (I've just been told by a Sunday supplement that within 35 years many colleges with enrollments of 100,000 to 200,000 will have become cities in their own rights.)

Johnny (Jonnie) expects none of the wonders of the College Experience, expect *in re* girls (boys). Johnny is amiably devoid of expectations. One might say that he goes where he's shoved. One might affirm with more tact that he lends himself amiably to the College Experience, having no better plans. That is what marks him as Johnny, not as a student. A student has a vocation for study. But there's really nothing that Johnny comes to campus burning to learn about.

"Real education," wrote Ezra Pound 30 years ago, "must ultimately be limited to men who INSIST on knowing; the rest is mere sheepherding."

The mind that insists on knowing is (alas) not to be identified by tests, which explains why, despite the well-publicized vigilance of admissions officers, the number of campus Johnnies keeps rising. A mind that insists on knowing has begun to focus its energies by the time it has been in the world 16 years. By 17 or 18—the age of a college freshman—it has learned the taste of knowledge and the sensation of reaching for more. It may spell erratically, if it is served (like Yeats) by a deficient visual memory. It may calculate imperfectly, if it is (like Einstein) more at home with concepts than with operations. There may be strange gaps in its information, since a young mind cannot be everywhere at once.

But what it does not know it will encounter with pleasure. And it *must* learn, as a cat must eat. It may not yet know where its need for knowledge is meant to be satisfied. It may tack about, sails taut, without regard for curricular symmetry, changing majors perhaps more than once. But its tireless curiosity is unmistakable. In time, if all goes well, it will accept training, and the lifelong responsibilities of keeping itself trained.

But Johnny has no such appetite, no such momentum. When Johnny applies his brand-new ball-point to his first blue book, each sentence comes out smudged with his unmistakable pawprint. "Newspaper comics are good because they put a rosy glow on the grayish realities of the mind": There you have Johnny ingenuously expressing the state of *his* mind—a gray place which Pogo can occasionally animate, and a place of Good Things and Bad Things where Pogo is a Good Thing.

"The three main groups of people are the well-educated, semieducated and semiuneducated." There is all mankind characterized (a feat that taxed Aristotle), complete with a category for Johnny himself; he never forgets himself.

I am not inventing these examples. A colleague of mine gleaned a dozen like them in a single afternoon, from freshman themes at a university that accepts only the top one-eighth of the high-school crop. What they illustrate isn't primarily the "inability to express oneself," i.e., technical difficulties with the English language. What they illustrate is something deeper, probably irremediable; a happy willingness to emulate the motions of thought, since a teacher is standing there expecting such motions, along with a nearly total want of experience of what the process of thinking feels like.

"And this is why we should have no prejudice against Negroes and other lower races." That mind, we may say with some confidence, doesn't insist upon knowing. It doesn't know even its own most blatant contradictions. "To analyze this theory, it can be broken down into two parts: men and women." That's what men and women are, for the nonce—they are the parts of Johnny's theory. "The result is a ridiculous fiasco under which the roof falls in." It is indeed, and one does not know whether to marvel more at the oppressive weight of that fiasco, crashing through the roof like a half-ton bear, or at the innocent ease with which Johnny, supposing ideas to be weightless, pats them to and fro like bubbles.

But examples don't define a problem which by its very nature arises out of sheer multitudinousness. The amiable dumbbell has for decades been a part of campus folklore, like the absentminded professor. It is when you multiply him by a million that he grows ominous, swamping the campus as with creeping molasses. His uncle of 40 years ago, Joe College, had no more interest in learning than Johnny has, but none of Johnny's baleful power. With a certain talent for grotesque stylization, he conducted his entertaining ballet of raccoon coats, hip flasks, and whiffenpoofery, while the business of the academy, a considerably more modest business than today, went on.

What has created the Johnny problem isn't some freakish metamorphosis of Joe College into numberless protozoa, but rather the nearly universal conviction that everybody ought to spend four years at college if it can possibly be managed.

Johnny's parents, needless to say, believe this. His state legislator, despite the fantastic costs, tries to believe it, since his constituents seem to. The prospective employer believes it: let Johnny check "none" where the personnel blank inquires after "college record," and Johnny will be lucky to be issued a pick and shovel, let alone a sample kit. Even the college, caught in competitions for funds (which tend to hinge on enrollments), has come to believe it believes it.

Meanwhile B.A.'s grow so common that employers who once demanded them now demand M.A.'s, and the Master's requirement in some fields (not just the academic) has been upgraded to the Ph. D. In the years since Robert M. Hutchins sardonically proposed that we achieve our desires with less trouble by granting every American citizen a B.A. at birth, we have moved closer and closer to a utopia in which everyone receives it at 21, in return for doing classroom time. One already hears talk of attendance being compulsory through age 20. In California, where problems tend to surface before New England need worry about them, the state population rose 50 percent in one decade, and the college population 82 percent. It grows easy to foresee the day when 50 percent of the population of California (and, after a suitable time lag, of Massachusetts, of New York, of Illinois and, yes of Montana) will be employed at teaching the other 50 percent, perhaps changing ends at the half.

Clearly something has got to bust, and no one doubts what: the idea of a university. As an institution for (in Thomas Jefferson's words) "the instruction of those who will come after us," it's already being trampled out of recognizable existence by hordes of Johnnies.

The real student, struggling against suffocation of the soul, draws back, or beefs about how "the class" is holding things up, or starts feeling superior (and energy expended in nourishing a feeling of superiority is wholly lost). At worst, from being eager he turns merely "sensitive," and allows his zeal to be leached away. He is deprived, and can rightfully resent being deprived, of the kind of company he deserves to expect at a place where, often at considerable sacrifice, he has elected to invest four years of his life.

The professors suffer too. For one thing, they are coming off the production line too rapidly (though the harried trustees, looking wildly around at teaching machines and television hookups say "Not rapidly enough!"). Since there's no way of growing scholars at a pace keyed to the amoebalike increase of Johnnies, substitutes have begun to be manufactured. As real students are swamped by Johnnies, real professors must coexist with a swarm of Johnny-professors.

And like the real students, the real professors grow obsessed with futility, and unless they succeed, as some do, in isolating themselves with advanced students, fall victim to the real occupational hazard of the profession: an inability to believe that anybody can be taught anything. I once heard of a man who was so startled by the discovery of a real student that, lest she slip over his horizon, he divorced his wife and married her. I don't believe that story, but it's indicative; the professor who told it to me found it believable.

There's no doubt that as a nation we settle for only the side effects and the fringe benefits of what we invest in universities: the products of physics labs and research stations, and the economic advantages, to which our economy has been attuned ever since the G. I. Bill, of keeping several million young people off the labor market as long as possible. We are getting even this, though, at the price of a colossal wastage of time and spirit—the time and spirit of the real students on whose behalf the system is allegedly being run. If by the year 2000, as President Clark Kerr of California expects, educational institutions will be the largest single force in the economy, and if attendance to the age of 20 is compulsory, as Dr. Dwayne Orton of I.B.M. expects, why then the economy will in the lifetime of most of us have begun devoting its principal energies to the maintenance of huge concentration camps for keeping Johnnies by the multimillion agreeably idle.

So do we kick out Johnny? Alas, things will never be that simple again. Our social and economic system has come to depend on Johnny, B.A., in ways that can probably never be unstitched. Moreover, the College Experience probably *is* the most important event in the lives of most of the people who undergo it, even of the hundreds of thousands who learn very little. It is their time of access to the intellectual traffic patterns that define the quality of American life. A Kansan and a Georgian who have both been to college —merely been there—will have more to say to one another than a Vermonter who has and a Vermonter who hasn't. The College Experience is our folk ritual for inducting our adolescents into the 20th century. As part of our established religion, it must be treated as immune from curtailment.

Very well, then: the College Experience for Johnny, in his Johnny-classrooms. But let us, in the name of sanity, allow the real students to have *their* version of the College Experience. That means either separate-but-equal facilities, or (better, I think), some college equivalent of the two-track high schools that already exist.

One way of arranging a two-track college with minimum disruption is to permit only the real students to pursue majors. The University of Toronto has been doing that for more than half a century. Two decades ago I was one of a group of 40 freshman English majors there. In the sophomore year there were 20 of us, in the junior year 10; there the ruthless cutting stopped. But the missing 30 were not slung out of school. All but a few hopeless cases were "permitted," as the official formula had it, "to transfer to the pass course," which meant that, if they wanted to stay on at college, they abandoned the major and enrolled in "pass arts."

Pass arts was a three-year humanities mixture, leading to the degree of B.A. And it wasn't a ghetto for dropouts; many students enrolled in it to start with. Its degree satisfied employers, parents and the Ontario College of Education. It satisfied Johnny just fine. It gave the university all the advantages of bigness, as the quality of the library testified. It wasn't conducive to snobbery or segregation; every honor student took a couple of pass courses a year, in subjects peripheral to his major.

It was, in short, a two-track system, with the tracks parallel, and with means for switching laggards onto the slow track.

Everyone, we agree, should have access to all the education he can absorb. Everyone who can absorb education deserves, I would add, a chance to absorb it, free from the distracting tramp of the million-footed Johnny. As colleges now operate, the idea that everybody should be sent to them is nonsense. The only hope is to start operating them differently, detached from the dogma that Johnny is by birthright a student. He needs, in fact, explicit treatment as a nonstudent. There's no inherent reason why the nation's universities shouldn't make special curricular arrangements for several million nonstudents, any more than there's an inherent reason why one of the nation's universities shouldn't be the world's largest purveyor of white mice. (One of them is.)

## STUDY QUESTIONS

1. According to Kenner, what has created the Johnny problem?
   Society says go to college

2. In what ways is Johnny different from the real student?
   Doesn't want to learn

3. Do you judge Kenner's proposal for the "Johnny problem" a practical solution? Would you be willing to take a "Johnny-curriculum"? No
   Yes

4. Compare Kenner's proposal with Hutchins' proposal ("Colleges Are Obsolete"). Soon well be with so many Johnnies

5. This essay originally appeared in a magazine designed for the general public. In what ways did Kenner direct his essay to this audience? Note the diction, sentence structure, organization, and general structure.
   Appealing to family ( Poco comic

*John William Gardner*

# COLLEGE AND THE ALTERNATIVES

John William Gardner (1912–       ) was born in Los Angeles, California.
After receiving his B.A. and M.A. from Stanford University and his Ph.D.
from the University of California at Berkeley, he taught psychology at
Connecticut College and at Mount Holyoke College. As an outspoken
critic of U.S. education, he has worked to bring about reforms in procedure
and curricula. Before he became Secretary of Health, Education, and Welfare in 1965, he was president of the Carnegie Corporation and the Carnegie Foundation for the Advancement of Teaching. In 1968 he published
*No Easy Victories,* a selection of essays.

## Who Should Go to College

ALL OF THE conflicting and confusing notions which
Americans have concerning equality, excellence and the
encouragement of talent may be observed with crystal
clarity in the current discussions of "who should go to college." In the years
ahead these discussions will become more heated. Pressure of enrollments
will make it far harder to get into the better colleges, and there will be a
lively debate over who has a "right" to a college education.

A good deal of this debate will center around issues of quality versus
quantity in education. Douglas Bush eloquently enunciated one extreme
position in the phrase, "Education for all is education for none." [1]

Arguments about quality in higher education tend to be heated and rather
pointless. There are many reasons why such conversations become muddled, the foremost being that they so often degenerate into arguments over
"elite" versus "mass" education. People who engage in these arguments are

[1] Douglas Bush, "Education for All Is Education for None," *New York Times Magazine,* January 9, 1955, p. 13.

like the two washerwomen Sydney Smith observed leaning out of their back windows and quarreling with each other across the alley: "They could never agree," Smith said, "because they were arguing from different premises." [2] In the case of arguments over "elite" versus "mass" education, I am convinced that both premises should be vacated, because behind the arguments is the assumption that a society must decide whether it wishes to educate a few people exceedingly well *or* to educate a great number of people rather badly.

This is an imaginary dilemma. It is possible to have excellence in education and at the same time to seek to educate everyone to the limit of his ability. A society such as ours has no choice but to seek the development of human potentialities at all levels. It takes more than an educated elite to run a complex, technological society. Every modern, industrialized society is learning that hard lesson.

The notion that so-called quality education and so-called mass education are mutually exclusive is woefully out of date. It would not have survived at all were there not a few remarkably archaic characters in our midst. We all know that some of the people calling most noisily for quality in education are those who were *never* reconciled to the widespread extension of educational opportunity. To such individuals there is something inherently vulgar about large numbers of people. At the other extreme are the fanatics who believe that the chief goal for higher education should be to get as many youngsters as possible—regardless of ability—into college classrooms. Such individuals regard quality as a concept smacking faintly of Louis XIV.

But neither extreme speaks for the American people, and neither expresses the true issues that pose themselves today. It would be fatal to allow ourselves to be tempted into an anachronistic debate. *We must seek excellence in a context of concern for all.* A democracy, no less than any other form of society, must foster excellence if it is to survive; and it should not allow the emotional scars of old battles to confuse it on this point.

Educating everyone up to the limit of his ability does not mean sending everyone to college. Part of any final answer to the college problem must be some revision of an altogether false emphasis which the American people are coming to place on college education. This false emphasis is the source of great difficulties for us. In Virginia they tell the story of the kindly Episcopal minister who was asked whether the Episcopal Church was the only path to salvation. The minister shook his head—a bit sadly, perhaps. "No, there are other paths," he said, and then added, "but no gentleman would choose them." Some of our attitudes toward college education verge dangerously on the same position.

There are some people who seem to favor almost limitless expansion of

[2] W. H. Auden (ed.), *Selected Writings of Sydney Smith,* Farrar, Straus & Giroux, Inc., 1956, p. xiv.

college attendance. One hears the phrase "everyone has a right to go to college." It is easy to dispose of this position in its extreme form. There are some youngsters whose mental deficiency is so severe that they cannot enter the first grade. There are a number of youngsters out of every hundred whose mental limitations make it impossible for them to get as far as junior high school. There are many more who can progress through high school only if they are placed in special programs which take into account their academic limitations. These "slow learners" could not complete high school if they were required to enroll in a college-preparatory curriculum.

It is true that some who fall in this group would not be there if it were not for social and economic handicaps. But for most of them, there is no convincing evidence that social handicaps are a major factor in their academic limitations. Children with severe or moderate intellectual limitations appear not infrequently in families which are able to give them every advantage, and in which the possibilities of treatment have been exhaustively explored. Such children can be helped by intelligent attention, but the hope that any major change can be accomplished in their academic limitations is usually doomed to disappointment.

With each higher grade an increasing number of youngsters find it difficult or impossible to keep up with the work. Some drop out. Some transfer to vocational or industrial arts programs. A great many never complete high school.

Presumably, college students should only be drawn from the group which is able to get through high school. So the question becomes: "Should all high school graduates go to college?" The answer most frequently heard is that "all should go to college who are qualified for it"—but what do we mean by *qualified?* Probably less than 1 per cent of the college-age population is qualified to attend the California Institute of Technology. There are other colleges where 10, 20, 40 or 60 per cent of the college-age population is qualified to attend.

It would be possible to create institutions with standards so low that 90 per cent of the college-age population could qualify. In order to do so it would be necessary only to water down the curriculum and provide simpler subjects. Pushed to its extreme, the logic of this position would lead us to the establishment of institutions at about the intellectual level of summer camps. We could then include almost all of the population in these make-believe colleges.

Let us pursue this depressing thought. If it were certain that almost all of the eighteen- to twenty-two-year-old population could benefit greatly by full-time attendance at "colleges" of this sort, no one could reasonably object. But one must look with extreme skepticism upon the notion that all high school graduates can profit by continued formal schooling. There is no question that they can profit by continued *education*. But the character of this education will vary from one youngster to the next. Some will profit by continued book learning; others by some kind of vocational training; still others by learning on the job. Others may require other kinds of growth experiences.

Because college has gained extraordinary prestige, we are tempted to assume that the only useful learning and growth comes from attending such an institution, listening to professors talk from platforms, and reproducing required information on occasions called examinations. This is an extremely constricting notion. Even in the case of intellectually gifted individuals, it is a mistake to assume that the only kind of learning they can accomplish is in school. Many gifted individuals might be better off if they could be exposed to alternative growth experiences.

In the case of the youngster who is not very talented academically, forced continuance of education may simply prolong a situation in which he is doomed to failure. Many a youngster of low ability has been kept on pointlessly in a school which taught him no vocation, exposed him to continuous failure and then sent him out into the world with a record which convinced employers that he must forever afterward be limited to unskilled or semiskilled work. This is not a sensible way to conserve human resources.

Properly understood, the college or university is the instrument of *one kind of further education of those whose capacities fit them for that kind of education.* It should not be regarded as the sole means of establishing one's human worth. It should not be seen as the unique key to happiness, self-respect and inner confidence.

We have all done our bit to foster these misconceptions. And the root of the difficulty is our bad habit of assuming that the only meaningful life is the "successful" life, defining success in terms of high personal attainment in the world's eyes. Today attendance at college has become virtually a prerequisite of high attainment in the world's eyes, so that it becomes, in the false value framework we have created, the only passport to a meaningful life. No wonder our colleges are crowded.

The crowding in our colleges is less regrettable than the confusion in our values. *Human dignity and worth should be assessed only in terms of those qualities of mind and spirit that are within the reach of every human being.*

This is not to say that we should not value achievement. We should value it exceedingly. It is simply to say that achievement should not be confused with human worth. Our recognition of the dignity and worth of the individual is based upon moral imperatives and should be of universal application. In other words, everyone has a "right" to that recognition. Being a college graduate involves qualities of mind which can never be universally possessed. Everyone does not have a right to be a college graduate, any more than everyone has a right to run a four-minute mile.

What we are really seeking is what James Conant had in mind when he

said that the American people are concerned not only for equality of opportunity but for equality of respect. Every human being wishes to be respected
regardless of his ability, and in moral terms we are bound to grant him that
right. The more we allow the impression to get abroad that only the college
man or woman is worthy of respect in our society, the more we contribute to
a fatal confusion which works to the injury of all concerned. If we make the
confusing assumption that college is the sole cradle of human dignity, need
we be surprised that every citizen demands to be rocked in that cradle?

## The Need for Institutional Diversity

But a scaling down of our emphasis on college education is only part of
the answer. Another important part of the answer must be a greatly increased emphasis upon individual differences, upon many kinds of talent,
upon the immensely varied ways in which individual potentialities may be
realized.

If we develop such an indomitable concern for individual differences, we
will learn to laugh at the assumption that a college education is the only
avenue to human dignity and social worth. We would educate some youngsters by sending them on to college. We would educate others in other ways.
We would develop an enormous variety of patterns to fit the enormous variety of individuals. And no pattern would be regarded as socially superior or
involving greater human dignity than any other pattern.

But the plain fact is that college education is firmly associated in the public mind with personal advancement, upward social mobility, market value
and self-esteem. And if enough of the American people believe that one
must attend college in order to be accorded respect and confidence, then the
very unanimity of opinion makes the generalization true.

It is particularly true, unfortunately, in the crude categories of the employment file. A cynical friend of mine said recently, "Everyone has two
personalities these days—the one under his hat and the one in his employment file. The latter is the most important—and it is made up of primitive
categories. Have you held too many jobs? (Never mind why.) Did you go to a
good college? (Never mind if you were the campus beachcomber.) Does
your job record show a steady rise in responsibilities? (Never mind if you
played politics every inch of the way.)"

If we are to do justice to individual differences, if we are to provide suitable education for each of the young men and women who crowd into our
colleges and universities, then we must cultivate diversity in our higher educational system to correspond to the diversity of the clientele. There is no
other way to handle within one system the enormously disparate human
capacities, levels of preparedness and motivations which flow into our colleges and universities.

But we cannot hope to create or to maintain such diversity unless we honor the various aspects of that diversity. Each of the different kinds of institutions has a significant part to play in creating the total pattern, and each should be allowed to play its role with honor and recognition.

We do not want all institutions to be alike. We want institutions to develop their individualities and to keep those individualities. None must be ashamed of its distinctive features so long as it is doing something that contributes importantly to the total pattern, and so long as it is striving for excellence in performance. The highly selective, small liberal arts college should not be afraid to remain small. The large urban institution should not be ashamed that it is large. The technical institute should not be apologetic about being a technical institute. Each institution should pride itself on the role that it has chosen to play and on the special contribution which it brings to the total pattern of American higher education.

Such diversity is the only possible answer to the fact of individual differences in ability and aspirations. And furthermore, it is the only means of achieving *quality* within a framework of quantity. For we must not forget the primacy of our concern for excellence. We must have diversity, but we must also expect that every institution which makes up that diversity will be striving, in its own way, for excellence. This may require a new way of thinking about excellence in higher education—a conception that would be applicable in terms of the objectives of the institution. As things now stand, the word *excellence* is all too often reserved for the dozen or two dozen institutions which stand at the very zenith of our higher education in terms of faculty distinction, selectivity of students and difficulty of curriculum. In these terms it is simply impossible to speak of a junior college, for example, as excellent. Yet sensible men can easily conceive of excellence in a junior college.

The traditionalist might say, "Of course! Let Princeton create a junior college and one would have an institution of unquestionable excellence!" That may be correct, but it may also lead us down precisely the wrong path. If Princeton Junior College were excellent, it might not be excellent in the most important way that a community college can be excellent. It might simply be a truncated version of Princeton. A comparably meaningless result would be achieved if General Motors tried to add to its line of low-priced cars by marketing the front half of a Cadillac.

We shall have to be more flexible than that in our conception of excellence. We must develop a point of view that permits each kind of institution to achieve excellence *in terms of its own objectives*.

In higher education as in everything else there is no excellent performance without high morale. No morale, no excellence! And in a great many of our colleges and universities the most stubborn enemy of high morale has

been a kind of hopelessness on the part of both administration and faculty
—hopelessness about ever achieving distinction as an institution. Not only
are such attitudes a corrosive influence on morale, they make it virtually
certain that the institution will never achieve even that kind of excellence
which is within its reach. For there *is* a kind of excellence within the reach of
every institution.

In short, we reject the notion that excellence is something that can only be
experienced in the most rarified strata of higher education. It may be experienced at every level and in every serious kind of higher education. And not
only may it be experienced everywhere, but we must *demand* it everywhere.
We must ask for excellence in every form which higher education takes. We
should not ask it lightly or amiably or good naturedly; we should demand it
vigorously and insistently. We should assert that a stubborn striving for excellence is the price of admission to reputable educational circles, and that
those institutions not characterized by this striving are the slatterns of
higher education.

We must make the same challenging demands of students. We must never
make the insolent and degrading assumption that young people unfitted for
the most demanding fields of intellectual endeavor are incapable of rigorous
attention to *some sort of standards*. It is an appalling error to assume—as
some of our institutions seem to have assumed—that young men and
women incapable of the highest standards of intellectual excellence are incapable of any standards whatsoever, and can properly be subjected to
shoddy, slovenly and trashy educational fare. College should be a demanding as well as an enriching experience—demanding for the brilliant youngster at a high level of expectation and for the less brilliant at a more modest
level.

It is no sin to let average as well as brilliant youngsters into college. It *is* a
sin to let any substantial portion of them—average or brilliant—drift
through college without effort, without growth and without a goal. That is
the real scandal in many of our institutions.

Though we must make enormous concessions to individual differences in
aptitude, we may properly expect that every form of education be such as to
stretch the individual to the utmost of his potentialities. And we must expect
each student to strive for excellence in terms of the kind of excellence that is
within his reach. Here again we must recognize that there may be excellence
or shoddiness in every line of human endeavor. We must learn to honor excellence (indeed to *demand* it) in every socially accepted human activity,
however humble the activity, and to scorn shoddiness, however exalted the
activity. As I said in another connection: "An excellent plumber is infinitely
more admirable than an incompetent philosopher. The society which scorns
excellence in plumbing because plumbing is a humble activity and tolerates

shoddiness in philosophy because it is an exalted activity will have neither good plumbing nor good philosophy. Neither its pipes nor its theories will hold water."

## Opportunities Other Than College

Not long ago the mother of two teen-age boys came to me for advice. "Roger made a fine record in high school," she explained, "and when he was a senior we had exciting discussions of all the colleges he was interested in. Now Bobby comes along with terrible grades, and when the question of his future arises a silence descends on the dinner table. It breaks my heart!"

I knew something about Bobby's scholastic limitations, which were notable, and I asked warily what I might do to help.

"The high school principal says that with his record no college will take him," she said, "and that if one did take him he wouldn't last. I can't reconcile myself to that!"

"Have you discussed any possibilities other than college?" I asked.

She shook her head. "His father says he can get him a job driving a delivery truck. But I think he just says that to jar Bobby."

It took some time for me to explain all that I thought was deplorable in her attitude and that of her husband. Parents of academically limited children should not act as though any outcome other than college is a fate worse than death. By doing so they rule out of discussion a world of significant possibilities; and the failure to think constructively about those possibilities is a disfavor to the young person.

The great prestige which college education has achieved in our society leads us to assume—quite incorrectly—that it is the only form of continued learning after high school. The assumption is that the young person either goes to college and continues to learn, or goes to work and stops learning. Most parents, deans, counselors—indeed the young people themselves—have given little or no thought to the many ways of learning and growing which do not involve college. The result is that the path to college appears to be the only exciting possibility, the only path to self-development. No wonder many who lack the qualifications for college insist on having a try at it.

*The young person who does not go on to college should look forward to just as active a period of growth and learning in the post-high school years as does the college youngster.*

The nature of this continued learning will depend on the young person's interests and capacities. The bright youngster who has stayed out of college for financial reasons will require a different kind of program from that of the youngster who stayed out for lack of ability.

The majority of young people—at least, of boys—who terminate their education short of college do so because they lack academic ability. Most have had unrewarding experiences in the classroom and have a negative attitude toward anything labeled "learning" or "education." Even if they are not bitter about their school experiences, they are likely to feel that, having tried that path and failed, their salvation lies elsewhere. *What they must recognize is that there are many kinds of further learning outside formal high school and college programs. The fact that they have not succeeded in high school simply means that they must continue their learning in other kinds of situations.*

The opportunities for further education of boys and girls who leave the formal educational system are numerous and varied.

Training programs within industrial corporations have expanded enormously and constitute a respectable proportion of all education today. Apprenticeship systems are not as universal as they used to be in the skilled crafts or trades, but they are still in operation in every major industry, and offer wide opportunities for the ambitious youngster. (He must be warned, however, that in some of the older crafts and trades entry is jealously guarded; indeed in some it is held within family lines as a hereditary right.)

A few labor unions have impressive educational programs. The International Ladies Garment Workers Union, for example, conducts European tours, sponsors lecture series and offers a wide variety of courses.

Various branches of government offer jobs to high school graduates which involve an opportunity to learn while working. The Armed Services offer training in a great many occupational specialties.

Night classes in the public schools are breaking all attendance records; and more than one quarter of present attendance is in trade courses for semi-skilled or unskilled workers. These courses offer a surprising range of interesting opportunities for the young person who wishes to test his aptitudes and to develop various skills.

There also exist, in the amazingly variegated pattern of American education, many special schools—art schools, music schools, nursing schools and the like—which should be considered by the young person not going on to college. The boy who wishes to become an X-ray technician and the girl who wishes to be a practical nurse, for example, will find a great many schools throughout the country at which they may receive training.

Correspondence study offers the most flexible opportunities for study beyond high school, but the young people who do not go on to college usually have little enthusiasm for paper-and-pencil work, and that is what correspondence study amounts to. For those who can overcome this handicap, there is an open door to almost any conceivable subject. One can study accountancy or blueprint reading, creative writing or diesel mechanics, watch repairing or dressmaking, fingerprinting or foreign languages, music or petroleum technology. Almost the only limits are one's own interest and ability.

Educational opportunities on radio and television continue to expand. In certain parts of the country the high school graduate can study a considerable range of subjects through this medium—e.g., salesmanship, typing, composition, reading improvement and foreign languages.

Finally, jobs themselves are a form of education. Today most young people have a wide choice of jobs. They should look at the array of jobs available not simply from the standpoint of money and convenience but from the standpoint of their own further growth. If the young man is willing to think hard about his own abilities and interests, and then to look at available jobs as opportunities for self-development, he can look forward to years of learning and growth at least as rewarding as anything a college student might experience.

The possibilities reviewed here are by no means exhaustive, but they suggest the diverse paths open to the noncollege student. Some youngsters will want to get as far away as possible from "book learning" and some will not. Some will want vocational education and others may wish to continue their general education. Some will shun anything labeled a "school" or "course." But all should somehow continue learning.

In order to help young people in this direction, the following steps are essential:

1. We must make available to young people far more information than they now have on post-high school opportunities other than college.

2. Parents, teachers and high school counselors must recognize that if the youngster who is not going to college is to continue his growth and learning he must receive as much sagacious help and counsel as a college-bound student.

3. We must do what we can to alter the negative attitude toward education held by many youngsters who fail to go on to college. They must understand that they have been exposed to only one kind of learning experience and that the failures and frustrations encountered in school are not necessarily predictive of failure in every other kind of learning.

4. We must enable the young person to understand that his stature as an individual and his value as a member of society depend upon continued learning—not just for four years or a decade, but throughout life.

## STUDY QUESTIONS

1. Although Mr. Gardner does not define excellence in this selection, what does he apparently mean by it?

2.  The author observes that "achievement should not be confused with human worth." Explain.

3.  Compare Gardner's views on the college experience with Kenner's ("Don't Send Johnny to College") and Hutchins' ("Colleges Are Obsolete").

4.  What is Gardner's solution to the problem created by the conflict of quality education and mass education?

5.  What kind of supporting evidence does the author use with his generalizations?

6.  Describe the general outline Gardner follows in this selection. Compare his prose style with that used by Kenner.

*Harold Taylor*

# QUALITY AND EQUALITY

Harold Taylor (1914–    ) was born in Toronto, Canada. He received his B.A. from the University of Toronto and his Ph.D. from the University of London. He has a distinguished record as an educator, and was president of Sarah Lawrence College from 1945 to 1959. He is the author of *On Education and Freedom* (1954), *Reluctant Rebel, Secret Diary of Robert Patrick*, and *Art and the Intellect* (1960).

"THE SCHOOLS are the golden avenue of opportunity for able youngsters, but by the same token they are the arena in which less able youngsters discover their limitations." John Gardner's book has to do with this plain fact. He wishes to make it plainer, to have the country face up to it and to have educators deal with it wisely.

The way to deal with it is not to assume that in school the able and the less able are two different species of human being, separated by inherent quali-

(A review of *Excellence* by John W. Gardner.) Reprinted with the permission of *Saturday Review* and the author.

ties that screen out those who can contribute to their society and those who can't. Nor is ability to be measured by whether or not a boy or girl is admitted to a well-known college.

"Properly understood," says Mr. Gardner, "college or university is merely the instrument of one kind of further education for those whose interests and capacities fit them for that kind of further education. It should not be regarded as the sole means of establishing one's human worth. It should not be seen as the unique key to happiness, self-respect, and inner confidence."

There are varieties of talent, of motivation, of aptitude, of achievement, of excellence, and it is up to the social system and its educational instruments to make the most of each of the varieties. Otherwise we will build, on the basis of a false educational philosophy, a society that betrays its democratic values by constructing a stratified order. In such an order it will be assumed that those who go to college are those who should run the society, and that the rest are to be considered, and therefore may come to consider themselves, inferiors who work at whatever they can.

Following this path, we quickly reach a point at which no one takes pride in his work because he thinks it is beneath him, and standards of excellence in every part of life are abandoned in favor of a grudging, niggling effort to get as much as possible for doing as little as possible.

The cure for this is not to abandon the ideal of equality, or to deplore and ignore the attitude of those who have little opportunity for social advancement. It is to invent new forms of education that can deal with the entire range of individual talent and ability, to assure that each has an honorable place in his society.

This is a problem that is not confined to the United States and its educational system. It is also at the center of the Soviet effort to blend together vocational training in the factories and on the farms with high school education. It shows itself in the riots of Indian students against their universities —institutions that are ill-adapted to educating the younger generation for productive careers in jobs that need doing.

Once you announce a creed of equality, forces are set in motion which can explode into violence or dissipate into lethargy unless an educational system is put into effect which actually provides a variety of opportunities for a variety of talents.

Mr. Gardner's book has the virtue of going directly to questions that are in the minds of educators, parents, teachers, and students in the schools and colleges and dealing with them sympathetically on the basis of his personal knowledge of the American system as it works. He puts the educational problems in their proper setting, that is, as the outcome of certain social, political, and economic conditions and ideas, and as the result of conflicting aims held by Americans.

We are proud to have thrown off the weight of hereditary privilege, says Mr. Gardner, and we admire both the successful man and the system that makes success a matter of individual performance rather than of birth. At the same time we create new problems for the man whose talent is not of a kind that does well in an intensely competitive society, yet whose abilities must have their own chance to find expression.

In guarding against the excesses of a competitive order where performance "may foster an atmosphere of raw striving" we become overprotective of those who are left behind in the competition, and we fall into sentimental postures in the way we treat children. We become hypocritical and refuse to deal honestly with differences in ability. The conflict between the sentiment of compassion and the reality of human capacity becomes direct when "it proves impossible to enable each to fill his potentialities without treating each differently."

In the matter of tests for ability and achievement, for example, it is crucial that a fair means be established for sorting out the more able from the less able. But intelligence testing cannot account for differences in background, and there is more to intelligence than the ability to pass intelligence tests.

Mr. Gardner suggests that we use testing devices with discretion, as a form of diagnosis as much as a criterion of judgment. We must hold to the doctrine of multiple chances by which the individual is given a variety of means and occasions to prove his worth through the whole of his education and through the whole of his life.

This means an enlightened approach to the welfare of the individual, not only through formal education but also through all the other institutions of a democratic society, from slum clearance projects and social welfare programs to hospitals, adoption services, business institutions, adult education, the church, and the home.

Some 1,873,000 boys and girls are graduating from high school this year: 880,000 will not go to college; 900,000 others have already dropped out of high school. Mr. Gardner is concerned about this cross-section of American youth. They are in the majority and will continue to be.

In the overemphasis on college preparation, academic grades, and competitive selection, too little attention has been paid to the educational needs of this majority, both before and after they take jobs and marry. Leadership, and standards of performance, Mr. Gardner points out, must come, not merely from what used to be called the educated classes, but from every segment of the entire society. That is, of course, if the society is to grow in strength and remain democratic. In his Carnegie Corporation presidential report of 1960, Mr. Gardner analyzes the problem, suggests solutions, and calls for action.

The present book provides an intellectual basis for such action on many fronts. It also provides a balanced, informed, and positive statement of democratic belief by a man who, in temperament, experience, and performance, has shown himself to be a gifted educator.

## J. Edward Dirks

# NEO-KNIGHTHOOD

J. Edward Dirks (1919–      ) was born in Iowa. He received a B.A. from the University of Dubuque and Yale University and his Ph.D. from Columbia. An ordained minister of the United Presbyterian Church, he has a distinguished record as a teacher of religious education. He has taught at Columbia University, Lake Forest College, and Yale Divinity School. He has been director of the commission on higher education for the National Council of Churches and was the founder and editor of *Christian Scholarly*. He is author of the book *The Critical Theology of Theodore Parker* (1947).

THIS IS A book dedicated to the proposition that excellence in all its forms and in all situations is attainable, even when it must be encouraged in a society which advocates the ideal of equality. In the realm of higher education as well as in the context of discussions concerning the image and prestige of America, the professed fear of a pervasive mediocrity, a lowering of standards of performance, and a persistent (sometimes a built-in) slovenliness reinforces the yearning for an elite and the domination of a group which rises to leadership. The author assumes that the demands of excellence and equality stand in this kind of conflict and internal contradiction, and that democracy has to overcome its equalitarian idealism if it is to be realistic about the need for excellence. This is the puzzle, then: how the very heart of democratic dogma can be maintained if at the same time Americans want to "let the best man win," identify, encourage and train their talented youth, and motivate toward leadership persons imbued with the idea of excellence.

(A review of *Excellence* by John W. Gardner.) Copyright 1961, Christian Century Foundation. Reprinted by permission from the May 17, 1961 issue of *The Christian Century*.

The book calls the nation to commit itself anew to the goal of being a democratic society—the kind of democratic society which insists on excellence, in which free men are capable of performing at the level of high standards, and which reckons with the tragedy of a lost or obscured national purpose. "The long-run challenge," says the author, president of Carnegie Corp. and of the Carnegie Foundation for the Advancement of Teaching, "is nothing less than a challenge to our sense of purpose, our vitality and our creativity as a people." And "if we fail to meet this challenge, the stratagems of the moment will not save us." Striving toward meaningful goals, pursuing excellence through devoted action, producing men and women of intelligence, imagination and courage, are among the challenges set forth in Mr. Gardner's essay. But, one may ask, just how is this to be done? What is to be expected of American people? The answer is straightforward: "If you believe in a free society, be worthy of a free society. Every good man strengthens society."

Despite the ringing appeals for "toning up" the nation, despite the author's own passion for excellence and his sense of the nation's passion for it, one reads the book with the feeling that something muscular, rigorous and disciplined is missing. The interpretation of the term "excellence" is vague; excellence remains an illusory ideal, demanding devotion, dedication and commitment to "the virtues of our society." To *pursue* and to *excel*—words with virtually identical meanings—can be encouraged when a clear goal is somewhere in sight, or when we know realistically enough what must certainly be avoided in our running! But the phrase "the highest standards of performance" is ambiguous as a referent and of little help amid all the other relativities of our society.

Nearly ten years ago Reinhold Niebuhr wrote a book which reflected on "the ironic element in the American situation." A part of this element was identified by him with the "extravagant emphasis in our culture upon the value and dignity of the individual and upon individual liberty as the final value of life" (*The Irony of American History*, p. 7). The ironic contradiction into which Niebuhr suggested we are placed is to be found in the fact that our culture does not really value the individual as much as it pretends, and that if justice is to be maintained and our survival assured, individual liberty cannot—contrary to our ideology—be unqualifiedly made the end of life. This is the necessary critique upon this book on excellence. But the structure of illusion built from our virtues has still not been clearly exposed, even in the state of threat through which we are passing. Our religious virtues and our national virtues tend to merge in this illusion; hence the religious roots of excellence are viewed as synonymous with the democratic roots of excellence.

However questionable may be the prescriptive sections of the book, it contains a valid analysis of the present situation in American culture—its "who cares?" attitudes, its wastefulness and consumer-consciousness, its persistent tendency to dismiss the importance of excellence in education, its lack of clarity regarding the social context which stimulates the pursuit of excellence. The flabbiness of our society is made visible; the dilemma of our democracy is acutely stated. Once we have passed through the prophetic and critical material, however, we need to permit our realism to continue into our pursuit of the ideal goals. If we lose it and lapse into a sentimental idealism, our espousal of the ideals of democracy will become absurd—as absurd as was Don Quixote's imitation of the ideals of medieval knight errantry. We cannot finally laugh at the betrayals of high performance (as we might at the illusions of the bogus knight), but with a profounder insight we can laugh at the contemporary anxiety which broods along over national goals and excellence (that is, at the bogus character of knighthood itself).

However great is the importance of our society's survival, the term "ironic" surely must be applied to our situation. The Christian prefers it because irony derives from the confidence that we can know the true God only where we have some awareness of the contradiction between his divine purposes and our human purposes, or even our highest aspirations. And the insights derived from such a recognition are nothing less than prerequisites for saving our civilization.

## STUDY QUESTIONS

1.  Compare and contrast Taylor's and Dirks' opinion of John W. Gardner's book *Excellence*. What does each single out for praise, and what does each point to as a fault or shortcoming?

2.  What is the general form each reviewer follows? Do they differ in degree or kind?

3.  Do they reveal any personal prejudices that may color their appraisal of the book? Who appears to be the more objective?

4.  On the basis of the experience you had with *Excellence* (you read "College and the Alternatives"), which reviewer appears to be more accurate in his appraisal? Is he necessarily the more convincing of the two?

*Graham Greene*

# THE LOST CHILDHOOD

Graham Greene (1904–       ) was born in Berkhamstead, England, and educated at Balliol College, Oxford. He holds an honorary Litt.D. from Cambridge University. Although a well-known playwright, essayist, and short-story writer, he is most famous for his novels and "entertainments." These include *Babbling April* (1925), *It's a Battlefield* (1934), *A Gun for Sale* (1936), *Brighton Rock* (1938), *The Power and the Glory* (1940), *The Ministry of Fear* (1943), *The Heart of the Matter* (1948), *The Third Man* (1950), *The End of the Affair* (1951), *The Quiet American* (1955), *Our Man in Havana* (1958), *A Burnt-out Case* (1961), and *The Comedians* (1966). His *Collected Essays* were published in 1969.

PERHAPS IT IS only in childhood that books have any deep influence on our lives. In later life we admire, we are entertained, we may modify some views we already hold, but we are more likely to find in books merely a confirmation of what is in our minds already: as in a love affair it is our own features that we see reflected flatteringly back.

But in childhood all books are books of divination, telling us about the future, and like the fortune teller who sees a long journey in the cards or death by water they influence the future. I suppose that is why books excited us so much. What do we ever get nowadays from reading to equal the excitement and the revelation in those first fourteen years? Of course I should be interested to hear that a new novel by Mr. E. M. Forster was going to appear this spring, but I could never compare that mild expectation of civilized pleasure with the missed heartbeat, the appalled glee I felt when I found on a library shelf a novel by Rider Haggard, Percy Westerman, Captain Brereton or Stanley Weyman which I had not read before. No, it is in those early years that I would look for the crisis, the moment when life took a new slant in its journey towards death.

I remember distinctly the suddenness with which a key turned in a lock
and I found I could read—not just the sentences in a reading book with the
syllables coupled like railway carriages, but a real book. It was paper-
covered with the picture of a boy, bound and gagged, dangling at the end of a
rope inside a well with the water rising above his waist—an adventure of
Dixon Brett, detective. All a long summer holiday I kept my secret, as I believed: I did not want anybody to know that I could read. I suppose I half
consciously realized even then that this was the dangerous moment. I was
safe so long as I could not read—the wheels had not begun to turn, but now
the future stood around on bookshelves everywhere waiting for the child to
choose—the life of a chartered accountant perhaps, a colonial civil servant, a planter in China, a steady job in a bank, happiness and misery, eventually one particular form of death, for surely we choose our death much as
we choose our job. It grows out of our acts and our evasions, out of our fears
and out of our moments of courage. I suppose my mother must have discovered my secret, for on the journey home I was presented for the train with
another real book, a copy of Ballantyne's *Coral Island* with only a single
picture to look at, a coloured frontispiece. But I would admit nothing. All
the long journey I stared at the one picture and never opened the book.

But there on the shelves at home (so many shelves for we were a large
family) the books waited—one book in particular, but before I reach that
one down let me take a few others at random from the shelf. Each was a
crystal in which the child dreamed that he saw life moving. Here in a cover
stamped dramatically in several colours was Captain Gilson's *The Pirate
Aeroplane*. I must have read that book six times at least—the story of a lost
civilization in the Sahara and of a villainous Yankee pirate with an aeroplane like a box kite and bombs the size of tennis balls who held the golden
city to ransom. It was saved by the hero, a young subaltern who crept up to
the pirate camp to put the aeroplane out of action. He was captured and
watched his enemies dig his grave. He was to be shot at dawn, and to pass
the time and keep his mind from uncomfortable thoughts the amiable
Yankee pirate played cards with him—the mild nursery game of Kuhn
Kan. The memory of that nocturnal game on the edge of life haunted me for
years, until I set it to rest at last in one of my own novels with a game of
poker played in remotely similar circumstances.

And here is *Sophy of Kravonia* by Anthony Hope—the story of a
kitchen-maid who became a queen. One of the first films I ever saw, about
1911, was made from that book, and I can hear still the rumble of the
Queen's guns crossing the high Kravonian pass beaten hollowly out on a
single piano. Then there was Stanley Weyman's *The Story of Francis
Cludde,* and above all other books at that time of my life *King Solomon's
Mines*.

This book did not perhaps provide the crisis, but it certainly influenced the future. If it had not been for that romantic tale of Allan Quatermain, Sir Henry Curtis, Captain Good, and, above all, the ancient witch Gagool, would I at nineteen have studied the appointments list of the Colonial Office and very nearly picked on the Nigerian Navy for a career? And later, when surely I ought to have known better, the odd African fixation remained. In 1935 I found myself sick with fever on a camp bed in a Liberian native's hut with a candle going out in an empty whisky bottle and a rat moving in the shadows. Wasn't it the incurable fascination of Gagool with her bare yellow skull, the wrinkled scalp that moved and contracted like the hood of a cobra, that led me to work all through 1942 in a little stuffy office in Freetown, Sierra Leone? There is not much in common between the land of the Kukuanas, behind the desert and the mountain range of Sheba's Breast, and a tin-roofed house on a bit of swamp where the vultures moved like domestic turkeys and the pi-dogs kept me awake on moonlight nights with their wailing, and the white woman yellowed by atebrin drove by to the club; but the two belonged at any rate to the same continent, and, however distantly, to the same region of the imagination—the region of uncertainty, of not knowing the way about. Once I came a little nearer to Gagool and her witch-hunters, one night in Zigita on the Liberian side of the French Guinea border, when my servants sat in their shuttered hut with their hands over their eyes and someone beat a drum and a whole town stayed behind closed doors while the big bush devil—whom it would mean blindness to see—moved between the huts.

But *King Solomon's Mines* could not finally satisfy. It was not the right answer. The key did not quite fit. Gagool I could recognize—didn't she wait for me in dreams every night in the passage by the linen cupboard, near the nursery door? and she continues to wait, when the mind is sick or tired, though now she is dressed in the theological garments of Despair and speaks in Spenser's accents:

> The longer life, I wrote the greater sin,
> The greater sin, the greater punishment.

Yes, Gagool has remained a permanent part of the imagination, but Quatermain and Curtis—weren't they, even when I was only ten years old, a little too good to be true? They were men of such unyielding integrity (they would only admit to a fault in order to show how it might be overcome) that the wavering personality of a child could not rest for long against those monumental shoulders. A child, after all, knows most of the game—it is only an attitude to it that he lacks. He is quite well aware of cowardice, shame, deception, disappointment. Sir Henry Curtis perched upon a rock bleeding from a dozen wounds but fighting on with the remnant of the Greys against the hordes of Twala was too heroic. These men were like Platonic ideas: they were not life as one had already begun to know it.

But when—perhaps I was fourteen by that time—I took Miss Marjorie Bowen's *The Viper of Milan* from the library shelf, the future for better or worse really struck. From that moment I began to write. All the other possible futures slid away: the potential civil servant, the don, the clerk had to look for other incarnations. Imitation after imitation of Miss Bowen's magnificent novel went into exercise books—stories of sixteenth-century Italy or twelfth-century England marked with enormous brutality and a despairing romanticism. It was as if I had been supplied once and for all with a subject.

Why? On the surface *The Viper of Milan* is only the story of a war between Gian Galeazzo Visconti, Duke of Milan, and Mastino della Scala, Duke of Verona, told with zest and cunning and an amazing pictorial sense. Why did it creep in and colour and explain the terrible living world of the stone stairs and the never quiet dormitory? It was no good in that real world to dream that one would ever be a Sir Henry Curtis, but della Scala who at last turned from an honesty that never paid and betrayed his friends and died dishonoured and a failure even at treachery—it was easier for a child to escape behind his mask. As for Visconti, with his beauty, his patience and his genius for evil, I had watched him pass by many a time in his black Sunday suit smelling of mothballs. His name was Carter. He exercised terror from a distance like a snowcloud over the young fields. Goodness has only once found a perfect incarnation in a human body and never will again, but evil can always find a home there. Human nature is not black and white but black and grey. I read all that in *The Viper of Milan* and I looked round and I saw that it was so.

There was another theme I found there. At the end of *The Viper of Milan* —you will remember if you have once read it—comes the great scene of complete success—della Scala is dead, Ferrara, Verona, Novara, Mantua have all fallen, the messengers pour in with news of fresh victories, the whole world outside is cracking up, and Visconti sits and jokes in the wine light. I was not on the classical side or I would have discovered, I suppose, in Greek literature instead of in Miss Bowen's novel the sense of doom that lies over success—the feeling that the pendulum is about to swing. That too made sense; one looked around and saw the doomed everywhere—the champion runner who one day would sag over the tape; the head of the school who would atone, poor devil, during forty dreary undistinguished years; the scholar . . . and when success began to touch oneself too, however mildly, one could only pray that failure would not be held off for too long.

One had lived for fourteen years in a wild jungle country without a map, but now the paths had been traced and naturally one had to follow them. But I think it was Miss Bowen's apparent zest that made me want to write. One could not read her without believing that to write was to live and to enjoy, and before one had discovered one's mistake it was too late—the first book one does enjoy. Anyway she had given me my pattern—religion might later explain it to me in other terms, but the pattern was already there—perfect evil walking the world where perfect good can never walk again, and only the pendulum ensures that after all in the end justice is done. Man is never satisfied, and often I have wished that my hand had not moved further than *King Solomon's Mines,* and that the future I had taken down from the nursery shelf had been a district office in Sierra Leone and twelve tours of malarial duty and a finishing dose of blackwater fever when the danger of retirement approached. What is the good of wishing? The books are always there, the moment of crisis waits, and now our children in their turn are taking down the future and opening the pages. In his poem "Germinal" A.E. wrote:

> In ancient shadows and twilights
>     Where childhood had strayed,
> The world's great sorrows were born
>     And its heroes were made.
> In the lost boyhood of Judas
>     Christ was betrayed.

## STUDY QUESTIONS

1.  Greene says that when he took Miss Marjorie Bowen's *The Vipers of Milan* from the library shelf, "The future for better or worse really struck." What does he mean by this?

2.  When Greene first discovered that he could read, why did he want to keep it a secret?

3.  How would you describe Greene's attitude toward his subject? What establishes the tone of this selection?

4.  In what way is the stanza that concludes the selection related to Greene's thesis?

5.  Has any book you read in your childhood had a lasting effect on you?

*Paul Goodman*

# THE NEW ARISTOCRATS

Paul Goodman (1911–      ) was born in New York City. He received his
B.A. from The City College of New York and his Ph.D. from the University of Chicago. An expert in city planning and the many problems inherent
in urban growth, he has lectured at the Massachusetts Institute of Technology, the University of Pennsylvania, Western Reserve University, Columbia University, and the University of California. He has taught at the Uni-
versity of Chicago, New York University, and Black Mountain University.
He is currently a practicing psychotherapist affiliated with the New York
Institute for Gestalt Therapy. A regular contributor to journals and magazines, Mr. Goodman has also written a number of books. His early works
include *Stop Light* (1942), a volume of poetry; and two novels, *The Grand
Piano* (1942) and *State of Nature* (1945). He is coauthor with his brother of
*Communitas* (1947, a work on city planning) and is author of *Gestalt Therapy* (1951). His recent books are *Structure of Literature* (1954) and *Growing Up Absurd* (1960). The latter has proved to be extremely popular, with
recent sales exceeding 1000 copies a week. He has also published *Hawk-
weed: Poems* (1967) and *Like a Conquered Province: The Moral Ambiguity of America* (1967).

℘REDICTIONS ABOUT the future of America during the next
generation are likely to be in one of two sharply contrasting moods. On the one hand, the orthodox liberals fore-
see a Great Society in which all will live in suburban comfort or the equivalent; given a Head Start and Job Training, Negroes will go to college like
everyone else, will be splendidly employed and live in integrated neighborhoods; billboards will be 200 yards off new highways, and the arts will flourish in many Lincoln Centers. On the other hand, gloomy social critics, and
orthodox conservatives, see that we are headed straight for 1984, when
everyone's life will be regimented from the cradle to the grave by the dic-
tator in Washington; administrative double talk and Newspeak will be the

only language; Negroes will be kept at bay by the police (according to the social critics) or will be the pampered shock troops of demagogs (according to the conservatives); we will all be serial numbers; civil liberties and independent enterprise will be no more.

Yet these predictions have much in common. They assume the continuation of the same trends and attitudes that are now in full sway. There will be increasing centralization in decision making, increasing mass education as we now know it, a stepped-up rate of technical growth and a growing Gross National Product, and more use of a technological style—of "planning" or "social engineering," depending on one's bias—with heavy use of computers. These same premises are seen by some as enriching and great, and by others as menacing and empty.

Oddly, however, both kinds of prediction describe the play and leave out Hamlet; namely, the next generation itself, the young people who are going to be the heirs to all this greatness or the slaves of this social engineering. I have not seen a single forecast that takes into account that present high school and college students will be of some importance in shaping society 20 years from now. Commencement speakers are eager to pass on the torch and they seem to be sure that there are ready hands to receive it. Yet the evidence is that students are not at all happy with the present trends and attitudes, whether the prediction is gloomy *or* rosy. For instance, in 1956, surveys showed that college students admired and wanted to work in big corporations, but last year (at Harvard) more seniors opted for the Peace Corps than for careers in business. Allow me a small personal example: My book *Growing Up Absurd* sells 1000 copies a week, of which the majority, my publisher guesses, are bought by high school students. This gives one pause; I wouldn't have thought they could read the words. Maybe they can't, but they get the message, that the conditions of our society are too inhuman to grow up in. For collegians that message is dated; they take it for granted.

I do not intend to predict what the future might look like if we take young people into account. I don't know (although I give plenty of advice, which they disregard). What I want to show, however, is that point by point, with remarkable precision, articulate students—and an indeterminate number of others—*live, feel and think in direct opposition to the premises on which both the rosy and the gloomy predictions are based*. It is so in their community life, their ethics and their politics. If only because of sheer numbers, the temper of young people must make a difference for the future. And it is whistling in the dark to think that their opposition is a "generational revolt" that will be absorbed as they grow older and wiser, for it is endemic in our system of things. If the planners continue to treat this temper as if it did not exist, the result will be still deeper alienation and worse ultimate disruption. My experience in Washington, as a Fellow of the Institute of Policy Studies, is that social and educational planners have about as much information of what happens on college campuses as the State Department has about Vietnam.

*Community:* About 50 percent of all Americans are now under 26. Of the college-age group, nearly 40 percent go to college—there are 6,000,000 in 2000 institutions. Of the present collegians, it is estimated that five percent are in some activity of the radical youth movement, usually "left" but sometimes "right." This does not seem a big proportion, but it has increased at least tenfold in the last decade, and it and the number of its alumni will certainly increase even more rapidly in the next years. We are thus speaking of several million people.

More important, they are the leaders. Radical collegians are not only middle class but they are also disproportionately the best academically and from the most prestigious schools. Unlike Negro youth, who are now causing such turmoil, collegians are a major economic force, looming large among the indispensable inheritors of the dominant power in society. And although—or perhaps because—they do not share a common ideology but rather a common sentiment and style, in showdown situations like the troubles in Berkeley, they have shown a remarkable solidarity and a common detestation for the liberal center, crossing even the apparent chasm between extreme right and extreme left.

A chief reason for their solidarity and their increase in numbers is mass higher education itself. For most, going to college has little academic value —indeed, one of their shared sentiments is resistance to being academically processed for the goals of the "system." In my opinion, about 15 percent, instead of 40 percent, ought to be in colleges; the rest, including most of the bright, would be better educated in other environments. Nevertheless, *the major colleges and universities are, in fact, many hundreds of physical and social communities of young people, with populations of a few thousand to 25,000, sharing a subculture, propagandizing one another and learning to distrust anybody over 30. Such collections of youth are a phenomenon unique in history.*

Consider some details from San Francisco State College, where I was hired as a teacher by the Associated Students last spring. With 15,000 students, the Associated Students collect $300,000 annually in dues, more than half of which is free and clear and which they use for untraditional purposes. These purposes include organizing a tenants' league, helping delinquents in a reformatory, running a tutorial program for Negro and Mexican children (with 300 collegian tutors), sponsoring a weekly television program on KQED, running an "experimental college" with offbeat courses, and hiring their own professors. They apply on their own for institutional grants from the Ford Foundation and the Poverty Program. In the fall of 1966, the experimental college registered 1600 students!

Or consider the college press, with its fairly captive audience of a couple of million, many of them daily. In a few cases, e.g., Harvard and Columbia, publication has gone off campus and is not under the tutelage of "faculty advisors." Increasingly, college papers subscribe to news services and print (and edit) national and international news; and they also use syndicated material, like Art Buchwald, Jules Feiffer, Russell Baker. Occasionally, the college paper is the chief daily of its town (e.g., the Cornell *Sun*). More important, there is a national student press service that could be a powerfully effective liaison for mobilizing opinion on common issues. Last winter I wrote a fortnightly column on student matters for a tiny college in Vermont, which the enterprising editor at once syndicated to 50 other college papers. On this model there could spring up a system of direct support, and control, of students' "own" authors, just as, of course, they now indirectly support them through magazines whose main circulation is collegiate.

Nor are these young people properly called "youth." The exigencies of the American system have kept them in tutelage, doing lessons, till 23 and 24 years of age, years past when young industrial workers used to walk union picket lines or when farmers carried angry pitchforks, or young men are now drafted into the Army. Thus, another cause of their shared resentment is the foolish attempt to arrest their maturation and regulate their social, sexual and political activity.

More than other middle-class generations, these young live a good deal by "interpersonal relations" and they are unusually careless, in their friendships, about status or getting ahead. I do not mean that they are especially affectionate or compassionate—they are averagely so—but they have been soaked in modern psychology, group therapy, sensitivity training; and as a style they go in for direct confrontation and sometimes brutal frankness. Add to this the lack of embarrassment due to animally uninhibited childhood, for their parents, by and large, were permissive about thumbsucking, toilet training, masturbation, informal dress, etc. They are the post-Freudian generation in this country—their parents were analyzed from 1920 to 1940. The effect of all this psychology—for example, long sessions of mutual analysis or jabber about LSD trips—can be tiresome, at least to me; but it is fatal to suburban squeamishness, race and moral prejudice, and to keeping up appearances. Still another cause of resentment at the colleges is the impersonality and distance of the teachers and the big classes that make dialog impossible. Students are avid for dialog. Sometimes this looks like clamoring for "attention," as our statesmen say about the demonstrators, but it is really insisting on being taken seriously as troubled human beings.

Middle-class privacy also tends to vanish. An innovation of the Beats was the community use of one another's pads, and this spirit of sharing has persisted in off-campus university communities, which are very different from paternalistic dormitories or fraternity row. In big cities there are rapidly growing bohemian student neighborhoods, usually—if only for the cheaper rent—located in racially mixed sections. Such neighborhoods, with their own coffeehouses and headquarters for student political clubs, cannot be controlled by campus administration. In the famous insurrection of Berkeley, Telegraph Avenue could easily rally 3000 students, ex-students, wives and pals. (The response of the University of California administration has been, characteristically, to try to root up the student neighborhood with Federally financed urban renewal.)

Inevitably, sexual activity and taking drugs loom overlarge in the public picture: for, whereas unkempt hair, odd company and radical politics may be disapproved, sex and drugs rouse middle-class anxiety, a more animal reaction. The statistics seem to show, however, that quantitatively there are not many more sexual goings on than since the Twenties. The difference is that the climate has finally become more honest and unhypocritical. Sexuality is affirmed as a part of life rather than as the Saturday religion of fraternity gang bangs covered by being drunk. Since there is more community altogether, sex tends to revert to the normalcy of back rural areas, with the beautiful difference of middle-class prudence and contraceptives. (Probably, since there is less moralism, there are more homosexual acts, though not, of course, any increase of homosexuality as a trait of character.) In the more earnest meaning of sex, love and marriage, however, the radical young still seem averagely messed up, no better than their parents. There is no remarkable surge of joy or poetry—the chief progress of the sexual revolution, so far, has been the freer treatment of small children that I mentioned above. The conditions of American society do not encourage manly responsibility and moral courage in men, and we simply do not know how to use the tenderness and motherliness of women. The present disposition of the radical young is to treat males and females alike; in my observation, this means that the women become camp followers, the opposite of the suburban situation in which they are tyrannical dolls. I don't know the answer.

Certainly the slogan "Make love, not war"—carried mainly by the girls —is political wisdom, if only because it costs less in taxes.

The community meaning of the widespread use of hallucinogenic drugs is ambiguous. (Few students use addictives; again, they are prudent.) I have heard students hotly defend the drugs as a means of spiritual and political freedom, or hotly condemn them as a quietist opiate of the people, or indifferently dismiss them as a matter of taste. I am myself not a hippie and I am unwilling to judge. It seems clear that the more they take pot, the less they get drunk, but I don't know if this is an advantage or a disadvantage. (I don't get drunk, either.) Certainly there is a difference between the quiet socializing of marijuana and the alcoholic socializing of the fraternities, suburbs and Washington. Also, being illegal and hard to procure, the drugs create conspiracy and a chasm between those who do and those who don't. As usual, the drug laws, like other moral laws, fail to eradicate the vice they intend to eradicate, but they produce disastrous secondary effects.

The LSD cult, especially, must be understood as part of a wave of religiosity in young persons that has included Zen, Christian and Jewish existentialism, a kind of psychoanalytic yoga, and the magic of the Book of Changes. On the campus, a young Protestant chaplain—or even a Catholic—is often the center of radical activity, which may include a forum for psychedelic theory as well as peace and Negro rights. Certainly the calculating rationalism of modern times is losing its self-evidence; and it is not the end of the world to flip. Personally, I don't like it when people flip, it is eerie; I like people to be in touch, and I think the heads are mistaken when they think they are communicating. Also, in our overtechnological society, I am intensely suspicious of Dr. Tim Leary's formula to "turn on, tune in and drop out" by chemical means. Yet by and large, the public repression in this field is grossly disproportionate to the occasional damage that has been proved; and frankly, the burden of proof is the other way: If we do not want young people to live in harmless dreams, we have to provide something better than the settled arithmetical delusions of Mr. McNamara, not to speak of Herman Kahn, author of *On Thermonuclear War*.

The shagginess and chosen poverty of student communities have nuances that might be immensely important for the future. We must remember that these are the young of the affluent society, used to a high standard of living and confident that, if and when they want, they can fit in and make good money. Having suffered little pressure of insecurity, they have little psychological need to climb; just as, coming from respectable homes, they feel no disgrace about sitting a few nights in jail. By confidence they are aristocrats —en masse. This, too, is unique in history. At the same time, the affluent standard of living that they have experienced at home is pretty synthetic and much of it useless and phony; whereas their chosen poverty is not degraded but decent, natural and in many ways more comfortable than their parents' standard, especially if they can always corral obvious goodies such as hi-fi equipment and motorcycles. Typically, they tour Europe on nothing, sleeping under bridges; but if they get really hungry, they can drop in at American Express to pick up their mail. Most of the major satisfactions of life— sex, paperback books, guitars, roaming, conversation, games and activist politics—in fact, cost little.

Thus, this is the first generation in America selective of its standard of living. If this attitude became general, it would be disastrous for the expanding Gross National Product. And there is obvious policy and defiance in their poverty and shagginess. They have been influenced by the voluntary poverty of the beat movement, which signified withdrawal from the trap of the affluent economy. Finally, by acquaintance they experience the harsher tone of the involuntary poverty of the Negroes and Spanish Americans whose neighborhoods they visit and with whom they are friends.

In a recent speech, Robert Hutchins pointed out that business can no longer recruit the bright young. He explained this by the fact that the universities are rich and can offer competitive rewards. But I do not think this is the essence, for we have seen that at Harvard, business cannot compete even with the Peace Corps. The essence is that the old drive to make a *lot* of money has lost its magnetism. Yet this does not seem to mean settling for security, for the young are increasingly risky. The magnet is a way of life that has meaning. This is a luxury of an aristocratic community.

*Ethics:*    The chief (conscious) drive of the radical young is their morality. As Michael Harrington, author of *The Other America,* has put it, "They drive you crazy with their morality," since for it they disregard prudence and politics, and they mercilessly condemn day-to-day casuistry as if it were all utterly phony. When politically minded student leaders, like the Students for a Democratic Society, try to engage in "tactics" and "the art of the possible," they may temporarily gain in numbers, but they swiftly lose influence and begin to disintegrate. Yet indignation or a point of honor will rally the young in droves.

Partly, the drive to morality is the natural ingenuousness of youth, freed of the role playing and status seeking of our society. As aristocrats, not driven by material or ulterior motives, they will budge for ideals or not at all. Partly their absolutism is a disgusted reaction to cynicism and the prevalent adult conviction that "Nothing can be done. You can't fight city hall. Modern life is too complex." But mostly, I think, it is the self-righteousness of an intelligent and innocent new generation in a world where my own generation has been patently stupid and incompetent. They have been brought up on a literature of devastating criticism that has gone unanswered because there is no answer.

The right comparison to them is the youth of the Reformation, of *Sturm und Drang,* and of Russia of the Seventies and Eighties, who were brought up on their own dissenting theologians, *philosophes* and intelligentsia. Let us remember that those students did, indeed, ultimately lead revolutions.

The philosophical words are "authenticity" and "commitment," from the existentialist vocabulary. And it cannot be denied that our dominant society is unusually inauthentic. Newspeak and double talk are the lingua franca of administrators, politicians, advertisers and the mass media. These official people are not even lying; rather, there is an unbridgeable chasm between the statements made "on the record" for systemic reasons or the image of the corporation, and what is intended and actually performed. I have seen mature graduate students crack up in giggles of anxiety listening to the Secretary of State expound our foreign policy; when I questioned them afterward, some said that he was like a mechanical man, others that he was demented. And most campus blowups have been finally caused by administrators' animal inability to speak plain. The students have faithfully observed due process and manfully stated their case, but the administrators simply cannot talk like human beings. At this point it suddenly becomes clear that they are confronting not a few radical dissenters but a solid mass of the young, maybe a majority.

Two things seem to solidify dissent: administrative double talk and the singling out of "ringleaders" for exemplary punishment. These make young people feel that they are not being taken seriously, and they are not.

In principle, "authenticity" is proved by "commitment." You must not merely talk but organize, collect money, burn your draft card, go South and be shot at, go to jail. And the young eagerly commit themselves. However, a lasting commitment is hard to achieve. There are a certain number of causes that are pretty authentic and warrant engaging in: Give Negroes the vote, desegregate a hotel or a bus, commute Chessman's sentence to the gas chamber, abolish grading and get the CIA out of the university, abolish HUAC, get out of Vietnam, legalize marijuana and homosexuality, unionize the grapepickers. But it is rarely the case that any particular authentic cause can really occupy the thought and energy of more than a few for more than a while. Students cool off and hop from issue to issue, then some become angry at the backsliders; others foolishly try to prove that civil liberties, for instance, are not so "important" as Negro civil rights, for instance, or that university reform is not so "important" as stopping the bombing of Hanoi. Others, disillusioned, sink into despair of human nature. And committed causes distressingly vanish from view at the June vacation, when the community disperses.

Shrewder psychologists among the young advocate getting involved only in what you "enjoy" and gravitate to—e.g., don't tutor unless you like kids —but this is a weak motive compared with indignation or justice.

The bother is that, except with a few political or religious personalities, the students' commitments do not spring from their own vocations and life ambitions; and they are not related in a coherent program for the reconstruction of society. This is not the fault of the students. Most of the present young have unusually little sense of vocation; perhaps 16 continuous years of doing lessons by compulsion has not been a good way to find one's identity. And there *is* no acceptable program of reconstruction—nobody has spelled it out—only vague criteria. Pathetically, much "definite commitment" is a self-deceptive way of filling the void of sense of vocation and utopian politics. Negroes, who are perforce really committed to their emancipation, notice this and say that their white allies are spiritually exploiting them.

It is a difficult period of history for the young to find vocation and identity. Most of the abiding human vocations and professions, arts and sciences, seem to them, and are (to a degree) corrupt or corrupted: law, business, the physical sciences, social work—these constitute the hated System. And higher education, both curriculum and professors, which ought to be helping them find themselves, also seems bought out by the System. Students know that something is wrong in their schooling and they agitate for university reform; but since they do not know what world they want to make, they do not know what to demand to be taught.

*Politics:*   It is not the task of age 18 to 25 to devise a coherent program of social reconstruction; for instance, to rethink our uses of technology, our methods of management, our city planning and international relations. They rightly accuse us of not providing them a program to work for. A small minority—I think increasing—turns to Marxism, as in the Thirties; but the Marxist theorists have also not thought of anything new and relevant to overripe societies. Most radical students, in my observation, listen to Marxist ideological speeches with polite lack of interest—"they are empty, man, empty"—and they are appalled by Marxist political bullying. On the other hand, they are disgusted with official anticommunism. By an inevitable backlash, since they think all American official speech is double talk, they disbelieve that Communist states are worse than our own.

What the American young do know, being themselves pushed around, itemized and processed, is that they have a right to a say in what affects them. They believe in democracy, which they have to call "participatory democracy," to distinguish it from double-talk democracy. Poignantly, in their ignorance of American history, they do not recognize that they are Congregationalists, town-meeting democrats, Jeffersonians, populists. But they know they want the opportunity to be responsible, to initiate and decide, instead of being mere personnel. Returning from their term overseas, the first thousand of the Peace Corps unanimously agreed that exercising responsibility and initiative had been the most worthwhile part of their experience, and they complained that back home they did not have the opportunity.

The primary area for seeking democracy would be, one would imagine, the universities, for that is where the students are and are coerced. And the radical students, who, we have seen, are among the best academically, have campaigned for *Lernfreiheit*—freedom from grading, excessive examination, compulsory attendance at lectures and prescribed subjects—and also for the ancient privilege of a say in designing the curriculum and evaluating the teachers. But unfortunately, as we have also seen, the majority of students do not care about higher education as such and are willing to put up with it as it is. They are in college for a variety of extrinsic reasons, from earning the degree as a union card to evading the draft. There is no mass base for university reform.

So instead of working in their own bailiwick, activist students have mainly sought participatory democracy for poor people, organizing rent strikes, opposing bureaucratic welfare procedures, and so forth. But there is an inherent dilemma in this. Negroes claim, perhaps correctly, that middle-class whites cannot understand their problems; if Negroes are going to run their own show, they have to dispense with white helpers. The present policy of the Student Nonviolent Coordinating Committee is that Negroes must solve their own peculiar problems, which are the only ones they care about and know anything about, and let their young white friends attend to changing the majority society. There is something in this. Certainly one would have expected Northern students to get their heads broken in the cafeteria at Tulane or the University of Mississippi, where they could talk with their peers face to face, as well as on the streets of country towns. And white Southern liberals have desperately needed more support than they have gotten.

But pushed too far, the rift with the middle-class students consigns poor people to a second-class humanity. The young Negroes cannot do without the universities, for there, finally, is where the showdown, the reconstruction of society, will be—although that showdown is not yet. Consider: Some pressing problems are universal; the poor must care about them, e.g., the atom bomb. Many pressing problems are grossly misconceived if looked at at short range from a poor man's point of view; only a broad human point of view can save Negroes from agitating for exactly the wrong things, as they have agitated for educational parks, when what is needed in schooling is a small human scale. Also, there is something spurious in Negro separatism, for a poor minority in a highly technological society will not engineer the housing and manufacture the cars that they intend to use. Finally, in fact, the Negroes are, perhaps unfortunately, much more American than Negro. Especially in the North, they are suckers for the whole American package, though it makes even less sense for them than for anybody else. The Negro subculture that is talked up has about the same value as the adolescent subculture; it has vitality and it does not add up to humanity.

As in other periods of moral change, only the young aristocrats and the intellectuals can *afford* to be disillusioned and profoundly radical. And in a high technology, only the students will be able to construct a program.

In their own action organizations, the young are almost fanatically opposed to top-down direction. In several remarkable cases, e.g., Tom Hayden, Bob Moses, Mario Savio, gifted and charismatic leaders have stepped down because their influence had become too strong. By disposition, without benefit of history, they are reinventing anarchist federation and a kind of Rosa Luxemburgian belief in spontaneous insurrection from below. In imitating Gandhian nonviolence, they do not like to submit to rigid discipline, but each one wants to make his own moral decision about getting his head broken. If the Army really gets around to drafting them, it will have its hands full.

All this, in my opinion, probably makes them immune to take-over by centralists like the Marxists. When Trotskyites, for instance, infiltrate an organization and try to control it, the rest go home and activity ceases. When left to their own improvisation, however, the students seem surprisingly able to mount quite massive efforts, using elaborate techniques of communication and expert sociology. By such means they will never get power. But, indeed, they do not want power, they want meaning.

*Parallel Institutions:*   The operative idea in participatory democracy is decentralizing, to multiply the number who are responsible, initiate and decide. In principle, there are two opposite ways of decentralizing: either by dividing overcentralized organizations where it can be shown that decentral organization is more efficient in economic, social and human costs, or at least not too inefficient; or by creating new small enterprises to fill needs that big organizations neglect or only pretend to fulfill.

Obviously, the first of these, to cut the present structures down to human size, is not in the power of the young. But it happens that it does require a vast amount of empirical research and academic analysis to find if, where and how decentralizing is feasible; and in current American academic style, there is no such research and analysis. So on 150 campuses, I have urged students to work on such problems. They seem fascinated, but I do not know if they are coming across. (To say it wryly, there is a fine organization called Students for a Democratic Society, but it is not enough evident that they are scholars for a democratic society.)

The other way of decentralizing, by creating parallel enterprises, better suits the student zeal for direct action, and they have applied it with energy and inventiveness. They have set up a dozen little "free universities" that I know about—probably there are many others—in or next to established institutions, to teach in a more personal way and to deal with contemporary subjects that are not yet standard curriculum, e.g., Castro's Cuba, Psychedelic Experience, Sensitivity Training, Theater of Participation. Some of these courses are action sociology, like organizing labor or community development. In poor neighborhoods, students have established a couple of radio stations, to broadcast local news and propaganda and to give poor people a chance to talk into a microphone. They have set up parallel community projects to combat the welfare bureaucracy and channelize needs and grievances. In the South, they have helped form "freedom" political machines, since the established machines are lily white. They have offered to organize international service projects as an alternative to serving in the Army. (I have not heard of any feasible attempts at productive cooperatives or planned urban communities of their own, and students do not seem at all interested in rural reconstruction, though they should be.)

Regarded coldly, such parallel projects are pitifully insignificant and doomed to pass away like so many little magazines. And, in fact, at present, the most intense discussions among student radicals, causing deep rifts, are on this theme. Some, following older thinkers like Michael Harrington and Bayard Rustin (director of a civil rights and poverty research institute) want to engage in "coalition politics," to become effective by combining with the labor unions and leftish liberals in the Democratic Party, to get control of some of the Federal money and to campaign for A. Philip Randolph's (president of the Brotherhood of Sleeping Car Porters) 185-billion-dollar budget to eliminate poverty. This involves, of course, soft-pedaling protests for peace, community action and university reform. Recent history, however, has certainly not favored this point of view. Federal money is drying up and radical coalition people who go to work for the Government get fired; nor is it evident that, if it were spent for liberal social engineering, Randolph's budget would make a better world—even if the money were voted.

Others, for example one wing of SDS, say that the use of participatory democracy and parallel institutions is not for themselves but to consolidate people into a political party; it is not to provide models for the reconstruction of society but, as a kind of initiation rite, to get into the big game of numbers and power. This seems to me to give up on the authenticity, meaning and beautiful spontaneous motivation that have, so far, been the real power of the radical young and the source of what influence they have had. And it presupposes that the young know where they want to go as a party, rather than in what direction they *are* going as a movement. But they don't know; they (and we) will have to find out by conflict.

In my opinion, it is better to regard the parallel institutions as a remarkable revival of a classical American movement, populism, that seemed to have been dead. It is now reviving on the streets and among citizens who storm city hall because they feel they have been pushed around; in such a movement, the young are natural leaders. The principle of populism, as in 1880, is to get out from under the thumb of the barons and do it yourself. And perhaps the important step is the first one, to prove that self-help is possible at all. There may be hope of bringing to life many of our routinized institutions if we surround them with humanly meaningful enterprises. The most telling criticism of an overgrown institution is a simpler one that works better.

This was John Dewey's vision of the young 60 years ago: He thought of an industrial society continually and democratically renewed by its next generation, freely educated and learning by doing. Progressive education, free-spirited but practical, was a typical populist conception. And it is useful to regard the student movement as progressive education at the college and graduate-school level; for at this level, learning by doing begins to be indistinguishable from vocation, profession and politics. It is the opposite of the mandarin establishment that now rules the country, and of the social engineering that is now called education. Maybe this time around, the populist movement will succeed and change what we mean by vocation, profession and politics.

So, describing radical students—and I do not know how many others—we have noticed their solidarity based on community rather than ideology, their style of direct and frank confrontation, their democratic inclusiveness and aristocratic carelessness of status, caste or getting ahead, their selectivity of the affluent standard of living, their effort to be authentic and committed to their causes rather than merely belonging, their determination to have a say and their refusal to be processed as standard items, their extreme distrust of top-down direction, their disposition to anarchist organization and direct action, their disillusion with the system of institutions, and their belief that they can carry on major social functions in improvised parallel enterprises.

Some of these traits, in my opinion, are natural to all unspoiled young people. All of them are certainly in contradiction to the dominant organization of American society. By and large, this is as yet the disposition of a minority, but it is the only articulate disposition that has emerged; and it has continually emerged for the past ten years. It is a response not merely to "issues," such as civil rights or Vietnam, but to deeply rooted defects in our present system, and it will have an influence in the future. It will make for a more decent society than the Great Society and it may well save us from 1984.

## STUDY QUESTIONS

1. Goodman notes that some of the traits of the new aristocrats are natural to all unspoiled young people. To what traits does he refer? Do you agree with him?

2. What are the characteristics of the new aristocrats? Why do they prefer poverty?

3. What is the attitude of the new aristocrats toward college?

4. What does Goodman mean by interpersonal relationships? What rhetorical method does he use to explain these relationships?

5. According to Goodman, what in our society has helped create the new aristocracy?

6. This essay originally appeared in *Playboy*. In what ways is this written for the *Playboy* audience?

*Clark Kerr*

# THE EXAGGERATED GENERATION

Clark Kerr (1911–    ), economist, university professor, and former university administrator, earned degrees from Swarthmore, Stanford University, and the University of California (Berkeley). After teaching in a number of universities, he became chancellor of the University of California (Berkeley) in 1952, and president in 1958. Resigning his office in 1967 at the height of the "free speech" movement on the Berkeley campus, he became Professor of Economics. In addition to his services to universities, he served both the Eisenhower and Kennedy administrations as an expert in labor and management affairs. He has written a number of books on labor relations and industrial management, including *Labor and Management in an Industrial Society* (1964). His influential *Uses of the University* was published in 1963.

THE CURRENT generation of college and university students is the most-berated, the most-praised—certainly the most talked-about—in America's history. The names are varied, even contradictory. They tend to reveal more of the biases of the observers than of the nature of the students.

To conservatives, this is a "discontented" generation—even though youth never had it so good; or a "distrustful" generation—distrustful of its elders, the schools, the Government, the Establishment, distrustful of all the elements that have brought the good life to Americans, and to young Americans in particular. University students of today are seen as "difficult" at best and "radical" at worst, disrupting society.

To liberals, students of today constitute a "generation of conscience" in a nation that badly needs a conscience; or a "prophetic minority" pointing the way for an evil society to evolve. Or they are said to be "committed" to reform and good works; or to constitute a "New Left," presumably carrying on the torch for the tired Old Left which sees in this new generation proof that it really was not defeated permanently and completely. Paul Goodman has called the students of today the "New Aristocrats"—"America's emergent power elite."

From a more neutral point of observation, today's youth has been called "cool" or "activist" or "alienated" or "permissive." The current generation is many of these things to some extent some of the time. It is, for example, certainly occasionally difficult; often committed to some cause or another; to a degree alienated. There are many facets to this generation, perhaps more than to any earlier generation. It is going in more directions and at a faster pace. Thus, any simple designation may hold an element of truth but not the whole truth.

Exaggeration is one word that figs this new generation. It has exaggerated itself. It has been exaggerated by the news media. It has been exaggerated and also used, for their own purposes, by the left and the right. And, as a result, seldom in history have so many people feared so much for so little reason from so few.

The exaggeration is the work of many people. The students themselves are responsible in the first instance; some of them have wanted it that way. A few highly visible minorities, on a relatively small number of campuses, have become symbolic to the public at large of a whole generation. The dress has, at times, been outlandish. The speech, on a few occasions, has been without taste. The behavior of some, with sex and drugs, has been outside established norms. These characteristics have created an impression of widespread Bohemianism distasteful to large elements of the public. To distaste has been added actual fear and anger over actions of the political activists.

The student activists might be called the "McLuhan Generation." Their style is geared to the TV cameras and the flashbulbs, the bullhorn, the microphone and the walkie-talkie. Electricity powers this new student guerrilla warfare. It pulls in information, sends out instructions and carries the message of dissident views to a huge audience.

The media have also played their role in the exaggeration. Berkeley in the fall of 1964 and again in December, 1966, offered an example. The crowds were uniformly reported as being far larger than they were. Herbert Jacobs, a lecturer in journalism at Berkeley, has compared TV and press reports with analyses of photographs of the crowds. Thus, when reports said that 8,000 or 10,000 students voted to strike in Sproul Hall Plaza in December, 1966, the actual number of people there was 2,000—and this number included wives, curious onlookers and nonstudents. Another count, on another occasion, showed a count of 2,400 actually present, when 6,000 to 7,000 had been reported.

"Crowdsmanship," as Jacobs calls it, is a game played by the sponsor, the police and the media alike. They all have an interest in raising the score.

Thus a demonstration becomes bigger and more violent than it really was. A sit-in becomes a riot, then a rebellion and finally the "revolution" at Berkeley.

I once said to some TV executives that, in the course of reporting history, they were changing it. They agreed, but said this was what their competition did—and what the public wanted.

Exaggerated accounts have, on occasion, produced exaggerated reactions. The Old Left has picked up each episode of campus protest around the nation and made it another omen of the second coming of the American Revolution. Its spokesmen saw these protests as involving more students, the students as more radical, the tactics as more effective and the "movement" as more permanent than the facts would seem to warrant. Some liberals went along, for they liked the goals, if not the methods; they wore their hearts on other people's picket signs.

The New Right, rising to the right of the Old Establishment, saw the long arm of Marx and trumpeted its discovery. The Old Establishment was the power structure and it did not like being pushed around; it liked law and order, and it did little to correct the exaggerations.

The middle class tended to be shocked. What it thought it saw of students disturbed it greatly—the biggest scare since the Korean war and Senator McCarthy. Politicians entered the game in more than one state to add their own misrepresentations. In California, "treason, drugs and sex" were said to be a part of the curriculum offered to the students on one campus, and student behavior was highlighted as involving an "orgy."

Amid these exaggerations, efforts to identify "cultures" and "typologies" of students are precarious at best. My own observation is that there are three main student types now vying to set the tone of campus life—Political Activists, Bohemians and the New Collegiates. These types, singly and together, constitute a minority of all students but contribute a majority of the off-campus impressions and impact of the modern generation.

*The Political Activists:*   The protest element of issue-by-issue demonstrations first arose out of opposition to the House Un-American Activities Committee, atomic testing, capital punishment and other similar issues in the late nineteen-fifties and early nineteen-sixties, but particularly reflects in its style and content the civil-rights movement and then the opposition to the war in Vietnam. It rises and falls as issues rise and fall, and it attracts more or fewer or different people as the issues change. The radical element on campus finds its origins particularly in the Depression of the nineteen-thirties and the more recent developments in Cuba and China, and its fractionalization relates to the historical point of origin of each of its components. It has been undergoing a current revival particularly as a corollary to the rise in protest sentiment. The protest element and the radical element together constitute the political activitists.

The activist students have wanted to influence the Establishment but have often ended up, partly because of exaggeration on all sides, by energizing the right, giving ammunition to their worst enemies. They have been, on some occasions, self-defeating prophets, better in the long run at building resistance than getting results, more adept at bringing the counterrevolution than at getting basic reforms, fated to achieve minor successes and major failures. A few of the activists, on the far left, wanted it this way, since they believed that destruction must precede reconstruction. But the great majority of activists wanted to do good things with and for the existing society.

*The Bohemians:* The Bohemian element in American universities is largely a product of the post-World War II period. It is basically incompatible, in its temperament and use of time, with hard academic work, and superficial evidence is a poor test of the real hold that this culture has on students. Yet this element is certainly growing and, given the conditions out of which it arises in modern society, it is almost bound to keep on growing. More fragmentation of life and less sense of purpose in the mass industrial society leads to more such behavior.

(Here we must note a subgroup, outside the campus itself but related to it. This comprises the nonstudents. It is a deviant group—deviant on politics, deviant on attitudes toward sex, morality, religion. Its members are children of affluence who often can make a life without having to make a living. They reflect the attraction of a large campus with its cultural programs, its political activism, its sense of freedom. They reflect the desire for the excitement without the hard work of intellectual pursuits. They reflect both Bohemianism and political activism—both of which reject the middle class. The period between emancipation from adult control and assumption of full adult responsibility can be prolonged almost indefinitely through nonstudent status. Left Banks are now found around a few of the great American universities. They will be found around more, and they will grow in size.)

*The New Collegiates:* Traditional collegiate culture took on its modern form before and after World War I with the development of intercollegiate athletics, formal student governments, debating clubs and the like. But, in terms of adherents, it has been losing ground rapidly since the G.I.'s came back to the campuses after World War II. What distinguishes the new collegiate culture is a sense of community service. It was hardly known in the nineteen-thirties and is particularly a product of the current decade, during which it has grown enormously.

In my student days at Swarthmore during the depths of the Depression, there were only two of us in my senior class who went to a Negro school in Philadelphia one morning a week to work on a Quaker project. Last fall, at the University of California, 8,000 students, or nearly 10 per cent of the total student body, engaged in projects such as these: tutoring Negro children in West Oakland; volunteer teaching in Watts; running a camp in the San Bernardino Mountains for disadvantaged children; serving as "Amigos Anonymous" in villages in Mexico; cleaning up freeways and parks as a beautification project around Berkeley; teaching in San Quentin prison; running summer schools for the children of migratory workers in the San Joaquin and Sacramento Valleys; helping to construct an orphanage in Baja California; working with delinquents in Riverside; providing free dental care to disadvantaged families in Northern California; "adopting" two orphanages in South Vietnam.

The report we issued on these and other projects was called "The Untold Story." The overtold story was about the "filthy nine" (only four of them students) who constituted the totality of the much-publicized Filthy Speech Movement on the Berkeley campus.

This generation, as a whole, has some characteristics that mark the influences that have shaped it. No one today would describe students, as Philip Jacobs did in 1957, as "gloriously contented" and "self-centered" and satisfied with the "American assembly line." They might better be described as "aggressive"—at home, on the campus, off the campus; "concerned"— about the meaning of life and the quality of society; "serious"—about their studies and their actions; "experimental"—in their way of life and their attack on problems; "impatient"—with an education that sometimes lacks relevance and a society that often practices hypocrisy.

This is a generation that was born under the sign of the bomb and suckled at the breast of TV. The bomb created a feeling that there was a time limit on getting a better world. Some students have another sense of urgency—to get something done before they disappear forever into the flatland of the suburb and the wasteland of the corporation.

TV brought to this generation at an early age, as the newspapers never did to children and young people in the past, a view of the whole world and all aspects of it. It became interested in all the world, including Mississippi and Vietnam, and saw vividly that participation was not something to be postponed until adult life. The means were there, through the electronic revolution, for students to be citizens, to be informed and to participate.

This generation was raised at home according to new manuals that stressed permissiveness, and at school under new views that stressed participation. Too often, its members arrived at colleges and universities which still reflected the old manuals and the old views, and both the students and the colleges were unprepared for the meeting.

The quality of education has been improved all along the line, particularly in the high schools and particularly since Sputnik I. There is a new emphasis on grades and on going into graduate work. The meritocracy is taking hold and school is the way to move up to avoid being moved down. The pressure is greater at all levels and students are better educated. Among other things, they are better educated in basic American principles like equality, freedom and the pursuit of happiness. And they see around them discrimination, restrictions on their freedoms, and poverty. They are troubled by the gap between aspiration and attainment. They were told all through high school about the sins of omission of the apathetic generation and the conformity of the "organization man" and exhorted to do otherwise. They are doing otherwise.

American society is now, by and large, affluent—students stay in school longer and fewer of them support themselves while going to school. One result is to reduce their dependence on the world of work and the sense of reality that goes with it. As Eric Hoffer said, "They haven't raised a blade of grass, they haven't laid a brick." They are also, frequently, less oriented toward getting a job after graduation, since that is taken for granted. Thus, materialistic considerations and pressures are less evident now that materialistic welfare is taken more or less for granted and also given a lower value.

The American society of the future troubles them. They have read "1984," "Brave New World," "Animal Farm," and they know about I.B.M. cards and automation. The sense of a world in which the individual counts for less and less weighs heavily. Conformity to Big Brother and to science seems not so very far off. There is a countermove toward individuality as against the requirements of "the system." This move toward individuality is speeded as the new religion and the new anthropology remove some of the restraints on personal behavior.

The Rebel, to use the terminology of Camus, accepts society but wants to improve it. He accepts restraint but not the status quo. He rejects the absolutism of much of the left but not the need for reform. He rejects violence and seeks the possible. Part of his motivation is religious; part relates to a desire for a better future. The Rebel approach is at the heart of the community-service element as well as of the protest tendency among college students.

Confrontation politics, which has often been the special form of student protest, seems to be becoming a less significant weapon. Civil-rights victories are farther in the background. The radicals have taken over much of the guidance of confrontations, and conservative, religious and moderate support has dropped away. Vietnam, of course, remains an issue over which protest can easily be organized, but the great wave of student confrontations now seems to be passing. The sense of protest will continue, and may even rise in intensity, but it will find expression less through confrontation and more through other means.

New leaders are arising from what I have characterized as the New Collegiate group. The New Collegiate type has as one of its characteristics devotion to the campus and willingness to work with and through the campus power structure. The New Collegiate leaders, including those active in fraternities and sororities, are pushing academic reform instead of athletics, political discussion instead of activities, community projects instead of dances—and they appeal to the new interests of the students. They do not wish to bring a campus to a grinding halt, but to halt neglect of students and give voice to community and national concerns. The New Collegiate leaders reflect the student interest in service and protest and give organized expression to it. And then a number of them go overseas and become Peace Corps participants.

Nobody pays much attention to them, but in my opinion they are setting the tone of this generation. The campus revolutionaries are never going to win; this is not a revolutionary country. And the alienated Bohemians are parasites. What is most significant about this generation is the very high proportion of the Peace Corps type.

Society faces the campus just as the campus faces society. A reappraisal by society of the new generation is in order—a reappraisal which recognizes the diversity and the essential goodwill of the students of today. The communications media have a special responsibility to present the facts for this reappraisal. The public should read and hear and see the news about university students with sophistication and some tolerance. The excesses of youth are nothing new in history.

Aristotle once wrote: "They [young people] have exalted notions, because they have not yet been humbled by life or learned its necessary limitations; moreover, their hopeful disposition makes them think themselves equal to great things—and that means having exalted notions. They would always rather do noble deeds than useful ones: Their lives are regulated more by moral feeling than by reasoning—all their mistakes are in the direction of doing things excessively and vehemently. They overdo everything—they love too much, hate too much, and the same with everything else."

## STUDY QUESTIONS

1. Kerr describes three student types that create the off-campus impression of the modern generation. Do these descriptions apply to types on your campus? Are there other types on your campus that are more influential than the ones Kerr notes?

2. From your perspective as a member of the modern generation, can you think of a more accurate name for your generation than the one Kerr uses?

3.  Kerr notes that the Bohemian group is growing and that unless conditions change it will continue to grow. Does this appear to be the case on your campus?

4.  Does Kerr's tone indicate his approval or disapproval of the modern generation or of any types in it?

5.  Does Kerr use any unsupported generalizations you could challenge?

# Paul Woodring

# EROS ON THE CAMPUS

Paul Woodring (1917–    ) is Distinguished Service Professor of the College of Western Washington State College and Editor-at-Large of the *Saturday Review*. He earned his undergraduate degree at Bowling Green University and his M.A. and Ph.D. degrees at Ohio State University. He taught in the public schools in Ohio before joining the ranks of college teachers. Before joining the staff of Western Washington State College he taught at Ohio State University. From 1960–1966 he was Education Editor of *Saturday Review*. He has written numerous articles and books about education; the latter includes *Let's Talk Some About Our Schools* (1953), *A Fourth of the Nation* (1957), and *New Directions in Teacher Education* (1965). Published in 1968, his latest book is *The Higher Learning in America: A Reassessment*.

## Has There Been a Sexual Revolution?

For as long as I can remember—and my memory for such things goes back into the 1920s—we have been hearing about something called a "sexual revolution." Students of the flapper era, who identified themselves with the "lost generation," dated the revolt from World War I. Undergraduates of the thirties believed that it began with the Depression, when many young people found marriage impossible and consequently looked for other sexual outlets. Those of the fifties thought the sexual revolution was an aftermath of World War II and began when returning veterans encountered patriotic coeds. Today's under-graduates firmly believe that the revolt started about 1960 when they were in junior high and that it somehow is related to both the threat of nuclear war and the invention of the pill.

All these views reveal the innocence of youth, for neither sexual activity nor the open discussion of it is as new as many students believe. In 1721, Harvard students formally debated the question "Whether it be fornication to lye with one's Sweetheart before Marriage." It is unlikely that there has ever been a generation of students to which sex was not a major interest or that did not include many individuals who violated the rules laid down for them by their elders and demanded that the rules be changed.

It requires no great knowledge of history to know that the sexual mores are no more relaxed today than they have been at many other times in man's long past and that the loosening and tightening of the restrictions on sexual activity go in cycles of irregular length that are related to a wide variety of social forces.

The present trend toward a loosening of restraints dates roughly from the beginning of the twentieth century. It is not so much a revolution as a persis-tent and growing reaction against the restrictive sexual morality that has variously and somewhat carelessly been described as "Puritanical," "Vic-torian," or "middle-class." The trend was accelerated by the invention of the automobile, improvement in the techniques of birth control, the disloca-tion of families resulting from the move from farms to cities, and the two world wars that took many young men away from the restraining influences of their home communities. Freer sexual activity was made to seem more necessary by careless reading of Freud and more normal (at least statisti-cally) by careful reading of Kinsey. It both gave rise to and fed upon the literature, motion pictures, and television programs of the twentieth cen-tury.

By 1920 students had discovered that a date in an automobile could be something quite different from one in the front parlor with Mother hovering in the background. Their parents were shocked to learn that young people were parking on country roads for purposes other than enjoying the moon-light. But the students who first made this discovery, and now are parents and grandparents, are shocked in turn to learn that students now have dates in dormitory rooms while the Dean of Women looks the other way. Perhaps the activities in either case do not differ greatly from what happened on back porches and in lawn swings in the nineties, but it seems to be generally agreed that the frequency has increased and that a larger proportion of today's adolescents participate freely in what has always been the favorite sport of the human race.

Whatever the change in activity—and no statistics on such a subject can be reliable—there has been a vast change in the kind of advice given to adolescents. A half-century ago the books of intimate advice for boys and girls told readers that any sexual activity outside marriage was sinful, and that premarital activity precluded the possibility of a happy marriage because no man respected a girl who allowed what were then called "liberties." Girls were advised that anything more intimate than handholding aroused the baser passions in a man and could lead to no good.

The books of advice read by teen-agers today are equally moral in their own way but the morality is different. Some sternly advise against all premarital intercourse, but the reasons given are often practical rather than ethical. Nearly all agree that some modest degree of petting and fondling is a normal way of showing deep affection and that such preliminary activities are a necessary prelude to a happy marriage. And every teen-ager has read at least one book in which a psychiatrist, psychologist, or possibly a minister sagely pontificates that while caution is advisable, no activity between two consenting adults is really sinful or necessarily harmful. Any reader over sixteen feels certain that he is an adult and that the consent can be obtained —if necessary with the aid of the book, which can be discussed on the next date.

Students are also aware that many "respectable" adults of this and other centuries, including quite possibly their own parents, have at times violated the conventional codes and seem to be none the worse for it. They have read the biographies of the mistresses of famous men and stories of clandestine affairs between individuals who have played a conspicuous part in history. They are aware of a conspicuous gap between the publicly announced morality and the actual behavior of men and women. Consequently they are not inclined to accept the restrictions that adults attempt to place upon their activities.

## The Dilemma

The dilemma faced by young people is clear enough. Males reach their period of greatest sexual vigor and desire at a time preceding marriage, when the doors to socially approved sexual activity are officially closed to them. But these doors, which have never been successfully locked and barred, have now been set aside by a more permissive society. Now that the fears of pregnancy and disease have been substantially reduced, there is even greater need than before for a code of ethics to guide behavior. But, in our pluralistic society, there is no clear-cut moral code for young people to follow.

The dilemma faced by girls is different but no less perplexing. Though some girls of college age have strong sexual urges, most of them are motivated more by the desire to be popular with boys and often by the desire to please one particular boy. They do not want to be considered old-fashioned, moralistic, or stuffy. When they find that other girls among their associates are engaging in sexual activities, and that the boys expect it, they find it difficult to give a socially acceptable reason for refusing.

Many of today's students would like to be conventional and law-abiding, but first they want the conventions and the laws changed to conform to the current practices. They are convinced that the older generation hypocritically gives lip service to a code in which it does not really believe and which it does not always follow. They differ from the students of the twenties and thirties in that while the earlier generation took pleasure in breaking the rules, the new generation demands that the rules be changed. Another difference is that among the older generation, even those who defended premarital sex insisted that it was justifiable only between two individuals deeply committed emotionally to each other, and that it should be of a continuing nature, while some of the college students today hold that neither commitment nor emotional involvement is necessary to sexual enjoyment. The thing to do, they say, is play it cool, avoid involvement, and live for the pleasure of the moment.

It is unlikely that so hedonistic a philosophy will be widely accepted, particularly by girls, most of whom see sex as a step toward a stable family life. Perhaps the younger generation eventually will develop its own code, though by the time it has done so it will probably have become the older generation and will experience the same difficulty older people always have faced in passing their own moral code on to the young.

## The New Morality

The new morality, if it is to be acceptable to a substantial majority of the people who are young today, must be one that appeals to people of many religious faiths as well as to those who are indifferent to religion. It must be acceptable to Catholics, Jews, Protestants of many denominations ranging from the Episcopalians to the fundamentalists, as well as to the agnostics and atheists who are found in substantial numbers on today's campuses. It must also be consistent with the knowledge now available from psychology, sociology, anthropology, and biology.

The fact that this seems a large order probably explains why a new morality to replace the old has been so slow in emerging. But unless it does, we are faced with the prospects of moral chaos, for the older sexual morality, based as it was on a combination of religion, tradition, and fears of pregnancy and disease, is not acceptable to most of the people in college today. No student who has studied the sexual practices that prevail in this and other cultures and that have prevailed at different times in history is likely to believe that monogamous marriage is the only outlet for sex that can be defended. He is almost certain to reject the view that all premarital or extramarital sex inevitably leads to guilt feelings, unhappiness, or neurosis. He knows that whether or not one will feel guilty about any kind of behavior depends on what he has been taught and what he has learned from previous experience. He knows that pregnancy can now be prevented by any intelligent adult willing to plan ahead, and he has more confidence than may be justified in his own ability to do the planning.

The view that men want to marry virgins is not nearly so popular with today's college boys as it is with men of lower cultural levels or as it was in Grandfather's day. Girls who know this no longer fear that premarital sexual experience will be a barrier to a happy marriage. No amount of lecturing on the part of older people is likely to change their conviction that some amount of premarital sex is both permissible and quite possibly a necessary prelude to a happy marriage. This does not mean that most of today's young people are or want to be promiscuous. Most of them believe that sex ought to mean something beyond the purely physical and that it ought to be a part of a continuing relationship. But they are convinced that sexual activities involving consenting adults should not be governed by law and that neither college officials nor the police and courts have a moral right to interfere, whatever the law may say. They are determined to bring about a change in the laws and regulations that are inconsistent with their views. And they have a considerable amount of support from older people, including many who are in responsible positions. The laws in England and in several of the United States are already undergoing change in the direction of greater permissiveness. Greater changes will come when those who are now in college reach voting age.

The Kinsey reports revealed that while adolescents, particularly boys, who lack a college education engage in overt sex earlier and more frequently than do those who go to college, the college students of both sexes much more often engage in "heavy petting" which leads to orgasm without actual intercourse. Some writers have said that such petting is the distinctive feature of dating behavior in the present generation, but anyone old enough to remember the flapper era of the twenties will recall that this term was used even then and that it meant just about what it does now. Petting, light or heavy, has been a part of dating behavior for a long time, but it probably is true that there has been a statistical increase in the variety called "heavy" and less moral opposition to it.

Insofar as they draw their conclusions from the printed word, today's students are influenced by the works of Albert Ellis, Kinsey, the Kronhausens, such recent medical reports as those of W. H. Masters and V. E. Johnson, and Hugh Hefner's "*Playboy* philosophy" of recreational sex far more than they are by the now-antiquated views of Havelock Ellis, Krafft-Ebing, Sigmund Freud, and Bertrand Russell. Older people who wish to guide them should be aware of these new sources of enlightenment even though it ob-

viously would be difficult for anyone to devise a workable code of behavior
from such an assortment of literary contributions.

Though a new code for sexual conduct clearly is needed, it cannot safely
be constructed by adolescents alone; for, as Richard Hettlinger reminds us
in *Living with Sex:* "There is no field of human activity in which it is so easy
to deceive oneself and to be convinced by arguments which are in fact nothing but rationalizations of clamant desires." In planning the new morality,
young people will need all the advice they can get from older people whose
desires presumably have cooled a bit and who can take a longer view. But,
being young, they are not likely to take it.

The new code must be based upon a clear recognition of the fact that most
educated and enlightened people of all ages look upon sexual desire as biologically, socially, and psychologically normal rather than as something
evil, dirty, or shameful. They reject as ridiculous the view that the desire to
produce offspring is the only legitimate motivation for sexual activities. Because they accept adolescent petting as normal and know that sex takes
many forms, they place less emphasis than their ancestors on the importance
of technical virginity. They are aware that sexual desire is strong in youth
and that efforts to postpone sexual activities until marriage are at best futile
and perhaps both unnecessary and undesirable.

But there is no agreement on what the new code should be, for there is a
solid nucleus of more conservative people on every college campus, and a
still larger number off campus, who think that it is essential that we preserve
some aspects of the traditional morality. Students holding such views and
living up to the older code can be found even on the campuses reputed to be
most liberal in their attitudes; a Reed professor recently was quoted as saying "There's a lot more virginity around here than you might expect."

One thing seems clear: the new code, to be acceptable, must grant equal
freedom to both sexes even though it still is true that it is the girls who have
the babies. Throughout the eighteenth and nineteenth centuries it was customary for college boys to have their first sexual experience with "town
girls" or prostitutes and then look for virgins of their own social class to
marry. Co-education has changed that. Today most of the college boys who
have premarital sex have it with girls of their own social and educational
level, often with the girls they eventually marry. The double standard is no
longer acceptable to either sex.

Early marriage, when it is combined with early parenthood, seems to create as many problems as it solves; the divorce rate among those who marry
in their teens is substantially higher than among those who marry later. But
it might be possible to provide for a new kind of temporary marriage that
would enable young couples to live together during their college years without subterfuge or hypocrisy and would provide a legitimate outlet for sexual
urges without all the responsibilities of conventional marriage.

Forty years ago, Judge Ben Lindsey of the juvenile courts of Denver proposed what he called "Companionate Marriage" whereby young couples might legally live together for a time with the understanding that divorce could be obtained by mutual consent so long as there were no children. The world was not ready for so drastic a solution; though Lindsey's plan was applauded by some it was roundly condemned by many and led to no action. But when Margaret Mead recently suggested a somewhat similar plan she met with much less opposition. Perhaps the nation is almost ready to accept such an arrangement, but it will surely take several decades to get the necessary laws through the state legislatures. In any case a good many of today's young people want a greater degree of freedom to experiment than would be provided for by any form of monogamous marriage.

Unless some solution is found we shall undoubtedly see a continued relaxation of standards, a growing contempt for the traditional rules and laws governing sexual activities, and still more confusion on the part of young people as to what is and what is not acceptable. If our society takes a downward trend, historians and archeologists of the future who dig up the remnants of our culture will probably conclude that a decline of sexual morality was a major cause of the deterioration. But if the culture continues to survive and flourish despite a greater degree of sexual freedom, tomorrow's historians will call attention to the fact that sexual freedom has been a characteristic of many of the greatest periods of human achievement. And they will find many examples to cite.

## STUDY QUESTIONS

1. Be prepared to discuss the author's claim that young people face a dilemma because there is no longer a clear cut moral code for them to follow. Do you agree with his position?

2. Why, according to the author, has a new morality been so slow in emerging?

3. This selection contains a number of unsupported generalizations about attitudes toward sex and sexual morality. Be prepared to challenge those you find invalid or misleading.

4. To what extent do you find the selection authoritative in tone and substance?

5. What are the basic differences between the attitudes of the older and the modern generation toward sex and morality?

*Herbert Gold*

# LETTER FROM A FAR FRAT

Herbert Gold (1924–      ) is a teacher who turned to a career in writing.
He earned both his B.A. and M.A. degrees at Columbia University and has
been awarded a Guggenheim Fellowship and an American Institute of Arts
and Letters Award. As a visiting professor, he has taught at Cornell University, the University of California (Berkeley) and Harvard University. His
novels include *Birth of a Hero* (1951), *The Prospect Before Me* (1954), *The
Man Who Was Not With It* (1956), *The Optimist* (1958), *Therefore Be Bold*
(1961), *Salt* (1963), and *Fathers* (1967). His short stories and articles have
appeared in various magazines.

If this is the era for assaulting university presidents and prancing nude in Harvard
houses, can life in a typical college fraternity still be the same? To the hop-
flavored surprise of Mr. Gold, author of FATHERS, THE MAN WHO WAS NOT WITH IT,
and other novels, the answer—at Chapel Hill, North Carolina, in any case—
proved to be, Yes.

WELL, THE Fraternity House still exists. I almost thought it
went out of fashion with Dick Powell and Jack Oakie and
the great homecoming games of early MGM musicals,
but by golly, the old beer-spraying, girl-harvesting, ear-splitting article can
still be found on, say, the campus of the University of North Carolina at
Chapel Hill, which is an excellent school with high standards. Because I was
a guest in the house, I'll invent a name for the occupants, Kappa Lambda Pi.

OK, on a Saturday night the fine old lovingly demolished mansion is surrounded by MG's, Sprites, American convertibles; the lawn is covered with
heartbreakingly—beautiful? well, cute—it's covered with girls, and
weaving about the girls are the boys, casting their spell, making time. The
band is an amplified rock group, good strong sound, tough and nonpsyche-

delic, out of Carrboro or the country surrounding—black, of course, and no one else is. The hospitality is immense and genuine. They are lovingly demolishing the place by hand; it's a local craft. Echo says, and echo replies: "Have a beer, have a brew. Here, have a swig. Hey, sir, have a drink of mine. Aw, come on, have fun with us, sir."

The boys of KLP are celebrating losing a game. On other nights they celebrate winning the game, or rush week, or the water shortage, or exam week, or the visit of Spiro T. Agnew to Raleigh, or it doesn't make any difference. The faucet in the kitchen is never turned off. Since there has been a prolonged drought and a crucial water shortage which threatens to shut down the school, it has seemed a fine joke to some good old boy to get out of various academic problems by doing his best to drain the lake. Some of the would-be adults in the house think this is childish behavior, he hadn't ought to do like that, but it's a matter of *esprit de corps*. It would be finking on a good buddy to interfere. When one fellow twisted the faucet shut, his good brother got red-eyed and sore, silent; but that's the limit of it. Well, it really means something to him, that water-lover. Hurtie tough-titty feelings. Anyway, they might get the emergency pipeline from Chapel Hill to Durham in time to relieve the reservoir. And in a democracy every man should be free, shouldn't he, to decide whether or not the town has any water?

During the festivities which I attended, sex and politics were the prime subjects. So far, so good. I've heard of them. Water and studying were a distraction from real life. The future is a slightly disagreeable consequence of the present, following it by association as "liver" follows "cirrhosis of the." The smell of beer, which I thought had disappeared from campuses, is making its last stand in North Carolina. Beer was a stranger to me (I've spent a lot of time at California colleges). A tall, sandy, snob-nosed brother called Boyce explained about things: "we can't be too cool, man. We can't operate like them Ivies, you know, smoke a joint and then zap her upstairs. We got to plan and work out a three-stage campaign, not like those Ivies up north, man. I prepped at Lawrenceville, I skied in Colorado, so I had that experience, those Ivies. We got to work a three-stage campaign, not cool, man, not like those Ivies, man, sir."

"I understand," I said, almost understanding.

"First stage, we got to dance a little, get 'em a little slushed up, you know, hot, not like those Ivies. That's first stage. Love 'em up a little. Then second stage: into the car. Sir, let me explain, that's trouble, getting 'em out of here and across the parking lot into the car. Now they want it as much as we do, don't misunderstand me, sir, just like those Ivy girls, they want it, but they stumble, they make it tough crossing the parking—OK, into the car, man. Then we have these apartments in town—"

"You mean you can't take the girls upstairs?"

He looked at me, shocked at my presumption. He offered me a swig from

his can. He defended Southern womanhood. "Here?" he asked. "In the
house? In front of all everybody?"

"I'm sorry," I said.

"Well, we drag 'em out the door and through the parking lot. Course lots
of times they yell and scream and laugh and throw up a lot, but we get 'em
out, because they want to as much as we do, you know, that's human nature.
So then we get 'em to our apartments in town, oh, maybe three, four of us
share an apartment, and then  . . ." A grin lit up his face. It was like the sun
rising over Georgia. "Man, can I just tell you what I did to that little girl over
there—see, that one? No, not that one, sir—you like her? Cindy?—no,
the one next to Cindy."

He pointed to a little flower of Southern womanhood stubbing out her
cigarette against the veneered wood atop the TV.

"You don't know her, do you? so it's all right if I tell you. But listen, sir, if
you'd like to meet her  . . ."

First, however, he described stage four in the three-stage plan.

I was also interested in his political views, but first we got involved about
this girl.

Oh, well, I have prurient interest, too.

"Come here, honey," Boyce called to the girl (not Cindy). She came over,
mussed and sulky, with a great hair-collector's mane of yellow hair, and
then shot me that marvelous easeful flirty Southern smile which nice girls
down there give not only their men but also girlfriends, pregnant ladies,
small animals, and the short-answer questions on a nursing exam. She had
liquid brown eyes, lovely, hysteric eyes, soft stalks with contact lenses
perched atop the irises. "I just been telling him what we did t'other night,
honey."

"Went to the movies," she said.

"No, not that night—"

"Saw *Disaster Angels,* with a revival of camp classic *Suddenly Last
Summer*—"

"No, the next night, night we had the party—"

"Oh, Boyce, you're a, you're a, you're a—"

He grinned while she suffered her failure of vocabulary. But she seemed
about to cry—hysteric, remember?—so he apologized gently, saying,
"Aw, honey, don't carry on like that. I didn't show him the Polaroids."

I was getting mired in interpersonal relations. It would be better all the
way around, including my development as a thinking human being and a
visiting writer, if I heard some of their views on wider topics.

Floyd Jones is an activist. He has been to Europe on his summer vacation.
He thinks about local option and states' rights (positive). Hair and hippies
mash around in his emotions (negative). In Europe he noticed the happy
faces in West Berlin, the unhappy ones in East Berlin, and that settled Com-

munism for him. It was all clear now, roger and over, and this led him straight back to American politics. "I met these German men in a bar," he told me, "good old boys, spoke good English, said why don't we kick the shit out of those hippies and draft-card burners." He had discussed everything from Vietnam to race with those happy faces, and they compacted together that Communism must be stopped.

Our conversation took place during the heat of the last political campaign, just after a Northerner, Curtis LeMay, native of my home state of Ohio, had been chosen to assist George Wallace in his mission. "He's a good old boy," said Floyd, as the dancers flailed about us. The cigarettes were falling into the carpet, the fastidious were drinking out of plastic-foam cups, the forthright were drinking out of their cans, and the group had me backed against the color TV. The sound was turned off, but the light show flickered and spattered against the screen. I reached behind to turn it off so that the radiation wouldn't catch me behind while the vocal emanations and renditions took me afront.

Floyd is the only man I know who was overjoyed by the three major candidates for the presidency. Hubie was a good old boy, loyal to London, a virtue all in itself, and of course Wallace had the clearest and finest ideas, but he personally was voting for Mr. Nixon. It's a class thing, he felt; a duty to live up to the word "responsible"; and Mr. Nixon's speeches nearly brought tears to his eyes. They were that sincere. Also, he hoped he'd kick the shit out of those draft-card burners and long-haired hippies.

"You really like all the candidates?"

"They're loyal Americans, aren't they? That's what I ask of a man."

I offered some objections to Floyd and the others, but mainly I tried to play Socratic Method—questions: Is this a happy country? Do you really think more weapons for the police are the "answers" to law and order? What is your conception of America's role? One very tall, horn-rimmed young man, with a look of poetic angularity about him, hung on my words, and I thought I had an ally. He too seemed puzzled by America circa 1968. He suddenly burst out: "Wha yo so gol-darned negative? What is this negative bit?" Astonished by his own anger, he added: "Sir?"

A few girls had joined us. One of them was Cindy—eyes afire, that old golf club menace in them. There was some kicking and giggling going on below the level of the conversation. It was stage one and a half of the campaign, I decided, not like those Ivies.

I must have asked a question, because the sensitive-looking brother burst out, "Course I wouldn't kick the shit out of 'em! I just say that!" Then he smiled shyly. "Wouldn't want to get my shoes dirty," and nudged me. "Aw, sir, I just say that. They got the right to free speech, too, so long as they don't go tearing down this country. You're not always so negative, are you, sir?"

It was time to be their buddy, I decided. I too had done my term at Fort Bragg and elsewhere, though this was before their birth. I reminisced about Fayetteville, North Carolina, which we called Fagleberg.

"You mean Fayettenam?" Floyd asked. "When they call me there, I'm going. If they cancel my deferment, sir, I'm going. But I'm going to try to finish my education first, and get into a good position, and if the Lord is good to me, I won't have to fight. I can tell what you're thinking, sir. I got strong feelings. But like I already explained, killing's just not in the American line."

He was wearing tight maroon pants and a white button-down short-sleeve shirt with notched vents at the sleeve. One of his Hush Puppies was unlaced. He leaned on me a little, partly out of friendship and desire to be understood, saying, "Now don't get me wrong, hear? They call me, I go. I got this deferment, no gol-darned evasion."

"I'm not a pacifist either," I said.

"But I never did meet any Marine from Veetnam committed an atrocity who enjoyed it, hear? Hear me, sir? We just got to defend the American perimeter, it's as simple as that. So I'll go, I'll go, sir, soon as they call me."

When it came time to part, two of the brothers insisted on walking me home to the Carolina Inn. It had rained gleaming Burgie flip-top friendship rings on the Carolina earth. The brothers scuffed along, bumping and uneasy about the discussion. The men of the KLP house have a complex feeling about life—a minority on this campus, a majority in their own hometowns, but are they a majority in America and the world? It is no longer easy to find the tides of right and float back and forth on them. Kappa Lambda Pi is in trouble as a way of life.

There was a shy moment in the fragrant Indian summer evening, hot rods and flowering trees and sweet echo of amplified rock from the Carrboro Rhythm Ramblers. Something had been left unsaid. Some generation gap had been left ajar, some culture gap unclosed, some stony silence in the metaphysics. We all wanted to be close and warm, and yet we were not close and warm. We had kidded around, but what else? In a world of making out OK, and getting bugged by it, we had made out all right, and gotten bugged by each other, just like the Ivies; and yet there must be something more than paltry victories in love and politics. There might be, for example, real victories. Stage five. Stage six. Stage seven.

On another part of the campus the 1 A.M. showing of underground art flicks was just beginning, and the Dandelion, a head shop, was just closing, and the Racial Confrontation group was continuing out under the famous Davie poplar. As we walked by, a tall black man in a denim suit, a refugee from Resurrection City, a pioneer of Freedom City, was smiling and saying softly, We're sick of trickeration, we won't stand still for extermination, so we got to have communication; and an earnest young white student said, But we got to talk it all out first so's not to frighten the other people; and the man from Resurrection City said, Son, that's trickeration . . .

One of my escorts shook his head, grinning. "Man, oh, man," he said to me. Some of these jerks were beyond his comprehension.

All over the campus the gritty Indian summer smell of autumn leaves was helping lovers and celebrants and reformers and late-night scholars fix the memory in their hearts, whether they knew it or not: *This is it, this was college in my time.*

As we walked along, beer fizzing in the jiggled cans, a member of my honor guard said, "It's just, sir, we didn't want you to get the one-sided impression about this school."

"I appreciate your hospitality," I said.

We were standing near the rocking chairs on the porch of the Carolina Inn (widows, conferences, and faculty visitors). "Don't get us wrong," he said. "We have strict rules at the house. We don't always live up to them, but we try not to be litterbugs. We might be Tarheels and we got a lousy team, but we have fun, too, sir." He gazed wearily back across campus to the traditional Davie poplar, famed in song and story. Chapel Hill's little Berkeley was still strolling and consulting near that spot. "Just didn't want you to go away thinking we're all a bunch of stupid intellectuals."

## STUDY QUESTIONS

1.  What characterizes the tone of this selection? Note details that reveal Gold's attitude toward his subject.

2.  What would you say is the sexual morality code of the Kappa Lambda Pi's?

3.  How does Gold's method of presentation serve his purpose better than a straight expository approach would?

4.  What is the serious purpose underlying Gold's playful account?

5.  What is the rhetorical effect of the last sentence in the essay?

*Sidney Hook*

# ACADEMIC FREEDOM
# AND STUDENT RIOTS

Sidney Hook (1902–    ), philosopher and educator, was born in New
York. At The City College of New York, where he received his B.S., he won
the Ward Medal for Logic. He received his M.A. and Ph.D. from Columbia
University. Currently he is chairman of the philosophy department at
Washington Square College, New York University. He has been an active
member of the Commission on Cultural Freedom and the Conference on
Methods and Philosophies, and he has been a recipient of a Guggenheim
fellowship.

$A$MERICANS ARE accustomed to reading about universities
as storm centers of political disturbance in Latin and Asiatic countries. In a country like the United States, how-
ever, most criticism of student bodies in the past has been directed against
their political apathy. The fact, therefore, that a building was seized by students at the Berkeley campus of the University of California, bringing all
administrative activities to a halt, that a strike was declared, paralyzing
teaching, and that the governor of the most populous state in the union, after
the arrest of some 800 students, felt it necessary to appeal for problems to be
solved "by evolution not revolution," should give not only educators but all
reflective citizens pause. It has focused attention upon a question of considerable complexity—the rights, and the responsibilities, of students.

Since so much of the controversy and agitation swirls around the slogans
of freedom, the first question to be asked is: Do students enjoy the right of
academic freedom? This depends on what is meant by academic freedom.
Perhaps the best short definition was offered by Arthur O. Lovejoy, founder,
together with John Dewey, of the American Association of University Professors.

"Academic freedom," he wrote, "is the freedom of the teacher or research worker in higher institutions of learning to investigate and discuss the problems of his science and to express his conclusions, whether through publications or the instruction of students, without interference from political or ecclesiastical authority, or from the administrative officials of the institution in which he is employed, unless his methods are found by qualified bodies of his own profession to be clearly incompetent or contrary to professional ethics."

A number of interesting implications may be drawn from this definition. First, academic freedom exists primarily for "teachers"—in the most comprehensive sense of that term. Strictly speaking, it makes no sense to talk of "academic freedom" for students. Students have a right to freedom to learn. The best guarantee of freedom to learn is academic freedom for those who teach them. Where teachers are deprived of academic freedom, students are *ipso facto* deprived of the freedom to learn.

The converse, however, is not true. It is simply false both in logic and in fact to assert that freedom to teach and freedom to learn are indivisible. Many things may interfere with the student's freedom to learn—poverty, racial discrimination, inadequate transportation—which have no direct relevance to academic freedom. The latter may flourish in institutions to which students are unjustly denied the opportunity to enter. The movement to abolish poverty, discrimination and other social evils in order to give students access to education and to effective freedom to learn flows from their *moral* rights as persons and from their *civil* rights as citizens. They are not corollaries of academic freedom. To deny this would make the university responsible for the entire state of society and its reform.

Second, academic freedom is not a civil right like freedom of speech. A teacher who is dropped or refused a post on grounds of incompetence, because, say, he indoctrinates his students with the belief that the earth is flat, or that the Elders of Zion are engaged in a conspiracy to destroy America, or that Communists are twentieth-century Jeffersonian democrats, is not being deprived of freedom of speech. He can still proclaim his discovery from the house tops. As a citizen he can talk nonsense without let or hindrance. But in order to talk "nonsense" in the academy with impunity—and strange things *can* be heard within it!—a teacher must win the right to do so by certification from his peers that he is competent and by having acquired tenure. What may sound like nonsense to the plain citizen may be the birth of a revolutionary discovery.

The same consideration applies to the student.

There is no direct connection between the student's freedom to learn and his freedom of speech. The controlling consideration must be his freedom to learn. If restrictions are placed on freedom of speech—aside from those which exist on the freedom of *all* citizens—they must be justified by the educational needs of the student and reasonable institutional provisions for its expression. It is one thing to set up a miniature Hyde Park on some corner of the campus and encourage students to use it; it is another to allow them to call a mass meeting on Prexy's lawn at dawn.

Third, responsibility for the certification of a teacher's competence, and for interpreting and applying the rules of tenure, must ultimately lie in the hands of the faculty. The faculty should also set the educational standards which students are required to measure up to. Students may be free to learn but sometimes they don't learn enough. Students too, therefore, must earn the right to continue as students. Higher education is not a civil right like the right to a fair trial or other Bill of Rights freedoms that do not have to be earned.

Fourth, an important aspect of the faculty's responsibility for the entire educational enterprise is ultimate control over the classrooms, meeting halls and other educational facilities of the campus and over the conditions of their use. This has a bearing, as we shall see, on some crucial questions.

The extent to which these principles are applied is affected by the fact that legal authority in American higher institutions of learning is vested either in boards of regents or in corporate boards of laymen. While there is no practicable way of reversing this historical trend, immense progress has been made in winning over those with legal authority to the acceptance of enlightened principles of academic freedom which in effect entrust educational policy to the faculties. This has been a gradual and sometimes painful development, but today academic freedom is in a more flourishing state than ever before in its history. It is only when one remembers how many and onerous were the religious, political and social restrictions upon the teacher's freedom in the past that one can grasp the remarkable progress that has been made.

What is true of the teacher's academic freedom is also true of the student's freedom to learn. My own lifetime spans a period from relative tyranny in the classroom to open inquiry. During my freshman year in college, I gave two reports in a class in political science. In the first, I defended Charles A. Beard's approach to the Constitution—to the manifest disapproval of the teacher. In the second, I argued that Calhoun's logic was superior to Webster's in their famous debates. This was too much for the instructor who ejected me from the class with the indignant observation: "When you aren't preaching sedition you are preaching secession!" That could hardly happen today. Although conditions are not uniform, almost everywhere the climate of opinion and practice is healthier than it used to be.

The issues that agitate campuses today are more likely to arise from the behavior of students than from actions of the faculty. Of these, some stem from rules governing the students' personal and social behavior, and some from efforts to regulate their extracurricular political activities both on and off campus.

Confusion, and sometimes needless controversy, arise from a failure to distinguish between the area of conduct in which students may justifiably exercise their rights as individual citizens and that which is related to the specific function of the college and to the business which presumably brings the student to school. To indicate the relevance of this distinction, let us examine some of the concrete issues that have provoked controversy in recent years.

The first concerns the personal morality of students. Unfortunately, personal morality for many people refers exclusively to sexual behavior, but, properly understood, it embraces every form of individual conduct whose consequences have some bearing on the welfare of others. On the assumption that in institutions of higher learning we are not dealing with children, standards of personal deportment should initially be left to the students themselves. In the interests of safety, however, it is necessary to establish rules and regulations governing the use of cars, liquor, smoking and visits to dormitories, but, wherever possible, these rules should be administered by the students themselves. Anything students can properly do for themselves as adults should be left to them. To student self-government, broad-based and representative, can be entrusted many of the functions incidental to organized student life in the college community—although the faculty cannot forgo exercising some oversight as a kind of appeals body to see that fair play is done.

Should students be permitted to organize political groups on campus or invite speakers of extremist political views to address them? This kind of problem has occasioned far more bitter controversy than problems of purely personal behavior. And failure to define the issue properly has prevented the right kind of questions from being asked and the relevant considerations brought to bear.

A student request which may have considerable *educational* validity may be wrongfully denied because it is mistakenly put forward as a political demand. This is particularly true with respect to who should be allowed to speak on a university campus. This has nothing to do with questions of free speech or academic freedom. Political speakers can reach students in many ways. If the faculties do not permit the use of college facilities to individuals outside of the academic community, they are not denying the civil right of freedom of speech to speakers, who can easily address students off-campus, or the civil right of freedom to listen to students, who can attend their meetings off-campus. This is a false issue.

The genuine issue is the *educational* one. It is on educational, not political, grounds that a valid case can be made for permitting recognized student organizations to invite speakers of their choice to the campus to discuss any topic, no matter how controversial. The educational process cannot and should not be confined merely to the classroom. Students should be encouraged to pursue their educational interests on their own initiative, and contemporary issues which convulse society are legitimate subjects of inquiry.

Faculties and administrations often suffer from educational timidity. They are unduly fearful when a speaker of extremist views is invited to the campus. If a college is doing its job properly, it doesn't require Fascists or Communists to instruct its students about Fascism or Communism. But so long as students want to hear such speakers—often to see them in the flesh and to find out how they tick mentally—there can be no reasonable educational objection to their appearance—particularly if it is made clear that such speakers do not represent the views of the student body or faculty.

If students and faculty cannot cope with the "arguments" of the Lincoln Rockwells and Gus Halls, then the college is failing badly in its educational task. In an open and honest forum, the cause of freedom and democracy can triumph over all challengers. And as for the vaunted "public image" (horrid phrase!) of the college, the prolonged controversy and newspaper publicity attendant upon banning a speaker is usually far more damaging than the one-day sensation provided by his appearance. For one thing seems assured by experience. A prolonged controversy over an invitation to an extremist almost always guarantees him an overflow audience when he does finally appear.

In the rare cases in which the need for control of student activities does arise, failure on the part of the faculty to draw the line means that it has abdicated from its educational responsibilities. For example, students, sometimes unfortunately abetted by junior faculty personnel, will occasionally try to break up meetings of speakers with whom they disagree. A self-respecting faculty cannot tolerate such activities. Similarly, if outside groups send professional organizers onto the campuses of large metropolitan universities to recruit students or to provoke incidents with the administration or faculties, they should be barred from access.

Then, too, small groups of students, zealots in some cause, will occasionally violate the rules of fair discussion and honest advocacy. I could fill a volume describing stratagems of this kind I have observed over a lifetime. A few students, for example, will organize a "Free Speech Forum" or something else with a libertarian flavor. Their first speaker will be Lincoln Rockwell or someone of his kidney. Thereafter, featured as "a reply" to Fascism, will come a succession of Communist speakers, sometimes paid from general student or school funds. The "educational" point of the forum is to build up Communism in its various disguises as the only real answer to Fascism.

Complaints about the absence of liberal speakers are met with the statement that liberals have been invited but refused to come. The evidence? A carbon copy of a letter to a liberal figure 2,000 miles or more distant, the original of which he may never have received. Where representatives of the student body are unable to prevent dishonest practices of this kind, the faculty is justified in stepping in.

The same general principles should govern student publications. On educational grounds, students should be encouraged to publish their own newspapers, periodicals and pamphlets, exchanging ideas, commenting on great issues, testing and challenging their teachers' views. But it would be ridiculous to say that this freedom is absolute and exempts them from restraints against slander and libel. Particularly obnoxious is the circulation of anonymous literature on campus defaming members of the student body or faculty.

Only those who believe it is possible to be liberal without being intelligent will affirm that the content of speech is always privileged irrespective of its effects.

The very fact that speech can be used not only for advocacy—which is permissible—but for incitement, defamation and slander—which is not —shows how absurd it is to hold that speech should never be restricted. There should be no prior censorship, of course, unless there is convincing evidence that a speaker plans to incite to violence. We do not have to wait for a mob actually to move to lynch someone before we stop the agitator inciting it.

The irony of the situation is that students in our mass institutions of learning suffer today far more from the failure of faculties to attend to the students' individual educational needs than from alleged suppressions of their freedom of speech. The students' freedom to learn is frustrated by crowding, inferior staffing and by the indifference of many faculties to the best methods of classroom teaching. Colleges still operate on the absurd assumption that anyone who knows anything can teach it properly. It is an open scandal that the worst teaching in the American system of education takes place at the college level.

In some universities, large introductory courses where skillful teaching is of critical importance in arousing student interest are turned over to young, inexperienced graduate assistants at the outset of their careers who stumble along by trial and error and groping imitation of the models of teaching they vaguely remember. No wonder they sometimes play up to students, joining them in their vague resentments against the educational establishment in a kind of compensatory camaraderie. Some observers believe that unless conditions change the real revolt on campus will some day be directed against the shoddy educational treatment to which students have been subjected. As the numbers of students grow the situation deteriorates.

A sense of proportion, a pinch of humor and a draft of common sense are wonderful specifics against friction, but they vanish when either students or faculty resort to ultimatums. Both sides have a mutual interest in keeping the educational enterprise going. When problems and difficulties arise they must be routed through recognized channels of petition, complaint and protest. The officially elected representatives of the student body should meet periodically with representatives of the faculty which, when grave issues are at stake, should sit as a committee of the whole.

Attempts by any group, even when it feels it has a legitimate grievance, to short-circuit official channels, to appeal over the heads of the representative student body for mass demonstrations or strikes, to threaten force and violence or to resort to so-called passive resistance should be condemned by both students and faculty. Such tactics are not only destructive of the atmosphere in which teaching and learning can take place, they prejudice the chances for reaching mutually satisfactory settlements.

The student "Free Speech Movement" at the University of California had every right to press for modification of university rules governing campus and off-campus activities. What was shocking, however, was its deliberate boycott and by-passing of the Associated Students, the elected representative organization of the student body. It neither used all the existing channels of protest nor sought to avail itself of the remedies open to it.

Even more shocking was the demagogic and odious comparison drawn by some students between the situation at the University, which, despite its restrictions, is still far more liberal than most, and the situation in Mississippi. And worst of all was the resort to tactics of mass civil disobedience which could only be justified in extreme situations in behalf of basic principles of freedom. Except in such situations, changes in the laws of a democratic community must be urged by practices within the law.

Almost as shocking as the action of the students in seizing University property was the failure of the faculty at Berkeley to condemn the action. Indeed, by failing to couple its call for an amnesty for students with a sharp rebuke for their actions, the faculty seemed to condone indirectly the students' behavior. Apparently those who wanted to be heroes were to be spared the consequences of their heroism.

The administration of the University also seems at fault in not anticipating developments on campus. Signs of student unrest and dissatisfaction were apparent many months ago. The faculty, therefore, should have been brought into the picture much earlier and entrusted with the formulation of rules of conduct, in consultation with official representatives of the student body, and with their subsequent enforcement.

The really disquieting aspect of the situation at the University of California, however, was the extremism of the student leaders, the lengths to which they were willing to go—at one point, bloodshed and possible loss of life seemed imminent—and the contemptuous and disingenuous account they gave of their behavior. One of them described their activities as "controversial measures to begin a dialogue." Student concern with the content and method of their education is sure to grow and should be encouraged. But if they are going to lie down, seize buildings and call strikes whenever their demands are not granted by faculty and administration, it bodes ill for the future.

Even before the events at Berkeley, I read literature distributed by a strong student group at the University of California calling for "the total elimination of course, grade and unit system of undergraduate learning" and urging other proposals—not all of them as silly. But what was definitely not silly or funny in the light of what has happened was the injunction to students to resort ultimately to "civil disobedience" to get their way! It is a safe bet to anyone who knows the psychology of students that once they get away with the tactic of civil disobedience in protesting a minor rule, their demands—and their conduct—will grow wilder and more unreasonable.

No service is done to students by flattering them or by giving them the impression they can acquire an education in any other way than by hard intellectual discipline—by accepting the logic of ideas and events. They cannot be encouraged too much to broaden their intellectual interests, and they certainly must not be discouraged from giving expression to their generous enthusiasms for civil rights, for human welfare, for peace with freedom. But good works off campus cannot be a substitute for good work on campus. Ultimately, the good causes our society always needs have a better chance of triumphing if their servitors equip themselves with the best education our colleges and universities can give them.

## STUDY QUESTIONS

1.  According to Hook, are there any restrictions on the students' right to learn? If so, what are they?

2.  What should be the criteria for allowing student organizations to invite speakers to the campus? What possible problems could arise from using this criteria?

3.  In his criticism of the Free Speech Movement at the University of California, what does Hook say about the faculty and the administration?

4.  How is it that the students' freedom to learn depends on the academic free-
    dom of the faculty but the converse is not true?

5.  In Hook's view, why is it unreasonable to give students unrestricted freedom
    of speech?

## Leo Rosten

## TO AN ANGRY YOUNG MAN

Leo Rosten (1908–      ), author and political scientist, earned his under-
graduate and his graduate degrees at the University of Chicago. He has
taught at the University of Chicago and the University of California
(Berkeley). At present he is a special correspondent and education adviser
for *Look* magazine. His books include *The Washington Correspondents*,
*The Education of Hyman Kaplan*, *The Straight Places*, *Hollywood: the
Movie Colony*, *The Movie Makers*, *The Dark Corner*, *The Return of
Hyman Kaplan*, *Captain Newman, M.D.*, *The Story Behind the Painting*,
*The Many Worlds of Leo Rosten*, and *A Most Private Intrigue*. A prolific
and versatile writer, as this list of books indicate, Rosten also is a regular
contributor to journals and magazines.

I HAVE BEEN GETTING lusty cheers and jeers for a rueful little paragraph I recently wrote about student riots. The
most eloquent (and savage) letter ended: "Drop dead!!!"
Another diatribe was signed "Columbia Senior." I wish I knew where to
send this reply to both:

Dear?:
    It will upset you to learn that I agree with many things you said. For in-
stance: "Don't question our sincerity!" I don't. You are about as sincere as
anyone can be. You are sincerely unhappy, sincerely frustrated and sincerely confused. You are also sincerely wrong about the few facts you cite,
and sincerely illogical in the violent conclusions you reach. Besides, what
does "sincerity" have to do with issues? Any insane asylum is full of sincere

patients. Hitler was undoubtedly sincere. So are the followers of Voliva, who think the world is sincerely flat.

I sadly agree that your college courses have been "outrageously irrelevant to the times"—because your letter reveals that you could not pass a freshman exam in at least three fields in which you pass such sweeping judgments: economics, history, political theory.

You say, "Destroy a system that has not abolished unemployment, exploitation and war!" By the same reasoning, you should blow up all hospitals (and perhaps execute all doctors, biologists and researchers): they have not abolished disease.

Before you destroy a system, propose another that *will* solve (not hide, shift or disguise) unemployment, "exploitation," war. Anyone can promise Utopia—without specifying a program. Tom Hayden, idol of the New Left, has said: "First we'll make the revolution—then we'll find out what for." Would you employ a plumber who rips out all the pipes in your house before he learned how to repair a leak?

You say, "The mass media are not telling us the truth." Then how and from whom did *you* learn the "evils" you correctly deplore? After all, your information comes from one or another organ of—the mass media.

"This society is only interested in higher prices and profits!" You apparently do not understand this society, or *a* society, or the function of prices (and profits) in *any* economy. Has it never occurred to you that the marketplace is a polling booth? That buying is voting? That no economic system is possible without *some* form of pricing, without some measure of efficacy or worth? Has it never occurred to you that profits are a form of *proof* (that something gives satisfaction to those who pay for it)? Perhaps you should examine the public *uses* that we make of private profits—through taxation.

The countries that follow your platitude, "production for use," *without exception* produce far less for their people to enjoy, of much shoddier quality, at much higher prices (measured by the hours of work needed to buy something). Don't you know that "Socialist" countries are smuggling "capitalist" incentives into their systems? Has it not dawned on you that wherever and whenever there is no free market, there is no free thought, no free art, no free politics, no free life?

You rage against "a heartless country in which the poor get poorer." Alas, poor Yoricks: The *decline* in poverty in the U.S. is among the more astonishing and hopeful facts of human history. (In 1900, about 90% of our population was poor; in 1920—50%; in 1930—34%; in 1968—15%). You will cry that 15% is outrageous. Agreed. The question is: How best abolish it? (A negative income tax makes more sense than anything your colleagues propose.)

"The middle class exploits the unemployed." Please examine that cliché. Would the middle class be worse off or better off if all the unemployed magically disappeared? Obviously, *much* better off: Think of the enormous saving in taxes, the enormous improvement in public services, the enormous benefits from refocused energies now used to ameliorate poverty's abominable toll.

You say your generation "wants to be understood." Well, so does mine. How much have you tried to understand others? You pillory us for injustices not of our making, frictions not of our choice, dilemmas that history (or our forebears or the sheer intractability of events) presented to us. You say we "failed" because you face so many awful problems. Will you then accept blame for all the problems that exist (and they will) when you are 20 years older? And how do you know that all problems are soluble? Or soluble swiftly? Or soluble peacefully? Or soluble, given the never-infinite resources, brains and experience any generation is endowed with?

I say that *you* are failing *us*—in failing to learn and respect discomforting facts; in failing to learn how to *think* (it is easier to complain); in using violence to shut down colleges; in shamefully denying the freedom of others to study and to teach; in barbarously slandering and abusing and shouting down those who disagree with you; in looting, stealing and defiling; in failing to see how much more complicated social problems are than you blindly assume; in acting out of an ignorance for which idealism is no excuse, and a hysteria for which youth is no defense. "Understanding"? You don't even understand that when you call me a "mother ------" you are projecting your unresolved incestuous wishes onto me. The technical name for such projection, in advanced form, is paranoia.

Again and again, you say, "the American people want" or "demand" or "insist." How do you know? *Every poll I have seen puts your position in a minority*. You just say, "the American people demand"—then add whatever *you* prefer. This is intellectually sloppy at best, and corrupt at worst.

You want to "wreck this slow, inefficient democratic system." It took the human race centuries of thought and pain and suffering and hard experiment to devise it. Democracy is not a "state" but a process; it is a way of solving human problems, a way of hobbling power, a way of protecting every minority from the awful, fatal tyranny of either the few or the many.

Whatever its imperfections, democracy is the only system man has discovered that makes possible *change without violence*. Do you really prefer bloodshed to debate? Quick dictates to slow law? This democracy made possible a great revolution in the past 35 years (a profound transfer of power, a distribution of wealth, an improvement of living and health) without "liquidating" millions, without suppressing free speech, without the obscenities of dogma enforced by terror.

This "slow, inefficient" system protects people like me against people like you; and (though you don't realize it) protects innocents like you against those "reactionary . . . fascist forces" you fear: They, like you, prefer "action to talk." As for "security"—at what price? The most "secure" of human institutions is a prison; would you choose to live in one?

You want "a society in which the young speak their minds against the Establishment." Where have the young more freely, recklessly and intransigently attacked "the Establishment"? (*Every* political order has one.) Wherever "our heroes—Marx, Mao, Ché" have prevailed, students, writers, teachers, scientists have been punished with hard labor or death—for what? For their opinions. Where but in "fake democracies" are mass demonstrations possible, or your bitter (and legitimate) dissent televised?

You rail against "leaders crazed with power," who "deceive the people." Your leaders are self-dramatizers who demand that power, which would craze them, and they deceive you in not telling you how they plan your "confrontations"—to force the police to use force, whose excesses I hate more than you do. *I*, unlike you, want no one put "up against the wall." No "cheap politician" more cynically deceived you than fanatical militants did—and will. Your support feeds their neurotic (because extremist) needs. Washington's " 'Non-Violent' Coordinating Committee" has engaged in gunfire for three days as I write this.

You say Marcuse "shows that capitalist freedom actually enslaves." (He doesn't "show"—he only *says*.) He certainly does not sound enslaved. And does mouthing fragments of 19th-century ideology (Marx, Bakunin) really liberate? And is not Marcuse 40 years "older than 30," your cutoff on credibility? Incidentally, would you trust your life to a surgeon under 30—who never finished medical school?

Your irrationality makes me wonder how you were ever admitted *into* Columbia. You confuse rhetoric with reasoning. Assertions are not facts. Passion is no substitute for knowledge. Slogans are not solutions. Your idealism takes no brains. And when you dismiss our differences with contempt, you become contemptible.

Very *sincerely* yours,
LEO ROSTEN

P.S. Please don't take any more courses in sociology, which seduces the immature into thinking they understand a problem if they discuss it in polysyllables. Jargon is not insight. Vocabulary is the opiate of radicals.

### STUDY QUESTIONS

1. What characterizes the author's tone in this selection? Does it appear that his intention is to antagonize?

2. The author employs a fairly conventional strategy in establishing his positions. What are the advantages of such strategy? What are the dangers?

3. If you were the Columbia Senior, what rebuttal could you offer to his reasoning in the fourth, fifth, and sixth paragraphs?

4. Does Rosten support any of his positions with arguments you find invalid or false?

*Jeremy Larner*

# ANOTHER PLANE IN ANOTHER SPHERE: THE COLLEGE DRUG SCENE

Jeremy Larner (1937–      ) was born in Olean, New York. He completed his undergraduate work at Brandeis University and attended the Graduate College of the University of California at Berkeley. He teaches at New York State University at Stony Brook, Long Island. His writings have appeared in the *Atlantic, Holiday, Nation,* and *Dissent.* He is coauthor of *The Addict in the Street.* His novel *Drive, He Said* won the Delta Award in 1965. His most recent books are *Answer* (1968), and *Poverty: Views From the Left* (1968), which he edited with Irving Howe.

Why do we try drugs? We really feel like we're limited so much. And we want to do so much. And we're always told we should try things and grow. It's part of the liberal arts education. It seems hypocritical of older people to tell us not to try certain things. We feel we can take care of ourselves.

W$_{\text{HILE THERE ARE}}$ no significant statistics—any more than there are on virginity, and for the same reasons—drug-taking is becoming increasingly popular on American campuses. A variety of drugs can now be easily obtained at any college which draws its students from metropolitan areas—which means that the problem is most acute at the biggest and best universities and at some of the most prestigious small colleges. Marijuana is generally the drug of choice: a young man from an Eastern college claims, "I have yet to see a college party anywhere in the last two years where at least one-third of the kids have not been turned on."

The local marijuana connection is usually a fellow classmate. But if a student wants other drugs, or if he uses marijuana in large quantities, he need not seek further than the circle of hangers-on who live in the university community without attending college. In brief, availability is such that nearly every contemporary student must make up his mind whether or not he wants to try drugs—because he will certainly have the chance.

For most students, marijuana is something to be tried once or twice, to see what it's like. Those who consider themselves hip with smoke reefers "socially," in the same spirit in which executives drink martinis. Of these social smokers, a few will get to the point where they are turning on every day; and it is these few who will also try other drugs—for example, amphetamine "pep pills" in quantities that can cause psychotic distortions, berserk outbreaks, and even cerebral hemorrhage. Heroin, barbiturates, and other "hard narcotics" are also available for the self-destructive; but as a rule the hip thing is to take drugs for "exploration" rather than escape.

When drug use first comes to light on a given campus, college officials tend to protect the school's reputation by expelling the culprits and even by turning them over to the police. Experienced administrators, however, are learning to make a distinction between trying drugs and selling them, and in the former case are more likely to use probation or a psychiatric referral as a means of correction. The fact that drugs are illegal does not in itself serve as a deterrent. Students of all generations have traditionally sought out forbidden activities as a valuable part of their college education. Thus choosing one's drug, or no drugs, is regarded as a personal decision, like choosing friends, books, or clothes, to be made on personal grounds quite apart from the opinions or threats of authorities.

The modern student will accept responsibility for the effects his actions have on others, but beyond that he sees all arbitrary limits as impositions of the status quo. Personal responsibility, to him, implies the freedom to take risks that involve only himself and his development. He feels that if parents and school officials really believe in that "free inquiry" which is supposedly the ideal of a liberal education, they must respect his right to conduct his own quest by his own rules.

The drugs most talked about in terms of questing are the powerfully mind-disturbing hallucinogens (peyote, mescaline, psilocybin, LSD). Most of the daily pot-smokers will sooner or later try the hallucinogens. Other students are also curious to try them, partly for "kicks," partly because they feel challenged, and partly because they are attracted by claims of mystic and psychological revelation. The most extravagant of these claims emanate from grown-up enthusiasts who are devoting their careers to popularizing the hallucinogens.

For many young Americans, college represents four years of free experiment between the restrictions of the parental family and the responsibilities of the marital family. The student is aware that every choice he makes—both occupationally and personally—may have a telling effect on the adult he will become. He is under pressure to "find himself"—and quickly.

Like other Americans, the college student may look for his "self" in the products he consumes. Universities that are organized like supermarkets will only encourage such unsatisfying searches. Students, moreover, are susceptible to an existentialist strain of the disease called "conspicuous consumption." Rerouting the pursuit of the material, they seek to consume pure experience. They hope that by choosing the right activities they can create an external confirmation of the power and beauty they would like to feel within.

Drugs, as we shall see, are products that supply the illusion of choice while they simultaneously minister to the anxieties that choosing creates. The increasing use of drugs may be seen as a reflection of an unconscious belief in the commercials that pound home the connection between a judicious drug choice and the relief of any mental or physical "symptom." Such assumptions are not easily overcome by a generation that is, after all, the first whose members are lifelong TV viewers, bombarded from infancy by suggestions of false needs.

## Marijuana

To us a muggle wasn't any more dangerous or habit-forming than those other great American vices, the five-cent Coke and the ice-cream cone, only it gave you more kicks for your money.

Us vipers began to know that we had a gang of things in common: we ate like starved cannibals who finally latch on to a missionary, and we laughed a whole lot and lazed around in an easygoing way, and we all decided that the muta had some aphrodisiac qualities too. . . . All the puffed-up strutting little people we saw around, jogging their self-important way along so chesty and chumpy, plotting and scheming and getting more wrinkled and jumpy all the time,. made us all howl. . . . We were on another plane in another sphere compared to the musicians who were bottle babies, always hitting the jug and then coming up brawling after they got loaded. We liked things to be easy and relaxed, mellow and mild, not loud or loutish, and the scowling chin-out tension of the lushhounds with their false courage didn't appeal to us.

This classic description—from *Really the Blues* (1946) by Mezz Mezzrow and Bernard Wolfe—will serve to convey the general relaxation of the marijuana high and the good fellowship which prevails in the society of satisfied vipers. The *LaGuardia Report*—published in 1944 and still the standard scientific text on the subject—confirms that marijuana is non-addicting. The *Report* warns that marijuana taken in excess may produce anxiety as well as pleasant feelings, and that psychotic episodes are not un-heard-of when the batch is strong and the smoker sensitive. The pleasurable response to pot is to some extent learned, and an experienced smoker will not continue once he has obtained the desired sensations. To quote the *Report:* "The description of the 'tea-pad parties' brings out clearly the convivial effect . . . and the absence of any rough or antagonistic behavior."

Obviously college administrators could not sanction pot, even if it were legal, any more than they sanction drinking. But students are contemptuous of the usual line about marijuana leading to heroin addiction. Since heroin is a depressant, its effects are entirely different from those described above, and are sought after by a different kind of person, one who is characteristically dissatisfied with marijuana. Commentators may fasten on the fact that heroin addicts "began" with pot, but it is just as accurate to say that they "began" with liquor. For most heroin addicts have at one time tried liquor as well as pot—and rejected both.

Since pot is outlawed, however, sooner or later a pot-smoker will come in contact with a connection who has other drugs for sale. This, to many students, represents the crucial difference between alcohol and marijuana. One drug is surrounded by accepted rituals, while consumption of the other is ipso facto connected with lawbreaking. Many feel that if marijuana were legalized, society would develop appropriate and enjoyable attitudes toward it. They feel that the comparison with alcohol is all in marijuana's favor. The White House Conference on Narcotic and Drug Abuse referred to alcohol as "the outstanding addictive drug in the United States." The country's five million alcoholics suffer from cirrhosis, nervous diseases, and even brain damage. Nicotine, too, has addictive properties, and cigarettes made from tobacco can cause lung cancer; whereas the *LaGuardia Report* tells us that "those who have been smoking marijuana for a period of years showed no mental or physical deterioration which may be attributed to the drug."

The upshot of misinformed fulminations about marijuana is that students in the know feel a certain superiority. They're entitled to smile when subjected to the liquor industry's 200-million-dollar annual barrage of advertising designed to link alcoholic intake with happiness, youth, and social power. They feel their product is better, cheaper, and less dangerous. And once they've tried pot and discovered that official warnings are based more on panic than fact, they are in a position to discredit apprehensions about any drug whatever.

## The Hallucinogens

The hallucinogens—of which the laboratory synthetic LSD is by far the most powerful—produce a stunning impact on the mind. Distortions of time and space, intense color phenomena, and delusions of death and grandeur are commonly experienced. All sorts of thoughts, feelings, memories, fears, dreams, and images are released, often with an overlay of euphoria. Some psychiatrists see the hallucinogens as potentially useful in the treatment of various mental disorders, though most regard the experimental work in this field to date as inconclusive. Psychoanalysts have for years rejected techniques of artificial release—such as hypnotism and "truth serums"—on the grounds that psychoanalysis is not identical with the mere unearthing of material.

LSD cultists feel that under the effect of a hallucinogen, the mind activates inborn knowledge long "repressed" by civilization, knowledge which reveals the mystic "oneness" of the universe. The individual personality is supposedly dissolved in "The Void," where space and time vanish and all is impersonal "ecstasy." This experience, along with the emergence of "repressed" psychic material, is supposed to help the individual gain a transcendent perspective with which to reorient himself to the "illusory" world of earthbound humanity.

It is claimed that the regular use of LSD increases individual development and lovingness toward others, and that therefore the drug should be freely available. An LSD millennium is seen as inevitable, bringing with it the dissolution of human conflict and the recognition of the cult leaders as prophets of a scientific, philosophic, and historical "breakthrough."

Most psychiatrists, however, are wary of dangerous reactions to the hallucinogens. There are many verified reports of students in whom a hallucinatory drug touched off a latent psychosis so severe that hospitalization was required. Prolonged psychotic states, depression, recurring hallucinations, and suicide attempts (some successful) have resulted from the use of LSD—in some cases months after the drug was taken. As for the effects of LSD on the personality, medical investigators have noted the following: 1) dissociation and detachment, 2) personal insensitivity, superiority, 3) religious and philosophical solipsism, 4) impulsivity, poor judgment.

These observations, to be sure, depend on the observer's point of view. One of the chief concerns of the dedicated drug-taker is precisely to repudiate the values, judgments, and most basic perceptions of the persons he believes to represent a monolithic and repressive authority. He does his best to perceive school officials, scientists, teachers, psychiatrists, and indeed anyone who does not appreciate "the drug experience," as an organized "Establishment" conspiring to suppress individual "freedom."

## *The Dedicated Drug-User*

It is now possible for a disaffected youngster to assume a highly developed role as drug-user. He usually begins with the perfection of a "cool" manner. The world is "too much"; his coolness announces that the cool one is invulnerable to involvement. He has taken the cure well in advance of the disease. To put it in consumer terms: desire is a weakness, because it expresses unfulfilled need. The cool one has found and taken the products that he needs.

To blow one's cool, then, is to reveal—to oneself as well as others—an inner lack. To maintain one's cool is to signify, "I've had it." The double meaning is intentional; for the cool one claims no great worldly future. He knows that his gestures are stylized; his pride is the masterly knowledge that in this world of appearances, style is all that matters. Unlike others whom he sees as self-deluded, the cool one suits his actions to his ideas. He has found a philosophy simple enough to live by (almost). In this sense, he alone has achieved the academic ideal.

There is, after all, a twisted idealism involved in submitting oneself to drug experiments. Erik Erikson, in "The Problem of Ego Identity," tells us that some young people respond to environmental pressures by trying to create a "negative identity." According to Erikson, "many a late adolescent, if faced with continuing diffusion, would rather *be nobody or somebody bad, or indeed, dead—and this totally, and by free choice—than be not-quite somebody*." (Italics his.) Drugs, in these terms, provide the idealist with a chance to control his own destiny and to go all the way. There is a distorted testing mechanism at work here; Erikson speaks of "a radical search for the rock bottom . . . a deliberate search"—as if the searcher could master a sense of unworthiness by seeking out and inflicting upon himself certain selected dangers. Drugs are like Russian roulette: if you survive, you must have something going for you. It shouldn't surprise us that one of the most common, popular, and easily induced drug delusions is the fantasy of rebirth.

If one is to be reborn, one needs replacements for the mortal, fallible parents and family whose existence dictates unendurable limitations. Says Erikson, "Young people often indicate in rather pathetic ways a feeling that only a merging with a 'leader' could save them. . . . the late adolescent wants to be an apprentice or a disciple, a follower, sex mate, or patient." The contemporary campus is replete with drug-givers who will gladly initiate the yearningly incomplete student into all of the above roles. The novice is then equipped with drug priests for parents and fellow acolytes for siblings. The members of the drug family are connected not by birth and mortality, but by destiny and salvation. They reinforce their new improved personalities with ceremonial rituals, an in-group language, and—above all—the taking of the sacrament.

Before long the initiate drug-taker is in turn initiating others. Their desire directed toward him helps to confirm him in his role of "holder" and to convince him that he is indeed in possession of something worthwhile. It is to his advantage that expectation and suggestibility play a tremendous role in an individual's reaction to drugs. He himself is no longer surprised by the sensations produced by powerful drugs; he has learned to enjoy them and to interpret them in accordance with his own desires. Therefore he can guide the initiate who is panicky under his first dose of, say, a hallucinogen, can calm him with lofty wisdom, and help him explain his experience in the language of the drug ideology.

As the drug-taker becomes drug-giver, he cultivates a transcendent personality. He views the world with the secret superiority of one who has access to something better. All of you are playing a game, he says in his every gesture, but you could be saved if you'd follow me. Reality for him is no longer the uncertainty of the ordinary world but the heightened visions he experiences when high. Should his would-be disciples reject their own visions as drug-induced delusions, he informs them that they are tied up in "ego games." For him, the only criteria for interpreting drug phenomena are the phenomena themselves.

The transcendent personality is particularly useful for a student supported by his parents or a technician performing a job he despises. Ordinarily such a situation would raise a crisis of identity centered around the problem of achieving independence and self-respect. But for the true holder, serving his drug postpones the questions, Who am I? and What can I do?

Further, those dedicated to drugs have avoided the ambiguities of democratic face-to-face personal relations. Clinging to an in-group solidarity, they divide the world into sages and fools, saints and devils, holders and seekers. Richard Blum, in his book *The Utopiates,* speculates that drug proselytizers are particularly afraid of seeking and being denied. So they reverse the process, becoming tempters and rejecters. For this writer, the essential point is that both seekers and tempters are still caught up in the infantile drama of power-testing. Unable to bear a grown-up world without absolute power, they have invented that power—and invested it both in drugs and in the parental figures who oppose drugs.

## Getting Hung Up

"David" is a brilliant student at an excellent college, well aware of the advantages he's had, and aware also that much is expected of him. Here, David tells of a recent experience which caused him to give up drugs entirely:

At the beginning of this year, I felt really low, I got completely bored with school, and I felt the teachers weren't giving me anything. I had been involved with a girl, but it ended at the end of the summer. And that was one of the things that really depressed me, you know, that I couldn't find anybody. Sex became a real drive, but since none of the chicks meant anything to me, sex itself became meaningless. I just didn't know what to do with myself. So I started smoking pot every day—to the point where I was high every minute.

Grass had become a crutch all of a sudden. I turned on before I went to class, before dinner, before skiing. I felt that everything could be better. It wasn't just music and girls; it was everything.

But after a few months, I got so I was tired all the time, my mouth was dry. I wasn't doing anything but getting high, and I couldn't get high anymore. I'd been dependent on getting high, and I wanted something to change. There had to be something that would *shake* me. No people were shaking me, no ideas were shaking me, and no course was shaking me. And no experiences were shaking me, so I said, what can shake me? LSD, maybe. So I thought I'd try LSD, to see if it shakes me into something new.

At this point David contacted a disturbed young friend who had been taking drugs heavily since he was fourteen. When David arrived, his friend had taken four times what is considered a heavy dose of LSD and had been hallucinating for five days. He gave David a black market sugar cube and told him it contained a heavy dose of LSD. After swallowing the cube, David found out that it held *twice* a heavy dose. "I think he was so far out of it he knew he wasn't coming back, and he wanted to take me with him."

So I took the cube. For a while it was nice, I'd lie down on the bed, hear some music, the music would sound nice, I'd see pretty colors dancing on the wall. But the fact that new and completely different, if not contradictory, ideas kept popping up in my mind, gradually began to depress me. I kept thinking I had the Answer to Life. I'd jump into one thing, then I'd say No, that's wrong; then another thing, then No, that's wrong . . . and finally I saw that the answers were just as illusory as the colors I saw on the wall.

And when I started to feel my mind flipping out of my body, I thought, Jesus Christ, I don't care how simple the pleasures would be, I'd rather be *back there*. I'd rather be in a boring state than where I am now, because I cannot live this way, I don't want to be like this. I'll commit suicide if necessary. I thought that this was going to go on continually, and I just couldn't cope with it.

Though inside himself David felt desperately hysterical, his outer manner was so remote that he couldn't convince the college doctor he needed help. Finally, after three days of hallucinations, David found a doctor who administered an antidote.

The LSD experience caused David to reconsider his way of using marijuana:

I realized afterwards that, as a result of smoking grass, the things that had been important to me were not only no longer important, I was incapable of doing them. I couldn't write, I couldn't think. I couldn't carry on normal relations with people. I saw how much time I'd been wasting. I mean, I sort of knew it all along. But when I took the LSD, I just had three days of intense fear and running around and nervous energy, and when I was brought back to earth, I said, God, your whole last few years have been like this! You haven't been doing anything; you've just been running around—and heading in toward a dead end. I hadn't been developing at all; I was just completely stagnant.

After telling his story, David gets into an argument with his roommate about a mutual friend who was once a brilliant musician but who now does nothing but stay high on pot all day long. David's roommate refers him to a long list of first-rate jazz musicians who are well-known vipers. David is forced to admit that the problem resides not in the marijuana itself but in the immaturity of his friend, who is "a weak, dependent person needing a crutch." The roommate presses further: isn't their musician friend just as well off staying high all day as he would be playing the piano? As long as he feels good, does it make any difference how he gets that way? David replies with some warmth:

No, my friend does *not* feel good—he could be happier with music than with pot. Because music never ceases to move and develop. Pot, instead of broadening and deepening, just becomes less than it was at the beginning. You could say the same about any drug: it's a dead end.

## The Mystique of "The Creative Experience"

Thousands of students would passionately object to David's separation of drugs and art. They would insist that drugs are indispensable for the understanding and creation of modern poetry, painting, music, fiction, and sculpture.

For reasons of social dislocation which the campus only mirrors, masses of the most confused, aimless, and sensitive young people are drawn to the arts and humanities. A common theme in the humanities is reverence for art—a reverence crudely reinforced by a society which has discovered the commodity value of culture. The student finds "great" art painstakingly analyzed by teachers who are masters of academic method. If he is not satisfied with mere learning, the student may be tempted to transcend the analysis and identify with the projected image of the artist. Art raises the possibility that one is possessed of a nonintellectual, unmeasurable, mysterious *something* that defies all academic categories. Under the circumstances, it is natural for the artistic student to be overly impressed with the notion that art is inspired by irrational mental states—even to the point where he regards insanity as a divine visitation.

For the would-be artist, drugs are a magic product advertising the separation of art from talent, time, judgment, and work. One turns on, and one has Visions. One digs music and painting with drug-heightened attention, and one has Revelations. If one tries to paint or write under the influence of drugs, the results are invariably disorganized and disappointing. Still, one has somehow been "creative." All that is necessary to call oneself an artist is to replace palpable creation with the notion of "the creative experience."

The trouble with "the creative experience" is that anyone can have it. But for those who cannot produce art itself, the drug ideology offers membership in an artistic consumer elite.

I recently met a young engineer who feels greater rapport with his girl when both are high. Every night they turn on while watching a TV movie and "really dig it." The engineer feels that everyone should smoke pot. "When I go out in the world looking for friends, the first question I ask myself is, do they smoke? Because if they don't they look at me like I'm a drug addict."

The engineer insists that he turns on not for escape but for "insight—to learn things about myself." As an example of his insight, he states that "ordinarily I have a masochistic streak: I let people get away with saying things they shouldn't. But when I'm high, I know what to answer."

The engineer's girl friend is an art student who claims she paints better when high. "I can paint and take in everything going on in the room at the same time." She enjoys the fact that so many of her friends use drugs. "You feel you're privileged—you're part of an artists' community."

College drug use reaches a peak at big city art schools. It's worth noting that at the art colleges young people in training to become fashion illustrators and advertising directors are exposed to a highly pretentious milieu. They make contact with future artists—and form an alliance between art and advertising which has proved effective in bringing visual art, more than any other, into the consumer market place. To be hip in the art world, one must now consume the newest thing in art in the same way one consumes drugs—for the latest sensation. Like "creative experience," the fabrication of "pop" art is within reach of anyone. And art fashions, like drug fashions, offer their consumers the justification of an in-group ideology.

## The American Dream

Ever since the discovery of the New World and the Frontier, Americans have been looking for an absolute truth. This truth is thought to be natural and good, yet often it is to be attained through technical developments. Our politicians reflect these assumptions whenever they resort to the apocalyptic view of history, in which the United States is to play a divinely ordained dramatic role in directing the "progress" of the rest of the world.

D. H. Lawrence once described Americans as "Some insisting on the plumbing, and some on saving the world: these being the two great American specialties." The LSD missionaries are out to do both at the same time —to save the world by tinkering with the internal plumbing. As in the drug ads, the idea is happiness and fulfillment through the ingestion of a synthesized additive. If drug evangelists combine proselytism with claims of mystic serenity, it's not because of any profound "paradox," but because they are, at bottom, American innocents.

Another American tradition—which can be encountered in any decent course in American literature—is the myth of the New Self. The myth is that a powerful experience can purge a hero of his past and release innate powers which have been hitherto suppressed by an unnatural society. The desire is to rid oneself entirely of fear and guilt. For the American student, drugs are the latest platform from which the New Self may be announced. The young user may rejoice in a mode of being which seems utterly to bypass his everyday problems in coming to terms with the world. He can occupy, for a while, "another plane in another sphere"—where everything depends upon himself and what he puts into his mouth.

Newness, by its nature, is temporary. Before long there may be a letdown, an impingement of the dreary "old" self who has survived somehow after all—then a need, as David puts it, for something to "shake" one. That something, for the modern student, is closer than the campus drugstore. It will be ready for him as often as he has to have it.

Eventually he may wonder why. Speaking of "insight"—as young "heads" are so prone to do—the deepest insight one could gain from drugs would be to discover, not one's essential greatness, but the reason one needed to take drugs in the first place. This knowledge comes from life rather than manufactured chemicals. As a matter of fact, there is a tendency for collegiate drug-users, such as David, to reach a peak and then abruptly leave the drug scene. But until an individual can understand his drug need in terms of his own psychology, drug use for him will continue to be one of those symptoms that perpetuates its causes.

## STUDY QUESTIONS

1.  What is the rhetorical effect of the way Larner begins and ends his essay?

2.  Would you describe Larner's prose voice as one that speaks with authority? How is the authority established and maintained?

3.   Do you believe he is correct in his account of why students try drugs?

4.   The author observes that most psychiatrists are wary of dangerous reactions to the hallucinogens. What are some of these reactions?

5.   What are popular views about the connection between the use of drugs and the understanding of poetry, music, and painting? What are Larner's opinions on this?

*Mark Schorer*

# TO THE WIND

Mark Schorer (1908–      ) was born in Sauk City, Wisconsin. He received his B.A. and Ph.D. from the University of Wisconsin, and his M.A. from Harvard University. He has taught in the English departments at Dartmouth College, Harvard University, and at present is Professor of English at the University of California at Berkeley. He is the author of many scholarly articles and a number of books, both fiction and nonfiction. Some of his books include *A House Too Old* (1935), *The Hermit Place* (1941), *The State of Mind* (1947), *William Blake: The Politics of Vision* (1946), *The Story* (1950), *The Wars of Love* (1954), *Sinclair Lewis: An American Life* (1961), and *World We Imagine: Selected Essays* (1968). He has been a Fulbright Scholar and a Guggenheim Fellow.

AT TWENTY-THREE, with a particular kind of education and experience, I did not know that the struggle with guilt is endless, and when I found myself embroiled in agonies of rationalization, the drama was short and factitious. If there is no other guilt, there is always the failure of imagination, which, among men, perhaps only Christ eluded.

At twenty-three, without any of the reasons one may legitimately have at fifty, I felt that childhood was the best time in life, and with empty, griefless eyes, I would look nostalgically back on my childhood as I imagined it. Only then, I thought, were you really free, without burdens; and thinking so, I would lapse into a reverie in which the world wavered into unreality and I found myself vividly reliving some trivial episode of my youth. Then I would feel that I was not merely remembering the past as something remote and vague, but actually living it, living through it as fully as the child had lived himself. Mistaking sentiment for sensuousness, I thought that I went through the past like a boy across a meadow in the sun, feeling the grass under the bare soles of his feet, the moist earth, the warm sun on his head, and in his heart the unknown song that we pretend a child forever sings.

I was remembering such a meadow when Jared Smith came to my office for the third time. A creek ran through the meadow, winding and turning, clear water running between steep banks of black earth, with shallow places where you could build a dam. I remembered a day when I followed this creek to its mouth at the river, wandering all of an afternoon along its banks in the long grass of the meadow, the earth moist and the sun warm.

Then Smith came in again, looking more grave than before. I didn't take him seriously. Too much of this sort of thing went on all of the time, and you came to expect it. Only most students were less persistent than Smith. This was the third time he had come about it, and I had grown increasingly impatient with him, so that now his state of near-hysteria did not move me. And if it had, there would still have been the fact that I could do nothing about it. His grades showed a certain average and I had turned that in for him; now the semester was over and the matter closed. Smith thought that if he could only make me see how important the thing was to him it would be easy enough for me to call someone up and say, "I've made an error. Jared Smith should have had a B instead of a C."

For the third time I tried to show him that this was impossible and I went over all his grades again, and all he kept saying was, "I see that, sir; I'm sure a C is exactly what I earned; but don't *you* see—"

Then he launched out into the whole tale again: he was a swimmer and he had given up swimming in order to put more time on his work; he broke with his fraternity in the middle of the term because it took up too much of the time that he wanted to give to his studies; he had sacrificed everything to studying and he had done well in everything except my course, but the C I gave him was enough to keep him out of the honorary society which was the only evidence he would ever have for his achievement.

"In high school they always thought I was stupid and I wanted to show them; I've got to have the grade because I've *got* to show them. You see, sir, they always thought I didn't have a brain at all, and now I've got to, I've *simply got to*—"

For the first time I began to see what an intense person he was, and at another time it might have surprised me, for I had come to think of him as a rather stolid youth. But now I was frankly bored. You read fifty or a hundred freshmen themes every week for nine months in the year and you soon find yourself without much interest in any one of your students; and you don't pay much attention to any individual's writing unless the student comes to you and takes it up with you himself. Smith had never asked for a conference, or even for any kind of casual assistance. Now I had gone over the whole matter three times and had tried each time to keep my patience, told him that I did think he was a high B student but that his writing simply didn't show it, that since the middle of the term it had been down to C and less almost consistently. Each time I said, "If you'd come to me before, we could have gone over your themes and perhaps straightened out your difficulty, but it's too late now to do anything about it except get the B next term. If you like, I'll see to it that you get another instructor, that is, if you think you'd do better with someone else—"

Against this he protested. "I know you've been fair with me, sir, but that isn't the point. The point is that you won't see now how important it is that I get a B. It means more than anything ever has, I've simply got to get it—"

I said again that he overemphasized grades, but that even if I agreed that making the honorary society was so important, I couldn't help him.

Finally he seemed to get the point. He looked at me steadily and then suddenly all the tenseness went from his body and he slumped down in the chair by my desk. He sat there for some minutes, completely dejected, staring at the floor, and at last got up and said, "All right. I'm sorry I bothered you. Thank you," and went out.

I haven't described him at all or tried to put down much about him beyond the facts of that last interview, because after he went out of my office that day, I never saw him again. And from this point on, the story is not Smith's but mine.

Late in the next afternoon a boy whom I had never seen before came rushing into my office. "You know Jared Smith?" he cried, and I, knowing somehow at once what had happened, feeling everything inside me contract in a spasm of faintness, said, "Yes, of course. Why?"

The boy stood with his mouth open, panting. "Sit down," I said.

At last it came. "His mother sent me. He committed suicide this afternoon. It's going to be in the papers—your name too. She asked me to say that the story didn't come from her and that she doesn't hold you responsible in any way."

I took hold of the edge of my desk and forced myself to say what seemed to be the most important thing at that moment, "Of course, I can't feel responsible."

A look of pain crossed the boy's blond face. He was quite young and very distressed. He said, "It's awful. It's too awful to think about!"

"Lord, yes!" I said. "You knew him well?"

He nodded.

"How did he do it?"

"Gas. There wasn't anyone at home. His mother was down-town at the movies. She came home and found him on the kitchen floor."

"Lord!"

I walked over to the window, looked down at the campus, and thought of the boy's body stretched out dead on a kitchen floor and gas still hissing from the stove. I felt myself struggling against something, I didn't know what or why, and wanted to turn round and tell his friend that I wasn't to blame, that nothing in the whole business could touch me. I did turn round, but I spoke quietly. "I'm terribly sorry. The whole thing is dreadful and please tell his mother that I can't say how sorry I am. But of course I'm *not* responsible. Any teacher is likely to have this sort of thing happen. Sometimes you can't possibly tell which students are hypersensitive, which hysterical—"

The look in the boy's face made me see that I was trying to defend myself (and before he spoke I asked myself, "Against what?"), and then he said, "He wasn't hysterical. I think you might have seen that he was sensitive." Scorn came into his eyes before he added, "But no one thinks you're to blame," and turned away from me.

Yet, when he looked back, his face was only sorrowful, his eyes bleached with loss, and when he got up to leave he offered me his hand. I thought for a second that I was going to lose my hold on the situation. Some gagged voice inside me was trying to protest that I didn't deserve this and that I couldn't be blamed. I thought that in the next moment I should be blubbering out that protest, and yet, when I took the boy's hand something else made me cold, almost rude. I said, "Thanks for coming. It was good of Mrs. Smith to send you. I don't mind the papers' running the story, because of course no one would blame me. Tell his mother how sorry I am. If she'd care to see me, I'd like very much to call." We looked at each other. His eyes were cold again, chilled by my voice.

"Good-bye," he said, and fled out as he had come, half-stumbling.

When you are young, I would keep thinking, remembering, you are free. I would think in the next three days (at night especially, and always remembering), when you are young you don't have to face such things, and that is the time. Waking in the night suddenly, feeling the presence of that boy in the room, in the shadows, somewhere in the hiding dark, I would remember such an incident as this:

*I am quite young—six or seven—and after supper one evening (it is summer; in the marshes along the river the frogs are setting up their monotonous croaking, soothing, comforting, a steady sound in the night that stabilizes the dark and makes it a friend) I leave the family assembled at table and go into a little-used parlor. I must be very tired—from a day of running in the bright, protecting sun—for I lie down on a sofa in the dark of the parlor (and this I seem never to have done before), and in the sleep that follows I hear voices and confusion and I have the feeling that there are many people somewhere near; but the voices are like the comforting croak-ing of the frogs, and I do not wake for a time, until abruptly I am snatched out of sleep and I find myself in my father's arms, and then in my mother's (and she is weeping with relief) and I see the faces of my brother and sister, looking at me with something like awe. Then slowly I awake, I see more people in the room, and I know that outside the house half the town is as-sembled. Then, from a mixed report from the whole family (breathless, broken, excited, relieved, all of it mingled with weeping and laughing, with kisses and quick embraces) I gather that I have been lost, that the whole town has been aroused, that for the two hours I have been asleep in the little-used parlor, where no one thought to look beyond a desperate glance into the dark, the search has been going on. Then all of us go out on the front porch and I am shown and the whole thing delights me. My mother still weeps beside me, remembering her fright in the midst of her happiness and gratitude.*

This was no new memory, suddenly recollected. It was part of a childhood that I lived with constantly, always there, always somehow adequate, where the memory of lying in a sun-bright meadow with the steady drone of bees in clover in my ears was enough to soften any blow. And so now again in those three days, those three nights especially, I found myself going back, not searching and yet remembering. In bed, with the ghost of that boy some-where in the room, powerful against me, I remembered this:

*Another summer day, late in the afternoon, and I am walking with an aunt to the cemetery a mile out of the village. On the way we pass a field of buckwheat, and my aunt stops in the path for a moment. "Buckwheat," she says, her arm lifted, and moves on, the flower-filled basket on her arm swinging a little as she walks, bumping now and again against her hip. At the cemetery we attend to the graves of relatives, snipping grass with the shears from the basket, pulling up weeds, arranging flowers under white headstones pink in the low summer sun, and when we start back to the vil-lage it is almost dusk. The air is very quiet now and cooler, the dust of the day settled. Once more we pass the buckwheat field and now, with a start, both of us smell in the air an incredible sweetness. We stop again and breathe the perfume of the buckwheat, stand still for perhaps five minutes —and then move on toward the village, marked in the dusk by a dozen yellow-lighted windows, friendly, home.*

But now, in the three dark nights, these memories were not strong. In the struggle that went on between the part of my brain that brought them up and the part that knew the boy was in the room, a thin ghost, pale, unhappy, accusing, the memories lost, until, on the third night, I found myself abruptly awake, sitting erect in my bed, perspiring, a scream that must have been mine echoing in my ears. In my fright I knew that I was helpless, that there was no escape from it, nothing with which to fight against it. Then my fear (and what was I fearing?) ebbed away, and I lay down again in the darkness and thought that now the boy was buried and that on the next day I would call on his mother. I would return the packet of his themes—the themes I had not dared to read again for fear that now I should see in them a whole cycle of hysteria that I had missed before, perhaps from careless reading—and then I would be done with the whole thing.

I fell asleep again. And next morning my childhood seemed far away. Now I remembered winter nights before the fire and the quiet sound of my father's voice reading aloud, but I *remembered* them only, as one remembers an image or a picture, not as something one is actually in. I remembered a pool where you fished for small perch, and a path leading up over a birch-covered hill and down to a strip of sandy beach by the river. But in these memories there was the threat of the end of something.

It was afternoon and time to go to the mother. Twice I had taken the rubber band from the packet of themes, twice brought myself to the point of reading them, but now, having decided, I stood by my desk and snapped the band firmly on the papers. I thought that if I read them and found nothing there—I remembered a theme called "War" (Jared Smith had been a pacifist) and another called "My Religious Views"—then I should be free and certain. But if I did find something there, some growing hysteria, some increasing despair (what *had* he said in the theme called "My Religious Views"?) then I might never be free. And I decided that I would rather be uncertain and slowly forget than know, and perhaps never be able to forget.

The mother let me into the apartment herself. She was a large woman, heavy and strong-looking, standing before me in the dark hall a great hulk of strength. I told her who I was and she said, "Oh-h-h," with a kind of long sigh, and then, "Please come in."

The room was all shadows and the windows were full of the gray beginning of the winter evening. The woman pulled a chair out of a corner and said, "Please sit down." Then she lit a lamp so that the light fell on me, and she stood over me, looking down, and said finally, "I didn't think of you as such a young man. I thought of you as somehow older. From Jared's accounts I thought that you'd been teaching for a long time. He felt at the end that you were treating him perfunctorily, as if every student were just another student and not a human being to you—any longer. But that could be true of the very young as well as of the older, couldn't it?"

She smiled and sat down across from me, her eyes quizzical and interested. It was almost as if I had come to have tea with her, as if in a moment we would begin to talk about literature. Her composure as she sat there made me feel my weakness.

I said, "Try to understand. We meet perhaps a hundred students a week, and we read a hundred themes, and it's difficult to do much with them individually. Especially if they don't come to you. He never did. I hardly knew him."

She leaned forward, concerned and apologetic. "Oh, I do understand that —quite! I didn't mean—"

"No, of course not. It was good of you to send the other boy to tell me. It would have been a blow if I'd just read about it in the papers or heard about it suddenly without some warning."

"Yes," she said. "I knew that."

"I've brought his themes. I thought you'd like to keep them. I can't tell you how upset I am about this."

"But, child," she said, smiling again. "I know you're not to blame. I know you couldn't have done anything about that grade. I told Jared so—"

"It isn't the grade," I said. "It's not having known him. It's not having seen in him the possibilities of the kind of hysteria that must have been behind his act. I should have seen that—if it was there. I certainly didn't. And now I don't know if it was there or not. I haven't had the courage to read his themes again, fearing that it might be. . . . Here they are." I leaned forward and gave them to her. She put them in her lap and folded her hands over them. I could see how calm she was by the steady rise and fall of her bosom, by the quiet hands in her lap.

Outside it had begun to snow very lightly. Through the window and the thin veil of snow I could see across a gray field to a bare tree standing beside a wooden fence, its empty branches reaching up into the dreary sky. I felt myself wavering away from the room and the woman across from me, to another tree in another place, an elm heavily laden with leaves, with great strong branches, with white clouds and a blue sky above it, and high in the tree somewhere, a platform with a boy lying on his stomach, reading, lost in the pages of a book, in the fabulous blue of the sky, in the almost mythical intricacies of branch and green, green leaf.

But the woman's voice wove itself into the myth (for now I knew that it was a myth, a dream of bliss that had never been, that could certainly never be again) and drew me from the imagined tree to the real tree and the dreary landscape outside, to the shadowy room, and to her hands, symbols of her quiet. She was saying, ". . . and of course, you must not let this disturb you, it might have happened to anyone. It was the merest chance that it happened to you. I hope that you will be able to see it that way. . . ."

"Yes, it might have happened to anyone else. But someone else might have seen what I failed to see, might have thought of Jared Smith as a person who was living too, who was alive, not just a hand that wrote themes, but a human being, with desires and a life to live. . . ."

(*The green of the tree, the fabulous strength of its branches, and the lost boy lost in the legend!*)

. . . with a home to go to and a childhood to remember, with burdens to bear (he bore them!) and a manhood to come to (he came to it!) . . . for if Jared Smith had ever had a childhood, he had put it behind him. He knew that it was no dream that he would meet in the hissing gas; he knew that in breathing in those fumes he was not losing himself in an impossible bliss but was taking on his burden and coming into his manhood.

The quiet voice again, ". . . always unstable, really, highly-strung, neurotic, I suppose, taking his disappointments terribly hard . . . no sense of proportion at all. . . . It was something I always feared. . . ."

Outside, the barren tree was lost in the winter evening. I got up. "I must go. It's late."

The mother rose with me. She put the packet of themes on a table and walked into the hall with me. I struggled into my coat. Then she put out her hand. "Thank you for coming."

I took her hand. It was cold. I said, "You're wonderful. Your composure—"

I felt her hand tighten in mine. She struggled to speak, and then, in a sudden, fearful sob, her voice was drowned in grief. Her whole body shook in a spasm of weeping as she sat abruptly on a little bench in the hall, weeping violently, sobs torn from her body with a fearful violence. She clamped her hands together between her knees and, swaying back and forth on the bench, spoke between her sobs, "Oh-h-h," (the long sigh tragic now) "I loved him, I loved him . . . you don't know, you don't *know* . . . there have been terrible moments . . . *you don't know!"*

The weeping of a frail, small woman I could have borne. But the racking violence of the grief in this woman, large and strong, as she sat rocking back and forth in the gloom, was more than I could bear. For a moment I had an impulse to share her grief, in the same violent sobbing to relieve myself in exhausting tears. But the second impulse was to flee, to leave her behind, to avoid the confession that tears from me would mean.

I opened the door and went out. In the street I ran through the snow and kept my head up, so that the wind could strike my face.

I ran blindly through the streets in no direction at all, and ran until my feet dragged, and yet would not stop. I pressed my eyes shut against the wind and went stumbling through drifts of snow that the sharpening wind was piling across the sidewalks. It was cold and the wind was biting, but I did not feel it. At last I came to a church, and saw it towering up into the sky, blacker than the night. I stood looking up at its great doorway and its steeple, and without thought I climbed its steps and sat down in the wide stone doorway, out of the wind. I had never been in the church, but out of some remote time I remembered nuns moving quietly across an altar, lighting tall candles, suffusing the white, glistening altar with a luminous warmth, giving to the stone images of pedestaled saints a soft, deceptive life. I had never knelt in a church, but now I thought that if I went in and knelt on a rail worn into grooves with many kneelings, if I could bury my head in my arms and empty my ears of the sound of weeping, I should find a penitent's peace. Then I began to say, "I am not to blame, God, I am *not,* I am *not . . .*" but no such peace came, and I wondered what I should do with this blame which was not mine but which I could not lose.

I thought of the confessional inside, at one side of the altar. If I could go in there and confess, and be forgiven, then I should be free again. *Confess! Confess!* something cried, some voice from the lost years, from the fabulous tree, from the fires on winter nights, some voice that came like the wind, sweeping across the sunny meadows, rippling the water of a child's dammed creek, *Confess!*

If I could confess, pour out my sins, empty myself of this pain . . . if I could!

*Confess! Confess!* the voice whistled, blowing through the branches of the unknown, the mythical tree, driving great billows of white cloud over a dream-blue sky.

But what? Confess what?

The voice answered (sadly now, soughing through the branches), *Confess . . . confess . . .*

But what? what—

Then, like an echo, weakly, from afar: *Confess . . .*

Yes, yes, but *what?*

And then the voice did not answer (*Oh, now the branches of the tree are bare and still, no longer the voice like the wind in the marvelous tree!*) and the silence tore me from that dream. I sat in the doorway, straining forward to hear an answer. But there was none and, suddenly ashamed and sobered, I leaned back against the door.

Something was ending. The desire to confess was but imagining that tree with its wonderful foliage that had never been. But the tree was dead, its branches bare, and all the lost years were dead, and the voice from the years was dead with them.

Then something had ended.

I went down the steps. The wind, sharper now than ever, came with a blast up the street, sweeping the snow before it. I stood in the empty street and let it blow at me and through me, blow the ashes of the years away into the dark sky.

Then I started back through the cold night, shivering, and resolved to go back to the woman's house. Something had ended, and I could go back to her and say that the blame was mine and that I took it, that, like her son, I had found a place to lay the burden.

The wind blew strong, scattering the years across the sky.

I went back. But nothing ends. We do not grow this way, in moments. And these moments, when self-righteousness hardens, are really the most treacherous of all. Then we exchange one naïveté for another, one dream for another dream. I had achieved the new shutters of a half-apprehended experience, the blinkers of an unreal moral courage.

Yet how was I to know, then, that the years as I imagined them scattering across the sky were as unreal as Shelley's dead and gaudy leaves of good?

## STUDY QUESTIONS

1.  Why did the author elect to tell the story in the first person instead of the third person? What is to be gained in this story by the first person point of view?

2.  What kind of boy was Jared? What are the sources in the story that give us information about Jared?

3.  Was the young instructor justified in his actions in regard to Jared?

4.  What feeling does the author expect the reader to have toward the young instructor? How is this indicated in the story?

5.  What function do the flashback memories of the young instructor have in the story?

6.  In the last two paragraphs, what does the young instructor tell us he has learned from the experience?

# Section Six

# Popular Culture

## "The Winter of Our Discontent"

*Elmo Roper*

# HOW CULTURALLY ACTIVE ARE AMERICANS?

Elmo Roper (1900–     ) was born in Hebron, Nebraska. He attended the University of Minnesota and the University of Edinburgh, and holds four honorary degrees. His distinguished record during World War II included service with the Office of Facts and Figures and the Office of Strategic Services. From 1935 to 1950 he was research director for the *Fortune Survey* of Public Service. The famed marketing consultant has taught at Columbia and serves as editor-at-large for the *Saturday Review*. His books include *You and Your Leaders* (1958).

IN AN ERA when culture is being promoted with all the enthusiasm once reserved for breakfast cereal and we are being reminded daily that ignorance is obsolete, how "cultural" are Americans? Where does learning rank in our range of interests?

The answers to some questions recently asked of a cross-section of adult Americans shed some light on our intellectual and cultural involvement. To begin with, respondents were offered a list of subjects and asked to name those in which they had "a good deal of interest." The results appear below:

| | |
|---|---|
| Religion | 49% |
| Sports | 47 |
| Music | 46 |
| Politics and government | 40 |
| International affairs | 37 |
| Cooking | 36 |
| Home decoration | 35 |
| History | 22 |
| Science | 20 |
| Literature | 19 |
| Art | 13 |
| No opinion | 7 |

Reprinted from *Saturday Review*, XLIX, May 14, 1966 by permission of the author.

Clearly, the egghead still has a long way to go before he replaces the baseball player as a national hero. Religion, sports, and music command the broadest appeal and top the list of interests. Politics and international affairs, interests that for various people have varying degrees of intellectual content, barely edge out the frankly down-to-earth concerns of home and kitchen. And at the very bottom lie the clearly intellectual and cultural subjects (with the exception of music, which may or may not reflect as deep a cultural interest), each mentioned by less than a quarter of the people interviewed: history by 22 percent, science by 20 percent, literature 19 percent, with art trailing off at 13 percent.

The next question inquired how often people read books that they felt would "advance their knowledge or education in some way." Twenty-two percent replied "frequently," 29 percent said they did so "occasionally," and 46 percent said "rarely" or "never." Another question found that 35 percent had less than twenty-five books in the home, and another 35 percent between twenty-five and 100, with only 27 percent owning more than 100 books (3 percent didn't know). Other questions also were asked about newspaper and magazine reading, and educational achievement.

Who, then, are the culturally and intellectually involved? Needless to say, the various indices do not all work in the same direction. While the heavy book *readers* are apt to be found among the young (20–34), the heaviest book *ownership* comes at a later age (35–55). Interest in international affairs goes up with age; interest in science is higher with youth. Among the intellectually involved, traditional sex differences in interests are very much in evidence, with women leaning toward such subjects as art and literature, men toward science and politics.

But perhaps the most interesting difference is that women, particularly college-educated women, have *more* interests than men. On the list of interests, seven items were singled out as subjects of a "good deal of interest" by 50 percent or more of college women. Among college men, only three items elicited that degree of interest. Also, the low point of intellectual interest for college women is science, which nevertheless is called interesting by 24 percent. The cultural "low" of college men is art, which at 18 percent is comparable with their interest in the female realm of home decorating (16 percent) and cooking (10 percent).

To get a rough measure of the general level of cultural and intellectual activity in the population, a scale was developed on which each respondent was given a score. Respondents were given one point each for such activities as regular reading of two or more newspapers or "fairly regular" reading of any leading news magazine or magazines with intellectual content such as *Harper's,* the *New Yorker,* or *Saturday Review;* one point each for expressing a "good deal of interest" in politics and government, international affairs, art, history, science or literature; five points each for "frequent" reading of books to advance knowledge or having more than 100 books in the home; two points for attending college; five points for graduating; and five points for taking academic, business or professional courses since graduating from college—with a maximum possible score of thirty-five points.

Using this measure of what might be loosely described as the "level of cultural activity," respondents fell into four main groups. Fifty-one percent received scores of from zero to three, and might be described as the "culturally inert." Another 26 percent received scores of from four to nine, and might therefore be considered "fairly inactive" culturally. Thirteen percent received scores of from ten to fifteen, and might be described as "fairly active." Only 10 percent received scores over fifteen (out of a possible thirty-five), thereby gaining the description of "culturally active"—the term is relative!

What is the relationship between cultural activity and formal education? If you're culturally active, does it mean you've been to college? And if you've been to college, are you thereby culturally active?

The answer to the first question is, by and large, yes. Only 1 percent of grade school people and only 4 percent of the high school educated fell into the culturally active category, whereas 26 percent of those who had had some college and 62 percent of people with college degrees received culturally active scores (abetted, of course, by the credit given for college in their scores).

But the answer to the second question is another thing. Before everyone who's been to college starts resting on his cultural laurels, thinking of the great gap that separates him from the lowly people who make up the rest of the population, let him take a look at the ranking of interests by those with college backgrounds:

Has a good deal of interest in:

| | |
|---|---|
| International affairs | 60% |
| Politics and government | 59 |
| Music | 56 |
| Sports | 53 |
| Religion | 49 |
| Literature | 39 |
| History | 37 |
| Science | 36 |
| Home decoration | 36 |
| Cooking | 31 |
| Art | 26 |

Political and international events replace religion, sports and music as the prime interests of the college educated. But pure cultural and intellectual interests still cluster, along with cooking and home décor, at the bottom of the list. Asked how often they read edifying books, 44 percent of college educated people answered "frequently"—which means that a majority read to learn infrequently after they leave the academic groves. Asked about book ownership (an easier test than book reading, and the books could be about anything), nearly one quarter (23 percent) of the college educated had less than fifty books in their homes, and just slightly over half (56 percent) owned more than 100 books.

All in all, it must be said that intellectual and cultural activity is still distinctly a minority taste. A college education is no guarantee of developed cultural or intellectual interests, although it certainly makes such interests more probable. In our national rush to get more and more people to college, it should perhaps be kept in mind that half the people who have gotten there show only minor intellectual after-effects. Regarding the other half who can be described as culturally and intellectually involved, the most important question is one that can not be answered by a survey. It is the depth and quality of that involvement.

Some years ago I wrote, "There is an urgent need—in fact a national survival need—for invigorating intellectual life, for upgrading the general regard for intellectual excellence. The United States must experience an intellectual renaissance or it will experience defeat. The time cannot be far off—if indeed it is not already here—when the *strength* of a nation, measured in terms of any kind of world competition, will depend less on the number of its bombs than on the number of its learned men."

The statement is equally valid today. Unquestionably, there have been changes in recent years in our attitude toward the intellectual life. But the changes have not gone far enough. There is no upsurge of intellectual interest in the young—except in the field of science. And too many people who consider themselves educated have really just gone through the motions. The question that should most concern our educators is not how far they can spread learning but how deep it goes.

## STUDY QUESTIONS

1.  Which of the subjects in Roper's list does he consider "cultural"? Are there any subjects you would add to the list?

2.  Why does Roper make a distinction between book *owners* and book *readers?* How do you account for the fact that the heavy book readers are between the ages of 20 and 24?

3. Roper lists three magazines "with intellectual content": *Harper's,* the *New Yorker,* and the *Saturday Review.* Having examined a copy of each of these magazines, do you agree? Does *Playboy* have intellectual content?

4. Does Roper in any way suggest that his rating scale is not an accurate measure of what it is supposed to measure?

5. What conclusions does Roper draw from his survey? Can you suggest other conclusions?

# *Frank Lloyd Wright*

## TALIESIN

Frank Lloyd Wright (1869–1959) was born at Richland Center, Wisconsin. He has been called "the greatest of all architects" as a result of the nearly 500 structures he designed and saw completed between 1890 and 1959. He was educated by serving as chief assistant to famed Chicago architect, Louis H. Sullivan. Founder of the "Prairie School" of architecture, he was first successful in Europe, particularly in Germany, where his works were published in 1910. For six years he lived in Tokyo, the site of one of his most famous structures—The Imperial Hotel. Among his other works are New York's Guggenheim Museum and the Johnson and Son administration building and tower. His books include *Modern Architecture* (1931), *An Autobiography* and *The Disappearing City* (1932), *Architecture and Modern Life* (1937), *An Organic Architecture* (1939), *A Testament* (1957), and *The Natural House* (1959).

TALIESIN WAS the name of a Welsh poet, a druid-bard who sang to Wales the glories of fine art. Many legends cling to that beloved reverend name in Wales.

Richard Hovey's charming masque, "Taliesin," had just made me acquainted with his image of the historic bard. Since all my relatives had Welsh names for their places, why not Taliesin for mine? . . . Literally the Welsh word means "shining brow."

This hill on which Taliesin now stands as "brow" was one of my favorite places when as a boy looking for pasque flowers I went there in March sun while snow still streaked the hillsides. When you are on the low hill-crown you are out in mid-air as though swinging in a plane, the Valley and two others dropping away from you leaving the tree-tops standing below all about you. And "Romeo and Juliet" still stood in plain view over to the southeast. The Hillside Home School was just over the ridge.

As a boy I had learned to know the ground-plan of the region in every line and feature. For me now its elevation is the modeling of the hills, the weaving and the fabric that clings to them, the look of it all in tender green or covered with snow or in full glow of summer that bursts into the glorious blaze of autumn. I still feel myself as much a part of it as the trees and birds and bees are, and the red barns. Or as the animals are, for that matter.

When family-life in Oak Park that spring of 1909 conspired against the freedom to which I had come to feel every soul was entitled, I had no choice, would I keep my self-respect, but go out a voluntary exile into the uncharted and unknown. Deprived of legal protection, I got my back against the wall in this way. I meant to live if I could an unconventional life. I turned to this hill in the Valley as my Grandfather before me had turned to America—as a hope and haven. But I was forgetful, for the time being, of Grandfather's Isaiah. His smiting and punishment.

And architecture by now was quite mine. It had come to me by actual experience and meant something out of this ground we call America. Architecture was something in league with the stones of the field, in sympathy with "the flower that fadeth and the grass that withereth." It had something of the prayerful consideration for the lilies of the field that was my gentle grandmother's: something natural to the great change that was America herself.

It was unthinkable to me, at least unbearable, that any house should be put *on* that beloved hill.

I knew well that no house should ever be *on* a hill or *on* anything. It should be *of* the hill. Belonging to it. Hill and house should live together each the happier for the other. That was the way everything found round about was naturally managed except when man did something. When he added his mite he became imitative and ugly. Why? Was there no natural house? I felt I had proved there was. Now I wanted a *natural* house to live in myself. I scanned the hills of the region where the rock came cropping out in strata to suggest buildings. How quiet and strong the rock-ledge masses looked with the dark red cedars and white birches, there, above the green slopes. They were all part of the countenance of southern Wisconsin.

I wished to be part of my beloved southern Wisconsin, too. I did not want to put my small part of it out of countenance. Architecture, after all, I have learned—or before all, I should say—is no less a weaving and a fabric than the trees are. And as anyone might see, a beech tree is a beech tree. It isn't trying to be an oak. Nor is a pine trying to be a birch, although each makes the other more beautiful when seen together.

The world had had appropriate buildings before—why not appropriate buildings now, more so than ever before? There must be some kind of house that would belong to that hill, as trees and the ledges of rock did; as Grandfather and Mother had belonged to it in their sense of it all.

There must be a natural house, not natural as caves and log-cabins were natural, but native in spirit and the making, having itself all that architecture had meant whenever it was alive in times past. Nothing at all I had ever seen would do. This country had changed all that old building into something inappropriate. Grandfather and Grandmother were something splendid in themselves that I couldn't imagine living in any period-houses I had ever seen or the ugly ones around there. Yes, there was a house that hill might marry and live happily with ever after. I fully intended to find it. I even saw for myself what it might be like. And I began to build it as the brow of that hill.

It was still a very young faith that undertook to build that house. It was the same faith, though, that plants twigs for orchards, vineslips for vineyards, and small whips to become beneficent shade trees. And it planted them all about!

I saw the hill-crown back of the house as one mass of apple trees in bloom, perfume drifting down the Valley, later the boughs bending to the ground with red and white and yellow spheres that make the apple tree no less beautiful than the orange tree. I saw plum trees, fragrant drifts of snow-white in the spring, loaded in August with blue and red and yellow plums, scattering them over the ground at a shake of the hand. I saw the rows on rows of berry bushes, necklaces of pink and green gooseberries hanging to the under side of the green branches. I saw thickly pendent clusters of rubies like tassels in the dark leaves of the currant bushes. I remembered the rich odor of black currants and looked forward to them in quantity.

Black cherries? White cherries? Those too.

There were to be strawberry beds, white, scarlet and green over the covering of clean wheat-straw.

And I saw abundant asparagus in rows and a stretch of great sumptuous rhubarb that would always be enough. I saw the vineyard now on the south slope of the hill, opulent vines loaded with purple, green and yellow grapes. Boys and girls coming in with baskets filled to overflowing to set about the rooms, like flowers. Melons lying thick in the trailing green on the hill slope. Bees humming over all, storing up honey in the white rows of hives beside the chicken yard.

And the herd that I would have! The gentle Holsteins and a monarch of a bull—a sleek glittering decoration of the fields and meadows as they moved about, grazing. The sheep grazing too on the upland slopes and hills, the plaintive bleat of little white lambs in spring.

Those grunting sows to turn all waste into solid gold.

I saw the spirited, well-schooled horses, black horses and chestnut mares with glossy coats and splendid strides, being saddled and led to the mounting-block for rides about the place and along the country lanes I loved —the best of companionship alongside. I saw sturdy teams ploughing in the fields. There would be the changing colors of the slopes, from seeding time to harvest. I saw the scarlet comb of the rooster and his hundreds of hens—their white eggs and the ducks upon the pond. Geese, too, and swans floating upon the water in the shadow of the trees.

I looked forward to peacocks Javanese and white on the low roofs of the buildings or calling from the walls of the courts. And from the vegetable gardens I walked into a deep cavern in the hill—modern equivalent of the rootcellar of my grandfather. I saw its wide sand floor planted with celery, piled high with squash and turnips, potatoes, carrots, onions, parsnips. Cabbages wrapped in paper and hanging from the roof. Apples, pears and grapes stored in wooden crates walled the cellar from floor to roof. And cream! All the cream the boy had been denied. Thick—so lifting it in a spoon it would float like an egg on the fragrant morning cup of coffee or ride on the scarlet strawberries.

Yes, Taliesin should be a garden and a farm behind a real workshop and a good home.

I saw it all, and planted it all and laid the foundation of the herd, flocks, stable and fowl as I laid the foundation of the house.

All these items of livelihood came back—improved from boyhood.

And so began a "shining brow" for the hill, the hill rising unbroken above it to crown the exuberance of life in all these rural riches.

There was a stone quarry on another hill a mile away, where the yellow sand-limestone uncovered lay in strata like outcropping ledges in the façades of the hills. The look of it was what I wanted for such masses as would rise from these native slopes. The teams of neighboring farmers soon began hauling the stone over to the hill, doubling the teams to get it to the top. Long cords of this native stone, five hundred or more from first to last, got up there ready to hand, as Father Larson, the old Norse stone mason working in the quarry beyond, blasted and quarried it out in great flakes. The slabs of stone went down for pavements of terraces and courts. Stone was sent along the slopes into great walls. Stone stepped up like ledges on to the hill and flung long arms in any direction that brought the house to the ground. The ground! My Grandfather's ground. It was lovingly felt as intimate in all this.

Finally it was not so easy to tell where pavements and walls left off and ground began. Especially on the hill-crown, which became a low-walled garden above the surrounding courts, reached by stone steps walled into the slopes. A clump of fine oaks that grew on the hilltop stood untouched on one side above the court. A great curved stone-walled seat enclosed the space just beneath them, and stone pavement stepped down to a spring or fountain that welled up into a pool at the center of the circle. Each court had its fountain and the winding stream below had a great dam. A thick stone wall was thrown across it, to make a pond at the very foot of the hill and raise the water in the valley to within sight from Taliesin. The water below the falls thus made was sent by hydraulic ram up to a big stone reservoir built into the higher hill, just behind and above the hilltop garden, to come down again into the fountains and go on down to the vegetable gardens on the slopes below the house.

Taliesin, of course, was to be an architect's workshop, a dwelling as well, for young workers who would come to assist. And it was a farm cottage for the farm help. Around a rear court were to be farm buildings, for Taliesin was to be a complete living unit genuine in point of comfort and beauty, yes, from pig to proprietor. The place was to be self-sustaining if not self-sufficient, and with its domain of two hundred acres was to be shelter, food, clothes and even entertainment within itself. It had to be its own light-plant, fuelyard, transportation and water system.

Taliesin was to be recreation ground for my children and their children perhaps for many generations more. This modest human programme in terms of rural Wisconsin arranged itself around the hilltop in a series of four varied courts leading one into the other, the courts all together forming a sort of drive along the hillside flanked by low buildings on one side and by flower gardens against the stone walls that retained the hill-crown on the other.

The hill-crown was thus saved and the buildings became a brow for the hill itself. The strata of fundamental stone-work kept reaching around and on into the four courts, and made them. Then stone, stratified, went into the lower house walls and up from the ground itself into the broad chimneys. This native stone prepared the way for the lighter plastered construction of the upper wood-walls. Taliesin was to be an abstract combination of stone and wood as they naturally met in the aspect of the hills around about. And the lines of the hills were the lines of the roofs, the slopes of the hills their slopes, the plastered surfaces of the light wood-walls, set back into shade beneath broad eaves, were like the flat stretches of sand in the river below and the same in color, for that is where the material that covered them came from.

The finished wood outside was the color of gray tree-trunks in violet light.

The shingles of the roof surfaces were left to weather silver-gray like the tree branches spreading below them.

The chimneys of the great stone fireplaces rose heavily through all, wherever there was a gathering place within, and there were many such places. They showed great rock-faces over deep openings inside.

Outside they were strong, quiet, rectangular rock-masses bespeaking strength and comfort within.

Country masons laid all the stone with the stone-quarry for a pattern and the architect for a teacher. The masons learned to lay the walls in the long, thin, flat ledges natural to the quarry, natural edges out. As often as they laid a stone they would stand back to judge the effect. They were soon as interested as sculptors fashioning a statue; one might imagine they were as they stepped back, head cocked one side, to get the general effect. Having arrived at some conclusion they would step forward and shove the stone more to their liking, seeming never to tire of this discrimination. Many of them were artistic for the first time, and liked it. There were many masons from first to last, all good. Perhaps old Dad Signola, in his youth a Czech, was the best of them until Philip Volk came. Philip worked away five years at the place as it grew from year to year—for it will never be finished. And with not much inharmonious discrepancy, one may see each mason's individuality in his work at Taliesin to this day. I frequently recall the man as I see his work.

At that time, to get this mass of material to the hilltop meant organizing man and horse-power. Trucks came along years later. Main strength and awkwardness, directed by commanding intelligence, got the better of the law of gravitation by the ton as sand, stone, gravel and timber went up into appointed places. Ben Davis was commander of these forces at this time. Ben was a creative cusser. He had to be. To listen to Ben back of all this movement was to take off your hat to a virtuoso. Men have cussed between every word, but Ben split the words and artistically worked in an oath between every syllable. One day Ben with five of his men was moving a big rock that suddenly got away from its edge and fell over flat, catching Ben's big toe. I shuddered for that rock as, hobbling slowly back and forth around it, Ben hissed and glared at it, threatening, eyeing and cussing it. He rose to such heights, plunged to such depths of vengeance as I had never suspected, even in Ben. No Marseillaise nor any damnation in the mouth of a Mosaic prophet ever exceeded Ben at this high spot in his career as a cusser. William Blake says exuberance is beauty. It would be profane perhaps to say that Ben at this moment was sublime. But he was.

And in Spring Green (the names in the region are mostly simple like Black Earth, Blue Mounds, Cross Plains, Lone Rock, Silver Creek) I found a carpenter. William Weston was a natural carpenter. He was a carpenter such as architects like to stand and watch work. I never saw him make a false or unnecessary movement. His hammer, extra light with a handle fashioned by himself, flashed to the right spot every time like the rapier of an expert swordsman. He with his nimble intelligence and swift sure hand was a gift to any architect. That William stayed with and by Taliesin through trials and tribulations the better part of fourteen years. America turns up a good mechanic around in country places every so often. Billy was one of them.

Winter came. A bitter one. The roof was on, plastering done, windows in, men working now inside. Evenings the men grouped around the open fire-places, throwing cord-wood into them to keep warm as the cold wind came up through the floor boards. All came to work from surrounding towns and had to be fed and bedded down on the place somewhere during the week. Saturday nights they went home with money for the week's work in pocket, or its equivalent in groceries and fixings from the village. Their reactions were picturesque. There was Johnnie Vaughn who was, I guess, a genius. I got him because he had gone into some kind of concrete business with an-other Irishman for a partner, and failed. Johnnie said, "We didn't fail sooner because we didn't have more business." I overheard this lank genius, he was looking after the carpenters, nagging Billy Little, who had been fore-man of several jobs in the city for me. Said Johnnie, "I built this place off a shingle." "Huh," said Billy, "that ain't nothin'. I built them places in Oak Park right off'd the air." No one ever got even a little over the rat-like per-spicacity of that little Billy Little.

Workmen never have enough drawings or explanations no matter how many they get—but this is the sort of slander an architect needs to hear occasionally.

The workmen took the work as a sort of adventure. It was adventure. In every realm. Especially in the financial realm. I kept working all the while to make the money come. It did. And we kept on inside with plenty of clean soft wood that could be left alone pretty much in plain surfaces. The stone, too, strong and protective inside, spoke for itself in certain piers and walls.

Inside floors, like the outside floors, were stone-paved or if not were laid with wide, dark-streaked cypress boards. The plaster in the walls was mixed with raw sienna in the box, went onto the walls natural, drying out tawny gold. Outside, the plastered walls were the same but grayer with cement. But in the *constitution* of the whole, in the way the walls rose from the plan and spaces were roofed over, was the chief interest of the whole house. The whole was supremely natural. The rooms went up into the roof, tent-like, and were ribanded overhead with marking-strips of waxed, soft wood. The house was set so sun came through the openings into every room sometime during the day. Walls opened everywhere to views as the windows swung out above the treetops, the tops of red, white and black oaks and wild cherry trees festooned with wild grape-vines. In spring, the perfume of the blos-soms came full through the windows, the birds singing there the while, from sunrise to sunset—all but the several white months of winter.

I wanted a home where icicles by invitation might beautify the eaves. So there were no gutters. And when the snow piled deep on the roofs and lay drifted in the courts, icicles came to hang staccato from the eaves. Prismatic crystal pendants sometimes six feet long, glittered between the landscape and the eyes inside. Taliesin in winter was a frosted palace roofed and walled with snow, hung with iridescent fringes, the plate-glass of the windows shone bright and warm through it all as the light of the huge fire-places lit them from the firesides within, and streams of wood-smoke from a dozen such places went straight up toward the stars.

The furnishings inside were simple and temperate. Thin tan-colored flax rugs covered the floors, later abandoned for the severer simplicity of the stone pavements and wide boards. Doors and windows were hung with modest, brown checkered fabrics. The furniture was home-made of the same wood as the trim, and mostly fitted into the trim. I got a compliment on this from old Dan Davis, a rich and "savin' " Welsh neighbor who saw we had made it ourselves. "Gosh-dang it, Frank," he said. "Ye're savin' too, ain't ye?" Although Mother Williams, another neighbor, who came to work for me, said "Savin'? He's nothin' of the sort. He could 'ave got it most as cheap ready-made from that Sears and Roebuck . . . I know."

A house of the North. The whole was low, wide and snug, a broad shelter seeking fellowship with its surroundings. A house that could open to the breezes of summer and become like an open camp if need be. With spring came music on the roofs, for there were few dead roof-spaces overhead, and the broad eaves so sheltered the windows that they were safely left open to the sweeping, soft air of the rain. Taliesin was grateful for care. Took what grooming it got with gratitude and repaid it all with interest.

Taliesin's order was such that when all was clean and in place its countenance beamed, wore a happy smile of well-being and welcome for all.

It was intensely human, I believe.

Although, thanks to "bigger and better publicity" among those who besieged it Saturdays and Sundays from near and far, came several characteristic ladies whose unusual enterprise got them as far as the upper half of the Dutch door, standing open to the living room. They couldn't see me. I was lying on a long walled-seat just inside. They poked in their heads and looked about with Oh's and Ah's. A pause. In the nasal twang of the more aggressive one, "I wonder . . . I wonder, now, if I'd like living in a regular home?"

The studio, lit by a bank of tall windows to the north, really was a group of four studies, one large, three small. And in their midst stood a stone fireproof vault for treasures. The plans, private papers, and such money as there was, took chances anywhere outside it. But the Taliesin library of Genroku embroidery and antique colored wood-block prints all stayed safely inside. As work and sojourn overseas continued, Chinese pottery and sculpture and Momoyama screens overflowed into the rooms where, in a few years, every single object used for decorative accent became an "antique" of rare quality.

If the eye rested on some ornament it could be sure of worthy entertainment. Hovering over these messengers to Taliesin from other civilizations and thousands of years ago, must have been spirits of peace and good-will? Their figures seemed to shed fraternal sense of kinship from their places in the stone or from the broad ledges where they rested.

Yes. It all actually happened as I have described it. It is all there now.

But the story of Taliesin, after all, is old: old as the human spirit. These ancient figures were traces of that spirit, left behind in the human procession as Time went on its way. They now came forward to rest and feel at home, that's all. So it seemed as you looked at them. But they were only the story within the story: ancient comment on the New.

The New lived for itself for their sake, as long ago they had lived, for its sake.

The storms of the north broke over the low-sweeping roofs that now sheltered a life in which hope purposefully lived at earnest work. The lightning in this region, always so crushing and severe, crashed (Isaiah) and Taliesin smiled. Taliesin was minding its own business, living up to its own obligations and to the past it could well understand. But the New, failing to recognize it as its own, still pursued and besieged, traduced and insulted it. Taliesin raged, wanted to talk back—and smiled. Taliesin was a "story" and therefore it and all in it had to run the gauntlet. But steadily it made its way through storm and stress, enduring all threats and slanderous curiosity for more than three years, and smiled—always. No one entering and feeling the repose of its spirit could ever believe in the storm of publicity that kept breaking outside because a kindred spirit—a woman—had taken refuge there for life.

## STUDY QUESTIONS

1. Where did Taliesin get its name? Was it an appropriate name for Wright's new school?

2. What does Wright mean in his statement that a house should not be *on* a hill, but *of* a hill? What details in Wright's description of Taliesin indicate that his architects' workshop was indeed *of* the hill?

3. Did Wright permit his workmen to be "creative" as they labored on Taliesin?

4. What storms does Wright discuss in his last paragraph?

5. Is there a rhetorical principle behind Wright's use of sentence fragments and one-sentence fragments?

*Ashley Montagu*

# FRANK LLOYD WRIGHT

Ashley Montagu (1905–    ) was born in England and became a United States citizen in 1940. An anthropologist and social biologist, he was educated at the Universities of London and Florence, and received his Ph.D. from Columbia University in 1937. He has taught at New York University, Rutgers-The State University, and the New School for Social Research. Since 1930 he has served as a legal expert on scientific problems related to race and, in 1949, helped draft the UNESCO statement on race. Among his books are *Coming into Being Among Australian Aborigines* (1937), *Man's Most Dangerous Myth: The Fallacy of Race* (1942), *The Natural Superiority of Women* (1953), *Life Before Birth* (1964), *The Idea of Race* (1965), and *Man and His First Two Million Years: A Brief Introduction to Anthropology* (1969).

THE LIFE of Frank Lloyd Wright as an architect could well serve as the point of departure for a discussion of what is both right and what is wrong with Americans. I do not say "with American judgment" or "American critical taste," for much more is involved than that. Wright, like the land of which he was a product, was full of promises, potential talents which by their very prodigality endangered their possessor. Talents require discipline, and the greater the talents, the greater the discipline required. What is talent? It is involvement. But involvement is not enough. What is necessary for substantive achievement is disciplined involvement, the devotion to the critical and systematic, the skillful organization of one's potentialities. Essentially this means the sharpening of one's wits on the whetstone of all the best that has been said, written, and done in the field of one's major interest. Genius can afford to take shortcuts. Frank Lloyd Wright not only considered himself to be a genius, but also imperiously demanded of others that they be in fealty bound to his own valuation of himself—a valuation to which most Americans readily acceded. Americans like their geniuses to be flamboyant, especially when they are homespun, as Frank Lloyd Wright was, the "Prairie Genius," a gross national product, if ever there was one.

But Frank Lloyd Wright was no genius. What was he then?

He was a huckster who had somehow blundered into architecture, a vainglorious man of overweening arrogance, effrontery, hardness, and insensitivity; a snake-oil salesman who talked convincingly of organic architecture but who, when it came to putting the talk into practice, committed the most atrocious blunders. I suppose the supreme early example of Wright's idea of organic form is the Tree House in a Chicago suburb. Here Wright built the house around the tree. I forget whether the tree stands in the hall or in the living room—it doesn't matter which. What does matter is that the house is a monument of ugliness and at the same time a monument to the gullibility of mankind and the impracticability of a plausible theory.

Nevertheless, Americans went on taking Wright at his own valuation for more than two generations. Was not Wright a genius, the greatest of American architects? Was he not always unconscionably late, and with never so much as an apology? Were not his houses the most talked about in America?

One of the most endearing qualities of Americans in their willingness to try almost everything. Those who could afford the luxury were willing to try the conjurations of Wright and pay for the experiment he called a house. The houses were not entirely wanting in magical qualities, but they were for the most part unlivable. The overhanging eaves shut out the light, making the bleak interiors even more dingy than they already were, a dinginess which was further emphasized by Wright's penchant for the darkest woods, with which the rooms were frequently paneled. As Henry Hope Reed, Jr., recently wrote, "Many of his houses, even in sunny Pasadena, are so dark that you need a miner's lamp to find your way about them. And, alas, the houses designed for 'the prairie' are always to be found in second-class suburbs where 'the far-reaching vistas' consist of views of the neighbors."

Wright built houses for cave dwellers, troglodytes, it would almost seem as a practical joke practiced by the High Priest of Ugliness and Contempt for Humanity.

Being a short man, Wright designed his rooms with very low ceilings. This barbarity was made to appear as a very great innovation. It was Wright "lowering the room on the American household." What in fact "the Isadora Duncan of American architecture" was actually doing was to play an egomaniacal joke on the American public. He would show them what organic architecture was, and if he were unable to add a cubit to his own stature, he would bring them down to his own dimensions. And so he produced elaborate versions of the cave and perpetrated what can be described only as the abysmal errors. "Organic architecture," forsooth!

The last of Wright's organic follies is among the worst of all his uglinesses, the Guggenheim Museum in New York. This has been appropriately dubbed a huge spiral of contempt for its contents. As anyone who has visited the museum knows, it is scarcely possible to hang a picture properly on its leaning walls, and what is worse, it is hardly possible to view a picture comfortably. It was Wright's final testament to his contempt for humanity.

The tragedy of Wright was that he was denied the discipline his fellow Americans might have given him through their criticism of his work, a criticism which might have prevented the development of that corrosive arrogance and self-blindness which made Frank Lloyd Wright the colossal failure he was.

## STUDY QUESTIONS

1.  If Montagu's thesis is stated in his first sentence, does his essay demonstrate the validity of that thesis?

2.  How does Montagu define *talent?* What does he mean by *involvement?*

3.  In what way is Wright a "flamboyant" personality?

4.  Montagu's criticism of Wright is severe. Is this criticism aimed at Wright himself or at Wright's work? What evidence does Montagu provide for his judgment of the Tree House? What other evidence could he have provided?

5.  Who does Montagu blame for Wright's "colossal failure" as an architect?

# ". . . BENJAMIN WILL SURVIVE. . . ."
# An Interview with Charles Webb,
# author of The Graduate

Charles Webb (1939–     ) was born in San Francisco, California, and grew up in Pasadena, where he now lives. He attended Williams College. *The Graduate,* his first novel, was published in 1964, but not until the film version was released in 1967, did the critical world turn its attention to Webb's book. He and his wife, Eve, have two sons. His second novel, *Love,*

*Roger,* was published in 1969 to high critical acclaim. This was followed by *Thoughts of a Young Stockbroker* (1969).

F. A. Macklin (1937–    ) was born in Philadelphia. He received both his B.A. (1960) and M.A. (1963) from Villanova University. An assistant professor of English at the University of Dayton, he is also editor of *Film Heritage* and film critic for the Dayton *Journal Herald.* His film criticism has been published in *Nation, New Leader, Commonweal, America, Film Quarterly, Film Comment,* and *College English.*

*Interviewer: F. A. Macklin.*

INTERVIEWER: J. D. Salinger is supposed to have refused to sell *The Catcher in the Rye* to the movies because "Holden wouldn't like it." How does Benjamin now feel about the sale of his story?

WEBB: I think Benjamin will survive the sweat-shirt ads, Peace Corps ads, and the other side effects that the movie has had upon him. As an individual, as originally conceived, his first concerns were with his relationships to the people immediately around him. This is not something that would change with accidental popular success, or whatever else might befall him.

INTERVIEWER: One often hears the statement that Dustin Hoffman *is* Benjamin. Does he fit with your view of the character?

WEBB: As the author, I don't feel that any single definition of the character of Benjamin could possibly be definitive. The one rendered by Dustin Hoffman was honestly and genuinely portrayed, and these are the reasons it succeeded to the extent that it did. This doesn't mean that someone else couldn't also have played the part in a convincing and moving manner.

INTERVIEWER: Jacob Brackman, in a long piece in *The New Yorker,* asked "Has Benjamin . . . checked out psychedelics, heavy sex, solitude, S.D.S., mysticism, and so on?" He says that many viewers assume Ben has. Has he?

WEBB: As far as the contemporary scene is concerned, which is something, in the novel especially, with which Benjamin is not concerned, (psychedelics, etc., which you mentioned) this is something in our environment which is constantly changing. There are other things which don't change, such as relationships between parents and children, males and females, and it was to these more classical elements of fiction that I, as the author, addressed myself in writing the novel.

INTERVIEWER: Is Benjamin a product of Eisenhower America, Kennedy America, or revolution America?

WEBB: Benjamin is a product of America, as are Kennedy, Eisenhower.

INTERVIEWER: One of the major questions about the film is Ben's motivation. In one of the funniest scenes in the book Ben tells his father about having slept with whores. The scene suggests that Ben does have a vital sexual appetite. There is a sexual motivation that is dropped from the film. Pauline Kael once scoffed at *Fantastic Voyage's* being only through the upper part of a man's body. It seems to me that the quick shots of Mrs. Robinson's discombobulated breasts equal this for safe boldness. Were you satisfied with the film's handling of Ben's "affair" with Mrs. Robinson?

WEBB: Regardless of how bold Hollywood may be, compared to earlier days, there are certain aspects of human behavior, sexual and otherwise, which do not translate from literature into film. One of these is the quality of human relationships.

INTERVIEWER: What is the motivation for Ben and Elaine's relationship?

WEBB: The motivation of Ben's and Elaine's relationship was a combination of things, including love, physical attraction and a desire, subconscious, to upset things.

INTERVIEWER: Stanley Kauffmann, in *The New Republic,* accuses you of using a trite device in allowing Ben to find out about the wedding in a note on a door. It seems to me that the device though obvious is easily possible. Do you feel that the film improves upon this?

WEBB: Stanley Kauffmann would perhaps best be left alone.

INTERVIEWER: Did the film do anything that you felt was an improvement on the book?

WEBB: No.

INTERVIEWER: In a letter to *The New Republic* you accused the film of failing to take a moral stance. You seemed to base your argument on the fact that in the film Benjamin does not reach Elaine until *after* the marriage ceremony while in the book he does arrive in time to prevent it. Why is this change crucial, and how does it invalidate the story's morality as you conceived it?

WEBB: There is a range of values, which can be called either human or moral, which, although under some skirmishing attacks at this time, have endured from the beginning of recorded history and which assumedly will continue to do so. Formalized arrangements between individuals is one of these. Benjamin, in the book, although unconsciously, recognized this fact of human nature. In the film version he was ignorant of it, therefore less intelligent and less sympathetic (perhaps more mod, however).

INTERVIEWER:   I know that a few viewers of the film have wept because of the annihilation of ritual when Benjamin invades the
church, while the majority laugh with glee. What is your response
to the two reactions?

WEBB:   The reason Ben goes in after Elaine in a Church is because
it is there he happens to find her. If he found her in a department
store, he would go in after her there (at that juncture of the story).
The particular building in which she is contained at that moment
is not relevant to his purposes.

INTERVIEWER:   Both Kauffmann and Hollis Alpert (*Saturday Review*)
have accused you of equating morality with marriage licences. In
your mind, is it the vows that are supreme?

WEBB:   In my mind, the vows are irrelevant.

INTERVIEWER:   Isn't annulment possible?

WEBB:   I'm not sure I understand what the basic issue is here, as regarding the possibility of annulment, etc. There are larger issues,
and perhaps these others could best be solved by qualified lawyers.

INTERVIEWER:   Why doesn't the fact that Ben arrives before sexual
consummation of the marriage compensate for the loss of the
formalized arrangement?

WEBB:   Sex is only peripherally connected to the moral issues. Therefore, Carl's, and Ben's, or anyone's, sexual relationship to Elaine is
not of central importance.

INTERVIEWER:   I agree that the ending of the film is vacillation as
you stated in your letter to *NR,* or at best it's badly done ambiguity, but I am surprised to see that you seem to see Ben as heroic
and effective. Is this the way you view him?

WEBB:   In his own way, in the attainment, one way or another, of
what he wants, I would say that Ben is both heroic and effective.

INTERVIEWER:   You consider the book's conclusion to be optimistic
rather than ironic?

WEBB:   Yes.

INTERVIEWER:   Why is Ben so noncommittal to Elaine's questioning
"Benjamin?" Why does he merely answer a dull "What" to her
appeal?

WEBB:   He has a plan.

INTERVIEWER:   Mike Nichols (the director) and you seem to differ de-
cisively about the film's ending. He has said that at the end Ben and
Elaine are destined to a future that is similar to their parents.
Your ending seems much more affirmative.

WEBB:   I think Mr. Nichols' comment that Ben and Elaine are destined to a future that is similar to their parents is not a well
thought-out one.

INTERVIEWER:   Nichols is unable to clarify his ending, if what he has said publicly is true—and it may not be. Most viewers (Kauffmann and Hollis Alpert, *SR*, included) see the ending as uplift. Many don't even realize the ceremony has taken place. Do you see the film's ending as uplift?

WEBB:   The ending means that Benjamin has, in his own way, achieved one of his goals. In his own way, I would hope, this would indicate, he will now go on to achieve more of them.

INTERVIEWER:   Can you give me some background on how the making of the film came about?

WEBB:   The making of the film came about by the producer finding the book on a book-stand and buying its rights from me.

INTERVIEWER:   What control, if any, did you have over the film?

WEBB:   The amount of control I had over the end result is open to interpretation.

INTERVIEWER:   Did you have any preferences for the director or actors?

WEBB:   I was pleased with the choice of director and the choice of actors and actresses.

INTERVIEWER:   If you had it to do all over again, would you?

WEBB:   Yes.

INTERVIEWER:   What are your plans? Do you have any film plans?

WEBB:   Right now I am going ahead with the sale of a novelette, and of a novel I wrote last summer, to Hollywood, I have been somewhat fearful of going ahead with these things, but from *The Graduate* experience feel I know enough of the ropes by now not to be overwhelmed, coerced into writing screenplays, or in other ways having time drawn away from my writing.

INTERVIEWER:   I have heard that you have a new novel *Loves Roger*.

WEBB:   The title of the book is *Love, Roger,* and the book is due to be published by Houghton Mifflin in the Spring of 1969.

INTERVIEWER:   If Mr. Nichols wanted to direct it and Mr. Turman to produce it what would be your reaction?

WEBB:   I would encourage it.

INTERVIEWER:   What's the novel about?

WEBB:   The story is about a young travel agent who lives in Boston. He meets a girl who is up from the South looking for a job, and she, and a third girl, a nursing student from Wisconsin who gives up school and comes to Boston, make up the three characters of the book.

INTERVIEWER:   What's the theme?

WEBB:   The theme is more or less one of the main character being in a position in which it seems as though he should be choosing between the two girls. However, he doesn't seem to choose. Instead, they all go along and in the end move into a house in the suburbs.

INTERVIEWER:   What about the leading character?

WEBB:   He is a middle-class, non-revolutionary character, likable (I hope), who aspires to be happy and stable in his life. He is naive, but naive on purpose, because he sees its benefits.

INTERVIEWER:   Would you prefer that your audience dismissed the film of *The Graduate,* responded to book and film as the same work, or tried to keep them separate?

WEBB:   Try to keep them separate.

INTERVIEWER:   *Film Heritage* has a feature in which it asks writers two questions about Hollywood and the artist. In summation, perhaps you can answer them. 1) Has Hollywood treated your work justly? 2) Can the serious writer's work survive in Hollywood?

WEBB:   I'm not sure I know the answer. My own work was treated as justly, I think, by Hollywood, as it is possible for an author's work to be treated. However, there are losses, as well as gains, in translating a novel into a movie, so that I suppose the only way of judging it would be to add up all the losses, balance them against the gains, and see where things stood. In my case, I think they balance out fairly evenly, so that, in the end, I wouldn't feel any more justified in making a sweeping denunciation of the industry than I would in saying it is the salvation of authors.

## STUDY QUESTIONS

1.   What are the "more classical elements of fiction" to which Webb says he addressed himself in writing *The Graduate?*

2.   Often, Webb seems to be side-stepping Macklin's questions. Is he? Why, then, are his answers phrased as they are?

3.   Why does Webb feel that the film version of his novel failed to take a moral stance? Do you agree?

4.   Webb says that Ben is both "heroic and effective." How would Webb define *heroic?* How is this related to Webb's agreeing that the film's ending is "uplift"?

5.   Webb says that the hero of his second novel is "a middle-class, nonrevolutionary character." He also says that Ben and Elaine had a "subconscious" desire "to upset things." Does Webb imply, then, that Ben and Elaine are revolutionary characters?

*Hollis Alpert*

# MIKE NICHOLS STRIKES AGAIN

Hollis Alpert (1916–      ) was born in Herkimer, New York. He was a student at the New School for Social Research in 1946–47. Although he achieved some success with novels—*The Summer Lovers* (1958) and *Some Other Time* (1960)—his reputation rests on his film criticism. His books on films and film history include *The Dreams and the Dreamers* (1962), *For Immediate Release* (1963), and *The Barrymores* (1964). With his colleague, Arthur Knight, he has written *The History of Sex in Cinema*, which was serialized in *Playboy*. The Screen Director's Guild gave him its Critics Award in 1957. Since 1950 he has been a film critic for the *Saturday Review*.

W̲E'RE GOING to have to talk about Mike Nichols again, in spite of the fact that this young man is no longer the conversation piece that he was a year or two ago. What else is there to say about him? We know how clever and knowledgeable he is, about his comic gifts, his strings of successes, his ability to handle a wide range of material, his adventurousness, his salutary effect on actors. So why bring him up again? Because now he has directed—and co-produced—*The Graduate,* based on the Charles Webb novel about the love pangs of a twenty-one-year-old, and has made the freshest, funniest, and most touching film of the year, and has filled it with delightful surprises, cheekiness, sex, satire, irreverence toward some of the most sacred of American cows, and, in addition, gives us the distinct feeling that the American film may never be quite the same again.

This is not to say that *The Graduate* is all glistening perfection. As a film director, Nichols still has some rough edges. His very zest for experimentation occasionally carries him a bit too far at times; he sometimes seizes a chance for an effect when the effect isn't altogether necessary. He punctuates a scene—a carryover from his stage habits. But these moments are few, and usually minor, and forgivable in view of the bounty he provides.

Working with a script provided for him by Calder Willingham and Buck Henry, he concentrates on a solemn young man, just out of four years of college in the East, who is now back at his California home—the epitome of upper-middle-class comfort. He's suspicious of all this bourgeois opulence, even more suspicious of the restless, alcoholic wife of his father's partner because she seems to have ill-diguised sexual designs on him. The suspicions are well founded, and soon enough his curiosity and sexual fantasies lead him into an affair with the woman—probably the funniest and maybe the saddest affair yet shown on the overexperienced screen. There's simply not the space to adequately describe what happens, except to say that scene after scene is a gem to be recalled in hilarious tranquility.

As the young man, Dustin Hoffman is the most delightful film hero of our generation. Slightly undersized, totally unsmiling, he stares his way through a series of horrendous, harrowing experiences which lead him from first sex to first real and true love. Unfortunately, the girl he encounters as first love happens to be the sweet, nice, intelligent, sensitive daughter of the woman he meets furtively in a Los Angeles hotel. He learns that there is no fury like that of a mother scorned, no hatred like that of a husband cuckolded by the boy his daughter loves. But the boy's love becomes blind faith and, eventually, mania; and faced with this, the girl, who has been spirited off to a hasty marriage with a suitable medical student, must make a decision. It would be unfair to reveal what happens. It has to be seen to be believed and appreciated.

As the mother, Anne Bancroft is close to miraculous; there isn't a note that she doesn't strike exactly right. The daughter is played winningly by Katharine Ross. For the minor roles, Nichols has fine performers— William Daniels as the boy's father, Elizabeth Wilson as his mother, Buck Henry as a room clerk. They're all effective, but because their appearances are brief, they run into Nichols's tendency to caricature. This does contribute to the fun, but tends to lessen the convincingness that Nichols elsewhere succeeds in obtaining. But it is close to ingratitude to mention minor deficiencies: a pop-up toaster that just shouldn't have popped up toast at a certain key moment; a tricky scene in the swimming pool. What is really nice about *The Graduate* is that Nichols, in spite of the remarkable breakthrough he makes in the traditional Hollywood mold, still seems to be learning. He can go farther. Meanwhile, hasten to catch up with *The Graduate*.

## STUDY QUESTIONS

1. Alpert says that "The Graduate" is full of sex, satire, and irreverence towards some of the most sacred of American cows. Which of these things does he proceed to discuss?

2. Alpert feels that Benjamin is suspicious of bourgeois opulence but "even more" suspicious of the restless, alcoholic wife of his father's partner. What is the effect of the words *even more?*

3. What does Alpert mean by "the overexperienced screen"?

4. Alpert describes Ben as a *totally unsmiling* boy who *stares his way* through a series of experiences which lead him from sex to a true love which becomes *blind faith* and then *mania.* What conclusions about Ben could be drawn from the italicized words?

5. What minor deficiencies does Alpert find in "The Graduate"?

*Stanley Kauffmann*

# CUM LAUDE

Stanley Kauffmann (1916–    ) was born in New York City. He has been an actor, a director, the film critic for the *New Republic,* and drama critic for the New York *Times.* While on the *Times* staff, he and Broadway producer David Merrick engaged in their now-famous feud. Kauffmann is presently associate literary editor for the *New Republic.* He is the author of seven novels, more than 40 plays, most of them one-acters, and books of film criticism. His books include *Hidden Hero* (1949), *The Tightrope* (1952), *Man of the World* (1956), *If It Be Love* (1960), and *A World on Film* (1966). In 1964 he received a Ford Foundation Traveling Fellowship and was named an honorary fellow of Morse College, Yale University.

Happy news. Mike Nichols' second film, *The Graduate,* proves that he is a genuine film director—one to be admired and concerned about. It also marks the screen debut, in the title role, of Dustin Hoffman, a young actor already known in the theatre as an exceptional talent, who here increases his reputation. Also, after many months of prattle about the "new" American film (mostly occasioned by the overrated *Bonnie and Clyde*), *The Graduate* gives some substance to the contention that American films are coming of age—of our age.

The screenplay, based on a novel by Charles Webb, was written by Calder Willingham and Buck Henry. The latter, like Nichols, is an experienced satiric performer. (Henry appears in this picture as a hotel clerk.) The dialogue is sharp, hip without rupturing itself in the effort, often moving, and frequently funny except for a few obtrusive gag lines. The story is about a young cop-out who—for well-dramatized reasons—cops at least partially in again.

Ben is a bright college graduate who returns to his wealthy parents' Hollywood home and flops—on his bed, on the rubber raft in the pool. Politely and dispassionately, he declines the options thrust at him by barbecue-pit society. The bored wife of his father's law partner seduces him. Ben is increasingly uncomfortable in the continuing affair, for moral reasons of an unpuritanical kind. (The bedroom scene in which Ben tries to get her to *talk* to him is a jewel.) The woman's daughter comes home from college, and against the mother's wishes, Ben takes her out. He falls in love with the girl —which is predictable but entirely credible. He is blackmailed into telling her about his affair with her mother and, in revulsion, the girl flees—back to Berkeley. Ben follows, hangs about the campus, almost gets her to marry him, loses her (through her father's interference), pursues her, and finally gets her. For once, a happy ending makes *us* feel happy.

To dispose at once of the tedious subject of frankness, I note that some of the language and bedroom details push that frontier (in American films) considerably ahead, but it is all so appropriate that it never has the slightest smack of daring, let alone opportunism. What is truly daring, and therefore refreshing, is the film's moral stance. Its acceptance of the fact that a young man might have an affair with a woman and still marry her daughter (a situation not exactly unheard of in America although not previously seen in American films) is part of the film's fundamental insistence: that life, today, in our world, is not worth living unless one can *prove* it day-by-day, by values that ring true day-by-day. Moral attitudes, far from relaxing, are getting stricter and stricter, and many of the shoddy moralistic acceptances that dictated mindless actions for decades are now being fiercely questioned. Ben is neither a laggard nor a lecher; he is, in the healthiest sense, a moralist— he wants to know the value of what he is doing. He does not rush into the affair with the mother out of any social rote of "scoring" any more than he avoids the daughter—because he has slept with her mother—out of any social rote of taboo. (In fact, although he is male and eventually succumbs, he sees the older woman's advances as a syndrome of a suspect society.) And the sexual dynamics of the story propels Ben past the sexual sphere; it forces him to assess and locate himself in *every* aspect.

Sheerly in terms of moral revolution, all this will seem pretty commonplace to readers of contemporary American fiction. But we are dealing here with an art form that, because of its inescapable broad-based appeal, follows well behind the front lines of moral exploration. In America it follows less closely than in some other countries, not because American audiences are necessarily less sophisticated than others (although they *are* less sophisticated than, say, Swedish audiences) but because the great expense of American production encourages a producer to cast the widest net possible. None of this is an apology for the film medium, it is a fact of the film's existence; one might as sensibly apologize for painting because it cannot be seen simultaneously by millions the way a film can. Thus the arrival of *The Graduate* can be viewed two ways. First, it is an index of moral change in a substantial segment of the American public, at least of an awakening of some doubts about past acceptances. Second, it is irrelevant that these changes are arriving in film a decade or two decades or a half century after the other arts, because their statement in film makes them intrinsically new and unique. If arts have textural differences and are not simply different envelopes for the same contents, then the *way* in which *The Graduate* affects us makes it quite a different work from the original novel (which I have not read) and from all the dozens of novels of moral disruption and exploration in recent years. Recently an Italian literary critic and teacher deplored to me the adulation of young people for films, saying that the "messages" they get from Bergman and Antonioni and Godard were stated by the novel and even the drama thirty or forty years ago. I tried (unsuccessfully) to point out that this is not really true: that if art as art has any validity at all, then the film's peculiar sensory avenues were giving those "old" insights a being they could not otherwise have.

This brings us to the central artist of this enterprise, Mike Nichols. In his first picture *Who's Afraid of Virginia Woolf?,* Nichols was shackled by a famous play and by the two powerhouse stars of our time; but considering these handicaps, he did a creditable job, particularly with his actors. In *The Graduate,* uninhibited by the need to reproduce a Broadway hit and with freedom to select his cast, he has moved fully into film. He is perceptive, imaginative, witty; he has a shrewd eye, both for beauty and for visual comment; he knows how to compose and to juxtapose; he has an innate sense of the manifold ways in which film can be better than *he* is and therefore how good he can be *through* it—including the powers of expansion and ellipsis.

From the very first moment, Nichols sets the key. We see Ben's face, large and absolutely alone. The camera pulls back, we see that he is in an airliner and a voice tells us that it is approaching Los Angeles; but Ben has been set for us as *alone.* We follow him through the air terminal, and he seems just as completely, even comfortably isolated in the crowd as he does later, in a scuba suit at the bottom of his family's swimming-pool, when he is huddling contentedly in an underwater corner while his twenty-first birthday party is being bulled along by his father up above.

Nichols understands sound. The device of overlapping is somewhat over-used (beginning the dialogue of the next scene under the end of the present scene), but in general this effect adds to the dissolution of clock time, creating a more subjective time. Nichols' use of non-verbal sound (something like Antonioni's) does a good deal to fix subliminally the cultural locus. For instance, a jet plane swooshes overhead—unremarked—as the married woman first invites Ben into her house.

In *Virginia Woolf* I thought I saw some influence of Kurosawa; I think so again here, particularly in such sequences as Ben's welcome-home party where the camera keeps close to Ben, panning with him as he weaves through the crowd, moving to another face only when Ben encounters it, as if Ben's attention controlled the camera's. As with Kurosawa, the effect is balletic; it seeks out quintessential rhythms in commonplace actions.

On the negative side, I disliked Nichols' recurrent affection for the splatter of headlights and sunspots on his lens; and his hang-up with a slightly heavy Godardian irony through objects. (The camera holds on a third-rate painting of a clown after the mistress walks out of the shot. When the girl leaves Ben in front of the monkey cage at the San Francisco zoo, the camera, too luckily, catches the sign on the cage: Do Not Tease.) And a couple of times Nichols puts his camera in places that merely make us aware of his cleverness in putting it there: inside the scuba helmet, inside an empty hotel-room closet looking past the hangers.

But the influences I have cited (there are others) only show that Nichols is alive, hungry, properly ambitious; the defects only show that he is not yet entirely sure of himself. Together, these matters show him still feeling his way toward a whole style of his own. What is important is his extraordinary basic talent: humane, deft, exuberant. And I want to make much of his ability to direct actors, a factor generally overlooked in appraising film directors. (Some famous directors—Hitchcock, for example—can do nothing with actors. They get what the actor can supply on his own. Sometimes—again like Hitchcock—these directors are not even aware of bad performances.) He has helped Anne Bancroft to a quiet, strong portrayal of the mistress, bitter and pitiful. With acuteness he has cast Elizabeth Wilson, a sensitive comedienne, as Ben's mother. From the very pretty Katharine Ross, Ben's girl, Nichols' has got a performance of sweetness, dignity, and a compassion that is simply engulfing. Only William Daniels, as Ben's father, made me a bit uneasy. His WASP caricature (he did a younger version in *Two for the Road*) is already becoming a staple item.

In the leading role, Nichols had the sense and the courage to cast Dustin Hoffman, unknown (to the screen) and unhandsome. Hoffman's face in it-

self is a proof of change in American films; it is hard to imagine him in leading roles a decade ago. How unimportant, how *interesting* this quickly becomes, because Hoffman is one of the best actors of his generation, subtle,
vital, and accurate. Certainly he is the best American film comedian since
Jack Lemmon, and, as theatregoers know, he has a much wider range than
Lemmon. (For instance, he was fine as a crabby, fortyish, 19th-century Russian clerk in Ronald Ribman's play *Journey of the Fifth Horse.*)

With tact and lovely understanding, Nichols and Hoffman and Miss Ross
—all three—show us how this boy and girl fall into a new kind of love: a
love based on recognition of identical loneliness on their side of a generational gap, a gap which—never mind how sillily it is often exploited in politics and pop culture—irrefutably exists. When her father is, understand-
ably, enraged at the news of his wife's affair with his prospective son-in-law
and hustles the girl off into another marriage, Ben's almost insane refusal to
let her go is his refusal to let go of the one reality he has found in a world that
otherwise exists behind a pane of glass. The cinema metaphors of the chase
after the girl—the endless driving, the jumping in and out of his sports car,
even his eventual running out of gas—have perhaps too much Keaton
about them; they make the film rise too close to the surface of mere physical-
ity; but at least the urgency never flags. At the wedding, when he finds it—
and of course it is in an ultra-modern church—there is a dubious hint of
crucifixion as Ben flings his outspread arms against the (literal) pane of
glass that separates him from life (the girl); but this is redeemed a minute
later when, with the girl, he grabs a large cross, swings it savagely to stave
off pursuers, then jams it through the handles of the front doors to lock the
crowd in behind them.

The pair jump on to a passing bus (she in her wedding dress still) and sit
in the back. The aged, uncomprehending passengers turn and stare at them.
(One last reminder!—of Lester's old-folks chorus in *The Knack.*) Ben and
his girl sit next to each other, breathing hard, not even laughing, just happy.
Nothing is solved—none of the things that bother Ben—by the fact of
their being together; but, for him, nothing would be worth solving without
her. We know that and she knows that, and all of us feel very, very good. The
chase and the last-minute rescue (just after the ceremony is finished) are
contrivances, but they are contrivances tending toward truth, not falsity,
which may be one definition of good art.

Paul Simon has written rock songs for the film, sung by Simon and Garfunkel, and as in many rock songs, these lyrics deal easily with such matters
as God, *Angst,* the "sound of silence," and social revision. But they *are* typical of the musical environment in which this boy and girl live.

Some elements of slickness and shininess in this wide-screen, color film
are disturbing. But despite them, despite the evident influences and defects,
the picture bears the imprint of a man, a whole man, warts and all: which is a

very different imprint from that of many of Nichols' highly praised, cagy, compromised American contemporaries. *All* the talents involved in *The Graduate* make it soar brightly above its shortcomings and, for reasons given, make it a milestone in American film history. Milestones do not guarantee that everything after them will be better, still they are ineradicable.

### STUDY QUESTIONS

1. According to Kauffmann, what is daring and refreshing about "The Graduate" 's "moral stance"? Why does he feel that the screen is necessarily "well behind" American fiction in its exploration of contemporary morality? How does he dispose of such criticism of the film?

2. What does Kauffmann feel Ben and Elaine's love is based on? Does he conclude that Ben and Elaine solve their problems? How does he explain his acceptance of the film's contrived ending?

3. Alpert used the word *mania* in discussing Ben. Does Kauffmann use any word with similar connotations?

4. What minor deficiencies does Kauffmann find in "The Graduate"? Are they the same deficiencies noted by Alpert—specifically or generally? Do Alpert and Kauffmann agree on the quality of the acting?

5. Why does Kauffmann feel that the musical score is appropriate?

*Brendan Gill*

# THE CURRENT CINEMA

Brendan Gill (1914–    ) was born in Hartford, Connecticut. He received a B.A. from Yale University in 1936. He has contributed to the *New Yorker* since 1936, and has been its film critic since 1960. His books include *The Trouble of One House* (1950) and *The Day the Money Stopped* (1957). In 1958 he and Maxwell Anderson collaborated on a play adaptation of the latter work.

THE CONTINUOUSLY felt presence back of "The Graduate"
is that of the director, Mike Nichols—a nervous, urban,
Eastern presence that encourages the movie, at a number
of critical moments, to shift from the sure footing of a full-length conventional comedy to the precarious jaunty jokiness of a night-club turn. (The authors of the screenplay are listed as Calder Willingham and Buck Henry. Not being familiar with Mr. Henry's work, I cannot judge the size of his contribution, but I know Mr. Willingham's work well, and I fail to detect much evidence of his hand.) Mr. Nichols is an exceedingly funny writer and actor, and I have no doubt that a skit by him and with him could, if he so wished, challenge the grandeur of "War and Peace," but "The Graduate" is not a skit, and his direction of it has rendered it somewhat more prankish and less savage than it should have been. Still, it is one of the liveliest gifts of the season, and I am not so unseasonable as to deny that it contains many admirable things including characters of novelty and substance, ably enacted. Dustin Hoffman makes a sensationally attractive movie debut as the troubled, virtuous hero. (Tarkington's Willy Baxter, fifty years later); Anne Bancroft is the sexually aggressive housewife who sets out to entrap him; Murray Hamilton is her cuckolded husband; and Katharine Ross is her daughter, who—preposterously, I must say—consents to marry a young dolt wildly unworthy of her. Luckily, our hero, in a slam-bang finish, snatches her from what may be called the very jaws of matrimony, and off they go in an orange bus, presumably to secure an annulment for the happy bride. The director of photography is Robert Surtees, whose use of telescopic long shots is itself an expression of wit and who makes mere blurrs blaze with meaning.

## STUDY QUESTIONS

1.  Gill's brief review is notably lacking in specificity, but he does call Nichols' direction "prankish." Does he thereby agree or disagree with Alpert and Kauffmann?

2.  Why does Gill feel Elaine's marriage to Ben is "preposterous"? What is a *dolt?* Gill says Ben is "wildly unworthy" of Elaine. What does he mean by *wildly?*

3.  Why might Gill presume that Ben and Elaine go off in an orange bus "to secure an annulment for the happy bride"?

*Stephen Farber and Estelle Changas*

# THE GRADUATE

Stephen Farber (1943–      ) was born in Cleveland, Ohio. He received his
B.A. from Amherst College, and M.A.'s in English and Theater Arts from,
respectively, the University of California at Berkeley and UCLA. He is currently Los Angeles editor of *Film Quarterly*, and has contributed articles on
the film to *Sight and Sound*, the *Hudson Review*, and *Film Quarterly*.

Estelle Changas (1939–      ) was born in Detroit, Michigan. She received
a B.A. in English from UCLA in 1962, and later attended graduate school
at the University of California at Berkeley. After teaching high school English for two years, she was accepted into the Graduate Division of the Motion Picture Department at UCLA, where she completed her M.A. Miss
Changas has served as a consultant for "An Oral History of the Motion
Picture in America," a project sponsored by the American Film Institute
and the National Endowment for the Humanities.

Director: Mike Nichols. Producer: Lawrence Turman. Screenplay by Calder Willingham & Buck Henry, from the novel by Charles Webb. Songs: Simon & Garfunkel. Photography: Robert Surtees. Embassy.

$\mathcal{M}$IKE NICHOLS'S name is so magical today that even if *The
Graduate* had been the worst movie of the year, people
would be buzzing reverently about it. As it is, *The Graduate* is only the most cleverly fashionable and confused movie of the year—
and the responses, from critics and customers alike, have been ecstatic. We
expected a lot—we're young, and so is Nichols; in addition to youth, he has
money, talent, intelligence, irreverence. And after lots of quickie exploitation films about teenyboppers and acidheads, *The Graduate* might have
been the first movie about today's youth to tell it like it is. But Nichols has

too much at stake to risk involving us. He's adored because he's hip and safe at the same time; his audiences know that he won't go too far.

*The Graduate* opens promisingly enough. Ben, a successful young Eastern college graduate, is returning home to Los Angeles, and Nichols immediately and effectively conveys his isolation by focusing exclusively on Dustin Hoffman's apprehensive face moving through the crowded LA airport. Nichols has said that he chose the thirty-year-old Hoffman (a talented comedian—to get that out of the way) to play his callow young hero because he had a face that suggested suffering. Hoffman himself thought there was something strange about the choice; he felt he wasn't suited to the part, which he described as "a young, conventional, squarejawed *Time* Magazine Man of the Year type." Hoffman was right of course. We soon learn that Ben, for all of his credentials and in spite of his vulnerable face, is clean-cut and stupid. He's supposed to be a champion college debater, but he can hardly form a sentence. In the first scenes he's thrown into his rich parents' cocktail and poolside parties; it's easy enough to caricature suburban phoniness, and we see quickly—Nichols provides a slick, superficial summary of anti-bourgeois satire of the last decade—everything that's wrong with LA society. But what does Ben see? He gapes a lot, but he never looks more than bewildered by what's going on. He certainly can't articulate any sort of protest. All he knows is that he wants his future to be "well . . . different. . . ." He really sweats to get that word out, but he doesn't seem capable of going further. When he's troubled, he stares into his bedroom aquarium.

Of course we're supposed to like Ben because he's victimized by all of those nasty, aging country clubbers. In the face of their boozing and their twaddle, he has a chunky innocence that is to endear him to us. Nothing is going on in his head, but because he's "mixed up," as he says at one point, and abused by his parents, audiences cluck over him and rush to give him credit for understanding anxieties that are actually beyond his grasp.

Nichols does use a few fine Simon and Garfunkel songs (written long before the film was conceived) to pump poetic and intellectual content into *The Graduate*. Because the songs, especially "The Sounds of Silence," are so concise, lyrical, eloquent, we're tempted to believe that the film contains their insights and that Ben understands them. We're supposed to assume that Ben shares Paul Simon's perceptions of "people talking without speaking, people hearing without listening" in a world whose "words of the prophet are written on the subway walls," but in truth Ben couldn't *begin* putting the world in that kind of order. He's only a beer-drinking *Time* magazine type, as Hoffman recognized, rather harmlessly stupid and awkward, but tricked up with a suffering face and an *Angst* ridden song intent on persuading us that he's an alienated generational hero. And audiences eager to believe that all young people are sensitive and alienated and that all old people are sell-outs or monsters gratefully permit Hoffman's manner-isms and Paul Simon's poetry to convince them of a depth in Ben that the part, as written, simply does not contain.

The film's best scenes are the early ones in which Ben is seduced by the wife of his father's partner (superbly played by Anne Bancroft—her per-formance is reason enough to see the film). Bancroft, a young man's deli-ciously provocative sexual fantasy come to life, makes us aware that there *is* something to be said for women over thirty. When she's on, Ben might just as well roll over and play dead. Bancroft is engagingly wicked as Mrs. Rob-inson; she is at once supremely confident of her sexual power and merci-lessly casual in the face of Ben's adolescent fear of her. Alone with him in her house, she takes calm delight in exposing her legs, while he ejaculates moral misgivings. Her sophistication enables her to see through his repeated protests: "You *want* me to seduce you, is that what you're trying to tell me, Benjamin?" she chants in poker-faced style. And finally, having trapped him in her daughter's bedroom, she remains utterly cool, while her daring flirta-tious assault, comically caught by rapid cuts from bare bosom to Ben's an-guished face, leaves him helplessly gasping, "Jesus Christ, Mrs. Robinson!"

Unfortunately, this is about the only scene which allows us to see that Ben is sexually attracted to Mrs. Robinson. Most of the time Nichols insists that Mrs. Robinson is repulsive because she is sexual and Benjamin lovable be-cause he is not. Sheer boredom, Ben confesses, is the only thing which brings him to her time after time. And later he explains that bedding down with Mrs. Robinson meant nothing; it was "just another thing that happened to me . . . just like shaking hands." Apparently we are to believe, as Stanley Kauffman has written, that Ben "sees the older woman's advances as a syn-drome of a suspect society," and that he deserves congratulations for his in-difference; what seems an astonishing blindness to Mrs. Robinson's very real sexiness is to be taken as a moral victory.

Ben's voice of morality, though, is rather unpleasantly self-righteous: "Do you think I'm proud that I spend my time with a broken-down alco-holic?" The scene in which he tries to liven up their evenings by getting Mrs. Robinson to *talk* to him has been much praised, and it *is* an interesting scene, though not for the reasons given, but because it presents Mrs. Robin-son with more complexity than usual. When, in the middle of their abortive conversation, she orders Ben not to take out her daughter, the only reason he can guess for the command is that she thinks he isn't good enough for Elaine, and he announces angrily that he considers this liaison "sick and perverted." Bancroft's face, marvelously expressive of deeply rooted social and personal discontents, makes clear to us that this is *not* Mrs. Robinson's reason, that her reasons are much more intense and tortured than Ben sus-pects—mostly, presumably, an envy of youth and a fear of being cast off for her daughter—and deserve his sympathy, not his moralistic outrage.

Ben is too insensitive to see that when she seems to acknowledge that she thinks her daughter too good for him, it's only out of desperation and confusion; she has feelings more intricate and disturbed than she knows how to explain to him. His rejection of her at this moment may look moral, but given the depth and the anguish of her emotional experience, it's a pretty ugly, unfeeling response. Mrs. Robinson's answer to Ben's plea that she talk to him—"I don't think we have much to say to each other"—proves to be quite accurate, but it doesn't expose her shallowness, as Nichols seems to have intended, it exposes *Ben's*. She has so much more self-awareness than he, and so many more real problems, why *should* she talk to him? Anne Bancroft is really too interesting for Nichols' sentimentalities about the generational gap, so he treats her characterization with no respect; after this scene, he turns her into a hideous witch, an evil Furie maniacally insistent on keeping Ben and her daughter apart. This goes along with the current urge to see the generational conflict as a coloring-book morality play—the young in white, the old in black—but it's a cheap dramatic trick.

What really wins the young audience to Ben is his compulsive pursuit of Mrs. Robinson's daughter Elaine in the second half of the film. His single-minded dedication to securing the girl he pines after may be the oldest staple of movie romance, but it is also manna to today's Love Generation. Elaine, though, is a problem. She's gorgeous, all right, she's earnest, and she smiles nicely, but what Ben sees in her beyond her lovely face is kept a secret from us. She does seem to be as clean-cut and stupid as he is. But since she wears her hair long and uncombed and goes to Berkeley (another put-on, much like Hoffman's suffering face), we're to assume that she's an extraordinary catch. Doesn't the fact that she dates and almost marries a smooth, starched medical student confirm the opposite? Ben, incidentally, doesn't even admit her physical attractiveness; his excuse for wanting her so desperately is that at last he has found someone he can talk to. What two such uninteresting people could talk about is a real stumper; and Nichols must have thought so too, for he bars us from one of their few conversations, placing them behind the windshield of Ben's convertible. Perhaps if Nichols were a more experienced film director, he could have convinced us of the vitality of Ben's and Elaine's love with some pungent, seductive visuals; but he relies only on modish out-of-focus shots of flowers and foliage (shots that looked a lot prettier in *Two for the Road* anyway).

All that does express their love is an old-fashioned Hollywood Kiss. On their first date, after treating her quite wretchedly, Ben tries to get her to stop crying and kisses her. And that does it. She forgets her humiliation and smiles. It's love at first sight, just like in the movies, but because the actors look casual and sensitive and alienated, audiences think their instant jello of a romance is "real." A little later Elaine learns of Ben's affair with her mother and flees back to Berkeley; he follows her there, and she comes to his room at night to ask why. But first she asks him to kiss her once more, and when he does, she's satisfied; her doubts are erased, and she's ready to marry him. It's all very reminiscent of Betty Grable cheerleader movies. And it's interesting that there seems to be no real sexual attraction between Ben and Elaine. Even their two or three kisses are awfully restrained. After receiving her second kiss, which looks about as exciting as a late-night cup of hot chocolate, Elaine darts quickly out of Ben's door. The movie is rather offensively prudish in splitting sex and love, implying that sexual relationships are sick and perverted, but that in a healthful Young Love relationship— why, sex is the furthest thing from the kids' minds. In this respect the film fits nicely with the flower talk about love, which for all of the bubbles and incense and the boast of promiscuity, is equally insipid, passionless, ultimately quite as sexless.

How bizarre it is that the vacuous Elaine, who has been so easily conned into marrying the fraternity's ace make-out king, can cause such a cataclysmic change in Ben. He throws off his lethargy, chases after her and breaks up her wedding at the last minute, bellowing an anguished "Elaine" as he beats against the glass that separates him from the congregation. A minute later, when Ben punches Elaine's father in the stomach, when he beats off the suburbanites with a giant cross and locks the door with it, the audience cheers vigorously—and to give Nichols his due, it's a pleasing, outrageous image. But it's much too glib to turn Ben suddenly into a rebel hero—this same Ben who's spent most of the film staring blankly into his aquarium and lounging by his pool, transformed by a kiss from a sweet little coed into a fighter for his generation. The motivation may be phony, but we can all laugh at how the old folks get theirs in the end.

*The Graduate,* like Nichols' film of *Virginia Woolf,* has been applauded for its boldness—never before in an American movie, it is said, could a hero have slept with a woman and married her daughter. The premise *is* arresting, but it's interesting how Nichols blunts it, makes it as easy as possible for his audiences to accept the outrageous. By minimizing Ben's participation in the affair with Mrs. Robinson, by suggesting that it's boring and unpleasant to him, and then by leaving sex out of the relationship with Elaine altogether, the film scampers away from a situation that would be truly challenging and compelling—a young man with strong sexual desire for mother and daughter. Ben doesn't have any sexual desires, apparently, and his unwilling involvement in the affair with Mrs. Robinson lets us off too comfortably. And at a time of much irrelevant nudity and bedroom talk in movies, this is one film that's entirely too fastidious; the absence of sex in *The Graduate* is a real failure (as it was in *The Family Way*) because the film is, to a large extent, *about* sexuality. But the urgency of Ben's triangular predicament is lost because we don't know much about what goes on in the bedroom, or even in Ben's fantasies. The incestuous longings that lie beneath the surface of the relationships are too uneasily sketched to carry much force. Any development of the oedipal rivalry between mother and daughter is also skimped. This hostility must be behind Mrs. Robinson's command that Ben not see Elaine, and if Elaine is human, she would have certain feelings of jealousy toward her mother. By making her outrage at Ben's affair *purely moral,* by ignoring its psychological content, the film misses an opportunity to explore its potentially explosive situation with depth and humanity—just as it cheated earlier by defining Ben's response to Mrs. Robinson in purely moral terms. Nichols titillates us with an intrigue that we haven't seen before in a movie, but he never gets close to feelings that would upset us. He knows how to startle, but he also knows how to please.

The movie as a whole is a Youth-grooving movie for old people. Nichols' young people have senile virtues—they're clean, innocent, upright, and cute too. Tired rich audiences can relax and say, "So *that's* what this youthful rebellion is all about; the kids want just what you and I want, Daddy—a happy marriage, a nice home, and they're really so well-behaved." Nichols doesn't risk showing young people who are doing truly daring, irreverent things, or even young people intelligent enough to seriously challenge the way old people live. All that ennobles Ben, after four years of college, is his virginity. He and Elaine are very bland, and that suits the old folks just fine; bankers and dowagers know that it's "in" to celebrate the young, and in *The Graduate* they can join the celebration with a minimum of fret or identification. The film is actually an insult to the young who aren't so goody-goody —young people who have complicated conflicts of loyalty and affection and who aren't able to make such a decisive moral rejection before they marry the most beautiful sweetheart of Sigma Chi.

Yet young people are falling for the film along with the old people, because it satisfies their most infantile fantasies of alienation and purity in a hostile world, their most simplistic notions of the generational gap, and their mushiest daydreams about the saving power of love. The movie swings on their side, though from a safe, rather patronizing position, and bleats that even when the middle-aged degenerates are cruelest, all you need is a closed-mouth kiss.

As for Nichols' film sense, he does seem to be learning. He still holds shots much too long or dresses them up much too self-consciously—as in the scuba-diving episode, a good idea ruined by clumsy direction. His images are mostly clichéd—not just blurs of flowers and sun-rippled water and car headlights reflecting on his lens, but even monkeys in the San Francisco zoo. He's good when you feel he's enjoying an unpretentiously silly, charming comic touch for its own sake, and he shows a nice eye for good natured satiric detail (he's hardly a caustic talent)—Mrs. Robinson watching *The Newlywed Game* on TV, a daffy, myopic lady organist at Elaine's wedding. And perhaps it's not fair to give the impression that the film fails because of expediency and calculated compromise; it may be that Nichols actually did not know what he was doing. He has stated recently, in an interview, that Ben and Elaine are not to be envied at film's conclusion, and that Ben will end up exactly like his parents—which suggests attempts at a more harshly sardonic point of view than the film manages to convey. Why do people cheer so exuberantly and walk out so happily if the film means to criticize Ben? Have they all missed the point? Whatever Nichols' intentions, *The Graduate* never really seems to be attacking the young people; all that can be said is that it celebrates them with a strange lack of conviction, which may once have been meant as savage irony, but comes across only as particularly hollow and ineffective film-making. Along with his handling of actors, Nichols' only real success in the movie is with the same sort of light-hearted, inconsequential farce routines he's provided for Neil Simon's comedies on Broadway; there's no point in encouraging him to believe that he's the seriocomic prophet of the plastic generation. Maybe Nichols does have the talent to do something more important—so far he has the energy and the ambition—but we're not going to find out as long as an evasive gimmicky hoax like *The Graduate* is trumpeted as a milestone in American film history.

## STUDY QUESTIONS

1.  Why do Farber and Changas call Benjamin *shallow?* What scene forces them to conclude that Mrs. Robinson is a more sensitive human being than Ben is?

2.  Why do they feel it significant that Nichols has not allowed the movie-goer to hear the conversation in Ben's convertible?

3.  Farber and Changas feel that the Benjamin—Mrs. Robinson—Elaine triangle is a "truly challenging and compelling" situation but that Nichols fails to grapple with it. How and why has he failed?

4.  In their last sentence, the reviewers call "The Graduate" "an evasive gimmicky hoax." Why *evasive? Gimmicky? Hoax?* Is *gimmicky* what Gill meant by *prankish?*

5.  Why do Farber and Changas feel that the musical score is inappropriate?

*Charles Webb*

# LETTER  TO  STANLEY  KAUFFMANN *

December 26, 1967

Dear Mr. Kauffmann,
    In the event that you should read my novel, *The Graduate,* I would appreciate hearing your views of it.

Sincerely,
Charles Webb

*Stanley Kauffmann*

# SECOND  LOOK

DOESN'T the film split in half? This is the recurrent question in a number of letters about *The Graduate*—although almost all correspondents start by saying they enjoyed it! I have now seen it again and have read the novel by Charles Webb on which it is based, and some further comment seems in order.

Reprinted by Permission of *The New Republic,* © 1967, 1968, Harrison-Blaine of New Jersey, Inc.

    * After Stanley Kauffmann's first review of "The Graduate" appeared in the *New Republic,* Webb wrote him this letter. Although the letter was not printed, Kauffmann's second review indirectly acknowledges it. The letter appears here with Webb's permission.

I like what I liked in the film even more, but now, having read the original, I can see a paradox about its shortcomings. (Many of which were noted
in my review.) Besides the fact that a great deal of Webb's good dialogue is
used in the screenplay, the structure of the first two-thirds of his book—
until Benjamin goes to Berkeley—is more or less the structure of the film.
The longest scene in the picture—the one in which Benjamin tries to get his
mistress to talk to him—is taken almost intact from the book. But Mike
Nichols and his screenwriters rightly sensed that the last third of the book
bogged down in a series of discussions, that Webb's device for Benjamin's
finding the place of Elaine's wedding was not only mechanical but visually
sterile, and that in general this last third had to be both compressed and
heightened. In reaction to the novel's weaknesses, they devised a conclusion
that has weaknesses of its own. But there is a vast difference between weakness and compromise.

Benjamin does *not* change, in my view, from the hero of a serious comedy
about a frustrated youth to the hero of a glossy romance; he changes *as Benjamin*. It is the difference between the women in his life that changes him.
Being the person he is, he could not have been assured with Mrs. Robinson
any more than he could have been ridiculous and uncommanding with
Elaine. We can actually see the change happen—the scene with Elaine at
the hamburger joint where he puts up the top of the car, closes the windows,
and talks. *Talks*—for the first time in the film. Those who insist that Mrs.
Robinson's Benjamin should be the same as Elaine's Benjamin are denying
the effect of love—particularly its effect on Benjamin, to whom it is not
only joy but escape from the nullity of his affair and the impending nullity of
himself.

There is even a cinematic hint early in the picture of the change that is to
come. Our first glimpse of Mrs. Robinson's nudity is a reflection in the glass
covering her daughter's portrait.

In character and in moral focus the film does not split, but there is a
fundamental weakness in the novel which the film tries, not quite successfully, to escape. The pivot of action shifts, after the story goes to Berkeley,
from Benjamin to Elaine. From then on, he knows what he wants; it is she
who has to work through an internal crisis. It was Nichols' job to dramatize
this crisis without abandoning his protagonist, to show the girl adjusting to
the shocking fact of Benjamin's affair with her mother, and to show it with,
so to speak, only a series of visits by her to the picture. To make it worse, the
environment—of the conventional campus romantic comedy—works
against the seriousness of the material. The library, the quad, the college
corridor have to be *overcome,* in a sense. Nichols never lets up his pressure
on what he feels the film is about, but the obliqueness of the action and the
associative drawbacks of the locale never quite cease to be difficulties. And,
as I noted, the final chase—though well done—does get thin.

But I think that, with some viewers, Nichols also suffers from his virtues. He has played to his strength, which is comedy; for, with all its touching moments and its essential seriousness, this is a very funny picture. A comedy about a young man and his father's partner's wife immediately seems adventurous; a comedy about a young man and a girl automatically gets shoved into a pigeonhole. This latter derogation seems to me unjust. We have only to remember (and to me it is unforgettable) that what is separating these young lovers is not a broken date or a trivial quarrel but a deep taboo in our society. For me, the end proof of the picture's genuine depth is the climax in the church, with Dustin Hoffman (even more moving the second time I saw him) screaming the girl's name from behind the glass wall. A light romance? That is a naked, last cry to the girl to free herself of the meaningless taboo, to join him in trying to find some possible new truth.

Yes, there are weaknesses. Yes, there are some really egregious gags. ("Are you looking for an affair?" the hotel clerk asks the confused Benjamin in the lobby.) But in cinematic skill, in intent, in sheer connection with us, *The Graduate* is, if I may repeat it, a milestone in American film history.

## STUDY QUESTIONS

1. In his second look at "The Graduate," Kauffmann focuses his attention on the second half of the film. What change occurs in Benjamin as a result of his discarding Mrs. Robinson for Elaine?

2. Why does Kauffmann feel that the conversation in the convertible is very important? How does his interpretation of this scene differ from that of Farber and Changas?

3. While Kauffmann admits that the film has some very funny moments, he is reluctant to label it as comedy. Where does he find "proof of the film's genuine depth"?

4. Does he, on second look, find new weaknesses in the film?

## Charles Webb and Stanley Kauffmann

# CORRESPONDENCE: "THE GRADUATE"

*Sirs:*

As the author of the novel, *The Graduate,* it has been extremely rewarding and gratifying to me to have had a film made of the book, and have the film so well received. Up till now I've made no criticisms of the film, either public or private. I would like to make one now, however, partially in response to the film itself and partially in response to two reviews of the film which Stanley Kauffmann wrote for *The New Republic.*

In a December 23 review he emphasizes the film's "moral stance." After considering the matter with care, I would have to say that my one greatest objection to the film is that it fails to take a moral stance.

In a February 10 review of the film, Mr. Kauffmann makes the point that the ending is proof of the picture's genuine depth. However, it is in the ending that the moral vacillation on the part of the film makers is, to me, most obvious. In the book the hero arrives at the church in time to rescue the girl before she's married. In the movie the hero arrives at the church after the vows have been spoken and drags her off anyway.

Benjamin Braddock, the hero, is a highly moral person as he is portrayed in the book. In the early portions he evinces a cynicism and defeatism which are clearly a reflection of the society he finds himself in. In the second half of the book he overcomes these feelings of self-defeat, or at least begins to. As a moral person he does not disrespect the institution of marriage. In the book the strength of the climax is that his moral attitudes make it necessary for him to reach the girl before she becomes the wife of somebody else, which he does. In the film version it makes no difference whether he gets there in time or not. As such, there is little difference between his relationship to Mrs. Robinson and his relationship to Elaine, both of them being essentially immoral.

*Charles Webb*
*So. Pasadena, Calif.*

*In reply* . . .

My first reaction to this letter was that it was written by Elaine May. But it comes from the same address, with the same signature, as an earlier letter from Mr. Webb after my first review, asking me to read his novel. I did so, and that was part of the reason for my second review.

Some authors are desecrated by film adaptation; some are lucky and don't always know it. In my second article I said that I thought Mike Nichols and his writers had sensed the novel's weaknesses and had tried to compensate for them. One such weakness was Mr. Webb's device by which Benjamin learns the place of Elaine's wedding, enabling him to get there in time to stop the ceremony. Nichols evidently felt the device was pat, the timing much too opportune, and the avoidance of difficulty (for the lovers) inconsistent with such moral confrontation as the film attempts. Nichols' solution is imperfect, but at least it avoids the destructive cliché of having Benjamin get there Just in Time. Equally important, Benjamin's desperation and Elaine's compassion are both heightened by the fact that the ceremony is over. And it is their feelings—not the question of the ceremony as such—that I said give that last scene its depth.

I still don't understand how the author of this novel, even though possibly upset at having been brushed off in all the furor about the film, can equate morality with marriage-licenses so absolutely. "There is little difference between his relationship to Mrs. Robinson and his relationship to Elaine, both of them being essentially immoral." . . . No, really, *is* it Elaine May?

                                                                *Stanley Kauffmann*

## STUDY QUESTIONS

1. According to Webb, how does Benjamin change in the second half of the novel?

2. What is Benjamin's attitude towards the institution of marriage?

3. Why does Webb think that, in the film version of his novel, Elaine is "essentially immoral"?

4. Why does Kauffman insist that the marriage ceremony, as such, is irrelevant?

5. Is he just in his accusation that Webb equates morality with marriage-licenses?

*Hollis Alpert*

# "THE GRADUATE" MAKES OUT

From a window of my apartment I have a view of a movie
house on Manhattan's East Side, where, ever since last
December, *The Graduate* has attracted long lines of patrons. During some of the coldest winter weekends, the lines extended
around the corner all the way down the block, much like those at the Radio
City Music Hall during holiday periods—except that the people waiting
for the next showing were not family groups but mostly young people in
their teens and early twenties. One night when it was eight degrees outside I
passed the line and noticed how little they seemed to be bothered by the
weather; they stomped their feet, they made cheerful chatter; it was as
though they all knew they were going to see something good, something
made for *them*. There were other cinemas nearby, but no one waited outside
in the cold. *The Graduate* was the film to see.

It still is, although now, with the warm weather, I notice that older people
have begun to intermix with the young crowd. Either *The Graduate* has
begun to reach deep into that amorphous audience that makes the large hits,
or the elders have become curious about the movie their offspring have been
going to see again and again. For that is what has been happening. *The
Graduate* is not merely a success; it has become a phenomenon of multiple
attendance by young people.

Letters from youthful admirers of the movie have been pouring in on
Dustin Hoffman, the talented thirty-year-old actor who plays the unprepos-
sessing twenty-one-year-old Benjamin Braddock. A strong theme of identification with Benjamin's particular parental and societal hang-ups runs
through these letters, as it also does in the letters to Mike Nichols, the director with an uncanny knack for forging hits. They've even been writing to
Joseph E. Levine, who backed and has been presenting the film. One boy
from Dallas wrote Levine, bragging that he had seen *The Graduate* more
than any of his friends, no less than fifteen times.

I have seen *The Graduate* three times—once at a preview, twice with audiences—thus satisfying, I hope, the Columbia graduate student who questioned my qualifications to assess the film after only one viewing. "But you must see it at *least* three times," she told me at a brunch given by her literature professor. "You see, it has meanings and nuances you don't get on just one viewing." She, and many others in her age group, cultishly attach all sorts of significance to the most minor of details. In the film's opening moments, for example, Benjamin is seen in the cabin of a huge jet, blank-faced among rows of blank faces. "Ladies and gentlemen," the captain's voice announces, "we are about to begin our descent into Los Angeles." My graduate student interpreted this as symbolic of Benjamin's arrival in his purgatory. Close to the end of the film, Benjamin is seen in an antiseptic church, outlined against a glass partition, his arms spread out. Many have interpreted this as suggesting a crucifixion theme, an interpretation, I have it on good authority, that was far from the minds of Mr. Nichols and Mr. Hoffman.

Viewers have made much of the symbolic use of glass and water in the film, signifying Benjamin's inability to get through, to communicate with the generation that has produced him. He peers through the glass of a tank at captive fish. At poolside, and in the pool, he looks out at his parents and their friends through the glass mask of a diving suit. At other times it is through sunglasses that he sees a home environment grown somewhat strange. Surely, Benjamin is alienated, but what is so odd here is that the generation-gappers who love the film regard this sense of estrangement as natural and normal, given the times and the middle-class values espoused by Benjamin's family and friends.

Hollywood has made strenuous attempts to appeal to the young film audience in the past, from Andy Hardy to Elvis Presley. There have been bikini beach parties, rock'n'roll orgies, Annette Funicello, and Peter Fonda on LSD, but the coin taken in from these usually cheap and sleazy quickies has been but a pittance compared to the returns from *The Graduate*. I need cite only the fact that *The Graduate* has already taken in more than $35,000,000 at the box office, after playing in only 350 of this country's theaters. Marlon Brando, the revered James Dean, and Presley never came near doing that. But this film, without the so-called stars for security, has now done better, financially speaking, than all but a dozen films of the past, and it still has thousands of drive-ins to play throughout the summer; it has yet to open anywhere abroad; and there are still those lines in front of the theater I see through my window. It is quite possible that *The Graduate* will become one of the three or four most profitable pictures *ever* made, perhaps as profitable as *The Sound of Music,* which has done so sensationally well that some critics renamed it *The Sound of Money.*

But how can these two industry landmarks be equated? *The Graduate* would appear to be squarely attacking all that *The Sound of Music* affirms so prettily: sugary sentiment, the sanctity of vows, whether religious or marital, the righteous rearing of children, melody over the mountains. The one has the well-scrubbed Julie Andrews and a dozen or so cute kids, all of them singing the Rodgers and Hammerstein lush gush as though it were the equal of Handel's *Messiah*. The other has the appealing but unhandsome Dustin Hoffman, Anne Bancroft playing a dissatisfied, alcoholic bitch of a wife, and a musical score by Paul Simon (performed by Simon and Garfunkel) that, contrasted with *The Sound of Music*'s sentimental reverence, chants: "And the people bowed and prayed/To the neon god they made . . ." Yet, a somewhat similar pattern of attendance has been noted about both films. The young audiences go to see *The Graduate* again and again. Housewives, matrons, women's clubbers went to see *The Sound of Music* again and again. We must hypothesize, then, that in this period of selective filmgoing there are at least two huge American audiences, there for the right picture, one made up of the seventeens to the twenty-fives, the other over thirty-five. The Motion Picture Association now advertises its more adult fare as "suggested for mature audiences," but one wonders which is the more mature.

I have encountered some members of my generation—let us loosely call it the over-forties—who haven't liked *The Graduate*. More than that, it made them angry. It was almost as though they felt themselves personally attacked, and it has occurred to me that their reaction is less objective and critical than emotional and, possibly, subliminal. These friends do worry about their children, they have brought them up well, given them opportunities of education and esthetic development, and they are quite certain they have managed to establish communication with their young. Their wives don't drink or seduce the neighbor's son. What's all this business about honesty and truth in *The Graduate?* The cards have been stacked against the middle-class parent and in favor of the rebellious "now" generation. They darkly hint at the commercial motives of Levine, Nichols, and company, who, it's true, hoped to come through at the box office, but had not the faintest notion they would come through so handsomely.

But *The Graduate* was not meant as an attack on a generation; it merely tells a *story,* as effectively as the makers knew how to do it. To understand the story it is necessary, however, to understand that Benjamin Braddock belongs to a milieu that has been termed the affluent society. He has never known financial insecurity—he has grown up among gadgets, among cars and swimming pools—and this he has taken so much for granted that it literally has no meaning for him. His parents, on the other hand, had presumably known hard times; they knew the value, for them, of money, of material success, of things. When Benjamin comes of age, literally and symbolically, he finds himself vaguely rejecting all that his parents hold so dear.

He finds himself a kind of object, the proud result of proper rearing, a reward of his parents' struggle in his behalf. Somehow, he feels, this is wrong,
but he doesn't yet know what is right. What guides and counselors does he
have? "Ben, I want to say one word to you, just one word," a friend of the
family breathes in his ear at a welcome-home party. Benjamin awaits the
word, among clinking glasses holding machine-made ice and good bourbon
and scotch. "Plastics," the fellow says, imparting the great secret to success
in our time. "There is a great future in plastics." The young audiences howl,
at least they did when I was there, and they're on the side of Benjamin and
the movie, which pokes fun at the plastic society and those who believe in it.

It is also interesting that while Benjamin tunes out for a while, he doesn't
turn on. He neither joins nor identifies with the hippies, the yippies, or the
weirdies; he is still thoroughly middle class, affluent variety. As he lazes
purposelessly in the California sun his thoughts turn heavily to those of sex
with Mrs. Robinson, whose frustrating marriage has borne her only one
good result, her lovely daughter, Elaine. Elaine will soon have the benefits
of her young womanhood, while the mother will sink into her bitter middle
age. Unconscious envy on Mrs. Robinson's part turns into willful determination, and she reveals herself in her nudity to Benjamin's unwilling gaze.
He first runs from her as from the very devil; after all, there are the proprieties, not to mention the taboos.

But then, he backs into the affair with Mrs. Robinson, who uses him for
the sex she doesn't get from Mr. Robinson. In only one moment does she
allow Benjamin to reach her; their intimacy is, literally, skin deep. When
Benjamin stupidly assumes that affection is necessary in a furtive affair, the
surprised Mrs. Robinson expels cigarette smoke into his mouth. She, too, is
aware of and insistent on the taboos; Benjamin is never, ever to take Elaine
out, for she assumes that by her actions she has cheapened both Benjamin
and herself.

And, of course, he does, forced into it by his unaware parents. Some critics have felt that the film breaks in two around this point, that the first half is
a "seriocomedy" and the second a kind of campus romance with a chase
finale. But this criticism seems to overlook the unifying fact of its all being
viewed and experienced through Benjamin, who is in a process of muddle,
change, and development. He is a truth-seeker, trying to cut through to some
acceptable level of meaning. He even tells the truth to the outraged Mr.
Robinson about the affair with Mrs. Robinson: "We got into bed with each
other. But it was nothing. It was nothing at all. We might—we might just as
well have been shaking hands."

One of the great appeals of the film to the young, and to the young in heart
of all ages, is Benjamin's honesty. The most important thing in common between Elaine and Benjamin is that they share the urge to see honestly and
clearly. But Elaine's emotions are still unstable. She allows herself to be

rushed into a hasty, secret marriage with an available suitor, appropriately enough a medical student, a candidate for surgeondom.

It is the ending of the film that has annoyed some, and delighted many others. If it were not for the ending, I doubt that *The Graduate* would have aroused as much enthusiastic favor as it has among the somewhat inchoately rebellious young. The distraught Benjamin, madly seeking his lost Elaine —the pure, the good, the holy—manages to reach the church, but not (as is invariably the case in a Doris Day movie) in time, upon which his hoarse, despairing appeal causes Elaine to leave her newly wedded groom, the assembled relatives, and to take a bus to nowhere in particular with Benjamin. To hold off the outraged parents, the attendants, and the minister, Benjamin grabs a large, golden cross and swings it menacingly, then uses it as a makeshift padlock on the church doors.

Curiously enough, the writer of the novel on which the film is based, Charles Webb, who was not much more than Benjamin's age at the time of writing, had fashioned a different ending—not *very* different, but crucial nevertheless. Benjamin, in the book, did arrive at the church in time, and there was no further "moral transgression" on his part involved, except, perhaps, for that bit of cross-wielding. It turns out that Mr. Webb was disturbed by the changed ending. He wrote a letter to *The New Republic,* complaining about critic Stanley Kauffmann's laudatory interpretation of the film, and particularly by what Kauffmann had approvingly termed the "film's moral stance." "As a moral person," Webb wrote, "he [Benjamin] does not disrespect the institution of marriage. In the book the strength of the climax is that his moral attitudes make it necessary for him to reach the girl before she becomes the wife of somebody else, which he does. In the film version it makes no difference whether he gets there in time or not. As such, there is little difference between his relationship to Mrs. Robinson and his relationship to Elaine, both of them being essentially immoral."

However, it *does* make a great deal of difference that in the film he does not get there in time, and the audiences have taken delight in just that fact. This film-bred, film-loving generation has seen that the ending is aimed, in a double-barreled kind of way, at what might be called general moral complacency in America, and also at Hollywood morality, which, from time immemorial, has felt it necessary to approve only the sexual love that occurs during the state of marriage, and that, up until only a decade ago, took place in twin beds, with at least one foot of the man on the floor.

Not only does Mr. Webb, in his letter, equate morality with marriage licenses, but he overlooks the fact that even in his novel Elaine would already have taken out a marriage license by the time Benjamin reached her. And there is a thing called consummation. The Nichols ending (relatively little story tampering was done otherwise) is a bold stroke that is not only effective but gives the story more meaning. We now see clearly Mrs. Robinson's tragedy, that she was unable to break out of the hollow formality, the prosperous smothering surface of her own marriage. "It's too late," she screams at her daughter, who is about to head for Benjamin. Upon which Elaine, seeing it all clearly for the first time, screams triumphantly back: "Not for *me.*"

But, if that old Production Code has been forsaken, if Doris Day has at last been soundly spanked for her virginal sins, hasn't morality triumphed after all? Of course it has. Mike Nichols, perhaps without fully realizing it, has lined up old Hollywood with avant-garde Hollywood. He has contrived a truly moral ending, and a most positive one at that. Honesty wins the day. Sex without love has been put in its place. Ancient taboos have been struck down. Material values have been shown to be hollow. As uninhibited and refreshing as *The Graduate* is, we are still left in fantasy land. "Most of us," a friend of mine ruefully commented, "still miss the bus."

On the other hand, perhaps the reason this newly mature generation has taken so to *The Graduate* is that it thinks, assumes, imagines it can make the bus. Mike Nichols told of meeting, recently, one of the leaders of the Columbia University rebellion. The student had loved *The Graduate,* as had his associates in rebellion. "In a way," he told Nichols, "it was what the strike was all about. Those kids had the nerve, they felt the necessity, to break the rules."

*The Graduate* represents a breakthrough of sorts in the Hollywood scheme of things, aside from its fine acting, its technical accomplishment, its vastly entertaining qualities. For it has taken aim, satirically, at the very establishment that produces most of our movies, mocked the morals and values it has long lived by. It is a final irony that it has thereby gained the large young audience it has been seeking and has been rewarded by a shower of gold.

## STUDY QUESTIONS

1. On what grounds does Alpert discard the crucifixion symbolism of the film's last scene?

2. Can you reconcile Farber and Changas' statement that "The Graduate" is a "Youth-grooving movie for old people" and Alpert's that it is a movie for those between 17 and 25.

3. How does Alpert answer Webb's charge about the film's conclusion?

4. According to Alpert, what is Mrs. Robinson's tragedy? Is she, then, a sympathetic character?

5. Alpert concludes that "The Graduate" demonstrates, among other things, the hollow material values of contemporary society. Where does he discuss this aspect of the film?

# *John Mason Brown*

# DISNEY AND THE DANE

John Mason Brown (1900–1969), critic, author, and lecturer, was born in Louisville, Kentucky. He took his B.A. at Harvard in 1923 and an L.H.D. at Williams in 1941; his honorary degrees include a Litt.D. from the University of Montana (1942), Clark University (1947), the University of Louisville (1948), Hofstra University (1954), and Long Island University (1963). He has taught at the University of Montana, Yale, Harvard, and Middlebury College, and has been drama critic for *Theater Arts Monthly,* the New York *Evening Post,* the New York *World-Telegram,* and the *Saturday Review.* He edited *The Portable Woollcott* (1946) and *The Portable Charles Lamb* (1949), and is the author of *The Modern Theater in Revolt* (1929), *Two on the Aisle* (1938), *Many a Watchful Night* (1944), *Seeing Things* (1946), and *Dramatis Personae* (1963).

Of COURSE, I wanted him to like it. I can't deny this. If I did, I would lie in my paternal teeth. Every parent knows the same hopes, the same fears when *that* afternoon at last comes around.

For both of us, this Saturday matinee was an adventure. For him, because it was the first time he had ever seen *Hamlet;* for me, because I was seeing it with him. And *Hamlet* shared with a boy of nine is *Hamlet* rediscovered.

He had seen other plays. *The Rose and the Ring,* for example, as done, and charmingly done, by the children of King-Coit School. This had been his initiation. In it he had found nothing to doubt, everything to believe, and suspense almost unbearable. But that had been at least five years back, when both he and the world were younger.

Since then he had seen *It Happens on Ice.* He had laughed at the clowns,

Reprinted in *Seeing Things* from *Saturday Review,* March 30, 1946. Reprinted here by permission of the author.

marveled at the spectacle, and in a voice filled with dread asked at the conclusion of each number, "Is it all over now?" He had also seen *Oklahoma!* He had come to it, Victrola-prepared, knowing all its songs, "Neat" was the word for *Oklahoma!*

But Maurice Evans in the GI *Hamlet*—this was something else. He did not know its song. My fingers were crossed. As I say, I hoped he would like it. You never know; you can never tell.

No form of cruelty is more cruel than exposing the young, when still too young, to books and plays ill-fated enough to have become classics. It is a murderous error; the kind of sulphurous mistake of more than paving-stone size, for which only good intentions can be responsible. The fact that both the living and the dead are equally defenseless against such foul play is the measure of its meanness.

To make a chore out of what should be a pleasure, to put the curse of obligation on what was meant to be absorbing, is to kill in the child the willingness to be pleased, and in the classic the ability to please. Masterpieces are masterpieces not because such grim conspirators as parents or teachers have told us that they are good. They are masterpieces because they tell us so themselves.

Yet they cannot be expected to speak for themselves until we are ready to hear them. Not to coin a phrase, there's the rub. For that happy conjunction of the man and the moment is as necessary for a book and its reader as Matthew Arnold knew it to be for the emergence of greatness in this world. When that moment will tick itself off, no one can foretell. It depends entirely upon the book and the individual.

Fortunately *Hamlet* can be approached on various levels. The difficulties of its language may pass unnoticed. Its inner anguishes may not be comprehended. Still it tells a story—and such a story. To the modern, no less than to the Elizabethan, its action remains the first of its excitements. The Ph.D.s move in only when the playgoers have moved out.

Quite naturally, one would expect a child to be more interested in what happens in the play than in what happens within the Prince's mind. But nowadays a boy comes to *Hamlet*—oh, perish the word!—"conditioned" in ways productive of unforeseeable results.

These war years, for example. They have accustomed him and his friends to every known weapon of mechanized destruction. After frequent newsreel exposures to, and hourly imitations of, the crash of buzz bombs, the drone of airplane motors, the rumble of tanks, the rat-tat-tat of machine guns, the swish of rockets, and the roar of navy guns, would a world seem unbearably tame in which death is brought about by mere poison or the quiet click of foils?

Then the comic books, those appalling polychrome termites which eat their way into every home, no matter how well guarded; into every weekly allowance, no matter how small; and into every budding mind, no matter how eager. They cannot be kept out. No doubt, in fairness they should not be. The young ought not to be exiled from an experience, common to their generation, which will one day prove a group memory. But what chance would Mary Arden's boy have against Blondie, or Superman? Was the Phantom the best homework for Shakespeare? Or Gandy and Sourpuss the proper preparation for Rosencrantz and Guildenstern? I must admit I wondered, more and more as that Saturday approached, with ever-increasing alarm.

And what about Disney, the greatest Walt the world has known since Whitman? In toy form in the nursery. In color in the comics. In books beyond counting. Above all, in the movies. Disney everywhere, Disney delectable because destructive. His creatures asking for no pity; creating pleasure by pain, living only to sock and, having socked or been socked, socking again. Could the Dane hope to compete with Donald Duck, Pluto, Monstro, the Big Bad Wolf, the Three Little Pigs, Dopey, and most particularly the redoubtable Mickey? Again I wondered. And hoped. And had my doubts.

How to unroll the red carpet for *Hamlet* was another question. I meant to prepare his mind for what he was to see without putting upon it the stigma of homework. I mentioned the play at breakfast for a week, naming it with as much excitement as if its title were synonymous with a fishing expedition, or a visit to the Hayden Planetarium, the Museum of Natural History, Schrafft's, or the Fleet.

Like many another apprehensive parent, I even fell back on the Lambs. Not for long—for only two pages, to be exact. I found my own eyes glazed as swiftly as his when I read that interminable first paragraph which begins, "Gertrude, Queen of Denmark, becoming a widow by the sudden death of King Hamlet, in less than two months after his death married his brother Claudius, which was noted by all people at the time for a strange act of indiscretion, or unfeelingness, or worse," etc. and etc.

Before I knew it, Saturday was upon us.

We lunched first. Not at home. At a restaurant. At Giovanni's, in feast-day style worthy of the event. While he sipped a preliminary Coke downstairs and I an old-fashioned, I tried in simpler language than the Lambs' to explain what he would see. It took more explanation than I had thought it would. I noticed that his eyes brightened whenever the Ghost was mentioned. Or whenever, in my narration, a cadaver bit the dust.

"Why don't they use pistols?" he asked while I was outlining the duel scene with its multiple jobs for the court mortician. It was only when I had described the poison foil, the poisoned wine, and the fury of the duel that he appeared to forgive Shakespeare for not having anticipated the age of the machine.

When he demanded, "They won't really be dead, will they?" I knew he was interested. For him, make-believe and reality were still blissfully, ter-rifyingly one—at least up to an uncertain point.

Traffic held us up so that we were a minute or so late in getting to the theatre. Hence we missed the first scene on the parapet. But a friendly Negro doorman did his bit for Shakespeare that afternoon.

"Yessuh," the doorman said to him, "the Ghost is walkin' now. It's too dark to go in there. You gotta wait. But never you fear—he'll walk again."

While we were waiting for the first scene to be over, I assured him for the tenth time that the Ghost was not real, and tried to tell him how the illusion of his disappearance would be achieved.

The auditorium was dark when, with other stragglers, we pushed our way in. After we reached our seats, I could hardly persuade him to take off his coat and muffler. His eyes were glued on the stage. I was pleased to see how, even for the young, *Hamlet* sweeps forward on its own feet without having to rely on footnotes.

He listened to every word. He was never bored. He sat far back in his seat, relaxed only during soliloquies. Whenever there was a threat of action, he pushed forward. Whenever the Ghost appeared, he stood up. Once, when an offstage cannon sounded in the darkness, he came close to turning a somersault into the lap of the woman who was sitting beyond him.

"Holy smokes, what's that?" he cried.

The intermission almost broke his heart. When I suggested that he go out with me while I had a cigarette, he was at first unwilling to leave. His was that nicest of nice fears. He was afraid they might start without waiting for the audience.

On the sidewalk we encountered the doorman for the second time. "Did you see the Ghost?" He beamed. "Well, you'll see him again. He ain't done walkin'."

On the way back to our seats came, "Is Mr. Maurice Evans married?"

"No," I replied, "I don't think so."

"Why doesn't he marry Ophelia?" he suggested. "She's a mighty pretty girl."

He was standing bolt upright during the whole of the play-within-the-play scene. The death of Polonius grieved him. "He's such a funny, nice old man; he made me laugh." But he started laughing again when Hamlet reached behind the curtains for Polonius's body, to say, "I'll lug the guts into the neighboring room."

He jumped as if dynamited at that moment when Laertes and his fol-lowers were storming the castle. And I almost had to hold him to prevent his crawling over the seat in front of him during the duel.

After Hamlet's body had been carried by the four captains up the stairs and the curtain had fallen, he stayed—taped to his seat—applauding. He applauded, and applauded, and applauded.

"How'd you like it?" I asked in the taxi, homeward bound.

"Gee, it was swell! I liked it better than *Oklahoma!*" Then a pause. "I liked it better than Donald Duck." Another pause—a long, reflective one. " 'A little more than kin, and less than kind.'—Gee! That's pretty, isn't it?"

### STUDY QUESTIONS

1. Why did Brown feel it so important that his son like *Hamlet?*

2. What does Brown say about the too-early introduction of the young to the classics? Do you agree? Who is responsible for this "foul" play?

3. What aspects of contemporary life condition the uninitiated theatergoer?

4. What does Brown mean when he calls Disney "delectable but destructive"?

5. Why did *Hamlet* appeal to the young eyes of Brown's son?

6. What was the ultimate proof that the boy had enjoyed the play?

*Marya Mannes*

# THE CONQUEST OF TRIGGER MORTIS

Marya Mannes (1904–    ) was born in New York City. She holds an honorary L.H.D. from Hood College, Maryland. From 1942 to 1945 she was an intelligence analyst for the United States government. Her television appearances, university lecture tours, and numerous periodical articles have made her a familiar figure to the American public. She has published *Message from a Stranger,* a novel (1948), *More in Anger* (1958), *Subverse,* satiric verse (1959), *The New York I Know* (1961), *But Will It Sell?* (1964), and *They,* a novel (1968).

THE RULING was passed in 1970, over the total opposition of the TV and radio networks and after ten years of controversy, six investigations, 483 juvenile murders, and the complete reorganization of the Federal Communications Commission.

What finally pushed it through was the discovery of *trigger mortis* in a number of American children born in widely separated areas. In this malformation the index finger is permanently hooked, forcing partial contraction of the whole hand in the position required for grasping a revolver. "The gun," said a distinguished anthropologist, "has become an extension of the American arm."

This mutation had been suspected some time before by others, who had found it worthy of note that in 1959, for instance, American toy manufacturers had sold more than $60 million worth of guns and revolvers and that on any given day on television between one and ten o'clock there were more than fifteen programs devoted to violence, and that in each of these programs a gun was fired at least once and usually several times. The only difference between the programs was that in some the shooting was done out of doors and often from horses and that in others it was done in hotel rooms, bars, or apartments. The first category was called Western and was considered a wholesome fight between good men and bad men in healthy country; the second was called Crime and Detective and was considered salubrious in its repeated implication that "crime does not pay," although the women and the interiors shown were usually expensive and the criminal's life, though short, a rich one.

Although this wholesale preoccupation with killing by gun coincided for many years with the highest rate of juvenile crime ever known in this country, and with open access to firearms for all who desired them, television and radio violence was considered by most experts of minimal importance as a contributory cause of youthful killing. Psychiatrists, social workers, program directors, advertisers, and sponsors had a handy set of arguments to prove their point. These (with translation appended) were the most popular:

Delinquency is a complex problem. No single factor is responsible. (Don't let's stick our necks out. Don't let's act. Don't let's lose money.)

It's all a matter of the home. (Blame the parents. Blame the neighborhood. Blame poverty.)

Crime and adventure programs are a necessary outlet for natural childhood aggressions. (Keep the little bastards quiet while Mummy fixes supper.)

We don't really know what influences children. (Let's wait till they kill somebody.)

Only disturbed or abnormal children are affected by what they see on programs. (And they are a minority. Let their psychiatrists worry about them.)

Everybody was very pleased with these conclusions, particularly the broadcasters, who could continue presenting thirty shootings a day secure in those sections of their old printed Code, which stated: ". . . such subjects as violence and sex shall be presented without undue emphasis and only as required by plot development or character delineation"; and "Television shall exercise care in . . . avoiding material which is excessively violent or would create morbid suspense, or other undesirable reactions in children." These same officials continued also to exercise care in not letting their own children look at the programs of violence which they broadcast.

So for years, and in spite of sporadic cries of alarm and protest from parents and a number of plain citizens, there were always enough experts to assure the public that crime and violence had nothing to do with crime and violence, and that gunplay was entertainment. Psychiatrists continued to say things like this about young killers: "The hostility, festering perhaps from the time he had been trained to the toilet, screamed for release," and educational groups came out periodically with reports on delinquency in which a suggested solution would be "to orient norm-violating individuals in the population towards a law-abiding lower-class way of life."

Dialogues like the following were frequent in Congressional investigations. This one occurred in a hearing of the Senate sub-committee on Juvenile Delinquency in 1954:

SENATOR: "In your opinion, what is the effect of these Western movies on children?"
EXPERT: "No one knows anything about it."
SENATOR: "Well, of course, you know that little children 6, 7, 8 years old now have belts with guns. Do you think that is due to the fact that they are seeing these Western movies and seeing all this shooting?"
EXPERT: "Oh, undoubtedly."

In the early 1950s, psychiatrist Fredric Wertham, from whose *The Circle of Guilt* the above was quoted, began a relentless campaign against what he called, in another book, *The Seduction of the Innocent*. Concentrating at first on horror and crime comics, the doctor moved inevitably into other fields of mass communication and provided impressive evidence along the way that although their gigantic dosage of violence could not be the sole factor in child criminality, it could certainly be considered a major one.

In attacking the slogan "It's all up to the home," he wrote: "Of course the home has a lot to do with it. But it is wrong to accuse the home as a cause in the usual abstract way, for the home is inseparable from other social circumstances to which it is itself vulnerable. . . . A hundred years ago the home could guard the children's safety; but with the new technological advances, the modern parent cannot possibly carry this responsibility. We need traffic regulations, school buses, school zones, and police to protect children from irresponsible drivers. Who will guard the child today from irresponsible adults who sell him incentives, blueprints, and weapons for delinquency?"

Wertham also countered the familiar claim that youthful violence was a result of wars by stating that it was not backed up by any scientific, concrete study and that neither the Second World War nor the Korean War explained the phenomenon: ". . . after the First World War the type of brutal violence currently committed on a large scale by the youngest children was almost unknown."

But Wertham was dismissed by many of his colleagues and much of the public as a man obsessed; too aggressively and intemperately committed to one cause—the rape of children's minds by mass communications—to be seriously considered. And the broadcasters and crime-comic publishers, first needled and exasperated by him, soon were able to view him with calm detachment as a crackpot. Thirty murders a day continued on the screen.

Then, early in 1959, the Nuffield Foundation in England put out a thick book called *Television and the Child,* by Hilde T. Himmelweit, A. N. Oppenheim, and Pamela Vince. For four years they examined thousands of children in five cities and of every class and background, and to this they joined a survey of American programming and viewing. They did not confine themselves to programming specifically for children, since it had long been obvious in England, as it was here, that children usually watched adult programs in preference. In more than four hundred pages of meticulous research, scientific detachment, and careful reasoning, they came to certain conclusions—the basis for a weight of further evidence that led, ten years later, to government intervention into broadcasting practices. Here are a few of their findings about the twenty percent of programs seen by children in their peak viewing hours that are devoted to aggression and violence:

"At the center of preoccupation with violence is the gun. Everyone has a gun ready for immediate use—even the barbers and storekeepers, who are not cowboys. People in Westerns take guns for granted. . . . Finally, while guns are used mostly for killing, they are also let off for fun. Nevertheless, guns spell power, they make people listen, and force them to do what is wanted.

"It is said that these programmes have two main desirable effects: they teach the lesson that crime does not pay; and they provide a harmless outlet through fantasy for the child's hostile feelings. We shall take issue with both statements. . . . The lesson as taught in these programmes is entirely negative (it is best not to offend against the law). . . . To present such a one-sided view, repeated week after week, is contrary to the recognized educational principle that a moral lesson, to be effective, must teach what should be done as well as what should not be done.

"More serious is the fact that . . . the child may equally well learn other, less desirable lessons from these programmes; that to shoot, bully, and cheat is allowed, provided one is on the right side of the law; and that relationships among people are built not on loyalty and affection but on fear and domination. . . ."

As for being a "harmless outlet for aggressive feelings," the authors— quoting the testimony of Dr. Eleanor E. Maccoby of Harvard that this discharge in fantasy alters nothing in the child's real life and so has no lasting values—write that when aggressive feelings exist, "They are not as a rule discharged on viewing crime and violence." "We cite three sets of data . . . [which] show that aggressive feelings are just as likely to be aroused as to be lessened through viewing these programmes—indeed, this seems more often to be the case." And, quoting Dr. Maccoby again, ". . . the very children who are presumably using the movie as an outlet for their aggressive feelings are the ones who carry away the aggressive content in their memories, for how long we do not know."

Miss Himmelweit and her colleagues sum up as follows: "It is suggested that crime and violence programmes increase tension and anxiety, increase maladjustment and delinquent behaviour, teach children techniques of crime, blunt their sensitivity to suffering and, related to this, suggest to them that conflict is best solved by aggression.

"Our findings and those of Maccoby suggest, then, that these programmes do not initiate aggressive, maladjusted, or delinquent behaviour, but may aid its expression. They may not affect a stable child, but they may evoke a response in the 5–10 percent of all children who are disturbed or at least emotionally labile, 'a group to be reckoned with by all the responsible people in the field of mass communications.' "

"We find . . . ," says the Nuffield Report, closing this chapter, "evidence that [these programs] may retard children's awareness of the serious consequences of violence in real life and may teach a greater acceptance of aggression as the normal, manly solution of conflict. . . . Just as a nation improves public hygiene when the evidence *suggests, without necessarily proving it* [my italics], that harm may otherwise result, so, we think there is need of remedial action here."

The Nuffield Report authors had obviously fallen into the error of blaming the industry instead of the child. For in most "acceptable" studies of television and its influence, wrote Wertham, "the assumption seems to be that when anything goes wrong the child must be morbid but the entertainment normal. Why not assume . . . that our children are normal, that they like adventure and imagination, that they can be stimulated to excitement, but that maybe something is wrong with what they are looking at? Why assume that they need death and destruction . . . ?"

Voices, voices, voices. "Beefs," "squawks," the broadcasters called these surges of protest year after year. And they would point with pride to the one children's program out of ten that was educational, the one out of twenty that had no shooting.

But their biggest defense became, in the end, their undoing. They had assured themselves that by removing the physical effects of violence, the violence was stripped of its harm. They showed no blood, no close-ups of agony, no open wounds, no last convulsions of a riddled body. Men were shot, they clapped their hands to their stomachs and either fell forwards or backwards as the camera panned away and returned to the gun. And while the broadcasters felt this a noble concession to the sensibilities of young viewers ("Brutality or physical agony," says the NBC Code, "is not presented in detail nor indicated by offensive sound or visual effects"), they were in actuality presenting, day after day, two great immoralities: that shooting is clean—and easy. To pull a trigger requires neither strength nor skill nor courage: it is the bullet that kills. And to kill with a gun is quick and painless. Hero or criminal, both were cowards who answered questions by pulling triggers. This was the daily lesson for sixty million children for twenty years.

Until, of course, the people finally rose. Some cool legal heads first managed to draft legislation banning the sale of pornographic and sensational printed material without in any way curbing individual liberty or preventing the sale of *Lady Chatterley's Lover* or Aristophanes. And then came the famous FCC ruling Bylaw A 41-632. In effect, this gave the FCC, by then reorganized into a body of able and dedicated communications experts who functioned in areas of human values as well as in electronics, the power to revoke the license of any broadcaster showing fictionalized killing, whether by gun or knife or bludgeon, without also displaying the natural consequences to the person killed. The bill as originally drawn was a forthright ban on all fictionalized killing except by direct bodily means, without weapons: killing had to involve strength, skill, and direct physical involvement. But after long wrangling, the later version was adopted as being less tainted by censorship and more practicable. For if a program showing a killing had to show a head blown to bits at close range, or blood gushing from mouth and nose, or a jagged stomach wound—all natural results of shooting—the sponsor would not sell many goods. It was therefore far easier to cut out guns entirely.

Far easier, that is, for everyone but the writers. After the law was put into effect, there was mass unemployment among the television writers in Hollywood and New York. They had relied so long on their collaborator, the gun, that they were incapable of writing a plot without it. As Wertham quoted an experienced TV crime writer: "You have to work backwards. You're given a violent situation and you have to work within that framework." Start with the murder and then fit in the people. And suddenly the poor writers had to think up situations where people and ideas provided the excitement instead of a Colt 45. It was a period of anguish none of them will forget.

But for every ten writers who became alcoholics or joined insurance firms, one began to tap resources he had never used and to write well and truly for the first time. And after a hiatus of incredible sterility, when frantic producers threw in anything innocuous, however old and poor, to fill up the time formerly used by crime plays and Westerns, television slowly began to get better and better, more inventive both in the uses of realism and fantasy.

A new generation of American children grew up with no appetite for guns and no illusions about the fun of painless killing. Instead they learned judo or, through compulsory strenuous exercises then conducted daily by their schools, became a race of confident acrobats, able to show their prowess in feats of skill, daring, and endurance without knifing, stomping, or shooting anyone.

Disarmament—at least of the young—was finally a fact.


## STUDY QUESTIONS

1. Define *trigger mortis*. What is *rigor mortis?*

2. What arguments were used to counteract the charge that television had contributed to the rising juvenile crime rate? How effective are Miss Mannes' parenthetical remarks in answering these arguments?

3. Why was Frederic Wertham's campaign dismissed by his colleagues and the public?

4. In self-defense, what modifications did the networks make?

5. In general, what is the tone of Miss Mannes' essay? Is it sarcastic? Satirical? Is the essay humorous?

Russell Lynes

# WHAT REVOLUTION
# IN MEN'S CLOTHES?

Russell Lynes (1910–      ) was born in Barrington, Massachusetts. He received a B.A. from Yale University in 1932 and holds an honorary A.F.D. from Union College, Schenectady, New York. Lynes is an associate fellow of Berkeley College, Yale University, and has been one of *Harper's* contributing editors since 1967. His books include *Highbrow, Lowbrow, Middlebrow* (1949), *Snobs* (1950), *Guests* (1951), *Tastemakers* (1954), *A Surfeit of Honey* (1957), *Cadwallader* (1959), *The Domesticated Americans* (1963), and *Confessions of a Dilettante* (1966).

ONE CAN HARDLY pick up a magazine or a newspaper without seeing a reference to the revolution in men's clothes.
I have been collecting material for several years on this so-called revolution, and the more I collect, the less like a revolution it seems to be. What I read is scarcely reinforced by what I see on the streets or among my contemporaries and my children's contemporaries or in men's shops. There seems to be a moderate shift in the nature of the way men dress, most men, that is, and the rate of change seems about the standard rate that has prevailed since the beginning of the Industrial Revolution a century and a half ago. Lapels change their width; the length of jackets goes up and down; waistcoats come and go; buttons move an inch in one direction or another; collars turn from high to low and back to high; hat brims expand and contract; neckties are wide and gaudy or narrow and bleak. But I can't see that there has been a revolution in clothes of any real consequence since the French Revolution, when fops were not only heedless but became headless. The only real revolutionary I can think of in my time was Raymond Duncan, who long survived his more famous sister, the dancer Isadora Duncan; he went about in homespun, skirted garments and wore a rope garland

around his head to restrain his long, gray hair. He did it out of some sort of conviction that modern men's clothes make no sense, and who can argue with that?

Something interesting, if not revolutionary, has obviously been going on, and I think it is worth considering why the changes are surprising enough to be thought of as a revolution.

The most obvious thing that has happened to male attire was rather surprisingly summed up for me by a narcotics-squad detective testifying before a New York County grand jury of which I was a member. Speaking of some individuals he had under surveillance on the street, he said, "One of them was an *apparently male* Puerto Rican . . ."

"Apparently male," indeed. There has, of course, been a great deal of comment in the last few years about how male fashions and female fashions are meeting at a center point where their inhabitants become indistinguishable. Like many people I am frequently misled by the long slim legs in tight pants, box jackets, and medium-long hair into thinking that what I am looking at (especially from behind) is not what I am looking at at all. But to say that this is a change in male fashion is to get the matter back-end to. It is a radical change in female fashion and a slight shift in what is considered tonsorially acceptable for men. Very long hair on men is still cause for sharp comment in many quarters, but moderately long hair is increasingly acceptable even to the conservative members of the community . . . any community. Very soon the American Civil Liberties Union, which has expended a good deal of energy on defending boys who have been thrown out of (or kept out of) high school because their hair is too long to suit the school principal, will be able to return to their more proper functions of defending more urgent causes.

What has caused the confusion between the sexes is the female affectation of male styles and not the other way around. Teen-age boys, for example, are not trying to look like Barbra Streisand, with their hair longish and down over one eye; Barbra (she wants everyone to know her as just Barbra) is trying to look like a teen-age boy, and the effect has been theatrically successful. She has made what is essentially a rather homely face into something remarkably attractive.

There has been a good deal of unnecessary and unjustified comment by the slowly vanishing crew-haircut crew about the sissy fashion of long hair. Actually, long tresses on men seems to be a socio-political rather than a sexual manifestation. There are sissies with long hair, I have no doubt, but homosexuals seem to incline more to tidy little bangs than to locks falling down over the backs of their necks. By and large, it seems to be true that homosexuals want to be conspicuous to each other but inconspicuous to the community in general. They have their own set of tonsorial signals which should not be confused with what is generally accepted as male fashions.

The long haircut, incidentally, is working a hardship on some factions of the barbering business. A *Wall Street Journal* reporter several months ago quoted a barber in New York whose shop is near Columbia University as saying, "This used to be a growing business. Now it's not. Long hair did it." And another barber in Manchester, Connecticut, says he specialized in the "nothin' haircut . . . nothin' off the top, nothin' off the sides, nothin' off the back." It is preferred by what he calls "Beatle types." Historically, of course, there is no connotation of sissiness in long hair for men. Davy Crockett and Buffalo Bill wore their hair long, but today's hair styles among the young are tending rather more toward styles popular with men at the height of the Italian Renaissance than anything that has come along since.

The feminization of male fashions has been criticized within the male clothing industry. George H. Richman, who is president of a major men's clothes manufacturing business that also has retail outlets, got himself in wrong with some of his colleagues by publicly deploring "creeping feminization in the men's and particularly the boys' wear in this country." To this the vice-president in charge of merchandizing for Hart Schaffner & Marx replied, "There's only an infinitesimal percentage of buyers and producers who take fashions to such an extreme you might charge a feminine trend." A guest columnist in *The Arizona Republic* of Phoenix expressed the opinion that a reputation for effeminate attire in high school can follow a boy through life; though the effeminate attire he describes ("long curled hair . . . extremely pointed shoes, and pants that are revealingly tight . . .") has perfectly good, indeed excellent, historic precedent as the most masculine of clothes.

What he is really talking about is not effeminacy but the revolt of the young against their parents' generation, which is another subject, another aspect of fashion, indeed. It can be argued that the elaborateness of dress, the concern with fancy details in shoes and scarves and shirts and jackets, is man trying to reclaim from women his right to plumage which he gave up at the time of the Industrial Revolution, when he wished to divorce himself from the frippery which was associated in the public mind with the old aristocracy. The Industrial Revolution man, as Quentin Bell [1] has pointed out, dressed in black like the chimneys of his factories, and his object of "conspicuous consumption" (Bell elaborates on Veblen) became his wife, whom he dressed in acres of silks and satins ornamented with miles of ruffles and bows. It took him more than a century to get sick of his smoke- (or soot-) colored garments, but he's no less a man for being bored with them. If some of the young are revolting to (and against) their parents and grandparents, it is because they have chosen to take a giant step in a corner of human male behavior where tiny steps have been the accepted practice.

There is a good deal of speculation in the press about what has caused the

[1] *On Human Finery.* A. A. Wyn, 1949.

change in men's fashions, who are the leaders who set the styles, if, of course, there is any great change.

The change is mostly among the young, and the source of their inspiration is said to be pop singers. John Crosby, writing in *The Observer* (London) quoted David Mlinaric, a designer and "one of the best-dressed young men in London," as saying, "The pop singers have the panache of the movie stars in the 'thirties. The pop singers and designers and film stars dress adventurously—and others have followed them."

Carnaby Street, in the West End in London, as every teen-ager who knows anything knows, is the Mecca of the "mod" fashions which became so popular that nearly every department store in America which caters to the young opened special shops for them. Though the fad has already declined somewhat, it was from there that the inspiration came for the "fancy floral-print cotton shirts," the "hip-hugging trousers with low belt lines," the jackets that were long and nipped in at the waist, the bell-bottom trousers, the high-heeled boots and gorgeous cuff links. In London, however, Carnaby Street is looked down upon with some disdain by the young men like Mlinaric who are the most conscientiously elegant and self-consciously fashionable young men in England, as producing rather shoddy wares of inferior materials and design. These young men, mostly in one way or another associated with the arts and therefore free of the confining conventions of the business world, regard themselves as dandies; their concern with what is in general socially acceptable is, if it exists at all, contemptuous. The scorn of dandyism for middle-class notions of suitability is far more like the beatnik scorn for middle-class morality, objectives, and conventions than either the dandy or the beatnik would be likely to recognize or, if he recognized it, admit.

But Carnaby Street and dandyism (some more accurately call it foppishness) are symptoms and not causes. The causes are in the changing social structure, in the nature of a society so affluent that it has the leisure to consume several wardrobes, on the one hand, and a society bored with itself (as England seems to be) on the other. It reflects as well changes in a society in which manual labor is continually giving way to automation and in which professionalism is increasingly in demand in every aspect of the economy. Clothes have always been a means of typecasting, a means of class identification, professional identification, regional identification, and even intellectual identification. The function of clothes in this respect has not changed; but the rules of the game have changed somewhat and will continue to change.

Let us leave the young aside for a moment, though we cannot ignore them in considering what has happened to the looks of their elders. Essentially, American men are extremely conservative in their dress and they change their habits slowly. What is suitable for the banker today and what was suitable forty years ago can be almost superimposed on each other. Like the military uniform, the bank uniform has given up the high, stiff collar; otherwise it remains, except for changes in details of lapels, width of trouser bottoms, and length of jacket almost precisely what it was in 1910.

In a catalogue of "Men's Nobby Clothes, made to measure" for the spring and summer of 1905, Magnus Brothers of Chicago shows page after page of suits which only the most meticulously up-to-date man would hesitate to wear to the office today. The double-breasted suits are three-button instead of two and the straight jackets are four-button instead of two or three, but the lapels are just about in today's fashion, so are the cuffless trousers. The dinner jackets have shawl collars, not notched lapels; short boxed topcoats are *au fait* for spring. The principal differences are in the width of hat brims, the length of overcoats, and the prices of everything. The suits cost from $10 to $20 (with "Rain-proof Overcoat, Fancy Vest, or Silk Umbrella FREE"); a Tuxedo Suit cost $30 to $40 and a Full Dress Suit (tailcoat) from $30 to $45. Clothes advertised by Hart Schaffner & Marx a couple of years later are a little more dashing and a little closer to what is being revived by Carnaby Street today as "Edwardian," than those offered by Magnus Brothers. The jackets are a little longer and some of them have piping on the lapels and down the front.

Most men dress most of the time to be inconspicuous, to draw as little attention to themselves as possible. No one, for example, notices a professor in tweeds, but a professor on campus in a dark business suit, white shirt with French cuffs, and a stickpin in his tie might be taken for a member of the board of trustees or of the upper echelons of the college administration. A man in tweeds in a New York business office is probably from the "creative" department of an advertising firm. Men's uniforms, in other words, vary only slightly and within a narrow range depending on how and where they work. The president of a Chicago or New York bank would be as much out of place in a tweed jacket and slacks as a man in a dinner jacket who turned up to read the gas meter. There are, to be sure, regional differences in what are considered suitable uniforms: California, for instance, and especially the southern part of the state, is a law unto itself; the light (even white) wide-brimmed hat is conventional for businessmen in the Southwest, and in Dallas men can reasonably wear tweed jackets to their offices; in Florida it is often difficult to tell the native real-estate man from the migrant vacationer in his winter plumage.

Obviously it is in the off-day or leisure or sports clothes that the greatest revolution has taken place, but it is not a new revolution at all. The trend to male "separates" (trousers and jackets that don't match) started (or I should say restarted; jackets and trousers of different materials were common in the last century) about twenty-five years ago in earnest; but just last year the number of sports coats that were sold increased from 12.5 million in 1965 to about 13.4 million. The number of suits, on the other hand, went down from 22.4 million in 1965 to about 21 million in 1966. More surprising, however, is the fact that, according to the *New York Times,* "More suits were made in 1953 than in 1966, even though the number of males in the country grew sharply during this thirteen-year period." Still more surprising, to me, and I would think to those who believe the American man to be increasingly clothes-conscious, is a statement by the clothing industry that "male apparel has been receiving a smaller share of the total consumer disposable income" than it did two decades ago.

It is quite possible, of course, that this diminishing percentage of income spent on clothes is attributable to the increased spending on equipment for leisure—for skis and outboards, for camping trailers and golf clubs and fishing tackle. Costumes for leisure are far less expensive for the average man than the clothes he needs for his office and for the formal aspects of his leisure. There is an interesting sidelight, however, on leisure clothes that is worth mentioning. Many men are inclined to wear as their leisure clothes the working uniform of other men. The businessman, for instance, wears blue jeans, the uniform of the farm or cowhand; the farmer, when he gets dressed up for his leisure, wears the uniform of the office worker, a business suit. (World War I uniforms, at the moment anyway, are dear to the hearts of teenagers who buy them, or copies of them, in Army and Navy stores.)

It is also in leisure clothes that the peacock in many men reveals itself, but even so, the efforts of the clothing industry to make men gorgeous has never quite succeeded. Do you remember in the mid-1950s when there was an attempt to get men into bright dinner jackets? Where are they now? An advertisement for a "tangerine double-breasted blazer" in *The New York Times Magazine* this February said, "Who says a tasteful outfit must be dull? And if you can't quite summon up the ego for Tangerine, how about Canary, Sky, or Skipper?" It does, as the ad implies, still take a great deal of summoning up of the ego for most men to wear flashing colors.

High style for mature men, like high style for the dashing young, comes to America from Europe as it has since the founding of the Republic, and before, and as it does for women. The influence of Italian tailors, so evident a few years ago (remember the silk suitings?) seems to have given way to the influence of Paris and London on those men whose closets bulge with thirty suits and fifty pairs of shoes. Pierre Cardin of Paris, whose reputation is based on *haute couture* for women, but who now runs a business that makes five times as much on men's clothes as on women's, is a current mentor of the fashionable (as opposed to the foppish) male, though much of what he advocates is greatly modified for the American scene. The jackets are long and tightly fitted, the waistcoats are high, and often have lapels, trousers are narrow and without cuffs, shirt collars spread wide (but are not long), and neckties are also wide but, compared with Carnaby Street fashions, they are rather subdued. Cardin's English counterpart, also a dressmaker, is Hardy Amies of Savile Row.

Their fashions are likely, however, to penetrate the general American market in greatly modified ways and very slowly. The primary influence on men's fashions comes, as it has not come in the past, from the young. It does not come from those young who are hopefully outrageous, from the black-leather jacket and surfing young or from the beats; it comes from the amused and urbane young who, without being foppish, have decided that there is more to dressing than putting on a shirt and a suit and a tie that nobody will notice and that their elders can certainly not complain about. What is evolving is not a revolution in men's clothes; it is an echoing of the past overlaid with a kind of humor and a sense of fun. Lord Chesterfield is quoted by Quentin Bell as saying, "The difference . . . between a man of sense and a fop is that the fop values himself upon his dress; and the man of sense laughs at it, at the same time that he knows he must not neglect it."

There are inevitably a great many people of my generation who think the young are going to hell in a basket because their hair is long, their shirts frilled, their trousers tight, their neckties loud as brass bands, and inevitably they will try to harness them, discourage them, lay down the law . . . keep them out of school, indeed. One is reminded of the "sumptuary laws" that have been enacted by almost every civilization at sometime or other to quell elaborateness of dress on grounds of extravagance, immorality, and the breaking down of social distinctions. As Mr. Bell says, ". . . the history of sumptuary laws is a history of dead letters."

## STUDY QUESTIONS

1. Russell Lynes seems to feel that "modern men's clothes make no sense." What does he mean by *no sense?* Do you agree?

2. According to Lynes, what has caused the confusion—of styles—between the sexes? How does Barbra Streisand demonstrate his point? Can you suggest other examples?

3. Lynes calls long hair on men "a socio-political rather than a sexual manifestation." What socio-political issues does he then discuss?

4. What is *typecasting?* How are clothes a means of typecasting? How is the matter of typecasting with clothes connected to Lynes' statement that "most men dress most of the time to be inconspicuous"?

5. What is a *fop,* as defined by Lord Chesterfield? As defined by a dictionary? Why might "a man of sense" laugh at his dress?

*Tom Wolfe*

# THE MARVELOUS MOUTH

Tom Wolfe (1931–      ) was born in Richmond, Virginia. He received his
B.A. from Washington and Lee (1951) and his Ph.D. from Yale (1957). He
has been a reporter for the Springfield, Mass. *Union,* the Washington *Post,*
and the *New York Herald-Tribune.* His essays were published in 1965
under the wildly improbable but singularly appropriate title of *The Kandy-
Kolored Tangerine-Flake Streamline Baby.* His most recent books are *The
Electric Kool-Aid Acid Test* and *The Pump House Gang* (1968). A talented
artist, his works have been exhibited in a one-man show.

ONE THING that stuck in my mind, for some reason, was the
way that Cassius Clay and his brother, Rudy, and their
high-school pal, Tuddie King, and Frankie Tucker, the
singer who was opening in Brooklyn, and Cassius' pride of "foxes," Sophia
Burton, Dottie, Frenchie, Barbara and the others, and Richie Pittman and
"Lou" Little, the football player, and everybody else up there in Cassius'
suite on the forty-second floor of the Americana Hotel kept telling time by
looking out the panorama window and down at the clock on top of the Paramount Building on Times Square. Everybody had a watch. Cassius, for example, is practically a watch fancier. But, every time, somebody would look
out the panorama window, across the City Lights scene you get from up high
in the Americana and down to the lit-up clock on that whacky Twenties-
modern polyhedron on top of the Paramount Building.

One minute Cassius would be out in the middle of the floor reenacting his
"High Noon" encounter with Sonny Liston in a Las Vegas casino. He has a
whole act about it, beginning with a pantomime of him shoving open the
swinging doors and standing there bowlegged, like a beer delivery man.
Then he plays the part of the crowd falling back and whispering, "It's Cassius Clay, Cassius Clay, Cassius Clay, Cassius Clay." Then he plays the part

of an effete Las Vegas hipster at the bar with his back turned, suddenly freezing in mid-drink, as the hush falls over the joint, and sliding his eyes around to see the duel. Then he plays the part of Cassius Clay stalking across the floor with his finger pointed at Sonny Liston and saying, "You big ugly bear," "You big ugly bear," about eighteen times, "I ain't gonna fight you on no September thirtieth, I'm gonna fight you right now. Right here. You too ugly to run loose, you big ugly bear. You so ugly, when you cry, the tears run down the back of your head. You so ugly, you have to sneak up on the mirror so it won't run off the wall," and so on, up to the point where Liston says, "Come over here and sit on my knee, little boy, and I'll give you your orange juice," and where Cassius pulls back his right and three guys hold him back and keep him from throwing it at Liston, "And I'm hollering, 'Lemme go,' and I'm telling them out the side of my mouth, You better *not* lemme go.' " All this time Frankie Tucker, the singer, is contorted across one of the Americana's neo-Louis XIV chairs, breaking up and exclaiming, "That's my man!"

The next minute Cassius is fooling around with Rudy's phonograph-and-speaker set and having some fun with the foxes. The foxes are seated around the room at ornamental intervals, all ya-ya length silk sheaths, long legs and slithery knees. Cassius takes one of Rudy's cool jazz records or an Aretha Franklin or something like that off the phonograph and puts on one of the 45-r.p.m. rock-and-roll records that the singers keep sending to him at the hotel.

"Those are Rudy's records, I don't *dig* that mess. I'm just a boy from Louisville"—he turns his eyes up at the foxes—"I dig rock and roll. Isn't that right?"

All the girls are hip, and therefore cool jazz fans currently, so most of them think the whole thing over for a few seconds before saying, "That's right."

Cassius puts a 45-r.p.m. on and says, "This old boy's an alley singer, nobody ever heard of him, he sings about beans and bread and all that old mess."

Cassius starts laughing at that and looking out over the city lights, out the panorama window. The girls aren't sure whether he is laughing with or at the alley singer.

Cassius scans the foxes and says, "This is *my* crowd. They don't dig that other mess, either."

The girls don't say anything.

"Is that your kinda music? I know it's *hers,*" he says, looking at Francine, who is sitting pretty still. "She's about to fall over."

And may be at this point somebody says, "What time is it?" And Rudy or somebody looks out the panorama window to the clock on the Paramount Building and says, "Ten minutes to ten."

Cassius had just come from the Columbia Records studio, across from the hotel at Seventh Avenue and 52nd, where he was making an album, *I Am the Greatest,* a long pastiche of poems and skits composed wholly in terms of his impending fight with Sonny Liston. The incessant rehearsing of his lines for two weeks, most of them lines he had sprung at random at press conferences and so forth over a period of a year and a half, had made Cassius aware, as probably nothing else, of the showman's role he was filling. And made him tempted by it.

After cutting up a little for Frankie Tucker and the foxes and everybody —showing them how he could *act, really*—he went over to one side of the living room and sat in a gangster-modern swivel chair and propped his feet up on the panorama-window ledge and talked a while. Everybody else was talking away in the background. Somebody had put the cool jazz back on and some husky girl with one of those augmented-sevenths voices was singing "Moon Over Miami."

"What's that club Leslie Uggams was at?" Cassius asked.

"The Metropole."

"The Metropole, that's right. That's one of the big ones out there, ain't it?"

His designation of the Metropole Café as "a big one" is an interesting thing in itself, but the key phrase is "out there." To Cassius, New York and the hot spots and the cool life are out there beyond his and Rudy's and Tuddie's suite at the Americana and beyond his frame of reference. Cassius does not come to New York as the hip celebrity, although it would be easy enough, but as a phenomenon. He treats Broadway as though these were still the days when the choirboys at Lindy's would spot a man in a white Palm Beach-brand suit heading up from 49th Street and say, "Here comes Winchell," or "Here comes Hellinger," or even the way Carl Van Vechten's Scarlet Creeper treated 125th Street in the days of the evening promenade. Cassius likes to get out amongst them.

About 10:15 P.M. he motioned to Sophia and started leaving the suite. All five girls got up and followed. The procession was spectacular even for Seventh Avenue on a crowded night with the chocolate-drink stands open. Cassius, six feet three, two hundred pounds, was wearing a black-and-white checked jacket, white tab-collared shirt and black tie, light gray Continental trousers, black pointed-toe Italian shoes, and walking with a very cocky walk. The girls were walking one or two steps behind, all five of them, dressed in slayingly high couture. There were high heels and garden-party hats. Down at the corner, at 52nd Street, right at the foot of the hotel, Cassius stopped, looked all around and began loosening up his shoulders, the way prizefighters do. This, I found out, is Cassius' signal, an unconscious signal, that he is now available for crowd collecting. He got none on that corner, but halfway down to 51st Street people started saying, "That's Cassius Clay, Cassius Clay, Cassius Clay, Cassius Clay," the way he had mimicked it back in the hotel. Cassius might have gotten his crowd at 51st Street —he was looking cocky and the girls were right behind him in a phalanx, looking gorgeous—but he headed on across the street, when the light changed, over to where two fellows he knew were standing a quarter of the way down the block.

"Here he comes. Whatta you say, champ?"

"Right, man. Hey," said Cassius, referring the girls to the taller and older of the two men, "I want you all to meet one of the greatest singers in New York." A pause there. "What is your name, man, I meet so many people here."

"Hi, Pinocchio," said one of the foxes, and the man smiled.

"Pinocchio," said Cassius. Then he said, "You see all these queens are with me?" He made a sweeping motion with his hand. The girls were around him on the sidewalk. "All these foxes."

"That's sump'n else, man."

Cassius could have gotten his crowd easily on the sidewalk outside the Metropole. When it's warm, there is always a mob out there looking in through the front doorway at the band strung out along the bandstand, which is really more of a shelf. If there is a rock-and-roll band, there will always be some Jersey teen-agers outside twisting their ilia to it. That night there was more of a Dixieland or jump band on, although Lionel Hampton was to come on later, and Cassius entered, by coincidence, while an old tune called "High Society" was playing. All the foxes filed in, a step or so behind. The Metropole Café has not seen many better entrances. Cassius looked gloriously bored.

The Metropole is probably the perfect place for a folk hero to show up at in New York. It is kind of a crossroads, or ideal type, of all the hot spots and live joints in the country. I can tell you two things about it that will help you understand what the Metropole is like, if you have never been there. First, the color motif is submarine green and Prussian blue, all reflected in huge wall-to-wall mirrors. If the stand-up beer crowd gets so thick you can't see over them to the bandstand, you can always watch through the mirror. Second, the place attracts high-livers of a sort that was there that night. I particularly remember one young guy, standing there at the bar in the submarine-green and Prussian-blue light with sunglasses on. He had on a roll-collar shirt, a silvery tie, a pale-gray suit of the Continental cut and pointed black shoes. He had a kingsize cigarette pasted on his lower lip, and when the band played "The Saints," he broke into a terribly "in" and hip grin, which brought the cigarette up horizontal. He clapped his hands and hammered his right heel in time to the drums and kept his eyes on the trumpet player the whole time. The thing is, kids don't even do that at Williams College anymore, but they do it at the Metropole.

This same kid came over to ask Cassius for his autograph at one point. He thought "The Saints" was hip, but he must not have thought autograph-hunting was very hip. He wanted an autograph, however. He handed Cassius a piece of paper for his autograph and said, "It's not for me, it's for a buddy of mine, he wants it." This did not score heavily with Cassius.

"Where's your pen?" he said.

"I don't have a pen," the kid said. "It's for a friend of mine."

"You ain't got no pen, man," said Cassius.

About a minute later the kid came back with a pen, and Cassius signed the piece of paper, and the kid said, "Thank you, Cassius, you're a gentleman." He said it very seriously. "It's for a buddy of mine. You're a real gentleman."

That was the tone of things that night in the Metropole. Everything was just a little off, the way Cassius saw it.

From the moment he walked into the doorway of the Metropole, people were trying to prod him into the act.

"You *really* think you can beat Sonny Liston, man?"

"Liston must fall in eight."

"You *really* mean that?"

"If he gives me any jive, he goes in five," Cassius said, but in a terribly matter-of-fact, recitative voice, all the while walking on ahead, with the foxes moseying in behind him, also gloriously bored.

His presence spread over the Metropole immediately. As I said, it is the perfect place for folk heroes, for there is no one in there who is not willing to be impressed. The management, a lot of guys in tuxedos with the kind of Hollywood black ties that tuck under the collars and are adorned with little pearl stickpins and such devices—the management was rushing up. A guy at the bar, well-dressed, came up behind Cassius and touched him lightly at about the level of the sixth rib and went back to the bar and told his girl, "That's Cassius Clay. I just touched him, no kidding."

They sat all the foxes down in a booth at about the middle of the Metropole Café and gave Cassius a chair by himself right next to them. Lionel Hampton came up with the huge smile he has and shook Cassius' hand and made a fuss over him without any jive about when Liston must fall. Cassius liked that. But then the crowd came around for autographs, and they wanted him to go into his act. It was a hell of a noisy place.

But the crowd at the Metropole hit several wrong notes. One was hit by a white man about fifty-five, obviously a Southerner from the way he talked, who came up to Clay from behind—people were gaggled around from all sides—and stuck the blank side of a Pennsylvania Railroad receipt, the kind you get when you buy your ticket on the train, in his face and said in a voice you could mulch the hollyhocks with:

"Here you are, boy, put your name right there."

It was more or less the same voice Mississippians use on a hot day when the colored messenger boy has come into the living room and is standing around nervously. "Go ahead, boy, sit down. Sit in that seat right there."

Cassius took the Pennsylvania Railroad receipt without looking up at the man, and held it for about ten seconds, just staring at it.

Then he said in a slightly accusing voice, "Where's your pen?"

"I don't have a pen, boy. Some of these people around here got a pen. Just put your name right there."

Cassius still didn't look up. He just said, "Man, there's one thing you gotta learn. You don't *ever* come around and ask a man for an autograph if you ain't got no pen."

The man retreated and more people pressed in.

Cassius treats the fact of color—but not race—casually. Sometimes, when he is into his act, he will look at somebody and say, "You know, man, you lucky, you seen me here in living color." One time, I remember, a CBS news crew was filming an interview with him in the Columbia Records Studio A, at 799 Seventh Avenue, when the cameraman said to the interviewer, who was moving in on Cassius with the microphone: "Hey, Jack, you're throwing too much shadow on Cassius. He's dark enough already."

All the white intellectuals in the room cringed. Cassius just laughed. In point of fact, he is not very dark at all.

But he does not go for any of the old presumptions, such as, "Put your name right there, boy."

Another wrong note was hit when a middle-aged couple came up. They were white. The woman struck you as a kind of Arkansas Blanche Dubois. They looked like they wanted autographs at first. They did in a way. They were both loaded. She had an incredible drunk smile that spread out soft and gooey like a can of Sherwin-Williams paint covering the world. She handed Cassius a piece of paper and a pencil and wanted him to write down both his name *and* her name. He had just about done that when she put her hand out very slowly to caress his cheek.

"Can I touch you?" she said. "I just want to touch you."

Cassius pulled his head back.

"Naw," he said. "My girl friends might get jealous."

He didn't call them foxes to her. He said it in a nice way. After she left, though, he let her have it. It was the only time I ever heard him say anything contemptuously of anyone.

"Can I *touch* you, can I *touch* you," he said. He could mimic her white Southern accent in a fairly devastating way.

"Naw, you can't touch me," he said, just as if he were answering her face to face. "Nobody can touch me."

As a matter of fact, Cassius is good at mimicking a variety of white Southern accents. He doesn't do it often, but when he does it, it has an extra wallop because he has a pronounced Negro accent of his own, which he makes no attempt to polish. He only turns it on heavier from time to time for comic effect. Once I heard him mimic both himself, a Louisville Negro, and newspapermen, Louisville whites, in one act.

I had asked him if the cocky act he was putting on all over the country, and in England for that matter, surprised the people who knew him back home. What I was getting at was whether he had been a cocky kid in Louisville back in the days before anybody ever heard of him. He changed the direction slightly.

"They believe anything you tell 'em about me back in Louisville. Newspapermen used to come around and I'd give 'em predictions and they'd say, 'What is this boy doing?'

"I had a fight with Lamar Clark, I believe it was, and I said [*Clay mimicking Clay, heavy, high-flown, bombastic Negro accent*]: 'Lamar will fall in two.' I knocked him out in two, and they said [*Clay mimicking drawling Kentucky Southern accent*]: 'Suht'n'ly dee-ud.' " (Certainly did.)

"I said, 'Miteff will fall in six.'

"They said, 'Suht'n'ly dee-ud.'

"I said, 'Warren will fall in four.'

"They said, 'Suht'n'ly dee-ud.' "

Clay had a lot better look on his face when people came by to admire what he had become rather than the funny act he puts on.

One young Negro, sharp-looking, as they say, in Continental clothes with a wonderful pair of Latin-American sunglasses, the kind that are narrow like the mask the Phantom wears in the comic strip, came by and didn't ask Cassius when Liston would fall. He shot an admiring, knowing look at the foxes, and said, "Who are all these girls, man?"

"Oh, they just the foxes," said Cassius.

"Man, I like your choice of foxes, I'm telling you," the kid said.

This tickled Cassius and he leaned over and told it to Sophia.

The kid, meantime, went around to the other side of the booth. He had a glorified version of how Cassius was living. He believed Cassius as he leaned over to the girls when the waiter came around and said, "You get anything you want. I own this place. I own all of New York." (Sophia gave him a derisive laugh for that.)

The kid leaned over to one of the girls and said: "Are you all his personal property?"

"What are you talking about, boy. What do you mean, his *personal property?*"

"You know, *his,*" said the kid. He was getting embarrassed, but he still had traces of a knowing look salivating around the edges.

"Why do we have to be his personal property?"

"Well, like, I mean, you know," said the kid. His mouth had disintegrated completely into an embarrassed grin by now, but his eyes were still darting around, as if to say, "Why don't they level with me. I'm a hip guy."

Cassius also liked it when a Negro he had met a couple of nights before, an older guy, came around and didn't ask when Liston would fall.

"I saw a crowd on the sidewalk out there, and I might have *known* you'd be inside," he told Cassius. "What's going on?"

"Oh, I'm just sitting here with the foxes," said Cassius.

"You sure are," the fellow said.

A young white kid with a crew cut said, "Are you afraid of Liston?"

Cassius said mechanically, "That big ugly bear? If I was worried I'd be out training and I'm out partying."

Cassius had a tall, pink drink. It was nothing but Hawaiian Punch, right out of the can.

"How you gonna beat him?"

"I'll beat that bear in eight rounds. I'm strong and I'm beautiful and I'll beat that bear in eight rounds."

"You promise?" said the kid. He said it very seriously and shook Cassius' hand, as though he were getting ready to go outside and drop off a couple of grand with his Weehawken bookmaker. He apparently squeezed pretty hard. This fellow being a fighter and all, a guy ought to shake hands like a man with him.

Cassius pulled his hand away suddenly and wrung it. "Don't ever squeeze a fighter's hand, man. That hand's worth about three hundred thousand dollars," he said, making a fist. "You don't have to shake hands, you doing good just to lay eyes on me."

The kid edged off with his buddy and he was saying, "He said, 'Don't ever squeeze a fighter's hand.' "

By now Cassius was looking slightly worse than gloriously bored.

"If they don't stop worrying me," he said, "I'm gonna get up and walk out of here."

Sophia leaned over and told me, "He doesn't mean that. He loves it."

Of all the girls, Sophia seemed to be closest to him. She found him amusing. She liked him.

"You know, he's really a normal boy," she told me. She threw her head to one side as if to dismiss Cassius' big front. "Oh, he's got a big mouth. But aside from that, he's a real normal boy."

The foxes were beginning to stare a little morosely into their Gin Fizzes and Brandy Alexanders and Sidecars, and even the stream of autograph seekers was slowing down. It was damned crowded and you could hardly hear yourself talk. Every now and then the drummer would go into one of those crazy sky-rocketing solos suitable for the Metropole, and the trumpet player would take the microphone and say, "That's what Cassius Clay is going to do to Sonny Liston's head!" and Cassius would holler, "Right!" but it was heavy weather. By this time Richie Pittman had dropped in, and Cassius motioned to him. They got up and went out "for some air." At the doorway there was a crowd on the sidewalk looking in at the bandstand, as always. They made a fuss over Cassius, but he just loosened his shoulders a little and made a few wisecracks. He and Richie started walking up toward the Americana.

It was after midnight, and at the foot of the hotel, where this paseo-style sidewalk pans out almost like a patio, there was a crowd gathered around. Cassius didn't miss that. They were watching three street musicians, colored boys, one with a makeshift bass—a washtub turned upside down with a cord coming up out of the bottom, forming a single string; a drum—a large tin-can bottom with spoons as sticks; and one guy dancing. They were playing "Pennies from Heaven," a pretty good number for three guys getting ready to pass the hat. Cassius just walked up to the edge of the crowd and stood there. One person noticed him, then another, and pretty soon the old "That's Cassius Clay, Cassius Clay, Cassius Clay" business started. Cassius' spirits were rising. "Pennies from Heaven" stopped, and the three colored boys looked a little nonplussed for a moment. The show was being stolen. Somebody had said something about "Sonny Liston," only this time Cassius had the 150-watt eyes turned on, and he was saying, "The only thing I'm worried about is, I don't want Sonny Liston trying to crash *my* victory party the way I crashed his. I'm gonna tell him right before the fight starts so he won't forget it, 'Sonny,' I'm gonna tell him, 'Sonny Liston, I don't want you trying to crash my victory party tonight, you hear that? I want you to hear that now, 'cause you ain't gonna be *able* to hear anything eight rounds from now.' And if he gives me any jive when I tell him that, if he gives me any jive, he must fall in five."

A soldier, a crank-sided kid who looked like he must have gone through the battered-child syndrome at about age four, came up to take the role of Cassius' chief debater. Cassius likes that when he faces a street crowd. He'll hold a press conference for anybody, even a soldier on leave on Seventh Avenue.

"Where you gonna go after Sonny Liston whips you?" the kid said. "I got some travel folders right here."

"Boy," said Cassius, "you talk about traveling. I want you to go to that fight, 'cause you gonna see the launching of a human satellite. Sonny Liston."

The crowd was laughing and carrying on.

"I got some travel folders," the kid said. "You better look 'em over. I can get you a mask, too."

"You gonna bet against me?" said Cassius.

"Every cent I can get my hands on," said the kid.

"Man," said Cassius, "you better save your money, 'cause there's gonna be a total eclipse of the Sonny."

Cassius was standing there looking like a million dollars, and Richie was standing by, sort of riding shotgun. By this time, the crowd was so big, it was spilling off the sidewalk into 52nd Street. All sorts of incredible people were moving up close, including sclerotic old men with big-lunch ties who edged in with jag-legged walks. A cop was out in the street going crazy, trying to prod everybody back on the sidewalk. A squad car drove up, and the cop on the street put on a real tough tone, "All right, goddamn it," he said to an old sclerotic creeper with a big-lunch tie, "get up on the sidewalk."

Cassius looked around at me as if to say, "See, man? That's only what I predicted"—which is to say, "When I walk down the street, the crowds, they have to call the police."

The autograph business had started now, and people were pushing in with paper and pens, but Cassius wheeled around toward the three colored boys, the musicians, and said, "Autographs are one dollar tonight. Everyone puts one dollar in there" (the musicians had a corduroy-ribbed box out in front of the tub) "gets the autograph of Cassius Clay, the world's strongest fighter, the world's most beautiful fighter, the onliest fighter who predicts when they will fall."

The colored boys took the cue and started up with "Pennies from Heaven" again. The kid who danced was doing the merengue by himself. The kid on the bass was flailing away like a madman. All the while Cassius was orating on the corner.

"Come on, man, don't put no fifty cents in there, get that old dollar bill outa there. Think at all you're getting free here, the music's so fine and here you got Cassius Clay right here in front of you in living color, the next heavyweight champion of the world, the man who's gon' put old man Liston in orbit."

The dollar bills started piling up in the box, and the solo merengue kid was dervishing around wilder still, and Cassius wouldn't let up.

"Yeah, they down there right now getting that Medicare ready for that old man, and if I hit him in the mouth he's gonna need Denticare. That poor ol' man he's so ugly, his wife drives him to the gym every morning 'fore the sun comes up, so nobody'll have to look at him 'round home. Come on, man, put yo' money in that box, people pay good money to hear this—"

The bass man was pounding away, and Cassius turned to me and said, behind his hand, "Man, you know one thing? If I get whipped, they gonna run me outa the country. You know that?"

Then he threw his head back and his arms out, as if he were falling backward. "Can you see me flat out on my back like this?"

The colored kids were playing "Pennies from Heaven," and Cassius Clay had his head thrown back and his arms out, laughing, and looking straight up at the top of the Americana Hotel.

### STUDY QUESTIONS

1.  Why does Wolfe begin so abruptly?

2.  Wolfe begins three consecutive paragraphs with "Cassius" and a verb in the present tense. What does he accomplish by this rhetorical parallelism?

3.  Is there any evidence that Clay does not take himself seriously, that he is amused by his public image? Can you tell Wolfe's attitude toward Clay?

4.  Sophie says Clay has a *big* mouth; Wolfe calls it *marvelous*. What does each mean?

5.  What is the point of Wolfe's final paragraph?

## *Eudora Welty*

# POWERHOUSE

Eudora Welty (1909–    ) was born in Jackson, Mississippi, where she now lives. She attended Mississippi State College for Women, the University of Wisconsin, and Columbia. Her first short stories were published in the 1930s in *The Southern Review;* her considerable skill resulted in Katherine Anne Porter writing the introduction to *A Curtain of Green* (1941). Miss Welty's other books include *The Robber Bridegroom* (1942), and *The Ponder Heart* (1954). She is a member of the National Institute of Arts and Letters and an honorary consultant in American letters of the Library of Congress.

POWERHOUSE is playing! He's here on tour, from the city— Powerhouse and His Keyboard—Powerhouse and His Tasmanians—all the things he calls himself! There's no one in the world like him. You can't tell what he is. He looks Asiatic, monkey, Babylonian, Peruvian, fanatic, devil. He has pale gray eyes, heavy lids, maybe horny like a lizard's, but big glowing eyes when they're open. He has feet size twelve, stomping both together on either side of the pedals. He's not coal black—beverage-colored; looks like a preacher when his mouth is shut, but then it opens—vast and obscene. And his mouth is going every minute, like a monkey's when it looks for fleas. Improvising, coming upon a very light and childish melody, *smooch*—he loves it with his mouth. Is it possible that he could be this! When you have him there performing for you, that's what you feel. You know people on a stage—and people of a darker race—so likely to be marvelous, frightening.

This is a white dance. Powerhouse is not a show-off like the Harlem boys —not drunk, not crazy, I think. He's in a trance; he's a person of joy, a fanatic. He listens as much as he performs—a look of hideous, powerful rapture on his face. Big arched eyebrows that never stop traveling. When he plays, he beats down piano and seat and wears them away. He is in motion every moment—what could be more obscene? There he is with his great head, big fat stomach, little round piston legs, and long yellow-sectioned strong fingers, at rest about the size of bananas. Of course you know how he sounds—you've heard him on records; but still you need to see him. He's going all the time, like skating around the skating rink or rowing a boat. It makes everybody crowd around, here in this shadowless steel-trussed hall with the rose-like posters of Nelson Eddy and the testimonial for the mind-reading horse in handwriting magnified five hundred times.

Powerhouse is so monstrous he sends everybody into oblivion. When any group, any performers, come to town, don't people always come out and hover near, leaning inward about them, to learn what it is? What is it? Listen. Remember how it was with the acrobats. Watch them carefully; hear the least word, especially what they say to one another, in another language; don't let them escape you—it's the only time for hallucination, the last time. They can't stay. They'll be somewhere else this time tomorrow.

Powerhouse has as much as possible done by signals. Everybody, laughing as if to hide a weakness, will sooner or later hand him up a written request. Powerhouse reads each one, studying with a secret face: that is the face which looks like a mask, anybody's; there is a moment when he makes a decision. Then a light slides under his eyelids and he says, "Ninety-two!" or some combination of figures—never a name. Before a number the band is all frantic, misbehaving, pushing, like children in a schoolroom, and he is the teacher getting silence. His hands over the keys, he says sternly, "You-all ready? You-all ready to do some serious walking?"—waits—then, STAMP. Quiet. STAMP, for the second time. This is absolute. Then a set of rhythmic kicks against the floor to communicate the tempo. Then, "Oh Lord," say the distended eyes from beyond the boundary of the trumpets;

"Hello and good-bye"—and they are all down the first note like a water-fall.

This note marks the end of any known discipline. Powerhouse seems to abandon them all; he himself seems lost—down in the song—yelling up like somebody in a whirlpool—not guiding them, hailing them only. But he knows, really. He cries out, but he must know exactly. "Mercy! . . . What I say! . . . Yeah!" and then drifting, listening,—"Where that skin-beater?" (wanting drums),—and starting up and pouring it out in the greatest delight and brutality. On the sweet pieces, such a leer for every-body! He looks down so benevolently upon all the faces and whispers the lyrics, and if you could hear him at this moment on "Marie, the Dawn Is Breaking"! He's going up the keyboard with a few fingers in some very de-rogatory triplet routine; he gets higher and higher, and then he looks over the end of the piano, as if over a cliff. But not in a show-off way: the song makes him do it.

He loves the way they all play, too—all those next to him. The far sec-tion of the band is all studious—wearing glasses, every one; they don't count. Only those playing around Powerhouse are the real ones. He has a bass fiddler from Vicksburg, black as pitch, named Valentine, who plays with his eyes shut and talking to himself, very young. Powerhouse has to keep encouraging him: "Go on, go on, give it up, bring it on out there!" When you heard him like that on records, did you know he was really plead-ing?

He calls Valentine out to take a solo.

"What you going to play?" Powerhouse looks out kindly from behind the piano; he opens his mouth and shows his tongue, listening.

Valentine looks down, drawing against his instrument, and says without a lip movement, "Honeysuckle Rose."

He has a clarinet player named Little Brother, and loves to listen to any-thing he does. He'll smile and say, "Beautiful!" Little Brother takes a step forward when he plays and stands at the very front, with the whites of his eyes like fishes swimming. Once when he played a low note Powerhouse muttered in dirty praise, "He went clear downstairs to get that one!"

After a long time, he holds up the number of fingers to tell the band how many choruses still to go—usually five. He keeps his directions down to signals.

It's a bad night outside. It's a white dance, and nobody dances, except a few straggling jitterbugs and two elderly couples; everybody just stands around the band and watches Powerhouse. Sometimes they steal glances at one another. Of course, you know how it is with *them*—they would play the same way, giving all they've got, for an audience of one. . . . When some-body, no matter who, gives everything, it makes people feel ashamed for him.

## II

Late at night, they play the one waltz they will ever consent to play. By request, "Pagan Love Song." Powerhouse's head rolls and sinks like a weight between his waving shoulders. He groans and his fingers drag into the keys heavily, holding on to the notes, retrieving. It is a sad song.

"You know what happened to me?" says Powerhouse.

Valentine hums a response, dreaming at the bass.

"I got a telegram my wife is dead," says Powerhouse, with wandering fingers.

"Uh-huh?"

His mouth gathers and forms a barbarous O, while his fingers walk up straight, unwillingly, three octaves.

"Gipsy? Why, how come her to die? Didn't you just phone her up in the night last night long distance?"

"Telegram say—here the words: 'Your wife is dead.' " He puts four-four over the three-four.

"Not but four words?" This is the drummer, an unpopular boy named Scoot, a disbelieving maniac.

Powerhouse is shaking his vast cheeks. "What the hell was she trying to do? What was she up to?"

"What name has it got signed, if you got a telegram?" Scoot is spitting away with those wire brushes.

Little Brother, the clarinet player, who cannot now speak, glares and tilts back.

"Uranus Knockwood is the name signed." Powerhouse lifts his eyes open. "Ever heard of him?" A bubble shoots out on his lip, like a plate on a counter.

Valentine is beating slowly on with his palm and scratching the strings with his long blue nails. He is fond of a waltz; Powerhouse interrupts him.

"I don't know him. Don't know who he is." Valentine shakes his head with the closed eyes, like an old mop.

"Say it again."

"Uranus Knockwood."

"That ain't Lenox Avenue."

"It ain't Broadway."

"Ain't ever seen it wrote out in any print, even for horse-racing."

"Hell, that's on a star, boy, ain't it?" Crash of the cymbals.

"What the hell was she up to?" Powerhouse shudders. "Tell me, tell me, tell me." He makes triplets, and begins a new chorus. He holds three fingers up.

"You say you got a telegram." This is Valentine, patient and sleepy, beginning again.

Powerhouse is elaborate. "Yas, the time I go out—go way downstairs along a long *corridor* to where they puts us. Coming back, steps out and hands me a telegram: 'Your wife is dead.' "

"Gipsy?" The drummer is like a spider over his drums.

"Aaaaaa!" shouts Powerhouse, flinging out both powerful arms for three whole beats to flex his muscles, then kneading a dough of bass notes. His eyes glitter. He plays the piano like a drum sometimes—why not?

"Gipsy? Such a dancer?"

"Why you don't hear it straight from your agent? Why it ain't come from headquarters? What you been doing, getting telegrams in the *corridor,* signed nobody?"

They all laugh. End of that chorus.

"What time is it?" Powerhouse calls. "What the hell place is this? Where is my watch and chain?"

"I hang it on you," whimpers Valentine. "It still there."

There it rides on Powerhouse's great stomach, down where he can never see it.

"Sure did hear some clock striking twelve while ago. Must be *midnight.*"

"It going to be intermission," Powerhouse declares, lifting up his finger with the signet ring.

He draws the chorus to an end. He pulls a big Northern hotel towel out of the deep pocket in his vast, special-cut tux pants and pushes his forehead into it.

"If she went and killed herself!" he says with a hidden face. "If she up and jumped out that window!" He gets to his feet, turning vaguely, wearing the towel on his head.

"Ha, ha!"

"Sheik, sheik!"

"She wouldn't do that." Little Brother sets down his clarinet like a precious vase, and speaks. He still looks like an East Indian queen, implacable, divine, and full of snakes. "You ain't going to expect people doing what they says over long distance."

"Come on!" roars Powerhouse. He is already at the back door; he has pulled it wide open, and with a wild, gathered-up face is smelling the terrible night.


## *III*

Powerhouse, Valentine, Scoot, and Little Brother step outside into the drenching rain.

"Well, they emptying buckets," says Powerhouse in a mollified voice. On the street he holds his hands out and turns up the blanched palms like sieves.

A hundred dark, ragged, silent, delighted Negroes have come around from under the eaves of the hall, and follow wherever they go.

"Watch out, Little Brother, don't shrink," says Powerhouse. "You just the right size now—clarinet don't suck you in. You got a dry throat, Little Brother, you in the desert?" He reaches into the pocket and pulls out a paper of mints. "Now hold 'em in your mouth—don't chew 'em. I don't carry around nothing without limit."

"Go in that joint and have beer," says Scoot, who walks ahead.

"Beer? Beer? You know what beer is? What do they say is beer? What's beer? Where I been?"

"Down yonder where it say World Cafe, that do?" They are across the tracks now.

Valentine patters over and holds open a screen door warped like a seashell, bitter in the wet, and they walk in, stained darker with the rain and leaving footprints. Inside, sheltered dry smells stand like screens around a table covered with a red-checkered cloth, in the centre of which flies hang onto an obelisk-shaped ketchup bottle. The midnight walls are checkered again with admonishing "Not Responsible" signs and black-figured smoky calendars. It is a waiting, silent, limp room. There is a burnt-out-looking nickelodeon, and right beside it a long-necked wall instrument labeled "Business Phone, Don't Keep Talking." Circled phone numbers are written up everywhere. There is a worn-out peacock feather hanging by a thread to an old, thin, pink, exposed light bulb, where it slowly turns around and around, whoever breathes.

A waitress watches.

"Come here, living statue, and get all this big order of beer we fixing to give."

"Never seen you before anywhere." The waitress moves and comes forward and slowly shows little gold leaves and tendrils over her teeth. She shoves up her shoulders and breasts. "How I going to know who you might be—robbers? Coming in out of the black night right at midnight, setting down so big at my table!"

"Boogers," says Powerhouse, his eyes opening lazily as in a cave.

The girl screams delicately with pleasure. Oh Lord, she likes talk and scares.

"Where you going to find enough beer to put out on this-here table?"

She runs to the kitchen with bent elbows and sliding steps.

"Here's a million nickels," says Powerhouse, pulling his hand out of his pocket and sprinkling coins out, all but the last one, which he makes vanish like a magician.

Valentine and Scoot take the money over to the nickelodeon, which is be-

ginning to look as battered as a slot machine, and read all the names of the
records out loud.

"Whose "Tuxedo Junction"?" asks Powerhouse.

"You know whose."

"Nickelodeon, I request you please to play 'Empty Bed Blues' and let
Bessie Smith sing."

Silence: they hold it, like a measure.

"Bring me all those nickels on back here," says Powerhouse. *"Look* at
that! What you tell me the name of this place?"

"White dance, week night, raining—Alligator, Mississippi—long ways
from home."

"Uh-huh."

"Sent for You Yesterday and Here You Come Today" plays.

The waitress, setting the tray of beer down on a back table, comes up taut
and apprehensive as a hen. "Says in the kitchen, back there putting their
eyes to little hole peeping out, that you is Mr. Powerhouse. . . . They
knows from a picture they seen."

"They seeing right tonight—that is him," says Little Brother.

"You him?"

"That is him in the flesh," says Scoot.

"Does you wish to touch him?" asks Valentine. "Because he don't bite."

"You passing through?"

"Now you got everything right."

She waits like a drop, hands languishing together in front.

"Babe, ain't you going to bring the beer?"

She brings it, and goes behind the cash register and smiles, turning different ways. The little fillet of gold in her mouth is gleaming.

"The Mississippi River's here," she says once.

Now all the watching Negroes press in gently and bright-eyed through the
door, as many as can get in. One is a little boy in a straw sombrero which has
been coated with aluminum paint all over. Powerhouse, Valentine, Scoot,
and Little Brother drink beer, and their eyelids come together like curtains.
The wall and the rain and the humble beautiful waitress waiting on them
and the other Negroes watching enclose them.

"Listen!" whispers Powerhouse, looking into the ketchup bottle and very
slowly spreading his performer's hands over the damp wrinkling cloth with
the red squares. "How it is. My wife gets missing me. Gipsy. She goes to the
window. She looks out and sees you know what. Street. Sign saying 'Hotel.'
People walking. Somebody looks up. Old man. She looks down, out the window. Well? . . . *Sssst! Plooey* What she do? Jump out and bust her brains
all over the world."

He opens his eyes.

"That's it," agrees Valentine. "You gets a telegram."

"Sure she misses you," Little Brother adds.

"Now, it's nighttime." How softly he tells them! "Sure. It's the nighttime. She say, 'What do I hear? Footsteps walking up the hall? That him?' Footsteps go on off. It's not me. I'm in Alligator, Mississippi; she's crazy. Shaking all over. Listens till her ears and all grow out like old music-box horns, but still she can't hear a thing. She says, 'All right! I'll jump out the window then.' Got on her nightgown. I know that nightgown, and she thinking there. Says, 'Ho hum, all right,' and jumps out the window. Is she mad at me! Is she crazy! She don't leave *nothing* behind her!"

"Ya! Ha!"

"Brains and insides everywhere—Lord, Lord."

All the watching Negroes stir in their delight, and to their higher delight he says affectionately, "Listen! Rats in here."

"That must be the way, Boss."

"Only, naw, Powerhouse, that ain't true. That sound too *bad*."

"Does? I even know who finds her," cries Powerhouse. "That no-good pussy-footed crooning creeper, that creeper that follow around after me, coming up like weeds behind me, following around after me everything I do and messing around on the trail I leave. Bets my numbers, sings my songs, gets close to my agent like a betsy-bug—when I going out he just coming in. I got him now! I got him spotted!"

"Know who he is?"

"Why, it's that old Uranus Knockwood!"

"Ya! Ha!"

"Yeah, and he coming now, he going to find Gipsy. There he is, coming around that corner, and Gipsy kadoodling down—oh-oh! Watch out! *Sssst-flooey!* See, there she is in her little old nightgown, and her insides and brains all scattered round."

A sigh fills the room.

"Hush about her brains. Hush about her insides."

"Ya! Ha! You talking about her brains and insides—old Uranus Knockwood," says Powerhouse, "look down and say, 'Lord!' He say, 'Look here what I'm walking in!' "

They all burst into halloos of laughter. Powerhouse's face looks like a big hot iron stove.

"Why, he picks her up and carries her off!" he says.

"Ya! Ha!"

"Carries her *back* around the corner . . ."

"Oh, Powerhouse!"

"You know him."

"Uranus Knockwood!"

"Yeahhh!"

"He take our wives when we gone!"

"He come in when we goes out!"

"Uh-huh!"

"He go out when we comes in!"

"Yeahhh!"

"He standing behind the door!"

"Old Uranus Knockwood!"

"You know him."

"Middle-size man."

"Wears a hat."

"That's him."

Everybody in the room moans with reassurance. The little boy in the fine silver hat opens a paper and divides out a jelly roll among his followers.

And out of the breathless ring somebody moves forward like a slave, leading a great logy Negro with bursting eyes, and says, "This-here is Sugar-Stick Thompson, that dove down to the bottom of July Creek and pulled up all those drownded white people fall out of a boat. Last summer—pulled up fourteen."

"Hello," says Powerhouse, turning and looking around at them all with his great daring face until they nearly suffocate.

Sugar-Stick, their instrument, cannot speak; he can only look back at the others.

"Can't even swim. Done it by holding his breath," says the fellow with the hero.

Powerhouse looks at him seekingly.

"I his half-brother," the fellow puts in.

They step back.

"Gipsy say," Powerhouse rumbles gently again, looking at *them,* " 'What is the use? I'm gonna jump out so far—so far—*Sssssst—*' "

"Don't, Boss, don't do it again," says Little Brother.

"It's awful," says the waitress. "I hates that Mr. Knockwoods. All that the truth?"

"Want to see the telegram I got from him?" Powerhouse's hand goes to the vast pocket.

"Now wait, now wait, Boss." They all watch him.

"It must be the real truth," says the waitress, sucking in her lower lip, her luminous eyes turning sadly, seeking the windows.

"No, Babe, it ain't the truth." His eyebrows fly up and he begins to whisper to her out of his vast oven mouth. His hand stays in his pocket. "Truth is something worse—I ain't said what, yet. It's something hasn't come to me, but I ain't saying it won't. And when it does, then want me to tell you?" He sniffs all at once, his eyes come open and turn up, almost too far. He is dreamily smiling.

"Don't, Boss. Don't, Powerhouse!"

"Yeahhh!"

"Oh!" The waitress screams.

"Go on, git out of here!" bellows Powerhouse, taking his hand out of his pocket and clapping after her red dress.

The ring of watchers breaks and falls away.

"*Look* at that! Intermission is up," says Powerhouse.

He folds money under a glass, and after they go out Valentine leans back in and drops a nickel in the nickelodeon behind them, and it lights up and begins to play, and the feather dangles still. That was going to be a Hawaiian piece.

"Take a telegram!" Powerhouse shouts suddenly up into the rain. "Take a answer.—Now what was that name?"

They get a little tired.

"Uranus Knockwood."

"You ought to know."

"Yas? Spell it to me."

They spell it all the ways it could be spelled. It puts them in a wonderful humor.

"Here's the answer. Here it is right here. 'What in the hell you talking about? Don't make any difference: I gotcha.' Name signed: Powerhouse."

"That going reach him, Powerhouse?" Valentine speaks in a maternal voice.

"Yas, yas."

All hushing, following him up the dark street at a distance, like old rained-on black ghosts, the Negroes are afraid they will die laughing.

Powerhouse throws back his vast head into the steaming rain, and a look of hopeful desire seems to blow somehow like a vapor from his own dilated nostrils over his face and bring a mist to his eyes.

"Reach him and come out the other side."

"That's it, Powerhouse, that's it. You got him now."

Powerhouse lets out a long sigh.

"But ain't you going back there to call up Gipsy long distance, the way you did last night in that other place? I seen a telephone. . . . Just to see if she there at home?"

There is a measure of silence. That is one crazy drummer that's going to get his neck broken some day.

"No," growls Powerhouse. "No! How many thousand times tonight I got to say *No?*"

He holds up his arm in the rain, like someone swearing.

"You sure-enough unroll your voice some night, it about reach up yonder to her," says Little Brother, dismayed.

They go on up the street, shaking the rain off and on them like birds.

## IV

Back in the dance hall they play "San" (99). The jitterbugs stiffen and start up like windmills stationed over the floor, and in their orbits (one circle, another, a long stretch and a zigzag) dance the elderly couples with old smoothness, undisturbed and stately.

When Powerhouse first came back from intermission (probably full of beer, everyone said) he got the band tuned up again not by striking the piano keys for the pitch: he just opened his mouth and gave falsetto howls—in A, D, and so on. They tuned by him. Then he took hold of the piano, like seeing it for the first time, and tested it for strength, hit it down in the bass, played an octave with his elbow, and opened it and examined its interior, and leaned on it with all his might. He played it for a few minutes with terrific force and got it under his power—then struck into something fragile and smiled. You couldn't remember any of the things he said—just inspired remarks that came out of his mouth like smoke.

They've requested "Somebody Loves Me," and he's already done twelve or fourteen choruses, piling them up nobody knows how, and it will be a wonder if he ever gets through. Now and then he calls and shouts, "Somebody loves me! Somebody loves me—I wonder who!" His mouth gets to be nothing but a volcano when he gets to the end.

"Somebody loves me—I wonder who!"

"Maybe—" He uses all his right hand on a trill.

"Maybe—" He pulls back his spread fingers and looks out upon the place where he is. A vast, impersonal, and yet furious grimace transfigures his wet face.

"—Maybe it's you!"

### STUDY QUESTIONS

1. Why does Miss Welty use the present tense? How would the use of the past tense change the effect of her story?

2. Miss Welty is careful to tell the reader exactly what numbers Powerhouse and his combo play. Is there any significance in these particular songs insofar as they contribute to the development of the plot?

3. Is Uranus Knockwood real? Did Gipsy really die?

4.  What is humorous about, "Brains and insides everywhere—Lord,
    Lord."?

5.  What is the reason for Powerhouse's "furious grimace"? What is the effect
    of the words *impersonal* and *transfigures?*

# E. H. Lacon Watson

# "TARZAN" AND LITERATURE [1]

E. H. Lacon Watson (1865–1948) was born in Sharnford, Leicestershire,
England. He was educated at the Winchester School and at Caius College,
Cambridge. His long career as a writer spanned two centuries. Among his
books were *The Unconscious Humorist and Other Essays* (1896), *Verses
Suggested and Original* (1896), *An Attic in Bohemia* (1897), *Benedictine*
(1898), *Christopher Deane* (1901), *Hints to Young Authors* (1902), *The
Templars* (1903), *A Conversational Tour in America* (1914), *Lectures to
Living Authors* (1925), *Lectures on Dead Authors* (1927), and *I Look Back
Seventy Years* (1938).

THERE is an age-long struggle always in progress between
the critic and the patron of art. Now and again, in the
world of books, it grows acute. There are some who can-
not endure to see false gods triumph. When a bad book sells in its tens of
thousands they raise despairing hands to heaven, and ask vainly what the
reviewers are doing that such things are permitted to happen. Are there indeed any real critics left, of the good old Macaulay breed, who were not
afraid or ashamed to say what they thought of illiterate rogues and vaga-
bonds who dared to print their thoughts between the sacred covers of a
book? Probably not; or, if there are, they no longer find their way into print.
Authorship in those ancient days was a close corporation: its shady courts
were guarded by efficient watch-dogs; unqualified intruders who dared to

Reprinted by permission of George Allen & Unwin Ltd. from the *Fortnightly Review*
119: 1035–45 (June 1, 1923).

[1] *Tarzan of the Apes, The Return of Tarzan, The Beasts of Tarzan, The Son of Tar-
zan, Tarzan and the Jewels of Opar, Jungle Tales of Tarzan, Tarzan the Untamed,
Tarzan the Terrible.*

attempt entrance without permission were lucky if they got off without a sharp nip or two in the region of the ankles. But it is now a long time since the gates were thrown open. Anyone can enter to-day: examinations in spelling or in grammar are no longer thought necessary. The prevailing school of criticism rather inclines to express regret for treasures the world may have lost through this old-fashioned determination to impose a certain standard of scholarship on would-be writers.

That danger, at least, hangs over us no longer. We encourage everyone to write and to publish, irrespective of his ability to string together two consecutive sentences. In fact, it would almost seem sometimes as though the success of a new book were assured in direct proportion to its illiteracy. Children of seven write romances on the leaves of an old exercise book: proud parents discover the treasure and hasten with it to a sympathetic publisher. In due course the new wonder blossoms forth, and another *Young Visiters* sells its tens of thousands. This is well enough for a passing jest. Periodically the infant prodigy has her vogue, rises into a brief popularity, and sinks again beneath the merciful waters of oblivion. The critic need not waste his time in blaming the ignorance of youth, about which, indeed, there may even linger a mild fragrance. But there is a mature and seasoned illiteracy, flourishing luxuriantly at the moment in certain quarters, to which he might reasonably apply his pruning-knife.

Here, for example, is Mr. Edgar Rice Burroughs, author of the "Tarzan," series, with which he appears to have reaped one of the greatest successes of modern times in the world of books. A short time ago it was difficult to get away from Tarzan: he pursued you on the railway bookstall, in the cinema palace, even (occasionally) in the Law Courts. I believe the name was registered, like that of a patent medicine. To call a performing chimpanzee Tarzan constituted a gross infringement of Mr. Burroughs's copyright.

Mr. Burroughs appears to specialise in two worlds. There are, as I write, eight of this Tarzan series "featuring," as they say on the films, the gigantic Ape-man. "Never," say the publishers on every available jacket, "never has such a character come to you from the pages of a book; never has the human brain conceived so strange a creation as Tarzan, the Ape-man." But now and again, possibly in search of variety, our author turns lightly from the African jungle to another planet. He runs also, it would seem, the Martian series—an absorbing series of Adventures and Romance forty-three million miles from Earth. It is hardly too much to say (and again I must acknowledge my indebtedness to the publishers) that this series is the boldest piece of imaginative fiction in this generation.

I confess I have not read this Martian series, nor, indeed, any single volume of it. For the present I have had enough to do in acquainting myself with the Ape-man's eight volumes of remarkable adventure. More, I have little doubt, are in active preparation, and I hope I may be excused for a natural weakness if signs of haste are discovered in this paper. Just now I am anxious to avoid reading any more about Tarzan, if possible. The worst of it is that Mr. Burroughs is still well under fifty years of age, and success seems to spur him on. His Ape-man did not burst upon the world before 1914: already we have these eight volumes, with three or four more of the Martian series as well, poured out upon our defenceless heads within a decade. It is hard to blame a young and energetic man, whose books appear to run through fourteen or fifteen large editions within a year or two, if he decides to exploit his lucky vein for all it is worth. Mr. Burroughs, I perceive on looking up his record, has been a gold-miner, as well as a storekeeper, a cowboy, and a policeman in Salt Lake City, but it is safe to say that he never made a luckier strike than when he drifted into the publisher's office with *Tarzan of the Apes* in his hand. There seems to be no reason why he should not go on working out this reef for many years to come, to his own profit and the pleasure of a large section of the public. For my part, having at length safely wound my way through the greater part of Tarzan's tangled career, I am inclined to offer my services as an unofficial guide to the young adventurer who intends to thread the maze. It may be a little difficult to construct a logical and consecutive story from the series as it stands, for in the hurry of the moment we cannot expect Mr. Burroughs to pause and recollect precisely what he may have said in a previous volume. But it may add to the pleasure of future readers if I provide them with a brief synopsis of the story of Tarzan so far as I have been able to follow it.

The whole affair begins when John, Lord Greystoke and his young wife leave England to take up a peculiarly delicate post in British West Africa. Mr. Burroughs, like so many of his tribe, cannot keep away from this dangerous ground of the British aristocracy; and it might be as well (not only for his sake but certain for indigenous writers) if some kindly gentleman were to bring out a handy manual settling once for all this pestilent matter of titles. I do not imagine, however, that Mr. Burroughs would pay much attention to this or any other handbook of useful information. He is one of those gallant spirits who break their way through whole zarebas of thorny detail, careless of the scratches they receive. "What is mere accuracy," they say, "as long as we get our main effects?" And so the reader may find himself slightly confused at first when he finds the author referring to Lord Greystoke frequently as plain John Clayton, and once at least as Sir John, while Lady Greystoke begins life as the Hon. Alice Rutherford and blossoms on her marriage into the Lady Alice. Clayton (or Greystoke) was "the type of Englishman that one likes best to associate with the noblest monuments of historic achievement upon a thousand victorious battlefields—a strong, virile man—mentally, morally, and physically." The sentence may not be pellucid; but it is clear that we are meant to admire this unfortunate peer, who sailed from Freetown in 1888 on a small barquantine, the *Fuwalda,* manned by a pack of bullying officers and a mutinous crew, and was never again seen alive by his fellow members of the House of Peers. Greystoke himself gets wind of coming trouble from one of the crew, but the captain refuses to listen to his warning.

> " 'I'm captain of this here ship,' he said, 'and from now on you keep your meddling nose out of my business.'
> "Greystoke never turned a hair, but stood eyeing the excited man with level gaze.
> " " 'Captain Billings,' he drawled finally, 'if you will pardon my candour, I might remark that you are something of an ass, don't you know.'
> "Whereupon he turned and left the cabin with the same indifferent ease that was habitual with him."

The indifferent ease of this typical British peer could not, however, delay the mutiny much longer. It came. "Short and grisly was the work" (Mr. Burroughs has hardly yet got into his fighting stride, so to speak), "but through it all John Clayton had stood leaning carelessly beside the companionway, puffing meditatively upon his pipe as though he had been but watching an indifferent cricket match." The officers are soon despatched and thrown overboard, but Greystoke is spared. The African coast is obligingly at hand, and himself, the Lady Alice, and "that other little life so soon to be launched amidst the hardships and grave dangers of a primeval world," are rowed ashore and deposited at the edge of the jungle, with an imposing array of diplomatic luggage. Then the small boats, having filled the ship's casks with fresh water, push out again toward the waiting *Fuwalda*.

> "As the boats moved slowly over the smooth waters of the bay, Clayton and his wife stood silently watching their departure—in the breasts of both a feeling of impending disaster and utter hopelessness.
> "And, behind them, over the edge of a low ridge, other eyes watched—close-set, wicked eyes, gleaming beneath shaggy brows."

I used once to think that film producers kept literary gentlemen of their own to invent the curious legends that are flashed on the screen between the more moving pictures—mercifully only for a brief instant. These legends are almost invariably faulty in grammar, or spelling, but then, as I say, they are hardly there long enough to be criticised. Since I read the Tarzan series, however, I have recognised that I did these imaginary gentlemen a wrong. They do not invent: they merely select from their authors. The works of Mr. Burroughs are almost entirely composed of suitable legends for the screen.

Lord Greystoke sets to work and builds a log cabin. Then comes a day when he is attacked by a huge bull-ape, which the Lady Alice contrives to kill with a chance shot from her husband's rifle. "That night a little son was born in the tiny cabin beside the primeval forest, while a leopard screamed before the door, and the deep notes of a lion's roar sounded from beyond the ridge." The young mother never quite recovered her pristine health. In effect, she dies a year later, the apes attack the cabin in a body, the unfortunate widower is slain, and Kala, the she-ape who has just lost her young one, annexes the young heir of Greystoke and leaves her own dead child in his cradle. Thus did Tarzan come into being, as a one-year-old child among the apes, somewhere about the year 1890. You perceive that he is not yet much over thirty years of age. Many more years of strange adventure probably lie before him. He is married, too, and has a son, of whom we have already heard remarkable tales. I see no reason why the Tarzan series should ever die: the right of continuing it will no doubt pass in due course to Mr. Burroughs's heirs and assigns.

I cannot follow young Tarzan through all his years of adolescence. They are told with a certain ingenuity, a really remarkable power of invention, and an immense courage. In the annals of fiction I confess that I have never seen a more high-spirited disregard for the probabilities than is displayed by Mr. Burroughs in these books, and especially in the later volumes. *Tarzan of the Apes* is itself pretty steep in parts, but it is a mere nothing to some of those that follow. The author has quite clearly said to himself something like this: "That jungle stuff of Kipling's was all right, but Rudyard did not know when he had a real good thing. The public will lap up any amount of that dope, strengthened a bit and with plenty of human love interest." And so he hastens to bring on the scene the fair Jane Porter, of the United States, with her father the comic professor Archimedes Q. Porter and his assistant comedian Samuel T. Philander, as well as William Cecil Clayton, eldest son of the reigning Lord Greystoke of England and heir to the title—unless Tarzan can prove his identity. This curiously assorted band have also had the misfortune to sail with a crew of villainous mutineers: they also chance to be put ashore close to the log cabin built by the late peer.

Tarzan by now was full-grown, a king of apes and men. He had killed old Tublat, his foster-father, with the aid of a hunting knife found in the old cabin: he had lassoed Sabor, the lioness, with the rope he had learned to plait from grass, and then killed her with poisoned arrows stolen from the natives: at length he had challenged Kerchak, chief of the anthropoid tribe, and slain him after a terrific struggle.

"Withdrawing the knife that had so often rendered him master of far mightier muscles than his own, Tarzan of the Apes placed his foot upon the neck of his vanquished enemy, and once again, loud through the forest, rang the fierce, wild cry of the conqueror.

"And thus came the young Lord Greystoke into his kingship of the Apes."

But soon he breaks away. Young Lord Greystoke lays down the kingship of the tribe. Something within him tells him that he is of finer clay than these others. He grows dissatisfied with his bull-apes, for he has somehow managed to learn how to read—a child's picture-book had been included in the luggage of his thoughtful parents, and when once he gained access to the old log cabin he used to sit for hours puzzling out the big capital letters. I suppose it was essential that he should have some means of communication with the next party of travellers marooned on the same spot, but the quickness with which Tarzan acquired the art of reading borders on the miraculous. In a short time we are told that Tarzan's growing discontent with the bull-apes was due to the limitations of their vocabulary. He could not talk with them "of the many new truths, and the great fields of thought that his reading had opened up before his longing eyes, or make known ambitions which stirred his soul." Samuel Smiles himself never immortalised an example of self-help comparable with this.

Something in the study of these picture books also warned the young English lord that it was time he acquired a certain amount of clothing. That was easily done, chiefly by robbing the tribe of natives nearest at hand. At the time of Jane Porter's arrival with her queer escort this is his picture:—

"About his neck hung the golden chain from which depended the diamond-encrusted locket of his mother, the Lady Alice. At his back was a quiver of arrows slung from a leathern shoulder-belt, another piece of loot from some vanquished black.

"The young Lord Greystoke was indeed a strange and warlike figure, his mass of black hair falling to his shoulders behind and cut with his hunting-knife to a rude bang upon his forehead, that it might not fall below his eyes."

With all this, the face was one of extraordinary beauty—a "perfect type of the strongly masculine, unmarred by dissipation, or brutal or degrading passions." The first sight of Jane Porter is sufficient for Tarzan. Henceforth he becomes the ready slave of her party, and he finds his work cut out shepherding the two extraordinarily silly scientists from the many dangers of the jungle. He watches the lady writing a letter to a friend, carries it off, and contrives to puzzle out the meaning—which is extremely creditable to one who had never before seen anything but the capital letters of a child's picture-book. Then he sits down to write his first love-letter in return. Just as he is about to deliver it, Jane is carried off by Terkoz, son of Tublat, Tarzan's own foster-brother, who has been expelled from the tribe for his bullying habits. Once before Terkoz has come across Tarzan's path, and been forced to crave his life. This time, with his loved one carried off to "a fate a thousand times worse than death," there can be no mercy. Tarzan pursues.

"When the long knife drank deep a dozen times of Terkoz's heart's blood, and the great carcase rolled lifeless upon the ground, it was a primeval woman who sprang forward with outstretched arms toward the primeval man who had fought for her and won her.

"And Tarzan?

"He did what no red-blooded man needs lessons in doing. He took his woman in his arms and smothered her upturned, panting lips with kisses.

"For a moment Jane Porter lay there with half-closed eyes. For a moment—the first in her young life—she knew the meaning of love."

It could not, naturally, be all as easy as that. Before Tarzan and Jane Porter are safely married many strange things have to happen. Not until the close of the second book in the series—*The Return of Tarzan*—can the fluttered nurse-maid go happily to bed with the knowledge that a double wedding is in full view. And, to tell the truth, if the fair Jane Porter Clayton, now Lady Greystoke (when the author can remember to give her the title), could have guessed one fraction of the horrid adventures that lay in store for the Ape-man's mate, she might well have delayed the inevitable union for a few volumes more.

It is in this second volume that Tarzan first crosses the path of MM. Rokoff and Paulvitch, two unamiable Russians who are destined to lead him and the Lady Jane a merry dance in our third book. In *The Return* we have Tarzan the perfectly appointed gentleman, speaking English and French as well as or better than most natives, and yet ready at a moment's notice to revert to the jungle, the eating of raw flesh, and the roaring of the terrible, fierce, wild challenge of the bull-ape. I fancy Mr. Burroughs is here guilty of an error of judgment in trying to make the most out of his two worlds. He continues persistently to refer to Lord Greystoke as "the ape-man," and repeatedly calls attention to the delight with which he sinks his strong teeth into the raw and bleeding flesh of the boar or deer that he has just killed; yet we are also to suppose him endowed with all the high sense of chivalry consonant with his birthright as an English nobleman. One year ago Tarzan was being painfully taught to speak French (from an English spelling-book) by Lieut. D'Arnot: now he seems to be able to bandy compliments in the best style of the old school. "To-morrow I shall be at home to Monsieur Tarzan at five," murmurs the fair Countess de Coude. "It will be an eternity until to-morrow at five," gracefully replies the ape-man. But then we must bear in mind that he learned to decipher and understand Jane Porter's letter to her girl friend, with all its allusions to various feminine and other mysteries, though he had no previous acquaintance with any other script than the printed capitals used in his child's picture-book. The ape-man cannot be judged by any ordinary standard.

It is in *The Beasts of Tarzan* that Mr. Burroughs really begins to show us what he can do. This book, the third in the famous series, is a mere orgy of terrible happenings. It narrates how "the wife and child of the famous Tarzan are abducted by his enemies. Their pursuit and rescue form a series of adventures so exciting that one gasps with astonishment." It is true. Quintilian would also stare and gasp could he see the manner of the telling. Nicolas Rokoff and his confederate Paulvitch do the kidnapping: by a stroke of luck they also capture Tarzan himself. Him they strip of his clothing and leave once more in the African jungle, with this note to comfort him. We are hardly surprised to read that "at first it made little impression on his sorrow-numbed senses, but finally the full purport of the hideous plot of revenge unfolded itself before his imagination."

"This will explain to you (the note said) the exact nature of my intentions relative to your offspring and to you. You were born an ape. You lived naked in the jungles—to your own we have returned you; but your son shall rise a step above his sire. It is the immutable law of evolution.

"The father was a beast, but the son shall be a man—he shall take the next ascending step in the scale of progress. He shall be no naked beast of the jungle, but shall wear a loin-cloth and copper anklets, and, perchance, a ring in his nose, for he is to be reared by men—a tribe of savage cannibals.

"I might have killed you, but that would have curtailed the full measure of the punishment you have earned at my hands.

"Dead, you could not have suffered in the knowledge of your son's plight; but living and in a place from which you may not escape to seek or succour your child, you shall suffer worse than death for all the years of your life in contemplation of the horrors of your son's existence.

"This, then, is to be a part of your punishment for having dared to pit yourself against—N. R.

"*P.S.*—The balance of your punishment has to do with what shall presently befall your wife—that I shall leave to your imagination."

We leave him for a moment to consider this while "from the jungle at his back fierce blood-shot eyes glared from beneath shaggy overhanging brows upon him."

"Where were the trained senses of the savage ape-man?
Where the acute hearing?
Where the uncanny sense of scent?"

And on that query the chapter, very judiciously, ends.

However, Lord Greystoke soon finds himself at home again in the jungle, killing lions and panthers with his bare hands as of old, breaking the neck of Molak, king of the apes, and only sparing Akut his successor in order to make him a vassal. Well may the author say, "Could his fellow peers of the House of Lords have seen him then they would have held up their noble hands in holy horror." But it is with Akut that Lord Greystoke begins to gather together his troop of assistants for the final stroke of vengeance. They comprise, towards the end of the book, the apes of Akut, a tame panther (rescued by Tarzan from a trap in the jungle), and Mugambi, the gigantic black warrior. *The Beasts of Tarzan* is packed with more exciting episodes to the page than you could well imagine. The end of Nicolas Rokoff is worthy of that consummate scoundrel.

". . . The fellow had retreated to the end of the bridge, where he now stood trembling and wide-eyed, facing the beast that moved slowly toward him.

"The panther crawled with belly to the planking, uttering uncanny mouthings. Rokoff stood as though petrified, his eyes protruding from their sockets, his mouth agape, and the cold sweat of terror clammy upon his brow.

"Before him was the panther, silent and crouched.

"Rokoff could not move. His knees trembled. His voice broke in inarticulate shrieks. With a last piercing wail he sank to his knees—and then Sheeta sprang."

The decease of Rokoff makes it necessary to provide another villain for *Tarzan and the Jewels of Opar*. This time he is a Belgian, Lieut. Albert Werper; in *Tarzan the Terrible* we have a German, Lieut. Obergatz. In this book—the last of the series up to the present date—Mr. Burroughs appears to have been led astray by the fertility of his own invention. Tarzan and the Lady Jane are captured, bound, and on the very eve of death so often that the most credulous of readers begins to weary. He gets bored with all the strange people that Tarzan discovers—Ta-den the white-tailed man, and Om-at the hairy black, belonging respectively to the Ho-don and the Waz-don. There is too much of this agglutinative formation of words.

"It is well," said Om-at. "Id-an, you are swift—carry word to the warriors of Kor-ul-ja that we fight the Kor-ul-lul upon the ridge and that Ab-on shall send a hundred men."

And at the long last we read:—

"So it was that Jane and Korak and Tarzan rode through the morass that hems Pal-ul-don, upon the back of a prehistoric triceratops, while the lesser reptiles of the swamp fled hissing in terror. . . . For a time they stood looking back over the land they had just quit—the land of Tor-o-don and *gryf;* of *ja* and *jato;* of Waz-don and Ho-don; a primitive land of terror and sudden death and peace and beauty; a land that they had all learned to love.

"And then they turned once more toward the north and with light hearts and brave hearts took up their long journey toward the land that is best of all—home."

It is with the material that I have attempted to describe that Mr. Rice Burroughs stepped into the position of a "best seller" in two continents.

Perhaps his success is not so surprising as it seems. In America they have always maintained that it is impossible to have too much of a good thing, and of late we in England appear to be accepting their canons of criticism. If you give an American sentiment, lay it on with a trowel: if you are writing a story of adventure, get your hair-breadth escapes in at the rate of one to every page. Sentiment and adventure are good things: in the eyes of an American they cannot possibly be overdone. If you have these in sufficient quantity, what else matters? Errors in grammar, split infinitives, the use of words in new and unauthorised meanings—these things may still annoy an occasional critic: to the mass of present-day readers they are not even negligible blemishes—they are passed by without notice. The really popular novel to-day must make no more demand on the intellect than the pictures on a film.

I am reminded of a story of the late Sir Walter Besant, to whom there came once for advice a lady with some remarkable experiences but no great literary talent. Sir Walter advised her to write a book. "But, whatever you do," he added, "keep your sentences short." It was good advice. The modern half-educated reader is incapable of understanding a paragraph containing more than a single sentence: the modern writer is apt to get into difficulties as soon as he ventures upon a subsidiary clause: thus we have two excellent reasons for keeping our paragraphs as short as possible. Mr. Burroughs does this throughout. He builds up his story by a series of short, sharp hammer-blows. And it is precisely this series of shocks that his public want. They are easy to assimilate—as easy as the pictures on a cinema reel. They startle: their appeal to the emotions is direct, and almost brutal. Unless something pretty violent is supplied there is a real danger of the reading public falling asleep over your book. Those old qualities, upon which the critic of old used to set some store—delicacy and restraint—are now worse than useless. If you desire to write a "best seller," keep your wit and wisdom (if you happen to possess any) well in the background.

For the educated reader seems likely to remain in a sad minority for many years to come. It is possible that his numbers may grow. But for the last twenty years or more he has been entirely swamped by the number of the half-educated—those who have contrived to assimilate just enough learning to enable them to enjoy a story, provided the sentences are not too long and make no demand for serious thought. Perhaps a time may come when these will feel the need for a higher form of entertainment, and begin to struggle forward to the conquest of another world, in which good workmanship, skill in character drawing, and some feeling for the dignity of letters may have a part. But I do not think a perusal of the works of Mr. Edgar Rice Burroughs is likely to lead them in this direction.

## STUDY QUESTIONS

1. How are the first two paragraphs of Watson's essay related to his discussion of the Tarzan books? How does the dictionary define *illiteracy?* As he uses it in the phrase, "a mature and seasoned illiteracy," how would Watson define it?

2. Watson has a very low opinion of the film and film producers. Why does he feel that the Tarzan books are eminently suited to the screen?

3. Generally, when a critic credits a novelist with "a certain ingenuity, a really remarkable power of invention, and an immense courage," he is complimenting the novelist. Clearly, Watson is not complimenting Burroughs. With what tone does Watson apply the description here quoted? What does he mean by *ingenuity, invention,* and *courage?*

4. What does Watson feel is characteristic of American reading taste? What is sacrificed in order to obtain generous amounts of "sentiment and adventure"?

5. Does the last paragraph provide a suitable conclusion to Watson's essay?


*Gore Vidal*

# THE WAKING DREAM: TARZAN REVISITED

Gore Vidal (1925–     ) was born in West Point, New York. He attended Phillips Exeter Academy. Vidal is equally famous for his novels, short stories, plays, and essays. Among Vidal's novels are *Williwaw* (1946), *In a Yellow Wood* (1947), *The City and the Pillar* (1948), *The Season of Comfort* (1949), *A Search for the King* and *Dark Green, Bright Red* (1950), *The Judgment of Paris* (1952), *Messiah* (1954), the highly acclaimed *Julian* (1964), *Washington, D.C.* (1967), and the highly controversial *Myra Breckenridge* (1968). *A Thirsty Evil,* his collection of short stories, was published in 1956. His successful plays include *Visit to a Small Planet* (1957), *The Best Man* (1960), and *Romulus* (1962). Collections of his essays have been published as *Rocking the Boat* (1962), *Sex, Death and Money* (1968), and *Reflections upon a Sinking Ship* (1969). Vidal has also written plays for the film and television. He was a Democratic–Liberal candidate for Congress in 1960.

THERE ARE SO many things the people who take polls never get around to asking. Fascinated as we all are to know what our countrymen think of great issues (approving, disapproving, "don't-knowing," with that same shrewd intelligence which made a primeval wilderness bloom with Howard Johnson signs), the pollsters never get around to asking the sort of interesting personal questions our new-Athenians might be able to answer knowledgeably. For instance, how many adults have an adventure serial running in their heads? How many consciously day dream, turning on a story in which the dreamer ceases to be an employee of IBM and becomes a handsome demigod moving through splendid palaces, saving maidens from monsters (or monsters from maidens: this is a jaded time). Most children tell themselves stories in which they figure as powerful figures, enjoying the pleasures not only of the adult world as they conceive it but a world of wonders unlike dull reality. Although this sort of Mittyesque daydreaming is supposed to cease in maturity, I suggest that more adults than we suspect are bemusedly wandering about with a full Technicolor extravaganza going on in their heads. Clad in tights, rapier in hand, the daydreamers drive their Jaguars at fantastic speeds through a glittering world of adoring love objects, mingling anachronistic historic worlds with science fiction. "Captain, the time-warp's been closed! We are now trapped in a parallel world, inhabited entirely by women, with three breasts." Though from what we can gather about these imaginary worlds, they tend to be more Adlerian than Freudian: The motor drive is the desire not for sex (other briefer fantasies take care of that) but for power, for the ability to dominate one's environment through physical strength. I state all this with perfect authority because I have just finished rereading several books by the master of American daydreamers, Edgar Rice Burroughs, whose works today, as anyone who goes into a drugstore or looks at a newsstand can see, have suddenly returned to great popularity.

When I was growing up, I read all twenty-three *Tarzan* books, as well as the ten *Mars* books. My own inner storytelling mechanism was vivid. At any one time, I had at least three serials going as well as a number of old faithful reruns. I used Burroughs as a source of raw material. When he went to the center of the earth à la Jules Verne (much too fancy a writer for one's taste), I immediately worked up a thirteen-part series, with myself as lead, and various friends as guest stars. Sometimes I used the master's material, but more often I adapted it freely to suit myself. One's daydreams tended to be Tarzanish prepuberty (physical strength and freedom) and Martian postpuberty (exotic worlds and subtle *combinaziones* to be worked out). After adolescence, if one's life is sufficiently interesting, the desire to tell oneself stories diminishes. My last serial ran into sponsor trouble when I was in the Second World War and was never renewed.

Until recently I assumed that most people were like myself: daydreaming ceases when the real world becomes interesting and reasonably manageable. Now I am not so certain. Pondering the life and success of Burroughs leads one to believe that a good many people find their lives so unsatisfactory that they go right on year after year telling themselves stories in which they are able to dominate their environment in a way that is not possible in this overorganized society.

"Most of the stories I wrote were the stories I told myself just before I went to sleep," said Edgar Rice Burroughs, describing his own work. He is a fascinating figure to contemplate, an archetype American dreamer. Born 1875, in Chicago, he was a drifter until he was thirty-six. Briefly, he served in the U.S. Cavalry; then he was a gold miner in Oregon, a cowboy in Idaho, a railroad policeman in Salt Lake City; he attempted several businesses that failed. He was perfectly in the old-American grain: The man who could take on almost any job, who liked to keep moving, who tried to get rich quick, but could never pull it off. And while he was drifting through the unsatisfactory real world, he consoled himself with an inner world where he was strong and handsome, adored by beautiful women and worshiped by exotic races. Burroughs might have gone to his death, an unknown daydreamer, if he had not started reading pulp fiction. He needed raw material for his own inner serials and once he had used up his favorite source, Rider Haggard, he turned to the magazines. He was appalled at how poor the stories were. They did not compare with his own imaginings. He was like a lover of pornography who, unable to find works which excite him, turns to writing them. Burroughs promptly wrote a serial about Mars and sold it to *Munsey's*. His fellow daydreamers recognized a master. In 1914 he published his first book, *Tarzan of the Apes* (Rousseau's noble savage reborn in Africa), and history was made. To date the Tarzan books have sold over twenty-five million copies in fifty-six languages. There is hardly an American male of my generation who has not at one time or another tried to master the victory cry of the great ape as it once bellowed forth from the androgynous chest of Johnny Weismuller, while a thousand arms and legs were broken by attempts to swing from tree to tree in the backyards of the republic. Between 1914 and his death in 1950, Burroughs, the squire of Tarzana, California (a prophet honored by his own land), produced over sixty books, while enjoying the unique status of being the first American writer to be a corporation.

Burroughs is said to have been a pleasant, unpretentious man who liked to ride and play golf. Not one to disturb his own unconscious with reality, he never set foot in Africa.

With a sense of recapturing childhood, I have just reread several Tarzan books. It is fascinating to see how much one recalls after a quarter century. At times the sense of *déjà vu* is overpowering. It is equally interesting to discover that one's memories of *Tarzan of the Apes* are mostly action scenes. The plot had slipped one's mind. It is a lot of plot, too. The beginning is worthy of Conrad. "I had this story from one who had no business to tell it to me, or to any other. I may credit the seductive influence of an old vintage upon the narrator for the beginning of it, and my own skeptical incredulity during the days that followed for the balance of the strange tale." It is 1888. The young Lord and Lady Greystoke are involved in a ship mutiny ("there was in the whole atmosphere of the craft that undefinable something which presages disaster"). They are put ashore on the west coast of Africa. They build a tree house. Here Burroughs is at his best. He tells you the size of the logs, the way to hang a door when you have no hinges, the problems of roofing. All his books are filled with interesting details on how things are made. The Greystokes have a child. They die. The "manchild" is taken up by Kala, a Great Ape, who brings him up as a member of her tribe of apes. Burroughs is a rather vague anthropologist. His apes have a language. They are carnivorous. They can, he suspects, mate with human beings. Tarzan grows up as an ape; he kills his first lion (with a full nelson); he teaches himself to read and write English by studying some books found in the cabin. The method he used, sad to say, is the currently fashionable "look-see." Though he can read and write, he cannot speak any language except that of the apes. He gets on well with the animal kingdom, with Tantor the elephant, Ska the vulture, Numa the lion (Kipling has added his grist to the Burroughs dream mill). Then white people arrive: Professor Archimedes Q. Porter and his daughter Jane. Also, a Frenchman named D'Arnot who teaches Tarzan to speak French, which is confusing. By coincidence, Jane's suitor is the current Lord Greystoke, who thinks the Greystoke baby is dead. Tarzan saves Jane from an ape. Then he puts on clothes and goes to Paris where he drinks absinthe. Next stop, America. In Wisconsin, he saves Jane Porter from a forest fire; then he nobly gives her up to Lord Greystoke, not revealing the fact that *he* is the real Lord Greystoke. Fortunately in the next volume, *The Return of Tarzan,* he marries Jane and they live happily ever after in Africa, raising a son John, who in turn grows up and has a son. Yet even as a grandfather, Tarzan continues to have adventures with people a foot high, with descendants of Atlantis, with the heirs of a Roman legion who think that Rome is still a success. All through these stories one gets the sense that one is daydreaming, too. Episode follows episode with no particular urgency. Tarzan is always knocked on the head and

taken captive; he always escapes; there is always a beautiful princess or high
priestess who loves him and assists him; there is always a loyal friend who
fights beside him, very much in the Queequeg tradition which Leslie Fiedler
assures us is the urning in the fuel supply of the American psyche. But no
matter how difficult the adventure, Tarzan, clad only in a loincloth with no
weapon save a knife (the style is contagious), wins against all odds and returns to his shadowy wife.

These books are clearly for men. I have yet to meet a woman who found
Tarzan interesting: no identification, as they say in series-land.

Stylistically, Burroughs is—how shall I put it?—uneven. He has moments of ornate pomp, when the darkness is "Cimmerian"; of redundancy,
"she was hideous and ugly"; of extraordinary dialogue: "Name of a name,"
shrieked Rokoff. "Pig, but you shall die for this!" Or Lady Greystoke to
Lord G.: "Duty is duty, my husband, and no amount of sophistries may
change it. I would be a poor wife for an English lord were I to be responsible
for his shirking a plain duty." Or the grandchild: "Muvver," he cried
"Dackie doe? Dackie doe?" "Let him come along," urged Tarzan. "Dare!"
exclaimed the boy turning triumphantly upon the governess, "Dackie do doe
yalk!" Burroughs' use of coincidence is shameless even for a pulp writer. In
one book he has three sets of characters shipwrecked at exactly the same
point on the shore of Africa. Even Burroughs finds this a bit much. "Could it
be possible [muses Tarzan] that fate had thrown him up at the very threshold of his own beloved jungle?" It was possible, of course; anything can happen in a daydream.

Though Burroughs is innocent of literature and cannot reproduce human
speech, he does have a gift very few writers of any kind possess: he can describe action vividly. I give away no trade secrets when I say that this is as
difficult for a Tolstoi as it is for a Burroughs (even William). Because it is so
hard, the craftier contemporary novelists usually prefer to tell their stories
in the first person, which is simply writing dialogue. In character, as it were,
the writer settles for an impression of what happened rather than creating
the sense of a happening. Tarzan *in action* is excellent.

There is something basic in the appeal of the 1914 Tarzan which makes
me think that he can still hold his own as a daydream figure, despite the
sophisticated challenge of his two contemporary competitors, Ian Fleming
and Mickey Spillane. For most adults, Tarzan (and John Carter of Mars)
can hardly compete with the conspicuous consumer consumption of James
Bond or the sickly violence of Mike Hammer, but for children and adolescents, the old appeal continues. All of us need the idea of a world alternative
to this one. From Plato's Republic to Opar to Bond-land, at every level, the
human imagination has tried to imagine something better for itself than the
existing society. Man left Eden when we got up off all fours, endowing most
of his descendants with nostalgia as well as chronic backache. In its naïve

way, the Tarzan legend returns us to that Eden where, free of clothes and the inhibitions of an oppressive society, a man can achieve in reverie his continuing need, which is, as William Faulkner put it in his high Confederate style, to prevail as well as endure. The current fascination with L.S.D. and non-addictive drugs—not to mention alcoholism—is all part of a general sense of frustration and boredom. The individual's desire to dominate his environment is not a desirable trait in a society which every day grows more and more confining. Since there are few legitimate releases for the average man, he must take to daydreaming. James Bond, Mike Hammer and Tarzan are all dream-selves, and the aim of each is to establish personal primacy in a world which in reality diminishes the individual. Among adults, increasing popularity of these lively inferior fictions strikes me as a most significant (and unbearably sad) phenomenon.

## STUDY QUESTIONS

1.  According to Vidal, what is the difference between an Adlerian and a Freudian imaginary world? Which of these worlds does Tarzan inhabit?

2.  Which scenes in the Tarzan books does Vidal find most memorable? Why?

3.  Why are men more interested in the Tarzan books than are women? Need one identify with a character in a literary work in order to find that work memorable?

4.  What are Burroughs' faults as a novelist? Why, then, is Vidal so kind to him?

5.  Is there any similarity between Tarzan and James Bond?

6.  Of what does Vidal feel Tarzan is a symbol?

## Joseph Wood Krutch

# MUST WRITERS HATE THE UNIVERSE?

Joseph Wood Krutch (1893–    ) was born in Knoxville, Tennessee. He received his B.A. (1915) from the University of Tennessee and his M.A. (1916) and Ph.D. (1932) from Columbia University. He has taught English, journalism, and drama at Columbia; lectured at the New School for Social Research; served as drama critic for the *Nation;* and acted as president of the New York Drama Critics Circle. Krutch now lives in Tucson, Arizona, and is a trustee of the Arizona-Sonora Desert Museum. He has edited the works of William Congreve, Eugene O'Neill, Marcel Proust, and Thomas Gray; and written critical studies of Restoration comedy, and of Samuel Johnson, Edgar Allan Poe, and Henry David Thoreau. Other books include *The Modern Temper* (1929), *The Desert Year* (1952), *The Measure of Man* (1954), *Grand Canyon* (1958), and the revised *Baja California, and the Geography of Hope* (1969).

THERE ARE not many nations so indefatigably given to honoring men of letters that a cabinet minister would preside over a ceremony in which the principal speaker eulogized a *poet maudit* upon whose newly erected monument was inscribed the poet's own clarion call to his fellows: "We have set out as pilgrims whose destination is perdition  .  .  .  across streets, across countries, and across reason itself." Simultaneously, and in accordance with a French custom which always reminds me of the monkish habit of digging up old bones to make way for new ones, the name of a street was changed from that of a forgotten worthy to Rue Guillaume Apollinaire.

The cabinet minister involved was André Malraux; the sculptor of the

From *And Even If You Do: Essays on Man, Manners, and Machines* by Joseph Wood Krutch. Appeared originally in *Saturday Review* 50: 19–21, 47 (May 6, 1967). Reprinted by permission of William Morrow and Company, Inc. Copyright © 1967 by Joseph Wood Krutch.

The translation of Baudelaire by Robert Lowell is reprinted with permission of Farrar, Straus & Giroux, Inc., from *Imitations* by Robert Lowell. Copyright © 1958, 1959, 1960, 1961 by Robert Lowell.

monument was Picasso; the honored poet, Guillaume Apollinaire, was that champion of, successively, Cubism, Dada, and Surrealism, among whose own best known works are the volume of poems called *Hard Liquor (Alcools),* the novel *The Assassinated Poet,* and the play *The Breasts of Tiresias.* One of his more notable pronouncements was the prediction that the dominant influence upon the twentieth century might well be that of the Marquis de Sade—a prophecy which, incidentally, seems in the course of being fulfilled.

Even if we had in this country a Minister of Arts, we cannot quite imagine him officially honoring a poet who urged painters as well as men of letters to set out resolutely on a road leading to that pit of hell, the descent into which —so an elder poet said—is easier than the road back again. No, one can't imagine an American Minister of Culture doing that. In fact, the proponents of government support to the arts are most likely to fear that we would be, officially at least, oppressively pure, genteel, and middlebrow.

But if we are not yet quite up to the French in this respect, there is no doubt that the avant-garde, even when perverse and sadistic, is no longer without honor even in rather surprising quarters, and that mass-circulation magazines give frequent and extensive treatment to movies, plays, novels, and poems which in one way or another—extravagant concern with usually abnormal sexuality, violence, cruelty, or at least the nihilism of the absurd—seem to be headed along the road which Apollinaire bid them take.

In March 1966, Cyril Connolly, a leading English critic, was commissioned by the ultrarespectable *Sunday Times* of London to make a list of the hundred literary works which best presented various aspects of modernism in intellectual literature. He headed his list with that same Guillaume Apollinaire whom the French Minister of Culture was so eager to honor, and though it is true that his list does include certain works which are neither beatnik, sadistic, existential, nor sexually perverse, at least a half—and perhaps two-thirds—of them might, I think, be classified as guideposts to perdition.

Among them—and remember these are not offered merely as striking works of literature but as typical of the modern spirit—are *Nadja (Nothing)* by the surrealist André Breton; *Journey to the End of the Night* by the pro-Nazi and violently anti-Semitic Céline; *The Immoralist* by Gide; *Là Bas* by Huysmans; *Cruel Stories* by Villiers de L'Isle-Adam; *Les Illuminations* by Rimbaud; and many others more or less in the same spirit of world-weariness, world-hatred, or perverse indulgence. And he finds the quintessence of modernity in Baudelaire as translated by Robert Lowell:

> Only when we drink poison are we
> well—

> We want, this fire so burns our brain
> tissue,
> To drown in the abyss—heaven or hell.
> Who cares? Through the unknown
> we'll find the new.

Readers curious enough to consult the full text with Connolly's own comments on individual works will find that he calls Baudelaire's poetry "a beam of light glowing for posterity," even though, it would seem, the poet himself declares that he does not care whether it points the way to a heaven or a hell. Connolly also states that Breton, one of his heroes, proposed to "wring the neck of literature" and quotes with apparent approval the following sentence, of which it is said "nothing more surrealist has ever been written": "Beautiful as the chance encounter on a dissecting table of an umbrella and a sewing machine."

Commenting on the list and Connolly's explanatory notes, *Time* (which certainly does not appeal to merely minority interests) remarks that though the list will seem perverse to many, it is, nevertheless, "an achievement in taste and learning."

I do not believe that more than a very small fraction of *Time*'s readers really share the convictions or admire the enterprises of such writers. Yet they are obviously much interested in them and they are timid about expressing any doubts. When they give deserved praise to, say, Tennessee Williams for his theatrical skill, they are half afraid of not taking seriously enough the implications of his extraordinary notions concerning sexual abnormality and are half convinced that their own normality needs to be apologized for. If a whole school of novelists (now a bit démodé) defines its conception of the good life as driving a stolen automobile at 90 miles an hour after a revivifying shot of heroin, almost nobody says merely, "Pooh," or, "Don't be silly."

Those of us who read such highbrow (or is it middlebrow?) weeklies as *The Nation* or *The New Leader* have come to expect a curious contrast between the front and the back of the book. Though the opening pages are full of schemes for improving the condition of this or that, the section devoted to the arts is occupied frequently by reviews of books, movies, paintings, and musical compositions which are bitterly cynical, pessimistic, and, by old-fashioned standards, obscene. This seems to reflect truly a similar contrast between the tastes and preoccupations of two different groups of "intellectuals." Most of them are either do-gooders on the one hand or, on the other, ready to entertain at least the possibility that the road to perdition is the wise one to take. If you are not a potential member of the Peace Corps, you are almost certainly a devotee of the absurd. You want either to rescue the underdeveloped countries or to explore once more the meaninglessness of the universe or the depravity of some version of the *dolce vita.* When *Time,* as it recently did, puts Sartre and Genet on its "best reading list" for a single week, neither of these writers can be said to be, by now, attractive to only a few.

Do I exaggerate either the violence, perversity, or nihilism of most of the most discussed modern writers or the tendency of even the mass magazines to select their works as the best or, sometimes, as only the most newsworthy books?

Let us look at a few excerpts from two or three publications which illustrate what I am driving at. Look first at a review in *The New Leader.* It concerned James Baldwin's so-called novel, *Another Country,* and it was written by the magazine's staff critic Stanley Edgar Hyman, who, though far from approving of the book, described it as follows:

The protagonist of *Another Country,* a young Negro jazz drummer named Rufus Scott, kills himself on page 88, and the rest of the book is taken up with the adventures and misadventures, mostly sexual, of the half-dozen people who had been close to him. Of the important characters, only Rufus and his sister Ida are Negro, but almost everything in the book that is powerful and convincing deals with Negro consciousness.

That consciousness, as the novel shows it, seethes with bitterness and race hate. "Let the liberal white bastards squirm" is Rufus's most charitable feeling towards Vivaldo, his best friend; his less charitable feeling is a passionate desire for the extinction of the white race by nuclear bombs. Ida is even fiercer. She regularly affirms, in language not quotable in this family magazine, the total sexual inadequacy of whites, as well as their moral sickness and physical repulsiveness. . . . The other Negroes in the book share this bitterness and hatred without exception. A big Negro pimp who lives by beating up and robbing the white customers of his Negro whore clearly does it out of principle; before robbing Vivaldo he stares at him "with a calm steady hatred, as remote and unanswerable as madness." The Silenski boys are beaten up by Negro boys unknown to them out of simple racial hostility and Richard, their father, automatically comments: "Little black bastards." Rufus's father, seeing his son's mangled corpse, remarks only: "They don't leave a man much, do they?" A musician who had been Rufus's friend, finding Ida out with a white man, calls her "black white man's whore" and threatens to mutilate her genitals twice, once for himself and once for Rufus.

Though *The New Leader'*s critic was by no means favorably impressed, the jacket of *Another Country* is able to cite the even better known and academically very respectable critic Mark Shorer, who called *Another Country* "powerful." Is that the adjective he would have chosen if this almost insane outburst of racism had been the work of some Southern Ku Klux Klanner— as it might easily be made to seem by reading "white" where Baldwin says "black" and "black" where he says "white"? Why is black racism "powerful," white disgusting?

Now for a movie, as admiringly described in *Time:*

The *Naked Prey* spills more beauty, blood, and savagery upon the screen than any African adventure drama since *Trader Horn.* Squeamish viewers will head for home in the first twenty minutes or so, when producer-director-star Cornell Wilde swiftly dooms three last century white hunters and a file of blacks, attacked and captured by a horde of warriors from a tribe they have insulted. One victim is basted with clay and turned over a spit, another is staked out as a victim of a cobra.

The only survivor is Wilde. In a primitive sporting gesture, the natives free the courageous white man without clothes, weapons, or water—and with ten stalwart young spearsmen poised to track him down. Hunted now, the hunter begins to run, and *Prey* gathers fierce momentum as a classic, single-minded epic of survival with no time out for faint-hearted blondes or false heroines.

It used to be said that the theater was often more searching, more bitter, and more "adult" than the movies ever dared to be. Today it can hardly keep up with them but it tries, as witnessed by this account of the latest play by a man widely regarded as Britain's leading playwright:

*A Bond Honoured,* British playwright John Osborne's adaptation of an atrocious horror show by seventeenth-century Spaniard Lope de Vega, has a hero who commits rape, murder, treason, multiple incest, and matricide, and blinds his father—after which he is crucified in precise imitation of Christ. London's critics cast one look at the tasteless mayhem at the Old Vic and held their noses. Whereupon Osborne, thirty-six, flipped his Angry Aging Man's lid, firing off telegrams to the London papers. Osborne declared an end to his "gentleman's agreement to ignore puny theater critics as bourgeois conventions. After ten years it is now war, open and frontal war, that will be as public as I and other men of earned reputations have the considerable power to make it."

The account is again from *Time* but its pooh-poohing of this masterpiece got an angry reply from Kenneth Tynan, the drama critic who was for a time the regular reviewer for *The New Yorker:*

Of the twelve newspaper critics, at least four held their breath. Herald Hobson in the *Sunday Times* said of Osborne: "He is not only our most important dramatist; he is also our chief prophet." According to Randall Bryden of the *Observer,* "The effect of *A Bond Honoured* in performance is marvelously theatrical." Allen Brien of the *Sunday Telegraph* thought it "a serious, ambitious, and valuable play which matures in the memory and fertilizes the imagination," while for Milton Shulman in the *Evening Standard* it was "a stunning parable with a magnificent theatrical impact."

Having glanced at a conspicuous American novel, a conspicuous movie, and a conspicuous play, let's look now at two serious American critics, taking first Leslie Fiedler. His well known contention is that the best American fiction from *Huckleberry Finn* to Hemingway and Faulkner is always concerned with a repressed homosexuality. In his most recent book he comes up with the following opinions:

[On the death of Ernest Hemingway] . . . One quarry was left him only, the single beast worthy of him; himself. And he took his shotgun in hand, probably renewing his lapsed allegiance to death and silence. With a single shot he redeemed his best work from his worst, his art from himself.

[Of President Kennedy and the arts] . . . John F. Kennedy, as Louis XV, seemed up to the moment of his assassination the true symbol of cultural blight; not only our first sexually viable President in a century, after a depressing series of uncle, grandfather, and grandmother figures, but the very embodiment of middlebrow culture climbing.

I have been leaning heavily on *Time* because it seems to me to be the publication which best gauges the interests, if not necessarily the opinions, of the largest number of literate Americans. But for a second critic—and, incidentally, an excellent example of the schizophrenia of the liberal weeklies—I will choose an essay by Susan Sontag, the most "in" of contemporary "far-out" critics. It was, paradoxically, published in *The Nation,* which has been for long the very paradigm of do-goodism. The article takes off from a discussion of Jack Smith's film *Flaming Creatures,* which is described thus:

A couple of women and a much larger number of men . . . frolic about, pose, posture, and dance with one another; enact various scenes of voluptuousness, sexual frenzy, romantic love, and vampirism . . . to the accompaniment of a sound track which includes . . . the chorale of flutish shrieks and screams which accompany the group rape of a bosomy woman, rape happily converting itself into an orgy. . . . shots of masturbation and oral sensuality. . . . *Flaming Creatures* is outrageous and it intends to be. But it is a beautiful film . . . a triumphant example of an esthetic vision of the world and such a vision is perhaps always, at its core, epicene.

Just why an esthetic vision of the world is perhaps always, at its core, homosexual is not explained and suggests the same reply which Chesterton made to the estheticism of the Nineties. The art of those who professed it, so they claimed, was morally neutral, but, said Chesterton, if it really were neutral it would often find itself dealing sympathetically with respectability, virtue, piety, and conventional behavior. The fact that it never did treat any of these things in even a neutral manner was sufficient proof that the art of its practitioners was not morally neutral but actually—to come back to Apollinaire again—an invitation to take the road to perdition.

If Miss Sontag does not explain why an esthetic vision must be epicene, she does undertake to explain why modern art must be "outrageous": "Art is always the sphere of freedom. In those difficult works of art we now call avant-garde, the artist consciously exercises his freedom." This argument is obviously parallel with that favorite of the Sartrian existentialists, namely, the contentions that: 1) the unmotivated act is the only positive assertion of freedom; and 2) the best unmotivated act is one of arbitrary cruelty. Why this should be so I have never understood, nor do I understand why the freedom of the artist can be demonstrated only by the outrageous. In the atmosphere of the present moment, the boldest position a creative or critical writer could take would be one championing not only morality but gentility and bourgeois respectability. Even the article which I am writing at this moment will probably be more contemptuously or even vituperatively dismissed than it would be if I were defending sadism, homosexuality, and nihilism.

Look at how "square" and "fuddy-duddy" the American Telephone & Telegraph Company can be, as demonstrated by recent full-page advertisements which answer the question posed in headline type: WHAT CAN YOU DO ABOUT OBSCENE, HARASSING, OR THREATENING TELEPHONE CALLS? Doesn't AT&T know that one of the simplest beginner's techniques for achieving existential freedom in a splendidly unmotivated act is to make an obscene telephone call? From that one can easily work up to the various vandalism so popular with teen-agers and, finally, to unmotivated murder. What can so triumphantly demonstrate an existential freedom as torturing and killing for kicks? Didn't Apollinaire himself say that de Sade was the freest man who ever lived?

What, precisely, is the road—or are the roads—which have led to the state of mind illustrated by the quotations in this article? I do not think that any analysis ending in a satisfactory answer to that question has ever been made. Someone with the stomach for it might undertake a study as nearly classic as Mario Praz's *The Romantic Agony,* which traces so brilliantly the origin and destination of 1890 decadence to which modernism is more closely parallel than is usually admitted, and of which it is, perhaps, only another phrase. Cyril Connolly has this to say:

[It] began as a revolt against the bourgeois in France, the Victorians in England, the Puritanism and materialism of America. The modern spirit was a combination of certain intellectual qualities inherited from the Enlightenment: lucidity, irony, skepticism, intellectual curiosity, combined with the impassioned intensity and enhanced sensibility of the Romantic, their rebellion and sense of technical experiment, their awareness of living in a tragic age.

All that is true enough and familiar enough but it doesn't go far enough. It does not explain why the most obvious and unique characteristics of the current avant-garde are not any of the characteristics of the Enlightenment or of any romanticism except that commonly called decadent. How, for instance, do lucidity, irony, skepticism, or even intellectual curiosity become preludes to "the century of de Sade"? How did an assault on Victorian complacency and hypocrisy end by practicing a sort of unmotivated vandalism? In London a recent city-wide series of "happenings" in which forty "artists" from ten nations took part was publicized as a reminder that "society will ignore the manifestations of destruction in art at its peril." Perhaps, as we say, the publicist had something there. Were certain members of the public justified when they objected to the performance of Juan Hidalgo, the representative from Spain, whose specialty, it seems, is cutting off the heads of chickens and flinging them at the audience?

I suppose that anyone who undertook to trace the development of modernism would have to begin by asking whether or not there is a single dominating characteristic of this latest development, any one which, at least by its frequent emphasis, seems to distinguish contemporary modernism from the movement out of which it is said to have grown. True, this modernism does indeed seem to be compounded of many simplicities and not all who represent it include all of them in their mixtures. Thus one distinguishing characteristic is the tendency to elevate raw sexual experience to a position of supreme importance so that the Quest for the Holy Grail becomes a quest for the perfect orgasm. Other characteristics are homosexuality, nihilism, and that impulse to self-destruction typified in the cult of drugs. Still another is that taste for violence which, as in the case of Baldwin, becomes unmistakably sadistic. If I had to answer the question, "What is most fundamental?" I should be inclined to say "the taste for violence." The belief that violence is the only appropriate response to an absurd world is the one element most often present in any individual's special version of the moment's avant-gardism.

Psychiatrists often say that suicide is frequently motivated by the desire for revenge against some person who, so the self-destroyer likes to believe, will be made to suffer. And psychiatrists are inclined to call this motive irrational. But in modern literature and modern criticism it is sometimes accepted as the ultimate rationality—as in these two examples:

In Friedrich Dürrenmatt's much discussed play *The Visit,* the principal character explains her conduct by saying, "The world made a whore of me, so I am turning the world into a brothel"; and in *The Nation* the reviewer of a novel calls the self-destruction of its hero "an alcoholic strike against humanity." In common-sense terms all such retaliations and revenges come under the head of biting off one's nose to spite one's face. But that seems to be what some modernists advocate.

Seldom, if ever before, has any of the arts been so dominated by an all-inclusive hatred. Once the writer hated individual "bad men." Then he began to hate instead the society which was supposed to be responsible for the creation of bad men. Now his hatred is directed not at individuals or their societies but at the universe in which bad men and bad societies are merely expressions of the fundamental evil of the universe itself.

It was once hoped that the iconoclasts who flourished during the early years of our century would clear the ground for higher ideals and truer values. Somewhat later it was argued that existentialism, having demonstrated that the universe was in itself morally and intellectually meaningless, now left man free to construct meanings and morals for himself and in his own image. What that has come down to, the Baldwins, the Burroughses, and the Jack Smiths have demonstrated in our language; the Apollinaires and the Genets, in theirs.

There is, of course, always the literature of social protest to which one may turn if one has had enough of sadism and the absurd. But sometimes the reviewers sound as though they were getting the same sort of sadistic kick in a less open way. Here, for example, is the way in which a recent novel is praised in (of all places) *Vogue:*

*The Fixer,* a brilliant new novel by Bernard Malamud, is harrowing. It is a dreadful story that cuts and lacerates without relief; it is a drama of ferocious injustice and then more injustice.

If anything except unrelieved violence in one form or another is "escapism"; if human nature, the world, and even the universe itself are what so many esteemed artists declare them to be, then what can anyone reasonable choose to do except escape in either life or literature—if he can? Perhaps that is why 18,000 people recently crowded a London exhibit devoted to memorabilia concerning the creator of Peter Rabbit.

## STUDY QUESTIONS

1. Does Krutch answer the question he poses in the title?

2. According to G. K. Chesterton, as paraphrased by Krutch, the advocates of art-for-art's-sake professed the moral neutrality of art. How did Chesterton disprove the validity of their statement? Does Krutch accept Chesterton's proof as valid? How might Chesterton define *neutral?*

3. What does Krutch feel is the most fundamental characteristic of "modernism"?

4. Does the selectivity of Krutch's examples help him prove his point? Is this an honest approach? A neutral approach?

5.  Krutch says that the contemporary arts are "dominated by an all-inclusive hatred." How does flower-children culture and its art refute Krutch's conclusions?

*Saul Bellow*

# MIND OVER CHATTER

Saul Bellow (1915–    ) was born in Quebec, Canada, the son of emigrant Russian parents. He attended the University of Chicago, received his B.A. from Northwestern University in 1937, and was awarded an honorary Litt.D. by Northwestern in 1962 and Bard College in 1963. Bellow now teaches at the University of Chicago. His novels include *Dangling Man* (1944), *Victim* (1947), *The Adventures of Augie March* (1953), *Seize the Day* (1956), *Henderson the Rain King* (1959), and *Herzog* (1964). Both *Augie March* and *Herzog* were awarded National Book Awards. *Mosby's Memoirs,* a collection of short stories, was published in 1968. Bellow's other honors include awards from the Ford and Guggenheim Foundations and the Prix International de Littérature.

THE FACT THAT there are so many weak, poor, and boring stories and novels written and published in America has been ascribed by our rebels to the horrible squareness of our institutions, the idiocy of power, the debasement of sexual instincts, and the failure of writers to be alienated enough. The poems and novels of these same rebellious spirits, and their theoretical statements, are grimy and gritty and very boring too, besides being nonsensical, and it is evident by now that polymorphous sexuality and vehement declarations of alienation are not going to produce great works of art either.

There is nothing left for us novelists to do but think. For unless we think, unless we make a clearer estimate of our condition, we will continue to write kid stuff, to fail in our function, we will lack serious interests and become truly irrelevant. Here the critics must share the blame, for they too have failed to describe the situation. Literature has for several generations been its own source, its own province, has lived upon its own traditions, and accepted a romantic separation or estrangement from the common world. This estrangement, though it produced some masterpieces, has by now enfeebled the novel.

The separatism of writers is accompanied by the more or less conscious acceptance of a theory of modern civilization. This theory says in effect that modern mass society is frightful, brutal, hostile to whatever is pure in the human spirit, a wasteland and a horror. To its ugliness, its bureaucratic regimes, its thefts, its lies, its wars, and its unparalleled cruelties, the artist can never be reconciled. This is one of the traditions on which contemporary literature has lived uncritically. But it is the task of artists and critics in their own day to look with their own eyes. Perhaps they will see evils even worse than those they have taken for granted, but they will at least be seeing for themselves. They will not, they can not, permit themselves, generation after generation, to hold views they have not individually examined. By refusing to look at civilization with our own eyes we lose the right to call ourselves artists; we have accepted what we ourselves condemn—received opinion, professionalism, snobbery and the formation of a caste. And unfortunately the postures of this caste, postures of liberation and independence and creativity, are attractive to poor souls dreaming everywhere of a fuller, freer life.

The writer is admired, the writer is envied. But what has he to say for himself? Why, he says, just as writers have said for more than a century, that he is cut off from the life of his own society, that he is despised by its overlords who are cynical about intellectuals and have nothing but contempt for the artist, and that he is without a true public, estranged. He dreams of ages when the poet or the painter expressed a perfect unit of time and place, had real acceptance, and enjoyed a vital harmony with his surroundings—he dreams of a golden age. In fact, without the golden age, there is no wasteland.

Well, this is no age of gold. It is only what it is. Can we do no more than complain about it? We writers have better choices. We can either shut up because the times are too bad, or continue writing because we have an instinct for it, a talent to develop, which even in these disfigured times we cannot suppress. Isolated professionalism is death. Without the common world the novelist is nothing but a curiosity and will find himself in a glass case along some dull museum corridor of the future.

Mechanization and bureaucracy are permanently with us. We cannot pretend the technological revolution has not occurred. We are its beneficiaries; we may also become its slaves. The first necessity, therefore, is to fight for justice and equality. The artist, along with everyone else, must fight for his life, for his freedom. This is not to advise the novelist to rush immediately into the political sphere. But to begin with he must begin to use his intelligence, long unused. If he is to reject politics, he must understand what he is rejecting. He must begin to think, and to think not merely of his own narrower interests and needs, but of the common world he has for so long failed to see. If he thinks his alienation has much significance, he is wrong. It is nine-tenths cant. If he thinks his rebellion significant, he is wrong again because the world is far more revolutionary in being simply what it is. In their attempts to imitate power, *Realpolitik,*[1] by violence or vehemence, writers simply make themselves foolish. The "romantic criminal" or desperado cannot get within miles of the significant human truth. It is with this truth that the writer must be concerned.

## STUDY QUESTIONS

1. Bellow's essay was a speech delivered at the presentation of the 1965 National Book Awards. How might the occasion have influenced both the form and content of "Mind over Chatter"?

2. On what points do Krutch and Bellow agree? Disagree?

3. According to Bellow, what has been the result of the novelist's and critic's estrangement from the common world?

4. With what task does Bellow charge the contemporary writer? What choices does he suggest are open to the writer?

5. What does Bellow mean by "the significant human truth"?

[1] Literally, realistic politics; the politics of violence.

# INDEX OF AUTHORS
# AND TITLES

*Academic Freedom and Student Riots,* 451
Alpert, Hollis, 508, 529
*Another Plane in Another Sphere: The College Drug Scene,* 463
*Argument Against Abolishing Christianity, An,* 44
Audubon, John James, 213

Baldwin, James, 133
Beerbohm, Max, 354
Bellow, Saul, 599
Benét, Stephen Vincent, 252
*Benjamin Franklin,* 11
*". . . Benjamin will Survive. . . ." An Interview with Charles Webb,* author of *The Graduate,* 502
*Bird and the Machine, The,* 236
*Bold and Arduous Project, A,* 3
*Books and Men,* 63
Brown, John Mason, 535
Buber, Martin, 63
*Buck Fanshaw's Funeral,* 347
*But What's a Dictionary For?,* 378

Carson, Rachel, 275
Changas, Estelle, 517

Clark, Walter Van Tilburg, 220
Cochran, Robert W., 92, 100
*College and the Alternatives,* 397
*Confessions of a Rebel: 1831,* 172
Connolly, Thomas E., 87, 98
*Conquest of Trigger Mortis, The,* 539
*Correspondence: "The Graduate,"* 527
Cox, Harvey, 21
*Crowded World, The,* 195
*Cum Laude,* 510
*Current Cinema, The,* 515

Darby, William J., 286
*Decline and Fall of English, The,* 326
Dirks, J. Edward, 410
*Disney and the Dane,* 535
*Don't Send Johnny to College,* 391
*Dream-Children,* 106

EBONY, 139
Eiseley, Loren C., 236, 282
*Eros on the Campus,* 438

Evans, Bergen, 378
*Everything That Rises Must Converge,* 152
*Exaggerated Generation, The,* 431


Farber, Stephen, 517
Faulkner, William, 143
Follett, Wilson, 369
Forster, E. M., 55
*For Two Cents Plain,* 101
*Frank Lloyd Wright,* 500
Franklin, Benjamin, 3


Gardner, John William, 397
Gill, Brendan, 515
Gold, Herbert, 445
Golden, Harry, 101
*Good-Bye to All T—T,* 344
Goodman, Paul, 418
Gove, Phillip B., 360
*Graduate, The,* 517
*Graduate" Makes Out; "The,* 529
Greene, Graham, 110, 413


Hamilton, Charles V., 177
*Hanging, A,* 114
Hawthorne, Nathaniel, 65, 76
*Hawthorne's Choice: The Veil or the Jaundiced Eye,* 92
*Hawthorne's "Young Goodman Brown": An Attack on Puritanic Calvinism,* 87
*Hell and Its Outskirts,* 338
*He Was There Before Coronado,* 244
*Hook,* 220
Hook, Sidney, 451
*How Culturally Active Are Americans?,* 487
*How Shall I Word It?,* 354

*How Young Goodman Brown Became Old Badman Brown,* 98
Huxley, Sir Julian, 195


*Introducing Anthropology,* 209
*"It Is Done" (Part IV, The Confessions of Nat Turner),* 165


Kauffmann, Stanley, 510, 524, 527
Kenner, Hugh, 391
Kerr, Clark, 431
Krutch, Joseph Wood, 32, 244, 590


Lamb, Charles, 106
Larner, Jeremy, 463
Lawrence, D. H., 11
*Letter From a Far Frat,* 445
*Letter to Stanley Kauffmann,* 524
*Looking for the Meat and Potatoes —Thoughts on Black Power,* 121
*Lord of the Dynamos, The,* 304
*Lost Childhood, The,* 413
Lynes, Russell, 546


Macklin, F. A., 502
MacDonald, Dwight, 326
Mailer, Norman, 121
Mannes, Marya, 539
*Marvelous Mouth, The,* 553
Mencken, H. L., 338
*Mike Nichols Strikes Again,* 508
*Mind Over Chatter,* 599
*Minister's Black Veil, The,* 76
*Modest Proposal, A,* 188
Montagu, Ashley, 209, 500
*Must Writers Hate the Universe?,* 590

*Neo-Knighthood,* 410
*New Aristocrats, The,* 418
*New Medicine and Its Weapons, The,* 264
NEWSWEEK, 264


*bligation to Endure, The,* 275
Connor, Flannery, 152
*n Being a Contemporary Christian,* 38
*On Fear: Deep South in Labor: Mississippi,* 143
*On Noise,* 203
Orwell, George, 114, 315
*Our Nat Turner and William Styron's Creation,* 177


*Politics and The English Language,* 315
*Powerhouse,* 563
Preface to *Webster's Third New International Dictionary,* 360


*Quality and Equality,* 407


*Reply,* 100
*Revolver in the Corner Cupboard, The,* 110
Roper, Elmo, 487
Rosten, Leo, 459
Russell, Bertrand, 291


*Sabotage in Springfield,* 369
Schopenhauer, Arthur, 203
Schorer, Mark, 474
*Science Has Spoiled My Supper,* 298

*Science to Save Us From Science, The,* 291
*Second Look,* 524
Sevareid, Eric, 181
*Sex and Secularization,* 21
*Silence, Miss Carson,* 286
Stegner, Wallace, 344
*Straight Men in a Crooked World,* 32
Styron, William, 165
Swift, Jonathan, 44, 188


*Taliesin,* 491
*"Tarzan" and Literature,* 574
Taylor, Harold, 407
TIME, 38
*To An Angry Young Man,* 459
*To the Wind,* 474
Twain, Mark, 347


*Unnameable Objects, Unspeakable Crimes,* 133
*Using a Plague to Fight a Plague,* 282


Vidal, Gore, 584


*Waking Dream: Tarzan Revisited, The,* 584
Watson, E. H. Lacon, 574
*We Aren't Superstitious,* 252
Webb, Charles, 502, 524, 527
Wells, H. G., 304
Welty, Eudora, 563
*What I Believe,* 55
*What Revolution in Men's Clothes?,* 546

*What Whites Can Learn From Negroes,* 139
*Wild Turkey, The,* 213
Wolfe, Tom, 553
Woodring, Paul, 438
Woodward, C. Vann, 172

*World Still Moves Our Way, The,* 181
Wright, Frank Lloyd, 491
Wylie, Philip, 298

*Young Goodman Brown,* 65